JUST, REASONABLE MULTICULTURALISM

This book explores the main challenges against multiculturalism. It aims to examine whether liberalism and multiculturalism are reconcilable, and what are the limits of liberal democratic interventions in illiberal affairs of minority cultures within democracy, when minorities engage in practices that inflict physical harm and non-physical harm on group members. In the process, this book addresses three questions: whether multiculturalism is bad for democracy, whether multiculturalism is bad for women and whether multiculturalism contributes to terrorism. *Just, Reasonable Multiculturalism* argues that liberalism and multiculturalism are reconcilable if a fair balance is struck between individual rights and group rights. Raphael Cohen-Almagor contends that reasonable multiculturalism can be achieved via mechanisms of deliberate democracy, compromise and, when necessary, coercion. Placing necessary checks on groups that discriminate against vulnerable third parties, the approach insists on the protection of basic human rights as well as on exit rights for individuals if and when they wish to leave their cultural groups.

RAPHAEL COHEN-ALMAGOR is Professor and Chair in Politics, and Founding Director of the Middle East Study Group, at the University of Hull. He has held teaching positions at Jerusalem, Haifa, UCLA and Johns Hopkins University. Previously he was Senior Fellow at the Woodrow Wilson International Center for Scholars and Distinguished Visiting Professor, Faculty of Laws, University College London. He is the author of many books, most recently *Confronting the Internet's Dark Side* (2015).

Just, Reasonable Multiculturalism

LIBERALISM, CULTURE AND COERCION

RAPHAEL COHEN-ALMAGOR

CAMBRIDGE
UNIVERSITY PRESS

CAMBRIDGE
UNIVERSITY PRESS

University Printing House, Cambridge CB2 8BS, United Kingdom

One Liberty Plaza, 20th Floor, New York, NY 10006, USA

477 Williamstown Road, Port Melbourne, VIC 3207, Australia

314–321, 3rd Floor, Plot 3, Splendor Forum, Jasola District Centre,
New Delhi – 110025, India

103 Penang Road, #05–06/07, Visioncrest Commercial, Singapore 238467

Cambridge University Press is part of the University of Cambridge.

It furthers the University's mission by disseminating knowledge in the pursuit of
education, learning, and research at the highest international levels of excellence.

www.cambridge.org
Information on this title: www.cambridge.org/9781108476140
DOI: 10.1017/9781108567213

First published 2021

A catalogue record for this publication is available from the British Library.

ISBN 978-1-108-47614-0 Hardback
ISBN 978-1-108-46983-8 Paperback

For Yehuda Elkana (1934–2012), Bhikhu Parekh and Will Kymlicka

Contents

Figures

Acknowledgements

This book is the result of many years of research and thinking. The journey started in 1992. I returned to Israel after four years in Oxford. The person who opened his arms and embraced me upon returning home was Yehuda Elkana (1934–2012), the then president of the Van Leer Jerusalem Institute. Yehuda gave me carte blanche to do whatever I wanted. I decided to join the European Project that studied cultural influences between Europe, Israel and Palestine. It was an interesting group of people, composed of Israeli-Jews, Israeli-Palestinians and two Germans. Our funding came from the Volkswagen Foundation which generously sponsored our three-year project.

This has been a fascinating journey during which I exchanged ideas and received support from many people. I acknowledge the guidance and support of my beloved mentors Isaiah Berlin (1909–97) and Geoffrey Marshall (1929–2003) at the early stages of thinking. Isaiah and Geoffrey were beacons of wit and knowledge up until their deaths. They supported the early formulation of my thinking and provided a sense of direction. Jack Hayward (1931–2017) provided me with many insights about French culture and complex heritage. Jack sparked my curiosity about France and was a driving force behind my decision to focus on the French secular struggle against multiculturalism. From 2008 until his death in December 2017 we had many conversations about France and Israel. On his deathbed, just a few days before he succumbed to cancer, Jack provided reflections on the origins of *laïcité*.

Will Kymlicka co-authored with me one of my early articles on multiculturalism and inspired my thinking on these complicated issues. Steve Newman, Geoffrey Brahm Levey, Bhikhu Parekh, Lester Grabbe and Gary Edles provided thoughtful critique and incisive comments on drafts of this manuscript. They furthered my thoughts with many sharp insights. I very much appreciate their incredible invest-ment in commenting on each and every chapter in minute detail. Several other scholars provided invaluable comments on specific chapters: Catherine Audard, Kristian Bartholin, Jean Baubérot, Alan Howard Brener, Emile Chabal, Naomi

Chazan, Brian Earp, Leonid Eidelman, Jonathan Fox, Raanan Gillon, Carole Goldberg, Amos Guiora, Tamar Herman, Myriam Hunter-Henin, Orit Ichilov, Allan Jacobs, Asa Kasher, Steven Kramer, Sam Lehman-Wilzig, Willem Lemmens, John Lotherington, Philippe Marliere, Eliahu Mazza, Nisar Mir, Christian Pihet, Uri Regev, Elyakim Rubinstein, Peter Schaber, Motti Schenhav, Colin Shindler, Tony Smith, Sammy Smooha, Stephanos Stavros, Avraham Steinberg, Wayne Sumner, Yofi Tirosh, Michel Troper, Andrew Winter and Ruvi Ziegler. I have learned a great deal from their wisdom, insights and experiences.

Many more people have helped me along the way, providing advice, information and other forms of assistance. Among them I wish to particularly note Bruce Ackerman, Scott Anderson, Soha Araf, Yonathan Arfi, Ehud Bandel, Izhar Be'er, Purushottama Bellimora, Haim Belmaker, Magali Bessone, Francois Boucher, David Chazan, David Chemla, Richard Oliver Collin, Dalia Dorner, Orly Erez-Likhovski, Itzik Galnoor, Dafna Gold-Malchior, Sophie Guérard de Latour, Manar Hassan, Anat Hoffman, Ruth Kaddari, Joel Alan Katz, Andy Knapp, Menny Mautner, Yonatan Melamed, Natan Nachmani, Robert Post, Frances Raday, Michal Rambau, Noya Rimalt, Philippe A. Schmidt, Tim Sellers, Bobby Silverman, Janet Spikes, Frank Stewart, Anna Triandafyllidou, Elliot Vaisrub Glassenberg, Patrick Weil, Karen Weisblatt, Dareen Yaacov, Alin Zaberowitz and Nick Zangwill.

Draft papers addressing different aspects of this research were presented at Queen's University Belfast, Northern Ireland; The Royal Irish Academy, Dublin; University of Toronto; University of Alberta; The Australian National University; Vrije Universiteit Amsterdam; The European University Institute, Florence; University of Copenhagen; Oxford University; St John's College, Cambridge; SOAS University of London; University of Manchester; Hull Guildhall; University College London (UCL); The Hastings Centre, New York; Arizona State University; University of California, Los Angeles and University of California, Berkeley; Johns Hopkins; The Woodrow Wilson Center, Washington, DC; University of Southern California; Antwerp University; University of Haifa; The European Project, Jerusalem; Tel Aviv University; The Hebrew University; Bar-Ilan University; The Adam Institute for Democracy and Peace, Jerusalem; Kinneret College, Galilee, Israel; Collegium Polonicum, Slubice, Poland; Balvant Parekh Centre for General Semantics, Vadodara, Malaviya National Institute of Technology Jaipur, and Gujarat National Law University, Gandhinagar, India. I thank the audiences at these talks for their criticism and suggestions.

I am also thankful to the University of Hull for providing me with invaluable resources to complete the book. Most of the book was written during my visiting professorship year at UCL Faculty of Laws. I am indebted to UCL scholars and library for the conducive conditions provided for writing.

An earlier version of Chapter 6 was published under the title 'Should Liberal Government Regulate Male Circumcision Performed in the Name of Jewish

Tradition?', *SN Social Sciences*, 1, 8 (2021). https://doi.org/10.1007/s43545-020-00011-7 (published online 9 November 2020). An earlier version of Chapter 10 was co-authored with Mohammed S. Wattad, 'The Legal Status of Israeli-Arabs/ Palestinians', *GNLU Law & Society Review*, 1 (March 2019): 1–28. My gratitude is granted for permissions to use the material.

The book is dedicated with gratitude and great appreciation to three people who influenced my research on multiculturalism more than anyone else: Yehuda Elkana, Bhikhu Parekh and Will Kymlicka. Yehuda was a true renaissance man with compassion, foresight and an inexhaustible thirst for knowledge. He generously supported the early phase of my research. Yehuda and I spent many hours together in Jerusalem and Tel Aviv, and on the road between these two cities, discussing culture, religion, peace and countless other subjects. Bhikhu was involved in the writing of this book, commenting on early drafts and providing intellectual guidance throughout. And Will has influenced and challenged my thinking on culture and religion since my Oxford days. His books are always on or next to my desk. This book is dedicated with gratitude to these three wise intellectuals.

Theory of Just, Reasonable Multiculturalism

1.

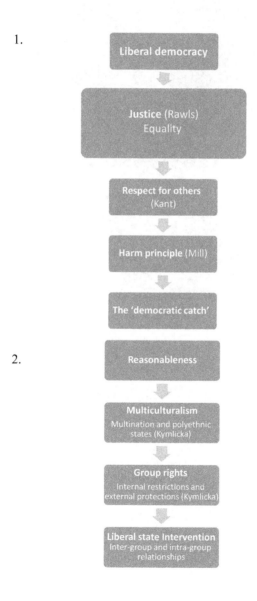

Liberal democracy

Justice (Rawls)
Equality

Respect for others
(Kant)

Harm principle (Mill)

The 'democratic catch'

2.

Reasonableness

Multiculturalism
Multination and polyethnic
states (Kymlicka)

Group rights
Internal restrictions and
external protections (Kymlicka)

Liberal state Intervention
Inter-group and intra-group
relationships

Theory of Just, Reasonable Multiculturalism

3.

Compromise
Principled and
tactical

Deliberative democracy
(Habermas)

4.

Coercion
Circumstantial and person-based
Benevolent and malevolent
Paternalistic
Via third party
Self- and other-regarding
Internalized and designated
Minority and majority

5.

Physical and non-physical harm
Freedom of religion and freedom from religion
Public v. private
Parenthood
Balancing

Introduction

Everything has its beauty but not everyone sees it.

Confucius

In 2008, British Prime Minister David Cameron said: 'State multiculturalism is a wrong-headed doctrine that has had disastrous results. It has fostered difference between communities ... it has stopped us from strengthening our collective identity. Indeed, it has deliberately weakened it.'[1] Cameron argued that multiculturalism means treating groups of people as monolithic blocks rather than individual citizens. It encourages difference and divisiveness rather than unity.

In October 2010, Chancellor Angela Merkel declared that 'the multicultural concept is a failure, an absolute failure'.[2] She acknowledged that the number of young people with a migration background was increasing and proposed a new and tougher approach to immigration: 'Those who want to have a part in our society', she said, 'must not only obey our laws and know the constitution, they must above all learn our language.'[3] Merkel maintained: 'it is right that a language test be taken in union-governed states. It is important that students who go to school understand their teachers ... And it is, without question, important and right to say that young

---

[1]   Andrew Sparrow, 'Cameron Attacks "State Multiculturalism"', *The Guardian* (26 February 2008), www.theguardian.com/politics/2008/feb/26/conservatives.race.

[2]   Chancellor Merkel's speech on 16 October 2010. See George Friedman, 'Germany and the Failure of Multiculturalism', *Stratfor* (19 October 2010), www.stratfor.com/weekly/20101018_germany_and_failure_multiculturalism?utm_source=GWeekly&utm_medium=email&utm_campaign=101019&utm_content=readmore&elq=98d2c1d56f644835bcad663c72d96ob1; Kate Connolly, 'Angela Merkel Declares Death of German Multiculturalism', *The Guardian* (17 October 2010), www.theguardian.com/world/2010/oct/17/angela-merkel-germany-multiculturalism-failures.

[3]   Rita Chin, *The Crisis of Multiculturalism in Europe* (Princeton, NJ: Princeton University Press, 2017): 237; Rita Chin, 'Thinking Difference in Post-war Germany', in Cornelia Wilhelm (ed.), *Migration, Memory, and Diversity: Germany from 1945 to the Present* (New York: Berghahn Books, 2018): chap. 8.

girls must attend school field trips and participate in gym classes, and that we do not believe in forced marriages – they are not compatible with our laws.'[4]

A year later, Cameron echoed Merkel's words by attacking the very notion of multiculturalism as encouragement for 'different cultures to live separate lives, apart from each other and apart from the mainstream'.[5] The British prime minister complained: 'When a white person holds objectionable views, racist views, we rightly condemn them. But when equally unacceptable views or practices come from someone who is not white, we have been too cautious … to stand up to them.'[6] Cameron referred to forced marriage as an example of problematic prac- tices. This hands-off tolerance, Cameron said, 'has only served to reinforce the sense that not enough is shared'.[7] All this left some young Muslims feeling rootless, and in search for a meaningful life they were radicalized, pushed to adopt extremist ideologies. Now for sure, Cameron qualified, 'they don't turn into terrorists over- night, but what we see – and what we see in so many European countries – is a process of radicalization'.[8]

Like Chancellor Merkel, Prime Minister Cameron went as far as saying that multiculturalism had failed and that it had fostered extremist ideology and radical- ization among British Muslims. Under the 'doctrine of state multiculturalism', different cultures have been encouraged to live separate lives, 'apart from each other and apart from the mainstream', and 'We have failed to provide a vision of society to which they feel they want to belong. We have even tolerated these segregated communities behaving in ways that run counter to our values.'[9]

Cameron proposed a new model of 'muscular liberalism' that would enforce the values of equality, law and freedom of speech. He pledged to withhold state funding from Muslim groups that discouraged community assimilation or refused to endorse women's rights. Cameron called upon Britain and other European countries to

---

[4] Ibid.
[5] David Cameron, speech and Munich Security Conference (5 February 2011).
[6] 'Full transcript | David Cameron | Speech on radicalisation and Islamic extremism | Munich | 5 February 2011', *New Statesman* (5 February 2011), www.newstatesman.com/blogs/the-staggers/ 2011/02/terrorism-islam-ideology.
[7] Ibid.
[8] Prime minister's speech at Munich Security Conference, *National Archives* (5 February 2011), http://webarchive.nationalarchives.gov.uk/20130109092234/http://number10.gov.uk/news/pms- speech-at-munich-security-conference/. For further discussion, Gurpreet Mahajan, 'Multiculturalism in the Age of Terror: Confronting the Challenges', *Political Studies Review*, 5 (2007): 317–336; Kent Roach, 'National Security, Multiculturalism and Muslim Minorities', *University of Toronto Legal Studies Series*, Research Paper No. 938451 (October 2006).
[9] Prime minister's speech at Munich Security Conference, *National Archives* (5 February 2011), http://webarchive.nationalarchives.gov.uk/20130109092234/http://number10.gov.uk/news/pms- speech-at-munich-security-conference/.

replace 'passive tolerance' with an 'unambiguous' and 'hard-nosed defence' of fundamental liberties, of democracy, of the rule of law, and of equal rights for all.[10]

The same year, 2011, a third world leader, French president Nicolas Sarkozy, declared that multiculturalism had failed, saying that: 'We have been too concerned about the identity of the person who was arriving and not enough about the identity of the country that was receiving him.'[11]

These are strong and powerful words, especially as they come from the leaders of three of the most important democracies in Europe. Is multiculturalism a failure? Does multiculturalism foster extremist ideology and terrorism? Is there a direct connection between multiculturalism and terror?

Multiculturalism was *en vogue* during the second half of the twentieth century as many Western democracies had witnessed minority cultures that demanded rights and recognition. Multiculturalism as a new field of studies emerged, examining the moral and political claims of a wide range of cultural groups, their self-determination and society's recognition of group rights. It pondered the proper ways to acknowledge differences and respond to cultural and religious diversity.

However, as the above statements demonstrate, the trend across Western democracies towards the increased recognition and accommodation of cultural diversity has been reversed. The concept of multiculturalism has been a subject of controversy and we witness reassertion of unitary citizenship.[12] Conflicts between liberal and illiberal countries, and conflicts between liberal and illiberal cultures within the liberal state, have yielded a backlash against multiculturalism. Government officials and policymakers expressed scepticism and criticism of multiculturalism, especially in the context of increased freedom of movement, immigration and the so-called 'war against terror'. While there are still some who endorse multiculturalism, celebrate cultural diversity and support the right of cultural groups to recognition, respect and resources, others have been voicing scathing criticisms. The critiques argue that multiculturalism is bad for liberal democracy, is bad for women and, as quoted from David Cameron, has contributed to terrorism.

OBJECTIVES

This book explores whether these challenges against multiculturalism are justified. Its primary objectives are twofold: to examine whether liberalism and

---

[10] Rita Chin, *The Crisis of Multiculturalism in Europe*: 283–284.

[11] 'Nicolas Sarkozy Declares Multiculturalism Had Failed', *The Telegraph* (11 February 2011), www.telegraph.co.uk/news/worldnews/europe/france/8317497/Nicolas-Sarkozy-declares-multi culturalism-had-failed.html.

[12] Christian Joppke, *Is Multiculturalism Dead? Crisis and Persistence in the Constitutional State* (Cambridge: Polity, 2016); Will Kymlicka, 'The Rise and Fall of Multiculturalism? New Debates on Inclusion and Accommodation in Diverse Societies', *International Social Science Journal* (November 2010): 97; David Brooks, 'The Death of Multiculturalism', *New York Times* (27 April 2006).

multiculturalism are reconcilable, and what are the limits of state interventions in affairs of illiberal minority subcultures within democracies.[13] In the process, I outline the theoretical assumptions underlying a liberal response to threats posed by cultural or religious groups whose norms entail different measures of harm. I do this by examining the importance of cultural, ethnic, national, religious and ideological norms and beliefs, and what part they play in requiring us to tolerate others out of respect. I proceed by formulating guidelines designed to prescribe boundaries to cultural practices and to safeguard the rights of individuals.

Historically, liberal democracies have hoped that the protection of basic individual rights would be enough to accommodate ethnocultural minorities. Indeed, the importance of individual civil and political rights in protecting minorities should be accentuated. Freedom of religion, association, expression, business, mobility and political organization enable individuals to form and maintain groups and associations, to adapt to changing circumstances, and to promote sectarian views and interests among the wider population. Common rights of citizenship may not be enough to accommodate all forms of cultural pluralism. In some cases, certain entitlements and group rights are justified. We need to examine how these group rights are related to individual rights.[14]

This book addresses the following questions: What should we do if group rights in a democracy come into conflict with individual rights? Can a democracy allow minority groups to restrict the individual rights of their members, or should it insist that all groups uphold liberal principles? Should democracy tolerate every norm that members of a cultural community carry with them, even if this means that harm might be inflicted upon some members of that cultural community? Do cultural norms possess enough weight to allow harm? May culture supply reasons for the toleration of behaviour that is regarded as unacceptable when evinced by other members of society who are not members of the considered subculture?

The discussion deals with real-life situations. In our men-dominated world, women are routinely discriminated against: suttee, witch-hunting, arranged and forced marriages including the sale of young daughters, discriminatory norms of marriage, divorce and property rights, gender segregation, denial of education, enforcement of a strict dress code, female infanticide, female genital mutilation (FGM), and murder for family honour are striking examples. Women are required to pay a high price for the whims of men. Hopefully the following discussion will bring about wider awareness that will have some positive bearing on the lives of the women concerned. The discussion will promote a debate on the liberal theory of

---

[13] By 'subculture' it is meant a community with certain distinguishing cultural practices living within a liberal democracy. 'Sub' relates only to its relative size compared to the larger community in which it resides.

[14] Will Kymlicka and Raphael Cohen-Almagor, 'Ethnocultural Minorities in Liberal Democracies', in Maria Baghramian and Attracta Ingram (eds), *Pluralism: The Philosophy and Politics of Diversity* (London: Routledge, 2000): 228–250.

neutrality so as to specify what should be allowed in a democratic society and what should be outlawed. Case studies are taken from the United States, Canada, the United Kingdom and some other Western European countries. The book also examines the situation in two countries, France and Israel, that do not adhere to Anglo-Saxon liberalism and employ coercive means vis-à-vis minorities in order to maintain national cohesion.

The book focuses on the relationships between cultural majorities and minorities. It does not discuss LGBTQ rights or the acceptability of specific cultural practices that involve animals (e.g., bullfighting). These important issues merit separate analysis.

TERMINOLOGY

The *state* is a political organization of society, a form of human association within geographic boundaries that has institutions that govern the people who reside in that territory. It comprises an executive, a legislature, security organizations and a bureaucracy that administers a vast number of institutions to answer ecological, human, animal and other needs and concerns. The state utilizes apparatuses of laws, procedures, norms and arrangements that establish order and security, promote certain values (national and international), enforce regulations, and settle disputes. A state is clearly more than a government as governments change while states endure. In this book, when I speak of states I refer to the body politics or to the governing body that devises and implements policies. The word *country* is used as a synonym.

This book is written from a liberal perspective. As the etymology of the word 'Liberalism' implies, liberals emphasize liberty. Liberalism's core principle is the protection of the individual, her rights, interests and choices. Governments are established to protect these rights, interests and choices. Liberalism aspires to provide individuals with the conditions to develop their autonomy and build their lives as they see appropriate. Liberals believe that human beings are endowed with reason and that they should enjoy the maximum possible freedom consistent with a like freedom for others. Liberalism speaks of respecting people qua people, as human beings, and of not harming others without appropriate justification. Thus, liberals speak of liberty as empowerment and liberty from constraints.[15] Liberal ideology also upholds the values of equality, not necessarily material equality but a basic moral equality. Liberalism endorses tolerance and highlights the importance of pluralism and diversity.

---

[15] Isaiah Berlin, *Liberty* (Oxford: Oxford University Press, 2002). See also Bruce Baum and Robert Nichols (eds), *Isaiah Berlin and the Politics of Freedom: 'Two Concepts of Liberty' 50 Years Later* (London: Routledge, 2015). For further discussion, see Jürgen Habermas, 'Equal Treatment of Cultures and the Limits of Postmodern Liberalism', *Journal of Political Philosophy*, 13(1): (2005): 1–28.

their faiths, arguing that their sacred sites and symbols should be revered or at least not be desecrated. In each of these cases, the duties generated by the right are duties owed to the group as a whole rather to its individual members.[24]

THEORETICAL FRAMEWORK

To tackle the above questions I have designed a theoretical framework that is both comprehensive and analytical. The theoretical framework is composed of four layers of analysis. It is grounded in liberal philosophy, benefiting from the thinking of prominent liberal thinkers. The theory of just, reasonable multiculturalism is not restricted to one school of thought. Rather, it is composed of principles from a range of liberal philosophies. The first layer is grounded in John Rawls' theory of justice, including his ideas about applying the veil of ignorance as an analytical tool for evaluation, and the concept of mutual respect. I am aware that there are some important differences between Rawls' *A Theory of Justice*[25] and *Political Liberalism*.[26] But the discussion here is not aimed to offer a comprehensive critical analysis of Rawls, something that many authors, including myself, have done extensively; instead, my aim is to build on some of his principles to compose a theory of just, reasonable multiculturalism. The Rawlsian theory is supplemented with Kantian ethics, and specifically Kant's ideas about respecting others, and perceiving people always as ends and never as mere means; with J. S. Mill's Harm Principle, and with my formulation of the 'democratic catch'.

The second layer develops the theory of reasonable multiculturalism. Here the concept of reasonableness is central. People can be said to be morally reasonable when they have an appropriate conception of themselves and their standing in relation to their fellows, and when they understand and accept the obligations and constraints upon their aspirations and behaviour which derive from that conception. Democratic moral reasonableness implies that all citizens possess moral dignity and that within the framework of a democratic polity every citizen must be treated with respect. In this context, different forms of cultural pluralism and of rights are explained. These are important for constructing bridges between liberalism and multiculturalism.

The second layer of analysis also adopts Will Kymlicka's two forms of cultural pluralism: 'multination' and 'polyethnic' states, and his formulation of two kinds of rights: 'internal restrictions' (the right of a group against its own members) and 'external protections' (the right of a group against the larger society). Again, I am fully aware that Kymlicka's two main writings, *Liberalism, Community, and*

---

[24] Peter Jones, 'Group Rights', in *Stanford Encyclopedia of Philosophy* (17 March 2016), https://plato.stanford.edu/entries/rights-group/.

[25] Rawls, *A Theory of Justice*.

[26] John Rawls, *Political Liberalism* (New York: Columbia University Press, 1993).

Culture[27] and *Multicultural Citizenship*[28] have some significant differences; but my aim is not to analyse these differences or to observe trajectories in Kymlicka's thinking. Instead, my aim is to constructively use some of his sharp principles as essential ingredients that supplement the first layer of the theory of just, reasonable multiculturalism. Like Kymlicka, I also try to reconcile between liberalism and multiculturalism.

The third layer provides the operational mechanisms for reasonable multiculturalism: compromise and deliberative democracy. Here I draw a distinction between principled and tactical compromise and explain that just, reasonable multiculturalism encourages exchange of ideas, consideration of the other and seeking the middle ground, and that it prefers deliberative democracy to coercion. In turn, the fourth layer examines the complex concept of coercion. Useful distinctions are made between circumstantial and person-based coercion, between benevolent and malevolent coercion, between self- and other-regarding coercion, between internalized and designated coercion, and between minority and majority coercion. I also explain the value and significance of paternalistic coercion. Paternalistic coercion is important for understanding the debate over Muslim dress in France.

The discussion is limited to democratic societies. The hypotheses put forward and the conclusions reached are based on the conception of democracy as it has emerged during the last eighty years or so. Liberal democracies promote the autonomy of the person, liberty, tolerance, participation in civic life, equality before the law and pluralism of different concepts of the good life. On the other hand, illiberal societies are based on authoritative conceptions and principles. Their set of principles does not encourage tolerance and pluralism and it often runs contrary to liberty and to the promotion of individual autonomy. Their governance involves excessive interference and coercion and thus one can assume that their behaviour in the scenarios presented *infra* would be totally different. France and Israel represent interesting cases because they are republican (France) and ethnic (Israel) democracies whose mode of conduct regarding religion is different from Anglo-Saxon liberalism.

The reader should not infer from this distinction between democracies and non-democracies that democracies are immune to problems and that citizens' rights and freedoms are secured in democracies. In each and every democracy we find violations of basic human rights concerning certain individuals and groups. There is no such thing as 'perfect' democracy. I illustrate this point with pertinent examples.

While liberalism assumes that its principles are universal in nature, the hypotheses advanced in this book and the conclusions reached are limited to modern democracies. While I think that the principles and values that are embraced and

---

[27] Will Kymlicka, *Liberalism, Community, and Culture* (Oxford: Clarendon Press, 1989).
[28] Kymlicka, *Multicultural Citizenship*. For further discussion, see Geoffrey Brahm Levey, 'Equality, Autonomy, and Cultural Rights', *Political Theory*, 25(2) (April 1997): 215–248.

promoted by liberal ideology should be universalized, I also acknowledge that theocracies, authoritarian regimes and totalitarian governments might not be persuaded to adopt liberalism. As for the two countries studied here, while France and Israel are liberal in some respects, they are not when freedom of religion is concerned. Both countries exhibit perfectionism rather than neutrality on religious matters. France is Christian, Israel is Jewish, and according to their respective governments so they should remain.

While the theory of just, reasonable multiculturalism is eclectic, it is based on solid and thoughtful foundations that together make a coherent whole, offering yardsticks as to when a liberal democracy should interfere in the illiberal and discriminatory practices of subcultures within a democracy.

PREMISES AND CONCEPTS

Between liberal democracy and multiculturalism there is an important dialectic. The motivation is to provide scope for diversity, to create bridges between cultures and to accommodate differences within certain boundaries set by liberal ideology as the locus is limited to democracy. This book is based on several underlying premises and concepts:

Respect for multiculturalism is respecting diversity, the mosaic of traditions and cultural pluralism within societies which enriches society and enhances our humanity as we allow people to promote their myriad conceptions of the good.

Compromise. Many of the issues that engulf society and create cleavages can be resolved via deliberations and compromises. Political and social conflicts can be mitigated and tamed by compromises. While politics is bound to include a conflictual dimension, liberal democracy is oriented towards a sustained quest for compromise.

Deliberative democracy. Governments should not behave like a bull in a china shop. A government should conduct its affairs vis-à-vis minority cultures with sensitivity and determination, setting reasonable ends, opening channels of communications and seeking accommodation and compromise that show respect both to the values of the state and to the minority cultures.

Freedom v. coercion. People would like to lead their lives as free and autonomous human beings. Instinctively coercion is foreign to us, and might be offensive to our sensibilities and lead to an increased sense of alienation and resentment. This is not to say that coercion is never employed in liberal democracies. But whenever coercion is employed it should be backed with firm, legitimate and reasonable justifications.

Gender equality. Men, women and transgender people should enjoy equal human and civil rights. Men are not inferior to women. Women are not inferior to men.[29] Transgender people are not inferior to men and women. Granted that men and women are biologically different, biology should not lead to a differentiation of rights and liberties. Countries that have perceived biology as the dictating factor have always been racist countries.

Religion is a matter of personal choice, faith and belief. Because religion provides an all-encompassing framework for all matters, people should be free to take what is appealing to them and reject aspects that are less appealing.

Consequently, *freedom of religion*, and *freedom from religion* are equally important. Both are matters of personal choice. Citizens in a democracy should enjoy the ability to choose one or the other. Each and every person should be allowed to choose her conception of the good, as she sees fit and appropriate for herself, as long as she does not harm others (see *Values* below).

Government intervention. Government should not restrict freedom because it assumes that one particular way of life is intrinsically better than others and that people who lead that way of life are better people. It is not up to government to impose one view on everyone.[30]

Public v. private. A clear distinction has to be made between the communal character of the state and personal matters. Personal matters are, by definition, personal. The state should limit its involvement in such matters to absolute minimum and intervene only when there are significant countervailing public interests.

Chain. We are the bridge between past and future. People are shaped by their birthplace, by their family and friends, by their upbringing and education. The past is of significance as people appreciate from where they are coming and believe this past is important in order to know where they are going.

Parenthood. It is often important for parents to bring up their children in accordance with their traditions and cultures. Parents certainly have a voice in the upbringing and education of their children. On many issues, until their children reach adulthood (commonly at 18 years old) parents decide for their children as they are assumed to represent the children's

---

[29] Susan Moller Okin, 'Feminism, Women's Human Rights, and Cultural Differences', *Hypatia*, 13(2) (Spring 1998): 32–52; Brian Barry, *Culture and Equality: An Egalitarian Critique of Multiculturalism* (Cambridge: Polity 2000); Ayelet Shachar, *Multicultural Jurisdictions: Cultural Differences and Women's Rights* (Cambridge: Cambridge University Press, 2001); Valerie Bryson, *Feminist Political Theory* (London: Palgrave, 2016).

[30] Ronald Dworkin, *Religion without God* (Cambridge, MA: Harvard University Press, 2013): 130.

best interests. However, while acknowledging the importance of parenthood as well as its duties and privileges, sometimes the right of the child might come into conflict with the right of the parents and this is where government interference might be warranted. The liberal state should protect vulnerable populations. It should protect women and it should also protect children.

Values. The two basic values enshrined in liberal democracies are respect for others and not harming others. We should strive to protect and promote these values. We uphold John Stuart Mill's Harm Principle which holds that the only purpose for which power can be rightfully exercised over any member of the community, against his or her will, is to prevent harm to others.[31] The Respect for Others Principle, derived from Kantian and Rawlsian philosophies, requires us to respect the dignity of people as human beings.

The democratic catch. One of the problems of any political system is that the principles that underlie and characterize it may also, through their application, endanger it and bring about its destruction. Democracy, in its liberal form, is no exception. It advocates liberty and tolerance and at the same time acknowledges the need to set boundaries to liberty. Moreover, because democracy is a relatively young phenomenon its practitioners lack experience in dealing with the pitfalls inherent in the working of the system. This is what I call the 'catch' of democracy.[32]

Balancing. Striking a balance between rights and liberties is challenging. There is no quick fix suitable for all societies. The balance must take into consideration history, politics and culture as well the pain and suffering of those who pay the price for belonging to a certain culture or religion and the consequences of intervention, or lack of intervention. These factors vary from one country to another as history and politics are distinct. The challenge is becoming more difficult as a result of globalization, immigration and the changing composition of societies.

THESIS

My thesis is that multiculturalism is not necessarily bad for women or for democracy, and that it is not conducive to terrorism. Multiculturalism enriches democracy in many respects and contributes to human development and autonomy. There is

---

[31] J.S. Mill, *Utilitarianism, Liberty, and Representative Government* (London: J.M. Dent, 1948), Everyman's edition, at 114 or *On Liberty*, www.utilitarianism.com/ol/three.html.

[32] Raphael Cohen-Almagor, *The Boundaries of Liberty and Tolerance* (Gainesville: The University Press of Florida, 1994); Raphael Cohen-Almagor, *Speech, Media, and Ethics: The Limits of Free Expression* (Houndmills and New York: Palgrave Macmillan, 2005); Raphael Cohen-Almagor, *The Scope of Tolerance* (London and New York: Routledge, 2006).

nothing inherently wrong in multiculturalism. Group rights, like individual rights, can be used to enhance human potential and they can also be abused. Both group rights and individual rights should be put in check and constrained by enacting justified and reasonable boundaries. If protections are in place to secure civic and human rights for all, then multiculturalism can serve the best interests of all, including minorities, women, children and other vulnerable populations.

National, cultural and ethnic memberships are significant in pursuing our essential interest in leading a good life; therefore, taking account of such memberships is an important part of giving equal consideration to the interests of each member of the community. I argue that it is possible to resolve the tensions between liberalism and multiculturalism, provided that a fair balance is struck between individual rights and group rights, and that reasonable multiculturalism can be achieved via mechanisms of deliberative democracy, reasonable compromise and justified forms of state coercion. Placing necessary checks and just, reasonable protective constraints on group coercion, my approach insists on the protection of basic human rights as well as on exit rights for individuals if and when they wish to leave their cultural groups. Emphasis is put on freedom from coercion, freedom *of* religion and freedom *from* religion, gender equality and on making a clear distinction between the communal character of the state and personal matters. Personal matters should remain so as much as possible. I will outline the boundaries of state intervention.

It is argued that it is justified to interfere in the business of its subcultures when excessive norms subvert the basic principles upon which a liberal society is founded. That is, democracy has the right to curtail norms that disrespect and cause harm to other persons (who may live inside or outside the given cultural community). It is easier for the liberal state to intervene when significant physical harm is inflicted on group members in the name of culture and tradition. The issues are more difficult and complicated when women and children are denied basic human rights in the name of culture. It is argued that liberal democracy should step in to protect people and to ensure their basic human rights. Considerations of substance (extent of harm) and context (time and place) should be taken into consideration.

BOOK STRUCTURE

The book examines the importance of cultural, ethnic, national, religious and ideological norms and beliefs in several countries. It proposes a comprehensive theoretical framework to the study of multiculturalism and then applies the theory to specific case studies. The book is composed of four parts:

Part I Chapters 1–4 comprise the theoretical part of the book. The concepts of liberal democracy, justice, reasonableness, multiculturalism, compromise, deliberative democracy and coercion constitute the foundations of the reasonable multiculturalism theory for reconciling tensions between liberalism and multiculturalism.

Chapters 5–8 apply the theoretical principles to analyse state intervention in cultural affairs of cultural groups within liberal democracies.

Part II   Chapters 5–6 examine cases in which groups inflict bodily harms on their own members.

Part III   Chapters 7–8 are concerned with the more complicated cases where groups inflict non-physical harm on women and children. These cases exhibit clashes between group rights and liberal individual rights. I question the extent that the discussed court rulings have suggested reasonable compromises to accommodate multiculturalism and to outline the limits of state interference in practices of illiberal communities that deny basic rights to women and children.

Part IV   Chapters 9–10 discuss two countries: France and Israel. In France, majority rule infringes on the rights of minorities. In Israel we witness majority coercion of minorities, and minority Jewish-Orthodox coercion of the Jewish secular majority. While Parts II and III outline instances in which liberal democracy is justified to intervene in group affairs in order to prevent harm to women and children, Part IV criticizes discriminatory and coercive state conduct vis-à-vis vulnerable minorities.

Multiculturalism is concerned with the ways to address cultural and religious claims and demands. Chapter 1 revolves around the questions: What does liberalism purport to include within the defence of neutrality? What scope is available for conceptions of the good to meet, to mingle and to rival each other? In order to answer these questions we need to understand what liberal democracy is about, what are its ground rules and how can we distinguish liberal democracies from illiberal societies. To address these important questions I avail myself of the Rawlsian justice as fairness theory which greatly influenced liberal discourse during the past century.

While Rawls' theory of justice is important it is yet insufficient. It needs to be supplemented with further ideas in order to construct a theory of just, reasonable multiculturalism. I proceed by an exploration of Kantian and Millian ethics, and the concept of the 'democratic catch'.

Chapter 2 aims to explain the concept of reasonable multiculturalism. Building on the Rawlsian notion of reasonableness, and on Will Kymlicka's formulation of multiculturalism, I start by outlining the mechanisms for reconciliation between liberalism and multiculturalism. The focus is on boundaries. What are the boundaries of multiculturalism within the framework of liberal democracy? And what are the boundaries of state interference in the business of minority cultures, when their norms and practices seem at odd with the underpinning values of liberal democracy? Reasonability assumes acceptance of the underpinning shared principles. Cultures that do not adhere to these principles are perceived as less reasonable. The extent of reasonability varies. But lacking reasonability does not immediately entail that the liberal majority should intervene in the business of the subcultures. Interference is warranted to restore justice. I discuss the concept of *mutual* respect, and distinguish between two forms of cultural pluralism – 'multination' and 'polyethnic' states – and between two kinds of rights that a group might claim: the first involves the right of a group against its own members; the second involves the right of a group against the larger society. Furthermore, the nature of liberal tolerance and the mechanisms of deliberative democracy are explained, the latter instrumental for resolving disputes in a liberal democracy in a civil, non-violent way.

Chapter 3 is concerned with the concepts of compromise and deliberative democracy. When compromise takes place between two or more parties, reciprocity must be present; that is, the concessions are mutual. It is argued that compromise and deliberative democracy are important in facilitating a healthy discourse between the majority and minorities about group rights and the extent of state interference in minority affairs. With proponents of discourse ethics, public reason and deliberative democracy, such as Jürgen Habermas,[33] Joshua Cohen,[34] Seyla Benhabib,[35] John Dryzek,[36] Amy Gutmann and Dennis F. Thompson,[37] it is argued that this is a desirable approach to negotiating and resolving conflicts. I agree with Monique Deveaux that deliberative democracy is an invaluable resource for thinking about how liberal democracies and minority cultural groups might mediate conflicts of culture.[38] In turn, Chapter 4 discusses the concept of coercion. Liberal democracies

---

[33] Jürgen Habermas, *Theory of Communicative Action* (Cambridge: Polity, 1986); Jürgen Habermas, *Between Facts and Norms* (Cambridge: Polity, 1996); Jürgen Habermas, 'Discourse Ethics: Notes on a Program of Philosophical Justification', in Fred Dallmayr and Seyla Benhabib (eds), *The Communicative Ethics Controversy* (Cambridge, MA: MIT Press, 1990).

[34] Joshua Cohen, 'Procedure and Substance in Deliberative Democracy', in James Bohman and William Rehg (eds), *Deliberative Democracy: Essays on Reason and Politics* (Cambridge, MA and London: MIT Press, 1997): 407–438; Joshua Cohen, 'Deliberation and Democratic Legitimacy', in Bohman and Rehg, *Deliberative Democracy*: 67–92, reprinted in Alan Hamlin and Philip Petit (eds), *The Good Polity: Normative Analysis of the State* (Oxford: Basil Blackwell, 1998): 17–34.

[35] Seyla Benhabib, 'Deliberative Rationality and Models of Democratic Legitimacy', *Constellations*, 1 (1994): 26–52.

[36] John S. Dryzek, *Deliberative Democracy and Beyond* (Oxford: Oxford University Press, 2002).

[37] Amy Gutmann and Dennis F. Thompson, *Democracy and Disagreement* (Cambridge, MA: Belknap Press, 1998); Amy Gutmann and Dennis F. Thompson, *Why Deliberative Democracy?* (Princeton, NJ: Princeton University Press, 2004).

[38] Monique Deveaux, *Gender and Justice in Multicultural Liberal States* (Oxford: Oxford University Press, 2009). See also Monique Deveaux, *Cultural Pluralism and Dilemmas of Justice* (Ithaca, NY: Cornell University Press, 2000): 138–179.

prefer to resolve disputes in non-coercive ways but sometimes setting limits via coercive mechanisms is unavoidable in order to maintain a just, well-ordered society.

Moving from theory to practice, the second part of the book considers concrete examples in which the above principles can be applied in delineating relationships between cultures and the scope of interference that a liberal society may apply in the business of illiberal subcultures. This part of the book is divided into four chapters. I first distinguish between two kinds of harm: physical and non-physical. Chapters 5 and 6 discuss interference in minority affairs when they engage in physical harm to others. Relevant considerations are the extent of harm, consent (or lack of) of those who are subjected to harm, parental care and responsibility, significance of religious and culture norms and values, and the extent to which a liberal society should intervene in group and individual affairs. I first analyse the practices of suttee, self-starvation, scarring, murder for family honour, female circumcision and FGM and in the following chapter examine male circumcision. The liberal culture is non-violent in nature and acts of physical harm startle us. It is argued that liberal democracy should examine several factors, including the underlying reasons for the infliction of harm and the possibility of exiting the community. Liberal democracy should interfere in the business of its subcultures when they inflict *significant* physical harm on its members. A great deal of attention is devoted to explaining what sorts of harm are significant.

One might question the need for discussing murder for family honour. Murder is murder. It should not be tolerated. I see a need for such discussion in order to accentuate the meeting point between strong liberals, who are generally opposed to government interference and who champion tolerance, and strong multiculturalists, who are generally supportive of group rights and cultural autonomy. I argue that responsible governments should perceive murder for family honour as ordinary murders and that if multiculturalism is used as an excuse for ignoring or minimizing the severity of the crime then this is an abuse of multiculturalism.

The question of state interference seems to be trickier when the harm is not physical. Chapter 7 examines North American court cases which dealt with the powers of tribes over their members and the denial of property from members who were expelled for apostasy, denial of education to women and forced marriages for girls and young women, while Chapter 8 analyses the denial of education from group members in order to preserve the community and make it difficult for members to integrate into the larger community. Can a community deny education to its children on religious grounds and by this effectively make their exiting from the community extremely difficult? The discussion focuses on Amish education. It is argued that Amish children have a right to adequate education, and that the liberal state should regulate and have oversight of their education. The liberal state is obligated to ensure that such schools provide their students with the training necessary for pursuit of a broad range of careers and for full citizenship in a pluralistic, democratic society.[39] Furthermore, while the impetus for researching this chapter was to learn about the consequences of denying education to children in the name of group rights, my research revealed that Amish isolation also results in physical harm to children. The stories about repeated child abuse increase the urgency for monitoring and aiding the Amish education system.

Joseph Raz wrote that one of the difficulties in making multiculturalism politically acceptable stems from the enmity between members of different cultural groups, accompanied by disapproval of the other culture 'for its decadence or vulgarity ... for its treatment of women, or something else'.[40] Such enmity, maintained Raz, is sometimes justified and sometimes it is due to ignorance and bigotry that can be eradicated.[41] The final part of this book examines two case studies of majority coercion: France and Israel. France is a secular, unitary democracy while Israel is the only Jewish democracy in the world. These two countries are interesting because, while democracies, France and Israel challenge the liberal discourse. The extent of liberalism in both countries is circumscribed. Both adopted discriminatory policies against their significant Muslim minorities. Both are lands of immigration and polyethnic states. Both France and Israel are in the process of continued deliberation with their respective minorities about their rights and freedoms. In the Democracy Index 2019, France is described as a full democracy while Israel is described as a flawed democracy.[42] In the Democracy Index of 2018, both countries were described as flawed rather than full democracies.[43] Interestingly, in 2018 France was ranked twenty-nine on the Index while Israel was ranked thirty.

Full democracies are countries in which basic political freedoms and civil liberties are respected and which tend to be underpinned by a political culture conducive to the flourishing of democracy. In full democracies the government is well-functioned, the media are independent and diverse, the judiciary is independent

[39] James G. Dwyer, *Religious Schools v. Children's Rights* (Ithaca, NY: Cornell University Press, 1998).
[40] Joseph Raz, 'Multiculturalism: A Liberal Perspective', *Dissent*, 4 (Winter 1994): 72.
[41] Ibid.
[42] *Democracy Index 2019: A Year of Democratic Setbacks and Popular Protest*, a report by the Economist Intelligence Unit, https://pages.eiu.com/rs/753-RIQ-438/images/Democracy%20Index%202019.pdf?mkt_tok=eyJpIjoiTldVeFpHTmhaakV5TldJNSIsInQiOiJyTkZVcHVNU2YoeExWZURKWTlSQUtBOVwvSE91XC9SS2FpR2tUendWNUNKViNcLzEwZlEyUXRxZDNHbnZNMGkoOEkod3ZaZndsK2U5ZohiYk4oMFArTolubVk3bkZGMGMipXRzhMb3hIS1VzdUk1aVBaOVR6TmpNaHdhU1wvWUd1SkRLTDUifQ%3D%3D.
[43] *Democracy Index 2018: Me Too? Political Participation, Protest and Democracy*, a report by the Economist Intelligence Unit, https://275rzy1ul4252pt1hv2dqyuf-wpengine.netdna-ssl.com/wp-content/uploads/2019/01/Democracy_Index_2018.pdf. *The Economist* explained that the key development that elevated France to the 'full democracy' category was the 'national debate' held in January–March 2019, in response to the 'gilets jaunes' protests that began in late 2018, with demonstrations across the country fuelled by anger at stagnant wages, cuts to public services and a sense that the government was out of touch with ordinary people. The national debate was an effort to engage with the public via democratic processes.

and judicial decisions are enforced, and there is an effective system of checks and balances. *Flawed democracies*, on the other hand, are countries that have free and fair elections and basic civil liberties are respected. However, flawed democracies have significant weaknesses, including problems in governance, an underdeveloped political culture and low levels of political participation.[44]

In France, coercion is employed to preserve and promote secularism. This urge to secure secularism has been fuelled in recent years by fearing terrorism. Terrorism has become a significant threat. It is also a threat for Israel, where coercion is employed to preserve and promote the Jewishness of the state. In both France and Israel critique of multiculturalism is prevalent, arguing that it is bad for women, bad for democracy and is related to terrorism.

A recent study that examined levels of government-based religious discrimination found that France exhibits the highest rate of government-based religious discrimination and hostility to religion among the European and Western democracies that were examined.[45] French *laïcité* is about separation between state and religion through state protection of individuals from the claims of religion. In recent years, the concept of *laïcité* fuelled French intolerance regarding its religious minorities, particularly Muslims. The tension between republicanism, neutrality and the spirit of *laïcité*, on the one hand, and the values of liberty, equality and solidarity, on the other, encapsulates today's hostility to multiculturalism. Chapter 9 probes the debates concerning cultural policies in the face of what its government perceives as a challenge to its national raison d'être, including those revolving around the burqa, the niqab and the burkini. Freedom of religion is restricted to the private sphere while secularism is celebrated in the public sphere. It is argued that the burqa and niqab ban is neither just nor reasonable in the eyes of these women and girls, their families and community, and that paternalism that holds that the ban is for the women's own good is a poor, coercive excuse. Claims for paternalistic coercion to protect adult women from their culture when they do not ask for protection are not sufficiently reasonable to receive vindication.

Chapter 10 examines Israel, a Jewish-ethnic democracy.[46] The framework of governance is democratic, but its underpinning concepts give precedence to Judaism over the Respect for Others Principle, and the Harm Principle. Israeli leaders have tried to settle tensions between Judaism and democracy at the expense of liberalism. Consequently, Israel has adopted illiberal policies and practices that

---

[44] *Democracy Index 2019*: 53.

[45] Jonathan Fox, *Thou Shalt Have No Other Gods before Me: Why Governments Discriminate against Religious Minorities* (New York: Cambridge University Press, 2020).

[46] Sammy Smooha, 'The Model of Ethnic Democracy: Israel as a Jewish and Democratic State', *Nations and Nationalism* 8(4) (October 2002): 475–503; Sammy Smooha, 'Types of Democracy and Modes of Conflict-Management in Ethnically Divided Societies', *Nations and Nationalism*, 8(4) (October 2002): 423–431; Sammy Smooha, 'Israel70 The Global Enigma', *Fathom* (July 2018), http://fathomjournal.org/israel70-the-global-enigma/.

are discriminatory in nature, preferring Jews over others. The institutional discrimination against the Palestinian minority is in the focus of attention. It is argued that if Israel aspires to be an egalitarian-liberal democracy it should respect secularism and not discriminate against non-Jews.

CONCLUSION

Liberal democracies have a long history of seeking to accommodate ethnocultural differences. With respect to national minorities, liberal democracies have accorded these groups some degree of regional political autonomy, so that they can maintain themselves as separate and self-governing, culturally and linguistically distinct societies. With respect to immigrants, liberal democracies have characteristically expected that these groups will integrate into mainstream institutions, but generally speaking have become more tolerant of the expression of immigrant identities and practices within these institutions.

Liberal democracies have been consistent in following these general patterns. Of course, countries vary in their cultural considerations and norms. Therefore, developing a comprehensive liberal theory of minority rights and outlining the extent of state interference in minority affairs is of the utmost importance for the future of liberal democracies. We need to set reasonable standards for reconciliation between liberalism and multiculturalism, between individual rights and group rights. This book, I hope, will promote a debate on what cultural conduct is allowed in a liberal democratic society and what should be reasonably excluded. This discussion is important not only in academic circles but also for judges and public policy decision-makers.

PART I

Theory

1

Just Liberal Democracy

At his best, man is the noblest of all animals; separated from law and justice he is the worst.

Aristotle

Justice is a contested concept. People have different conceptions of justice, and the ideology that underpins its understanding is of great significance. In this chapter I start laying the theoretical principles that underpin just, reasonable multiculturalism. As my aim is to formulate a just way for accommodating different, sometimes incompatible interests of various groups and individuals, I first explain what liberal democracy is and the difference between formal and speculative democracy. Then I outline the concept of justice. In the process I avail myself of the teachings of liberal philosophers, mainly Immanuel Kant, John Stuart Mill and John Rawls. I elucidate two important concepts without which it is impossible to imagine any liberal democracy: respect for others, inspired by Kantian and Rawlsian philosophies, and the Harm Principle derived from Millian ethics. It is the Harm Principle that guides us in prescribing boundaries to conduct. The necessity in introducing boundaries is further explained by the concept of the 'democratic catch'.

LIBERAL DEMOCRACY

Liberalism was a product of the climate of opinion that emerged at the time of the Renaissance and the Reformation. As the political expression of the new individualism, it was a political declaration of faith in the autonomy of human reason and the essential goodness of man. In the nineteenth century, John Stuart Mill wrote in chapter 4 of *On Liberty*, 'Of the Limits to the Authority of Society over the Individual', that people may take advice from others but the final decision should be made by them. Each person should be the final judge of her action: 'Considerations to aid his judgment, urgings to strengthen his will, may be offered to him and even pushed at him by others; but he is the final judge. Any errors that he is likely to commit against advice and warning are far outweighed by the evil of allowing others to constrain him to what they think to be his good.'[1] The belief in human reason and in the essential goodness of humanity reflected the political, social, religious and economic aspirations of the rising commercial classes. The liberal ideology grew in its influence and prominence. Thus, in *The Rise of European Liberalism*, Harold Laski argues that liberalism has been, over the last four centuries, 'the outstanding doctrine of Western Civilization'.[2]

The preservation of individual rights and the emancipation of the individual from public control mean that all people in liberal democracy enjoy the same equal rights. No group is preferred over others. The majority decides the identity of government, but it should not undermine equal rights for all. In opposition to feudalism, liberalism established the legal equality of all citizens and challenged the right of the monarch to govern except in the interests of the citizens. Thus, Crawford Brough Macpherson wrote,

> Liberalism had always meant freeing the individual from the outdated restraints of old established institutions. By the time liberalism emerged as liberal democracy this became a claim to free all individuals equally and to free them to use and develop their human capacities fully.[3]

It is from the concept of a person as an autonomous individual, whose actions are the product of choice and purpose, that the philosophy of a free society is constructed.[4] The liberal society makes the common good available not to a privileged class but to all, so far as the capacity of each permits the individual to share it. The end of such a society, according to the Millian view, is to increase the capacities by which the individual can contribute to the common good.

To facilitate and promote individualism, many defenders of liberalism argue that liberal policies should refrain from identifying essential interests with a particular

---

[1] J.S. Mill, *Utilitarianism, Liberty, and Representative Government* (London: J.M. Dent, 1948): Everyman's edition, 133.

[2] H.J. Laski, *The Rise of European Liberalism: An Essay in Interpretation* (London: Unwin Books, 1962): 5. See also Edmund Fawcett, *Liberalism: The Life of an Idea* (Princeton, NJ: Princeton University Press, 2018); Daniel Ziblatt, *Conservative Parties and the Birth of Democracy* (Cambridge: Cambridge University Press, 2017); Steven Vincent, *Benjamin Constant and the Birth of French Liberalism* (London: Palgrave, 2011); L.T. Hobhouse, *Liberalism* (London: Oxford University Press, 1945).

[3] C.B. Macpherson, *The Life and Times of Liberal Democracy* (Oxford: Oxford University Press, 1977): 21. This same argument also appears in F.A. Hayek's writing, where he says that libertarians start from the basic assumption that the comprehension of social reality, from a scientific *or* ethical point of view, necessitates an entirely individualistic orientation. See F.A. Hayek, *The Counter-Revolution of Science* (New York: Glencoe Free Press, 1955): 36–43, www.archive.org/stream/counterrevolutio0030197mbp/counterrevolutio0030197mbp_djvu.txt.

[4] John Christman, 'Autonomy in Moral and Political Philosophy', *The Stanford Encyclopedia of Philosophy* (Spring 2018 Edition), Edward N. Zalta (ed.), https://plato.stanford.edu/archives/spr2018/entries/autonomy-moral/.

conception of the good life, and shrink from the possibility that the government, which could be associated with one or more fragments of society, might impose its values on others, either by propagation or by force.[5] Neutrality ensures that every person will be able to pursue her conception of the good. The assumption is that should governments not be neutral regarding the plurality of convictions that prevail in society, then their bias could generate intolerance.[6] Neutrality is also a contested concept among liberals. While neutrality is a guiding principle, it is not immune to qualifications.

Conceptually, one should note, the idea of neutrality is strongly connected with pluralism. The idea of pluralism is an essential element of democracy, an indispensable feature for having the potential for a good life. Methodologically, the idea of neutrality is placed within the broader concept of anti-perfectionism. While perfectionism holds that the state may promote a specific conception of the good, anti-perfectionism perceives this promotion as illegitimate. The implementation and promotion of conceptions of the good, though worthy in themselves, are not regarded as a legitimate matter for governmental action.[7] Governments ought to acknowledge that each person has her own interest in acting according to her own convictions; that each person must enjoy autonomy and have the freedom to hold her ideals.

Thus, liberals argue that democracies should allow citizens freedom to develop their own conceptions.[8] Bearing in mind that neutrality proscribes any attempts on

---

[5] Robert Nozick, *Anarchy, State and Utopia* (New York: Basic Books, 1974): 33, 48–51, 271–274; Bruce A. Ackerman, *Social Justice in the Liberal State* (New Haven and London: Yale University Press, 1980): 11–12, 347–378; Ronald M. Dworkin, 'Why Liberals Should Believe in Equality?', *New York Review of Books*, 30(1) (1983): 32–4; Ronald M. Dworkin, *A Matter of Principle* (Oxford: Clarendon Press, 1985): 191–194, 205; Ronald M. Dworkin, *Justice for Hedgehogs* (Cambridge, MA: Belknap, 2011); Will Kymlicka, *Liberalism, Community, and Culture* (Oxford: Clarendon Press, 1989), esp. 76–85, 95–96; Will Kymlicka, 'Liberal Individualism and Liberal Neutrality', *Ethics*, 99(4) (1989): 883–905, esp. 899–905; Peter De Marneffe, 'Liberalism, Liberty, and Neutrality', *Philosophy & Public Affairs*, 19(3) (1990): 253–274; C. Edwin Baker, *Human Liberty and Freedom of Speech* (New York: Oxford University Press, 1992); Floyd Abrams, *The Soul of the First Amendment* (New Haven, CT: Yale University Press, 2017).

[6] Collis Tahzib, 'Perfectionism: Political not Metaphysical', *Philosophy & Public Affairs*, 47(2) (2019): 144–178; Thomas Hurka, *Perfectionism* (Oxford: Oxford University Press, 1993); George Sher, *Beyond Neutrality* (Cambridge: Cambridge University Press, 1997); Raphael Cohen-Almagor, *The Boundaries of Liberty and Tolerance* (Gainesville: The University Press of Florida, 1994); Raphael Cohen-Almagor, *The Scope of Tolerance* (London and New York: Routledge, 2006).

[7] Joseph Raz, *The Morality of Freedom* (Oxford: Clarendon Press, 1986): 110. For an elaborated discussion, see Raphael Cohen-Almagor, 'Between Neutrality and Perfectionism', *The Canadian Journal of Law & Jurisprudence*, 7(2) (1994): 217–36.

[8] John Rawls, *A Theory of Justice* (Oxford: Oxford University Press, 1971): 327–328, 446–452; John Rawls, *Political Liberalism* (New York: Columbia University Press, 1993): 190–195; Dworkin, *A Matter of Principle*; Charles Larmore, *Patterns of Moral Complexity* (Cambridge: Cambridge University Press, 1987); Ronald Dworkin, *Sovereign Virtue* (Cambridge, MA: Harvard University Press, 2000); T.M. Scanlon, *What We Owe to Each Other* (Cambridge, MA:

the part of governments to force others to lead lives in which they do not believe, a question arises whether neutrality should oblige governments to remain silent in the face of such phenomena as suttee (also spelled 'sati') and FGM (both practices are discussed in Chapter 5), or prohibit abortions even when there is a danger to the life of the mother,[9] or abandon the elderly.[10] The question, then, is whether or not every norm that any culture values or considers to be of importance is to have a lasting place in the framework of a liberal society.

The term 'democracy' has been used in conjunction with the terms 'monarchy' and 'aristocracy', and this trilogy has been employed to discern situations of monopoly, of oligopoly and of equality. A state is democratic not 'if' but in so far as the great mass of the population can exercise an effective influence on the process of decision-making. Thus, it implies that democracy is a matter of degree and not a fixed concept, and that it is more useful to think in terms of a scale than to attempt to lay down conditions for democracy. The same is true for the notion of liberal society. The democratic creed is concerned not only with majority rule but also with preserving the rights of minorities. Here let me mention Lord Acton who states that the most certain test by which we may judge whether a country is truly free is the amount of security enjoyed by minorities.[11]

Democracy is about procedure and structure. Like any form of government, democracy is a system of government in which political power is exercised by the state over individuals within it. The term is derived from the Greek words *demos* δῆμος (the people), and *kratos* Κράτος (power), meaning the rule of the people: political authority rests with the people and is exercised in order to establish, modify or abolish the system of power. Democracy involves non-governmental as well as

Belknap, 2000); Corey Brettschneider, *When the State Speaks, What Should It Say?* (Princeton, NJ: Princeton University Press, 2012); Alan Patten, 'Liberal Neutrality: A Reinterpretation and Defense', *Journal of Political Philosophy*, 20(3) (2012): 249–272.

9 Noya Rimalt, 'When Rights Don't Talk: Abortion Law and the Politics of Compromise', *Yale Journal of Law & Feminism*, 28 (2016–2017): 327–79; *Whole Woman's Health v. Hellerstedt*, 136 S. Ct. 2292 (2016); Rebecca B. Reingold and Lawrence O. Gostin, 'Women's Health and Abortion Rights: *Whole Woman's Health v Hellerstedt*', JAMA, 316(9) (2016): 925–6; John A. Robertson, 'Whole Woman's HealthHellerstedt and the Future of Abortion Regulation', *UC Irvine Law Review*, 7 (2017): 623–651; Raphael Cohen-Almagor and Yehuda Snir, 'The Decision Making Process of the Abortion High Committees', *Ha'refuah* (*Medicine*, The Journal of the Israeli Physicians Association), 138(12) (15 June 2000): 1009–1014 (Hebrew); *Roe v. Wade*, 410 U.S. 113 (1973).

10 In various Eskimo tribes individuals have recourse to suicide because of old age and a feeling that their social usefulness is ended, and to spare families the burden of caring for an unproductive member; other causes might be terminating a condition of serious illness, remorse, unrequited love and the prospect of starvation. A close relative is usually asked to act as executioner, but if the relative refuses the individual has to take his or her own life or ritually appease the spirits who already anticipate his or her end. See David Landy, 'Death: Anthropological Perspective', in Warren T. Reich (ed.), *Encyclopedia of Bioethics* (New York: The Free Press, 1978): Vol. 1, p. 224.

11 Baron John Emerich Edward Dalberg-Acton, *Essays on Freedom and Power* (Boston, MA: Beacon, 1948).

governmental decision-making. The growth of democracy has been associated with the flow of opinions, with free discussion of political issues, with the right to differ concerning them and with the settlement of the differences, not by sheer force but rather by resorting to notions of discovering what 'the will of the people' is.

Democracy can be considered as a way of administering and facilitating discussion among people, parties and organizations that hold different, at times conflicting, interests. The aim is not to secure complete agreement on every question, though democracy certainly welcomes crystallization of consensus and agreement. Democracy does not demand the creation of a society which consists of people who parrot the decisions of the governing body, but rather it accepts the right to be different, recognizing that there can be a range of opinions. This acceptance implies, in turn, an agreement on the ways in which these differences could be settled in practice. Therefore the commonly accepted principle is compromise, a principle whereby that which divides is rejected in favour of that which unites the people. However, this is not to say that compromise is a self-sufficient principle that can be divorced from moral or other considerations. Compromise between two or more groups is not to come at the expense of the rights of others. I elaborate on this in Chapter 3.

At the heart of democratic theory lies the principle of popular will. Political power belongs to the public as a whole and not merely to a single person or a particular limited group of people. The citizens participate in influencing and shaping the policies which concern their lives. They share the duties and rights of political life; they possess citizenship burdens and benefits, rights and liberties; they initiate policies and govern the political authority. Each citizen is granted one vote to elect representatives who execute the general will. Participation in the political processes and representation of the public are essential for the working of democracy, so much so that the modern form of democracy is often called participatory democracy.[12] The state is regarded as an organization whose aim is to serve the given society, and to make it more of a community. Separation of powers ensures checks and balances between the powerful democratic agencies. In a democracy this means making the community freer and of a participatory character.

Democracy provides a framework of governance aiming to entertain as many public interests as possible, to resolve conflicts and to offer just accommodations. Historically considered, there is an intimate relation between democracy and liberalism. While democracy is significantly older than liberalism, democracy has been sustained by liberalism as a theory of government and society. Most modern democracies sustain and promote liberal values.

---

[12] Carole Pateman, *Participation and Democratic Theory* (Cambridge: Cambridge University Press, 1970); Michael Menser, *We Decide! Theories and Cases in Participatory Democracy* (Philadelphia: Temple University Press, 2018); Nils Hertting and Clarissa Kugelberg (eds), *Local Participatory Governance and Representative Democracy* (London: Routledge, 2017); Thomas Zittel and Dieter Fuchs (eds), *Participatory Democracy and Political Participation* (London: Routledge, 2006).

2. Difference Principle. Social and economic inequalities should be arranged so that they are both (a) to the greatest benefit of the least advantaged persons, and (b) attached to offices and positions open to all under conditions of equality of opportunity.[22] The Difference Principle means that society may undertake projects that require giving some persons more power, income, status, etc. than others; for example, paying physicians and upper-level managers more than assembly-line operatives, provided that the following conditions are met:

(a) the project will make life better off for the people who are now worst off, for example by raising the living standards of everyone in the community and empowering the least advantaged persons to the extent consistent with their well-being; and

(b) access to the privileged positions is not blocked by discrimination according to irrelevant criteria. All social primary goods are to be distributed equally unless good reasons, working for the advantage of the least favoured, are introduced.[23]

The *second stage* is a constitutional convention in which the veil of ignorance is partly lifted, so that people can know what societies they belong to; but, nevertheless, they are still unaware which people they are. At this second stage they choose a constitution, which includes the two principles of justice. The constitution will provide some form of majority rule, since it must secure equal liberties of voting, and equal opportunities for competing for governmental posts.[24]

The *third stage* is that of legislation. The legislators are still ignorant of their personal circumstances. To be just, the laws must comply only with the two principles of justice and the constitution. Finally, at the *fourth stage* judges apply the laws, and then the veil of ignorance is totally removed.[25]

According to Rawls, the liberties of equal citizenship in a just society are taken as settled; the rights secured by justice are not subjected to political bargaining or to the calculus of social welfare.[26] An injustice is tolerable only when it is necessary to avoid an even greater injustice. Being first virtues of human activities, truth and justice are uncompromising. Behind the veil of ignorance, when one does not know one's gender, culture, nationality, religion or any other dividing factors, one would wish to ensure that justice prevails across the board, without discrimination or any form of favouritism. Justice knows no cultural boundaries. Applying the veil of ignorance would lead to a just and reasonable society.

---

[22] Ibid., 302.
[23] Ibid., 303.
[24] Ibid., section 2:10, at 54–60.
[25] Ibid., chapter 4, at 195–257.
[26] Ibid., 3–4.

OVERLAPPING CONSENSUS

Rawls' theory of justice as fairness is a moral conception that provides us with an account of the cooperative virtues suitable for a political doctrine in view of the conditions and requirements of a constitutional regime. It is a theory of an 'overlapping consensus' between different groups and individuals with divergent doctrines as to the fair procedures for making political demands in a democratic society, where mutual respect, toleration and fairness must be the norm. In *Political Liberalism*, Rawls explains that by an 'overlapping consensus' he means a consensus that is affirmed by the opposing religious, philosophical and moral doctrines likely to thrive over generations in a more or less just constitutional democracy. Such a consensus is moral both in its object and grounds, and so is distinct from a consensus founded solely on group or self-interest. It supposes agreement about the underpinning ideas of society as a fair system of cooperation and of citizens as reasonable, rational, free and equal.[27]

Rawls believes that the democratic public culture is obligated to pursue forms of social cooperation which can be achieved on a basis of mutual respect. This cooperation involves the acceptance of common procedures to regulate political conduct. Citizens are to be accorded equal respect in their pursuit of their idea of the good. Rawls' concept of justice is independent of and prior to the concept of goodness in that its principles limit the conceptions of the good that are permissible. Rawls' ideal polity would not be congenial to those whose conception of the good is inconsiderate and coercive, inflicts damage on others or derives profit at the expense of others. The constitution of such controversial beliefs is unjust as it does not enable individuals to make their shared institutions and basic arrangements mutually acceptable. Mutual respect would allow social cooperation among individuals who affirm fundamentally different conceptions of the good. Rawls does not exclude religious groups with strong beliefs who may demand strict conformity and allegiance from their members, but he could not endorse the formation of a theocracy.[28]

Gutmann and Thompson explain that mutual respect requires a favourable attitude towards, and constructive engagement with, the persons with whom one disagrees and consists in an excellence of character that permits a democracy to flourish in the face of fundamental moral disagreement.[29] Persons, as moral agents, have their conceptions of a moral life, and accordingly determine what they deem to

---

[27] Rawls, *Political Liberalism*, 149.

[28] Rawls, *A Theory of Justice*, sects. 33–35; John Rawls, 'Fairness to Goodness', *Philosophical Review*, 84 (1975): sect. VI; John Rawls, 'Representation of Freedom and Equality', *Journal of Philosophy*, 77(9) (1980): sect. II; John Rawls, 'Justice as Fairness: Political Not Metaphysical', *Philosophy & Public Affairs*, 14(3) (1985): sect. VI; John Rawls, 'The Priority of Right and Ideas of the Good', *Philosophy & Public Affairs*, 17(4) (1988): sect. VII; Rawls, *Political Liberalism*, 197–198.

[29] Amy Gutmann and Dennis Thompson, *Democracy and Disagreement* (Cambridge, MA: Belknap, 1996): 79.

be the most valuable or best form of life worth leading. It is emphasized that one's conception of the good does not have to be compatible with moral excellence. It does not mean a conception of justice. The assumption is that a conception of the good comprises a basic part of our overall moral scheme and that it is public insofar as it is something we advance as good for others as well as for ourselves.

The Rawlsian conception of justice provides a good starting point for developing a doctrine of *just*, reasonable multiculturalism. Notwithstanding its reputation for being indifferent to identity recognition, the Rawlsian theory of justice contains some important ingredients: an aspiration to establish a just constitution; emphasis on equality; the idea of the veil of ignorance that should guide us in our understanding of the other; the desire for overlapping consensus; the understanding that it is impossible to establish a democratic polity that would include all conceptions of the good; and the insistence on mutual respect. The argument in support of *mutual* respect is crucial for achieving a well-ordered society.

In a reasonable and well-ordered society, people are generally disposed to cooperate with each other. They are disposed to cooperate by virtue of their mutual basic concern and respect for each other, or by virtue of one's attachment to an identity or project one shares with the other. People strive to accommodate and find ways to live together. Citizens of a reasonable and well-ordered society have some degree of solidarity and good will that underpin the whole societal structure. They share the burdens and responsibilities of collective self-governance and they share a basic commitment to democracy.[30]

To argue that some conceptions of the good may have no place requires a recognition that *there are* some values that underlie a liberal society, that cause members of that society to view some other conceptions as disagreeable. It is important to complement communal solidarity with the institutional protection of individuals. Some norms and moral codes must be shared by members of the community, despite their cultural differences. This is not to say that one dominant culture, or one dominant conception of the good exists, but that some basic norms should be safeguarded in order to make the working of a liberal democratic system possible and to ensure its survival. These accepted norms, by virtue of their existence, enable each individual and group to pursue their beliefs, as long as convictions are not contradictory to them. These norms set limitations on the range of values that society can respect. Neutrality is prescribed to ensure standoff from support for what, prima facie, is perceived to be valuable and moral conceptions of the good. The qualification 'so far as it is socially possible' implies a place for some restrictions on citizens and organizations to maintain the framework of society,

---

[30] Jürgen Habermas, *The Structural Transformations of the Public Sphere* (Cambridge, MA: MIT Press, 1989): 27–31; Henry S. Richardson, *Democratic Autonomy: Public Reasoning about the Ends of Policy* (Oxford: Oxford University Press, 2002): 155; Jeffrey C. Alexander, *The Civic Sphere* (New York: Oxford University Press, 2006): 13–50.

but when introduced they require some justification. The justifications for restrictions should not be abusive but reasonable, measured and well considered. Racism, hate speech, political and ideological extremism, gun violence and terrorism continue to test the parameters and boundaries of liberalism.

LIMITING CONCEPTIONS OF THE GOOD

Irreconcilable and incommensurable conceptions of the good often occur. Having diverse ideals, in light of which people lead different ways of life, is the normal condition.[31] Generally speaking, this variety is perceived to be a good thing; to quote Rawls, it is rational for members of a just society to want their plans to be different.[32] For, as Rawls explains, human beings have talents and abilities the totality of which is unrealizable by any one person or group of persons. We not only benefit from the complementary nature of our developed inclinations, but we take pleasure in one another's activities.[33] Hence, liberal inclination is to allow citizens to follow their conceptions of the good rather than being obliged to live with convictions they do not uphold.[34]

This is to mean that not *all* conceptions of the good should be open as options to be pursued in a liberal democratic society. It is possible to be liberal and exclusionary at the same time. Liberal democracy should not remain neutral when third parties, especially vulnerable third parties, are harmed. Quite the opposite. Liberals argue that it is the responsibility of liberal democracy to protect vulnerable groups in society.[35] Not every norm that any religion or culture values or deems important may be permitted to endure within the democratic framework. The question, then, is which conceptions it is just and reasonable to exclude?

Rawls explicitly argues that by virtue of its culture and institutions, 'any society will prove uncongenial to some ways of life'.[36] A decent society accepts certain

---

[31] Rawls, *Political Liberalism*, 190–195; Nozick, *Anarchy, State and Utopia*; Ackerman, *Social Justice in the Liberal State*; R.M. Dworkin, 'Why Liberals Should Believe in Equality?' *New York Review of Books*, 30(1) (1983): 32–34, at 32; Dworkin, *A Matter of Principle*; Will Kymlicka, *Liberalism, Community, and Culture*; Will Kymlicka, *Multicultural Citizenship: A Liberal Theory of Minority Rights* (Oxford: Oxford University Press, 1995).

[32] John Rawls, 'A Well-Ordered Society', in P. Laslett and J. Fishkin (eds), *Philosophy, Politics, and Society* (Oxford: Basil Blackwell, 1979): 6–20; John Rawls, 'The Idea of an Overlapping Consensus', *Oxford Journal of Legal Studies*, 7(1) (1987): 1–25.

[33] Rawls, *A Theory of Justice*, 448.

[34] Ackerman, *Social Justice in the Liberal State*.

[35] Susan Mendus, *Toleration and the Limits of Liberalism* (London: Macmillan, 1989); Cohen-Almagor, *The Scope of Tolerance*; Steven J. Heyman, *Free Speech and Human Dignity* (New Haven, CT: Yale University Press, 2008); Jeremy Waldron, *The Harm in Hate Speech* (Cambridge, MA: Harvard University Press, 2012).

[36] Rawls, 'The Priority of Right and Ideas of the Good', 265–266; Rawls, *Political Liberalism*, 197. See also John Rawls, 'Fairness to Goodness', *Philosophical Review*, 84 (1975): 536–554, sect. VI; Rawls, 'Representation of Freedom and Equality', 535–554, sect. II. Isaiah Berlin holds that we cannot conceive a situation which would allow joint realization of all values in one society.

moral and legal requirements in order to maintain civility and justice. Its citizens recognize that non-liberal societies fail to treat people as truly free and equal and therefore concede that non-liberal societies are always properly subject to some form of sanction.[37]

This issue of limiting some conceptions of the good is reiterated in *Political Liberalism*, where Rawls argues that some conceptions will die out in a just constitutional regime. He distinguishes between comprehensive doctrines and *reasonable* comprehensive doctrines. Comprehensive doctrines include conceptions of what is of value in human life, as well as ideals of personal virtue and character, of friendship and of familial and associational relationships. They include the major religious, philosophical and moral aspects of human life; they organize and characterize recognized values, and they normally belong to, or draw upon, a tradition of thought and doctrine.[38] Reasonable comprehensive doctrines accept the essentials of a democratic regime[39] and some form of political argument for toleration.[40]

The most basic norms democracy has to secure are, in my opinion, respecting others as human beings (under the Respect for Others Principle), and not to inflict harm upon others (under the Millian Harm Principle).[41] I shall now turn to explain these basic norms by referring to the writings of Immanuel Kant and John Stuart Mill.

KANTIAN RESPECT FOR OTHERS PRINCIPLE

Kantian ethics is based upon reflexive self-consciousness. It speaks of respecting people as rational beings, and of autonomy in terms of self-legislation. The ability to be motivated by reason alone is called by Kant the autonomy of the will, to be contrasted with the 'heteronomy' of the action whose will is subject to external causes. An autonomous agent is someone who is able to overcome the promptings of all heteronomous counsels, such as those of self-interest, emotion and desire, should they be in conflict with reason. Only an autonomous being perceives genuine ends

There are logical, psychological and sociological limits on what range of values one society can respect in the lives of some of its citizens. Isaiah Berlin, 'The Pursuit of the Ideal', in Isaiah Berlin, *The Crooked Timber of Humanity* (Princeton, NJ: Princeton University Press, 2013). See also Bernard Williams's introduction to Berlin's *Concepts and Categories* (Oxford: Oxford University Press, 1980): xi–xviii and Brian Barry, *Theories of Justice* (London: Harvester, 1989).

37 Rawls, *The Law of Peoples* (Cambridge, MA: Harvard University Press, 2002): 60.

38 Rawls, *Political Liberalism*, 58–66. See also Amy Gutmann (ed.), *Multiculturalism: Examining the Politics of Recognition* (Princeton, NJ: Princeton University Press, 1994).

39 Rawls, *Political Liberalism*, xvi. See also Joseph Raz, 'Multiculturalism: A Liberal Perspective', *Dissent*, 4 (Winter 1994): 75.

40 Rawls, *The Law of Peoples*, 176.

41 Raphael Cohen-Almagor, *Speech, Media, and Ethics: The Limits of Free Expression* (Houndmills and New York: Palgrave Macmillan, 2005); Raphael Cohen-Almagor, *Confronting the Internet's Dark Side: Moral and Social Responsibility on the Free Highway* (New York and Washington, DC: Cambridge University Press and Woodrow Wilson Center Press, 2015).

of action (as opposed to mere objects of desire), and only such a being deserves our esteem, as the embodiment of rational choice. The autonomy of the will, Kant argues, 'is the sole principle of all moral laws, and of all duties which conform to them; on the other hand, heteronomy of the will not only cannot be the basis of any obligation, but is, on the contrary, opposed to the principle thereof, and to the morality of will'.[42] Autonomy is the foundation of human dignity and the source of liberal morality.

The notion of obligation instructs us how to behave. According to Kant, an action has moral worth only if it is performed from a sense of duty. Duty rather than purpose is the fundamental concept of ethics. It is the practical unconditional necessity of action and, therefore, it holds for all rational beings. Thus, it can be a law for all human wills. The moment one sets up a Categorical Imperative for oneself ('Act on maxims that can at the same time have themselves as universal laws of nature as their object'; that gives us the formula for an 'absolutely good will'[43]) and submits to it, one is then governed by reason; when reason becomes the master of one's desires, one is capable of imposing certain limitations on oneself. Duty commands us to accept moral codes because they are just, regardless of the other's attitude towards them. This deontological ethics proscribes a set of actions, with the effect of constraining our range of options, not because the results will be useful, but because this set of actions is incompatible with the concept of justice.[44] Transgression of the rights of others intends to make use of them merely as means, without considering that, as rational beings, they must always be esteemed at the same time as ends.

According to Kant, it is only through morality that a rational being can be a law-giving member in the realm of ends, and it is only through morality that a rational being can be an end in herself. Kant distinguishes between relative value and intrinsic value, explaining that people have intrinsic value, namely dignity. Kant identifies dignity with moral capacity, arguing that human beings are infinitely above any price: 'to compare it with, or weigh it against, things that have price would be to violate its holiness, as it were'.[45] In other words, 'morality, and humanity

---

[42] Immanuel Kant, *Critique of Practical Reason*, http://philosophy.eserver.org/kant/critique-of-practical-reaso.txt. For further deliberation, see Lawrence Jost and Julian Wuerth (eds), *Perfecting Virtue: New Essays on Kantian Ethics and Virtue Ethics* (Cambridge: Cambridge University Press, 2011).

[43] Immanuel Kant, *Groundwork for the Metaphysic of Morals*, chapter 2, www.redfuzzyjesus.com/files/kant-groundwork-for-the-metaphysics-of-morals.pdf. For discussion of the Categorical Imperative, see Robert Paul Wolff (ed.), *Kant* (London: Macmillan, 1968): 211–336; Paul Guyer, *Kant's System of Nature and Freedom* (Oxford: Clarendon Press, 2005): 146–168.

[44] Kant, *Foundations of the Metaphysics of Morals* (Indianapolis, IN: Bobbs-Merrill, 1969): 54–55. See also Paul Dietrichson, 'What Does Kant Mean by "Acting from Duty"?', in Wolff, *Kant*, 314–330.

[45] Immanuel Kant, *Foundations of the Metaphysics of Morals* (Indianapolis, IN: Bobbs-Merrill Educational Publishers, 1969) or www.redfuzzyjesus.com/files/kant-groundwork-for-the-metaphysics-of-morals.pdf.

insofar as it is capable of morality, is that which alone has dignity'.[46] Kant explains that such beings are not merely 'subjective ends' whose existence as a result of our action has value for us, but are 'objective ends', that is, things whose existence is an end in itself.[47] Each person has dignity and moral worth. People should be respected qua being persons. The concept of dignity is universal. Dignity cannot be qualified due to one's gender, race, religion, culture, class or any other characteristics, and it requires us to take responsibility for our conduct. As Dworkin suggests, the concept of dignity needs to be associated with the responsibilities each person must take for her own life vis-à-vis herself and others. Dignity requires owning up to what one has done.[48] 'The buck stops here', writes Dworkin, is an important piece of ethical wisdom.[49] At the same time, and in accordance with the Rawlsian conception, we insist on the requirement of mutuality. We ought to show respect for those who respect others.

I am invoking Kantian ethics in order to place dignity and respect for others as constitutive elements of a just, reasonable theory of multiculturalism. Following Kant, we may distinguish between *dignity as recognition* and *dignity as liability*. *Dignity as recognition* is about us recognizing the inner spark of the soul that we all possess, the inherent quality of the person. It is not given from the outside but rather is intrinsic to the bearer of dignity. People possess dignity as an inner source of worth. It is impossible to put a price tag on humans because this would denigrate them into mere objects. Kant unequivocally instructed: 'Man and, in general, every rational being exists as an end in himself and not merely as a means to be arbitrarily used by this or that will.'[50] In all their actions, humans must always be regarded as an end.

Dignity as liability requires us all to respect persons qua persons. People deserve to be accorded a certain treatment from birth. We are endowed with dignity and have the right to be treated with dignity. While people cannot expect genuine *concern* from fellow humans, we can expect *respect* from others.

---

[46] Immanuel Kant, *Groundwork of the Metaphysics of Morals*, https://cpb-us-w2.wpmucdn.com/blog.nus.edu.sg/dist/c/1868/files/2012/12/Kant-Groundwork-ngopby.pdf.

[47] Kant, *Groundwork of the Metaphysic of Morals*. For further discussion, see Ino Augsberg, '"The Moral Feeling within Me": On Kant's Concept of Human Freedom and Dignity as Auto-Heteronomy', in Dieter Grimm, Alexandra Kemmerer and Christoph Möllers (eds), *Human Dignity in Context* (Munich: Hart, 2018): 55–68.

[48] Dworkin asserts that people who blame others or society at large for their own mistakes, or who absolve themselves of any responsibility for their conduct by blaming genetic determinism, lack dignity. Dworkin, *Justice for Hedgehogs*, chap. 8.

[49] Dworkin, *Justice for Hedgehogs*, 210–211.

[50] Immanuel Kant, *Foundations of the Metaphysics of Morals* (Indianapolis, IN: Bobbs-Merrill Educational Publishers, 1969) or www.earlymoderntexts.com/assets/pdfs/kant1785.pdf. For further discussion, see Graham Bird (ed.), *A Companion to Kant* (Oxford: Blackwell, 2006); Samuel Moyn, 'The Secret History of Constitutional Dignity', in C. McCrudden (ed.), *Understanding Human Dignity* (Oxford: Oxford University Press, 2015): 95–121.

In patriarchal cultures, where honour is important and gender differences accentuated, women do not have a claim to honour as individuals. Their honour, and the honour of their families, are intertwined. They lack dignity as recognition as their inner spark is secondary. The concept of dignity as liability receives a twist by which females are not endowed with dignity which put liability on others to grant them respect. Instead, females themselves are liability. Their conduct is closely inspected so as to ensure that they do not dishonour and shame the family. This issue is discussed in the application part of this book (Chapters 5–10).

Per Kant, the Respect for Others Principle is formulated in positive terms. It prescribes people to respect those who respect them, but we cannot infer from it that, under all circumstances, people should disrespect those who disrespect them. The boundaries of tolerance are determined by the qualification of not harming others that is added to the Respect for Others Principle. Under the Harm Principle, restrictions on liberty may be prescribed when there are clear threats of immediate violence against some individuals or groups.[51] A similar idea was pronounced by Rabbi Hillel in his dictum: 'What is hateful to you do not do unto your fellow people.'[52]

Kantian ethics is deontological. Utilitarianism is consequentialist. The theory of just, reasonable multiculturalism adopts elements of both theories. These elements supplement each other. The theory promotes the ideas of the dignity of the person, perceiving each person as an end, showing respect for others, and refraining from harming others.

THE MILLIAN HARM PRINCIPLE

The Millian Harm Principle holds that something is eligible for restriction only if it causes harm to others. People may interfere with the other's liberty of action in order to protect themselves and to prevent injury to themselves or to others. Mill wrote in *On Liberty*: 'Acts of whatever kind, which, without justifiable cause, do harm to others, may be, and in the more important cases absolutely require to be, controlled by the unfavourable sentiments, and, when needful, by the active interference of mankind.'[53] Whether an act ought to be restricted remains to be calculated. Hence, in some situations, people are culpable not because of the act that they have performed, though this act might be morally wrong, but because of its

---

[51] To quote Mill, the end for which 'mankind are warranted, individually or collectively, in interfering with the liberty of action of any of their number, is self-protection'. J.S. Mill, *On Liberty*, in Mill, *Utilitarianism, Liberty and Representative Government*, 72–73. See also pp. 114, 138.

[52] 'The Golden Rule', *Think Humanism*, www.thinkhumanism.com/the-golden-rule.html. For further discussion, see Philipp Gisbertz, 'Overcoming Doctrinal School Thought: A Unifying Approach to Human Dignity', *Ratio Juris*, 31(2) (2018): 196–207.

[53] Mill, *On Liberty*, 72–73, 114. See also p. 138, or www.bartleby.com/130/3.html.

circumstances and its consequences. While Kant spoke of unqualified, imperative moral duties, Mill's philosophy is discretionary. Together the Kantian and Millian arguments make a forceful plea for moral, responsible conduct: always perceive others as ends in themselves rather than means to something and avoid harming others.

Upholding the Respect for Others Principle and the Harm Principle safeguards the rights of those who might find themselves in a disadvantageous position in society, such as women; ethnic, religious, national and cultural minorities; homosexuals, transgenders and others. Here I should clarify that since not all cases of disrespect are cases of harm (disobeying one's parents need not be harmful) and apparently not all cases of harm are cases of disrespect (deserved punishment is required in some sense), the formulation would be logically inconsistent were it to state 'respect those who do not harm others'. This would be a rather mixed, or unbalanced, mutuality principle. Therefore, I maintain that the mutuality principle speaks only of respect, and that it supplements the requirement of not harming others, but it does not and cannot stand by itself. Furthermore, the liberty which is granted by democracy is not to injure and to prejudice someone else's liberty. This, I suggest, is the idea of 'significant liberty', in the sense that one's liberty is significant for creating and maintaining one's views and actions if one does not interfere with and damage the other's liberty. People are free and autonomous creators, but they neither live in isolation nor in a vacuum; they live within humanity and must consider the effects of their deeds on the significant liberties of others.

When the doer's action inflicts harm upon others, interference in her liberty is vindicated if:

1. The action violates distinct and assignable obligations to another person.[54] Mill clarified that an action can be seen to violate such an obligation when
   a. the degree of harmfulness is weighty enough to outweigh the loss of freedom incurred as a result of the interference, *and*
   b. the damage is definite.[55]

In other words (a) + (b) are conducive to identify (1). Upholding the Respect for Others Principle and the Harm Principle safeguards the rights of those who are in a disadvantageous position in society.

---

[54] The degree and the probability of the harm still do not explain Mill's intention when speaking of 'assignable obligation' (*On Liberty*, 137). We may assume that by 'assignable' Mill meant 'undoubted': an obligation that one can clearly attribute to another.

[55] For further discussion, see Raphael Cohen-Almagor, 'Ends and Means in J.S. Mill's Utilitarian Theory', *The Anglo-American Law Review*, 26(2) (1997): 141–174; Raphael Cohen-Almagor, *Speech, Media, and Ethics: The Limits of Free Expression*; Raphael Cohen-Almagor, 'JS Mill's Boundaries of Freedom of Expression: A Critique', *Philosophy*, 92(4) (October 2017): 565–596.

John Rawls and John Stuart Mill, like many other liberals, are reluctant to elaborate on the limits of one's autonomy in liberal democracy. They feel much more comfortable speaking about the principles that underlie democracy and devote much less detailed discussion to the exceptions to the rules. Liberals prefer to speak of the general rules – liberty, tolerance (John Stuart Mill,[56] Alf Ross,[57] Alexander Meiklejohn,[58] Lee Bollinger[59]), justice (John Rawls,[60] Brian Barry,[61] Michael Walzer[62]) and rights (Hugo Black,[63] Aryeh Neier,[64] Ronald Dworkin,[65] Joel Feinberg,[66] Wayne Sumner,[67] among others). They all wish to promote liberty and tolerance; to urge governments not to apply partisan considerations that affirm principally their own interests and conceptions; to seek ways to accommodate different ways of life; and to reach compromises by which the system will respect variety and pluralism and at the same time continue to uphold the rationale of democracy which may be summarized by the twofold dictum: do not harm others; promote respect for others. All of them largely tend to ignore what I term the 'democratic catch'. Let me explain.

THE 'DEMOCRATIC CATCH'

One of the problems of any political system is that the principles which underlie and characterize it might also, through their application, endanger it and bring about its destruction. Democracy, in its liberal form, is no exception. Moreover, because democracy is a relatively young phenomenon, having been crystalized only after World War I, it lacks experience in dealing with the pitfalls involved in the working of the system. This is what I call the 'democratic catch'.

Any political system – theocratic, liberal, Marxist, Leninist, Maoist, etc. – is based on a given set of principles. The working of these principles is designed to promote values, which those systems hold dear. However, these same principles might endanger the very foundations of the political systems. The case is clear when authoritarian systems are pondered over. Any form of government that is based on

---

[56] Mill, *Utilitarianism, Liberty, and Representative Government*.

[57] Alf Ross, *Why Democracy?* (Cambridge, MA: Harvard University Press, 1952).

[58] Alexander Meiklejohn, *Political Freedom* (New York: Oxford University Press, 1965).

[59] Lee C. Bollinger, *The Tolerant Society* (Oxford: Clarendon Press, 1986).

[60] Rawls, *A Theory of Justice*; Rawls, *Political Liberalism*.

[61] Brian Barry, *Theories of Justice* (London: Harvester, 1989).

[62] Michael Walzer, *Spheres of Justice: A Defence of Pluralism and Equality* (New York: Basic Books, 1983).

[63] Hugo L. Black, 'The Bill of Rights', *New York University Law Review*, 35 (1960): 865–881.

[64] Aryeh Neier, *Defending My Enemy* (New York: E.P. Dutton, 1979).

[65] Ronald M. Dworkin, *Taking Rights Seriously* (London: Duckworth, 1977); Dworkin, *A Matter of Principle*.

[66] Joel Feinberg, *Rights, Justice, and the Bounds of Liberty* (Princeton, NJ: Princeton University Press, 1980).

[67] L.W. Sumner, *The Moral Foundations of Rights* (Oxford: Oxford University Press, 1987).

coercion is objectionable. One can presume that, if given the opportunity, the people would rebel against the oppressor and retain their liberty. People would like to live their lives as free human beings, with dignity, free from subjugation, pain and suffering. Thus, we can assume that despots will survive as long as they are successful in upholding and monitoring an efficient machinery of internal police, intelligence agencies and security offices whose role is to deny freedom. The very principles of the oppressing system, be it dictatorship (rule of one), oligarchy (rule of few), theocracy (rule of religious sages) or fascism (rule of one who embodies the state) are those that will open the way for its destruction. One can do almost anything with bayonets, but one cannot sit on them. Sitting on bayonets for a long time will cause bleeding, and eventually will exhaust the regime's energies and consume its power. The very principles designed to bolster the power of the one, or of the few, at the expense of the many, would lead eventually to the system's destruction.

While clearly the foundations of authoritarian coercion bring about the destruction of the system, the case seems to be different for democracies, where governance is based on liberty and tolerance. Unlike forms of oppression that deny basic human rights, undermine the dignity of the person and harm others, liberal democracy sustains and promotes human rights, the dignity of the person, and its motto is not to harm others. Democracy is the only political system that perceives tolerance as a virtue, that embodies a normative stance geared to promote equal respect and self-determination when the latter results in allocation of resources and involves some form of legal commitment. But a close examination of the democratic foundations reveals that in this case too, the very foundations of the system might bring about its destruction.[68]

Liberty is a basic liberal democratic principle. Liberal democracy is based on granting people freedom to advance themselves, to develop their capacities, to enrich their world, to self-govern. Liberalism puts the individual at the centre of attention: everything revolves around the individual. Everything stems from the individual. Everything is directed for the individual to promote and advance her autonomy. However, this liberty is not without constraints. People are autonomous to advance themselves and cultivate their freedoms as long as they do not hurt others. There should be boundaries to liberty, otherwise we might be left with no liberty. Liberty is not a recipe for anarchy. Thus, there is a difficult balance to maintain: the government should provide opportunities for freedom and at the same time maintain law and order. Too much freedom might destroy the system. Too little might lead to lack of trust in the system.

Furthermore, there is also a tension between equality and liberty. Some people are so preoccupied in their endeavour to achieve equal status in society, often via finance, that they neglect protecting their basic liberties. Instead of investing in

---

[68] Cohen-Almagor, *The Boundaries of Liberty and Tolerance*; Raphael Cohen-Almagor, *The Democratic Catch* (Tel Aviv: Maariv, 2007) (Hebrew).

public matters, and in checks and balances against governmental potential or real abuse of power, some people invest their energies in partisan initiatives to increase their wealth. In *Democracy in America*, Alexis de Tocqueville observed, 'liberty is not the chief and constant object of their desires; equality is their idol: they make rapid and sudden efforts to obtain liberty, and if they miss their aim resign themselves to their disappointment; but nothing can satisfy them except equality, and rather than lose it they resolve to perish'.[69] Democracy needs to maintain a balance between equality and freedom, and to protect human rights as well as individual rights.

Another cherished democratic principle is tolerance. Tolerance stems from certain underpinning values we hold dear. Therefore, tolerance is not neutral. Nor can tolerance be equated with apathy or indifference. Tolerance is composed of three main components: (1) a strong disapproving attitude towards a certain conduct, action or speech; (2) power or authority to curtail the disturbing conduct; and (3) moral overriding principles which sway the doer not to exert her power or authority to curtail the said conduct. From this formulation, tolerance cannot be considered as indifference, for the doer *does* have strong reservations regarding the conduct. He or she cares greatly about the issue but nevertheless applies self-restraint. Tolerance could not also be equated with the concept of neutrality because neutrality is perceived as a specific requirement of justice and, in this respect, its meaning is akin to that of impartiality. Tolerance, on the other hand, assumes that the agents are very partial regarding the phenomenon they consider.[70]

In a democracy, government is said to tolerate people, providing others with scope to develop themselves and their respective ways of life.[71] However, here again the important proviso is to tolerate as long as the tolerated do not damage others. Tolerance should not be exploited by extreme, intolerant groups, to destroy the very foundations that prescribe tolerance. As Karl Popper said, it is absurd to assume that we should tolerate the intolerant no matter what. If we extend unqualified tolerance to the intolerant, then the tolerant people might be destroyed, and tolerance with them.[72] Here again the delicate task is to maintain a balance between tolerance and intolerance, otherwise the very foundation of tolerance might provide the intolerant with the tools to destroy democracy.

---

[69] Alexis de Tocqueville, *Democracy in America* (The Pennsylvania State University, 2002), http:// seas3.elte.hu/coursematerial/LojkoMiklos/Alexis-de-Tocqueville-Democracy-in-America.pdf : 72.

[70] Cohen-Almagor, *The Scope of Tolerance*, 26–27. For further discussion, see Dario Castiglione (ed.), *Toleration, Neutrality and Democracy* (Dordrecht: Springer, 2011); Michael Kühler, 'Can a Value-Neutral Liberal State Still Be Tolerant?', *Critical Review of International Social and Political Philosophy* (2019), https://doi.org/10.1080/13698230.2019.1616878.

[71] Cohen-Almagor, *The Scope of Tolerance*; Teresa M. Bejan, *Mere Civility: Disagreement and the Limits of Toleration* (Cambridge, MA: Harvard University Press, 2017).

[72] K.R. Popper, *The Open Society and Its Enemies* (London: Routledge and Kegan Paul, 1962): Vol. 1, p. 265.

are uncertain about the appropriate means to be utilized in order to fight down explicit antidemocratic and illiberal practices. Chapter 2 takes us a step forward by probing further the concept of reasonable multiculturalism. Liberalism assumes that justice knows no race, no colour, no religion. The Rawlsian metaphor is one of a veil of ignorance. Justice should be blind to these considerations. However, multiculturalism endorses group rights and demands recognition of racial differences, of colour differences and of religious differences. Multiculturalism asks special considerations due to race, colour and religion. It holds that these differences are significant, and that groups are entitled to certain just considerations in recognition of pluralism.

Furthermore, liberalism emphasizes individual rights whereas multiculturalism supports group rights. What if the latter conceptions of the good are not reasonable? Toleration supported by liberal neutrality might not be just. Tolerating group rights might trump individual rights. Reasonable pluralism that is able to construe 'overlapping consensus' on the social and political framework needs to establish and preserve a just and stable democracy.[75] Chapter 2 lays the second tier of the theory of reasonable multiculturalism by explaining the concepts of reasonableness and multiculturalism.

---

[75] Shaun P. Young, 'Exercising Political Power Reasonably', in Shaun P. Young (ed.), *Reasonableness in Liberal Political Philosophy* (Abingdon: Routledge, 2009): 149.

2

Reasonable Multiculturalism

Share our similarities, celebrate our differences.

M. Scott Peck

What is the meaning of reasonable multiculturalism? In a private conversation, Bhikhu Parekh explained the complexity of reasonableness using the following story. When he served as the chairman of the Commission on the Future of Multi-Ethnic Britain (1998–2000) a group of Muslim representatives petitioned his commission to recognize that women are not equal to men. They thought their petition was reasonable. When the commission refused their petition, they thought its members were unreasonable. They were guided by religious-moral principles which they accepted as given, without dispute, and they expected the commission to do the same. The commission was guided by other moral principles, not necessarily religious, and they wished to devise a reasonable policy for Britain, one that would reflect British values and ways of life. Here the clash was unavoidable and irreconcilable. Both camps thought they were reasonable and regarded the other as unreasonable.

After explaining the concept of just liberal democracy, this chapter explains the substance of reasonable multiculturalism within the liberal framework. When one looks at rituals around the globe, it is almost always the case that females are discriminated against and even tortured and killed in the name of culture and religion: female infanticide, FGM, suttee and murder for family honour are such examples. Women are required to pay a high price for the norm of male dominance. Group rights are invoked by theocratic and patriarchal cultures where women are oppressed, and religious orthodoxy enforced. Indeed, one of the main attacks on multiculturalism is that it is bad for women. At the same time, there is also a danger that claims for group rights might override law and order. In the name of preserving culture and protecting a sense of community, a demand is raised against society not to interfere even when the most atrocious things take place. Some groups claim that the preservation of their cultural norms should take precedence over state law. What would be a reasonable response to challenges posed by discriminatory groups?

This chapter aims to establish a middle ground between liberal reasoning and multiculturalists who see multiculturalism as an alternative to liberalism and who believe that protecting the group's culture trumps otherwise generally applicable laws.[1] I do this by advocating the concept of reasonableness. Building on the Rawlsian notion of reasonableness, and on Will Kymlicka's formulation of multi-culturalism, I delineate the boundaries of multiculturalism within the framework of liberal democracy. The state may have justifiable grounds to interfere in the business of illiberal minority cultures when their norms and practices are at odds with the underpinning values of liberal democracy.

REASONABLENESS

The *Oxford English Dictionary* defines 'reasonableness' as 'The quality of being as much as is appropriate or fair.'[2] Reasonable decision-makers are expected to consider alternatives for actions, to estimate short- and long-term consequences, and to weigh the pros and cons. John Rawls' concept of reasonableness is normative, loaded with a strong moral notion as he writes that people are reasonable when they behave fairly, seek cooperation with others and assume that others act in the same way.[3] In the Rawlsian just framework, members of society give moral weight to securing an agreement. They weigh different interests and values that may come into conflict. When such a conflict arises, people seek a fair compromise that balances between prospects and risks. Conflicts are not necessarily intractable, and dissent can be peacefully resolved via democratic deliberation. Reasonability is important because it provides a solution to conflicts and brings about stability.

The concept of reasonableness is essential to Rawlsian political liberalism because public exchange and reasoning would yield legitimacy.[4] Rawls maintains that a modern democratic society is characterized not simply by a pluralism of comprehensive religious, philosophical and moral doctrines but by a pluralism of incompatible yet reasonable comprehensive doctrines. Political liberalism assumes that this plurality is the result of the exercise of human reason within the framework of

---

[1]   Charles Taylor, *Multiculturalism and the Politics of Recognition* (Princeton, NJ: Princeton University Press, 1992); Charles Taylor, 'The Politics of Recognition', in Amy Gutmann (ed.), *Multiculturalism: Examining the Politics of Recognition* (Princeton, NJ: Princeton University Press, 1994): 25–73; James Tully, *Strange Multiplicity: Constitutionalism in an Age of Diversity* (Cambridge: Cambridge University Press, 1995).

[2]   The *Oxford English Dictionary*, https://en.oxforddictionaries.com/definition/reasonableness.

[3]   John Rawls, *Political Liberalism* (New York: Columbia University Press, 1993): 49.

[4]   The concept of 'reasonableness' plays an important role also in Brian Barry's *Theories of Justice* (London: Harvester, 1989) and in Thomas Scanlon's 'Contractualism and Utilitarianism', in Amartya Kumar Sen and Bernard Arthur Owen Williams (eds), *Utilitarianism and Beyond* (Cambridge: Cambridge University Press, 1982): 103–110. For general discussion, see Shaun P. Young (ed.), *Reasonableness in Liberal Political Philosophy* (Abingdon: Routledge, 2009).

democratic constitutional institutions. Political liberalism also assumes that these doctrines do not reject the essentials of a democratic regime.[5]

Etymologically, the terms 'rational' and 'reasonable' are near synonymous. Each derives from the Latin word *ratio* that means reason.[6] Rawls distinguishes between the rational and the reasonable. The rational applies to a single agent 'with the powers of judgement and deliberation in seeking ends and interests'.[7] The rational applies to how these ends and interests are adopted and affirmed as well as to how they are given priority. It also applies to the choice of means, in which case it is guided by the suitability of means to ends.[8] Rational agents lack a *'particular* form of moral sensibility that underlies the desire to engage in fair cooperation as such'.[9] However, they share the idea of fair social cooperation.

Rawls explains that reasonable people propose principles and standards they deem to be fair and cooperative. People would abide to them willingly because they seem just and because they believe that other reasonable people will perceive them in the same way as fair and just. Rawls writes: 'The reasonable is an element of the idea of society as a system of fair cooperation.'[10] Reciprocity brings people to accept reasonable fair terms of conduct. Reciprocity is a device of representation of their original position. It is a key for deciding what is reasonable, and what is questionable and thus merits close reflection and possibly limitation.

For Rawls, political actions, doctrines and principles should be deemed reasonable when people presume that human beings are properly treated as free and equal, that the right takes priority over the good and that social inequalities are almost wholly the result of contingencies for which people cannot properly be held accountable.[11] According to Rawls, principles are reasonable rather than true. They are principles that reasonable individuals would find morally binding. Just political principles are reasonable. They enable access, social processes and political mobilization. Rawls further suggests that reasonable people acknowledge that there can be multiple comprehensive doctrines. They think it is unreasonable to use political power to repress views merely because these are different from the ones they hold.[12] They think that terms of cooperation can be established and accepted by all provided that these terms are fair.[13]

---

[5] Rawls, *Political Liberalism*, xvi.
[6] Michele Mangini, 'Toward a Theory of Reasonableness', *Ratio Juris*, 31(2) (2018): 216.
[7] Rawls, *Political Liberalism*, 50.
[8] Ibid., 50.
[9] Ibid., 51 (my emphasis).
[10] Ibid., 49–50.
[11] Thomas A. Spragens Jr., 'Democratic Reasonableness', in Young, *Reasonableness in Liberal Political Philosophy*, 89.
[12] Rawls, *Political Liberalism*, 60.
[13] Ibid., 53. For further discussion, see Sebastiano Maffettone, 'Political Liberalism: Reasonableness and Democratic Practice', *Philosophy and Social Criticism*, 30(5–6) (2004): 541–577; Edward Andrew and Peter Lindsay, 'Are the Judgements of Conscience Unreasonable?', in Young, *Reasonableness in Liberal Political Philosophy*, 130.

The concept of reasonableness is of great relevance and importance for addressing the question whether liberalism and multiculturalism are reconcilable. My thesis is that liberalism and multiculturalism are reconcilable provided that multiculturalism is reasonable. The assumptions are that people are rational beings who are capable of reason, that they seek to secure a stable and just system of governance that would respect their own basic rights as well as the rights of others. People recognize the need for common life and the compulsion of living together.

The reasonableness of a cultural rite is determined by its significance for the cultural group. If it is crucial for the livelihood of the group then it is of obvious importance to the group, notwithstanding what outsiders may think about that rite. Similarly, the rite is significant when it is an integral part of social and family life, perceived as important for maintaining the group's heritage and the way the group defines itself. Conversely, cultural rites that have no value for the group and for others are not reasonable. However, there can be cultural rites that are of importance to the group but have no value or utility for society at large. They may be reasonable to the group in question but unreasonable and possibly offensive in the eyes of outsiders. This is when a conflict arises, and the scope of tolerance afforded to the group is questioned.

We can differentiate between moral reasonableness, legal reasonableness, social reasonableness and political reasonableness. By *moral reasonableness* it is meant that people apply reason based on moral principles to define the margins of the acceptable. This is an inward-looking process. *Legal reasonableness* relates to the legal institutions and mechanisms aimed to secure human goods for the benefit of all. The law helps to anchor and promote moral principles and thus there is a strong connection between moral and legal reasonableness. According to the European Court of Justice, public authorities must weigh public and private interests and choose measures that imply the least burden on private interests. Courts are required to balance between interests and examine the suitability of means, their necessity and their proportionality.[14] By *social reasonableness* it is meant that citizens determine through application of reason which comprehensive doctrines of justice are reasonable. What is socially reasonable would apply to them as well as to others. By *political reasonableness* it is meant that citizens, politicians and various groups apply reason in deciding the political conceptions that would support the comprehensive and reasonable doctrines of justice. The result would lead to reasonable policies for all.

People can be said to be morally reasonable when they have an appropriate conception of themselves and their standing in relation to their fellow people, and when they understand and accept the obligations and constraints upon their aspirations and behaviour which derive from that conception. Reasonableness consists in equitableness whereby an individual respects other persons' rights as well as her

---

[14] Mangini, 'Toward a Theory of Reasonableness, 208–230.

own.[15] People act in accord with norms of procedural reasonableness when they understand and comply with the requirements of their practices and institutionalized relationships logically appropriate to the norms of moral reasonableness and the purposes of their political association.[16] Social policies and acts of political associations are reasonable when they embody sound judgement of practical reason within the constraints of moral reasonableness. Democratic moral reasonableness implies that one's identification with a certain culture or religion does not diminish one's universal entitlement to dignity and respect. Reasonable people are able to devise forms of mediation that would ensure the stability of governance.

Furthermore, people are reasonable when they behave and respond in ways that seem suitable to the situation at hand and to the powers, rights and responsibilities which they bear. Balancing as a method and proportionality as a measure are important. People need to weigh and balance relevant interests and apply appropriate measures. The employed means should be proportionate to the ends we wish to attain. Doctrines are reasonable when they are comporting properly to the understandings of their relevant empirical realities and the moral criteria that seem appropriate. Reciprocity is the central norm both for fair terms of social cooperation and for the legitimacy of government authority. The requirement of reciprocity, derivative from our insistence on mutual respect (see Chapter 1), is also central to the liberal principle of legitimacy. Morally appropriate exercises of government must be defensible based on just practices which are acceptable to citizens or to the majority of them.[17]

A reasonable governance framework would accommodate the demands of reasonable people situated in an environment of reasonable pluralism and reasonable disagreement. Reasonable people strive to accommodate differences in order to reach a stable political consensus on social and political principles. Reasonableness includes patience, tolerance and reciprocity. We assume that cultures are not homogenous. Within cultures there are different strands, different interpretations of the norms and different understandings of the implications dictated by culture in the working of everyday life. We assume that most people are capable of reasoning and making choices. People may opt not to exercise their capacity to reason, but most people possess this capacity, to varying degrees. As discussed *supra*, in liberal societies the general expectation is that all accept the underpinning principles of respect for others, and not harming others: don't do to others what you don't want them to do to you.

The Supreme Court of Canada grappled with reasonableness in the *Multani* case. The case concerned Gurbaj and his father Balvir Singh Multani, orthodox

---

[15] Alan Gewirth, 'The Rationality of Reasonableness', *Synthese*, 57(2) (1983): 225–247.
[16] Thomas A. Spragens Jr, 'Democratic Reasonableness', in Young, *Reasonableness in Liberal Political Philosophy*, 91.
[17] Ibid., 92.

Sikhs who believed that their religion required them to wear a kirpan (a metal dagger) at all times, including at school. The school governing board objected, arguing that the school code of conduct prohibited the carrying of weapons. The Multanis appealed all the way to the Supreme Court. The court, *per* McLachlin C.J. and Bastarache, Binnie, Fish and Charron JJ., resolved that the decision to establish an absolute prohibition against wearing a kirpan does not fall within a range of reasonable alternatives.[18] The risk that the kirpan will be used for violent purposes is very low, especially if the kirpan is worn under the cloths in a secure way. While the board should work to ensure a reasonable level of safety at the school, the evidence revealed that there was not a single violent incident related to the presence of kirpans in schools. Reasonableness requires that the existence of concerns relating to safety must be unequivocally established for the infringement of a constitutional right to be justified. Furthermore, there are many objects in schools that could be used to commit violent acts and that are much more easily obtained, including scissors, pencils and baseball bats. The court also dismissed the argument that the kirpan is a symbol of violence. This argument is contradicted by the evidence regarding the symbolic nature of the kirpan. This argument is disrespectful to believers in the Sikh religion and it does not consider Canadian values based on multiculturalism.[19]

The court emphasized that religious tolerance is a very important value of Canadian society. The board decision was unreasonable because it did not sufficiently consider either the right to freedom of religion or the proposed accommodation measure. The decision to establish an absolute prohibition against wearing a kirpan was not within a range of reasonable alternatives and it failed to meet the constitutional standard. 'A total prohibition against wearing a kirpan to school undermines the value of this religious symbol and sends students the message that some religious practices do not merit the same protection as others.'[20] The court held that 'Accommodating G and allowing him to wear his kirpan under certain conditions demonstrates the importance that our society attaches to protecting freedom of religion and to showing respect for its minorities.'[21]

MULTICULTURALISM

Multiculturalism appeared on the Western social and political agenda in the 1960s, in response to cultural diversity and demands that were brought up by national minorities, indigenous peoples and immigrants.[22] Multiculturalism perceives

---

[18] *Multani v. Commission scolaire Marguerite-Bourgeoys*, [2006] 1 S.C.R. 256, 2006 SCC 6.

[19] Ibid.

[20] Ibid.

[21] Ibid. For further discussion, see Brian Leiter, *Why Tolerate Religion?* (Princeton, NJ: Princeton University Press, 2014).

[22] Will Kymlicka, 'The Essentialist Critique of Multiculturalism: Theories, Policies, Ethos', in Varun Uberoi and Tariq Modood (eds), *Multiculturalism Rethought* (Edinburgh: Edinburgh

individuals as social beings whose identity has been shaped by past generations and continues to be shaped by us as individuals. It is impossible to understand and analyse social life at the individual level and talk about human identity independently of the group in which one lives. We are all part of a long chain of history and tradition; therefore, the basic concepts of social analysis should include both individuals and groups. Individuals sometimes form new groups that give new meaning to their identity. Often time, however, the group precedes the individuals and is playing a crucial role in forming their identity. Therefore, the analysis cannot begin with individuals and their organization rights in isolation of already pre-existing and well-established group rights.

The critique of multiculturalism perceives it as legitimacy to contradict the liberal (in France, Republican) way of life. The critique follows the following logic:

Liberal democracy puts *the individual* at the centre of attention.
The state is perceived as the means, a sophisticated instrument to enable individual development and autonomy.
In contrast, multiculturalism puts *the group* at the centre of attention.
The tension is inevitable as group claims might trump individual claims.
Fostering a society with shared common values and commitments requires unity. Democracy requires a *demos* (people).
When the *demos* is divided into cultural groups, democracy is undermined.
Thus, liberal democracy should cultivate and cherish values that are compatible with individual rights rather than assist with the fostering of many cultural rights which bring about division and fracture society.[23] Kukathas called governments to refrain from pursuing cultural integration and adopt instead a 'politics of indifference' towards minority groups.[24]

Alternatively, reasonable multiculturalism recognizes that societies are composed of multiple conceptions of the good and that not all demands are answerable. Reasonable multiculturalism assumes that society members have the good will to make living together possible and that they are willing to make reasonable accommodations. In a reasonable multicultural society all people have their own goals and all stand ready to propose fair terms that others may reasonably be expected to accept, so that all may benefit and improve on what every individual can do on his or her own.[25] Compromise is required because complete agreement might not be

University Press, 2015): 209–249; Bhikhu Parekh, *Ethnocentric Political Theory* (Cham: Palgrave, 2019): 161.

[23] Chandran Kukathas, 'Is Multiculturalism Bad for Democracy?', www.academia.edu/12540718/Is_multiculturalism_bad_for_democracy.

[24] Chandran Kukathas, *The Liberal Archipelago: A Theory of Diversity and Freedom* (Oxford: Oxford University Press, 2007): 15. See also Brian Barry, *Culture and Equality: An Egalitarian Critique of Multiculturalism* (Cambridge, MA: Harvard University Press, 2001).

[25] Rawls, *Political Liberalism*, 54.

possible but functional agreement done in good faith is still doable. I will elaborate on the concept of compromise in Chapter 3.

Following the reasoning developed earlier, it is argued that the fair terms that constitute reasonableness are respect for others and not harming others. These are the moral binders that hold a stable liberal democracy together. These moral binders enable the reconciliation of different conceptions of the good based on competing religions and cultures within a societal vision of justice shared by all. Reasonable doctrines develop a sense of civic responsibility to society as a whole, beyond group affiliation. Reasonable multiculturalism operates via mechanisms of dispute resolution to settle differences and conflicts if and when these arise. It is proposed that deliberative democracy facilitates communication and exchange of ideas to explain the reasonable, how and why different ways of life can coexist within a liberal democratic framework of government. Via open deliberation and open disputation of the limits of the reasonable and the boundaries of tolerance, the challenge of plurality of cultures will transform into a source of value. The concept of deliberative democracy is elaborated and explained in Chapter 3.

Rawls believes that social cooperation is possible due to two moral powers: a capacity for a sense of justice and a capacity for conception of the good. Rawls did not devote much attention to culture and his just society is depicted as homogenous. A more realistic picture of liberal democracies consists of a plurality of cultures, whose freedoms ought to be secured by the elected government. Indeed, liberal democracies are all multinational states, or polyethnic states, or both. Liberal democracies consist of a variety of national, religious or cultural groups. Wars, imperialist inclinations and conquests, the industrial revolution, commerce relationships, immigration, the development of more rapid modes of transportation, mass communication and the internet were the notable factors that made the idea of culturally homogeneous society obsolete.

CULTURE AS PRIMARY GOOD

Within the context of the Rawlsian original position, among the particular facts of which people are aware is cultural membership. Using the veil of ignorance analytic metaphor, people in the original position know that they are representatives of cultural communities, but they do not know to which culture they belong. Neither do they know whether the contingencies of culture are to their advantage or to their disadvantage. Hence, they would accept that each and every person may be able to associate with their cultural association. They would reject any sort of political and religious fundamentalism that urges that the best community is one in which only some preferred practices are allowed.[26] Granting cultural membership the status of primary good will not provide fundamentalists with claims to further

---

[26] John Rawls, A *Theory of Justice* (Oxford: Oxford University Press, 1971), sect. 24.

their aims because we insist on safeguarding liberal principles and on the requirements of mutuality, reciprocity and reasonableness. Each person should have a
share of the communal resources. Thus, promotion of fundamentalist politics
conflicts with the primary good of cultural membership because it negates meaningful individual choice.[27]

Notwithstanding Rawls' recognition that culture and institutions may cause
people to reject some convictions, and that the cultural context of choice is
important in deciding ways of life, Rawls does not explicitly state that culture is a
primary good nor does he single out culture as a necessary social condition to enable
people to pursue their determinate conceptions of the good life and to develop and
exercise their moral powers. However, a close analysis of Rawls' argument for liberty
as a primary good could imply that it is also an argument for cultural membership as
a primary good. Rawls does not make this argument clear because his model of the
nation state is quite simplified, on many occasions characterizing political community without paying adequate attention to cultural differences. He seems to assume
that opportunities and powers, leisure time and certain mental states, and even a
sense of one's own worth, can be detached from cultural considerations. He also
appears to presume that only religious groups possess intensity of beliefs and a set of
conceptions that binds all members. Ronald Dworkin appears to hold the same
basic view.[28]

Culture and tradition are important. People can accept a certain sense of justice
and develop mutual reasonable accommodations in the context of their given
historical, social and cultural conditions. For many people culture and tradition
define who they are. Know from where you are coming in order to know where you
are going is a common motto of many. Members of minority cultures within a larger
society may have affinities to both larger society and the minority group. To a
significant extent, cultural membership shapes one's identity and provides more
meaning to one's activities as part of a collective effort. Kymlicka rightly argues that
some minority cultures need protection from the economic or political decisions of
the majority culture if they are to provide this context for their members. For
example, cultural minorities may need veto power over certain decisions regarding
language and culture and may need to limit the mobility of migrants or immigrants

---

[27] Will Kymlicka, *Liberalism, Community, and Culture* (Oxford: Clarendon Press, 1989): 172. For
further discussion, see Bhikhu Parekh, *Rethinking Multiculturalism* (Houndmills: Palgrave,
2000): 99–109.

[28] The term 'culture' is absent from *Political Liberalism*'s index. Ronald M. Dworkin, *Taking
Rights Seriously* (London: Duckworth, 1977); Ronald M. Dworkin, *A Matter of Principle*
(Oxford: Clarendon Press, 1985); Ronald M. Dworkin, *Justice for Hedgehogs* (Cambridge,
MA: Belknap, 2011). For further critique and discussion, see Parekh, *Rethinking
Multiculturalism*, 80–90, and Bhikhu Parekh, *Debating India: Essays on Indian Political
Discourse* (Oxford: Oxford University Press, 2016); Joseph Raz, 'Multiculturalism', *Ratio Juris*,
11(3) (September 1998): 193–205, and generally Joseph Raz, *The Morality of Freedom* (Oxford:
Clarendon Press, 1986).

into their homelands. Such rights are held by French Canadians and by Aboriginal peoples in Canada, the United States and Australia.[29]

Deciding how to lead our lives is, in the first instance, a matter of exploring the possibilities made available to us by our culture. In trying to reach a morally justified decision our starting point is that all people matter, and matter equally. From a liberal point of view, liberal democracies that fail to accord substantial civil rights to members of minority cultures are deficient. Loss of cultural membership might inflict a profound harm on minority cultures. Our capacity to form and revise our conception of the good, without coercion, is intimately tied to our cultural membership, our language, the way we organize our community and the norms we have been adopting.

Kymlicka articulates different kinds of groups and different kinds of 'group rights'. He offers two helpful distinctions: between *multination states* and *polyethnic states*, and between *internal restrictions* and *external protections*. The concept of *internal restrictions* concerns the rights of a group against dissenting members of the same group, whereas the concept of *external protections* concerns the rights of a group against the society at large.[30] I explicate *infra*.

TWO FORMS OF CULTURAL PLURALISM

Common rights of citizenship might be insufficient to accommodate all forms of ethnocultural diversity. In some cases certain 'collective' or 'group-differentiated' rights are also required. Liberal thinkers, including Thomas Hobbes (1588–1679), John Locke (1632–1704), Jean-Jacques Rousseau (1712–1778), the American Founding Fathers (eighteenth century), J. S. Mill (1806–1873) and John Rawls (1921–2002) only spoke about individual rights and liberties. Individual rights need protection from the power of the state. Rights of groups did not occupy their minds. However, within liberal democracies cultural groups wish to enjoy recognition of group-differentiated rights. Their demands raise vital questions: How are these group rights related to individual rights? What should we do when group rights come into conflict with individual rights? Can a liberal democracy allow minority groups to

---

[29] Will Kymlicka, 'The Rights of Minority Cultures, Reply to Kukathas', *Political Theory*, 20(1) (1992): 140–146, at 140. See also Will Kymlicka, *Citizenship in Diverse Societies* (Oxford: Oxford University Press, 2000) and Will Kymlicka (ed.), *The Rights of Minority Cultures* (Oxford: Oxford University Press, 1995); Mark D. Walters, 'The Jurisprudence of Reconciliation: Aboriginal Rights in Canada', in Will Kymlicka and Bashir Bashir (eds), *The Politics of Reconciliation in Multicultural Societies* (New York: Oxford University Press, 2010): 165–191. On the importance of language, see Daniel Bell, *Communitarianism and Its Critics* (Oxford: Clarendon Press, 1993): 156–207.

[30] Will Kymlicka, *Multicultural Citizenship: A Liberal Theory of Minority* (Oxford: Oxford University Press, 2000). For critique of Kymlicka's distinction between internal restrictions and external protections, see Geoffrey Brahm Levey, 'Equality, Autonomy, and Cultural Rights', *Political Theory*, 25(2) (April 1997): 215–248; Annamari Vitikainen, *The Limits of Liberal Multiculturalism* (Houndmills: Palgrave, 2015): 45–72.

restrict the individual rights of their members? Should liberal democracies insist that all groups uphold liberal principles?

All liberal democracies contain some degree of ethnocultural diversity and therefore they are all 'multicultural'. But the patterns of ethnocultural diversity vary from one society to another, and these variations are important in understanding minority cultures' claims. Offering a complete typology of the different forms of ethnocultural diversity is outside the scope of this book. A basic distinction is drawn between two forms of cultural pluralism: 'multination' and 'polyethnic' states.

Multination States

Many countries are multinational, containing more than one nation. By 'nation' it is meant a historical community, more or less institutionally complete, occupying a given territory or homeland, sharing a distinct language and culture. A 'nation' in this sociological sense is closely related to the idea of a 'people' or a 'culture'.[31]

If a nation's homeland becomes incorporated into a larger state, then it becomes what we will call a 'national minority'. National minority is a *minority* of citizens of the country (nationals of the state) who have certain *ethnic*, linguistic or religious characteristics which are different from those of the majority. Incorporation of national minorities into a larger state has typically been an involuntary process. Some national minorities have been invaded and conquered by another nation; others have been ceded from one imperial power to another; yet others have had their homeland overrun by colonizing settlers. But some multination states have arisen voluntarily, when different cultures agree to form a federation for their mutual benefit.[32] The Native Americans, Canadian First Nations, Australian Aborigines, Māori of New Zealand, Catalonia and the Basque country in Spain, Welsh and Scots in Britain, Kurds in Turkey and Israeli Arabs/Palestinians are just a few examples of national minorities.[33]

The notion of citizenship is commonly perceived as an institutional status from within by which a person can address governments and other citizens and make

---

[31] Will Kymlicka and Raphael Cohen-Almagor, 'Democracy and Multiculturalism', in Raphael Cohen-Almagor (ed.), *Challenges to Democracy* (Aldershot: Ashgate, 2000): 89–118; Will Kymlicka and Raphael Cohen-Almagor, 'Ethnocultural Minorities in Liberal Democracies', in Maria Baghramian and Attracta Ingram (eds), *Pluralism: The Philosophy and Politics of Diversity* (London: Routledge, 2000): 228–250.

[32] Kymlicka, *Multicultural Citizenship*, chap. 2; Parekh, *Ethnocentric Political Theory*, 117–119.

[33] The European Framework Convention for the Protection of National Minorities (Strasbourg, 1995), which is the most comprehensive multilateral treaty devoted to minority rights, contains no definition of 'national minority' as member states were unable to agree on terminology. The convention sets out principles relating to persons belonging to national minorities in the sphere of public life, such as freedom of peaceful assembly, freedom of association, freedom of expression, freedom of thought, conscience and religion, and access to the media, as well as in the sphere of freedoms relating to language, education, transfrontier co-operation, etc. www.coe.int/en/web/conventions/full-list/-/conventions/rms/090000168007cdac.

claims about human rights. All who possess the status are equal with respect to rights and duties with which the status is endowed. In North America national minorities include Native Americans, Puerto Ricans and descendants of the Mexicans living in the south-west before 1848 in the United States, and the Aboriginal peoples and the Quebecois in Canada. In Israel roughly 21 per cent of the population are Palestinian Arabs.[34] In Europe some countries are multinational, either because they have forcibly incorporated indigenous populations (e.g., Norway and Finland which contain communities of Lapps, known also as Sami. In Norway the Sami community is considerably larger), or because they were formed by the more or less voluntary federation of two or more European cultures (e.g., Belgium and Switzerland). However they were incorporated, national minorities have typically sought to maintain or enhance their political autonomy, either through outright secession or through some form of regional autonomy.[35]

Polyethnic States

As mentioned, a major source of diversity is immigration, particularly where large numbers of individuals and families are admitted from other countries and allowed to maintain some of their ethnic particularity. With the rise of capitalism, many people changed their place of dwelling in pursuit of a better life. An increasing number of countries now contain sizeable immigrant communities. These immigrant groups are not nations and do not occupy homelands. Immigrant groups should be able to maintain at least some of their culturally distinct ways of life within the framework of the larger society. Cultural policies with respect to these groups may include policies against discrimination, funding for private associations such as religious community centres, recognition of their cultural heritage and norms, and guaranteeing their representation in state institutions.

The three main countries of immigration outside of Europe – Australia, Canada and the United States – had preferred an 'Anglo-conformity' model of immigration. Immigrants were expected to assimilate to existing cultural norms, and, over time, become indistinguishable from native-born citizens in their speech, dress, leisure activities, cuisine, family size and so on. However, beginning in the last century it was increasingly accepted that this assimilationist model was unrealistic and unjust. All three countries gradually adopted a more tolerant or 'multicultural' approach, which allows and indeed encourages immigrants to uphold various aspects of their

---

[34] TOI Staff, 'Israel's Population Tops 9 Million, Including 45% of World Jewry', *Times of Israel* (6 May 2019), www.timesofisrael.com/israels-population-tops-9-million-including-45-of-world-jewry/.

[35] D. Elazar, *Exploring Federalism* (Tuscaloosa: University of Alabama Press, 1987); Will Kymlicka, 'Federalismo, Nacionalismo y Multiculturalismo', *Revista Internacional de Filosofía Política*, 7 (1996): 20–54; Arend Lijphart, *Patterns of Democracy: Government Forms and Performance in Thirty-six Countries* (New Haven, CT: Yale University Press, 2012).

ethnic heritage. Immigrants are free to maintain their old customs regarding food, dress and recreation, and to associate with each other to sustain these practices. This is not regarded as unpatriotic or contradictory to the credo of the nation.[36]

In these Anglo-Saxon societies, immigrant groups actively participate in the social and political institutions of the larger society. They mix with native-born citizens in common educational, economic, legal and political institutions, all of which operate in the majority's dominant language. Their distinctiveness is manifested primarily in their family lives and in their various activities in voluntary associations of their choice. Because they lack separate institutions operating in their own language, and because they do not occupy homelands, few if any immigrant groups think of themselves as 'nations' or claim rights to self-government. In the United States minorities have asserted that the Americanism to which they are committed is more authentic and they are 'more patriotic' than the White Anglo-Saxon Protestant (WASP) elite.[37]

Multiculturalism for immigrants, therefore, is best understood not as a rejection of linguistic and institutional integration, but as a change in the terms of integration. Immigrants are still expected to learn the majority's language, and to integrate into common institutions. Indeed, learning English is a mandatory part of children's education in Australia and the United States.[38] In Israel the Hebrew language is mandatory in Jewish schools, and in Canada children must learn either of the two official languages (French or English). Germany offers integration classes that teach immigrants German language, history, culture and the basics about its legal system.[39] In turn, the British Nationality Act 1981 is a very detailed piece of legislation that requires immigrants who wish to undergo the process of naturalization to satisfy a residency requirement of at least five years. New citizens are required to demonstrate not only knowledge of English but also knowledge about life in the United Kingdom, via a citizenship test that was introduced in 2005. One may expect that such a citizenship test includes questions about history, culture, norms, values,

---

[36] Kymlicka and Cohen-Almagor, 'Ethnocultural Minorities in Liberal Democracies'; Will Kymlicka, 'Liberal Theories of Multiculturalism', in Lukas Meyer, Stanley Paulson and Thomas Pogge (eds), *Rights, Culture and the Law* (Oxford: Oxford University Press, 2003): 229–250.

[37] Edward Ashbee, *American Society Today* (Manchester: Manchester University Press, 2002): 108.

[38] In the USA, English Language Exemptions state: 'You Are Exempt From The English Language Requirement, But Are Still Required To Take The Civics Test If You Are:

Age 50 or older at the time of filing for naturalization and have lived as a permanent resident (green card holder) in the United States for 20 years (commonly referred to as the '50/20' exception). OR

Age 55 or older at the time of filing for naturalization and have lived as a permanent resident in the United States for 15 years' (commonly referred to as the '55/15' exception). See US Citizenship and Immiration Services, www.uscis.gov/us-citizenship/citizenship-through-naturalization/exceptions-accommodations.

[39] Thom Brooks, *Becoming British: UK Citizenship Examined* (London: Biteback, 2016): 145.

politics, geography and institutions. However, the 'Life in the UK' test attracted criticisms as many of the questions are deemed irrelevant to life in the UK.[40] In addition, there are wide-ranging good character requirements that demand applicants to have clean criminal record and good standing in society.[41] Similar requirements exist in France, where those applying via residency need to prove they can speak adequate French, have an adequate knowledge of France – its culture, history and politics, and have integrated into and appreciate the French way of life. They also need to show they have a clean criminal record (for those who have less than ten years' residence in France), that their tax payments are up to date, and that they are financially sustainable.[42] While immigrants are expected to integrate into their chosen society, liberalism does not see it necessary or fair to insist on cultural assimilation. On the contrary, it seems fair to reform common institutions to accommodate immigrant groups.[43] In this respect, liberalism is in tandem with multiculturalism.

In addition to multination and polyethnic states there are other kinds of ethnocultural diversity as many groups are neither immigrants nor national minorities. Take, for instance, European travellers[44] or guest workers in Europe and in Israel.[45] I focus on national minorities and on immigrants because they are the most common in liberal democracies, and also because liberal democracies have, over the years, learned a great deal about how to accommodate these forms of diversity.

Europe has always experienced significant population movements, but recent decades have seen a change from generally short-term immigration motivated by a search for work, to immigration for purposes of family reunification or to seek asylum. Since the mid-1980s there has been an unprecedented increase in the number of requests for asylum in European Union (EU) countries.[46] This trend has become more marked since the collapse of the communist bloc and the outbreak of war in Yugoslavia, and even more so following the so-called Arab

[40] Thom Brooks, 'The "Life in the United Kingdom" Citizenship Test: Is It Unfit for Purpose?' (13 June 2013), http://dx.doi.org/10.2139/ssrn.2280329.

[41] Thom Brooks, *Becoming British*, 38; British Nationality Act 1981, www.legislation.gov.uk/ukpga/1981/61.

[42] 'The Common Questions about French Citizenship You Need Answering', *The Local* (7 March 2018), www.thelocal.fr/20180307/common-questions-about-gaining-french-nationality.

[43] Will Kymlicka, 'Ethnic Associations and Democratic Citizenship', in Amy Gutmann (ed.) *Freedom of Association* (Princeton, NJ: Princeton University Press, 1998): 177–213.

[44] Becky Taylor, 'Britain's Gypsy Travellers: a People on the Outside', *History Today*, 61(6) (2011), www.historytoday.com/becky-taylor/britains-gypsy-travellers-people-outside.

[45] D. Cinar, 'From Aliens to Citizens: A Comparative Analysis of Rules of Transition', in Rainer Baubock (ed.), *From Aliens to Citizens: Redefining the Legal Status of Immigrants* (Aldershot: Avebury, 1994): 49–72; Nermin Abadan-Unat, *Turks in Europe: From Guest Worker to Transnational Citizen* (New York: Berghahn Books, 2011); Lidia Averbukh, 'Foreign Workers in Israel: How Ethno-Nationalism prevents Structures of Representation', *Momentum Quarterly*, 5(2) (2016): 88–96.

[46] 'A Welcoming Europe?', www.europarl.europa.eu/external/html/welcomingeurope/default_en .htm; see also 'History of International Migration', University of Leiden (2008), www.let .leidenuniv.nl/history/migration/chapter10.html.

Spring that spread across the Middle East in 2011. Violent uprisings, armed rebellions and civil wars have prompted the biggest migrant wave since World War II. Bloodshed in Syria, Libya and Iraq, severe repression in Eritrea, and instability across much of the Arab world have all contributed to the displacement of millions of refugees. More than a million migrants and refugees crossed into Europe in 2015, mostly from war-torn countries such as Syria, Afghanistan and Iraq.[47] The year of 2015 was a peak year in the number of people who sought refuge in Europe with more than 1,321,000 asylum applications. The twenty-eight member states of the EU granted protection status to 646,060 asylum seekers in 2018.[48] In 2017, the highest number of persons granted protection status was registered in Germany (325,370), ahead of France (40,575), Italy (35,130), Austria (33,925) and Sweden (31,235).[49]

Citizens of EU member states have freedom to travel and freedom of movement within the EU's internal borders. In 2017 a total of 4.4 million people immigrated to one of the EU-28 member states, while at least 3.1 million emigrants were reported to have left an EU member state;[50] 2.4 million immigrants entered the EU from non-EU countries; 22.3 million people (4.4 per cent) of the 512.4 million people living in the EU on 1 January 2018 were non-EU citizens. EU member states granted citizenship to 825,000 people in 2017.[51]

It is expected that countries that welcome immigrants and foreign workers provide them with proper treatment and adequate social welfare services, ensure their security and protect their rights in accordance with the provisions of the relevant international conventions and recommendations of the International Labour Organization. More specifically, governments should work to prevent discrimination in the labour markets, to combat prejudice against foreign workers and to assist them in the reunion of their families. In addition, liberal governments should let

---

[47] BBC, 'Migrant Crisis: Migration to Europe Explained in Seven Charts', *BBC News* (4 March 2016), www.bbc.co.uk/news/world-europe-34131911; Demetrios G. Papademetriou and Susan Fratzke, 'Top 10 of 2016 – Issue #1: Dawn of New Migration Reality Brings Focus on Borders, Returns, and Integration', *Migration Policy Institute* (20 December 2016), www.migrationpolicy .org/article/top-10–2016-issue-1-dawn-new-migration-reality-brings-focus-borders-returns-and; 'Moving Europe beyond Crisis', *Migration Policy Institute*, www.migrationpolicy.org/pro grams/moving-europe-beyond-crisis?gclid=CjoKEQiA7qLDBRD9xJ7PscDCu5IBEiQAqo3BxI 3D9lBOpoWf4HaXhg1rlvMYmG7uDe2cKB9QhsMaZcAaAljX8P8HAQ. For critical discussion, see Ruvi Ziegler, 'Asylum Seekers Are Now Political Pawns in a Disharmonious EU', *The Conversation* (13 June 2018), https://theconversation.com/asylum-seekers-are-now-political-pawns-in-a-disharmonious-eu-98260.

[48] Renata Palen, 'Asylum Decisions in the EU: EU Member States Granted Protection to More than Half a Million Asylum Seekers in 2017', *Eurostat Press Office* (19 April 2018), https://ec .europa.eu/eurostat/documents/2995521/8817675/3–19042018-AP-EN.pdf/748e8fae-2cfb-4e75-a3 88-f06f6ce8ff58.

[49] Ibid.

[50] 'Migration and Migrant Population Statistics', *Eurostat* (March 2019), https://ec.europa.eu/ eurostat/statistics-explained/pdfscache/1275.pdf.

[51] 'Migration and Migrant Population Statistics', *Eurostat* (2017), http://ec.europa.eu/eurostat/ statistics-explained/index.php/Migration_and_migrant_population_statistics.

immigrants preserve their cultural heritage, their language and their conception of the good. This is in conformity with the provisions of the UN Charter (especially Article 55).[52] But safeguarding cultural heritage does not entail justification of norms that harm others and that disrespect other groups in society.

Liberal democracies have a long history of seeking to accommodate ethnocultural differences. With respect to national minorities, liberal democracies have typically accorded these groups some degree of regional political autonomy, so that they can maintain themselves as separate and self-governing, culturally and linguistically distinct, societies. Generally speaking, liberal democracies have become more tolerant of the expression of immigrant identities and practices within these institutions. You can gauge the viability of a democracy by the way it treats its minorities. At the same time, moral and religious freedoms follow from the Principle of Equal Liberty, and, assuming the priority of this principle, the only grounds for denying equal liberties is to avoid an even greater injustice and even greater loss of liberty. Individual liberty is valuable to the extent that in order to secure an extensive system of overall liberties for everyone we may restrict a basic liberty of some sects. Thus, for example, if members of a cultural group who wish to immigrate to a liberal democracy insist on maintaining female infanticide then the government has legitimate grounds to deny them entry. The principles of respect for others and not harming others that underpin reasonable multiculturalism provide grounds for and set limits to liberty and tolerance. Otherwise democracy might not be able to triumph over its own 'catch': the very principles that underlie democracy might bring its end.

TWO KINDS OF GROUP RIGHTS

Both immigrant groups and national minorities raise demands to recognize their ethnocultural identities and practices. These demands are often described, by both their defenders and critics, in the language of 'group rights'. Questions arise as to whether these demands are reasonable and legitimate. Defenders of multiculturalism would describe them as *supplementing* individual rights, and hence as enriching and extending traditional liberal principles to deal with new challenges, whereas critics would argue that group rights involve *restricting* individual rights, and hence as threatening basic liberal democratic principles.[53]

Consider two kinds of rights that a group might claim: the first involves the right of a group against its own members; the second involves the right of a group against the larger society. Both kinds of collective rights can be seen as protecting the stability of national, ethnic or religious groups. The first kind is intended to protect

---

[52] See *World Population Plan of Action* in Report of the United Nations World Population Conference (1974), U.N. Doc. E/CONF 60/19, paras 55–56, at 16–17.

[53] Will Kymlicka and Raphael Cohen-Almagor, 'Democracy and Multiculturalism', reprinted in Raphael Cohen-Almagor (ed.), *Challenges to Democracy: Essays in Honour and Memory of Isaiah Berlin* (Aldershot: Ashgate Publishing Ltd., 2000).

the group from internal dissent whereas the second is intended to protect the group from the impact of external pressures. Kymlicka calls the first 'internal restrictions', and the second 'external protections'.[54]

A sociological look at different societies reveals that many groups seek the right to legally restrict the freedom of their own members. This is in order to maintain cultural cohesion or solidarity. Such restrictions are contested. Their legitimacy might be suspect. Groups may impose certain restrictions as conditions for membership in *voluntary* associations, but it is unjust to restrict the liberty of members without ample justifications. From a liberal point of view, under the Respect for Others Principle (see Chapter 1), whoever exercises political power in a community must respect the civil, religious and political rights of all its members. Furthermore, an exit right should be available for dissenting members who no longer wish to be associated with the group. People in democratic societies should be free to move in and out of their cultural communities without penalties. They should not be coerced to stay in order to serve the partisan interests of others.

Liberal democracy cannot reasonably be expected to endure without question norms that deny respect to people and that are designed to harm others, notwithstanding whether those norms are dictated by some cultures. According to Rawls, a workable conception of political justice must allow for a diversity of doctrines and the plurality of conflicting, indeed incommensurable, conceptions of the meaning, value and purpose of human life affirmed by members of existing democratic societies.[55] But given the profound differences in beliefs and conceptions of the good, we must recognize that, just as on questions of religious and moral doctrine, public agreement on the basic questions of philosophy cannot be reached without the state's infringement of basic liberties.[56] Rawls explains that conceptions that directly conflict with the principles of justice should be excluded. Rawls further asserts that if a conception of the good is unable to persist and gain adherents under institutions of equal freedom and mutual toleration, we must question whether it is a viable conception of the good, and whether its passing is to be regretted.[57] Rawls explicitly argues that no social world exists that does not exclude some ways of life that realize in special ways some essential values.

---

[54] The distinction between these two kinds of collective rights is developed in depth in Kymlicka, *Multicultural Citizenship*, chap. 3.

[55] John Rawls, 'The Idea of an Overlapping Consensus', *Oxford Journal of Legal Studies*, 7(1) (1987): 1–25, at 4. For further discussion, see Jeffrey Reitz and Raymond Breton, *Multiculturalism and Social Cohesion: Potentials and Challenges of Diversity* (New York: Springer, 2009).

[56] John Rawls, 'Justice as Fairness: Political not Metaphysical', *Philosophy & Public Affairs*, 14(3) (1985): 223–251, at 225–230.

[57] John Rawls, 'The Priority of Right and Ideas of the Good', *Philosophy & Public Affairs*, 17(4) (1988): 266. For further discussion on the connected question of stability in society see Rawls, *Political Liberalism*, 140–144.

social acceptability of both means and ends, methods and solutions, and account-ability. Following Kymlicka, two forms of cultural pluralism, 'multination' and 'polyethnic' states, are formulated as well as the distinction between 'internal restrictions' and 'external protections'.

Rawls' and Kymlicka's arguments are designed to protect fundamental rights and liberties for all, the majority and the minority (or minorities) alike. Note the fear of coercion that underlies the arguments. Kymlicka stresses the fear of majority coercion. Rawls specifically fears religious coercion and objects to the formation of a theocracy, for some people lack intensity of religious beliefs.[62]

Rawls implies that some norms and moral codes must be shared by members of the community, despite their cultural differences. These accepted norms, by virtue of their existence, enable each individual and group to pursue their way of life, as long as convictions are not contradictory to them. These norms set limitations on the range of values that society can respect.

Several factors are relevant in deciding when state intervention is warranted, including:

- the nature of the proposed interference – the severity of rights violations within the minority community;
- the existence of historical agreements which base the national minority's claim for some sort of autonomy;
- the extent of division within the community on the issue of restricting individual rights;
- the existence of any treaty obligations (e.g., historical promises made to immigrant groups);
- the extent to which formalized dispute resolution mechanisms exist within the community;
- the extent to which these mechanisms are seen as legitimate by group members;
- the ability of dissenting group members to leave the community if they so desire.[63]

Furthermore, if the right violation within a minority community is gross, for example, when members of the group are murdered or tortured, the liberal state is justified to intervene even if historically those minority groups enjoyed cultural autonomy. Norms and standards that might have been acceptable in the past might

---

[62] Rawls, *A Theory of Justice*, 216–221.
[63] Kymlicka and Cohen-Almagor, 'Ethnocultural Minorities in Liberal Democracies', 228–250. See also Kymlicka, *Multicultural Citizenship*, 165–70; Will Kymlicka and Bashir Bashir (eds), *The Politics of Reconciliation in Multicultural Societies* (New York: Oxford University Press, 2010); Geoffrey Brahm Levey, 'Liberal Autonomy as a Pluralistic Value', *The Monist*, 95(1) (2012): 103–126; Ayelet Shachar, 'Group Identity and Women's Rights in Family Law: The Perils of Multicultural Accommodation', *Journal of Political Philosophy*, 6(3) (1998): 285–305.

not be acceptable today. Norms do change with time, for instance with regard to homosexuality and presently regarding gender relationships as a result of the Me Too Movement.[64]

This chapter opened with Bhikhu Parekh's story. In his experience, holding on to 'reasonableness' as the sole yardstick was insufficient. The commission resolved that a consensus was not always possible and that on this matter an overlapping consensus was beyond reach. Accepting the Muslim petition would have undermined the delicate equilibrium in society and betray what the British deem fair and just. Chapters 3 and 4 present the third and last layer of the theory of reasonable multiculturalism. While Chapter 3 outlines the advantages of compromise and deliberative democracy as preferred methods to reconcile differences and overcome social disputes, Chapter 4 outlines the concept of coercion and explains why coercion should have a limited role in a society that is based on reasonable liberal multiculturalism. Yet coercion might be necessary to prevent the continuation of an abuse of power and denying basic human rights to vulnerable third parties.

---

[64] Me Too Movement, https://metoomvmt.org.

3

Compromise and Deliberative Democracy

All government, indeed every human benefit and enjoyment, every virtue and every prudent act is founded on compromise and barter.

Edmund Burke

'Compromise' isn't supposed to be a dirty word. It is, in fact, how representative democracy works.

Joe Kennedy III

Abe is a Jehovah's Witness. His son was involved in a serious car accident and was rushed to hospital. Abe arrived at the hospital shortly thereafter and is told by the physicians that his son needs a blood transfusion or he will die. Abe explains that his religion prohibits taking or giving blood transfusions and that his son would rather die than be denied a place in heaven. Can Abe compel the medical team, and his son, to follow his conception of the good? Is there a possible compromise between Abe's stern religious convictions and the physicians who wish to save life?

The aim of this chapter is to analyse the concepts of compromise and deliberative democracy. Groups employ both compromise and deliberation in their dealings with other groups as well as in their dealings with members of their own groups. In politics there are constant bargaining and compromises between different groups and organizations as well as between government and citizens. In liberal democracy the need for compromise is a constant necessity. When compromise is perceived as the preferred strategy, tolerance plays a major role in the decision-making process.

I draw a distinction between *principled* and *tactical* compromise. I speak on the need to promote coexistence through compromise, based on mutual respect and genuine concessions between different fragments of society. I also see it as important to extend civic education through discussions and open deliberation. Participatory and deliberative democracy is a preferred non-coercive way to resolve conflict.

66

COMPROMISE

According to the *Oxford English Dictionary*, 'compromise' is a 'settlement of a dispute by which each side gives up something it has asked for and neither side gets all it has asked for'.[1] Every compromise requires a quid pro quo. Following deliberation and discussion, a settlement is agreed upon by consent. Through scrutiny of the quid pro quo, agents deliberate the nature and amount of concessions required of them.[2] The parties explore the margins of appreciation and look for a space where they can share their positions with others.

Compromise entails flexibility and foregoing rigidity. The settlement may be reached through direct negotiations without any external interference or assistance, or by various forms of mediation, facilitation or arbitration that involve a third party who is not a disputant. Mediators need to maintain equitable treatment of the adversaries and drive forward a process by which gaps are bridged and agreements replace division. Unlike mediation, facilitation does not focus so much on substance but on enhancing the understanding of the perceptions, interests and needs of the disputants or on preparing the negotiations and generating an amicable atmosphere conducive to making compromises. Facilitators need to ensure that the negotiating parties are treated equitably and have equal representation at the negotiation table. The team leaders need to be in the same or very similar ranking.

Arbitration is a contract-based dispute resolution mechanism where parties to a dispute agree to appoint an impartial third party for resolution to adjudicate and find a solution. It is essential that the third party is acceptable by all parties to the dispute, and that it is not coerced or imposed on one or more of the sides.

Negotiation is the art of compromise. Communication is essential. When compromise takes place between two or more parties the emphasis is on reciprocity, that is, the concessions are mutual. The parties need to have mutual respect, listen actively and acknowledge what is being said. As explained in Chapter 1, mutual respect involves the acceptance of common procedures. Mutuality is derived from the endorsement of autonomy and our enshrined belief in the dignity of the person. It guides us to make concessions in order to make living together possible. Compromise is made when each side values more the things that can be achieved than the things they are required to give up. People give up the desirable for the necessary, acknowledging the social, cultural, moral and/or political constraints.

Good faith is essential. We respect each other as autonomous human beings who exercise self-determination to live according to our life plans. In turn we respect each other in order to help realize what we want to be. Each individual is a bearer of

---

[1] *Oxford Advanced Learner's Dictionary of Current English*, s.v. 'compromise'.

[2] Chiara Lepora, 'On Compromise and Being Compromised', *Journal of Political Philosophy*, 20 (1) (2012): 1–22, at 7.

rights and a source of claims against other persons, just because the resolution of the others is theirs, made by them as free agents.[3]

Compromise has preconditions. The discussion presupposes that some forms of communication and cooperation take place between the involved parties (notice that compromise requires some kind of cooperation, but not all forms of cooperation require compromise), and that the parties speak the same language, in the sense that they share some basic norms which form the grounds for potential understanding. When divergences become so fundamental that they can no longer be compounded, then no compromise can be reached.[4] There is simply nothing to talk about. Thus, to reach an agreement or some form of understanding, an appeal to common norms has to be made. Sides to a given dispute may recognize the force or sincerity of the opponent's view and – while not agreeing with their position – they still accept their right to hold it.

Conflicts are sometimes deep and bitter to the extent that parties do not recognize each other and are unwilling to sit together for negotiations. For instance, sovereign democracies often are unwilling to negotiate directly with terrorist organizations. The divides and gaps seem to be too wide and the parties opt to continue fighting each other. Thus, sitting at the negotiation table should not be taken for granted. This act in itself shows willingness to make concessions.

When parties negotiate it is important to distinguish between the underlying interests and other considerations. 'Other considerations' might be 'noise': excuses, rhetoric that the parties employ to promote their cause, immaterial arguments, diversions and other tactics deemed practical in pursuing the ends. Consider the following: suppose that you wish to send your children to the best school while your spouse is worried about the children coping in a highly competitive environment and prefers to send them to the local community school. Both parties should explain why they wish to send the children to a particular school and what are the worries and concerns if this were to happen. Reasoning that involves distance of school from home, traffic, school uniform, expenses, etc. might be raised but they are immaterial. If and when they are raised they only distract the conversation rather than focusing on the real interests of the parents.

Fisher and Ury bring another example. Two men argue in a library. One wants the window open while the other wants it closed. They bicker back and forth about how much to leave it open. The librarian asks one why he wants the window open.

---

[3] In 'Two Kinds of Respect', *Ethics*, 88 (1977): 36–49, Stephen Darwall distinguished between *recognition respect* and *appraisal respect*: the former being respect we ought to have to all human beings, while the latter means having a positive attitude towards a person above and beyond mere respect for her as a person. Here I am using the term 'respect' to mean recognition respect. See also Stephen Darwall, 'Honor, History, and Relationship: Essays in Second-Personal Ethics II', *Oxford Scholarship Online* (January 2014).

[4] Paul A. Sabatier and Hank C. Jenkins-Smith (eds), *Policy Change and Learning* (Boulder, CO: Westview Press, 1993), chaps 2 and 3.

'To get some fresh air', he answers. She then asks the other guy why he wants it closed. 'To avoid the draft', he replies. The librarian opens a big window in the adjacent room, bringing in fresh air without a draft. The librarian could not have reached that solution if she had focused only on the men's positions. Instead she observed their underlying interests of fresh air and no draft. The difference between positions and interests is crucial.[5]

Some suggestions for compromise are reasonable and acceptable whereas others are not. The act of compromise needs to be *directly related to the end the parties wish to achieve*. Xi-Sun loves the yellow dress. Her husband prefers the light blue dress. They compromise on a third, turquoise dress. This compromise might be reasonable and acceptable to both sides. Another example concerns an American Supreme Court case in which religion and security came into conflict. Gregory Holt, a Muslim prison inmate also known as Abdul Maalik Muhammad, wished to grow a beard as required by his faith. The prison objected on the ground that beards might be used to hide contraband, such as SIM cards, and because of potential identity problems when inmates grow and shave their beards. Holt suggested a compromise: to allow him to grow a half-inch beard. This compromise would address security concerns and would enable Holt to live according to his religion. However, prison officials denied his request, and the warden told Holt: '[Y]ou will abide by [Arkansas Department of Correction] policies and if you choose to disobey, you can suffer the consequences.'[6] Holt thought that the warden was unreasonable and appealed all the way to the Supreme Court. The court, *per* Justices Alito, Sotomayor and Ginsburg, accepted Holt's compromise and ordered the prison to allow Holt to grow a small beard. While acknowledging the prison's compelling interest in staunching the flow of contraband into and within its facilities, the court was not convinced that this interest would be seriously compromised by allowing an inmate to grow a half-inch beard. It was 'almost preposterous to think that [the petitioner] could hide contraband' in such a short beard.[7] The court also noted that the prison authorities did not demand that inmates have shaved heads or short crew cuts, thus it is easier to hide contraband in the hair than in a half-inch beard.[8] Furthermore, the court dismissed the potential identity problem claim by pointing out that the prison did not enforce restrictions on growing moustaches, head hair or quarter-inch beards for medical reasons. The court failed to understand why Holt's request evoked security concerns whereas head or other facial hair did not raise serious security concerns.[9]

---

[5] Roger Fisher, and William Ury, *Getting to Yes: Negotiating Agreement without Giving In* (London: Random House, 1991): 41.

[6] *Holt v. Hobbs*, 574 US 352, 135 S. Court 853 (2015).

[7] Ibid.

[8] Ibid.

[9] Ibid. For further discussion, see Brian Hutler, 'Compromise and Religious Freedom', *Law and Philosophy*, 39 (2020): 180–185.

I agree with the court's decision. Holt's suggestion reasonably balanced between his religious commitment and justified security considerations. He would have liked to have a full beard. Holt said that although he believed that his faith required him not to trim his beard at all, he proposed a solution that would make the prison's security claims irrelevant. Accommodating Holt was justified as his dignity as a believer was at issue. Holt felt he was obliged to fulfil a divine commandment. The warden's stubbornness was misplaced. I should also note that Justice Ginsburg, in her concurring opinion, said that accommodating Holt's request 'would not detrimentally affect others who do not share petitioner's belief'.[10]

Now consider unreasonable suggestions for compromise. A British couple are deliberating the destination of their summer vacation in 2016. David prefers Israel whereas Viagem prefers Turkey. Compromising on war-torn Syria on the grounds that it is geographically situated between Israel and Turkey would be unreasonable and unacceptable to both David and Viagem. Or suppose that a person, Thomaso, suffers from a kidney failure. His brother Louis (Lo in short) would be the perfect match donor but he refuses to sacrifice one of his kidneys to save his brother. Instead, Lo is willing to donate another organ: his cornea. This is not a reasonable or helpful compromise. It has nothing to do with Thomaso's condition and the end he wishes to achieve.

In compromise, interests are accommodated rather than regulated. When we are sensitive to the rights of the other then we will prefer settlement to coercion, and we will be more willing to acknowledge the need for concessions in order to reach an agreement. Different types of conflict will generate different sorts of compromise, according to the nature of the diversity at issue, the content and context of the dispute, and the complexion of the groups involved.

Political conflicts are usually divided into three categories: conflicts over scarce resources, ideological conflicts involving rival-rights claims and the collision of opposed identities, each seeking recognition. Whereas splitting the difference entails mutual concession, compromises over ideological and identity issues prove more challenging and require constructing a distinctive position to accommodate the various claims, values and ideals at stake.[11]

In politics, compromise suggests adapting to the realities of the situation at hand, meeting opponents somewhere in the middle and promoting the public good by sacrificing certain demands or preferences.[12] However, there are some matters on which it might be extremely difficult, even impossible, to reach a compromise. I have mentioned blood transfusions for Jehovah's Witnesses. Another issue is male

---

[10] *Holt v. Hobbs*, 574 US 352, 135 S. Court 853 (2015).

[11] Richard Bellamy, *Liberalism and Pluralism* (London and New York: Routledge, 1999): 103–104. For further discussion, see Martin Benjamin, *Splitting the Difference* (Lawrence: University Press of Kansas, 1990).

[12] April Carter, *Direct Action and Liberal Democracy* (London: Routledge & Kegan Paul, 1973): 144.

circumcision that is practised in Jewish, Muslim and certain Christian communities (see Chapter 6). Yet another is abortion.[13] Some religious groups are vehemently opposed to abortion under any circumstances. In the United States, the Supreme Court precedent *Roe v. Wade*[14] attracted criticisms from both pro-life and pro-choice activists. The former argue that the decision effectively allows the murdering of innocent children, while the latter assert that the decision does not give due weight to the wishes of the woman who is solely responsible for what is inside her body. The state should not interfere. Indeed, a person who believes in the sanctity of life no matter what would principally object to abortion and also to deciding the moment of one's death (euthanasia, suicide, assisted suicide and physician-assisted suicide). People who take issue with this position may seek a compromise, trying to persuade the opponent to recognize some considerations that, to their mind, play a major part in such grave decisions. For instance, regarding abortion they would try to persuade that abortion might be available if conducted at an early stage of pregnancy and when the reason is compelling, say rape. With regard to assisted suicide they would insist that it should be available when the patient voluntarily asks for that, without any pressure, the prognosis for some recovery is nil and the patient is suffering miserably.

Yet it might be the case that all arguments would fail to persuade the sanctity-of-life believers. Among orthodox religious groups sanctity of life is conceived in absolutist terms, that is, it means exactly that: sanctity of life, period. This viewpoint upholds an unqualified ban on all forms of life termination. This issue is taken outside the realm of politics. The only power who may take life is the Almighty, he and he alone (vitalists will speak of nature instead of God). People should not decide such issues for themselves, and no considerations are ever compelling enough to persuade otherwise. If liberals insist on securing compromise then they might find themselves in an undesirable situation in which they are pushed to concede infringement of basic human rights.

Compromise is not only a matter of two or more parties dealing with a common subject of concern or resources. Sometimes a compromise is made by one side regarding its aims, in deciding how to allocate the available means and in determining priorities. Compromise may mean a rational acquiescence in the fact that others not yet prepared either to embrace new ideas or to change their ways of life in conformity to this new idea. The originator of the new idea shrinks from coercion and does not wish to force others to accept something they are not ready to embrace.[15]

---

[13] Simon Cabulea May, 'Principled Compromise and the Abortion Controversy', *Philosophy & Public Affairs*, 33(4) (September 2005): 317–348. For further discussion, see Klemens Kappel, 'How Moral Disagreement May Ground Principled Moral Compromise', *Politics, Philosophy and Economics*, 17(1) (2017): 75–96.

[14] 410 U.S. 113 (1973).

[15] John Morley, *On Compromise* (London: Macmillan, 1923): 171–172.

Compromise, then, often is required between the different demands, needs and ideas that are to be pursued and satisfied, and between what is believed in and the circumstances. In short, people compromise between the 'ought' and the 'is', between what they aspire to and what is given in reality. In this connection the given circumstances, incompatible goals, scarcity of resources, uncertainty, complexity of the subject involved, availability of means and pressure precipitated by time may induce a party to compromise in making a decision. A relevant distinction is between *principled* and *tactical* compromise.

PRINCIPLED COMPROMISE

When genuine compromise is reached, a sense of relief and of real achievement is shared by the parties to the agreement. A principled genuine compromise is a mutual recognition by the parties of each other's rights, which leads them to make concessions and to seek constructive solutions, possibly by meeting halfway. Principled compromise may mean the acceptance of compromise as a matter of principle and it may also mean compromise that results from a principled, moral position. Justice as fairness comes into play.

Fair compromise entails readiness of the parties in concern to make reasonable concessions, and not merely tactical concessions, in order to establish a common ground that may satisfy all parties. Being reasonable in discussion means being open to listening to others, being open to changing one's mind and taking part in a deliberative exchange in which people air ideas in civility, according due respect to other participants.

When parties craft justifications for their positions and concessions, the negotiations are deliberative. The mechanism of deliberation is discussed below. When parties are accepting the compromise as a matter of principle, they genuinely participate in the debate with their counterpart with the willingness to recognize the other's interests and together establish a common ground. Both sides respect the personal autonomy, or dignity, of their counterpart.[16] This, however, does not necessarily mean that compromise should only be on principled matters, or that the parties compromise only on principles. In this context a further distinction is in order between changing one's mind on a given issue and adhering to the same

---

[16] Patrick Dobel, *Compromise and Political Action* (Savage, MD: Rowman and Littlefield, 1990), esp. p. 80. For further discussion, see Arthur Kuflik, 'Morality and Compromise', in J. Roland Pennock and John W. Chapman (eds), *Nomos XXI: Compromise in Ethics, Law and Politics* (New York: New York University Press, 1979): 38–65; Anton Ford, 'Third Parties to Compromise', and Amy J. Cohen, 'On Compromise, Negotiation and Loss', both in Jack Knight (ed.), *Nomos LIX: Compromise* (New York: New York University Press, 2018): 53–79, at 70–73, and 100–149, at 105–109. respectively; Ingolf U. Dalferth, 'Religion, Morality and Being Human: The Controversial Status of Human Dignity', in Dieter Grimm, Alexandra Kemmerer and Christoph Möllers (eds), *Human Dignity in Context* (Munich: Hart, 2018): 55–106.

position but conceding to accept a very different arrangement in a specific situation. Let me explain by considering the following examples.

In many cultures, the prevailing belief is that women's dignity is best preserved when they remain at home, taking care of housing chores. Batlan and Samantha are a married couple. Batlan likes to play video games. This is what he does all day, and he is quite good at it. Practice does matter to the extent that his friends call him 'Number 1!', a title Batlan carries with pride. Samantha does not have the time to play video games. She is busy taking care of the house, of Batlan and of the children. She does not particularly like cooking, cleaning and ironing, but this is Batlan's expectation of her. She used to argue in the past. It did not go well. The arguments quickly escalated into abuse and sometimes included not only pouring verbal but also physical violence. Samantha knows that her situation is anything but just and fair. No compromise is possible with Batlan. Her situation is coercive, the subject of Chapter 4.

Now consider another married couple, Elda and Oxana. Elda believes that one of the woman's roles is to be in charge of cooking and of feeding the family. This is how he was brought up. Elda lived all his life in an environment where women cooked for their men and families. When he grew up he fell in love with Oxana, a strong-minded feminist woman. After extensive debates with Oxana, Elda changed his mind. He came to realize that there is not a natural mechanism that tunnels women to kitchens, that there is nothing inherent, no sacred bond that connects women to cooking. Some women don't like to cook. Some men love to cook. And, in any event, if he wanted to connect his life with Oxana's life, nothing short of complete equality in allocating house chores will do. She made it very clear as a precondition for living together. Elda renounced his previous stance and accepted a new, equality-based position.

Finally, consider the case of Bur and Sarah. Like Elda, Bur also grew up believing that one of many woman's roles is to cook. Women, he always said, are made for cooking. It is one of their major rights and duties. He falls in love with Sarah who has many qualities, but cooking is not one of them. For the first years of marriage Bur insisted that Sarah will cook no matter what. Sarah had no strong feeling about the issue. She was willing to cook to the best of her limited abilities. Still the result was fury, resentment and unhappiness: the kids constantly complained about the food; Bur had to force himself to eat the delicacies that Sarah prepared. Sarah was unhappy to receive all the complaints and nagging comments. After some time, Bur realized that a change should be made: for the sake of their home peacefulness he was willing to do take away, to hire a cook and to find ways to keep Sarah outside the kitchen. Sarah, for her part, realizing the importance her husband assigned to 'mom's cooking' said she would prepare breakfast during the weekends. Eggs and pancakes she can do. Unlike Elda, Bur still believes it is one of the woman's roles to cook for their families, but this principle is not valid for his wife. Sarah is simply unable to cook as he wants her to. He does not renounce his position. He acknowledged that it will not work in his specific family. But it should be the case for women in general.

In the first and second examples, Batlan and Samantha, Elda and Oxana did not compromise. Samantha gave up fighting while Elda changed his mind. Bur and Sarah, on the other hand, did compromise. Sarah took upon herself a certain cooking responsibility. Bur did not revoke his previous stance and found himself required to make accommodations in order to continue living with the woman he loves and with his family. Bur still believed in his cherished principle that the kitchen is made for women. The cooks he hired were all women. He compromised with Sarah realizing that the principle will not do for their family. Bur and Sarah continued to believe that the agreed upon course of action was suboptimal, but each accepted that resolving the problem provided enough reason to accept the suboptimal outcome.[17] The compromise was made in good faith and both sides reconciled themselves to the results.

Let me now discuss compromise that results from a principled, moral position. This kind of compromise is not conditional. It does not depend on circumstances. It is made in good faith and both sides reconcile themselves to the results. The parties have respect for each other, and they acknowledge the reasonableness and legitimacy of the other side's argument while insisting that their own argument is entitled to enjoy a comparable consideration. Thus, for instance, while a religious minority may respect the majority's religion, it expects similar recognition of its own way of life.

Simon May makes three further points. First, principled reasons for moral compromise are usually thought to arise only when moral disagreement is reasonable.[18] Second, principled reasons for compromise are thought to have normative significance for everyone as they offer a common ground for reconciliation.[19] This is especially true when different sides accept the maxim of peaceful 'live and let live'. Third, not all intrinsic appeals to moral disagreement are used as reasons for moral compromise.[20] Parties to a debate may hold a different understanding of the concept of justice and/or of a community and/or group rights and would appeal to common features of what might be considered a just solution. Daniel Weinstock adds that such compromises are morally necessary as a result of the shortfalls that separate democratic institutions from democratic ideals, and they express a desirable form of democratic community.[21] Of course, principled compromises designed to promote a

---

[17] See Hutler, 'Compromise and Religious Freedom', 181.

[18] May, 'Principled Compromise and the Abortion Controversy', at 321.

[19] Ibid., 322.

[20] Ibid. For further discussion, see Peter Jones and Ian O'Flynn, 'Can a Compromise Be Fair?', *Politics, Philosophy & Economics*, 12(2) (2012): 115–135.

[21] Daniel Weinstock, 'On the Possibility of Principled Moral Compromise', *Critical Review of International Social and Political Philosophy*, 16(4) (2013): 537–556. See also Christian F. Rostbøll and Theresa Scavenius (eds), *Compromise and Disagreement in Contemporary Political Theory* (London: Routledge, 2017).

certain moral value may also take into account circumstances and likely outcomes of the compromise so as to optimize the extent that compromise is required.

A true story, shared by my friends, D and J, may serve as an example for principled compromise. D was brought up in a traditional Catholic family in Israel. J was brought up in a Jewish family in the United States. They met in Israel, fell in love and decided to marry. Neither D nor J wanted to convert to another religion. They could not marry in any of the Israeli religious courts as those insist that the couple must be of the same religious denomination. They agreed to marry in a civil ceremony in Cyprus, as civil marriage is not allowed in Israel. A civil ceremony abroad is the only legal option for a mixed couple in Israel. Israel recognizes and registers such ceremonies based on international law principles. But for D and J it was also important to start their lives together with respect for and acceptance of each other's traditions and beliefs, and to give their families an opportunity to share in their marriage, taking into consideration their feelings and concerns. D and J understood that the future would require complicated decisions regarding how to raise their children and how to navigate between two cultures and religions, so a good start would be to establish trust and begin to build good relationships with both families. After long deliberations, D and J decided to have two additional, subsequent wedding celebrations: a blessing ceremony in a Christian church in Jerusalem with family and friends, and another ceremony with a Jewish Reform rabbi in Florida, where J's home-bound mother resided.

Both D and J had to undergo a challenging process. They reached their joint decisions after much deliberation and soul searching, looking for satisfactory solutions with which they could live. The priest who conducted their Christian ceremony chose the wording with the couple, including phrases from the Catholic traditional ceremony, and also some Hebrew and Aramaic hymns. The Reform rabbi delivered a biblical blessing revered by both traditions. D and J received support from their families as well as from two clerics, the Christian priest and a modern Orthodox rabbi who provided guidance. They made compromises and accommodations based on mutual respect because they were bound together by their mutual love, for which they have been paying a price as the environment in which they lived is not always tolerant with regard to intermarriage, and also because they shared responsibility for the successful pursuit of their goal to live together as a couple and to raise their children together. Both D and J understood this was a test for them as a couple, one of many, as their bond was likely to attract attention and criticism from many who object to such inter-religious bonding.

Principled genuine compromise should be sought in many social matters. On some matters it might be extremely difficult, even impossible, to reach a compromise that would be acceptable to all sides of the dispute. But we should appreciate the genuine attempt on the part of participants to reach some sort of compromise, of workable formula that will answer some of the demands and interests of the proponents as well as of the opposition.

Simon May argues categorically that moral compromise in political life is only ever warranted for pragmatic reasons.[22] As a student of politics I concede that political decisions are motivated first and foremost by interests. However, I disagree that *all* decisions are *always* divorced from moral considerations and are made solely for partisan interests. Decisions that have to do with welfare, housing, human rights, women rights and minority rights, among others, are not merely pragmatic. I have worked with politicians in Israel, the United States and the United Kingdom and can testify that some of them are motivated, at least on some issues, by a genuine desire to do good to others. In those instances their own good was secondary. Kantian considerations of viewing people as ends, of respecting others, of affinity and sympathy, and of egalitarianism do play a part.

At times, parties that push for an egalitarian agenda need to compromise as a result of resource constraints, considerations that have to do with maintaining a coalition among other pragmatic reasons, *and also* because their agenda comes into conflict with other values that are deemed of importance to the negotiation parties. For instance, one party may push for expanding the liberties of minorities while another promotes societal security. Both sides respect the moral position of the other: promoting minority rights for one and the safeguarding of life and limb for the other. The compromise should be made in good faith and both sides agree to accept the results. The parties acknowledge the reasonableness and legitimacy of the other side's demands while insisting that their own agenda is entitled to have a comparable consideration. The compromise they seek to secure promotes certain moral values and is also prudential, acknowledging that it is better to meet halfway than to stick to the existing policy.[23]

Consideration for the other may dictate refraining from opening non-Kosher shops that sell pork in Jewish-orthodox districts as well as from placing billboards advertising provocative images of bathing suits in the same districts. Public roads that pass solely through such religious neighbourhoods should be closed during Shabbat, the Jewish day of rest. The case is much more complicated when public roads pass through religious *and* secular neighbourhoods. Then there is a need to strike a fair balance between competing interests, aiming to reconcile between the religious desire to keep those roads closed during Shabbat as well as during hours of prayers in other days of the week, and the free movement of the secular residents.[24]

---

[22] May, 'Principled Compromise and the Abortion Controversy', at 317. See also Simon C. May, 'Moral Compromise, Civic Friendship, and Political Reconciliation', *Critical Review of International Social and Political Philosophy*, 14(5) (2011): 581–602.

[23] For another example, see Weinstock, 'On the Possibility of Principled Moral Compromise', 553. See also Michele Mangini, 'Toward a Theory of Reasonableness', *Ratio Juris*, 31(2) (2018): 214.

[24] A case in point is H.C. (High Court of Justice) 5016/96, 5025/96, 5090/96, 5434/96 *Horev v. Minister of Transport* (Jerusalem, April 1997) (Hebrew). Another interesting case concerns the opening of shops in Tel Aviv during Shabbat. While striking a balance between competing interests – honouring the Shabbat versus freedom of occupation, the Supreme Court decided

FIGURE 3.1. The Western Wall, Jewish Quarter, Old City, Jerusalem, Israel (Gonzalo Azumendi/Stone/Getty Images).

THE WESTERN WALL

Another area of contention concerns the Western (known also as the Wailing) Wall, the *Kotel* (Figure 3.1). Since 1988, a group called Women of the Wall is fighting for the introduction of a new, pluralistic and *equal* section of the Western Wall, which is one of the holiest places for Jewish prayers.[25] Unlike the current separated men's and women's prayer sections, they demand that this section should *not* be administered by the Orthodox Rabbi of the *Kotel*. The pluralistic section would be governed under the auspices of a group of leaders from all Jewish denominations, with fair representation for women. The mission of Women of the Wall is to achieve the social and legal recognition of their right, as women, to wear prayer shawls (*tallit*) and *Tefillin* (Jewish phylacteries), pray (*Tefillah*) and read from the Torah collectively and out loud at the Western Wall.[26] After a long struggle the women were able

that merchants should be free to open their shops on Shabbat: H.C. 3660/17 *Association of Merchants and the Self – Employed v. Minister of the Interior* (Jerusalem, October 2017) (Hebrew).

[25] The Wall, known as the Western Wall and the Wailing Wall, is the only structure remaining from the Holy Temple, rebuilt in glorious style and splendour by King Herod and destroyed by the Romans in 70 AD.

[26] Women of the Wall, http://womenofthewall.org.il/about/faq/; Yuval Jobani and Nahshon Perez, *Women of the Wall: Navigating Religion in Sacred Sites* (Oxford: Oxford University Press, 2017); Rivka Haut, 'Women of the Wall: Fighting for the Right to Pray', *The Jofa Journal*,

to secure rights to *tallit*, *Tefillin* and *Tefillah* but they are unable to read at the *Kotel* from a Torah scroll. As the *Kotel* is the most unsuitable place in the world to wage religious rivalries, a compromise needs to be found so all Jews, notwithstanding their interpretations of *Halacha*, will be able to pray freely in accordance with their beliefs. Instead, these women were verbally and physically attacked by men who think that the 'defiant' women overstep their assigned boundaries.

The case was considered by the Supreme Court several times but divisions within the court prevented the raising of a clear voice in support of women's equality in this delicate religious affair. In the final hearing, with an expanded panel of nine justices, the court held that the Women of the Wall were entitled to pray in the manner of their choice in the Western Wall compound, but in order to prevent injury to the sensitivities of other worshippers the court suggested a compromise according to which the government would make arrangements for them in another prayer area at an adjacent site called Robinson's Arch. The Women of the Wall were opposed to this proposal as they wish to pray in the manner they see appropriate at the women's section, adjacent to the men's section in front of the Western Wall.[27] In 2016 the Israeli government passed a resolution that authorized the construction of a new plaza built where men and women can pray together at the Western Wall in Jerusalem's Old City. Two other sections will remain segregated by gender. This decision meant that, for the first time ever, men and women would have been able to pray side by side at Judaism's holiest site.[28] However, the Orthodox and ultra-Orthodox immediately voiced their protest against the decision, saying that it only created conflict and dispute. Clashes, at times violent, between Women of the Wall and Orthodox and ultra-Orthodox opposition are recurrent.

The feminists challenge the Orthodox establishment. Their fight is just and reasonable. It is also most difficult. On each and every issue that is regarded as 'man's domain', be it praying rituals, membership in religious bodies or the ordination of women rabbis, women face strong resistance as they challenge an intricate and complex web of entrenched norms that for the Orthodoxy define Jewish

10(2) (Fall 2012): 9–10; Frances Raday, 'Claiming Equal Religious Personhood: Women of the Wall's Constitutional Saga', in W. Brugger and M. Karayanni (eds), *Religion in the Public Sphere: A Comparative Analysis of German, Israeli, American and International Law* (Berlin: Max Plank, 2007): 255–298.

[27] H.C.J. 1025/89, 955/89, 699/89 *Anat Hoffman v. The Jerusalem Municipality and Others*, P.D. 48(1), 678; H.C.J. 257/89 *Anat Hoffman v. Commissioner of the Western Wall*, P.D. 48 (2) 265; H.C.J. 3358/95 *Anat Hoffman v. Director General of Prime Minister's Office*, P.D. 54(2) 345; H.C.J. 4128/00 *Director General of Prime Minister's Office v. Anat Hoffman*, P.D. 57(3) 289; Raphael Cohen-Almagor, 'Israel and International Human Rights', in Frederick P. Forsythe (ed.), *Encyclopedia of Human Rights* (New York: Oxford University Press, 2009), 3: 247–257; Frances Raday, 'Women of the Wall', *Jewish Women's Archive*, http://jwa.org/encyclopedia/article/women-of-wall.

[28] Paul Goldman, 'Israel to Build Area for Men, Women to Pray Together at Wailing Wall', *NBC News* (1 February 2016), www.nbcnews.com/news/world/israel-build-area-men-women-pray-together-wailing-wall-n508551.

identity.[29] While we can discern some progress in religious gender equality in education, prayer rituals, public leadership and domestic family abuse, the success is modest. Powerful religious sectors still do not appreciate female creativity, spirituality, intelligence and engagement, and wish to minimize women's role in society.

In March 2013 the attorney general issued a scathing report against the phenomenon of gender segregation and the exclusion of women. Its unequivocal conclusion was that these discriminatory practices undermine the very foundations of Israeli democracy which recognizes the inherent value of every human being. Tolerance must be shown towards lifestyles of different communities. The exclusion of women as equal participants in civil life is unacceptable. The report also dismissed the *Haredi* argument that maintaining segregated arrangements in the public sphere is required for the preservation of its unique character.[30] The attorney general instructed municipalities, religious services, bus companies, health clinics and public institutions to take active steps to ensure gender equality. While some services have changed their practices and stopped gender segregation and discrimination, others are slow to respond.[31] This divide between the foundations of Israeli democracy and the practice of religious communities harms women and undermines Israeli democracy.

TACTICAL COMPROMISE

Because disputes frequently involve conflicts of personality, of character and of distinct interests, settlements might turn out to be no more than a temporary arrangement, reached as a result of constraints related to time. This type of compromise is not the result of an effort to bridge the gap between rival groups. Instead it is a compromise which at least one side is forced to accept under given circumstances or is driven to accept believing no further gains could be achieved in the given circumstances. There is no genuine willingness to give up part of the interests involved but only to postpone the deadlines for their achievement. If any compromise occurs here, it is within one party, and not between different parties. The essential component of compromise, namely mutuality, is lacking.[32]

---

[29] Leah Shakdiel, 'Women of the Wall: Radical Feminism as an Opportunity for a New Discourse in Israel', *Journal of Israeli History*, 21(1) (2002): 126–163; Yael Israel-Cohen, *Between Feminism and Orthodox Judaism* (Leiden: Brill, 2015): 49–78. For further discussion, see Valerie Bryson, *Feminist Political Theory* (London: Palgrave, 2016): 268–297.

[30] Orly Erez-Likhovski and Riki Shapira-Rosenberg, *Excluded, for God's Sake* (Jerusalem: Israel Religious Action Center and Israel Movement for Reform and Progressive Judaism, 2013–2014): 7–8.

[31] Ibid., 23–26, 29–31, 33–41, 51–58, 75–81.

[32] May speaks of goal-based pragmatic compromise where people compromise and concede as much as they need to secure a certain goal. This compromise is instrumental and strategic. Furthermore, pragmatic reasons for compromise only have normative significance for those sympathetic to the goals the compromise facilitates. See May, 'Principled Compromise and the Abortion Controversy', 320.

Here a distinction can be made between tactical compromise that still respects the rights of the opponents, and tactical compromise that is based on deceit. As for the first type, political partisans make tactical compromises all the time. That does not mean they fail to respect their negotiating partners, only that they deem their ultimate goals too important to surrender. Thus, for example, minority groups make tactical compromises, accepting less sweeping legislation than they desire about, say, the level of their representation in local and national parliaments, hoping that later they can win enough votes to pass a more comprehensive voting reform.

The second type of tactical compromise is unethical. It involves one side that does not respect the partner for negotiation as a rights-bearers. That side would have no qualms about violating the common understanding and trying to gain a further advantage at the expense of its opponent should a proper opportunity occur. This is what I call deceitful tactical compromise, to which agents resort without giving up any of their aims. It is not reached in good faith. In other words, deceitful tactical compromise lacks respect for the other and it is a form of a lie in the sense that the deceitful person will break the terms of the bargain when the right occasion presents itself.

In international relations, possibly the best example of deceitful tactical compromise is the 1938 Munich summit. In March that year Austria was declared a province of Germany and Hitler marched into Vienna. Then he set his eyes on Czechoslovakia. Part of that country, the Sudetenland which bordered Germany, was populated mostly by Germans who resented living under Czech officials and police, many of whom spoke poor German. They were excited over Austria's absorption into Germany and demanded political equality and autonomy. The Czechoslovakian government rejected their demands. Hitler wished to rescue the Sudeten Germans, and war between the two countries seemed inevitable. Mussolini responded to an appeal to mediate in order to forestall war, and on 29 September 1938 Mussolini, Hitler, Britain's Prime Minister Neville Chamberlain and France's premier, Edouard Daladier, agreed to meet in Munich. President Edvard Beneš of Czechoslovakia was not invited to the summit. Munich is the destructive symbol of deceitful tactical compromise and illustrates the dangers that lie when one side is willing to make genuine concessions while the other is stealing for time.[33] While Chamberlain and Daladier thought they reached a compromise with Hitler, the latter was deceitful. Hitler led Chamberlain and Daladier to believe that he was willing to make concessions when in fact he was not.

On crucial matters it is enough to make one such deceit to gain a reputation of someone who cannot be trusted. After that, those deceitful persons would find it

---

[33] For further discussion, see Donald McIntosh, 'Coercion and International Politics: A Theoretical Analysis', and Robert Jarvis, 'Bargaining and Bargaining Tactics', both in J. Roland Pennock and John W. Chapman (eds), *Nomos XIV: Coercion* (Chicago and New York: Aldine – Atherton, Inc., 1972): 243–271 and 272–288 respectively; Eric Beerbohm, 'The Problem of Clean Hands', in Knight, *Nomos LIX: Compromise*, 1–52.

difficult to regain others' respect. Robert Mnookin speaks of 'devils' with whom people find it difficult to negotiate because people are not able to trust those 'devils', fear that they might harm them or are unable to verify the devils' good faith in fulfilling their said obligations.[34] Avishai Margalit terms agreements that cause harm or injustice to one of the sides rotten compromises.[35] He argues that such compromises should be prohibited in all circumstances.[36]

An example might be the obligation of all public schools in England to teach English and the breaking of this obligation by some Jewish ultra-religious schools that were said to accept this obligation, like any other school, but with time reverted to teaching in other languages without informing the education authorities. It appears that the leaders of the schools were insincere in accepting the terms of the British Department of Education.[37] They were said to accept a compromise in order to enable them to open their schools but it is questionable whether they acted in good faith, with the intention to abide by the terms. It seems that all they did was to make a tactical compromise. The compromise was between them and themselves. With time, they abandoned what was agreed upon.

Sometimes compromise is made through the use of coercion. Again, this is not a genuine compromise as one of the sides to the agreement lacks the ability to resist. This situation happens when the two sides are unequal in power. The majority in a given society may reach an agreement with a minority culture that the latter would forfeit an important asset, declared to be of national importance, without proper compensation. The majority simply exercised its power over the weak minority. There were so-called negotiations between the two sides, but they were a façade. The result leads to anger and frustration among the minority group that feels deprived of something that is very important to them. In this instance, questions arise about the moral legitimacy of the action. The issue is whether such a coerced compromise is compatible with integrity and with justice in some sense. Compromise should be considered and reached according to the content of the demands, regarding their substance and meaning, and with due care to the interests

---

[34] Robert Mnookin, *Bargaining with the Devil* (New York: Simon and Schuster, 2011).

[35] Avishai Margalit, *On Compromise and Rotten Compromise* (Princeton, NJ: Princeton University Press, 2010).

[36] Ibid., 3. Margalit speaks of 'sanguine compromise' which is an agreement that involves painful recognition of the other side, a giving up of dreams and making mutual concessions that express recognition of the other's viewpoint, and is not based on coercion. 'A sanguine compromise is not necessarily the proverbial compromise of meeting halfway, yet it does mean splitting the difference not too far from some central value.' See Avishai Margalit, 'Indecent Compromise, Decent Peace', *The Tanner Lectures on Human Values*, Stanford University (4–5 May 2005), https://tannerlectures.utah.edu/_documents/a-to-z/m/Margalit_2006.pdf. Principled compromise, discussed above, is somewhat similar.

[37] Siobhan Fenton, 'Illegal Jewish Schools: Department of Education Knew about Council Faith School Cover-up as Thousands of Pupils "Disappeared"', *The Independent* (3 April 2016), www.independent.co.uk/news/uk/home-news/illegal-jewish-schools-department-of-education-knew-about-council-faith-school-cover-up-as-thousands-a6965516.html.

of both sides. If the values at stake contradict basic rights, and/or inflict harm on society or part of it, then the term 'compromise' is a mere euphemism. A better term to describe the situation is exploitation. The fact that a power is engaged with the making of forced compromises does not imply that might makes right. A majority may resort to exploitative conduct and the mere fact that a considerable number of people are involved does not make their actions just. It only makes the situation more terrible.

Democracy is not simply a matter of counting heads. It is about free discussion, a willingness to recognize the other's rights and respecting differences of opinion. It is a way of administering discussion between different persons who hold different interests. The aim is not to secure complete agreement on every question, though democracy certainly welcomes crystallization of consensus and agreement. If, however, unanimous agreement cannot be reached regarding a certain decision, then relevant minorities can bring about their considerations as to why they should not consent to or comply with these directives. This process has to be done through the deliberative mechanisms of democracy: free exchange of opinions, and open, mutual criticism. When majority and minorities are engaged in discussion, the breadth of opinion is further broadened by the inclusion of new elements, or by the modification of old ones. Moreover, the understanding which induces minorities to make concessions to the prevailing views must be shared by the majority as well. From time to time the majority too must make some concessions to the will of minorities, so the sense of community that keeps majority and minorities together will not be dissolved. Therefore the commonly accepted treaty is compromise, a principle whereby that which divides is rejected in favour of that which unites the people. This is not to say that compromise is a self-sufficient principle that can be divorced from moral or other considerations. Compromise between two or more groups is not to come at the expense of the rights of others. Deliberation helps in the elucidation of interests and goals.

DELIBERATIVE DEMOCRACY

Kant, Mill and Rawls stressed the importance of deliberation, exchanging ideas and voicing critique. The freedom to reason and to argue publicly about social concerns is a necessary condition of legitimate and sound government and legislation. In *Critique of Pure Reason*, Kant explained that the critique of reason leads to science, whereas dogmatic use of percepts, without criticism, leads to groundless assertions.[38] Both Mill and Kant believed that in the absence of open criticism people will hold beliefs as mere lifeless doctrine. Mill wrote that without the free exchange of ideas, the common views would be rigid, lack adaptability and soon turn into dead dogma. However true an opinion may be, if it is not fully, frequently and fearlessly discussed,

---

[38] Immanuel Kant, *Critique of Pure Reason* (1781), www.earlymoderntexts.com/assets/pdfs/kant1781part1.pdf.

it will cease to be held as a 'living truth'.[39] Kant wrote: 'Only through criticism can we cut the roots of materialism, fatalism, atheism, agnosticism, fanaticism, and superstition, all of which can do harm to everyone.'[40] Rawls' just polity presupposes freedom of thought, conscience, speech and assembly.[41] Rawls spoke of a process of deliberative rationality through which people develop their life plans and ascertain the best course of action to fulfil their desires.[42] Freedom to reason and deliberate publicly is vital for protecting people's rights.

According to Jürgen Habermas, each and every person should receive a threefold recognition: 'they should receive equal protection and equal respect in their integrity as irreplaceable individuals, as members of ethnic or cultural groups, and as citizens, that is, as members of the political community'.[43] Democracy does not demand the creation of a society which consists of people who parrot decisions of the governing body, but rather it demands acceptance of the right to be different, to accept that there can be a range of opinions. This acceptance implies, in turn, an agreement on the ways in which these differences could be resolved.

In deliberative democracy discussions are held between different persons who hold various interests. People weigh considerations, consolidate judgement and convey their reasons for a particular course of action. Public discussion is perceived to be a common good. People address the problems they are facing together. As members of the same polity they assume that they have common interests and that they can reach agreement on principles and policies. Political leaders have moral obligation and responsibility to tease out just, reasonable policies through the mechanisms of compromise and deliberation, based on respect, the acknowledgement of plural interests and the desire to reach a consensus or at least satisfactory arrangements. Respect for different conceptions of the good, and a commitment to moderation, have to be promoted.

The essence of democratic legitimacy should be sought in the ability of all citizens to collectively engage in authentic deliberation about their conduct. Deliberative democracy presents an ideal of political autonomy based on the practical reasoning expressed in an open and accountable discourse, leading to an agreed judgement on substantive policy issues concerning the common good. Habermas notes that the success of deliberative democracy depends on the institutionalization of the corresponding procedures and conditions of communication and on the interplay of deliberative processes and informed public opinions.[44]

---

[39] J.S. Mill, *On Liberty*, 95.
[40] Kant, *Critique of Pure Reason* (1781), www.earlymoderntexts.com/assets/pdfs/kant1781part1.pdf.
[41] Rawls, *A Theory of Justice*, 225.
[42] Ibid., sect. 64, 416–424.
[43] Jürgen Habermas, *Between Facts and Norms* (Cambridge: Polity, 1996): 496.
[44] Habermas, *Between Facts and Norms*, 298. See also Jürgen Habermas, *Moral Consciousness and Communicative Action* (Cambridge, MA: MIT Press, 1990); David Miller, 'Deliberative Democracy and Social Choice', *Political Studies*, 40 (August 1992): 54–67; C.S. Nino, *The Constitution of Deliberative Democracy* (New Haven, CT: Yale University Press, 1996); Jon

Deliberative democracy implies a strong meaning of inclusion and political equality which, when implemented, increases the likelihood that democratic decisions will promote justice. Democracy is not only a means through which citizens can promote their interests and hold the power of rulers in check. It is also a means of collective problem-solving which depends for its legitimacy on the expression of diverse opinions. Inclusiveness promotes free exchange of views and better understanding of diverse interests.[45]

Monique Deveaux speaks of a government's conscious effort to encourage frank deliberation about citizens' needs-based and interest-based disagreements. Such deliberations would reflect the key motivating concerns behind cultural disputes. A politically focused framework for mediating cultural conflicts would bring to the fore the practical, strategic and intracultural nature of many disputes about social customs and their legitimacy in liberal democracies. Deliberative procedures would provide open and also secure spaces for dissenting voices and present criticisms of particular practices and arrangements within communities.[46]

Inclusiveness, openness, candidness and transparency are keys for successful deliberations. Open deliberations directly involve citizens in the decision-making processes on matters of public concern. This requires the setting of public reason institutions by which knowledge is exchanged and ideas crystallized via critical reflections. Democratic procedures establish a network of pragmatic considerations and a constant flow of relevant information. People present their cases in persuasive ways, trying to bring others to accept their proposals. Processes of deliberation take place through an exchange of information among parties who introduce and critically test proposals. Each participant has an equal voice in the process and tries to find reasons that are persuasive to all so as to promote the common good.[47]

Elster, *Deliberative Democracy* (Cambridge: Cambridge University Press, 1998); Amy Gutmann and Dennis F. Thompson, *Why Deliberative Democracy?* (Princeton, NJ: Princeton University Press, 2004); Amy Gutmann and Dennis F. Thompson, 'Reflections on Deliberative Democracy', in André Bächtiger, John S. Dryzek, et al. (eds), *The Oxford Handbook of Deliberative Democracy* (Oxford: Oxford University Press, 2018): 900–912; Stephen Macedo, *Deliberative Politics: Essays on Democracy and Disagreement* (New York: Oxford University Press, 1999); James S. Fishkin and Peter Laslett, *Debating Deliberative Democracy* (Oxford: Wiley-Blackwell, 2003); John S. Dryzek, *Deliberative Democracy and Beyond* (Oxford: Oxford University Press, 2002); John S. Dryzek, *Foundations and Frontiers of Deliberative Governance* (New York: Oxford University Press, 2012); Maurizio Passerin, *Democracy as Public Deliberation* (Piscataway, NJ: Transaction Publishers, 2006).

45 Young, *Inclusion and Democracy*, 6; Judith Squires, 'Culture, Equality and Diversity', in Paul Kelly (ed.), *Multiculturalism Reconsidered* (Cambridge: Polity, 2002): 114–132; Jorge Valadez, *Deliberative Democracy, Political Legitimacy, and Self-Determination in Multicultural Societies* (London: Routledge, 2018).

46 Monique Deveaux, *Gender and Justice in Multicultural Liberal States* (Oxford: Oxford University Press, 2009): 96–107.

47 Joshua Cohen, 'Deliberation and Democratic Legitimacy', in Alan Hamlin and Philip Petit (eds), *The Good Polity* (Oxford: Blackwell, 1989): 22–23; Jürgen Habermas, *Between Facts and Norms* (Cambridge: Polity, 1998): 304–308.

Deliberation may lead people to seek more data, or prompt them to avoid seeking further information. Information may affect their mental, cognitive and emotional systems, helping people consolidate their short- and long-term objectives. A genuine attempt to reach consensus should be made before a formal decision is attempted. This often occurs by way of refining and weeding out options. Participants aim that the informal mutual agreement will be translated into an explicit and effective decision that is shared by those who are party to it.[48] Now, I am not saying that the deliberative process always yields success. Granted that sometimes it does not. But I argue that we should try to converse, and persuade via the free exchange of ideas, deliberation and open contestations of views.

Mutual recognition, respect and concern for others, and equal protection, are essential. Deliberative democracy enables an understanding of cultures as continually creating, recreating and renegotiating the imagined boundaries between 'us' and 'them'.[49] Securing and promoting human rights are desired goals, especially of vulnerable populations. Instilling trust via means of deliberative democracy and public engagement ensures democratic legitimacy.[50]

When mutual recognition, respect and concern for others and equal protection are absent, compromise might be beyond reach. Observing the democratic catch, mechanisms of self-defence will come into play to ensure that liberty and tolerance are not abused to destroy democracy. Thus, for instance, violent ideological and/or religious movements that vow to abuse democracy in order to undermine it if they come to power should be fought against. It would not be prudent to strive to compromise with, for example, fascist movements as any compromises they may make would only be tactical. These kinds of movements are unlikely to change and reform because violence is embedded firmly within their ideology. It would be a mistake to try and reach compromises with them. Those movements should be denied access to a compromise as they challenge the very grounds upon which liberal democracy is based.[51]

CONCLUSION

I opened this chapter with the example of Abe, the Jehovah's Witness who wishes to deny a blood transfusion to his injured son. This example raises an ethical dilemma.

---

[48] Henry S. Richardson, *Democratic Autonomy: Public Reasoning about the Ends of Policy* (Oxford: Oxford University Press, 2002): 166.

[49] Seyla Benhabib, *The Claims of Culture: Equality and Diversity in the Global Era* (Princeton, NJ: Princeton University Press, 2002).

[50] John Ferejohn, 'Deliberation and Citizen Interests', in Bächtiger, Dryzek, et al. *The Oxford Handbook of Deliberative Democracy*, 420–431; Monique Deveaux, *Gender and Justice in Multicultural Liberal States* (Oxford: Oxford University Press, 2009); Matthew Festenstein, *Negotiating Diversity: Culture, Deliberation, Trust* (Cambridge: Polity, 2005).

[51] Raphael Cohen-Almagor, 'Disqualification of Lists in Israel (1948–1984): Retrospect and Appraisal', *Law and Philosophy*, 13(1) (1994): 43–95; Raphael Cohen-Almagor, 'Disqualification of Political Parties in Israel: 1988–1996', *Emory International Law Review*, 11 (1) (1997): 67–109.

On the one hand, we need to respect Abe's set of beliefs. On the other hand, physicians who are trained to save lives would not be at ease in denying a patient a life-saving treatment when that treatment is readily available. The further complication is that Abe is not asking to deny treatment from himself but from his son. To what extent has he the power over his son and the physicians to compel them to live by his conception of the good? Applying Rawls' veil of ignorance, what would be a just and fair solution? Is Abe's demand reasonable? Can there be any compromise between the parties?

Abe is not simply demanding special recognition of his rights; he is rejecting a wide range of assumptions that underpin liberal democracies, first and foremost those concerning the dignity of the person, respect for human life and the duty of physicians to save life and not stand idly by when they have the ability to help. Abe is not in the same discursive realm as liberals who seek to mediate disputes and foster compromise. In the framework of liberal democracy the principles of respect for others and not harming others as well as the accepted medical norms that accentuate the obligation of physicians to save life dictate helping Abe's son.[52] Humane medicine and just doctoring warrant blood transfusion for Abe's son. By contrast, an LGBTQ activist demanding equal access to healthcare and the recognition of gay marriage is making claims that fit squarely within – and, indeed, are derived from – the liberal democratic tradition of respect for others and not harming others. The potential for a reasonable discussion and compromise is therefore much greater.

The compromise process involves communication between the parties. It is a conscious process in which there is a degree of moral acknowledgement of the other party.[53] Both sides understand this is the right thing to do. Compromise may also be the result of expediency. The parties understand that they may gain more by the compromise than by entering into a prolonged state of conflict that would demand much more resources from them or may require an intervention of a third party that may impose on them a disliked state of affairs. The process should be perceived as fair and legitimate by all parties. Democracies are advised to enhance and promote civic education which includes discussions on the merits of tolerance, based on mutual respect for others, and of compromise, based on mutual genuine concessions between different groups in society.

When parties are unable to reach a compromise or when a compromise breaks down after agreement, sometimes one of the sides to a given dispute might resort to coercion, aiming to force its perspective on the opponent. Other times, when

---

[52] For a different perspective, see Chandran Kukathas, 'Cultural Toleration', *Nomos*, 39 (1997): 69–104.

[53] Martin Golding, 'The Nature of Compromise: A Preliminary Inquiry', in J. Roland Pennock and John W. Chapman (eds), *Nomos XXI: Compromise in Ethics, Law and Politics* (New York: New York University Press, 1979): 16.

coercion fails, the side who wished to coerce at first is pushed to make concessions and to compromise, realizing that coercion will not do. When coercion is preferred over compromise, the relationships are based on domination, on actions that repress autonomy rather than enabling it to flourish. Chapter 4 elaborates on the concept of coercion.

4

Coercion

One who uses coercion is guilty of deliberate violence. Coercion is inhuman.

Mahatma Gandhi

Some years ago the Israeli daily newspaper *Yedioth Ahronoth* reported on one Bedouin girl who ran away from home to escape both female circumcision and coerced planned marriage. The girl was quoted as saying: 'I lost confidence in all people around me. My loving mother became my number 1 enemy. I did not trust my friends, or my sisters. There were moments when I thought about killing myself.'[1] The girl maintained that she heard horrible stories about circumcision from girls who experienced it, and that she believed the worst of those stories. When she approached her father as a last hope, and the latter had referred her back to her mother, she ran away to her sister who lived in the north of Israel. She was 15-and-a-half years old at the time. This act of running away from her tribe constitutes enough reason for murder for family honour. Bedouin girls who wish to escape their lot have a mountain to climb as they aim to free themselves from tribal compulsion.

The word 'coercion' comes from the Latin *coercere*, meaning 'to surrender', and even more suggestively from two older Latin words, *arca* ('box' or 'coffin') and *arcere* ('to shut in'). 'Coercere' means to repress, to contain, to restrain. Either the restraint is exercised in the interest of security, as when a person takes refuge in an ark, places relics in an *arca*, experiences arctation or protects arcane knowledge; or the restraint is exercised directly by an outside agent, as when a person coarcted or submits to coarctation.[2] To coerce is to narrow the space of free movement and action, lessening one's self-sovereignty and self-mastery. A common form of coercion occurs

---

[1] Shlomo Abramowitz, 'The Bedouin Girls Scream Silently', *Yedioth Ahronoth* (15 May 1992): 45–50 (Seven Days Supp.).
[2] Michael A. Weinstein, 'Coercion, Space, and the Modes of Human Domination', in J. Roland Pennock and John W. Chapman (eds), *Nomos XIV: Coercion* (Chicago and New York: Aldine – Atherton, Inc., 1972): 64–65.

when a person (P) is threatening another person (Q) to bring about negative consequences if Q does not do a certain conduct (A) ('You'd better leave now or later you get fired'). Coercion might limit space ('You are not allowed to leave this room'; 'You are prohibited from entering this territory'); restrict choices or opportunities (A offers B options X, Y and Z and/or explicitly prohibits options M, N and O); enforce certain conduct or prohibiting another ('You must/must not do T'); or suppress desires or wishes ('I will not allow you to be what you want to be'). Coercion may involve threats, intimidation, sanctions, manipulation, demoralization, blackmail and restriction ('You don't receive any property if you leave, or if you marry outside the tribe.' Discussed in Chapter 7). It may or may not involve physical violence. Belittling people's abilities ('You are not capable of doing M'; 'You are not worthy of holding position F') and subjecting people to emotional manipulation ('I will harm myself if you don't return to me'), emotional blackmail ('Show me your love by doing G') or psychological pressure are all forms of coercion designed to push people to do things they otherwise most probably would not do.

Coerced people are not free to exercise their autonomy. Their voluntariness is being compromised. Coercion undermines self-rule and voluntariness because the doer is unable to freely reflect on choices and preferences. She is left with no option but the one (or few) the coercer chooses for her.[3] Voluntary thinking and action are essential for developing one's autonomy and, in this common usage, autonomy and coercion are defined by each other's absence: one is autonomous if one is not coerced, and to the extent that one is coerced one is not autonomous.[4]

There are some similarities between compromise and coercion. Both involve two or more parties who are in conflict and whose relationships are complex and uneasy. The parties in both compromise and coercion use communication to convey their interests, wishes, incentives, offers and threats. Parties may engage in the process of compromise and coercion themselves or via a third party. However, compromise and coercion are also different in some very important respects. In compromise, the parties make concessions. This is not a prerequisite to coercion. In coercion, the sense of justice, of seeing the other as an end in itself, of mutual respect, of avoiding harm – all these might be (but not necessarily be) absent. The coercer may impose its will on the coerced without diminishing its initial demands. The motives for coercion are important, whether it is used to promote human rights, social welfare or any other public good, or it is done to deny human rights and/or public good. While the former may still be considered moral, the latter is not because then

---

[3] Wertheimer argues that one acts voluntarily only when one's motivations are internal to the self or internal to the self in a certain way. See Alan Wertheimer, *Coercion* (Princeton, NJ: Princeton University Press, 1987): 287–306, esp. p. 291. See also Nicos Stavropoulos, 'The Relevance of Coercion: Some Preliminaries', *Ratio Juris*, 22(3) (September 2009): 339–358.

[4] Willard Gaylin and Bruce Jennings, *The Perversion of Autonomy* (New York: The Free Press, 1996): 154. See generally Gerald Dworkin, *The Theory and Practice of Autonomy* (Cambridge: Cambridge University Press, 1988).

people are infringed of their right to pursue their conception of the good autonomously.[5] When people are no longer autonomous to decide on their way of life but are forced to follow a certain scheme, which they do not consider to be a conception of the good life, we need to examine whether the causes for coercion are just and reasonable. In this book this issue arises time and again as multicultural claims might be based on coercion, and liberal interventions in the cultural practices of illiberal subcultures might also be coercive. The standards that guide us to decide what is just and reasonable were established in the preceding chapters.

In coercion, compliance is sought. The relationships are clearly unequal and asymmetric. If and when a third party is involved, that third party does not necessarily aim to treat the parties fairly and equally. When coercion is established there might be a sense of satisfaction and achievement in the camp of the coercer, while there might be anger and frustration among the coerced. A forced state of affairs is hardly fair and amicable. The relationships will remain tenuous and difficult as long as the state of coercion is maintained. Principled compromise and brute forms of coercion are in striking opposition. I elaborate *infra*.

Persons, as moral agents, have their conceptions of a moral life, and accordingly determine what they deem to be the most valuable or best form of life worth leading. It is emphasized that one's conception of the good does not have to be just or reasonable. When coercion is involved, and people are no longer autonomous to decide on their way of life, they are unable to act from principles that they would consent to as free and equal rational beings.[6] They are then forced to follow a scheme, which they might not consider to be a conception of the good life.

People resent coercion and, when possible, rebel against it. The mere characterization of something as coercive yields a negative reaction. But if the same thing would be characterized differently, in softer terms explaining its logic and necessity, the reaction might be different. Education is a case in point, discussed *infra*. Paying taxes is another. The state justly requires its citizens to accept certain obligations for the benefit of all. It is legitimate to ask people to take part in necessary social institutions, such as juries and security forces.

In this chapter I differentiate between circumstantial coercion and person-based coercion, between coercion and brute forms of oppression, and between benevolent and malevolent coercion. I then discuss the coercer's intentions and specifically address the issues of paternalistic coercion, coercion via a third party and self-coercion, proceeding by making two useful distinctions: between internalized and designated coercion, and between coercion enforced by a minority versus coercion imposed by a majority. These distinctions are helpful for the understanding of just, reasonable multiculturalism. Their application is discussed throughout the book.

[5]   Raphael Cohen-Almagor, 'On Compromise and Coercion', *Ratio Juris*, 19(4) (2006): 434–455.
[6]   John Rawls, *A Theory of Justice* (Oxford: Oxford University Press, 1971): 516.

CIRCUMSTANTIAL COERCION AND
PERSON-BASED COERCION

We may distinguish between *circumstances-based coercion* and *person-based coercion*. The relevant question regarding circumstances-based coercion is: What caused this situation? The relevant question regarding person-based coercion is: Who caused this situation? Both affect one's liberty and restrict one's choice. Both might put people in an uncomfortable position. Consider a university that enacts a bylaw, enforcing all staff to live within a parameter of 50 km around the university. Consequently people are forced to move homes, relocating their families away from their familiar surroundings and from their nearby extended family and friends. Many may resent the move and the need to accommodate themselves to the changing circumstances. While the bylaw is enacted, of course, by people, the coercion is circumstantial.

As for person-based coercion, consider Chantalle who wants something from Jess. She demands that Jess give it to her or she would reveal a secret that Jess wishes to remain confidential. Chantalle coerces Jess into accepting the terms or else she will speak and cause Jess agony, even more agony than is caused by putting Jess in a compromising position where she is subjected to potentially prolonged and sustained blackmail. People concede to coercion when they think that, on balance, they lose less by succumbing to the coercer. Coercion does not work when people can free themselves from it without a substantial penalty. In the context of group rights and multiculturalism, coercion is invoked through social pressure, with significant group penalties if and when individuals do not do what is expected of them. Coercion is widely held to be a matter of significance in human life, and with good reason. It gives one agent the ability to directly alter or impede the conduct of another. Coerced people could not be held culpable for conduct they are forced to perform. Note in this context that while coercion is a form of power not all exercises of power are exercises of coercion.[7]

When we speak of coercion it is essential that one party successfully affects another party's choice of actions by either a constraining action (leaving one's community) or by communicating to the other a credible threat – by which is meant an announced conditional intention to degrade the latter's prospects for acting, posing demands regarding the threatened person's (or persons') future actions and/or inaction. The perceived threat – be it physical, psychological or

---

[7] As McCloskey notes, power may be exercised via the use of force, by manipulation, conditioning, pressure; by rational, non-rational, irrational persuasion, propaganda; by behaviour-modification devices, operations consented to, drugs freely or un-freely used, hypnosis, brainwashing applied with or without the help of force; by the use of inducements, personal charisma, as well as in many other ways. McCloskey rightly argues that while various of these forms of power are loosely characterized as forms of coercion, coercion proper should be distinguished from all these forms of power. See H.J. McCloskey, 'Coercion: Its Nature and Significance', *Southern Journal of Philosophy*, 18(3) (Fall 1980): 335.

emotional – is often more important than the actual threat. When a person does something because of threats, the will of another is predominant, whereas when she does something because of offers this is not so.[8]

Coercion is sometimes the only viable means available by which one can affect the behaviour of other agents as it impacts on one's vital interests, such as one's bodily security, possession of property or ability to move about in the world. Correspondingly it is a means that others can use to change one's own activities for their particular ends and in so doing undermine these very same interests.

There is a presumption against coercion. Other things being equal, a non-coercive rule, policy or action is preferable and morally superior to a coercive one.[9] Other things being equal, we prefer offers and compromises to threats. In other words, generally speaking people shrink from coercion and would like to lead their lives free of compulsion. Authoritarian societies aggressively fight to undermine political opponents while liberal societies encourage pluralism of ideas and provide avenues to empower opposition. Theocracy attempts to provide strict answers to all questions and concerns, often resorting to exclamation marks, whereas liberal societies have no qualms about presenting questions with no definite answers, challenging common truisms, presenting competing ideas, admitting human infallibility and even celebrating heresy.

While liberals resent coercion they accept the necessity of regulation. When one speaks, the other keeps quiet. Then the other responds and the civil exchange continues in mutual respect. Deliberation is dependent on arguing, listening and responding. For instance, one day the peace movement may hold a parade in the major square of the city, and the following day the anti-peace movement may hold its own parade at the same square. No movement is coerced into accepting the other's way of life. No movement is silenced or censored.

In *The Law of Peoples*, John Rawls drew a distinction between liberal and illiberal societies. Liberal societies are pluralistic and peaceful; they are governed by reasonable people who protect basic human rights. These rights include providing a certain minimum to the means of subsistence, security, liberty and personal property as well as to formal equality and self-respect as expressed by the rules of natural justice.[10] Liberal peoples are reasonable and rational. Their conduct, laws and

---

[8]   Robert Nozick, 'Coercion', in Sidney Morgenbesser, Patrick Suppes and Morton White (eds), *Philosophy, Science, and Method: Essays in Honor of Ernest Nagel* (New York: St. Martin's Press, 1969): 459; Michael Gorr, 'Toward a Theory of Coercion', *Canadian Journal of Philosophy*, 16(3) (September 1986): 395. For discussion on the distinction between coercive threats and conditional offers, see Craig L. Carr, 'Coercion and Freedom', *American Philosophical Quarterly*, 25(1) (January 1988): 59–67.

[9]   Virginia Held, 'Coercion and Coercive Offers', in Pennock and Chapman, *Nomos XIV*, 61.

[10] John Rawls, *The Law of Peoples* (Cambridge, MA: Harvard University Press, 2002): chap. 2. For further discussion, see Richard Rorty, 'Justice as a Larger Loyalty', *Ethical Perspectives*, 4 (1997): 139–151.

policies are guided by a sense of political justice.[11] Equal citizens as a collective body exercise political and reasonable coercive powers in legislating laws and in constructing their constitution.[12] In contrast, non-liberal societies fail to treat their people as truly free and equal. The values of liberty, equality and fairness are not deeply enshrined. The basic norms of respect for others and not harming others are undermined. Authoritarian societies aggressively fight to undermine political opponents while liberal societies encourage pluralism of ideas and provide avenues to empower opposition. In authoritarian societies the distribution of rights is not done in a just and fair way.

There might be certain forms of coercion in the framework of liberal democracy, which I discuss shortly. In non-liberal societies coercion might be the general rule. Military occupation, civil oppression, slavery and apartheid employ *brute forms of oppression*. They are, by definition, unjust, lack respect for fundamental human rights and dehumanize the oppressed. They also dehumanize the oppressors, transforming them into cruel and heartless beings who lack the basic components of dignity, compassion and civility. Brute oppression desensitizes the oppressing public, making the public accept it as part of life, convincing them that this abnormality is necessary and can, even should, be maintained. Abnormal situations force people to do unjust and unreasonable things. Under a coercive structure, bad things are inevitable.

However, denouncing all forms of coercion and disparaging coercion per se is too simplistic as it is not necessarily malevolent. I disagree with Wolff who holds that coercion is intrinsically evil, that it is by definition degrading, stripping people from their personhood.[13] Here Wolff falls into the familiar liberal fallacy that perceives all people as rational and autonomous beings who are capable of deciding for themselves and of carrying out their life plans as they desire. This is not the case. There are instances in which we must resort to coercion. The agents' intentions and motives are important. Indeed, they are vital for assessing the coercer's conduct.

COERCER'S INTENTIONS

Laws contain a certain coercive element in them. This, in itself, does not make them inherently bad or unjust. A relevant question is: Whose interests is coercion designed to promote – those of the coercer, of the coerced or of society at large? Coercion that is benevolent, aiming to better human condition, might be positive.

---

[11] Rawls, *The Law of Peoples*, 25.
[12] John Rawls, *Political Liberalism* (New York: Columbia University Press, 1993): 214. For further discussion, see Michele M. Moody-Adams, 'Democratic Conflict and the political Morality of Compromise', in Jack Knight (ed.), *Nomos LIX: Compromise* (New York: New York University Press, 2018): 186–219.
[13] Robert Paul Wolff, 'Is Coercion "Ethically Neutral"?', in Pennock and Chapman, *Nomos XIV*, 146.

Coercion that is malevolent, aimed at unjustly undermining the coerced and advancing the coercer's partisan interests, is negative. However, there can be instances in which coercion is conducted to serve the best interests of the coercer and yet be considered as legitimate.

For instance, coercion can be resorted to as a mechanism of self-defence. Consider the following: Sofo declares his wish to kill Franco. As Sofo approaches Franco with a gun in his hand, Franco succeeds in subduing Sofo and threatens to stab him with a knife if Sofo does not drop his gun. This is an act of coercion. Given the circumstances, the act was not intrinsically evil. It is a justified act of self-defence.

Coercion can also be used to protect weaker individuals from stronger ones. This other-regarding coercion is motivated by benevolence. Immanuel Kant associates coercion and punishment with the executive authority of the state's ruler. Governments enact laws and resort to coercive means to force the lawless to respect the rights of others. Coercion might be a hindrance to freedom, but it can also be used to prevent other rights violations. In the latter case coercion might be justified.[14] Such state coercion is compatible with the maximal freedom demanded in the principle of right because it does not reduce freedom but instead provides the necessary background conditions needed to secure freedom.[15] State coercive powers are necessary to secure order and justice. Laws that are designed to keep order and to promote certain moral codes (do not murder, do not steal, do not break into other people's homes, etc.) limit freedom but are not perceived as wrong. Quite the opposite: they are an essential glue to maintain the fabric of society and to enshrine a sense of justice. To take an example from the field of multiculturalism, liberal democracies are resorting to coercive measures and uphold heavy penalties in their fight to uproot certain practices from society, such as FGM and murder for family honour. Liberal morals put restraints on multicultural freedom when that freedom seems to be at odds with what liberals perceive as fundamental human rights. Are these coercive measures unreasonable? This is the focus of Chapter 5 where I start applying the just, reasonable multiculturalism theory to specific case studies.

PATERNALISTIC COERCION

Another other-regarding, benevolent form of coercion is exhibited by parents when they bring up and educate their children. Parents use coercion to educate young

---

[14] Immanuel Kant, *The Metaphysics of Morals* (New York: Cambridge University Press, 1996). See also Scott Anderson, 'Coercion', *Stanford Encyclopedia of Philosophy* (2011), https://plato.stanford.edu/entries/coercion/; Arthur Ripstein, 'Authority and Coercion', *Philosophy & Public Affairs*, 32(1) (January 2004): 2–35; Cheyney C. Ryan, 'The Normative Concept of Coercion', *Mind*, 89(356) (October 1980): 481–498.

[15] Frederick Rauscher, 'Kant's Social and Political Philosophy', *Stanford Encyclopedia of Philosophy* (2016), https://plato.stanford.edu/entries/kant-social-political/. For further discussion, see Colin Bird, 'Coercion and Public Justification', *Politics, Philosophy & Economics*, 13(3) (2014): 189–214.

children on how to live, things they should do and things they should refrain from doing. Parents use coercion to protect children from themselves and from others as well as from their hazardous surroundings. Studies have shown that children aged 7 to 12 have difficulties in identifying and describing risks and benefits. Children lack the experience and thus the capacity to process relevant data. They do not differentiate between cause and effect.[16] Only in later stages of adolescence are minors able to acquire the ability to plan ahead, understand what steps should be taken to meet their goals and acquire more developed decision-making capacities.[17] Brain studies suggest that the adolescent's decision-making capacity fluctuates. Notwithstanding raging hormones, risky behaviour and rebellious tendencies, teenagers are unable to consistently make decisions as adults do. This explains why adolescents are three or four times more likely to die than children past infancy.[18]

Adolescents perceive rewards associated with taking risks to be particularly great. This can result in decisions that are detrimental to their health.[19] Before adulthood there is less crosstalk between the brain systems that regulate rational decision-making and those that regulate emotional arousal. During adolescence, impulse control is lacking and so are capabilities to plan ahead and compare the costs and benefits of alternatives. Laurence Steinberg explains that this is one reason that susceptibility to peer pressure declines as adolescents grow into adulthood. With maturity, individuals become better able to put the brakes on an impulse that is aroused by their friends.[20] But during adolescence, susceptibility to taking risks and to peer pressure can be injurious.

Parents need to resort to various means to educate their children – coercion included when deemed necessary, for instance, to stay away from electrical wires and running cars. Carefree attitude would be considered careless if not criminal. Of course, the identity of the coercer is relevant for us to make a judgement about the legitimacy of the coercing act. An act of parents over their child might be considered legitimate while the same act, conducted by the state over the child, even if proclaimed to be done for their own good, might be considered as illegitimate

[16] R. Abramovitch, J.L. Freedman, K. Henry, et al., 'Children's Capacity to Agree to Psychological Research: Knowledge of Risks and Benefits and Voluntariness', *Ethics and Behaviour*, 5 (1995): 25–48; T.L. Kuther, 'Medical Decision-Making and Minors: Issues on Consent and Assent', *Adolescence*, 38(150) (2003) (Summer): 346–349.

[17] D. Verstraeten, 'Level of Realism in Adolescent Future Time Perspective', *Human Development*, 23 (1980): 177–191. See also A. Iltis, 'Parents, Adolescence and Consent for Research Participation', *Journal of Medicine and Philosophy*, 38 (2013): 332–346.

[18] K. Powell, 'How Does the Teenage Brain Work?', *Nature*, 442 (2006) (August): 865.

[19] E. Wilhelms and V. Reyna, 'Fuzzy Trace Theory and Medical Decisions by Minors: Differences in Reasoning between Adolescents and Adults', *Journal of Medicine and Philosophy*, 38 (2013): 268–282, at 271.

[20] L. Steinberg, 'Does Recent Research on Adolescent Brain Development Inform the Mature Minor Doctrine?', *Journal of Medicine and Philosophy*, 38 (2013): 256–267, 261. See also Raphael Cohen-Almagor, 'Should the Euthanasia Act in Belgium Include Minors?', *Perspectives in Biology and Medicine*, 61(2) (Spring 2018): 230–248.

and unjustifiable. On the whole we would like to keep the integrity of the family and safeguard its privacy against state intrusion. There should be very compelling reasons to persuade us to forego the privacy of the family and allow the state room to interfere. We need to manage coercion carefully and reasonably. Liberals are suspicious of state powers and how they are put into use, for good reasons. We are wary of powerful agents.[21]

Kant and Mill supported compulsory education for the benefit of the child. Kant wrote: 'The child should be allowed perfect liberty, while at the same time he must be taught to respect the liberty of others, and submit himself to a restraint which will lead to a right use of future liberty.'[22] John Stuart Mill, the great liberal champion of liberty, supported compulsory education. In his mind governments must provide proper facilities for education designed for the benefit of society as a whole, and it is 'one of most sacred duties of the parents' to ensure education for their children.[23] Mill acknowledged that compulsory education contradicted the freedom one enjoyed in choosing for oneself and one's children the form and level of education. Education is both a means towards liberty and one of the ends for which liberty existed.[24] Education is essential for good government,[25] and for according equal rights to men and women. Furthermore, education is beneficial to the child and also to society because it teaches the child social norms which are useful to all. I elaborate in the context of Amish education in Chapter 8.

Mill insisted that parents, especially fathers, were responsible for the proper education of their children and he wanted to compel them to take responsibility. He suggested introducing an examination at a certain age by which children manifest their reading ability. If the child was unable to read, the father had to explain why his child did not meet the required level of reading. If the explanation was deemed unsatisfactory, the father 'might be subjected to a moderate fine'.[26] And if a father, either from idleness or any other avoidable cause, fails to perform his legal duties, for instance supporting his children, 'it is no tyranny to force him to fulfil that obligation, by compulsory labour, if no other means are available'.[27]

Indeed, welfare states commonly reason today that they know better what is good for their citizens, thus enforcing a certain level of education upon them. Liberal

[21] Scott Anderson, *Coercion, Agents and Ethics* (PhD dissertation, University of Chicago, 2002): chap. 2. See also Scott Anderson, 'The Enforcement Approach to Coercion', *Journal of Ethics and Social Philosophy*, 5(1) (October 2010): 1–31.

[22] Immanuel Kant, *Kant on Education: Ueber Pädagogik* (Boston: D.C. Health & Co. Publishers 1900): 28.

[23] J.S. Mill, *Utilitarianism, Liberty and Representative Government* (London: J.M. Dent, 1948): 160.

[24] Mill, *Utilitarianism, Liberty and Representative Government*, 160–162.

[25] J.S. Mill, *Dissertations and Discussions* (London: Longmans, Green, Reader & Dyer, 1859), III, 1–46.

[26] Mill, *On Liberty*, 162.

[27] Ibid., 153.

democracies invoke mandatory education and most people – adolescents and their parents – accept it. Compulsory education may seem to be an invasion of individual rights, but in the final analysis it may guarantee more freedom than it destroys. For if ignorance may be viewed as a type of unfreedom, education increases the number of options and possibilities that are open for people to pursue their interests.

In France the education system is a primary instrument to shape a unified, Republican identity. Public schools have played a major role in counteracting religious prejudice and in inculcating French national values. Dogmatism and traditionalism are left behind the school gates and students inside the school are able to entertain, in a free and secular atmosphere, values of progress and justice. School teachers and administrators are to protect this environment.[28] They should ensure that distinctions are eliminated, and students of diverse backgrounds are taught what is needed for the development of a common civic identity.

Since the Revolution, France has used its school system to make French citizens out of people from the country's many different regions: Corsica, the Basque areas, Provence, Brittany, Gascony, Savoie (Italian), Alsace-Lorraine. In the late nineteenth century the process intensified under the influence of a centralist state.[29] Laws on schools were passed during the July monarchy (1830–1848), the Second Republic (1848–1851) and the Second Empire (1851–1871). In 2003, former Socialist Prime Minister Laurent Fabius described public schools by saying: '[T]he school is not just one among many places; it is the place where we mold our little citizens. There are three legs: *laïcité*, Republic, school; these are the three legs on which we stand.'[30] Two years later, in 2005, a framework law was passed stating that education is a national priority, and that the system should guarantee that all students acquire a common set of knowledge and skills that will give them equal opportunities in professional life. These principles were reaffirmed by the 2013 reform (law no. 2013-595 of 8 July 2013) and related decrees.[31]

Public education was perceived as a key in the rivalry between religion and the progressive ideas of the revolution. Against dogmatic and intolerant religions, Catholicism and Islam, the French have developed a quaternity of values: *liberté*, *égalité*, *fraternité* and *laïcité*. In the Republic's earlier days Catholicism was seen as an enemy of progress and liberty as well as hostile to the idea of substantive democracy. More recently, Islam attracts the same criticism. To recall (Chapter 1),

---

[28] Donald N. Baker and Patrick J. Harrigan (eds), *The Making of Frenchmen: Current Directions in the History of Education in France, 1679–1979* (Ontario: Historical Reflections, Vol. 7, Nos. 2–3, 1980); Anne Corbett and Bob Moon (eds), *Education in France: Continuity and Change in the Mitterrand Years 1981–1995* (London: Routledge, 1996).

[29] Johannes Willms, 'France Unveiled: Making Muslims into Citizens?', *Open Democracy* (26 February 2004), www.opendemocracy.net/en/article_1753jsp/.

[30] T. Jeremy Gunn, 'Religious Freedom and Laicite: A Comparison of the United States and France', *BYU Law Review*, 2 (2004): 454.

[31] Arianna Caporali, 'Educational Policies: France', *Population Europe Resource Finder and Archive* (2014), www.perfar.eu/policy/education/france.

in substantive democracy the opinion of the majority is respected, yet minorities are protected, and the majority does not misuse its power to abuse the minorities. In France the idea entails the *laique* state, neutrality towards all religions, independent of all clergy, especially Catholic clergy, detached from all theological concepts promoting universal values. The problem, however, is that implementation of *laïcité* is contradictory to the trinity of the French Revolution. If you wish to remain true to *liberté, égalité, fraternité*, then the by-product is tolerance of difference whereas the French have adopted statism that trumps individual freedoms. Such manifestions are allowed at the home and in places of prayer (Chapter 9).

COERCION VIA THIRD PARTY

Sometime people lack the ability to coerce others directly. Conflicts often become triadic when the two sides are unable to resolve their differences. Then the coercer may try to exert pressure by a third party who is susceptible to its influence and has some leverage on the target for coercion.

Coercion via third party is useful when the target is too strong. Then the party that wishes to sway the target to comply with certain demands may need a stronger party, with broader abilities, to join in and exert its power. Coercion via third party is useful also when the target is evasive. The target might operate in the underground, away from the public eye. Those who may wish to coerce it to discontinue a certain practice may require the assistance of a third party that has better communication with the target or is better positioned to influence it. Third parties, of course, have their own interests. We may distinguish various forms of relationship between two sides vis-à-vis a third party:

1. Shared interests. The two parties see eye to eye. They have a good relationship. Trust between them is good. Both have something to gain from coercing the target. The third party can coerce the target and the first party can give the third party something that the latter wants in return. Collaboration will enhance their relationship and contribute to their standing and status.
1a. Shared interest. The two parties see eye to eye and have a good relationship. None has the ability to coerce the target, but they believe that together they will be able to do it. Both are interested in collaboration.
2. Lukewarm shared interests. The two parties have a lukewarm relationship. Trust between them is limited but both sides are interested to further their relationship. The third party has the ability to coerce the target and the first party has the ability to give the third party something that the latter wants in return. While the third party does not have an urgency to engage in coercion against the target, it still perceives some

potential gains. In this case, the offer made by the first party is likely to determine the level of the third party's involvement and commitment.

2a. Lukewarm shared interests. As above but none has the ability to coerce the target alone. Both sides are willing to explore working together and see whether they have enough to build upon to exercise co-coercion.

3. No shared interests. The third party can coerce the target and the first party has the ability to give the third party something that the latter wants in return. However, the two parties are not sufficiently familiar with each other. They do not have shared interests or are not aware of having such shared interests. They have never worked together. The third party does not have a real, urgent interest to coerce the target. In this case, the first party needs to invest in trying to influence the third party to change its perception and make it realize that they do have common interests if not directly vis-à-vis the target then in other spheres. The first party will try to engage with the third party, provoke its interest, make an attractive offer, build some trust and motivate the third party to engage in coercion.

3a. No shared interests. As above but none can coerce the target alone. The first party will strive to convince the third party to collaborate in coercing the target.[32]

In Chapter 5 I suggest using third-party coercion in the context of communities that practice FGM.

SELF-COERCION

Can a person forfeit her own freedom and become a slave? Both Kant and Mill answer in the negative. Kant believed that human beings are objects of respect. People are objective ends whose existence is important and cannot be substituted for another end.[33] This principle of humanity and of every rational creature as an end in itself is the supreme limiting condition on freedom of the actions of each individual and therefore one cannot subject oneself to serfdom.

Kant emphasized the importance of morality, humanity and autonomy. As explained in Chapter 1, according to Kant people do not have mere relative worth that can be exchanged as a commodity. In turn, the concept of autonomy is inseparably connected with the idea of freedom. Autonomy is related to the universal principle of morality, which ideally is the ground of all actions of rational beings.[34] In *Towards Perpetual Peace*, Kant denounced colonial conquest and

---

[32] For further discussion, see Wendy Pearlman and Boaz Atzili, *Triadic Coercion* (New York: Columbia University Press, 2018).

[33] Immanuel Kant, *Foundations of the Metaphysics of Morals and What Is Enlightenment?* (Indianapolis: Bobbs-Merrill Educational Publishing, 1959): 46–47.

[34] Ibid., 71.

slavery as uncivilized, cruel and brutal practices: 'The inhospitality of coastal people (e.g. those on the Barbary coast) in robbing ships that come near or making slaves of stranded travelers, and the inhospitality of desert people (e.g. the Bedouin Arabs) who see the approach of nomadic tribes as conferring the right to plunder them, is thus opposed to the natural law.'[35]

Similarly, Mill urged that one did not have the right to impede one's own freedom in an irreversible way, which would impede one's personal sovereignty. Any contract of even a voluntary servitude would be 'null and void'.[36] Mill explained that in this extreme case the state is legitimate to limit the power of the individual to forego his own lot in life and that no law should permit slavery, for by selling oneself to slavery one abdicates the very purpose which is the justification of allowing one to dispose of oneself: 'The principle of freedom cannot require that he should be free not to be free. It is not freedom to be allowed to alienate his freedom.'[37] Liberty does not mean that every person, regardless of character or capacity, should claim to do as she pleases without respect to the common good.[38]

Mill implicitly assumed that one who decides to become a slave is not rational enough to have full responsibility for one's future life. Therefore, the state was legitimate in not respecting such contracts, and in liberating the individual from the situation in which she entered without realizing its absolute implications. Mill maintained that an exception to the doctrine that individuals are the best judges of their own affairs occurs when 'an individual attempts to decide irrevocably now, what will be the best for his interest at some future and distant time'.[39]

The underpinning rational is that liberty is important, but it must be contained. People cannot uphold liberty as a licence to do as they please with little thinking about the consequences of their conduct. If the conduct inflicts pain upon oneself, Mill advocated moral reproach. But people should not be punished simply for developing an addiction to bad habits such as drinking, taking drugs, gambling or visiting prostitutes. Mill distinguished between harm to self and harm to others,

---

[35] Immanuel Kant, *Toward Perpetual Peace: A Philosophical Sketch*, www.earlymoderntexts.com/assets/pdfs/kant1795_1.pdf.

[36] Mill, *On Liberty*, 157. See also Raphael Cohen-Almagor, 'Between Autonomy and State Regulation: J.S. Mill's Elastic Paternalism', *Philosophy*, 87(4) (October 2012): 557–582.

[37] Mill, *On Liberty*, 158. For further discussion, see R.J. Arneson, 'Mill versus Paternalism', *Ethics*, 90 (July 1980): 470–489; John D. Hodson, 'Mill, Paternalism and Slavery', *Analysis*, 41 (1981): 60–62.

[38] Mary Agnes Hamilton, *John Stuart Mill* (London: Hamish Hamilton, 1933), 76; John Gray, *Mill on Liberty: A Defence* (London: Routledge and Paul, 1983): 94. See also Kalle Grill and Jason Hanna (eds), *Routledge Handbook of the Philosophy of Paternalism* (London: Routledge, 2018).

[39] J.S. Mill, 'The Grounds and Limits of the Laissez-Faire or Non-interference Principle', in Ronald Fletcher (ed.), *John Stuart Mill* (London: Michael Joseph, 1971): 322. For further discussion, see Ben Saunders, 'Reformulating Mill's Harm Principle', *Mind*, 125(500) (October 2016): 1005–1032.

allowing more latitude to self-harm.[40] If the conduct damages others, then liberty needs to be restrained. Intervention in one's liberty is warranted if the benefits of doing so outweigh the costs. Thus, if because of their addiction people are unable to pay their debts and unable to support and educate their children, then they are deservedly reprobated and 'might be justly punished'.[41] In short, wrote Mill, whenever there is a definite damage, 'or a definite risk of damage', either to an individual or to the public at large, 'the case is taken out of the province of liberty, and placed in that of morality or law'.[42] With Mill, I argue that coercion can be legitimate also when it is exercised over people who do not secure basic reasoning and planning capacities.[43] Like Mill I think that those who exercise coercion are obligated to ensure that their coercion is legitimate. I also think that special caution is required when the coerced are vulnerable people. Vulnerability is a cause for concern and certainly not a window for exploitation.

At the same time, I think Mill went too far in endorsing laws which prohibit marriage unless the parties provide evidence to show that they have the means to support a family.[44] While Mill thought that such laws do not exceed the legitimate powers of the state, I think they are objectionable and violate individual liberty. This coercive paternalism contravenes the underpinning liberal principles of respect for others and not harming others.

What about suicide? According to Mill, if a given action primarily concerns the acting individual, then she should enjoy freedom to inflict upon herself harm as every person is the best judge in her own affairs. Mill explained his reasoning by formulating the example of the unsafe bridge:

> If either a public officer or anyone else saw a person starting to cross a bridge that was known to be unsafe, and there was no time to warn him of his danger, they might seize him and pull him back without any real infringement of his liberty; for liberty consists in doing what one desires, and he doesn't desire to fall into the river. Nevertheless, when there is not a certainty of trouble but only a risk of it, no-one but the person himself can judge whether in this case he has a strong enough motive to make it worthwhile to run the risk; and so I think he ought only to be warned of the danger, not forcibly prevented from exposing himself to it.[45]

Mill qualified this assertion by maintaining that he assumed that the individual who wishes to cross the bridge is capable to reason. Thus, Mill excluded children, or delirious persons, or persons in some state of excitement or preoccupation that won't

---

[40] Mill, *On Liberty*, 136–140.

[41] Ibid., 138.

[42] Ibid., 138, 153. For further analysis, see D.G. Brown, 'Mill on Harm to Others' Interests', *Political Studies*, 26 (1978): 395–399.

[43] For a contrary view, see Nicole Hassoun, 'Coercion, Legitimacy and Global Justice', *Carnegie Mellon University Research Showcase* (2009).

[44] Mill, *On Liberty*, 163.

[45] Ibid., chap. 5.

let them think carefully. But people who are prima facie reasonable may commit suicide if they so wish, and agencies of the liberal state should not actively take it upon themselves to stop them from doing so. Autonomy and liberty are that important in the liberal thinking that they enable people to put an end to their autonomy and liberties.

INTERNALIZED AND DESIGNATED COERCION

Inter and intracultural relationships pose further problems and dilemmas. When a given subculture in society denies some freedoms and rights to a certain group living in that same culture, we may feel that some form of coercion is being exercised. For example, if a religious sect denies rights and liberties to its female members, that sect may continue doing so because it is assumed that all members of that group internalized the system of beliefs that legitimizes the exclusion of rights from women as part of the socialization process of the group. It is further assumed that all members of that group conform to and abide by the particular way of life that guides and directs members of the said group. They are subjected to a system of manipulation that is working against the basic interests of the group inside the community not to be harmed and to enjoy equal respect. The discriminated members of the community do not feel that they are being coerced to follow a certain conception. They internalize cultural norms that are coercive by nature. Outsiders may claim that a whole-encompassing system of manipulation, rationalization and legitimization is being utilized to make women accept their denial of rights. But in most cases this view may only be the view of outsiders, not of the persons concerned. If at all, one may argue that women of that sect are experiencing *internalized coercion*.[46] Unlike the common form of coercion where (P) is threatening (Q) to bring about negative consequences if Q does not do a certain conduct (A), in internalized coercion a group (G) is enshrining norms that bring the group to believe that certain discriminatory practices against part of the group are legitimate and even necessary for the preservation of G.

Is internalized coercion reasonable? This is a difficult question. Prima facie, those who are subjected to it may not see it as coercive. They willingly accept the social conditions to which they are subjected. They may not feel that their options are being restricted, and they voluntarily abide by the restricting cultural codes. Those who are subjected to internalized coercion may accept the reasoning and justifications that are part of their culture. They may perceive the upkeep of tradition as more important than the personal freedoms they are asked to sacrifice. It might be the case that they are not even aware of their sacrifice. For many of those who are subjected to this form of coercion their way of life, their conception of the good, is a

[46] I first developed the idea of internalized and designated coercion in Cohen-Almagor, 'On Compromise and Coercion'.

form of just, reasonable multiculturalism. It is coercive because some form of manipulation is involved to overcome potentially resisting will. The manipulation makes that which is perceived to be objectionable by people outside the group an accepted and legitimate practice by members of the said group.

The moral coercion of group opinion is persuasive and overbearing. Tradition and historical memory may keep internalized coercion alive even when it is clearly unjust in the eyes of outsiders. Liberal attempts to intervene in order to end discriminatory relationships might face objections and vilification as an unjust, coercive colonialism. Attempts to free people from coercion might be regarded as vile and insensitive coercion. Thus, the boundaries of liberal intervention in a subculture's internal affairs should be delineated with great caution.

Concrete difficulties arise when some women in the said cultural or religious group fail to internalize fully the system of norms that discriminates against them. Upon realizing that they are being denied fundamental rights, they might wish – for instance – to opt out of their community. This is the example of the Bedouin girl that opened this chapter. If members are allowed to opt out, no question arises. If not allowed, then a case may arise for state interference to overrule this individualistic, designated coercion that aims to deny women freedom to leave their community. Then threats of physical harm, perhaps of significant economic loss that would leave the girl in question in a dependent situation, are used. I call this form of coercion *designated coercion*. Unlike internalized coercion it is not concerned with machinery aiming to convince the entire cultural group of an irrefutable truth; instead it is designed to exert pressure on uncertain, 'confused' individuals so as to bring them back to their community.

The case of Bedouin women in Israel is discussed in Chapter 5. There are communities in which FGM is being practised and most of the girls in these communities grow to believe that this practice is essential for their integration as women in their communities.[47] Because this cultural norm is backed by the elder women who lead by example, most girls do not object to the practice and accept it as is, as part of their growing up.[48] They are not aware of the system of manipulation

---

[47] Sami A. Aldeeb Abu Sahlieh, 'To Mutilate in the Name of Jehovah or Allah: Legitimization of Male and Female Circumcision', *Medicine and Law*, 13(4) (1994): 575–622; American Academy of Pediatrics, Committee on Bioethics, 'Ritual Genital Cutting of Female Minors', *Pediatrics*, 125(5) (May 2010), http://pediatrics.aappublications.org/content/125/5/1088; Rosie Duivenbode and Aasim I. Padela, 'The Problem of Female Genital Cutting: Bridging Secular and Islamic Bioethical Perspectives', *Perspectives in Biology and Medicine*, 62(2) (Spring 2019): 273–300; S. Creighton and L.-M. Liao (eds), *Female Genital Cosmetic Surgery: Solution to What Problem?* (Cambridge: Cambridge University Press, 2019).

[48] Robyn Cenry Smith, 'Female Circumcision: Bringing Women's Perspectives into the International Debate', *Southern California Law Review*, 65 (1992): 2449–2504; J. Whitehorn, O. Ayonrinde and S. Maingay, 'Female Genital Mutilation: Cultural and Psychological Implications', *Sexual & Relationship Therapy*, 17(2) (May 2002): 161–170; Ben Mathews, 'Female Genital Mutilation: Australian Law, Policy and Practical Challenges for Doctors', *Medical Journal of Australia*, 194(3) (2011): 139–141; The Public Policy Advisory Network on

and the coercion that is internalized into their way of life and conception of the good. However, when girls object to the practice and wish to protect their woman-hood, then designated coercion is employed to safeguard the norms of the community and to 'educate' the 'stray weeds'. This form of coercion is unjustified, and the state is warranted to interfere and to rescue the helpless girls who wish to retain their femininity and sexuality and have the power and the will to fight against their superiors and tradition. It is one of the roles of the liberal state to stand by weak parties who seek defence and help to safeguard their human rights.

COERCION BY MINORITY AND BY MAJORITY

Rawls speaks of a case where one group wants to make the entire community accept its own conception of the good. He has in mind political parties in democratic states whose doctrines commit them to suppressing constitutional liberties when they have the power.[49] He supports objection and state intervention to prevent this scenario in order to protect the rights of individuals who disassociate themselves from the intensive and all-embracing conception of the given cultural group. A case in point is the religious coercion practised by the Orthodox minority in Israel over society as a whole.[50]

Adhering to the principles of respecting others, and not harming others, the constant challenge for all democracies is to secure human rights for all, the powerful as well as the powerless. The lack of separation between state and religion in Israel leads to discrimination against non-Orthodox Jews in the private sphere, in conduct-ing their most personal issues of marriage and divorce. Secular Jews and Jews of non-Orthodox denominations are coerced by the Orthodox minority establishment. The Chief Rabbinate, the supreme rabbinic authority for Judaism in Israel, enjoys a monopoly on all matters relating to personal status. This body has a clear bias against non-Orthodox movements. At the centre of this illiberal system of governance is Jewish law, *Halacha*, not the individual. All Jews need to conform to the Orthodox way of life. There is no pluralism and equality between different dominations of

Female Genital Surgeries in Africa, 'Seven Things to Know about Female Genital Surgeries in Africa', *Hastings Center Report*, 6 (2012): 19–27; Jane Muthumbi, Joar Svanemyr, Elisa Scolaro, Marleen Temmerman, and Lale Say, 'Female Genital Mutilation: A Literature Review of the Current Status of Legislation and Policies in 27 African Countries and Yemen', *African Journal of Reproductive Health*, 19(3) (2015): 32–40; Chizoma Millicent Ndikom, Feyintoluwa Anne Ogungbenro and Olajumoke Adetoun Ojeleye, 'Perception and Practice of Female Genital Cutting among Mothers in Ibadan, Nigeria', *International Journal of Nursing & Health Science*, 4(6) (2017): 71–80.

[49] Rawls, *A Theory of Justice*, 216. See generally Timo Airaksinen, *Ethics of Coercion and Authority* (Pittsburg, PA: University of Pittsburgh Press, 1988); Hillel Steiner, *Essay on Rights* (Oxford: Blackwell, 1994): 22–32.

[50] Raphael Cohen-Almagor, 'The Monopoly of Jewish Orthodoxy in Israel and Its Effects on the Governance of Religious Diversity', in Anna Triandafyllidou and Tariq Modood (eds), *The Problem of Religious Diversity* (Edinburgh: Edinburgh University Press, 2017): 250–272.

Judaism. Respect for Reform and Conservative ways of life is scarce. Orthodox and ultra-Orthodox religious figures coerce others to follow their conception of the good.[51]

Reform and Conservative marriages performed inside Israel are not recognized by the state, led on religious matters by the Orthodoxy. This does not deter over 1,000 couples a year from asking a Reform rabbi (male and female) to officiate at their wedding.[52] Most couples, after having a Jewish Reform or Conservative ceremony in Israel, go overseas to places such as Greece, Cyprus, sometimes other European countries and even the United States to conduct a civil ceremony (see the story of D and J in Chapter 3). This marriage is recognized in Israel for marriage registration purposes.

Israelis who travel abroad to marry are not necessarily affiliated with the Reform and Conservative movements. They simply object to coercion and do not wish to have any religious stamp on a very personal civic conduct. It is estimated that one in six of Jewish couples marry abroad.[53] The 2013 Religion-and-State Index showed that two-thirds of secular Israelis would prefer not to marry in an Orthodox ceremony, if they were free to choose.[54] The 2019 Religion-and-State Index showed that 68 per cent of the public support equal status to Orthodox, Conservative and Reform denominations.[55] Furthermore, couples who decide to go their separate ways, including those who married in a civil marriage abroad, are still required to divorce

[51] Frances Raday, 'Religion, Multiculturalism and Equality: The Israeli Case', *Israel Yearbook on Human Rights*, 25 (1995): 193–241; F. Raday, 'Self-determination and Minority Rights', *Fordham International Law Journal*, 26(3) (2002): 453–499; Raphael Cohen-Almagor, 'Israeli Democracy, Religion and the Practice of *Halizah* in Jewish Law', *UCLA Women's Law Journal*, 11(1) (Fall/Winter 2000): 45–65; Tamar Hermann and Chanan Cohen, 'Reform and Conservative Jews in Israel: A Profile and Attitudes', Israel Democracy Institute (30 June 2013), http://en.idi.org.il/analysis/articles/the-reform-and-conservative-movements-in-israel-a-profile-and-attitudes

[52] I thank Yonatan Melamed for this information. In recent years some 50,000 couples marry each and every year. In 2013, there were 52,705 marriages. In 2017, 50,029 marriages. Israel Bureau of Statistics, www.cbs.gov.il/reader/?MIval=cw_usr_view_SHTML&ID=889; www.cbs.gov.il/he/mediarelease/pages/2019/2019-לקט-נתונים-לרגל-טו-באב-תשעט.aspx (Hebrew).

[53] 'One in Six Marriages Involving Jews Are Conducted Abroad', *Hiddush* (21 August 2014) (Hebrew).

[54] 'One in Six Marriages Involving Jews Are Conducted Abroad', *Hiddush* (21 August 2014) (Hebrew). The National Council of Jewish Women (NCJW) has called on the government of Israel to adopt a system of civil marriage and divorce: 'NCJW is committed to the letter and spirit of respect for democratic values and civil liberties. The monopoly of authority given to Orthodox rabbinical courts in Israel regarding issues of personal status, particularly marriage, weakens rather than strengthens the state itself by causing disunity, disrespect for the law, and even hostility among Israelis and between Israel and Jews abroad. In addition, twenty percent of the Israeli population is made up of members of minority groups whose marriages are similarly governed by the religious authorities of each faith, and who, as a result, face marital issues of their own. As a result, hundreds of thousands of Israeli citizens are denied the right of marriage solely based on issues of religion.' See 'NCJW Board Calls for Civil Marriage in Israel' (3 April 2013) www.ncjw.org/content_9812.cfm.

[55] Uri Regev, 'The 2019 Religion-and-State Index', *Hiddush* (2019) (Hebrew).

in a religious court. Most Israelis are not aware of this.[56] Only when couples separate do they realize that they are forced to undergo a discriminatory ritual in rabbinical courts that are of little significance for them.[57] Thus, the present situation infringes basic human rights, freedom of religion, freedom of conscience and equality.

The *halachic* coercion brings about continued agony and a great deal of hardship that alienate many parts of the population from the state and its institutions. Secular people are required to abide by a set of norms and *halachic* regulation that are not part of their worldview. Designated coercion is employed against those who protest against *halachic* dictates.

A minority culture should not force its ideas upon the entire community. This form of *minority coercion* is repudiated by Rawls just as he rejects *majority coercion*. Democracy is a form of government that secures the rights of all, majority and minority alike. We oppose majority rule when it does not protect the rights of minorities, and likewise we object to minority coercion when that does not respect the rights of the majority. Democracy is a majority rule *while respecting rights of minorities*. Throughout the book it is argued that democracy should come to the help of vulnerable populations when their human rights are violated.

Speaking of safeguards and constraints, a pertinent distinction is the one between *substantial* or *irrevocable* safeguards and constraints, and *contingent* or *alterable* ones. The first category consists of safeguards and constraints that are non-consequentialist, prescribed by the most fundamental principles of liberalism: they present hard-and-fast restraints as a rule, urging that some things lie beyond society's capacity to tolerate.

Government should grant each person equal concern and respect, and promote the view that each person matters, that she or he matters equally. This also means that government should secure each person's fundamental rights and liberties, first and foremost the right to life and the right not to be harmed by others, no matter whether the offender is a member of another community, the same community or the same cultural minority. Stranger or relative, neither may set herself above the law by resorting to cultural justifications.

---

[56] Sixty-two per cent of the Jewish population are unaware that even those who are married in civil ceremonies abroad may only get legally divorced in Israeli rabbinical courts. The 2015 Israel Religion and State Index, 'Marriage Freedom in Israel by the Numbers', *Hiddush* (2016), marriage.hiddush.org.

[57] The *Halachic* ceremony of granting a *gett*, the bill of divorce, is conducted by men. The wife has to wait outside the courtroom while the judge, his assistants and the witnesses, all men, participate in the procedure that is foreign to secular women. The wife is called to the courtroom only in the final stage in order to receive the *gett*. See Libby Rosenthal, 'When a Group of Men Mocks You in the Rabbinical Court', *Ynet* (27 May 2019) (Hebrew), www.ynet .co.il/articles/o,7340,L-5516022,00.html?fbclid=IwAR3KY43wmnEe4nQnbo1AKeiHZkIxEMoR olpgyojJGTt4LNBW6ncY5wixfRQ; Zvi Triger, 'Freedom from Religion in Israel: Civil Marriage and Cohabitation of Jews enter the Rabbinical Courts', *Israel Studies Review*, 27(2) (2012): 1–17, at 1.

The second category consists of contingent safeguards and constraints. Here the view is that some safeguards and constraints may be removed when circumstances change, therefore they are introduced conditionally: they are a matter of time, place and manner. If the circumstances are altered, the safeguards and constraints may be removed. This category includes familiar controversies on issues such as conscientious objection, alcoholism, drugs, capital punishment, sexual intercourse, abortion, euthanasia and paternalism in matters of safety. This is not to say that wide consensus is attainable with regard to every one of the above subjects. Some people will surely argue that some of these are matters of principle and should never be permitted (say capital punishment) or prohibited (say sexual intercourse between consenting men), regardless of the circumstances. But since prophecy is not guaranteed to philosophers, we cannot dismiss out of hand the notion of possible debate in future circumstances that are hard to envisage.

CONCLUSION

Coercion yields one winner, at least for a short term. Compromise, on the other hand, if conducted in the genuine sense of the word, yields at least two winners. Coercion lasts as long as the powerful maintain power over the opponent who – if she feels the coercion is unjustified and negates her best interest – will be looking for the right opportunity to regain autonomy. Compromise lasts as long as the parties communicate and maintain trust and good will between them. They need not feel that they sacrificed part of their autonomy. Generally speaking, democracies should resort to mechanisms of compromise and deliberation before they employ coercion.

The distinctions employed are instructive. I distinguished between circumstantial coercion and human coercion, between coercion and brute forms of oppression, and between benevolent and malevolent coercion, highlighting specifically the need for paternalistic coercion. I spoke of self- and other-regarding forms of coercion and when they are deemed justified and provided further distinctions between internalized and designated coercion, and between minority and majority coercion. I explained that majority coercion is not necessarily more justified than minority coercion. Might does not make right. Democracies should come to the help of designated individuals whose basic liberties are infringed by the exercise of coercive methods employed by intolerant and illiberal elements among the community in which they live. The constant challenge for all democracies is to secure human rights for all, the powerful as well as the powerless, for those who are able to take care of themselves and for those who are struggling to maintain their independence and autonomy.

Now that I have fully developed the different layers of the theory of reasonable multiculturalism based on Rawlsian theory, Kantian ethics, Millian ethics, the 'democratic catch' and on the concepts of reasonableness, cultural pluralism, group rights, compromise, deliberative democracy and coercion, the remainder of the book addresses concrete contentious topics. The theoretical framework will provide tools for analysis. In Parts II and III, I examine state interference in the conduct of its illiberal subcultures when, first, physical harm is involved and, then, when non-physical harm is at issue.

PART II

Interference in Minority Affairs: Physical Harm

5

Murder and Torture for Tradition and Honour

We have certainly honored the children of Adam and carried them on the land and sea and provided for them of the good things and preferred them over much of what We have created, with [definite] preference.

The Holy Quran, Surah Al-Isra (17:70)

A leading feminist, Susan Okin, argued that multiculturalism is bad for women. According to Okin, most cultures have as one of their principal aims the control of women. Many culturally based customs aim to control women and render them servile to men's desires and interests. Sometimes, Okin maintained, culture is so closely linked with the control of women that they are virtually equated. Some minority cultures claim special group rights to enable sustained discrimination against women. Such discriminatory cultures do not believe that women should be recognized as having human dignity equal to that of men. They deny women the opportunity to live as meaningful and as freely chosen lives as men.[1]

Thus, if multiculturalism is so bad for women then we should stop promoting it. Okin thinks that preserving cultural minority rights is not a positive thing. In the spirit of liberalism, she argues that we should perceive people as individuals and not as part of a group. But does upholding group rights necessarily exacerbate existing violations of basic human rights? Does multiculturalism necessarily hinder liberal democracy? Is it possible to promote group rights without undermining women's rights?

This chapter and Chapters 7–10 grapple with these questions. Coming to terms with multiculturalism requires reasonable compromises. These should be such that

---

[1]   Susan Moller Okin, *Is Multiculturalism Bad for Women?* (Princeton, NJ: Princeton University Press, 1999). See also Martha Nussbaum, *Sex and Social Justice* (New York: Oxford University Press, 2000); Ayelet Shachar, 'Feminism and Multiculturalism: Mapping the Terrain', in Anthony Simon Laden and David Owen (eds), *Multiculturalism and Political Theory* (Cambridge: Cambridge University Press, 2007): 115–147.

would not undermine the values of liberal democracy and would not unjustly offend women and their basic rights. Liberal democracy cannot and should not claim complete cultural neutrality. Dignity of the person assumes that all humans are equally worthy of respect. For Kant, what commanded respect in us was our status as rational agents, capable of directing our lives through principles, perceiving all people qua people as ends rather than means (see Chapter 1). In this chapter I argue that intervention is justified in the case of gross and systematic violations of human rights, such as murder, slavery, expulsion or inflicting severe bodily harm on certain individuals or groups. Such norms are considered by liberal standards to be intrinsically wrong, wrong by their very nature. Physical harm includes cases of widow burning, female infanticide, murder for family honour and harsh forms of female circumcision, deformation or alteration which are rightly termed 'female genital mutilation' (FGM). The practice of FGM inflicts significant pain and has lasting negative effects on its subjects. I emphasize that the context is liberal democracy. Thus, all the cases I analyse in this chapter as well as in Chapters 6–8 have to do with illiberal communities that wish to pursue their illiberal practices in the liberal state. The question relates to the bounds of state intervention to curtail, or limit, those practices. We need to consider the internal restrictions – the right of a group against its own members as well as the external protections – and the right of a group against the larger society.

For starters, my concern is with two specific matters in which (1) cultural norms justify the taking of a person's life, and (2) autonomy is irreversibly curtailed by the infliction of bodily damage. Should we tolerate things such as decreeing death on oneself or on others? Should we tolerate ritual circumcision of male and female children? Do these norms have a place in a liberal society? As some of these concerns have to do with children, how should we weigh parental rights to decide the future of their children versus children's rights?

In attempting to answer these questions, first it must be stressed that the right to bodily integrity is the most personal and arguably most important of all human rights. It is the right to decide what happens to one's body, the right to object to unwanted interference and not to be subjected to abuse or assault. In 1765, William Blackstone wrote that 'every man's person being sacred, and no other having a right to meddle with it, in any the slightest manner'.[2] It is incumbent on the liberal state to protect the right to bodily integrity especially when vulnerable parties are concerned.

Second, we need to distinguish between cases in which one is inflicting pain or death upon oneself, and cases in which one is inflicting damage upon others. This distinction is made in the framework of the traditional liberal dichotomy between self- and other-regarding conduct. Here I follow in the footsteps of John Stuart Mill.

---

[2] William Blackstone, *Commentaries on the Laws of England* (London: Bichard Taylor, 1830, 17th ed.) Vol 3, at 120, www.llmc.com/docDisplay5.aspx?set=74037&volume=0003&part=001.

True as it is that almost no action can be absolutely personal – in the sense that it does not concern other members of the community, for no person is an island unto herself – nevertheless, if a given action primarily concerns the acting individual, Mill will categorize it as self-regarding and will argue against interference. Mill prescribed interference in another's *self-regarding* conduct when:

1. doers are likely to harm themselves, *and*
2. sufficient grounds exist to believe that doers do not have an interest in doing so, *and*
3. the circumstances are such that the time factor is pressing, and the opportunity to deliberate is denied doers.[3]

Whereas interference in people's liberty is vindicated if their action inflicts harm *upon others*, in situations when the action violates distinct and assignable obligations to another person, the degree of harmfulness is weighty enough to outweigh the loss of freedom incurred as a result of the interference, and the damage is definite (see Chapters 1 and 4).

The considerations we have in mind concern the severity of harm, the subjects to the harm and the level of interference. The more severe the damage, the heavier is the moral requirement of the liberal state to interfere to stop that harm. Harm inflicted on others is more problematic than harm inflicted upon oneself. The issue of harm to others is particularly problematic when the subjects belong to vulnerable populations. In this category, women and children (including babies) are of particular concern. Compared to men, the abilities of children and women to protect themselves are more limited.[4] As children are under the control of adults who are their legal caregivers, the liberal state has a prima facie obligation to intervene when those adults are causing children unnecessary or unjust pain and suffering. Here a balance has to be struck between the individual rights of children and group rights to maintain community tradition and cohesion.

SELF-REGARDING HARM

Consider the following self-harm that may result in death: the permissibility of the Jainas' practice of sallekhana or santhara in relation to the dying. This practice

---

3   J.S. Mill, *On Liberty*, chaps 4 and 5, particularly the example of the unsafe bridge at pp. 151–152. See my discussion in Chapter 4 *supra*. For discussion on Mill's paternalism, see Raphael Cohen-Almagor, 'Between Autonomy and State Regulation: J.S. Mill's Elastic Paternalism', *Philosophy*, 87(4) (October 2012): 557–582.

4   Frank H. Stewart, *Honor* (Chicago: University of Chicago Press, 1994); Robert Ludbrook, 'The Child's Ability to Bodily Integrity', *Current Issues in Criminal Justice*, 7(2) (1995): 123–132; Amir H. Jafri, *Honour Killing* (Oxford: Oxford University Press, 2008); Jane Murray, Beth Blue Swadener and Kylie Smith (eds), *The Routledge International Handbook of Young Children's Rights* (London: Routledge, 2019); Rebecca Budde and Urszula Markowska-Manista (eds), *Childhood and Children's Rights between Research and Activism* (Weisbaden: Springer, 2020).

permits members of the community, under certain circumstances, to actively welcome impending death in a non-violent manner. Community members in the late stages of their lives may decide that they want to die and undertake the vow of terminal fast.[5] This is seen as the ultimate way to expunge all sins and karma, liberating the soul from the eternal cycle of birth, death and rebirth. A Jain woman monk explained: 'You have to understand that for us death is full of excitement. You embrace sallekhana not out of despair with your old life, but to gain and attain something new. It's just as exciting as visiting a new landscape or a new country: we feel excited at a new life, full of possibilities.'[6]

The Jains see a great difference between suicide and sallekhana. While suicide is a great sin, the result of despair, sallekhana is a triumph over death, an expression of hope. With suicide death is full of pain and suffering, while sallekhana is beautiful, with no elements of distress or cruelty. Should liberal democracies intervene to stop this practice?

To address this question, it is emphasized in line with the Millian reasoning that sallekhana refers to voluntary self-harm. It is about a self-regarding act made out of a belief in the purity and beauty of accepting upon oneself the practice of terminal fasting. The assumption is that the person who chooses sallekhana is of sound mind and is not acting under the influence of another person.

Second, fasting is common in many religions. Christianity, Islam and Judaism all direct believers to fast on certain occasions, though none of these major religions instructs fasting till death. None is pushing the practice to such an extreme.

Third, no society encourages suicide. Suicide is self-defeating. If suicide is to be encouraged, the state may then be seen to suggest that living in this state is not an attractive proposition. The state is unable to make life comfortable for its citizens. Through mechanisms of education and deliberation, liberal democracies should evince messages that support living a meaningful life.

Fourth, liberal democracies should not punish individuals for attempting to commit suicide.[7] The thinking is that individuals who contemplate suicide require help rather than punishment. Thus, while liberal democracies do not encourage suicide and promote ideas about quality of life and finding meaning in life, and explain why life is worth living, my view is that those who attempt suicide already punished themselves and do not deserve further penalty.

---

[5] Purushottama Bilimoria, 'The Jaina Ethic of Voluntary Death', *Bioethics*, 6(4) (1992): 331–355, esp. 333.

[6] Soutik Biswas, 'Should India's Jains Be Given the Choice to Die?', *BBC* (21 August 2015), www .bbc.co.uk/news/world-asia-india-33998688. For further discussion, see Thomas Hill, *Autonomy and Self-respect* (Cambridge: Cambridge University Press, 1991): 85–103.

[7] Emily Reynolds, 'Criminalising People Who Attempt Suicide Is Unjust and Dangerous', *The Guardian* (4 June 2019), www.theguardian.com/commentisfree/2019/jun/04/suicide-attempt-criminalised-unjust-dangerous.

Now consider practices such as suttee (also spelled sati, 'burning of the widow'). 'Suttee' in Sanskrit literally means virtuous or good woman, but the term has come to refer to the immolation of a wife on her husband's funeral pyre or to the woman who performs that rite (Anumarana). According to Hindu custom, the Hindu wife who follows her husband to death fulfils her social and religious duty as a woman. She avoids the potent stigma of Hindu widowhood, destroys her own and her husband's sins and attains the status of a benevolent goddess who blesses her family with prosperity and well-being.[8] Some may argue that, following Mill, such a widow should be free to terminate her life if she so wishes. Let me present three opinions in this regard.

One person, Zavit, may say that cultural groups that practice suttee do not think they are disrespecting their women; they believe they are acting appropriately to the nature and circumstances of women. Furthermore, women of those cultures accept these norms as part of their cultural structure; through those norms they define themselves and their place in the world, making sense of their lives.

Another person, Norma, may say that notwithstanding people's willingness, even desire, to belong to their culture, norms of this kind should be excluded; those norms had lost their validity in a liberal society. Suttee undercuts the concept of dignity as recognition. Individuals want to belong to their culture, but they do not necessarily accept all norms as valid within the society in which they now live.

A third person, Taluy, may accept Norma's reasoning in part. Taluy might distinguish between two situations. The first situation is one in which individuals immigrate to a liberal country and then Norma's reasoning is valid. Indian immigrants who wish to live their lives in England are required to forego the norm. This is because they themselves decided to live within the liberal framework. The situation is different when a liberal state expands and colonializes other communities who find themselves under a liberal sovereignty. This was the case of India that found itself under British rule. This is also the case of the Inuit community in Alaska and of the Native Americans in North America, who found themselves under American colonial rule, and this is also the case of the Bedouins who found themselves, not by their own free will, under Israeli rule. Taluy would say that in those cases the liberal state should not add the sin of so-called 'benevolent' paternalism to the evil of expansion and colonialism. Therefore, no justification exists to forbid cultural norms such as deserting elderly people in the icy wasteland. In other words, Taluy argues that the question is one of choice and time precedence. We should allow the prohibition of cultural norms when individuals voluntarily migrate to a liberal state. But we should not bar cultural norms, however distasteful and harmful we might see

---

8   Edward Thompson, *Suttee: A Historical and Philosophical Enquiry into the Hindu Rite of Widow-Burning* (New York: Houghton Mifflin, 1928); Sakuntal Narasimhan, *Sati: Widow Burning in India* (New York: Anchor, 1992); Holly Baker Reynolds, book review of *Sati: Widow Burning in India, Harvard Women's Law Journal*, 12 (Spring 1989): 277–286.

them, in the case where cultural minorities lived their lives peacefully and the liberal state expanded and forced itself upon them.

In the case of immigrants who come to a country knowing its laws, imposing liberal principles as embodied in general laws is unobjectionable in the eyes of liberal multiculturalists. This can be seen as part of the terms of admission to a liberal polity, and immigrants have no basis for denying that the state has legitimate authority over them.[9] But the situation is more complicated with national minorities, particularly if (1) they were involuntarily incorporated into the larger state (as the Palestinians claim with regard to their incorporation into the Jewish state; see Chapter 10), and (2) they have their own internal governance, with their own internal mechanisms for dispute resolution (see Chapter 7). In these circumstances the legitimate scope for coercive intervention by the state may be contested. Whether this contestation is reasonable and justified is open for debate, but deliberation should ensue.

When women are pressured to perform suttee, this destroys women's right to seek meaningful choice for themselves. It also violates the two basic liberal norms of not harming others and of *mutual* respect for others as enunciated by the Respect for Others Principle (see Chapter 1). The argument that the woman gave her consent before she was burnt to death does not hold water as, unlike the case of the Jainas, questions arise regarding the free will of women who were burnt to death. It points to circumstances-based coercion (Chapter 4), social pressure and the failure of the community to help and shelter those women. Suttee happened because the community's coercive expectations were subtly coded in the martyrdom-like agency of the widowed.[10] Her free will had been compromised. Recoursing to Hindu terminology, this form of termination of life involves more than merely internalized coercion and it violates the basic principle of *ahimsa* (virtue of non-injury) towards all life. It 'presents something of an embarrassment to Indians from across a broad spectrum'.[11] The practice of suttee is repugnant even in the eyes of Hindu members.

---

[9] Things are more complicated if an immigrant group was exempted from liberal requirements when it arrived, and so has been able to maintain certain illiberal institutions for many years or generations (e.g., the Amish in the United States). These groups were given certain assurances about their right to maintain separate institutions, and so have built and maintained self-contained enclaves that depend on certain internal restrictions. Had those assurances not been given, these groups might have emigrated to some other country. It seems that these groups do have a stronger claim to maintain internal restrictions than newly arriving immigrants. I discuss the Amish in Chapter 8.

[10] Purushottama Bilimoria, 'The Enlightenment Paradigm of Native Right and Hybridity of Cultural Rights in British India', in Michael Barnhardt (ed.), *Varieties of Ethical Reflection: New Directions for Ethics in a Global Context* (Lanham, MD: Lexington Books, 2002): 235–262.

[11] Bilimoria, 'The Jaina Ethic of Voluntary Death', 344–345. For further discussion, see K. Sangari and S. Vaid, 'Sati in Modern India: A Report', *Economic and Political Weekly*, 16 (31) (1 August 1981): 1284–1288.

SCARRING

Now let us consider self-harm to young people; not to death but involving significant pain inflicted on these people as a result of social pressure. The issue concerns scarring parts of the body, sometimes as part of rites common in some African cultures,[12] sometimes for a host of other reasons. In some cultures, scarring is performed by adolescents who wish to undergo the rite of passage and be recognized as men by their own community. If boys are able to endure the pain of initiation, they prove their entitlement to manhood. Henderson argues that Africans viewed their tribal markings as an extension of their native selves, a fleshly embodiment of tribal customs and histories.[13] The scars are no less than 'a mark of grandeur'.[14] In certain tribes, cicatrization is done to mark association with the tribe.[15] It was done on men and women on different parts of the body. Sometimes marks were used to indicate that the man killed another in action, or that a woman had aborted her child. The practice of marking a killer is supposed to prevent the spirit of the deceased from troubling the killer. Women self-harm themselves by marking distinct beauty spots.[16]

Slavery and the forced displacement of Africans from their native land as well as their cultural heritage bring some people to scar themselves (Figure 5.1). During the days of the slave trade, public auctions of people included humiliating close inspection of 'merchandise' by potential buyers. They were looking for scars and bruises that would lower the slave's market value. Thus, self-inflicted scarring is an act of rebellion and memorialization. The body speaks, reminds us of the evils of the past and embodies political, cultural and personal discourse.[17]

While liberals might be troubled by this cultural rite that subject people to pain, and while liberals would acknowledge that members of these cultures would find it difficult to refuse undergoing scarring as they would be put between a rock and a hard place, I fail to find sufficient reasons to bar this practice in order to preserve the integrity of the body. Western revulsion in the case of scarring may reflect squeamishness. Here external protections aimed at protecting group identity are defensible. It is problematic to object to scarring when societal norms put great

---

[12] Roland Garve, Miriam Garve, Jens C. Turp, et al., 'Scarification in Sub-Saharan Africa: Social Skin, Remedy and Medical Import', *Tropical Medicine & International Health*, 22(6) (2017), www.researchgate.net/publication/315800896_Scarification_in_sub-Saharan_Africa_Social_skin_remedy_and_medical_import.

[13] Carol E. Henderson, *Scarring the Black Body: Race and Representation in African American Literature* (Columbia: University of Missouri Press, 2002): 29.

[14] Ibid., 30.

[15] Cicatrisation means contraction of tissue, formed at a wound site by fibroblasts, reducing the size of the wound while distorting tissue. It relates to scar formation of a healing wound.

[16] G.A. Turner, 'Some of the Tribal Marks of the South African Native Races', paper read before the Transvaal Medical Society, *Transvaal Medical Journal* (February 1911): 13–14.

[17] Henderson, *Scarring the Black Body*, 39.

FIGURE 5.1. Scarring for beauty (Tara Moore/Stone/Getty Images).

pressure on women to change their bodies, resort to painful procedures, expecting them to shave the majority of their body hair and embark on 'beauty' diets. Furthermore, tattooing has become commonplace and this is also not a pain-free procedure. Granted that scarring is more painful than tattooing but the degree of pain is not the only consideration. Liberal interference is more likely to hurt the community than to 'rescue' these members. To my mind there are no countervailing strong reasons to go against the group's culture and norms. The severity of harm does not warrant intervention.

The customs of scarring and self-starvation should not be promoted and encouraged by the liberal state, but since the subcultures possess historical claims and strongly believe in their traditional practices and norms, they should have a right to cultural autonomy. Having said that, the formation of *elaborate* patterns of scarring is very painful and might result in fatal consequences owing to the wounds having become septic.[18] Elaborate marking are usually not self-harm but are done by others. The Golden Mean requires deliberation and moderation. The liberal state should also advise and propagate the importance of adequate standards of hygiene. The use of dirty instruments might result in developing and transferring diseases.

[18] Turner, 'Some of the Tribal Marks of the South African Native Races', 14.

Now let me consider cases of other-regarding harm. Unlike the previous cases, consent is not alleged or sought. Illiberal groups adopt norms that are clearly harmful to others. The targets are often women who are expected to yield and accept those harmful norms.

MURDER FOR FAMILY HONOUR

The subjugation, exploitation and commodification of women are ancient and widespread. Throughout history women have been humiliated and treated brutally. Women have been viewed as the embodiment of sin, misfortune, disgrace and shame. In most societies women had hardly any rights or social position.[19] Most ancient legal codes have conceded the right to offended husbands to divorce, torture or even kill their wives.[20]

Patriarchal cultures maintain mores that help sustain the male rule and domination. One of the ways to do this is by instilling an honour/shame system. Women who are raised in such cultures know the strict regimen of honour, what is expected of them and what the consequences of shame are. Controlling women's sexuality is a prime concern for both men and women. Preserving women's purity is a high priority on the agenda. As extreme violence might be employed as punishment for transgression of cultural norms, women are, generally speaking, compliant in accepting their subordinate position.[21]

In these cultures, family honour is violated when an unmarried woman is suspected of having intimate relationships with a man, or when a married woman is suspected of adultery. In Arabic, the term 'ird denotes honour surrounding female chastity and self-restraint; 'ird implies both respect and disdain.[22] The issue of consent is secondary or even irrelevant. Family honour is violated also when a woman is a victim of rape or incest, especially when the conduct becomes public knowledge. To salvage family honour, a member of the family or the community murders the sinner.[23] Cases where the murder of kin is justified as an avenue to restore honour occur in some Muslim communities as well as in Sardinia and Sicily.[24]

---

[19] Jafri, *Honour Killing*, 27.

[20] Ibid., 140.

[21] Nancy V. Baker, Peter R. Gregware and Margery A. Cassidy, 'Family Killing Fields: Honor Rationales in the Murder of Women', *Violence Against Women*, 5(2) (1999): 180.

[22] Aref Abu-Rabia, 'Family Honor Killings: Between Custom and State Law', *The Open Psychology Journal*, 4(Suppl. 1-M4) (2011): 34.

[23] Ilsa M. Glazer and Wahiba Abu Ras, 'On Aggression, Human Rights, and Hegemonic Discourse: The Case of a Murder for Family Honor in Israel', *Sex Roles*, 30(3/4) (1994): 274; Joseph Ginat, *Blood Revenge* (Tel Aviv: Haifa University Press and Zmora-Bitan, 2000) (Hebrew): 181.

[24] Abu-Rabia, 'Family Honor Killings', 35.

Chastity and promiscuity are not the only reasons for redeeming family, especially male honour. Women were murdered when they refused to obey or violated traditional mores or for being 'too Western'.[25] Western values challenge tradition and are perceived as threats in certain communities. These include growing independence on the part of women, being not subservient enough, refusing to wear traditional clothing, pursuing education and a career outside the home, having friends or boyfriends outside the community, refusing to marry the person who was the designated groom, wanting to choose one's own husband or wishing to leave one's husband.[26] Female conduct as well as the *perception* of their conduct is important. Girls and women should ensure that they are not subjects of gossip and hearsay that might smear their names and, *ipso facto*, discredit and shame their families. Girls and women are expected to keep their dignity, and the dignity of their families, intact.

In liberal thought the concept of dignity refers to a worth or value that flows from an inner source. People should be able to control their destiny, maintain their autonomy, not be humiliated and perceive themselves with honour. According to Kant, it is only through morality that a rational being can be an agent in the realm of ends. Through morality we become ends in ourselves. People have intrinsic value, that is, dignity, infinitely above any price.[27] Each person has moral worth. People should never be exploited. Dignity cannot be qualified due to one's gender, culture or any other characteristics, and it requires us to take responsibility for our actions.

The concept of dignity as recognition is explained in Chapter 1. People have inherent dignity. If this were not the case, people would simply be the bearers of instrumental value like all other objects in the world. Instead, human beings are set apart and treated in special ways. Human beings are precious; our lives are appreciated and should be protected.

The UN estimates 5,000 women are murdered each year in the name of 'honour'. Such murders have been documented in many countries, including Bangladesh, Belgium, Brazil, Canada, Denmark, Ecuador, Egypt, Germany, India, Iran, Iraq, Israel, Italy, Jordan, Morocco, The Netherlands, Norway, Pakistan, Peru, Sweden, Switzerland, Syria, Turkey, Uganda, the United Kingdom, and the United States. While 'honour' crime is committed predominantly against women and girls,

---

[25] J.G. Peristiany (ed.), *Honour and Shame: The Values of Mediterranean Society* (London: Weidenfeld & Nicholson, 1965); Manar Hasan, 'The Politics of Honor: Patriarchy, the State and the Murder of Women in the Name of Family Honor', *Journal of Israeli History*, 21(1–2) (2002): 31.

[26] Phyllis Chesler, 'Worldwide Trends in Honor Killings', *Middle East Quarterly*, 17(2) (Spring 2010): 3–11.

[27] Kant, *Groundwork of the Metaphysic of Morals*. For further discussion, see Ino Augsberg, '"The Moral Feeling within Me": On Kant's Concept of Human Freedom and Dignity as Auto-heteronomy', in Dieter Grimm, Alexandra Kemmerer and Christoph Möllers (eds), *Human Dignity in Context* (Munich: Hart, 2018): 55–68.

'honour' crime is also on the rise against LGBT people, particularly gay men.[28] Often the victims are young women in their twenties. Chesler's study that reviewed 230 murders (she terms them 'honour-killings') showed that the worldwide average age of victims was 23 year old, and that over half of these victims were daughters and sisters, and about a quarter were wives and girlfriends, of the perpetrators. The remainder included mothers, aunts, nieces, cousins, uncles or non-relatives. Worldwide, two-thirds of the victims were killed by their families of origin. Substantial number of the victims were tortured. In North America, over one-third of the victims were tortured, while in Europe two-thirds were tortured.[29]

Murder, by definition, is both wrong and other-regarding. The reason, 'for family honour', does not justify it. This practice is employed by some patriarchal cultural communities in order to perpetuate male control and preserve his honour. Control was damaged, or lost, due to a woman's conduct; the way to restore order and to reclaim honour is to murder the woman. This is a mechanism of brute justice and deterrence against other women.

In Israel, murder for family honour takes place most notably in the Bedouin and Druze communities, sometimes also in the Christian community, as a control mechanism to 'protect the community' against 'misbehaving' girls who do not follow the dictates of their elders. In these communities, honour is frequently more important than life, and culture more important than law. Reports show that women were assassinated because they were accused of not conforming to prevailing moral codes.[30] Violation of the sexual norm by a married woman constitutes a tribal sin and automatically calls for her murder. As for single women, accusation is always based on the breach of the norm that a girl or unmarried woman who has 'sinned' must be punished by death unless she marries her sexual partner. If, for some reason, marriage does not take place and the woman is subjected to public accusation, one of her relatives will have to kill her whether or not the family wishes to execute this harsh punishment. As the matter is part of the tribal social fabric, family preferences have no significance.[31] Girls in their early teens might be murdered for the mere 'sin' of shaking hands with boys from other families.[32] In some instances, women were murdered due to their independence, initiative and resolve; daring to enter a sphere that is governed by men and thus embarrassing their families. Women's refusal to stop smoking, to stop working outside the home or to follow family dictates

---

[28] Chesler, 'Worldwide Trends in Honor Killings', 3–11; Amnesty International, 'The Horror of "Honor Killings", Even in US', www.amnestyusa.org/the-horror-of-honor-killings-even-in-us/; Cees Maris and Sawitri Saharso, 'Honour Killing: A Reflection on Gender, Culture and Violence', *Netherlands Journal of Social Sciences*, 37(1) (2001): 52–73.

[29] Chesler, 'Worldwide Trends in Honor Killings'.

[30] Mohammad M. Idriss and Tahir Abbas (eds), *Honour, Violence, Women and Islam* (London: Routledge, 2010); G.M. Kressel, 'Sororicide/Filiacide: Homicide for Family Honour', *Current Anthropology*, 22(2) (1981): 141–158. On different types of Bedouin honour, see Stewart, *Honor*.

[31] Abu-Rabia, 'Family Honor Killings', 38.

[32] Hasan, 'The Politics of Honor', 19.

as to whom they should marry may serve as grounds for murder to preserve family honour.[33] By murdering their daughters or sisters, the men prove the control the natal family has over its women.[34]

Many men of these communities see such instances of murder for family honour as 'internal matters', meaning that society should not interfere. They wish to erect external protections against societal intervention in their affairs. Recognizing phenomenology, the power of words in establishing reality, those who somehow 'understand' or condone the practice do not use the term 'murder'. They would resort to other terms, such as 'killing' or 'homicide'. In these communities a connection of silence surrounds the issue. Victims who escaped death are often reluctant to testify against their families.[35] On some occasions, the act of murder is disguised as a suicide, and it needs some investigation to clear things up and resolve the case. When girls do not step forward and acts of murder are committed, sometime the police are reluctant to interfere, perceiving these crimes as the decision-makers of these communities want, that is, as 'internal affairs' to be resolved within the specific community. Ipso facto, the result of this outlook might be that an offence against family honour (*intihak el-hurma*) serves as an adequate justification for taking life.[36]

Cultural considerations should not override the rule of law and people should not take the law into their own hands. Notwithstanding whether it is conducted by indigenous people or by immigrants, murder is murder is murder. Murder performed for traditional reasons is still murder. No cultural claims can redeem the severity of the crime. There is nothing dignified or honourable in the practice of murder for family honour. The term 'honour' is misplaced. It diminishes the victim and serves criminals by providing them with a legitimate reason which some perceive as an understandable excuse for murder.

In the United Kingdom, 'honour'-based violence is a significant problem impacting thousands of victims.[37] It is estimated that twelve murders for family honour take place each and every year. Figures from the Crown Prosecution Service

---

[33] Ibid., 30–31; Maris and Saharso, 'Honour Killing', 52–73.

[34] Raphael Cohen-Almagor, 'Female Circumcision and Murder for Family Honour among Minorities in Israel', in Kirsten Schulze, Martin Stokes and Colm Campbell (eds), *Nationalism, Minorities and Diasporas: Identities and Rights in the Middle East* (London: I.B. Tauris, 1996): 178. See also Rana Husseini, *Murder in the Name of Honor* (London: Oneworld, 2009).

[35] Dana Weiller-Polak and Dana Yarkezi, 'Conspiracy of Silence: How 10 Women, of the Same Family, Were Murdered and Disappeared in 14 Years', *Walla* (26 October 2014) (Hebrew), https://news.walla.co.il/item/2795932; see also Yoni Mendel, 'Silence on Desecration of Family Honour', *Walla* (7 July 2007) (Hebrew), https://news.walla.co.il/item/1131435.

[36] Ginat, *Blood Revenge*, 179–245; Gideon M. Kressel and Unni Wikan, 'More on Honour and Shame', *Man*, 23(1) (March 1988): 167–170. See Shelley Saywell's documentary *Crimes of Honour* (1999), http://icarusfilms.com/if-cri.

[37] Hannah Summers, '"Honour Killing" Term Must Not Be Banned, Says Woman Raped on Wedding Day', *The Independent* (2 February 2017), www.independent.co.uk/news/uk/home-news/honour-killing-latest-rape-victim-wedding-day-term-a7559971.html.

show that in 2013–2014 there were 123 successful prosecutions for crimes of honour-based abuse. The offences include coercive control, forced marriage and subsequent repeated rape, FGM, assault, threats to kill, attempted murder and murder. In 2017–2018, there were seventy-one convictions on these grounds.[38]

In both the United Kingdom and Israel, the state's response to murder for family honour was not always swift and the police at times lacked interest to act. Women are often invisible from protective agencies and social services.[39] One critique of British law enforcement argued: 'Thousands of crimes of honour-based crimes are going undetected and therefore unpunished. Perpetrators are not being held to account. The fall in prosecutions is massively concerning given more victims than ever are coming forward. It sends a message to communities that you can almost get away with it.'[40] Multicultural respect for diversity and cultural differences unwittingly engendered non-interference and led to neglect in the state's responsibility to protect vulnerable populations.[41]

In Israel, at times it was easier to commute a sentence or obtain an early release from prison in cases of crime for blood revenge or for reasons of family honour. Unfortunately, there were occasions in which the Israeli police and legal authorities showed 'understanding' of the culture that warrants murder or behaved irresponsibly. For instance, while knowing that an unmarried girl might be murdered if her family knew that she was pregnant or gave birth, they still failed to protect her. Some reports claim that the police delivered girls straight into the hands of their murderers.[42] Unlike common murderers, murderers for family honour were entitled to a pardon.[43] This forgiving attitude has helped to perpetuate an unjust and abominable practice that no liberal society should tolerate.

I find it worrying to read the following: 'The partial recognition by the state of traditional customs may indeed contribute to their continuity. But more probably the responsiveness shown limits the alienation of the traditional communities within the modern state.'[44] This line of reasoning could be interpreted as legitimizing

---

[38] Maya Oppenheim, 'Convictions for Honour Crimes Including FGM, Rape and Forced Marriage Plummet amid National Police Crackdown', *The Independent* (22 July 2019), www .independent.co.uk/news/uk/home-news/honour-crimes-women-fgm-murder-abuse-convic tions-cps-a9001321.html; Emma Lake, 'Honour Crimes: What Is an Honour Killing and How Common Are the Horrific Crimes in the UK?', *The Sun* (17 September 2018), www.thesun.co .uk/news/4091357/what-is-honour-killing-murder-uk/.

[39] Omri Efraim and Hasan Shaalan, 'Murder of Arab Women in Israel: :Women Are Targeted''', *YNET* (27 October 2016) (Hebrew), www.ynet.co.il/articles/0,7340,L-4870581,00.html.

[40] Oppenheim, 'Convictions for honour crimes'.

[41] Veena Meetoo and Heidi Safia Mirza, 'There Is Nothing "Honourable" about Honour Killings': Gender, Violence and the Limits of Multiculturalism', *Women's Studies International Forum*, 30 (2007): 188–193.

[42] Hasan, 'The Politics of Honor', 19–20.

[43] Ibid., 1–37.

[44] Joseph Ginat, *Blood Disputes among Bedouin and Rural Arabs in Israel* (Pittsburgh: University of Pittsburgh Press, in cooperation with Jerusalem Institute for Israel Studies, 1987): 27.

crime, equating what the state deems murder with the fear of Bedouin alienation from Israeli society. While alienation is bad for the Bedouins and it also goes against the interests of the state of Israel, mitigating it should not be done by turning a blind eye to murder. The way to address Bedouin alienation is to eliminate discrimination and strive for equal rights for all, not by acceding to immoral codes of practice that undermine the raison d'être of the state. I elaborate on this in Chapter 10.

Things, however, have changed for the better in recent years. Education, campaigns for the rights of women, deliberative mechanisms facilitated by human rights organizations and raising media awareness to women's concerns have made a positive impact. Concrete steps were taken to deter and to punish criminals who hide behind culture to justify heinous and utterly unjust deeds. Increasingly, Israel shows more sensitivity to human life than to cultural norms. Its authorities are more anxious to protect fundamental moral codes and basic human rights than to protect partisan interests.

In 2005, the Israel Supreme Court considered the case of Taha Najar, who murdered his sister because she wished to travel alone to Egypt. According to his moral code, this was not allowed as Samia, his sister, was unmarried and unmarried women do not travel alone. Taha tried to get Samia to change her mind, and when he failed he stabbed Samia eleven times. He was convicted and sentenced in a court of law and then appealed to the Supreme Court to mitigate his sentence. The court, *per* Justice Elyakim Rubinstein, dismissed his appeal arguing that 'honour' is not an excuse for murder. Rubinstein held that it was the role of the Sheikh, the leader of the tribe to which Taha belonged, as well as the role of the education system, to see that such 'twisted' honour norms that legitimize murder be uprooted.[45] This was a premeditated murder that has no excuse.

Indeed, courts of justice should not, prima facie, make religious distinctions and, generally speaking, should not pass judgement on religious beliefs. Religious norms are entitled to equal respect so long as they are legally and socially acceptable, within the Rawlsian overlapping consensus (see Chapter 1) and not immoral or socially obnoxious, defeating the underpinning norms of respecting others and not harming others.

Prominent political leaders of the Israeli Arab/Palestinian minority have protested and condemned murder for family honour. Member of Knesset Ahmad Tibi asked to speak of 'murder of women' instead of honour killing as 'There is no honor in murder based on family honor. There is anti-honor.'[46] A person who takes life is a criminal. No one has the right to be the judge and the executor. Member of Knesset Ibrahim Sarsur who was the head of the Islamic Movement in Israel said, 'there is no linkage between this despicable murder and Islam. Islam, Islamic law, and even

---

[45] *Taha Najar v. State of Israel*. Criminal Appeal 10828/03. Israel Supreme Court (2 May 2005).
[46] Abu-Rabia, 'Family Honor Killings', 40.

Islamic punitive law ... reject out of hand murder of this kind.'[47] While sexual relations outside marriage are objectionable, no one has the right to take the law into one's own hands. Such murders emanate from custom, not Islam.[48]

The case of murder poses no moral dilemma. It is clearly wrong, unjust and unreasonable. It is both morally and legally reasonable to expect the state to strive to eradicate the practice. Even if a woman followed her heart and 'sinned' by going against the wishes of her family or by dishonouring her husband, her punishment should not be murder. People of those cultural communities understand this when the issue concerns men who sin; somehow, the standards for women are far more demanding, and their punishment is drastic. Rawls explains that the principles of any *reasonable* political conceptions must impose restrictions on permissible comprehensive views, and the basic institutions of a just society inevitably encourage some ways of life and discourage others, or even exclude them altogether.[49] The state is certainly justified in curtailing this phenomenon and delivering a clear message: this issue is beyond negotiations and squarely outside the scope of tolerance.

As the preservation of human rights and the protection of vulnerable populations are at the heart of liberal democracy, governments are obliged to resort to multiple mechanisms to aid women in danger:

- Education. Raising the issue early in primary schools, denouncing the practice and explaining that murder has no place in a civilized society, and that such practice dishonours the murderer and his family. Education is essential especially in schools where immigrants from relevant countries study.
- Deliberation. As mentioned (Chapter 3), the freedom to reason and to deliberate publicly about social concerns is a necessary condition of legitimate policies and legislation. Using methods of deliberative democracy, the values of gender equality, respect for others and not harming others should be accentuated. Social workers and other stakeholders involved in family welfare should engage with men and women in the relevant communities in the attempt to delegitimize the practice while elucidating a zero-tolerance policy and the existence of harsh penalties for those who violate state law. Murderous cultural norms do not override law or precede law.
- Support. Providing counselling to women who are under pressure to behave in accordance with coercive standards. Vulnerable women who suffer abuse should receive adequate mental support.

---

[47] Ibid., 41.
[48] Ibid.
[49] Rawls, *Political Liberalism*, 195. See also Joseph Raz, *Ethics in the Public Domain: Essays in the Morality of Law and Politics* (Oxford: Clarendon Press, 1995): 184–187.

- Protection. Mental support might not be enough. In some cases physical support is also needed. Women who are threatened and who fear for their lives as they wish to break free from their coercive communities should be provided with exit opportunities. Alternative accommodation, shelter homes and, when needed, suitable supporting arrangements similar to the witness protection scheme should be provided for women in duress.
- Shame. As honour is an important component of this brutal practice, public shaming of perpetrators is a useful way to fight against it. Murdering one's own daughter is not a source of pride but shame. It is a shame that a young life were taken. It is a shame that a father robbed himself of the joy of his own daughter. It is a shame that the father and his family will have to live with the consequences of this misguided action.
- Legislation. The law should be clear, explicit and not open to interpretation. It should include harsh and deterring penalties for murder, making it clear that honour reasoning is baseless and unacceptable.
- Law enforcement. Law should be enforced, otherwise it is unworthy of the paper on which it is written. Prosecution of offenders should be swift and effective.

I have mentioned (Chapter 2) that Rawls does not explicitly state that culture is a primary good. At the same time, behind the veil of ignorance we can safely assume that reasonable people will not choose to have murder for family honour as a norm. People who do not know their gender would be reluctant to concede having such a practice. There are boundaries to liberty and tolerance otherwise the very principles of liberal democracy might undermine its existence. Recognizing the 'democratic catch', we should not allow 'internal group affairs' to trump law. Murder for family honour is beyond the scope of tolerance.

Now let me examine the case of inflicting harm on a girl's genitalia in the name of culture. This practice is referred to by different names, depending on the viewpoint of those discussing it, thus a note on terminology is in order. Those opposing these rituals call them 'genital torture' and 'female genital mutilation'. These terms convey urgency to take active steps of intervention, aiming to curtail the practice. Those who view the rituals in more neutral terms call them 'female circumcision' or 'female genital cutting' (FGC). The terms 'circumcision' and 'cutting' suggest drawing a comparison between male and female versions of the practice.

I am a firm believer in phenomenology. I believe that reality is shaped by the terms we use. Terminology should be exact, appropriate for describing phenomena and procedures, and respectful of the people concerned. I use the term 'circumcision' to refer to a moderate form of female cutting of sexual organs, and the term 'female genital mutilation' (FGM) to refer to a harsh form of circumcision. The term 'mutilation' is, of course, value-laden, indicating the infliction of severe physical pain on and damage of the female body. Mutilation amounts to torture. Communities that engage with FGM torture their girls. Liberal democracy should establish substantial safeguards to prevent FGM.

An interesting question is whether it is reasonable to allow female circumcision to the same extent that societies allow male circumcision. Why is male circumcision generally accepted in liberal democracies, while female circumcision is not?

FEMALE CIRCUMCISION AND FGM

Female circumcision is an ancient cultural practice involving inflicting damage on the external female genitalia for cultural reasons. Those who vindicate this practice view it as crucial to the continued survival of tribal groups as separate cultural entities and so it should be autonomous and free from state interference.[50] FGM is a far more elaborate and harsher procedure that amounts to torture. The World Health Organization (WHO) defines FGM as 'all procedures that involve partial or total removal of the external female genitalia or other injury to the female genital organs for non-medical reasons'.[51]

The WHO classifies FGM into four major categories:[52]

- Type 1. Often referred to as *clitoridectomy*, this is the partial or total removal of the clitoris (a small, sensitive and erectile part of the female genitals), and in very rare cases only the prepuce (the fold of skin surrounding the clitoris).[53]
- Type 2. Often referred to as *excision*, this is the partial or total removal of the clitoris and the labia minora (the inner folds of the vulva), with or without excision of the labia majora (the outer folds of skin of the vulva). The vast majority of female cutting performed in Africa is of type 1 or 2.[54]

---

[50] Robyn Cenry Smith, 'Female Circumcision: Bringing Women's Perspectives into the International Debate', *Southern California Law Review*, 65 (1992): 2449–2504.

[51] WHO, 'Female Genital Mutilation' (31 January 2018), www.who.int/en/news-room/fact-sheets/detail/female-genital-mutilation. See also WHO, *Global Strategy to Stop Health-Care Providers from Performing Female Genital Mutilation* (Geneva: WHO, 2010).

[52] WHO, 'Female Genital Mutilation'.

[53] In his comments, Earp notes (email received 24 October 2019) that there are no forms of FGM that remove the total clitoris. The WHO is just flatly wrong on this and perpetuates a seriously mistaken view of female sexual anatomy, equating the external, visible portion of the clitoris with the entire clitoris, thereby diminishing the anatomical and sexual significance of the latter. Most of the clitoris is underneath the skin like an iceberg and excising it requires major surgery which does not occur in any recognized form of FGM. For further critique of the WHO categorization, see B.D. Earp, 'Protecting Children from Medically Unnecessary Genital Cutting without Stigmatizing Women's Bodies: Implications for Sexual Pleasure and Pain', *Archives of Sexual Behavior* (April 2020).

[54] Duivenbode and Padela, 'The Problem of Female Genital Cutting', 276.

- Type 3. Often referred to as *infibulation*, this is the narrowing of the vaginal opening through the creation of a covering seal. The seal is formed by cutting and repositioning the labia minora, or labia majora, sometimes through stitching, with or without removal of the clitoris (clitoridectomy). Infibulation, when the entire visible part of the clitoris and some or all of the labia minora are excised, and incisions are made in the labia majora to create raw surfaces, is the most severe form of FGM. According to estimates, one in five of the women and girls genitally cut has undergone this most severe form of FGM.[55]
- Type 4. This includes all other harmful procedures to the female genitalia for non-medical purposes, for example pricking, piercing, incising, scraping and cauterizing the genital area.[56]

The European Institute for Gender Equality holds that Female Genital Mutilation (FGM) is 'an expression of deeply entrenched gender inequalities, grounded in a mix of cultural, religious and social factors inherent within patriarchal families and communities'.[57] The practice sustains gender inequalities and maintains power structures based on gender in societies where 'women and their "honour" are valued as the objects and properties of men'.[58]

In the following discussion, when I resort to the term "FGM" I refer to the first three harsh categories that involve excessive cutting of female genitalia and inflict on its subjects severe bodily and psychological harm. At times, to emphasize that I do not refer to type 4 that varies in severity, I will write excessive forms of FGM. FGM has no known health benefits. While there is evidence of a significant decline in the prevalence for FGM among children across countries and regions, many communities in thirty countries still practice it, especially in North and West Africa but also in Asia,[59] Latin America[60] and the Middle East.[61] It is estimated that three million

---

[55] Celia W. Dugger, 'Report Finds Gradual Fall in Female Genital Cutting in Africa', *New York Times* (22 July 2013), www.nytimes.com/2013/07/23/health/report-finds-gradual-fall-in-female-genital-cutting-in-africa.html?nl=todaysheadlines&emc=edit_th_20130723&_r=0&page wanted=print.

[56] Arora and Jacobs offer a different categorization based on the extent of disability caused by the procedure. See Kavita Shah Arora and Allan J. Jacobs, 'Female Genital Alteration: A Compromise Solution', *Journal of Medical Ethics*, 42(3) (2016): 148–154.

[57] European Institute for Gender Equality (EIGE), *Female Genital Mutilation in the European Union and Croatia* (Belgium: EIGE, 2013): 23.

[58] Ibid.

[59] Small communities within India and Pakistan, primarily the Dawoodi Bohra, while Thai and Malay Muslims practice ritual nicking fairly widely.

[60] Natalio Cosoy, '"Cut with a Blade": Colombia Indigenous Groups Discuss FGM', *BBC* (12 October 2016), www.bbc.com/news/world-latin-america-37374006; 'A Silent Epidemic: The Fight to End Female Genital Mutilation in Colombia', *UN Population Fund* (9 February 2016), www.unfpa.org/news/silent-epidemic-fight-end-female-genital-mutilation-colombia.

[61] Jane Muthumbi, Joar Svanemyr, Elisa Scolaro, Marleen Temmerman and Lale Say, 'Female Genital Mutilation: A Literature Review of the Current Status of Legislation and Policies in

girls and women worldwide are at risk each year. About 200 million women are estimated to be living with the consequences.[62] In Africa, gender identity formation and aesthetic considerations underlie the practice.[63] In the Western world, FGM is practised by asylum seekers and immigrants. An estimated 513,000 women and girls have immigrated to the United States from African countries that practice FGM. They are at risk of been subjected to FGM.[64] Western countries prohibit this practice but families who send their daughters abroad to undergo female circumcision often are not prosecuted.[65]

Shahvisi and Earp argue that the majority of women within populations of prevalence who have themselves been cut report their continuing support for the practice.[66] They stress the distinction between consensual and non-consensual practices, voicing support for the permissibility of consensual practice and arguing that non-consensual genital cutting that is not medically necessary is morally wrong. Shahvisi and Earp, who prefer to use the term FGC as they find the term 'mutilation' biased against the practice,[67] maintain that it is plausible that there may be

---

27 African Countries and Yemen', *African Journal of Reproductive Health*, 19(3) (2015): 32–40; Ngianga-Bakwin Kandala, Martinsixtus C. Ezejimofor, Olalekan A. Uthman, et al., 'Secular Trends in the Prevalence of Female Genital Mutilation/Cutting among Girls: A Systematic Analysis', *BMJ Global Health*, 3(5) (2018), https://gh.bmj.com/content/3/5/e000549; Samuel Kimani, Tammary Esho, Violet Kimani, et al., 'Female Genital Mutilation/Cutting: Innovative Training Approach for Nurse-Midwives in High Prevalent Settings', *Obstetrics and Gynecology International* (2018), https://doi.org/10.1155/2018/5043512; Eva Ontiveros, 'What Is FGM, Where Does It Happen and Why?', *BBC* (6 February 2019), www.bbc.com/news/world-47131052.

[62] WHO, 'Female Genital Mutilation'.

[63] Duivenbode and Padela, 'The Problem of Female Genital Cutting', 275; The Public Policy Advisory Network on Female Genital Surgeries in Africa, 'Seven Things to Know about Female Genital Surgeries in Africa', *Hastings Center Report*, 6 (2012): 19–27.

[64] Ranit Mishori, Nicole Warren and Rebecca Reingold, 'Female Genital Mutilation or Cutting', *American Family Physician*, 97(1) (January 2018): 49.

[65] Human Rights Council, 'Promotion and Protection of All Human Rights, Civil, Political, Economic, Social and Cultural Rights, Including the Right to Development', *Report of the Special Rapporteur on Torture and Other Cruel, Inhuman or Degrading Treatment or Punishment* (15 January 2008); Ylva K. Hernlund and Bettina K. Shell-Duncan (eds), *Transcultural Bodies: Female Genital Cutting in Global Context* (Piscataway, NJ: Rutgers University Press, 2007).

[66] Arianne Shahvisi and Brian D. Earp, 'The Law and Ethics of Female Genital Cutting', in S. Creighton and L.-M. Liao (eds), *Female Genital Cosmetic Surgery: Solution to What Problem?* (Cambridge: Cambridge University Press, 2019), www.researchgate.net/publication/322287554_The_law_and_ethics_of_female_genital_cutting.

[67] In comments on a draft of this chapter Earp writes that, like murder being 'immoral killing' (when what is precisely under dispute is whether a certain kind of killing is immoral), calling medically unnecessary female genital cutting 'mutilation' defines away the very thing that is in dispute (those who value ritual female genital cutting obviously do not typically regard it as mutilating, but rather as a form of culturally contextualized bodily enhancement). It is not that 'mutilation' is 'biased' against the many practices that the WHO defines in one lump category; rather, it defines the very thing that is disputed between different moral frameworks. Similarly, consider a debate between pro-choice and an anti-abortion persons having a conversation and the anti-abortion person says, 'Why do you support baby murder?' Obviously that is not the way

potentially severe adverse consequences to the mental health of women who are 'denied' FGC if they live within a community that supports the practice, identifies with the practice and perceives it as 'normal' or even 'beautiful'.[68] It is, indeed, plausible to think that women who underwent FGM would condone it more than women who did not undergo the practice as a self-defence mechanism. Their lives would be more difficult if they were to complain and constantly feel bitter about their lot. It should be noted that the UNICEF report that Shahvisi and Earp quote in support of their argument indicates that attitudes towards the practice have changed significantly, with reported support for FGM/C in Ethiopia halving, from 60 per cent in 2000 to 31 per cent in 2005.[69] In Sudan in 2006, 51 per cent of women between 15 and 49 years of age thought that the practice should continue, compared to 79 per cent in 1989–1990. Women's intention to cut their daughters decreased from 82 per cent to 54 per cent.[70] The report further shows that in Senegal the percentage of women who support continuation of FGM was much higher among women who have been cut (53 per cent) compared to women who have not been cut (2 per cent).[71]

What is the relationship between FGM and religion? FGM is practised by some people of the Muslim faith. FGM is also practised in some Christian communities (Copts, Orthodox and Protestants) and among Ethiopian Jews.[72] With regard to Islam, this religion like all other major religions incorporates a large corpus of writings. The Quran is the most important book of all and it does not explicitly mention female circumcision or male circumcision. Still, both practices are commonplace among many Muslim communities. Circumcision signifies a rite of passage from girlhood to womanhood and is a way of preserving group identity, preventing wantonness and preserving the virginity of a future bride. The most common reason women give for continuing genital cutting is to gain social acceptance.[73]

---

that the pro-choice person views abortion, so such a conversation cannot even get off the ground. Email of 24 October 2019. For further discussion, see Fuambai Ahmadu, 'Ain't I a Woman Too?', in Hernlund and Shell-Duncan, *Transcultural Bodies*, 278–310.

[68] Shahvisi and Earp, 'The Law and Ethics of Female Genital Cutting'. A similar argument is made by Rosie Duivenbode and Aasim I. Padela, 'Female Genital Cutting (FGC) and the Cultural Boundaries of Medical Practice', *American Journal of Bioethics*, 19(3) (2019): 3–6.

[69] UNICEF, *The Dynamics of Social Change: Towards the Abandonment of Female Genital Mutilation/Cutting in Five African Countries* (Florence: UNICEF, 2010): 24.

[70] Ibid., 40.

[71] Ibid., 10. While the framework of my analysis is limited to the democratic world, it is important to note these patterns as some members of these communities may immigrate to the West and bring this ritual with them.

[72] Vincenzo Puppo, 'Female Genital Mutilation and Cutting: An Anatomical Review and Alternative Rites', *Clinical Anatomy*, 30(1) (January 2017): 81–88; Nimrod Grisaru, Simcha Lezer and R.H. Belmaker, 'Ritual Female Genital Surgery Among Ethiopian Jews', *Archives of Sexual Behavior*, 26(2) (1997): 211–215.

[73] Celia W. Dugger, 'Report Finds Gradual Fall in Female Genital Cutting in Africa', *New York Times* (22 July 2013), www.nytimes.com/2013/07/23/health/report-finds-gradual-fall-in-female-

The issue is debated among Muslim scholars because while there is no conclusive directive that instructs this practice, there is also no explicit statement instructing that the practice is prohibited. Circumcision is underlined in the Sunnah, which is the body of traditional, social and legal custom and practice of the Islamic community, based on the record of the teachings, deeds and pronouncements, permissions and disapprovals of the Prophet Muhammad.

Some religious scholars argue that if the Prophet wanted female circumcision to be an integral aspect of Islam, as is male circumcision, he would have said that clearly. Other scholars rely on the *hadiths* (sayings about the life of the Prophet), where four relevant statements are quoted which suggest at least the permissibility of the practice. One says: 'Five are the acts quite akin to fitrah [pure human creation or nature]: circumcision, shaving the pubic areas, cutting the nails, plucking the hair under the armpits, and clipping (or shaving) the moustache.'[74] Sahih Muslim, Book 3, Hadith 684, instructs: 'When anyone sits amidst four parts (of the woman) and the circumcised parts touch each other a bath becomes obligatory.' Another *hadith* recounts a discussion between Prophet Muhammad and Um Habibah (or Um 'Atiyyah), a woman known as an exciser of female slaves. The Prophet asked her if she kept practising her profession. She answered affirmatively, adding: 'unless it is forbidden, and you order me to stop doing it'. Muhammad replied: 'Yes, it is allowed. Come closer so I can teach you: if you cut, do not overdo it.'[75] From this we may infer that women are allowed to enjoy at least some sexual pleasure and therefore severe forms of FGM that are aimed at suppressing women's sexuality are not to be allowed. Muhammad is also quoted as saying: 'Circumcision is a law for men and a preservation of honour for women',[76] and that circumcision is one of the norms of purity and that only circumcised men can go on pilgrimage.[77] There are those who interpreted the *hadiths* to mean that circumcision, any circumcision, is religiously virtuous as it brings about purity.[78] Others contended that Islamic female circumcision is limited to the partial or total removal of the clitoral hood (clitoridotomy) and does *not* involve the clitoris.[79]

---

genital-cutting-in-africa.html?nl=todaysheadlines&emc=edit_th_20130723&_r=o&page wanted=print.

[74] Jens Kutscher, 'Towards a Solution Concerning Female Genital Mutilation? An Approach from within according to Islamic Legal Opinions', *Scripta Instituti Donneriani Aboensis*, 23 (2011): 224.

[75] Sami A. Aldeeb Abu Sahlieh, 'To Mutilate in the Name of Jehovah or Allah: Legitimization of Male and Female Circumcision', *Medicine and Law*, 13 (1994): 581.

[76] Ibid. See also BBC, 'Circumcision of Boys' (13 August 2009), www.bbc.co.uk/religion/religions/islam/islamethics/malecircumcision.shtml.

[77] Abu Sahlieh, 'To Mutilate in the Name of Jehovah or Allah', 581.

[78] Kavita Shah Arora and Allan J. Jacobs, 'Female Genital Alteration: A Compromise Solution', *Journal of Medical Ethics*, 42(3) (2016): 148–154.

[79] Duivenbode and Padela, 'The Problem of Female Genital Cutting', 286.

The subjects of FGM are young girls.[80] The practice reassures the husband that he is the first and only man to engage in coitus with the woman. This is perceived to be essential both for the man's pride and status as well as for the woman's respectability.[81] In some communities where FGM is practised, members hold uncircumcised women in contempt as immoral freaks. The cutting is aimed to preserve sexual dignity, chastity and fidelity, and to promote family honour. In many communities the external part of the clitoris is considered to be phallic. Its removal is a symbolic denial of masculinity and an affirmation of the 'feminine within', aesthetically enhancing the genitals to be more attractive, smooth and clean.[82] In many communities, the clitoris is considered to be ugly and threatening to the male organ and even to endanger the baby during delivery. 'The clitoris and labia, considered to be the masculine parts, are seen as dangerous and poisonous organs and must be removed for health reasons. It is believed that they will kill a baby during birth and will also cause trouble to the man during intercourse.'[83]

Brian Earp argues that in many of the same communities where the clitoris is seen as 'ugly and masculine', the foreskin of the penis is seen as a 'feminine' appendage which encloses like a vagina/womb, such that its removal more clearly delineates the 'androgynous' children's genitalia into the clearly male/female dichotomous adult genitalia. Without discussing the complete symbolic system whereby both boys and girls are considered to have androgynous genitalia with organs from the 'opposite' sex, it is impossible to understand the 'meanings' of either male or female genital cutting. Earp further maintains that virtually all societies that practice FGC also practice male genital cutting and hold the males to similar ostracizing and stigmatizing norms for failing to undergo the rite.[84]

It is also believed that a woman's genitalia, if left uncut, will produce offensive discharges: an uncut woman is considered polluted and unclean. Some believe that cutting is instrumental to increase fertility.[85] In addition, FGM confers a

---

[80] Shahvisi and Earp, 'The Law and Ethics of Female Genital Cutting'.

[81] In Western societies an unmarried woman can have sexual intercourse and then be reinfibulated just prior to marriage to disguise the fact from her husband.

[82] The Public Policy Advisory Network on Female Genital Surgeries in Africa, 'Seven Things to Know about Female Genital Surgeries in Africa', 23.

[83] Written evidence submitted by the Hawa Trust, Home Affairs Committee: Written Evidence Female Genital Mutilation (13 May 2014), www.parliament.uk/documents/commons-committees/home-affairs/FGM-written-evidence.pdf.

[84] Brian Earp's comments on a draft of this chapter (24 October 2019); Brian D. Earp, 'Between Moral Relativism and Moral Hypocrisy: Reframing the Debate on "FGM"', *Kennedy Institute of Ethics Journal*, 26(2) (July 2016): 105–144.

[85] Valerie Oosterveld, 'Refugee Status for Female Circumcision Fugitives: Building a Canadian Precedent', *University of Toronto Faculty of Law Review*, 51(2) (Spring 1993): 277–303, at 281–283; Kirsten Lee, 'Female Genital Mutilation: Medical Aspects and the Rights of Children', *The International Journal of Children's Rights*, 2(1) (1994): 35–44, at 36.

desired social status on the girl and her family; it is associated with beauty, and it furthers marriage goals as it is believed that FGM enhances sexual pleasure for men.[86]

The clitoris has important procreative (reproductive) and recreative (pleasure) functions. Clitoridectomies create not only sexual disability but also a reproductive disability.[87] Often, for those who experience especially the severe forms of FGM, the cutting results in physical (gynaecological and obstetric) and psychological problems. Research conducted among migrant women in Europe showed that women living with FGM can experience recurrent sexual, psychological and physiological problems.[88] The physical problems include severe pain, shock due to pain or haemorrhage, infection, cysts and abscesses, damage to the urethra and anus, difficulty urinating, incontinence, problems in menstruating, malformation and scarring of the genitalia, physical trauma with sexual intercourse, increased vulnerability to lethal viruses, difficulty in childbirth[89] and increased likelihood of sterility and infant mortality. Infibulation is often associated with long-term gynaecologic or urinary tract difficulties.[90] Sometimes genital tissue is stitched again several times, including after childbirth, hence the women go through repeated opening and closing procedures, further increasing both immediate and long-term risks. The psychological problems include depression, anxiety, post-traumatic stress disorder, low self-esteem, flashbacks and self-harm and psychological trauma with sexual intercourse.[91] FGM increases the risk for both mother and child before and during

---

[86] Committee on Bioethics, 'Ritual Genital Cutting of Female Minors'; Vincenzo Puppo, 'Female Genital Mutilation and Cutting: An Anatomical Review and Alternative Rites', *Clinical Anatomy*, 30(1) (January 2017): 81–88.

[87] Roy J. Levin, 'The Clitoris – An Appraisal of Its Reproductive Function during the Fertile Years: Why Was It, and Still Is, Overlooked in Accounts of Female Sexual Arousal?', *Clinical Anatomy* (5 November 2019).

[88] Helen Baillot, Nina Murray, Elaine Connelly and Natasha Howard, 'Addressing Female Genital Mutilation in Europe: A Scoping Review of Approaches to Participation, Prevention, Protection, and Provision of Services', *International Journal for Equity in Health*, 17(1) (2018): 21.

[89] L. Almroth, S. Elmusharaf, N. El Hadi, et al., 'Primary Infertility after Genital Mutilation in Girlhood in Sudan: A Case-Control Study', *Lancet*, 366(9483) (2005): 385–391.

[90] Committee on Bioethics, 'Ritual Genital Cutting of Female Minors'; Dan Reisel and Sarah. M. Creighton, 'Long Term Health Consequences of Female Genital Mutilation (FGM)', *Maturitas*, 80(1) (2015): 48–51.

[91] NHS, 'Female Genital Mutilation (FGM)' (16 June 2016), www.nhs.uk/conditions/female-genital-mutilation-fgm/; Chizoma Millicent Ndikom, Feyintoluwa Anne Ogungbenro and Olajumoke Adetoun Ojeleye, 'Perception and Practice of Female Genital Cutting Among Mothers in Ibadan, Nigeria', *International Journal of Nursing & Health Science*, 4(6) (2017): 71–80; J. Whitehorn, O. Ayonrinde and S. Maingay, 'Female Genital Mutilation: Cultural and Psychological Implications', *Sexual & Relationship Therapy*, 17(2) (May 2002): 161–170; Stephen A. James, 'Reconciling International Human Rights and Cultural Relativism: The Case of Female Circumcision', *Bioethics*, 8(1) (January 1994): 9–10; BBC, 'FGM Summit: Parents to Be Prosecuted under New Measures', *BBC.com* (22 July 2014); WHO, 'Female Genital Mutilation'.

childbirth, including higher incidences of caesarean section and post-partum haemorrhage. Thus, the operation, even in the condoning cultures' own terms, is
dysfunctional and it violates the basic human rights of both females and children.

Some severe forms of FGM deny women the ability of full enjoyment of clitoral
stimulation and orgasm, generating frustration that influences not only their sex lives
but also their entire well-being as autonomous, imaginative human beings. Women
with FGM scored significantly lower on sexual function and desire than women
without FGM. They reported significantly more dyspareunia.[92] It is argued (not only
by feminists) that FGM is designed, at least in part, to maintain male control over
women's lives, and that this practice denies the individual the ability of being a
woman, of being a person[93] Moreover, research conducted where this norm is
practised showed significant mortality from infibulation under dirty conditions.[94]
Some girls died from blood loss or infection as a direct result of the procedure.[95]
The high-FGM-prevalence countries also have high maternal mortality ratios and
high numbers of maternal death. Additionally, due to damage to the sex organs,
sexual intercourse can result in the laceration of tissue, which greatly increases the
risk of HIV transmission.[96]

As FGM is illegal in the Western world, its underground performance might be
risky as the sensitive procedure might be conducted in unsafe and unregulated
environment and conditions. A question then arises why girls consent to this
practice. One answer is made in the framework that emphasizes the power of
tradition. Another answer speaks of the inability of the young women to resist social
and economic pressures. A third answer resorts to practical reasoning: uncircumcised women are not considered suitable for marriage. Consequently many women

---

[92] Jasmine Abdulcadir, Diomidis Botsikas, Mylène Bolmont, et al., 'Sexual Anatomy and
Function in Women With and Without Genital Mutilation: A Cross-Sectional Study',
Journal of Sexual Medicine, 13(2) (2016): 226–237.

[93] Article 1 of the Convention on the Elimination of All Forms of Discrimination Against Women
(1979) provides that '"discrimination against women" shall mean any ... restriction made on
the basis of sex which has the effect or purpose of impairing or nullifying the ... enjoyment or
exercise by women ... of human rights and fundamental freedoms in the political, economic,
social, cultural ... or any other field'. G.A. Res. 180, 34th Sess., Supp. No. 46, Art. 1, at 194,
U.N. Doc. A/34/180 (1980). This may be understood to secure the right of women to sexual and
corporal integrity. Cf. Smith, 'Female Circumcision', 2494.

[94] Patricia A. Broussard, 'The Importation of Female Genital Mutilation to the West: The
Cruelest Cut of All', *University of San Francisco Law Review*, 44 (2010): 792; UN Population
Fund, 'Female Genital Mutilation (FGM) Frequently Asked Questions' (February 2018), www
.unfpa.org/resources/female-genital-mutilation-fgm-frequently-asked-questions.

[95] Human Rights Council, 'Promotion and Protection of All Human Rights, Civil, Political,
Economic, Social and Cultural Rights, Including the Right to Development', *Report of the
Special Rapporteur on Torture and Other Cruel, Inhuman or Degrading Treatment or
Punishment* (15 January 2008).

[96] UN Population Fund, 'Female Genital Mutilation (FGM) Frequently Asked Questions'.

are forced to undergo circumcision to avoid becoming social and economic outcasts.[97] They experience what I termed internalized coercion (see Chapter 4).

In 2008, the Special Rapporteur on Torture defined FGM as a form of torture. The Special Rapporteur stressed that, from a human rights perspective, the 'medicalization' of FGM, whereby girls are cut by trained personnel rather than by traditional practitioners, does not in any way make the practice more acceptable.[98] In December 2012, the UN General Assembly approved a resolution calling for all member states to ban the practice.[99] A year prior, in 2011, the Council of Europe Convention on preventing and combating violence against women and domestic violence (known as the 'Istanbul Convention') recognized FGM as also a European issue and included a specific Article (38) on the criminalization of FGM.[100] On 7 February 2018, the European Parliament passed a resolution on zero tolerance for FGM.[101] In the United States, the Federal Prohibition of Female Genital Mutilation Act (1995) forbids and sets penalties for knowingly circumcising, excising or infibulating any part of the labia majora, labia minora or clitoris of another person who has not reached the age of 18, 'except where this is necessary to the health of the person on whom it is performed by a person licensed as a medical practitioner'; or it is performed on 'a person in labor or who has just given birth if performed for medical purposes'.[102] In addition, as of 2018, 27 US states have made specific laws that bar FGM.[103] The Canadian Criminal Code has prohibited FGM since 1997.[104] Similarly, Australian law clearly proscribes the performance of any type of FGM, including clitoridectomy, excision of any other part of the genitalia, infibulation and

---

[97] Kay Boulware-Miller, 'Female Circumcision: Challenges to the Practice as a Human Rights Violation', *Harvard Women's Law Journal*, 8 (1985): 155–177.

[98] Human Rights Council, 'Promotion and Protection of All Human Rights'.

[99] UN General Assembly, GA/11331 (20 December 2012).

[100] Council of Europe Convention on preventing and combating violence against women and domestic violence (Istanbul Convention) Female Genital Mutilation, https://rm.coe.int/CoERMPublicCommonSearchServices/DisplayDCTMContent?documentId=090000168046eb24.

[101] The European Parliament, Strasbourg 2017/2936(RSP), www.europarl.europa.eu/sides/getDoc.do?pubRef=-//EP//TEXT+TA+P8-TA-2018-0033+0+DOC+XML+V0//EN&language=GA. For further discussion, see Brian D. Earp, 'Zero Tolerance for Genital Mutilation: A Review of Moral Justifications', *Current Sexual Health Reports* (2021).

[102] Federal Prohibition of Female Genital Mutilation Act (1995), H.R. 941, 104th Cong. (1st Sess. 1995). www.congress.gov/bill/104th-congress/house-bill/941.

[103] However, only eleven of the twenty-seven states with anti-FGM laws have specific provisions which bar the transportation of a child out of the state to perform FGM. Maya Oppenheim, 'Campaigners Say Tens of Thousands of Girls at Risk after US Law Banning Female Genital Mutilation Declared Unconstitutional', *The Independent* (21 November 2018), www.independent.co.uk/news/world/americas/fgm-us-law-female-ban-genital-mutilation-detroit-jumana-nagawala-a8645476.html.

[104] Canada Criminal Code, R.S.C. ch. C-46, section 268(3), amended in 1997 S.C. ch. 16, section 5, http://evaw-global-database.unwomen.org/fr/countries/americas/canada/1997/act-to-amend-the-criminal-code.

any other mutilation of the genitalia, on a child or an adult.[105] In many European countries, including Austria,[106] Belgium,[107] Cyprus,[108] Denmark,[109] France,[110] Italy,[111] Norway[112] Portugal,[113] Spain,[114] Sweden[115] and the United

---

[105] Ben Mathews, 'Female Genital Mutilation: Australian Law, Policy and Practical Challenges for Doctors', *Medical Journal of Australia*, 194(3) (2011): 139–141, www.mja.com.au/journal/2011/194/3/female-genital-mutilation-australian-law-policy-and-practical-challenges-doctors.

[106] Article 90(3) of the Austrian Penal Code (2002) stipulates: 'It is not possible to consent to a mutilation or other injury of the genitals that may cause a lasting impairment of sexual sensitivity.' The person performing the operation therefore remains liable to punishment, even if the woman gives her consent (for whatever reason) to the operation. See Legislation in the Member States of the Council of Europe in the Field of Violence against Women (2008): 39.

[107] Article 409 of the Belgian Penal Code (27 March 2001) holds that a prison sentence of three to five years will be enforced on 'all persons participating, facilitating or encouraging all forms of female genital mutilations or any attempt to do so, with or without consent of the person concerned. Any attempt will be punished with a term of imprisonment from eight days to one year', https://gams.be/en/fgm-2/the-law/.

[108] Article 233A, Section 1, of the Cypriot Penal Code prohibits FGM, defined as 'any form of cutting or mutilation of the major or minor lips of the vagina or of the clitoris of the genitalia', https://uefgm.org/index.php/legislative-framework-cy/.

[109] Denmark enacted a criminal law applicable to clitoridectomy, excision and infibulation in 2003. Els Leye, Jessika Deblonde, José García-Añón, et al., 'An Analysis of the Implementation of Laws with Regard to Female Genital Mutilation in Europe', *Crime Law Social Change*, 47 (2007): 1–31; Yasmine Ergas, 'Regulating Religion beyond Borders: The Case of FGM/C', in Jean L. Cohen and Cécile Laborde (eds), *Religion, Secularism, and Constitutional Democracy* (New York: Columbia University Press, 2016): 66–88, at 70.

[110] French law was revised in 1984 to the effect that female circumcision is considered a criminal act. In addition, the French penal code bans all forms of physical abuse against children.

[111] Law no. 7/2006 introduces two articles in the Criminal Code: 583 bis (Female Genital Mutilation Practices, and 583 ter (Ancillary Penalties). Art. 583 bis establishes punishment by imprisonment from four to twelve years to anyone who, without any therapeutic need, would cause mutilation to female genitals. The second paragraph sanctions three to seven years' imprisonment to anyone who, without any therapeutic needs, would cause harms to female genitals different from the ones listed in the previous paragraph and bringing to physical or psychological illness. E. Turillazzi and V. Fineschi, 'Female Genital Mutilation: The Ethical Impact of the New Italian Law', *Journal of Medical Ethics*, 33 (2007): 98–101, and https://eige.europa.eu/gender-based-violence/resources/italy/italian-law-ndeg7-2006-introducing-article-583-bis-female-genital-mutilation-practices-and-article-583-ter-ancillary.

[112] Norway adopted a specific criminal law in 1996, and altered the law on 23 May 2004 to include the statutory *duty to report* for professionals and employees in various public services and religious communities. Broussard, 'The Importation of Female Genital Mutilation to the West', 812.

[113] Following Portugal's ratification of the Istanbul Convention in August 2015, FGM is a specified crime under Law no. 83/2015 of the Portuguese Penal Code. According to Article 144 A on Female Genital Mutilation, the perpetrator of FGM may be sentenced to a prison term of two to ten years, https://uefgm.org/index.php/legislative-framework-pt/.

[114] The Spanish Criminal Code includes specific regulation on FGM. Spain has also ratified the Council of Europe Istanbul Convention, https://uefgm.org/wp-content/uploads/2016/11/COUNTRY-INFO-PAGES_SPAIN_HIGH-1.pdf.

[115] Sweden outlawed female circumcision in 1982 (law no. 316). Carlbom S. Johnsdotter, *FGM in Sweden: Swedish Legislation Regarding 'Female Genital Mutilation' and Implementation of the Law* (Research Report in Sociology) (Department of Sociology, Lund University, 2004); Sara

Kingdom,[116] FGM is unlawful but is still performed in African and Asian immigrant communities. In Britain alone, one study estimated that 137,000 women and girls who have migrated to England and Wales are living with the consequences of FGM.[117] Recalling the moment she was cut, Leyla Hussein, 32, from London, said: 'Your whole body is in pain, the scream that you scream meant I lost my voice for a couple of days. The moment your genitals are cut, a part of your soul dies.'[118] Another British woman said: 'I don't think there's any word I can use to describe that moment. They grab you with a woman holding each leg and another holding your head and chest so you can't move.'[119]

Although FGM amounts to torture, Britain is unable to eradicate the practice completely. From time to time news concerning this conduct break out and triggers debate,[120] but only in February 2019 a woman whose 3-year-old daughter was subjected to FGM became the first person in the United Kingdom to be convicted

Johnsdotter, 'Meaning Well While Doing Harm: Compulsory Genital Examinations in Swedish African Girls', *Sexual and Reproductive Health Matters*, 27(2) (2019): 1–13.

[116] The United Kingdom outlawed the practice by Prohibition of Female Circumcision Act 1985, www.legislation.gov.uk/ukpga/1985/38/section/1 and Female Genital Mutilation Act 2003, www .legislation.gov.uk/ukpga/2003/31/contents. Prior to these Acts the practice was seemingly unlawful under sections 18 and 20 of the Offences Against the Person Act of 1861. See Lisa R. Avalos, 'Female Genital Mutilation and Designer Vaginas in Britain: Crafting an Effective Legal and Policy Framework', *Vanderbilt Journal of Transnational Law* (1 May 2015), www.thefreelibrary.com/Female+genital+mutilation+and+designer+vaginas+in +Britain%3A+crafting. . .-a0421625965. See also R.D. Mackay, 'Is Female Circumcision Unlawful?', *Criminal Law Review* (November 1983): 717–722.

[117] Lizzie Dearden, 'FGM: Number of Child Victims and Girls at Risk Doubles in Year in England and Wales', *The Independent* (30 November 2018), www.independent.co.uk/news/ uk/home-news/fgm-female-genital-mutilation-uk-girls-number-doubles-year-england-wales-a866 0036.html.

[118] Lucy Waterlow, '"I Screamed So Hard I Lost My Voice for Days": Victims of Female Genital Mutilation Speak Out as It's Revealed Thousands of Brits Are Still Planning to Cut their Daughters', *Mail Online* (11 March 2015), www.dailymail.co.uk/femail/article-2989409/Victims-female-genital-mutilation-speak-s-revealed-thousands-Brits-planning-cut-da ughters.html.

[119] Ibid.

[120] Sandra Laville, 'First FGM Prosecution: How the Case Came to Court', *The Guardian* (4 February 2015), www.theguardian.com/society/2015/feb/04/first-female-genital-mutilation-pros ecution-dhanuson-dharmasena-fgm; BBC, 'FGM Summit: Cameron Calls for End "In This Generation"', *BBC.com* (22 July 2014), www.bbc.co.uk/news/uk-28412179; Louise Ridley, 'FGM Trial: Why Has No-one Ever Been Convicted in Britain, Despite the Practice Being Illegal for 30 Years?', *The Huffington Press* (4 February 2015), www.huffingtonpost.co .uk/2015/02/04/fgm-police-lead-mak-chishty-convictions-charges-evidence-illegal_n_5747672 .html; Martin Beckford and Debbie McCann, 'Just Four Cases of Female Genital Mutilation Have Been Carried Out in Britain as Experts Admit Figure Is "Lower than Expected"', *Mail Online* (25 March 2018), www.dailymail.co.uk/health/article-5540921/Four-cases-female-geni tal-mutilation-carried-Britain.html.

for the practice since it was criminalized in 1985.[121] She was jailed for eleven years for the FGM.[122]

In France, the Aminata Diop case of 1991 attracted attention. This case involved a 20-year-old girl from Mali who was about to be married. Before the marriage took place, her family and fiancé insisted that she be circumcised. When Diop refused to undergo this procedure her father beat her and subsequently she fled from Mali to France and requested asylum as a refugee under the terms of the Geneva Convention. The French Commission for Appeals of Refugees recognized that the threat or practice of genital mutilation is a form of persecution and that Diop consequently fell within the definition of 'refugee' set out in the Geneva Convention. Diop, however, was not granted this status for procedural reasons: Diop had failed to appeal for help from the Mali authorities and therefore had not exhausted local remedies.[123]

Underlying my reasoning is the rationale of the rights of adolescents and caring for those who are not able to defend their interests. The assumption of moral equality of persons rules out the idea that children are the unqualified property of their parents. Children are beings with their own moral status, whose interests must be considered equally by government. So the liberty of parents does not extend to treating their children in any way they please. Parents are not at liberty to deny their children a decent future. They should not be allowed to inflict severe bodily damage upon their children just as they should not be allowed to abuse them. FGM should be prohibited, just as we proscribe torturing children, selling them into slavery or prostitution, or starving them. Children have rights that set limits on what parents (or governments) can do to them. Principle 2 of the Declaration of the Rights of the Child holds: 'The child shall enjoy special protection, and shall be given opportunities and facilities, by law and by other means, to enable him to develop physically, mentally, morally, spiritually and socially in a healthy and normal manner and in conditions of freedom and dignity.'[124] The power of parents over children, therefore, is a trust, and if the trust is violated the powers can be taken away by the state.

This line of reasoning rules out one common defence of FGM which holds that to proscribe the practice would violate the religious or cultural liberty of the parents. I believe that, in case of excessive forms of FGM, this cannot be held as an acceptable argument since parental liberty is limited by the interests and moral

---

[121] Lizzie Dearden, 'FGM Conviction: Mother of Girl, 3, becomes First Person Found Guilty of Female Genital Mutilation in UK', *The Independent* (1 February 2019), www.independent.co.uk/news/uk/crime/fgm-first-uk-conviction-mother-three-year-old-female-genital-mutilation-witchcraft-london-a8758641.html.

[122] 'Mother Jailed for Female Genital Mutilation on Three-Year-Old', *BBC* (8 March 2019), www.bbc.co.uk/news/uk-england-london-47502089.

[123] Re *Aminata Diop*, French Commission for Appeals of Refugees, recours No. 164.078 (September 1991). See also Oosterveld, 'Refugee Status for Female Circumcision Fugitives', 278–279.

[124] G.A. Res. 1386, 14th Sess., Supp. No. 16, at 19 U.N. Doc. A/4354 (1959).

standing of the child. Posing substantial constraints on harsh forms of FGM does not merely reflect Western hang-ups or squeamishness about sexuality. Notice that the two major considerations emphasized are the fact that children are involved and the degree of damage. If the practice occurred after women reached the age of majority, and so took place with their informed consent, then the case would be somewhat different. Adults can waive their rights, and some may argue that FGM could be one example of that. But where children are involved the government must decide whether the practice is acceptable on the basis of the best evidence available on its effect on the long-term health and well-being of the children involved. This latter point brings me to the second consideration. The particular sort of mutilation involved dramatically undermines a woman's ability to enjoy basic goods of sexuality and intimacy.

The question then arises, however, whether we should object to minor ritual forms of female circumcision, physically similar to or less invasive than male circumcision, when the girls in question appear not to object to this practice, and the harm involved might be smaller than the harm of state interference. The American Academy of Pediatrics Committee on Bioethics calls these practices FGC, arguing that it would be wrong to call them 'mutilation'.[125] From a Western liberal moral point of view, all forms of female circumcision may be viewed as morally detestable. But we are required to balance the different interests involved, including the external protections, the severity of rights violations within the minority community, the inbuilt reluctance to allow government interference in internal community affairs and the view that such interference is justified and reasonable only when the rights' violation and inflicted harm are significant. Upon balancing, we may come to conclude against state interference when the minor excision is symbolic. With time, without explicit state interference, the practice may die out. The Israeli experience may serve as an example.

FEMALE CIRCUMCISION IN ISRAEL

I studied the prevalence of female circumcision in Israel during the 1990s.[126] Then it was practised in six Bedouin tribes in the south of the country. These tribes originated from Saudi Arabia and Sudan. All (or almost all) women of those tribes underwent this procedure. No instances of mutilation of the labia majora or clitoris were found. On most (if not all) occasions they experienced a very moderate form of ritual circumcision. Physical exams of parental women showed scars on the prepuce of the clitoris or on the labia about 1 cm in length, indicating that a ritual incision had been made but without removal of tissue. Almost all of the women interviewed

---

[125] Committee on Bioethics, 'Ritual Genital Cutting of Female Minors'.
[126] Cohen-Almagor, 'Female Circumcision and Murder for Family Honour among Minorities in Israel', 171–187.

in the study, including educated women, intended to continue the practice by performing cutting on their daughters.[127]

The ceremony took place when the girls were between the ages of 12 and 17, sometime before the girl's marriage. It was always conducted by women. The primary decision-maker for the procedure was the mother. Elderly women known as the 'traditional surgeons' performed it.[128] Men were not involved. Water and soap were used to clean the external genitalia. It was believed that urine functions like iodine to heal the wound. A razor was used to perform the circumcision, without anesthesia. All the women reported bleeding and pain at the time of the cutting.[129] Although the circumcision was conducted in poor hygienic conditions, the number of complications reported by hospitals was low. Part of the reason was that the Bedouins perceived female circumcision as something private and consequently approached hospitals only as a last resort. More often than not they would not admit the cause of the infection and of the medical complications. All of the women reported pain on intercourse in the months after marriage, but none felt this was related to the cutting.[130]

Bedouin women believed that this conduct contributed to their tidiness and purified them. Women who did not undergo circumcision could not become good bakers and cooks. According to the Bedouin folk, the bread uncircumcised women bake, the food they cook, even the tea and the coffee they brew, are all 'not good', 'impure', 'not tasty', etc.[131] Most girls accepted this belief and conformed to the practice. They did not feel that they were coerced to perform it. Like women in other communities, Bedouin women had experienced internalized coercion.

In 1999, another study among the Bedouin population in southern Israel confirmed that the ritual was a symbolic operation without major mutilation. While the procedure had no apparent effect on their mental health, Bedouin women after the procedure reported difficulties in mother–daughter relationships and trust.[132]

In 2008, follow-up research was conducted. A total of 132 women were examined, and the researchers did not identify a single case of scarring of the kind reported during the 1990s. Eight women heard that this ritual was still practised. Thus, it is

---

[127] R.H. Belmaker, 'Successful Cultural Change: The Example of Female Circumcision among Israeli Bedouins and Israeli Jews from Ethiopia', *Israel Journal of Psychiatry and Related Sciences*, 49(3) (2012): 179–180; A. Asali, N. Khamaysi, Y. Aburabia, et al., 'Ritual Female Genital Surgery among Bedouin in Israel', *Archives of Sexual Behavior*, 24(5) (1995): 571–575.

[128] Ibid.

[129] Ibid.; Gideon M. Kressel, *Descent through Males* (Wiesbaden: Otto Harrassowitz, 1992): 208–211.

[130] R.H. Belmaker, 'Successful Cultural Change', 180.

[131] Ibid., 179; R. Belmaker, 'Female Genital Mutilation: Successful Social Change Exemplified by Israeli Bedouin and Ethiopian Jews', *Asian Journal of Psychiatry*, 4S1 (2011): S1; Kressel, *Descent through Males*, 210.

[132] Julia Applebaum, Hagit Cohen, Michael Matar, et al., 'Symptoms of Posttraumatic Stress Disorder after Ritual Female Genital Surgery among Bedouin in Israel: Myth or Reality?', *Primary Care Companion to the Journal of Clinical Psychiatry*, 10(6) (2008): 453–456.

possible that isolated incidents may have occurred but the systematic cultural rite had disappeared.[133] The researchers explained that Bedouins have become more Westernized.[134] I would say that the Bedouin have re-evaluated their position and altered their customs. Their health care, school attendance, school achievements and literacy have improved over time.[135] The community decided that circumcision should be discontinued. Similar developments take place in many immigrant communities that post-immigration to Western countries largely gave up the practice.

Another study examined 113 Jewish women who immigrated to Israel from Ethiopia, where FGM is practised among Christian, Muslim and Jewish groups. On physical examination, 27 per cent of the women had full or partial amputation of the clitoris, 10 per cent had scars on the female genitalia, while the rest had no evidence of incision or ablation.[136] All women said that they did not intend to continue this practice with their own daughters. They stated that this was a practice that would be left behind in their country of origin. They decided to abandon it upon arrival in Israel.[137]

In 2014, in a response by the state of Israel to a questionnaire that followed Human Rights Council Resolution 27/22 concerning the intensification of global efforts to eliminate FGM, the government of Israel informed that the practice 'has been eradicated completely in recent years'.[138] An inspection by the Ministry of Health of different health facilities, in particular of health clinics and hospitals in the Negev area, indicated that no instances of FGM were recorded during the last decade.

What can we learn from the Israeli experience? Rawls asserts that if a conception of the good is unable to persist and gain adherents under institutions of equal freedom and mutual toleration, then we may question its viability.[139] The Bedouin live within Israeli society and are influenced by its values and way of life. They might have come to the realization that change was required. They acquired a sufficient sense of justice to question the reasonableness of female circumcision and its place within the group. The same is true for the Ethiopian women.

The researchers could not pinpoint with certainty the reasons that brought about the change. They noted that health variables such as infant mortality, mean birth

---

[133] S. Halila, R.H. Belmaker, Y. Abu Rabia, et al., 'Disappearance of Female Genital Mutilation from the Bedouin Population of Southern Israel', *Journal of Sexual Medicine*, 6(1) (2009): 70–73.

[134] Ibid.

[135] Ibid., 71–72; Belmaker, 'Successful Cultural Change', 180–181.

[136] Ibid., 182.

[137] Ibid., 182–183.

[138] Israel Ministry of Justice, 'Female Genital Mutilation', *Response by the State of Israel to the Questionnaire for Member States Following Human Rights Council Resolution 27/22* (17 December 2014).

[139] John Rawls, 'The Priority of Right and Ideas of the Good', *Philosophy & Public Affairs*, 17(4) (1988): 251–276, at 266; Rawls, *Political Liberalism*, 140–144.

weight and educational variables such as percentage attending school, number of school years completed and literacy have continued to improve in the Bedouin population over the years and that these may be associated with the decline in female circumcision.[140] In addition, the media and public opinion in both the Jewish and Arab populations were against the practice.

It is necessary to continue research on this issue and review it from time to time. It would be good news to reaffirm the disappearance of female circumcision. The issue has to be put on the public agenda. Upon reaching the conclusion that the best interests of the circumcised girls justify state intervention (because, for instance, the severity of the excision has increased, and/or complaints about designated coercion are becoming frequent), then these interests should serve as a trump card to override tradition and cultural considerations. Upon reflection, however, when we come to evaluate the practice of female circumcision among Bedouins, it seems that the girls' best interests were better served by the state of Israel's abstention from interference. Punitive measures against *de minimis* cutting might cause more harm than toleration of the practice.[141]

In countries where FGM is illegal, the liberal state should fight against it by all the tools it has, employing mechanisms of deliberative democracy, incentives and sticks. The state should deny the practice any legitimacy and publicize the relevant penalties for deterrence. Liberal democracies should address this concern with sensitivity and diligence, finding the least harmful ways for intervention. As FGM is practised in the liberal world mainly by immigrants from Africa, the liberal state should engage with the governments of the home countries, relying on careful evidence and possibly employing third-party pressure and coercion to bring about change (see Chapter 4). While the focus of this book is on Western democracies, it can be assumed that countries like the United States and the United Kingdom have leverage on African countries and if norm change can be brought about in Africa, Western democracies would be less troubled by the practice on their own soil. In accordance with the principles discussed in Chapter 4, I presume that if Western democracies will present African countries with attractive rewards for cooperation, governments will then exert various modes of pressure on local tribes, per their own interests and sensitivities, to bring about change.

In countries where FGM is not illegal, the state could offer to train women and grant them official authorization as circumcisers. The training will include, *inter alia*, studies of sterilization and methods to reduce pain and handle severe bleeding. The government could offer to pay the trained circumcisers for each circumcision as an incentive. In both male and female circumcision, cases were recorded in

[140] Halila, Belmaker, Abu Rabia, et al., 'Disappearance of Female Genital Mutilation from the Bedouin Population of Southern Israel'; Belmaker, 'Successful Cultural Change'.
[141] For further discussion, see Allan J. Jacobs and Kavita Shah Arora, 'Punishment of Minor Female Genital Ritual Procedures: Is the Perfect the Enemy of the Good?', *Developing World Bioethics*, 17(2) (2017): 134–140.

which the operation was botched or there were significant complications.[142] This risk should be addressed especially when the practice is conducted in the traditional, non-hospital settings of migrant communities in Western countries.

People who perform the custom should not be condemned as they are performing the circumcision in good faith. While the information should include data on the physical and psychological harms of FGM, the concept of responsibility rather than blame should be highlighted. Who should drive change? The best interests of the community require cooperation between men and women to drive this change together, introduce new community norms that would work for the benefit of all. Cooperation with leaders of the community is essential as change preferably should arise out of internal community recognition of its desirability. Empowering the community will contribute to empowering women. Because social acceptability is the major reason for women to perform and accept FGM, men should be required to pledge that FGM is no longer the requirement and, even better if possible, that they would not marry women who underwent FGM.

It is important to engage in dialogue with the men and women of the FGM communities, exploring the underlying reasons for the practice. If the reason is to diminish women's sexuality, to express male chauvinism, to lower the standard of female members of the community or to undermine them in any other way, the liberal state should clarify, in bold terms that are not open to interpretation, that FGM is unacceptable. Once one has decided to come and live in the liberal world, one must accept its enshrined values and laws. There is no negotiation that would mean that the liberal state would accept brute discrimination of women and their torture. The liberal state should use all the tools in its disposal, including education, public debate, social pressure and legal intervention in requiring all group members to abide by the existing law to ensure that FGM is not part of the place.

However, if the main reason is to maintain tradition, then negotiations can be opened about the ways and means by which it is possible to do this while maintaining the values and laws of the state. Tradition can be maintained by a minor and symbolic scar on female genitals. If women consent to FGM to gain social acceptability, it is important to bring about a change of norm by which men of the community explain to the women that this rite is no longer necessary.

In line with the American Academy of Pediatrics' position, medical associations should instruct their members not to perform FGM, actively seek to dissuade families from carrying out harmful forms of FGM and provide girls and their parents with compassionate education about the harms of FGM while remaining sensitive to the cultural and religious reasons that motivate parents to seek this procedure for

---

[142] Helen A. Weiss, Natasha Larke, Daniel Halperin, et al., 'Complications of Circumcision in Male Neonates, Infants and Children: A Systematic Review', *BMC Urology*, 10 (2010): 2, www .ncbi.nlm.nih.gov/pmc/articles/PMC2835667/; Efua Dorkenoo, *Cutting the Rose* (London: Minority Rights Group, 1994).

their daughters.[143] Through open deliberations, constructive compromises and reasonable accommodations should be sought to bring about positive change and secure just women's rights.

CONCLUSION

I opened this chapter with Susan Okin's negative view of multiculturalism. Her view reflects a profound liberal feminism that is insensitive to multiculturalism. Dismissing multiculturalism and group rights by simply saying that most cultures are patriarchal and therefore discriminatory to women does not solve women's plight and does not promote human rights and women's rights. All that Okin does is to highlight the gap between Western liberal feminism and non-Western cultures. A comprehensive concept of just, reasonable multiculturalism would help women develop their autonomous will vis-à-vis their communities and urge the liberal state to develop the appropriate mechanisms of reconciliation based on mutual respect and harm reduction.

The purpose of the discussion was to suggest that (1) we should distinguish between self- and other-regarding harm. (2) Liberal democracy is justified to inter-fere in the illiberal conduct of its subcultures when those exact significant injury to others. Not every norm that a culture values may be permitted to endure within the democratic framework. (3) Democracy may prevent certain conduct because the conception that some illiberal groups perceive as a conception of the good essen-tially conflicts with basic liberal democratic norms. (4) Some cultural norms such as suttee, slavery, female infanticide, murder for family honour and FGM are incom-patible with basic liberal democratic principles. These practices have no justifica-tion in liberal democracy. No group claim can reasonably rationalize it today in the confines of liberal democracy. (5) Gender violence is embedded in honour-based societies that wish to maintain family and community control over individual behaviour, especially that of women. Such violence should not be tolerated in a liberal democracy. (6) We should distinguish between female circumcision and FGM according to the extent of harm inflicted on girls. (7) The right to enjoy sexual pleasure is not limited only to men. This good should not be arbitrarily denied to women through an act of genital mutilation that occurs before they are able to give their informed consent. (8) While every idea possesses a claim to equal validity within a democratic society, considerations of context, intentions, rights, respect for others and not harming others must be considered, and they may require the introduction of constraints.

There are many ways to strengthen mechanisms for respecting individual rights in a consensual way, without simply imposing liberal values on national minorities. Coercive intervention in the internal affairs of a national minority is justified in the

---

[143] Committee on Bioethics, 'Ritual Genital Cutting of Female Minors'.

case of a gross and systematic violation of human rights, such as inflicting severe bodily injuries on certain individuals or expulsions of people. The intention behind imposing these restrictive provisions is to sustain and promote basic human rights.

Reasonable multiculturalism assumes that in society there are disagreements between different cultural groups. Some disagreements are reasonable. Because they are reasonable, they can be resolved by reasonable people who employ reasonable standards of compromise. When cultural practices are unreasonable and amount to torture, compromise should be eschewed in favour of state coercion to clearly flag that that practice has no place in society. Clear substantial safeguards and constraints should be erected. We should object to FGM in liberal democracies even if women accept it as part of their culture, perceiving such support as a form of internalized coercion. FGM cannot be reconciled with the raison d'être of liberal democracy and the values we hold dear (see Chapter 1). This is simply not to be done. While some may tolerate FGM when consenting adult women are concerned, I think that FGM is beyond the scope of tolerance in a liberal democracy. Permitting it would amount to acceding to voluntary torture which is unacceptable.

It has been argued that if we curtail FGM then we should also curtail male circumcision. By and large, both practices are conducted without sufficient medical reasons on young children who do not and cannot give informed consent due to certain norms, values and beliefs that the child may not accept at a later age. Both practices inflict bodily damage on sensitive bodily organs.[144] People have muddied the water by using the terms FGM and female circumcision interchangeably. I argue that FGM should be explicitly outlawed. In the case of female circumcision, a minor scar on the major labia is arguably no more harmful than male circumcision and cannot be considered as more mutilating to the body. Communities that internalize the belief in the need for such rituals may perceive them as important for the communities in question. Chapter 6 unfolds the complexity of the analogy between male and female circumcision. Here, again, on balance are considerations pertaining to respecting cultural and religious traditions while protecting the rights of the child.

---

[144] Brussels Collaboration on Bodily Integrity, 'Medically Unnecessary Genital Cutting and the Rights of the Child: Moving toward Consensus', *American Journal of Bioethics*, 19(10) (2019): 17–28.

6

Male Circumcision in the Name of Tradition and Good Health

If we are to achieve a richer culture, rich in contrasting values, we must recognize the whole gamut of human potentialities, and so weave a less arbitrary social fabric, one in which each diverse gift will find a fitting place.

Margaret Mead

When Judith and Joel Cohen's son, Mishmar, was born, they did not consider the option of not circumcising him. This option was not on the cards. As Jews, circumcision is an integral and important part of their tradition. Circumcision signifies the lasting bond between God and the Jewish people. For many Jews, notwithstanding whether or not they believe in God, if they acknowledge the importance of tradition and believe in one's association with the Jewish people, circumcision is to be done.

While Judith and Joel did not question its necessity, they did debate how the circumcision should be performed: by a *mohel* (circumciser, a traditional person whose profession is to perform circumcision) or by a physician; with or without injections to relieve pain; in hospital or outside of hospital. At the ceremony itself, both Judith and Joel identified with Mishmar's pain. Judith could not stand it and went out of the room. Joel stayed behind; one of them needed to be there for Mishmar. After the cutting, the *mohel* gave Mishmar some wine drops to mitigate the pain. It took some time and effort to stop Mishmar's crying. Later Judith and Joel asked themselves whether circumcision was necessary as they felt uncomfortable with the painful imposition on their son. Ten years later, when their second son was born, they went through the similar process of decision-making, with the same result. Mishmar's brother was also subjected to circumcision, and Judith and Joel were in pain watching and hearing his suffering. Tradition is powerful.

This chapter opens with some preliminary data about male circumcision and then explains its importance in Islam and in Judaism. I examine the medical justifications for male circumcision and the risks involved in the practice;

subsequently, I discuss the critique of male circumcision, and the differences between this practice, female circumcision and FGM. I also highlight the points of agreement and disagreement between those supporting and opposing the ritual and insist that male circumcision should be performed by using adequate pain relief.

MALE CIRCUMCISION

The word 'circumcision' comes from the Latin *circum* (meaning 'around') and *cædere* ('to cut'). Debates over male circumcision involve important yet conflicting considerations. It is argued that the practice violates the rights of children, including their right to health and bodily integrity[1] and their right to an open future.[2] Children have rights in trust—rights that they cannot yet exercise, but which they will exercise upon reaching maturity. Thus, Darby argues that children's rights require that the decision whether to circumcise be deferred until adulthood.[3] Parents should not foreclose or pre-empt their children's future options. Earp makes a similar argument, adding that if people grow up to dissociate from their parents' culture or religion, or to reject those norms or values, they might feel harmed or even mutilated by the circumcision. Therefore, circumcision is warranted only when it is medically necessary, or near that threshold.[4] Parents should enable their children the greatest possible scope for exercising personal life choices in adulthood.[5] The rights of the child need to be weighed against parental rights over their children, and against group rights to maintain tradition and practice this controversial ritual.

Circumcision is a cultural rite that is of importance to the group but not necessarily to society at large. The ritual is reasonable to the group in question but unreasonable, possibly offensive, in the eyes of outsiders. When such a debate arises,

[1] S.K. Hellsten, 'Rationalising Circumcision: From Tradition to Fashion, from Public Health to Individual Freedom – Critical Notes on Cultural Persistence of the Practice of Genital Mutilation', *Journal of Medical Ethics*, 30 (2004): 248–253; Wim Dekkers, Cor Hoffer and Jean-Pierre Wils, 'Bodily Integrity and Male and Female Circumcision', *Medicine Health Care and Philosophy*, 8(2) (2005): 179–191; Joseph Mazor, 'The Child's Interests and the Case for the Permissibility of Male Infant Circumcision', *Journal of Medical Ethics*, 39(7) (2013): 421–428; J. Steven Svoboda, 'Circumcision of Male Infants as a Human Rights Violation', *Journal of Medical Ethics*, 39(7) (2013): 469–474; Eliyahu Ungar-Sargon, 'On the Impermissibility of Infant Male Circumcision: A Response to Mazor', *Journal of Medical Ethics*, 41(2) (2015): 186–190.

[2] Robert J.L. Darby, 'The Child's Right to an Open Future: Is the Principle Applicable to Non-therapeutic Circumcision?', *Journal of Medical Ethics*, 39 (2013): 463–468; Eldar Sarajlic, 'Can Culture Justify Infant Circumcision?', *Res Publica*, 20(4) (November 2014): 327–343.

[3] Darby, 'The Child's Right to an Open Future'.

[4] Brian D. Earp, 'The Child's Right to Bodily Integrity', in David Edmonds (ed.), *Ethics and the Contemporary World* (Abingdon and New York: Routledge, 2019): 229–230; Brian D. Earp, 'In Defence of Genital Autonomy for Children', Journal of *Medical Ethics*, 41(3) (2016): 158–163.

[5] Darby, 'The Child's Right to an Open Future', 463. See also Joel Feinberg, 'The Child's Right to an Open Future', in J. Feinberg, *Freedom and Fulfilment: Philosophical Essays* (Princeton, NJ: Princeton University Press, 1992): 76–97.

the scope of tolerance afforded to the group is questioned. Circumcision is a controversial ritual because it exerts pain in a psychosexually significant and sensitive (both physical and symbolic) part of the body that is usually construed in Western societies as 'private', 'discreet', 'sensitive' and 'intimate'. The subjects are young children who did not freely consent to this act.[6] The act might undermine the children's well-being. All forms of ritual circumcision wish to put a physical mark of tradition and belonging to a community while exacting a price from the children involved. Parents believe that the ritual is done for their children's good notwithstanding the pain, risk and suffering involved. Cultural and religious justifications are employed to convince members of the community as well as outsiders that circumcision is reasonable and just.

Male circumcision is a common practice in Islamic and Jewish communities, and it is also practised by many Christian communities and tribes all over the world. It is estimated that 37 to 39 per cent of the men in the world are circumcised. In Afghanistan, Comoros, Gabon, the Gaza Strip, Iran, Mauritania, Morocco, Tajikistan, Tunisia, the West Bank, Western Sahara and Yemen, the circumcision rate is estimated to be 99 per cent and above.[7] In the Western world, male circumcision is far less popular. The striking exceptions are Israel and the United States. In Israel, the overwhelming majority of Jewish babies are circumcised. According to Rabbi Professor Avraham Steinberg, a medical ethicist, paediatric neurologist and an authority in this field, 97 per cent of Jewish male babies are circumcised.[8] In the United States, while the male circumcision rates had dropped the majority of babies still undergo circumcision. In 1979, 64.5 per cent of male babies were circumcised while in 2010, 58.3 per cent underwent the practice.[9]

In the United States, the popularity of circumcision dates back 140 years to Dr Lewis Sayre, one of the founders of the American Medical Association. Sayre believed that many medical conditions had their root in a dysfunction in the genital area, and that circumcision could be used to treat a wide array of problems, from depression to mental health issues, syphilis and epilepsy. Circumcision was also promoted as a way of discouraging masturbation and was regarded as clean and hygienic. It was particularly popular among the higher classes. Sayre's theories were later discredited, but not before they were accepted in other English-speaking countries, in particular in the United Kingdom, Canada, Australia and New

---

[6] J. Goodman, 'Jewish Circumcision: An Alternative Perspective', *BJU International*, 83 Supp. 1 (1999): 22–27.

[7] Brian J. Morris, Richard G. Wamai, Esther B. Henebeng, et al., 'Estimation of Country-Specific and Global Prevalence of Male Circumcision', *Population Health Metrics*, 14(4) (2016), https://pophealthmetrics.biomedcentral.com/articles/10.1186/s12963-016-0073-5.

[8] Professor Avraham Steinberg's personal communication (29 November 2019).

[9] Julie Vadnal, 'Why Fewer Guys Are Getting Circumcised', *Cosmopolitan* (21 August 2018), www.cosmopolitan.com/sex-love/a22094429/why-fewer-guys-are-getting-circumcised/.

Zealand.[10] In the United States today, non-religious circumcision is usually performed in hospital when the infant is a few days old. While in the USA, Egypt, Saudi Arabia, the Gulf States and the Republic of Korea circumcision is provided almost exclusively by medically trained professionals, in North Africa, Pakistan, Indonesia, Israel and rural Turkey the majority of providers are not medically trained.[11]

Male circumcision consists of the removal of the prepuce, or foreskin, the tissue covering the head(glans) of the penis. The foreskin is freed from the head of the penis, and part of the foreskin is excised.[12] The foreskin contains nerve endings that are important for the enjoyment of sexual pleasure. Its glands produce lubricants that protect both the head of the penis and the female vagina.[13] The circumcision generally heals in a week. Circumcision of infants and pre-pubertal boys is simpler than circumcision of older boys and adults, because the penis is relatively underdeveloped and the foreskin less vascular, and because suturing is usually not necessary. Healing tends to be quick and chances of complication are low.[14]

In Chapter 5 I argued that the right to bodily integrity is the most personal and arguably most important of all human rights. This right should not be compromised without ample justification. Let me now examine the religious and medical justifications for male circumcision. In both Islam and Judaism, this rite is significant. It is an integral part of social and family life, perceived as contributing to communal heritage and the way communities define themselves.

MALE CIRCUMCISION IN ISLAM

Muslims are the largest single religious group that practices male circumcision. About 70 per cent of the circumcised males are Muslim.[15] For the majority of

---

[10] George C. Denniston, Frederick Mansfield Hodges and Marilyn Fayre Milos (eds), *Male and Female Circumcision: Medical, Legal and Ethical Considerations in Pediatric Practice* (New York: Kluwer Academic/Plenum Publishers, 1999); David Gollaher, *Circumcision: A History of the World's Most Controversial Surgery* (New York: Basic Books, 2000); Cordelia Hebblethwaite, 'Circumcision, the Ultimate Parenting Dilemma', *BBC* (21 August 2012), www.bbc.co.uk/news/magazine-19072761; J. Steven Svoboda, 'Circumcision of Male Infants as a Human Rights Violation', *Journal of Medical Ethics*, 39 (7) (2013): 469–474.

[11] WHO, *Neonatal and Child Male Circumcision: A Global Review* (April 2010): 5.

[12] J.M. Hutson, 'Circumcision: A Surgeon's Perspective', *Journal of Medical Ethics*, 30 (2004): 238–240; J.R. Taylor, A.P. Lockwood and A.J. Taylor, 'The Prepuce: Specialized Mucosa of the Penis and Its Loss to Circumcision', *British Journal of Urology*, 77(2) (1996): 291–295.

[13] Men's Health Forum, 'Circumcision FAQs', www.menshealthforum.org.uk/circumcision-faqs.

[14] WHO, *Manual for Male Circumcision under Local Anaesthesia*, Version 3.1 (December 2009): chap. 6; WHO, *Neonatal and Child Male Circumcision*, 46; Task Force on Circumcision, 'Male Circumcision', *Pediatrics*, 130(3) (September 2012), http://pediatrics.aappublications.org/content/130/3/e756. Earp argues that the procedure is simpler for the operator; it's not necessarily better for the individual undergoing the procedure. A. Myers and B.D. Earp, 'What Is the Best Age to Circumcise? A Medical and Ethical Analysis', *Bioethics* (February 2020).

[15] WHO, *Neonatal and Child Male Circumcision*, 7; Neta Achituv, 'Blood Circumcision', *Haaretz* (14 June 2012) (Hebrew).

Muslims, circumcision is seen as an introduction to the Islamic faith and a sign of belonging to the Muslim community. To Muslims it is a sign of submission to God, and it is also known as *tahara*, meaning purification or cleanliness. It is essential that every Muslim man washes before praying. It is important that no urine is left on the body.[16]

There is no fixed age for Islamic ritual circumcision. The age varies depending on denomination, country, community, region and family. The preferred age is often seven although some Muslims are circumcised as early as the seventh day after birth and as late as puberty. In Asia, circumcision commonly takes place from the age of 1 to the age of 11 years. In North Africa and the Middle East, the ages for this practice range between 5 and 11 years. In the Philippines, circumcision typically occurs at 10–14 years. There is no equivalent of a Jewish *mohel* (circumciser). In Britain, circumcisions are usually conducted in clinics and hospitals. The circumciser is not required to be a Muslim but he must be medically trained.[17]

MALE CIRCUMCISION IN JUDAISM

To Jews, male circumcision represents the covenant between Abraham and God; 98 per cent of male Jews are circumcised (Figure 6.1).[18] The Bible instructs that every Jewish boy needs to be circumcised. In the Book of Genesis, chapter 17, it is told that when Abram was 99 years old, God appeared before him and said to him: 'I will make a covenant between us and I will give you many, many descendants.' Abram fell on his face, and God continued:

> My covenant is with you; you will be the ancestor of many nations. And because I have made you the ancestor of many nations, your name will no longer be Abram but Abraham. I will make you very fertile. I will produce nations from you, and kings will come from you. I will set up my covenant with you and your descendants after you in every generation as an enduring covenant. I will be your God and your descendants' God after you. I will give you and your descendants the land in which you are immigrants, the whole land of Canaan, as an enduring possession. And I will be their God.[19]

[16] 'Circumcision of Boys', *BBC* (13 August 2009), www.bbc.co.uk/religion/religions/islam/isla methics/malecircumcision.shtml.

[17] Sami A. Aldeeb Abu Sahlieh, 'To Mutilate in the Name of Jehovah or Allah: Legitimization of Male and Female Circumcision', *Medicine and Law*, 13 (1994): 581; WHO, *Neonatal and Child Male Circumcision*, 76; WHO, *Male Circumcision: Global Trends and Determinants of Prevalence, Safety and Acceptability*, World Health Organization and Joint United Nations Programme on HIV/AIDS (2007): 4–6.

[18] Achituv, 'Blood Circumcision'; Michelle Boorstein, 'A Small but Growing Number of Jews Are Questioning the Ancient Ritual of Circumcision', *Washington Post* (28 December 2013), www .washingtonpost.com/local/a-small-but-growing-number-of-jews-are-questioning-the-ancient-ritual-of-circumcision/2013/12/25/d24c5a4e-6403–11e3-aa81-e1dab1360323_story.html.

[19] Genesis 17.

FIGURE 6.1. Male circumcision (Menahem Kahana/Staff/Getty Images).

This is a very important paragraph for the Jewish people that explicitly outlines the eternal connection between God and the Jewish people. To mark this milestone, and also to ensure that each and every generation is aware of this Covenant, God instructed Abraham to circumcise every male:

> You must circumcise the flesh of your foreskins, and it will be a symbol of the covenant between us. On the eighth day after birth, every male in every generation must be circumcised, including those who are not your own children: those born in your household and those purchased with silver from foreigners. Be sure you circumcise those born in your household and those purchased with your silver. Your flesh will embody my covenant as an enduring covenant. Any uncircumcised male whose flesh of his foreskin remains uncircumcised will be cut off from his people. He has broken my covenant.[20]

The language is clear, and it is phrased as a command that is not open to dispute or interpretation. Jews must do this, or they will be cut off the Jewish people. Thus, the importance of circumcision to Jews cannot be underestimated. There are many people who are not necessarily religious but still identify themselves as culturally Jewish. Their tradition, their culture, their way of life is to some extent Jewish. They

[20] Genesis 17.

identify with Judaism more than they do with any other religion; even if they are secular, they still define themselves as secular *Jews*.[21] Most Jews in the world observe this symbolic ritual because they wish to maintain their association with the Jewish community.

A major Jewish sage, Moses ben Maimon, commonly known as Maimonides, also referred to by the acronym Rambam, was a twelfth-century Jewish philosopher, astronomer and physician. In his book, *The Guide for the Perplexed*, Maimonides explained the logic behind male circumcision by saying that there are primarily two reasons for circumcision. First, its object is to limit sexual intercourse, and thus cause man to be moderate. This commandment has not been enjoined as a complement to a deficient physical creation, but 'as a means for perfecting man's moral shortcomings'.[22] The bodily injury caused by circumcision does not interrupt any vital function, nor does it destroy the power of generation, but it does counteract excessive lust; for 'there is no doubt that circumcision weakens the power of sexual excitement, and sometimes lessens the natural enjoyment; the organ necessarily becomes weak when it loses blood and is deprived of its covering from the begin-ning'.[23] Jewish sages remind that the first person to perform this commandment was Abraham who was well known for fearing sin.

Second, this commandment gives to male Jews a common bodily sign, so that it is impossible for a non-Jew to say that he belongs to the Jewish people for some ulterior motive, and also it gives Jews a common sign of togetherness, connecting all Jews with the belief in God's Unity. Maimonides considers this purpose to be 'perhaps more important' than circumcision's effect on libido.[24]

Maimonides explains that this law can only be kept and perpetuated if circumci-sion is performed when the child is of a very young age because of three reasons. First, if the operation were postponed until the boy had grown up, he would perhaps not submit to it. Second, 'the young child has not much pain, because the skin is tender, and the imagination weak'.[25] Adults, on the other hand, 'are in dread and fear of things which they imagine as coming'.[26] Third, when a child is very young, 'the parents do not think much of him; because the image of the child, that leads the parents to love him, has not yet taken a firm root in their minds. That image becomes stronger by the continual sight; it grows with the development of the child.'[27]

---

[21] Mazor argues that boys who grow up in a community that endorses the ritual would most likely choose to become circumcised as an adult. Joseph Mazor, 'The Child's Interests and the Case for the Permissibility of Male Infant Circumcision', 421–428.

[22] Moses Maimonides, *A Guide for the Perplexed* (1186): chap. 49, p. 378, https://oll.libertyfund .org/titles/maimonides-a-guide-for-the-perplexed.

[23] Ibid.

[24] Ibid.

[25] Ibid, at 379.

[26] Ibid.

[27] Ibid.

Recent research refuted the second assumption, suggesting that babies experience pain much like adults. Research at the University of Oxford found that eighteen of the twenty brain regions active in adults experiencing pain were active in babies. Scans also showed that babies' brains had the same response to a weak 'poke' as adults did to a stimulus four times as strong. Not only do babies experience pain much like adults but that they also have a much lower pain threshold.[28]

THE PRACTICE OF CIRCUMCISION FOR MEDICAL REASONS

The use of circumcision for medical or health reasons is in much debate. The American Academy of Pediatrics asserted that the health benefits of newborn male circumcision outweigh the risks, but the benefits are not great enough to recommend universal circumcision. Circumcision makes it easier to keep the end of the penis clean. Consequently, there is some evidence that circumcision has health benefits, including a decreased risk of urinary tract infections, a reduced risk of some sexually transmitted diseases in men, protection against penile tumour and a reduced risk of cervical cancer in female sex partners.[29] The WHO holds that there is compelling evidence that male circumcision reduces the risk of heterosexually acquired HIV infection in men by approximately 60 per cent.[30] The British National Health Service (NHS) explains in its recent guidelines that medical reasons for men to undergo circumcision include:[31]

Tight foreskin (phimosis), where the foreskin is too tight to be pulled back over the head of the penis (glans). This can sometimes cause pain when the penis is erect and, in rare cases, passing urine may be difficult.

Recurrent balanitis, where the foreskin and head of the penis become inflamed and infected.

Paraphimosis, where the foreskin cannot be returned to its original position after being pulled back, causing the head of the penis to become swollen

---

[28] Sezgi Goksan, Caroline Hartley, Faith Emery, et al., 'fMRI Reveals Neural Activity Overlap between Adult and Infant Pain', *eLife* (2015): 4; University of Oxford, 'Babies Feel Pain "Like Adults": Most Babies Not Given Pain Meds for Surgery', *Science Daily* (21 April 2015), www.sciencedaily.com/releases/2015/04/150421084812.htm. See also 'Pain and Your Infant: Medical Procedures, Circumcision and Teething', *Michigan Medicine* (2020), www.med.umich.edu/yourchild/topics/paininf.htm.

[29] Task Force on Circumcision, 'Male Circumcision', *Pediatrics*, 130(3) (September 2012), http://pediatrics.aappublications.org/content/130/3/e756. For a critique, see B.D. Earp and D.M. Shaw, 'Cultural Bias in American Medicine: The Case of Infant Male Circumcision', *Journal of Pediatric Ethics*, 1(1) (2017): 8–26.

[30] WHO, 'Male Circumcision for HIV Prevention', www.who.int/hiv/topics/malecircumcision/en/. See also WHO, *Male Circumcision*, 1.

[31] '"Circumcision", Information about Your Procedure', British Association of Urological Surgeons (BAUS), Leaflet No: 16/077 (June 2017), www.baus.org.uk/_userfiles/pages/files/Patients/Leaflets/Circumcision.pdf.

and painful. Immediate treatment is then needed to avoid serious complications, such as restricted blood flow to the penis.

Balanitis xerotica obliterans which causes phimosis and, in some cases, also
affects the head of the penis, which can become scarred and inflamed.

Cancer of the penis, a very rare type of cancer that can occur in men, where
a red patch, wart-like growth or ulcer appears on the end of the penis or
under the foreskin.[32]

The NHS instructs that, in most cases, circumcision will only be recommended
when other, less invasive and less risky treatments have been tried and have not
worked.[33]

Arik V. Marcell of Johns Hopkins University argued that substantial science shows
that male circumcision is beneficial not only in early life but later in life when men
become sexually active – with lower risk of acquiring HIV, syphilis, human papillo-
mavirus and genital herpes, lower risk of cervical cancer in sexual partners and lower
risk of penile cancer over a lifetime. Marcell maintained that African studies found
that being circumcised reduces the risk of HIV transmission by approximately 50 per
cent.[34]

RISKS OF MALE CIRCUMCISION

While liberal democracies are intolerant of FGM, they are tolerant of male circumcision. Therefore, the practice is not performed underground but within the confines of the law. Consequently, there are no exacerbating factors that play a
significant role when illegal practices are performed in secret to the detriment of
the subjects. Generally speaking, male circumcision is performed with appropriate
and hygienic instruments in an appropriate setting.

As in any surgical procedure, there are risks associated with circumcision.
According to Professor Avraham Steinberg, some 75,000 male circumcisions are
practised in Israel each and every year. The average number of complications each

---

[32] A. Wolbarst, 'Circumcision and Penile Cancer', *The Lancet*, 1(5655) (16 January 1932): 150–153;
W.D. Dunsmuir and E.M. Gordon, 'The History of Circumcision', *BJU International*, 83,
Suppl. 1 (1999): 1–12; Natasha L. Larke, Sara L. Thomas, Isabel dos Santos Silva, et al., 'Male
Circumcision and Penile Cancer: A Systematic Review and Meta-analysis', *Cancer Causes
Control*, 22(8) (2011): 1097–1110. For a survey of medical benefits of male circumcision, see
Michael Benatar and David Benatar, 'Between Prophylaxis and Child Abuse: The Ethics of
Neonatal Male Circumcision', *American Journal of Bioethics*, 3(2) (2003): 38–41.

[33] 'Circumcision in Men', *NHS* (5 November 2018), www.nhs.uk/conditions/circumcision-in-
men/. For supportive views of male circumcision, see A.A.R. Tobian and R.H. Gray, 'The
Medical Benefits of Male Circumcision', *JAMA*, 306(13) (2011): 1479–1480 and their reply to
critique, *JAMA*, 307(5) (2012): 457; Jeffrey D. Klausner and Brian J. Morris, 'Benefits of Male
Circumcision', *JAMA*, 307(5) (2012): 455–456.

[34] Arik V. Marcell, 'Greater Benefits of Infant Circumcision', *Johns Hopkins Medicine* (15
October 2012), www.hopkinsmedicine.org/news/articles/greater-benefits-of-infant-circumcision.

year is forty, mostly involving bleeding that is easily treated without leaving any permanent damage.[35] In the United Kingdom some 30,000 ritual circumcisions are performed every year, and Wheeler and Malone argue that only a few children were subsequently admitted to hospitals for treatment resulting from complications.[36] Another study by Fox et al. suggests that over an eight-year period 1,266 post-circumcision problems were reported by NHS authorities and that many of those complications were relatively minor.[37] An American study showed that the incidence of male circumcision-associated adverse events was slightly less than 0.5 per cent.[38] While acknowledging that complication rates from routine circumcision are low, critics argue that the chances of these complications being mutilatory, infective or haemorrhagic are high and potentially catastrophic. Critics further argue that death, gangrene and total or partial amputation are known adverse outcomes.[39]

CRITIQUE OF THE PRACTICE

Those associated with the holistic view hold that every organ of the body has a function, the foreskin included, and that we should not interfere with nature or God's creation. They maintain that the 'cleanliness of the penis' argument might have been true in certain eras but it is not nowadays, when we have baths and running water that provide us with simple procedures to keep ourselves clean and tidy. Brian Earp argues that uncircumcised males have no difficulty in washing the glans; it takes about one second to retract the foreskin.[40] Critics of male circumcision argue that the practice is painful and psychologically damaging.[41] Cutting the foreskin results in thickening and progressive desensitization of the

[35] Personal communication (14 June 2019). Further information in Hebrew at www.itim.org.il/פיקוח-על-עבודת-המוהלים-בישראל-2/.

[36] Robert Wheeler and Pat Malone, 'Male Circumcision: Risk versus Benefit', *Archives of Disease in Childhood*, 98 (2013): 322.

[37] Marie Fox, Michael Thomson and Joshua Warburton, 'Non-therapeutic Male Genital Cutting and Harm: Law, Policy and Evidence from U.K. Hospitals', *Bioethics*, 33 (2019): 471–472.

[38] Charbel El Bcheraoui, Xinjian Zhang, Christopher S. Cooper, et al. 'Rates of Adverse Events Associated with Male Circumcision in US Medical Settings, 2001 to 2010', *JAMA Pediatrics*, 168(7) (2014): 625–634.

[39] M. Fox and M. Thomson, 'A Covenant with the Status Quo? Male Circumcision and the New BMA Guidance to Doctors', *Journal of Medical Ethics*, 31(2005): 463–469; B.D. Earp, V. Allareddy, V. Allaredy and A.T. Rotta, 'Factors Associated with Early Deaths Following Neonatal Male Circumcision in the United States, 2001–2010', *Clinical Pediatrics*, 57(13) (2018): 1532–1540; Eran Elhaik, 'Neonatal Circumcision and Prematurity Are Associated with Sudden Infant Death Syndrome (SITS)', *Journal of Clinical and Translational Research*, 4(2) (2019): 136–151.

[40] Earp's comments on a draft of this chapter. Email 24 October 2019.

[41] G.J. Boyle, R. Goldman, J.S. Svoboda and E. Fernandez, 'Male Circumcision: Pain, Trauma and Psychosexual Sequelae', *Journal of Health Psychology*, 7(3) (2002): 329–343.

the circumcision of a boy unable to voice consent is unlawful as it is contrary to the best interests of the child.[54]

The ruling outraged both the Muslim and Jewish communities.[55] The German parliament reacted swiftly. On 12 December 2012 it passed a law allowing infant male circumcision for religious reasons when performed by a trained practitioner.[56] Notwithstanding, in October 2013 the Council of Europe passed a resolution condemning the practice as a 'violation of the physical integrity of children' and calling for a public debate in order to ban the practice 'before a child is old enough to be consulted'.[57] Norway, Sweden, Denmark, Finland and Iceland joined forces to call for a ban. While the incidence of male circumcision is relatively rare in all Scandinavian countries (0.82 per cent in Finland, 3 per cent in Norway, 5.1 per cent in Sweden, 0.1 per cent in Iceland, 5.3 per cent in Denmark[58]), these countries find the practice as such problematic. However, no European country has introduced a ban on male circumcision. In Iceland, a legislator took concrete steps to prohibit the practice for non-medical reasons. It was not specifically a bill to outlaw circumcision; rather, it was a proposal to change the wording of the law forbidding medically unnecessary FGC from 'girls' to 'children'. According to the proposal, a penalty of up to six years in prison should be imposed on anyone carrying out a circumcision for non-medical reasons.[59] The proposal was dropped following widespread criticism, including from European Jewish leaders.[60] The ban was proposed by Silja Dögg Gunnarsdóttir of the Progressive Party who failed to understand the religious-cultural importance of the practice and consequently failed to consult Iceland's tiny

[54] Bijan Fateh-Moghadam, 'Criminalizing Male Circumcision? Case Note: Landgericht Cologne, Judgment of 7 May 2012 – No. 151, Ns 169/11', *German Law Journal*, 13(9) (2012): 1134.

[55] Geoffrey Brahm Levey, 'Thinking about Infant Male Circumcision after the Cologne Court Decision', *Global Discourse*, 3(2) (2013): 326–331.

[56] Michael Germann and Clemens Wackernagel, 'The Circumcision Debate from a German Constitutional Perspective', *Oxford Journal of Law and Religion*, 4 (2015): 443–444.

[57] Jeremy Laurance, 'Circumcision: A Necessary Cut or Bodily Harm?', *The Independent* (6 May 2014), www.independent.co.uk/life-style/health-and-families/features/circumcision-a-necessary-cut-or-bodily-harm-9328250.html.

[58] Brian J. Morris, Richard G. Wamai, Esther B. Henebeng, et al., 'Estimation of Country-Specific and Global Prevalence of Male Circumcision', *Population Health Metrics*, 14(4) (2016), https://pophealthmetrics.biomedcentral.com/articles/10.1186/s12963-016-0073-5; The Danish National Board of Health estimates that 1,000 to 2,000 boys are ritually circumcised every year. Josefine Fagt, 'Det siger Sundhedsstyrelsen og reglerne om omskæring af drenge', *DR* (10 January 2018), www.dr.dk/nyheder/indland/det-siger-sundhedsstyrelsen-og-reglerne-om-omskaering-af-drenge.

[59] Harriet Sherwood, 'Iceland Law to Outlaw Male Circumcision Sparks Row over Religious Freedom', *The Observer* (18 February 2018), www.theguardian.com/society/2018/feb/18/iceland-ban-male-circumcision-first-european-country.

[60] Mattha Busby, 'Danish Parliament to Consider Becoming First Country to Ban Circumcision of Boys', *The Independent* (3 June 2018), www.independent.co.uk/news/world/europe/denmark-boyhood-circumcision-petition-danish-parliament-debate-a8381366.html.

Jewish and Muslim communities. She certainly did not anticipate the uproar that ensued.[61]

In Denmark, a citizens' petition calling for the introduction of a minimum age of 18 for circumcision to protect 'children's fundamental rights' was put forth. The petition described circumcision as a form of abuse and corporal punishment, equating it with FGM.[62] I examine this proposition below.

MALE CIRCUMCISION AND FGM

If we advocate the rights of children, similar reasoning to that pronounced in regard to FGM may lead us to object to male circumcision as well. Critics of both male circumcision and FGM argue that these practices are unjustified. The vast majority of the boys and girls who are subjected to these procedures are healthy. They are not patients. There is no need to excise their healthy organs. Both procedures are harmful to children and damage their bodily integrity. Both practices are unjustified paternal mechanisms designed to decrease lust. Furthermore, in most cases the issue of consent is irrelevant. Parents are making the decision for the male infants and for the young girls. Since the practice is conducted involuntarily when the children are of a very young age, this invasive and coercive rite effectively ties them to a certain culture or religion for life by deforming their bodies. It has negligible if any medical benefits, certainly in Western societies.[63]

Critics further argue that circumcision as such constitutes child abuse since it is painful, medically unwarranted mutilation and disfigurement. The practice damages the sexual satisfaction of circumcised women, circumcised men and also their partners, and makes the reaching of orgasm more difficult.[64] Principally, any impingement on bodily integrity constitutes an assault, an intolerable injury to the dignity of the person.[65] From a legal perspective, both male circumcision and FGM

---

[61] Michael Cook, 'Iceland Dumps Proposed Ban on Male Circumcision', *BioEdge* (13 May 2018), www.bioedge.org/bioethics/iceland-dumps-proposed-ban-on-male-circumcision/12690.

[62] JTA, 'Danish Parliament Committee Approves Draft Resolution to Ban Circumcision', *Haaretz* (30 September 2018), www.haaretz.com/world-news/europe/danish-parliament-com mittee-approves-draft-resolution-to-ban-circumcision-1.6514879. See also Vilhjálmur Örn Vilhjálmsson, 'How is Fighting Circumcision Denmark's Priority in 2020?', *Times of Israel* (6 September 2020), https://blogs.timesofisrael.com/how-is-fighting-circumcision-denmarks-pri ority-in-2020/?utm_source=The+Daily+Edition&utm_campaign=daily-edition-2020–09–06& utm_medium=email.

[63] Hanoch Ben-Yami, 'Circumcision: What Should Be Done?', *Journal of Medical Ethics*, 39 (7) (2013): 459–462.

[64] Ben-Yami, 'Circumcision: What should be done?'; Earp, 'Female Genital Mutilation and Male Circumcision'; Jasmine Abdulcadir, Diomidis Botsikas, Mylène Bolmont, et al., 'Sexual Anatomy and Function in Women with and without Genital Mutilation: A Cross-Sectional Study', *Journal of Sexual Medicine*, 13(2) (2016): 226–237.

[65] Martha C. Nussbaum, *Women and Human Development* (Cambridge: Cambridge University Press, 2000); Reinhard Merkel and Holm Putzke, 'After Cologne: Male Circumcision and the

violate core human rights documents: the Universal Declaration of Human Rights, the Convention on the Rights of the Child, the International Covenant on Civil and Political Rights and the Convention Against Torture.[66] Consequently, at the very least, so critics argue, in order to protect the rights of children circumcision should be postponed until the age of maturity;[67] then males will decide whether or not they want to go through this ceremony.

Scholars like Brian Earp[68] who draw analogies between male circumcision and female circumcision argue that in both the parents are deciding for their children, thinking about their children's best interests which include bonding and maintaining the community. But the children's best interests also include their physical and mental well-being, their enjoyment of a supportive environment and their social and economic welfare. Weighing the different considerations, Earp is opposed to all forms of child genital cutting, male and female alike. A *fortiori*, non-consensual nicking, piercing or any other form of genital cutting or alteration wrong the child irrespective of the level of harm caused, insofar as they are not medically required. The child's fundamental human rights, the dignity and worth of the human person, are to be preserved and promoted.[69]

However, there are major differences that distinguish male circumcision from FGM when performed in the Western world. These differences soothe the objections raised against male circumcision.

To start with, excessive forms of female circumcision, termed FGM, involve excising the visible part of the clitoris, the female organ that is most analogous to the male organ. Excising a part or all of a girl's clitoris is more like cutting off part or all of the boy's penis than removing his foreskin. There are reasons for calling excessive forms of female circumcision FGM. The extent, scope and depth of the excision do matter. Severe bodily harm amounts to torture and is unjustifiable. Like torture, FGM involves the deliberate infliction of extreme pain and suffering. The

---

Law – Parental Right, Religious Liberty or Criminal Assault?', *Journal of Medical Ethics*, 39 (7) (2013): 444–449.

[66] Somerville, *The Ethical Canary*; Matthew Thomas Johnson, 'Religious Circumcision, Invasive Rites, Neutrality and Equality: Bearing the Burdens and Consequences of Belief', *Journal of Medical Ethics*, 39(7) (2013): 450–455; J. Steven Svoboda, 'Circumcision of Male Infants as a Human Rights Violation', *Journal of Medical Ethics*, 39 (7) (2013): 469–474.

[67] Earp, 'Female Genital Mutilation and Male Circumcision'.

[68] Ibid. For further discussion, see Abu Sahlieh, 'To Mutilate in the Name of Jehovah or Allah'; George C. Denniston, Frederick Mansfield Hodges and Marilyn Fayre Milos (eds), *Male and Female Circumcision: Medical, Legal and Ethical Considerations in Pediatric Practice* (New York: Kluwer Academic/Plenum Publishers, 1999); Kavita Shah Arora and Jacobs Allan J., 'Female Genital Alteration: A Compromise Solution', *Journal of Medical Ethics*, 42(3) (2016): 148–154.

[69] United Nations Human Rights, *Convention on the Rights of the Child*, adopted and opened for signature, ratification and accession by General Assembly resolution 44/25 of 20 November 1989 entry into force 2 September 1990, in accordance with article 49, www.ohchr.org/en/professionalinterest/pages/crc.aspx.

pain is usually exacerbated by rudimentary tools and lack of anaesthesia. Many girls suffer physical and psychological trauma as well as exhaustion from screaming. As mentioned in Chapter 5, FGM can result in death through severe bleeding leading to haemorrhagic shock, neurogenic shock as a result of pain and trauma, and overwhelming infection and septicaemia. When the severe forms of FGM do not result in death, they result in an ongoing torture throughout life.[70] FGM does not only change the body, it is also a life-changing operation. No wonder that women described it as if their whole life had stopped there and then.[71]

Second, while male circumcision is regarded as a religious initiation rite in Islam and in Judaism, this is not true of FGM where the ritual is opened to interpretation. Some argue that 'there is clearly no basis whatsoever in any religion for the practice' of female circumcision.[72] As explained in Chapter 5, canonical Islamic texts offer relatively little justification for the practice.[73]

Third, the health consequences of FGM are entirely to the girl's disadvantage and there appears to be no medical reason for this operation. No medical expert disputes the argument that FGM inflicts major injury,[74] while many medical experts argue

---

[70] Human Rights Council, 'Promotion and Protection of All Human Rights, Civil, Political, Economic, Social and Cultural Rights, Including the Right to Development', *Report of the Special Rapporteur on Torture and Other Cruel, Inhuman or Degrading Treatment or Punishment* (15 January 2008).

[71] Abu Sahlieh, 'To Mutilate in the Name of Jehovah or Allah', 578.

[72] R.D. Mackay, 'Is Female Circumcision Unlawful?', *Criminal Law Review* (November 1983): 717–722, at 719; Kirsten Lee, 'Female Genital Mutilation: Medical Aspects and the Rights of Children', 36.

[73] Ali Gomaa, 'The Islamic View on Female Circumcision', *African Journal of Urology*, 19(3) (September 2013): 123–126, www.sciencedirect.com/science/article/pii/S1110570413000313; Eric K. Silverman, 'Anthropology and Circumcision', *Annual Review of Anthropology*, 33 (2004): 419–445.

[74] 'Female Genital Mutilation', *WHO Fact sheet* (2020), www.who.int/news-room/fact-sheets/detail/female-genital-mutilation; Social Care, Local Government and Care Partnership, *Female Genital Mutilation Risk and Safeguarding: Guidance for Professionals* (London 2016); Binaifer A. Davar, 'Women: Female Genital Mutilation', *Texas Journal of Women & the Law*, 6 (1997): 257–271; Lee, 'Female Genital Mutilation', 35. For further discussion on female circumcision, see William E. Brigman, 'Circumcision as Child Abuse: The Legal and Constitutional Issues', *Journal of Family Law*, 23(3) (1984–1985): 337–357; Amy Stern, 'Female Genital Mutilation: United States Asylum Laws Are in Need of Reform', *American University Journal of Gender & the Law*, 6 (1997): 89–111; Beth Ann Gillia, 'Female Genital Mutilation: A Form of Persecution', *New Mexico Law Review*, 27 (1997): 579–614; Joanne A. Liu, 'When Law and Culture Clash: Female Genital Mutilation, a Traditional Practice Gaining Recognition as a Global Concern', *New York International Law Review*, 11 (1998): 71–95; Gregory A. Kelson, 'Female Circumcision in the Modern Age: Should Female Circumcision Now Be Considered Grounds for Asylum in the United States?', *Buffalo Human Rights Law Review*, 4 (1998): 185–209; Carol M. Messito, 'Regulating Rites: Legal Responses to Female Genital Mutilation in the West', *In the Public Interest*, 16 (1997–1998): 33–77; Gerry Mackie, 'Ending Footbinding and Infibulation: A Convention Account', *American Sociological Review*, 61 (December 1996): 999–1017; Sarah Webber and Toby Schonfeld, 'Cutting History, Cutting Culture: Female Circumcision in the United States', *American Journal of Bioethics*, 3(2) (2003): 65–66.

that male circumcision cannot be considered an infringement upon the health or rights of boys and young men as it rarely implies permanent damage to health. Some argue that male circumcision has positive effects on those circumcised, in that it lessens the possibility of penile cancer and infections, and contributes to the cleanliness of the penis.[75] In sub-Saharan Africa, circumcision is used as a means of combating HIV transmission. There is evidence that circumcision reduces the risk of heterosexual men acquiring HIV and therefore male circumcision is encouraged as part of HIV prevention programmes in some African countries with high rates of HIV.[76] R. V. Short argues that male circumcision is 'a life saver' that can also 'bring about major improvements to both male and female reproductive health'.[77] Current epidemiological evidence clearly supports the promotion of male circumcision for HIV prevention, especially in populations with a high HIV prevalence and low circumcision rates.[78]

Fourth, FGM is associated with sexual control and diminution. While some argue that male circumcision causes sexual diminution, the practice is not performed for reasons of gender repression. To the best of my knowledge, no one made the claim (often rehearsed when FGM is concerned) that male circumcision reflects deep-rooted preconceptions and prejudices about the lower status of men. Unlike FGM, claims are not made that male circumcision is an oppressive tradition designed to subjugate males.

One of the reasons for FGM is to increase male sexual pleasure during intercourse, because of the confined space and added friction.[79] FGM's main purpose is to keep women 'controlled', and to diminish their identity as sexual beings. Male circumcision does not imply the end of a healthy sex life for a man. The purpose of circumcision varies in different communities, but it has roots in many religious beliefs that base the practice in cleanliness of self and purification.[80]

---

[75] Task Force on Circumcision, 'Male Circumcision', *Pediatrics*, 130(3) (September 2012), http://pediatrics.aappublications.org/content/130/3/e756.

[76] Helen A. Weiss, Maria A. Quigley and Richard J. Hayes, 'Male Circumcision and Risk of HIV Infection in Sub-Saharan Africa: A Systematic Review and Meta-analysis', *AIDS*, 14 (2002): 2361–2370; Matthew Thomas Johnson, 'Religious Circumcision, Invasive Rites, Neutrality and Equality: Bearing the Burdens and Consequences of Belief', *Journal of Medical Ethics*, 39 (7) (2013): 450–455; 'Circumcision in Men', *NHS* (5 November 2018), www.nhs.uk/conditions/circumcision-in-men/. For critique, see G.W. Dowsett and M. Couch, 'Male Circumcision and HIV Prevention: Is There Really Enough of the Right Kind of Evidence?', *Reproductive Health Matters*, 15(29) (2007): 33–44.

[77] R.V. Short, 'Male Circumcision: A Scientific Perspective', *Journal of Medical Ethics*, 30 (3) (2004): 241.

[78] Emiola Oluwabunmi Olapade-Olaopa, Mudasiru Adebayo Salami and Taiwo Akeem Lawal, 'Male Circumcision and Global HIV/AIDS Epidemic Challenges', *African Journal of Urology*, 25 (2019): 3.

[79] American Academy of Pediatrics, Committee on Bioethics, 'Ritual Genital Cutting of Female Minors', *Pediatrics*, 125(5) (May 2010), http://pediatrics.aappublications.org/content/125/5/1088.

[80] Ellen Gruenbaum, 'Socio-Cultural Dynamics of Female Genital Cutting: Research Findings, Gaps, and Directions', *Culture, Health & Sexuality*, 7(5) (September–October 2005): 437.

It is not about control and subjugation. Excessive forms of FGM rob sexuality and diminish women's ability to enjoy one of the most natural and pleasurable parts of life.

Fifth, a major way by which people manifest their love to others is physical. If, as a result of circumcision, women cannot express their love, these women are not living a life that is completely human as the procedure diminishes their human potential. If women are reluctant and afraid to have intercourse due to the resulting pain, then one of the principled ways we have for physical pleasure is denied to them. This reasoning is, by and large, irrelevant regarding male circumcision. Men who underwent circumcision are not reluctant to have sexual intercourse as a result of the procedure. They do not suffer pain during intercourse.

Sixth, in some communities, most notably Jewish communities and in the United States, male circumcision is performed at a very young age, commonly when the male is only a few days old.[81] Circumcised people know that this ritual was performed on them but they do not have any recollections of the event. The ritual is arguably more traumatic to the parents than to the babies; whereas FGM is commonly performed at a later stage of a woman's life, at late childhood or in adolescence. Women remember this ritual, especially the excessive forms of FGM. The lives of circumcised girls are saturated in a physical trauma. These girls are frequently reminded of the practice that is causing them great pain and suffering.

Seventh, due to the different perception of FGM and male circumcision in the Western world, problems of poor hygiene and complications are reported more in cases of FGM than in male circumcision as the extent of excision, the tools used for the female excision, the sanitary conditions, the pain relief methods and the training of the circumcisers vary greatly to the detriment of the girls. As FGM is commonly illegal in the Western world, it might be carried out with rudimentary tools, usually razors, knives, scissors, scalpels or pieces of glass (see Chapter 5). Most often the excision is performed without any form of anesthesia or antiseptics.[82] Circumcision undertaken by inexperienced providers with inadequate instruments, or with poor aftercare, can result in serious complications. On the other hand, in male circumcision there are specialized circumcision devices and the operation can be performed surgically, with anesthesia. Furthermore, neonatal circumcision is a simpler and much safer procedure than adolescent or adult circumcision. According to the WHO, circumcision of male babies results in 'a very low rate of adverse events, which are usually minor (0.2–0.4%)'.[83]

---

[81] Early in the twentieth century the age of circumcision differed from one tribe to another in South Africa, before puberty and during adolescence. See G.A. Turner, 'Some of the Tribal Marks of the South African Native Races', paper read before the Transvaal Medical Society, *Transvaal Medical Journal* (February 1911): 4.

[82] NHS, 'Female Genital Mutilation (FGM)' (16 June 2016), www.nhs.uk/conditions/female-genital-mutilation-fgm/.

[83] WHO, *Male Circumcision*, 17.

Eighth, in many communities opting out is a possibility. Male circumcision is conducted without coercing the parents. Parents who wish to refrain from the ritual are able to do so. They and their children might be subjected to social stigma for not following the custom but it is up to them to weigh the arguments for and against, to deliberate and to make a decision. As Israel exemplifies, the Jewish community does not disintegrate when some members decide not to subject their children to circumcision.[84] Opting out of practising circumcision if parents so wish should be an option for all members of communities where circumcision is practised.

Furthermore, most experts agree that male circumcision rarely involves long-term damage to those concerned; that no psychological damage is inflicted by this practice when the trauma occurs in a very early age;[85] that the operation is conducted in a sterile environment, so the possibility of complications is very slight; and that the persons conducting the operation are well trained and well equipped to circumcise. Similar reasoning may guide us in the case of female circumcision. If a moderate form of female circumcision were conducted through a deliberative process with the girls, in a conducive environment and by well-trained and well-equipped people, then there would be a case against prohibiting female circumcision. But the liberal state cannot allow the extreme forms of FGM, nor can it allow this procedure to be carried out by people who may have experience but lack any medical expertise, that is, people who see it proper to use kitchen knives, old razor blades, broken glass or sharp stones to perform the operation.

POINTS OF AGREEMENT AND DISAGREEMENT BETWEEN PROPONENTS AND CRITICS OF MALE CIRCUMCISION

Proponents and critics of male circumcision agree on some things and disagree on many others.[86] They acknowledge that male circumcision is practised primarily for

---

[84] Rani Kasher, 'It's 2017: Time to Talk about Circumcision', *Haaretz* (23 August 2017), www .haaretz.com/opinion/.premium-its-2017-time-to-talk-about-circumcision-1.5445192.

[85] There are some indications that infants who underwent circumcision without anaesthesia show post-traumatic disorders in the first six months of their lives. They tend to be more nervous, they cry more and become stressful as a result of minor stimulations. Achituv, 'Blood Circumcision'.

[86] Benatar and Benatar, 'Between Prophylaxis and Child Abuse', 35–48; British Medical Association, 'The Law and Ethics of Male Circumcision: Guidance for Doctors', *Journal of Medical Ethics*, 30(3) (2004): 259–263; Bennett Foddy, 'Medical, Religious and Social Reasons for and against an Ancient Rite', *Journal of Medical Ethics*, 39(7) (2013): 415; Brian D. Earp, 'The Ethics of Infant Male Circumcision', *Journal of Medical Ethics*, 39(7) (2013): 418–420; Allan J. Jacobs and Kavita S. Arora, 'Ritual Male Infant Circumcision and Human Rights', *American Journal of Bioethics*, 15(2) (2015): 30–39; B.C. Earp and R. Darby, 'Does Science Support Infant Circumcision?', *The Skeptic*, 25(3) (2015): 23–30; Brian J. Morris, John N. Krieger, Jeffrey D. Klausner and Beth E. Rivin, 'The Ethical Course Is to Recommend Infant Male Circumcision: Arguments Disparaging American Academy of Pediatrics Affirmative Policy Do Not Withstand Scrutiny', *Journal of Law Medicine & Ethics*, 45 (2017): 647–663; Joseph Mazor, 'On the Strength of Children's Right to Bodily Integrity: The Case of Circumcision', *Journal of Applied Philosophy*, 36(1) (February 2019): 1–16.

cultural and religious reasons, not for medical reasons. Proponents and critics view circumcision for medical reasons as uncontroversial. So is consensual circumcision at an adult age. They also do not underestimate the importance of male circumcision for the relevant communities. Most ardent critics of male circumcision, who see some similarities between the practice and FGM, still acknowledge discerning significant differences. Only a small minority use the term 'male genital mutilation'.[87] Even the most critical voices of male circumcision do not suggest putting a blanket ban on the practice as they understand that such a ban, very much like the 1920–1933 prohibition laws in the United States,[88] would not be effective.

Male circumcision is essential to Islamic and Jewish identity. It is a defining moment in the lives of members of these communities. People who practice male circumcision are not necessarily religious. Still, they associate themselves with Islam or Judaism as a culture. They define themselves as Muslims, or Jews, as a way of life and circumcision is one of the ways in which they inject meaningfulness into their group association. Circumcision is part of who they are. The ritual is a vital component of the cycle of life: birth, entering adulthood, entering life-in-partnership, death; each is signified with an accompanying ritual: circumcision, Bar Mitzvah (Bat Mitzvah for girls), wedding and funeral. One need not be religious to regard these rituals as quintessential, defining moments in one's life. Banning such a powerful defining sentiment that withstood the test of time for thousands of years would be a major blow to the communities in question and also to the wider communities at large as friction and conflict would be unavoidable.

Proponents and critics of male circumcision debate whether the practice is morally acceptable. They disagree on whether there are substantial similarities between male and female circumcision. Proponents clearly demarcate the practices by calling the one male circumcision and the other FGM. A senior leader in the Jewish British community asked me to refrain from using the term 'female circumcision' to avoid any association with male circumcision. Proponents and critics disagree whether there is an absolute right to bodily integrity. Proponents and critics disagree on issues pertaining to parental responsibilities and paternalism, whether parents should have the power to deform the integrity of the children's bodies and how to assess children's best interests. They reach contrasting results when they balance the right of parents to determine their children's communal association vis-à-vis children's rights. They assign different weight to harm as well as to medical risks and to non-medical benefits. The different weights to risks and benefits conform to their underlying views about the practices.

---

[87] S.K. Hellsten, 'Rationalising Circumcision: From Tradition to Fashion, from Public Health to Individual Freedom – Critical Notes on Cultural Persistence of the Practice of Genital Mutilation', *Journal of Medical Ethics*, 30 (2004): 248–253; Matthew Johnson, 'Male Genital Mutilation: Beyond the Tolerable?', *Ethnicities*, 10(2) (2010): 181–207.

[88] Between 1920 and 1933 the United States imposed legal prohibition on the manufacture, sale and transportation of alcoholic beverages.

While there are medical justifications for male circumcision, these are usually brought by supporters of the practice who wish to reinforce their position. Proponents and critics disagree about the significance of medical reasons for circumcision and about the injuries resulting from the practice. They disagree on whether the potential complications resulting from the procedure are significant.[89] They disagree as to whether circumcision contributes to the cleanliness of the penis. They also disagree about the extent of reduction in sexual pleasure and the trauma that male circumcision might cause to its subjects.[90] Furthermore, proponents do not necessarily see reduction in sexual drive as a bad thing. They also disagree whether the issue of consent is important and what steps the state should take.

These are all, prima facie, reasonable disagreements. The issue presents a hard case for which there are a number of interpretations, and a number of possible solutions. Here is what I suggest.

A PROPOSAL

Any form of circumcision is painful. Our reproduction organs are most sensitive and even slight scars can cause discomfort and agony. It is our responsibility to devise procedures that are as pain-free as possible in the safest possible environment. What form of state interference would seem reasonable?

We need to recognize that male circumcision is deeply rooted in tradition. Finding a compromise over ideological and identity issues is most challenging. The communities that adopted the practice see male circumcision as a significant component of their identity. These communities have legitimate, strong historical claims for autonomy. Some liberals may claim that male circumcision is not morally justified. But we do not have legitimate grounds to enforce our morality upon the group because *significant* bodily damage is rarely inflicted upon those who are circumcised, because no straightforward coercion is employed (as distinct from internalized coercion) against parents who refuse to circumcise their boys and because of the historical claims for cultural autonomy that the said groups possess.

---

[89] El Bcheraoui, Zhang, Cooper, et al., 'Rates of Adverse Events Associated with Male Circumcision in US Medical Settings, 2001 to 2010'; H.A. Weiss, N. Larke, D. Halperin *et al*, 'Complications of Circumcision in Male Neonates, Infants and Children: a systematic review', *BMC Urology*, 10 (2010).

[90] Jacobs and Arora presented evidence suggesting that there was no overall loss of sexual satisfaction in circumcised populations. See 'Ritual Male Infant Circumcision and Human Rights': 32. See also J. Steven Svoboda, 'Promoting Genital autonomy by Exploring Commonalities between Male, Female, Intersex, and Cosmetic Female Genital Cutting', *Global Discourse*, 3(2) (2013): 237–255; Sara Johnsdotter, 'Discourses on sexual Pleasure after Genital Modifications: the fallacy of genital determinism (a response to J. Steven Svoboda', *Global Discourse*, 3(2) (2013): 256–265; Robert Van Howe, 'Infant Male Circumcision in the Public Square: applying the public reason of John Rawls', *Global Discourse*, 3(2) (2013): 214–229; Susan Mendus, 'Infant Male Circumcision in the Public Square: applying the public reason of John Rawls (a reply to Robert Van Howe)', *Global Discourse*, 3(2) (2013): 230–233.

The case would be different if evidence showed that families were to feel that they were being coerced to follow a certain conception of the good and were not allowed to leave their community. That is, the case would be different if these families were subject to *designated coercion*.

Evidence suggests that children should be circumcised in the early days or weeks of life, when the circumcision is safest and unlikely to leave any trauma on the young infant.[91] While the issue of consent is important, on this particular matter of male circumcision there are weighty countervailing considerations that compellingly convince to perform circumcision in infancy. The health benefits include better hygiene; protection against urinary tract infection; eliminating the risk of balanitis and phimosis in childhood and after puberty which impedes micturition and results in difficult and painful erections in adolescence and adulthood as well as reduced likelihood of penile inflammation, HIV, genital herpes and other sexually transmitted infections (STIs).[92] In the future female sexual partners of males, infant circumcision means they too will be at reduced risk of STIs and cervical cancer. Furthermore, the infant is less mobile and, therefore, it is easier to preform anesthesia; the procedure is simpler; healing is quicker; the cosmetic outcome is superior; and cost-effectiveness is high, as is acceptability of the procedure. Moreover, psychological consequences for circumcision performed later in childhood are avoided as well as absence from work or school.[93]

Thus, circumcision is commonly decided by parents. The British Medical Association is supportive of allowing parents to make choices for their children, and believes that 'neither society nor doctors should interfere unjustifiably in the relationship between parents and their children'.[94] At the same time, parental judgement should consider the child's best interests. While the liberal state has an obligation to protect vulnerable third parties, I am not confident that less harm will be caused by prohibiting male circumcision than by permitting it. Given the importance of the practice, making it illegal would only drive it underground. Orthodox (and also not-so-Orthodox) Muslims and Jews will continue to practice male circumcision as it is an integral and essential part of their religion and tradition. Driving the practice underground would increase the overall harms to children. The circumcisers might be unprofessional and are likely to be operating in

---

[91] El Bcheraoui, Zhang, Cooper, et al., 'Rates of Adverse Events Associated with Male Circumcision in US Medical Settings, 2001 to 2010'.

[92] David A. Cooper, Alex D. Wodak, and Brian J. Morris, 'The Case for Boosting Infant Male Circumcision in the Face of Rising Heterosexual Transmission of HIV', *The Medical Journal of Australia*, 193 (2010): 318–319; Brian J. Morris, Sean E. Kennedy, Alex D. Wodak, et al., 'Early Infant Male Circumcision: Systematic Review, Risk–Benefit Analysis, and Progress in Policy', *World Journal of Clinical Pediatrics*, 6(1) (8 February 2017): 89–102.

[93] Brian J. Morris, Jake H. Waskett, Joya Banerjee, et al., 'A "Snip" in Time: What Is the Best Age to Circumcise?', *BMC Pediatrics*, 12 (2012): 20, www.ncbi.nlm.nih.gov/pmc/articles/PMC3359221/.

[94] British Medical Association, 'The Law and Ethics of Male Circumcision'.

poor conditions, detrimental to the child's health. Furthermore, if penalties against parents are imposed in the form of fines, losing parental custody or imprisonment, the welfare of the child would be negatively impinged.

The state should have as little say as possible in personal matters. Earlier I established that it should intervene in weighty cases such as murder for family honour and FGM. Here the damage to the circumcised is much less grave. I am not convinced that at least part of the critique of male circumcision is accurate. I do not think that circumcision is psychologically damaging and an oppressive tradition designed to subjugate the individual and his sexuality.[95] While physical pain is inflicted on male babies, it is unlikely that they will remember the circumcision in the long run. Granted that babies should receive adequate pain relief medication during the procedure and for the days ahead. As it takes approximately a week for the wound to heal, parents should be advised to ensure minimal contact with the wound as this may cause pain, including when it comes into contact with the baby's urine. Parents should be mindful to alleviate the pain as much as they possibly can by attending to the baby's needs swiftly. As for psychological pain, the event is arguably more distressing to the parents and other family members than to the infants.[96] Yet, as the example of Judith and Joel Cohen that opened this chapter shows, not all adults need to be present during the circumcision.

Parents should be free to opt out and decide not to circumcise their children. In non-Orthodox Jewish communities, some parents opt out without been subject to penalties. Parents should also be free to decide that circumcision will be performed by special physicians in a medical setting and with various forms of anesthesia. Weighing the pros and cons of intervention, it is argued that barring the practice will do very little good, outweighed by the harm caused by state interference.

Male circumcision and minor forms of female circumcision in countries where this ritual is allowed should be performed with local anaesthesia. Subjects of the rituals should not suffer needlessly when analgesics are available. In this context, the KNMG's position paper emphasized that circumcision is a surgical procedure and, therefore, it should be performed only by qualified healthcare professionals who follow all applicable scientific guidelines. This entails, *inter alia*, that 'circumcisions can only be carried out under local or general anaesthetic, after thorough and precise advice and information has been given to the child's parents'.[97] The KNMG emphasized that this practice is not medically necessary and carries a risk

---

[95] Boyle, Goldman, Svoboda and Fernandez, 'Male Circumcision'.

[96] Some speculate that circumcision may lead to persistent traumatic consequences for the infants. See Merkel and Putzke, 'After Cologne'; Gregory J. Boyle, 'Circumcision of Infants and Children: Short-Term Trauma and Long-Term Psychosexual Harm', *Advances in Sexual Medicine*, 5(2) (2015): 22–38. See also A. Taddio, J. Katz, A.L. Ilersich, and G. Koren, 'Effect of Neonatal Circumcision on Pain Response during Subsequent Routine Vaccination', *The Lancet*, 349 (1997): 599–603.

[97] Royal Dutch Medical Association (KNMG), *Non-therapeutic Circumcision of Male Minors*, 4.

of complications. This means that 'extra-stringent requirements must be established with regard to this type of information and advice'.[98]

The KNMG recommended (1) local anaesthesia (2) that the procedure be performed by a qualified healthcare professional. As for the first recommendation, it has been argued that circumcision of neonates and children without suitable anaesthesia is unacceptable and is of great moral concern.[99] Local or regional anaesthesia for neonatal circumcision requires a certain skill in anaesthesia to monitor the infant and intervene if the anaesthesia is inadequate. Anaesthesia with lignocaine-prilocaine cream is insufficient while injected anaesthesia is painful due to the injection but it is comprehensive.[100] The WHO recommends local anaesthesia with dorsal penile nerve block (DPNB). The WHO holds that circumcision with EMLA (eutectic mixture of local anaesthetics) 5 per cent cream is safe and provides effective anaesthesia when applied correctly but not as effective as DPNB.[101] Other studies suggest that newborns circumcised with the dorsal block and *subcutaneous* ring block in combination with the concentrated oral sucrose had the lowest pain scores. This combination is said to be the most effective anaesthetic and, therefore, the preferred option.[102] However, this view is contested.

In his comments on a draft of this chapter, Avraham Steinberg writes that the state should not intervene in a religious process as long as there is no damage to the babies. In his view, the main reason that the issue has arisen in recent years is the execution of circumcisions in hospitals by young and inexperienced interns. Consequently there were complaints about continuous pain and suffering. In contrast, *halachic* circumcision performed by skilled circumcisers (*mohalim*) takes a very short time, and the degree of pain does not require anaesthesia by injection. The injections are painful in themselves. Steinberg thinks that if the state would

---

[98] Ibid.

[99] Benatar and Benatar, 'Between Prophylaxis and Child Abuse', 43; B.R. Paix, and S.E. Peterson, 'Circumcision of Neonates and Children without Appropriate Anaesthesia Is Unacceptable Practice', *Anaesthesia and Intensive Care*, 40 (2012): 511–516; Steven J. Svoboda, 'Circumcision of Male Infants as a Human Rights Violation', *Journal of Medical Ethics*, 39(7) (2013): 469–474.

[100] Paix and Peterson, 'Circumcision of Neonates and Children without Appropriate Anaesthesia Is Unacceptable Practice'.

[101] WHO, *Manual for Male Circumcision under Local Anaesthesia*, Version 3.1 (December 2009): chap. 6; WHO, *Neonatal and Child Male Circumcision: A Global Review* (April 2010): 11. See also Michael Rosen, 'Anesthesia for Ritual Circumcision in Neonates', *Paediatrics Anaesthesia*, 20 (2010): 1126; Allan J. Jacobs and Kavita S. Arora, 'Ritual Male Infant Circumcision and Human Rights', *American Journal of Bioethics*, 15(2) (2015): 31.

[102] Ivy S. Razmus, Madelyn E. Dalton and David Wilson, 'Pain Management for Newborn Circumcision', *Pediatric Nursing*, 30(5) (January 2004): 414–417; Rana Sharara-Chami, Zavi Lakissian, Lama Charafeddine, et al., 'Combination Analgesia for Neonatal Circumcision: A Randomized Controlled Trial', *Pediatrics*, 140(6) (December 2017), https://pediatrics.aappublications.org/content/140/6/e20171935. See also J. Lander, B. Brady-Fryer, J.B. Metcalf, et al., 'Comparison of Ring Block, Dorsal Penile Nerve Block, and Topical Anesthesia for Neonatal Circumcision', *Journal of the American Medical Association*, 278(24) (1997): 2157–2162.

insist on anaesthesia by injection, the result would be pirated circumcisions as many parents would opt to still approach the traditional *mohalim*. Also, the circumcision costs would skyrocket. The state of Israel will not fund the practice for the entire population. Moreover, the cumulative experience in Israel shows that in comparison to circumcisions conducted by physicians in other countries, no differences were found in the number of complications;[103] thus, there is no real benefit to performing the circumcision only by physicians.

Professor Leonid Eidelman, chair of anaesthesia at the Rabin Medical Center in Israel, former president of the World Medical Association and past president of the Israel Medical Association, agrees that a penal block is not preferable to non-invasive anaesthesia. Like Steinberg, Eidelman explains that the injection itself hurts. It requires skill and might be dangerous to the baby if not done properly. There were cases where the injection was too deep, in the wrong place and/or with an excessive dose. In Eidelman's view the best way to perform male circumcision is to apply the EMLA ointment a few hours prior the procedure, apply it again during the procedure while giving the baby sugar to suck which relaxes the baby and mitigates the pain. After the operation, the baby should be given some pain relief, love and attention. Eidelman testified that when he circumcised his grandson he called on a physician to perform the operation, and while the physician was qualified to use invasive forms of anaesthesia, Eidelman asked him to resort to the above method.[104]

Concurrently, Dr Nisar Mir argues that there is not one method that is clearly preferable to another. Dr Mir, who is a retired consultant paediatrician/neonatologist, assistant coroner in Cheshire, the United Kingdom, and formerly professor and head of the Department of Paediatrics at the King Saud University College of Medicine, said that there is no need for injection. Dr Mir explains that in the first month of life infants are at a higher risk of surgery and anaesthesia-related adverse events when compared with older children. Analgesia and anaesthesia for neonates require a good knowledge of neonatal and transitional physiology combined with skills in airway maintenance, vascular access and prompt management of unexpected adverse events or complications. A blood loss of about 25 ml in a 3 kg baby is equivalent to a loss of nearly 10 per cent of the infant's total blood volume and sepsis-related mortality is threefold higher in neonates on account of immature host defence mechanisms.[105] Both Mir and Eidelman argue that inhalation anaesthesia

---

[103] Personal communication (14 June 2019). See also Avraham Steinberg, 'Anaesthesia in Circumcision, Medical and Halachic Perspectives', *Shana Be'Shana* (2001) (Hebrew); Avraham Steinberg, 'Anesthesia in Circumcision: Medical and Halachic Consideration', *Jewish Medical Ethics*, 6 (2007): 15–25; Edward Reichman and Fred Rosner, 'The Use of Anesthesia in Circumcision: A Re-evaluation of the Halakhic Sources', *Tradition: A Journal of Orthodox Jewish Thought*, 34(3) (Fall 2000): 6–26.

[104] Professor Leonid Eidelman, personal conversation (16 August 2020).

[105] Dr Nisar Mir, personal conversation (17 August 2020); S. Ratiuddin, M.E. El-Awad and N.A. Mir, 'Bacterial Meningitis: T Cell Activation and Immunoregulatory CD4+ T Cell Subset Alteration', *Allergy & Clinical Immunology*, 93(4) (1994): 793–798.

is very effective. *Decision Support in Medicine* similarly holds that for infants and small children, mask induction with oxygen/nitrous oxide/sevoflurane is preferred.[106]

As for the second KNMG recommendation that male circumcision should be performed by a qualified healthcare professional, this recommendation will face objections and criticisms. As mentioned above, in quite a few parts of the world, including Israel, the procedure is performed in the main by circumcisers who are not medically trained. According to Dr Mir, in the British NHS there are not many physicians who perform circumcision.[107] Insisting on regional anaesthesia by injection would exclude *mohalim* as they do not have the required knowledge and skill. In Dr Mir's opinion, the circumciser need not necessarily be a physician. Experience matters no less than credentials. A circumciser who performs the procedure a few times a day is more qualified than a physician who does it once a year. However, the circumciser needs to have formal training and accreditation for performing the procedure and there needs to be a system of audit and monitoring of the practice to ensure that all agreed safety standards are followed.[108] According to Rabbi Professor Avraham Steinberg, Jewish law (*Halacha*) proscribes full anaesthesia and permits local anaesthesia provided that it is not injected.[109] Steinberg explains that *Halacha* objects to anaesthesia by injection because this procedure carries unnecessary risks, is painful no less than the circumcision and prevents *mohalim* from conducting the ceremony as they have been doing for the past 3,000 years.[110]

In Israel, circumcision is not considered a surgical procedure, but a religious act.[111] Circumcisers are not under the responsibility of the Ministry of Health although they are performing a surgical procedure. The vast majority of circumcisers are *mohalim* who learn their profession from former circumcisers, sometimes from their fathers. They need not learn medicine and they are regulated and monitored by a designated interministerial committee, where the Ministry of Health has a representative, under the responsibility of the Chief Rabbinate which administers religious matters. Only a third of male circumcisions is performed by physicians under anesthesia.[112] Some of these physicians are also registered *mohalim*.

---

[106] Decision Support in Medicine, 'Anesthesiology: Circumcision', *Clinical Pain Advisor* (2017), www.clinicalpainadvisor.com/home/decision-support-in-medicine/anesthesiology/circumci sion/.

[107] Dr Nisar Mir, personal conversation (17 August 2020).

[108] Ibid.

[109] Personal communication (10 January 2019).

[110] Personal communication (29 November 2019).

[111] In his comments on a draft of this paper, Professor Leonid Eidelman qualified by saying that hundreds, may be thousands of circumcisions were performed on adults and children of different age in Israel after 1990 as surgical procedures in operating rooms. Eidelman referred to the great immigration wave from Russia to Israel.

[112] Achituv, 'Blood Circumcision'. Professor Steinberg doubts that these data are correct. Personal communication (14 June 2019). Steinberg argues that only 40 of the 400 *mohalim* who were

Some are not. Steinberg advised that if the physician is not a registered *mohel*, the religious decree (mitzvah) of circumcision is not fulfilled.[113]

To address this delicate dilemma a reasonable balancing act is required that would make the procedure safe and as pain-free as possible for the babies, and would not offend religious sentiments. The proposal should seek to find a middle ground between tradition and protecting the rights of the child. My motivation for this proposal is reasonable, just and humane. These are my recommendations:

- Both parents should be involved and give consent for non-therapeutic circumcision. Parents are free to opt out and may decide not to circumcise their children.

- It is recommended to perform circumcision at a very young age. This is for the reasons stipulated by Maimonides (see sectin 'Male Circumcision in Judaism') but also for medical reasons. Circumcision beyond infancy is riskier as the procedure is more complex, takes more time and the likelihood of complications is higher. A comprehensive study showed that the incidences of probable adverse events were approximately twentyfold and tenfold greater for males circumcised at age 1 to 9 years and at 10 years or older, respectively, compared with boys circumcised at an age younger than 1 year.[114] If circumcision is conducted at the adulthood stage of the boy's life, he should be involved in the decision-making process and have the ability to refuse undergoing the procedure if he so wishes.

- Male circumcision should be performed by someone who is fully qualified, who is familiar with the procedure and who can sort out potential complications.

- Male circumcision has been performed in Judaism for many generations. Traditional, Orthodox and ultra-Orthodox Jews will find it difficult to accept the transfer of responsibility solely to physicians. Therefore, in the spirit of compromise, professional circumcisers, *mohalim*, could also practice the ritual. They should be fully trained and qualified to relieve human suffering. The state should administer and licence the procedure, ensuring that only people with the right qualifications could perform circumcision.

---

registered are physicians (personal communication, 29 November 2019). An updated list of *mohalim* is available at www.gov.il/he/departments/general/mohalim_list (Hebrew).

[113] Personal communication (10 January 2019).

[114] El Bcheraoui, Zhang, Cooper, et al., 'Rates of Adverse Events Associated with Male Circumcision in US Medical Settings, 2001 to 2010'. For a critical view, see Morten Frisch and Brian D. Earp, 'Circumcision of Male Infants and Children as a Public Health Measure in Developed Countries: A Critical Assessment of Recent Evidence', *Global Public Health*, 13(5) (2018): 626–641.

- Some physicians may refuse to perform non-therapeutic circumcisions for reasons of conscience. Conscientious objection is certainly a reasonable and valid ground for physicians to opt out.[115]
- Before the procedure, the circumciser should ensure that the baby is healthy, of good size, has no medical concerns, and that there are no defects in the penal structure. The circumciser needs to ensure that the baby is fit for surgery.[116]
- Professional circumcisers should discuss the potential harms and benefits of circumcision with the parents or legal guardians.
- The procedure should be done in the appropriate hygienic setting, with appropriate clean, antiseptic instruments, preferably in a medical centre or near such a medical facility to which it would be possible to rush the baby in case of complications. Some babies have a low pain threshold. Their blood pressure might drop as a result. Bleeding and seizures are also among the possible complications. Therefore, it is useful to have nearby qualified medical professionals who know what to do in the minority of cases where there are complications.
- The circumciser should enquire about known intolerance to anaesthesia or medication in the close family.
- The procedure should be conducted with local anaesthesia. If performed by a qualified physician, ring block (or inhalation anaesthesia) combined with oral sucrose and EMLA cream is required. If performed by a qualified circumciser, non-invasive local anaesthesia and oral sucrose are required.
- I have mentioned that according to some studies the combination of dorsal block, subcutaneous ring block and concentrated oral sucrose had the lowest pain scores and is therefore perceived to be the most effective anaesthetic for male circumcision. Some countries may consider training circumcisers to perform this procedure. According to this proposal, *mohalim* will not be required to study for a medical degree with specialization in anaesthesia. Instead, they will be required to participate in a designated course on anaesthesia for male circumcision. Such a course will be much shorter compared to studying for a medical degree. It will still require a hundred hours of training, and that twenty to thirty procedures should be done under direct supervision. The training should encompass some neuroanatomy and physiology, anatomy and

[115] British Medical Association, 'The Law and Ethics of Male Circumcision'.

[116] WHO, *Manual for Male Circumcision under Local Anaesthesia*, Version 3.1 (December 2009): chap. 6, www.who.int/hiv/pub/malecircumcision/who_mc_local_anaesthesia.pdf. See also J.G. Lenhart, N.M. Lenhart, A. Reid and B.K. Chong, 'Local Anesthesia for Circumcision: Which Technique Is Most Effective?', *The Journal of the American Board of Family Practice*, 10 (1) (1997): 13–19.

physiology of the male reproductive tract, pharmacology of anesthetic agents and agents for treating complications. The medicine involved should include circumcision, local anesthesia and their complications, as well as how to address these complications. Each country will specify the knowledge and skills that training should achieve in order to receive an official accreditation. Each national medical association will ensure that only people with the right qualifications will be able to perform male circumcision with this elaborate and skilful form of anesthesia. The length of training might vary from nation to nation depending on the risk-averseness of government and other political considerations.

- After the procedure, adequate pain control such as paracetamol in a proper dose is required.[117]
- Auditing is required. Circumcisers should report all cases of male circumcision that they perform. Mechanisms of quality control should be in place to monitor the number of explained complications.
- Parents, religious authorities, medical professionals, human rights activists and other stakeholders should engage in a constructive debate in the spirit of deliberative democracy about the pros and cons, benefits and risks of circumcision.

CONCLUSION

The purpose of the discussion was to suggest that (1) there are some valid analogies between female and male circumcision; (2) there are significant differences between male circumcision and FGM; and (3) male circumcision should be conducted in a humane fashion, making it as pain-free to its subjects as it is possible. Balancing between group rights and the rights of the child, it is essential to avoid unnecessary suffering. In this context, let me acknowledge and reject the view that argues for *intentional* affliction of suffering on the child, wishing the baby to suffer. Some rabbinical authorities argue that circumcision requires some amount of pain while others contest this assertion. R. Meir Arik, known by his pseudonym Imrei Yosher, argued that pain is an integral part of the circumcision. Abraham endured pain to increase his reward and he set a precedent. Because Abraham suffered pain so we should not introduce any mitigating innovations to negate this aspect of circumcision.[118] The majority of halachic authorities, however, disagree with Rabbi Arik and hold that pain is not a necessary requirement of circumcision.[119] After all, Abraham was an adult and gave his consent. The issue remains contested and here religious

---

[117] Professor Eidelman noted that it is easy to overdose.
[118] Reichman and Rosner, 'The Use of Anesthesia in Circumcision', 13.
[119] Ibid., 15. See also Questions and Answers, www.eretzhemdah.org/newsletterArticle.asp?lang=he&pageid=48&cat=1&newsletter=295&article=1083 (Hebrew).

belief comes into conflict with the rights of the child as well as the rights of the parents. Article 37 of the Convention on the Rights of the Child (1990) holds: 'No child shall be subjected to torture or other cruel, inhuman or degrading treatment or punishment.'[120] Acknowledging the importance of non-therapeutic circumcision as a religious and cultural rite does not entail that we are required to concede to torture. It is one of the liberal state's obligations to protect the best interests of vulnerable third parties.

The chapter was opened with the illustrative example of Mishmar Cohen who was subjected to traditional circumcision. While cultural groups have external protections against the larger community, these protections should be reasonable. They should not dictate inflicting unnecessary pain on children. Behind the veil of ignorance, parents would opt to conduct the ritual with minimum pain for their sons. Their sons' crying also inflicts pain on them. I hope my proposal will lead to an open debate with the communities through means of deliberative democracy, where the need for adequate analgesia is explained, and the rights of the child are safeguarded.

So far I have discussed state intervention when physical harm is concerned. I now move on to discuss whether the liberal state may justly intervene in the illiberal practices of subcultures that inflict non-physical harm on designated group members. While physical harm is easily discernible, non-physical harm is not. This makes the debate even more complicated.

---

[120] *Convention on the Rights of the Child* (1990), www.ohchr.org/en/professionalinterest/pages/crc .aspx.

PART III

Interference in Minority Affairs: Non-physical Harm

7

Discrimination of Women and Apostates

[T]he full and complete development of a country, the welfare of the world and the cause of peace require the maximum participation of women on equal terms with men in all fields.

Preamble of the Convention on the Elimination of All Forms of
Discrimination against Women, 1979

In Chapter 5 I argued for state intervention in a very limited range of cases that involves the taking of life, grave risk to life and torture. This view is endorsed as a matter of moral principle. No cultural claims should constitute justification for the taking of life and as a barrier against state control aimed at saving life from death and torture. Cases involving less severe injuries are contested. The state cannot and should not control *everything*. It is better to limit its immediate control to the most obvious and undisputed matters. Internal restrictions may be inconsistent with liberal principles, but it does not yet follow that liberals should impose their views on minorities that do not accept some or all of these liberal principles. What is needed is case by case investigation in accordance with the theoretical framework that underpins this book.

In this chapter and Chapter 8 I examine the limits of state interference in proscribing cultural norms by considering gender discrimination, the right of people to leave their community free of penalties, denying women and children appropriate education and forced or arranged marriages for girls and young women. By 'appropriate' I mean education that will enable individuals comfortable integration into the wider society if they so wish. Practices that force children to marry at a very young age and denial of education to vulnerable populations constitute serious harms. The discussion opens by reflecting on the discriminatory practices of a Pueblo tribe against its women and analysing an American court case, *Santa Clara Pueblo v. Martinez*.[1] A Canadian case, *Hofer v. Hofer*,[2] illustrates the

---

[1]   *Santa Clara Pueblo v. Martinez* 436 US 49 (1978).
[2]   *Hofer et al. v. Hofer et al.* (1970) S.C.R. 958.

problematics of denying reasonable exit rights to members who may wish to leave their community. Subsequently, the discussion turns to the issue of arranged marriages of girls and young women. A case in point concerns the Jewish-Yemenite immigrants who came to Israel during the 1950s.

In each of these cases the question is whether a dominant culture has a right to interfere in the business of a cultural minority, if one or more of their practices or norms cause some harm to members of that same minority culture. Groups employed internal restrictions and erected external protections to protect themselves. In the name of culture and religion, they deny women basic human rights and undermine their ability to develop themselves as autonomous beings. As explained in Chapter 1, Rawls has argued that the various conceptions of justice are the outgrowth of different notions of society against the background of opposing views of the natural necessities and opportunities of human life. A conception of social justice is to be regarded as providing in the first instance a standard whereby the distributive aspects of the basic structure of society are to be assessed.[3] It is accentuated that the context of analysis is democracy, where respect for others and not harming others are enshrined as basic tenets. Following Susan Moller Okin, it is argued that practices and arrangements that serve to undermine women's equal dignity and equal access to opportunities are incompatible with these two basic tenets.[4]

One of the underlying premises of this book is gender equality (see Introduction). The Universal Declaration of Human Rights, 1948 (UDHR) is the normative foundation of human rights discourse.[5] The preamble to the declaration explains the need to protect human rights, in reference to the historic fact that 'disregard and contempt for human rights have resulted in barbarous acts which have outraged the conscience of mankind'.[6] The two major international human rights legal instruments that derived from the UDHR are the International Covenant on Civil and Political Rights, 1966[7] and the International Covenant of Economic, Social and Cultural Rights, 1966.[8] Other important conventions are the 1967 International Convention for Elimination of All Forms of Discrimination against Women,[9] the

---

[3] John Rawls, *A Theory of Justice* (Oxford: Oxford University Press, 1971), 7.

[4] Susan Moller Okin, 'Is Multiculturalism Bad for Women?', in Joshua Cohen, Matthew Howard and Martha C. Nussbaum (eds), *Is Multiculturalism Bad for Women?* (Princeton, NJ: Princeton University Press, 1999): 9–24.

[5] The Universal Declaration of Human Rights (1948), www.un.org/en/universal-declaration-human-rights/.

[6] Ibid.

[7] International Covenant of Civil and Political Rights (1966), www.ohchr.org/en/professionalin terest/pages/ccpr.aspx.

[8] International Covenant of Economic, Social and Cultural Rights (1966), www.ohchr.org/EN/Professionalinterest/Pages/CESCR.aspx.

[9] International Convention for Elimination of All Forms of Discrimination against Women (1967), www.ipu.org/PDF/publications/cedaw_en.pdf.

1981 Declaration on the Elimination of all Forms of Intolerance and of Discrimination Based on Religion or Belief[10] and the 1990 Convention on the Rights of the Child.[11] They are all aimed at safeguarding the inalienable rights of women and children, who are perceived as vulnerable and therefore in need of protection. Specifically, Article 26 of the International Covenant of Economic, Social and Cultural Rights holds:

> All persons are equal before the law and are entitled without any discrimination to the equal protection of the law. In this respect, the law shall prohibit any discrimination and guarantee to all persons equal and effective protection against discrimination on any ground such as race, colour, sex, language, religion, political or other opinion, national or social origin, property, birth or other status.[12]

GENDER DISCRIMINATION: THE CASE OF THE PUEBLO INDIAN COMMUNITIES

It is estimated that 370 million people in ninety countries are indigenous people.[13] An indigenous position is distinctive and incorporates an expectation of control over the nature and pace of adaptation to modernity and global forces. This is due to historical reasons. Most of the indigenous groups experienced great suffering at the hands of the white men who colonialized them, took their lands and exploited them. Many indigenous people were forced to forfeit their sources of subsistence. The colonializing powers dispossessed and subjugated the local communities by brute force, showing little regard to the indigenous just claims on land and natural resources.

During the twentieth century, many Western countries recognized the evil that their forefathers brought on the indigenous people. Repenting, they have aimed to compensate them in various ways. The old-school repressive methods have been reversed. Instead of trying to suppress indigenous cultures, liberal democracies have been acknowledging cultural value and importance. Steps were taken to accommodate cultural rights. In the United States, some Pueblo Indian communities enjoy extensive rights of self-government. They limit freedom of conscience of their own

---

[10] Declaration on the Elimination of All Forms of Intolerance and of Discrimination Based on Religion or Belief (1981).

[11] Convention on the Rights of the Child, adopted and opened for signature, ratification and accession by General Assembly resolution 44/25 of 20 November 1989, entry into force 2 September 1990, www.ohchr.org/en/professionalinterest/pages/crc.aspx.

[12] International Covenant on Civil and Political Rights, adopted and opened for signature, ratification and accession by General Assembly resolution 2200A (XXI) of 16 December 1966, entry into force 23 March 1976, in accordance with Article 49, www.ohchr.org/en/professionalinterest/pages/ccpr.aspx.

[13] Alexander Kedar, Ahmad Amara and Oren Yiftachel, *Emptied Lands: A Legal Geography of Bedouin Rights in the Negev* (Stanford: Stanford University Press, 2018): 160.

members and employ sexually discriminatory membership rules that negate the liberal principles of respect for others, and not harming others. Similarly, some immigrant groups and religious minorities use 'multiculturalism' as a pretext for imposing traditional patriarchal practices on women and children. Some immigrant and religious groups demand the right to stop their children (particularly girls) from receiving a proper education, so as to reduce the chances that the child will leave the community; some other communities uphold compulsory arranged marriages.

Pueblo peoples are thought to be the descendants of the prehistoric Ancestral Pueblo (Anasazi) culture. This Native American tribe has been in existence for more than 600 years. They established villages in New Mexico along the Rio Grande and in northern Arizona.[14] Practices of some Pueblo Indian communities in the United States discriminate in the distribution of housing against members who have abandoned the traditional tribal religion. They also discriminate against women who have married outside the tribe. If female members marry outside the tribe, their children are denied membership. But if men marry outside the tribe, the children are members.[15] Should the American federal government have the authority to step in?

Many liberals have assumed that all governments within a country should be subject to a single Bill of Rights, adjudicated and enforced by a single Supreme Court. Hence many American liberals supported legislation to make tribal governments subject to the federal Bill of Rights, even though Indian tribes have historically been exempted from having to comply with the Bill of Rights, and their internal decisions have not been subject to Supreme Court review.[16]

In 1968, the American Congress passed the Indian Civil Rights Act (ICRA)[17] which recognized tribes' sovereignty and their right to self-government but stated that tribes are subject to constitutional guidelines resembling the Bill of Rights. This legislation was widely opposed by Indian groups who perceived it as an unjust federal intrusion into tribal affairs, and for understandable reasons.[18] The assumption that all governments within a country should be subject to a single Bill of

---

[14] 'Ancestral Pueblo culture', *Britannica*, www.britannica.com/topic/Ancestral-Pueblo-culture.

[15] This discriminatory rule was upheld in *Santa Clara Pueblo v. Martinez* 436 US 49 (1978), discussed *infra*. For further discussion, see A. Shachar, *Multicultural Jurisdictions: Cultural Differences and Women's Rights* (Cambridge: Cambridge University Press, 2001); J. Resnik, 'Dependent Sovereigns: Indian Tribes, States, and the Federal Courts', *University of Chicago Law Review*, 56 (1989): 671–759.

[16] F. Svensson, 'Liberal Democracy and Group Rights: The Legacy of Individualism and Its Impact on American Indian Tribes', *Political Studies*, 27(3) (1979): 421–439.

[17] The Indian Civil Rights Act of 1968 (ICRA), 25 U.S.C.§§ 1301–1304 (ICRA), www.courts.ca .gov/documents/Indian-Civil-Rights-Act-of-1968.pdf.

[18] Carla Christofferson, 'Tribal Courts' Failure to Protect Native American Women: A Reevaluation of the Indian Civil Rights Act', *Yale Law Journal*, 101(1) (1991): 169–185; D. Schneiderman, 'Human Rights, Fundamental Differences? Multiple Charters in a New Partnership', in Guy Laforest and Roger Gibbins (eds), *Beyond the Impasse: Toward Reconciliation* (Montreal: Institute for Research in Public Policy, 1998): 147–185.

Rights, enforced by a common Supreme Court, was perceived inappropriate in the eyes of the Pueblo and other incorporated indigenous groups. After all, the indigenous population preceded the establishment of the United States. Most of their valuable assets were taken away from them by the colonizing power.

Since the nineteenth century, Indian tribes were recognized by the courts as having a distinct political society. They are domestic dependent nations, capable of managing their own affairs and of governing themselves; yet they are dependent on the United States to whom the relation resembles that of a ward to a guardian.[19] Still, Indian tribes are neither states nor arms of the federal government, therefore many Indian leaders argued that Indian governments should be exempt from the Bill of Rights, not in order to impose illiberal internal restrictions within Indian communities but to defend the external protections of Indians vis-à-vis the larger society. They feared that their rights to land, or to guaranteed representation, which help reduce their vulnerability to the economic and political pressure of the larger society, could be struck down as violating the equality provisions of the Bill of Rights. Also, Indian leaders fear that white judges may interpret certain rights (e.g., democratic rights) in ways that are culturally biased. Hence many Indian groups seek exemption from the Bill of Rights, affirm their commitment to the basic human rights and freedoms which underlie the American constitution and wish to enjoy social and legal responsibilities for their communal affairs.[20]

Spinner-Halev argues that avoiding the injustice of imposing reform on an oppressed group is often more important than avoiding the injustice of gender discrimination.[21] The American Supreme Court legitimized the acts of colonization and conquest, which dispossessed the Pueblo of their property and power. The Pueblo have never had any representation on the Supreme Court. Thus, the American federal constitution and courts do not enjoy obvious legitimacy in the eyes of an involuntarily incorporated indigenous group. Why should the Pueblo

---

[19] Ray A. Brown, 'The Indian Problem and the Law', *Yale Law Journal*, 39(3) (1930): 307–331.

[20] The basic attitude of the American Supreme Court towards Indian sovereignty was determined by Chief Justice John Marshall's judgement in *Johnson v. M'Intosh*, 21 U.S. (8 Wheat.) 543 (1823). In this judgement, Marshall said that 'Conquest gives title which the courts of the conqueror cannot deny', the validity of which 'has never been questioned by our courts' (pp. 587–588). Marshall's approach continues to determine the court's approach to Indian rights, not just in the United States but also in other settler societies such as Canada and Australia. On this, see D.E. Wilkins, '*Johnson v. M'Intosh Revisited*: Through the Eyes of *Mitchel v. United States*', *American Indian Law Review*, 19(1) (1994): 159–181, esp. pp. 161–168; and R. Williams Jr, 'Sovereignty, Racism, Human Rights: Indian Self-Determination and the Postmodern World Legal System', *Review of Constitutional Studies*, 2 (1995): 146–202; Charles Wilkinson, *Blood Struggle: The Rise of Modern Indian Nations* (Boston: W.W. Norton, 2006); Rebecca Tsosie, 'Reconceptualizing Tribal Rights: Can Self-Determination Be Actualized within the U.S. Constitutional Structure?', *Lewis & Clark Law Review*, 15(4) (2011): 923–950.

[21] Jeff Spinner-Halev, 'Feminism, Multiculturalism, Oppression, and the State', *Ethics*, 112 (October 2001): 84–113.

agree to have their internal decisions reviewed by a body which is, in effect, the court of their conquerors?

The Pueblo have their own internal constitution and courts, which prevent the arbitrary exercise of political power. To be sure, while the Pueblo constitution is not liberal, it is a form of constitutional government. As Graham Walker notes, it is a mistake to conflate the ideas of liberalism and constitutionalism.[22] There is a genuine category of non-liberal constitutionalism, which provides meaningful checks on political authority and preserves the basic elements of natural justice, and which thereby helps ensure that governments maintain their legitimacy in the eyes of their subjects.

In an earlier article, Kymlicka and I argued that the liberal state should not intervene in indigenous affairs because they have strong claims for self-government. Balancing group rights and gender rights, we gave more weight to the former.[23] Kymlicka has long been arguing that liberal societies should extend group rights and special arrangements to cultural communities – especially to disadvantaged national minorities and some polyethnic or immigrant groups – as a matter of liberal justice.[24] Upon further reflection, in recent years I have revised my opinion thinking that there is a scope for state interference to redress gender injustice. Let me explain by reflecting on the landmark case regarding the federal government's jurisdiction over Indian tribes.

DENYING BASIC RIGHTS TO WOMEN: *SANTA CLARA PUEBLO V. MARTINEZ*

Santa Clara Pueblo is one of nineteen pueblos in New Mexico. They share a long history of contact and struggle with Spain, Mexico and the United States.[25] In *Santa Clara Pueblo v. Martinez*, the Supreme Court contended with the issues of Indian autonomy and gender discrimination.[26] Julia Martinez and one of her children, Audrey Martinez, challenged the Santa Clara Pueblo membership ordinance that disqualified Martinez's children because she had married outside the tribe. Tribal members qualify for property rights, shares in the profits of tribal industries and

---

[22] Graham Walker, 'The Idea of Non-liberal Constitutionalism', in Ian Shapiro and Will Kymlicka (eds), *Ethnicity and Group Rights* (New York: New York University Press, 2000): 154–184.

[23] Will Kymlicka and Raphael Cohen-Almagor, 'Democracy and Multiculturalism', in Raphael Cohen-Almagor (ed.), *Challenges to Democracy* (London: Ashgate, 2000): 106–108.

[24] Will Kymlicka, *Liberalism, Community, and Culture* (Oxford: Clarendon Press, 1989); Will Kymlicka, 'Do We Need a Liberal Theory of Minority Rights? Reply to Carens, Young, Parekh and Forst', *Constellations*, 4(1) (1997): 72–87; Will Kymlicka, *Multicultural Citizenship: A Liberal Theory of Minority* (Oxford: Oxford University Press, 2000): 35–48.

[25] Gloria Valencia-Weber, 'Three Stories in One: The Story of Santa Clara Pueblo v. Martinez', in C. Goldberg, K.K. Washburn and P.P. Frickey (eds), *Indian Law Stories* (New York: Thomson Reuters/Foundation Press 2011): 456.

[26] *Santa Clara Pueblo v. Martinez* 436 US 49 (1978).

certain paying jobs on the Pueblo. The same ordinance did not place similar restrictions on men. Martinez appealed to the American justice system, seeking declaratory and injunctive relief, claiming that this ordinance discriminated against her on basis of gender, in contravention of the ICRA which states that no Indian tribe in exercising powers of self-government shall 'deny to any person within its jurisdiction the equal protection of its laws or deprive any person of liberty or property without due process of law'.[27] Although the Martinez children were raised on the reservation and continued to reside there as adults, they were denied basic rights. As a result of their exclusion from membership they were not eligible to vote in tribal elections or to hold secular tribal offices. They had no right to remain on the reservation in the event of their mother's death, or to inherit their mother's home or her possessory interests in the communal lands. The Pueblo successfully erected external protections to exclusively reserve land for their own community and did not wish to forfeit possession. Land for them is a source of cultural identity, not mere real estate.[28] Respondent Julia Martinez engaged with the tribe elders in an attempt to change the membership rule, but to no avail. Then she appealed to the courts, seeking justice. She was certified to represent a class consisting of all women who were members of the Santa Clara Pueblo and who had married men who were not members of the Pueblo, while Audrey Martinez was certified as the class representative of all children born to marriages between Santa Claran women and men who were not members of the Pueblo.[29]

The Santa Clara Pueblo argued that the 1968 ICRA did not authorize civil actions in federal court for relief against a tribe or its officials. The Supreme Court, *per* Justice Thurgood Marshall who delivered the opinion of the Court, in which Justices Burger, Brennan, Stewart, Powell, Stevens and Rehnquist joined (Justice Blackman took no part in the consideration or decision of the case) agreed, guaranteeing strong tribal autonomy except when Congress provided for federal judicial review. Marshall J. conceded that Indian tribes have been recognized as possessing common law immunity from suit traditionally enjoyed by sovereign powers.[30] The Pueblo successfully campaigned for external protections for devolution of powers to enable them to make decisions regarding their community. The court emphasized that the role of courts in adjusting relations between and among tribes and their members is restrained. The tribes are better suited to understand their own culture. Congress retains authority expressly to authorize civil actions for relief if the tribes themselves prove deficient in applying and enforcing its

---

[27] The Indian Civil Rights Act of 1968 (ICRA), 25 U.S.C.§§ 1301–1304 (ICRA), www.courts.ca .gov/documents/Indian-Civil-Rights-Act-of-1968.pdf.

[28] Valencia-Weber, 'Three Stories in One', 458.

[29] *Santa Clara Pueblo v. Martinez* 436 US 49 (1978), at 53. See also Nell Jessup Newton, 'Federal Power over Indians: Its Sources, Scope and Limitations', *University of Pennsylvania Law Review*, 132(2) (1984): 195–288.

[30] *Santa Clara Pueblo v. Martinez* 436 US 49 (1978), at 58.

substantive provisions. 'But unless and until Congress makes clear its intention to permit the additional intrusion on tribal sovereignty that adjudication of such actions in a federal forum would represent', the court is constrained to find that the ICRA 'does not impliedly authorize actions for declaratory or injunctive relief against either the tribe or its officers'.[31]

Justice White disagreed. In his dissent he wrote that the majority of the court had substantially undermined the goal of the ICRA, in particular its purpose to protect 'individual Indians from arbitrary and unjust actions of tribal governments'.[32] While acknowledging that Indian tribes have had special status in American law, White J. did not think that the tribe was insular from state scrutiny.[33] He thought that in this case there was a need to interfere in the Pueblo's affairs because its membership law was unjust. White J. reminded his fellow justices that the ICRA in itself was an intrusion into tribal affairs. Thus, he thought that the federal courts have jurisdiction to consider the merits of the respondents' claims.[34]

I side with Justice White. The non-liberal constitutionalism of the Santa Clara Pueblo is unjust from the point of view of liberal principles. The court judgement left Native American women with a general right but without recourse for remedy. The Pueblo courts were left to uphold their rules which discriminated against women (as well as Christians). Clearly, for the federal courts to overturn the decisions of the Pueblo courts and impose liberal principles is a problematic move. We need to seek a solution that would take into account the risk of denigrating the group's own system of government and courts, the high levels of legitimacy of the governance system in the eyes of its own members as well as rights of women and children, and the liberal goal of arriving at a just and reasonable formula. Reasonableness consists in equitableness whereby an individual respects other persons' rights as well as her own.[35] In this case, mutual respect is clearly lacking. The severity of rights violations within the minority group, the insufficient dispute resolution mechanisms and the inability of individuals to leave the community if they so desire without penalty justify state intervention to uphold the dissenters' basic rights.

While acknowledging that imposing liberal principles on self-governing indigenous groups is problematic, and that attempts to impose liberal principles might backfire since they are perceived as a form of aggression or paternalistic colonialism, it is unjust to accept that it is, according to the Pueblo, a matter of cultural survival to

---

[31] Ibid., 72. For further discussion, see Gloria Valencia-Weber, 'Santa Clara Pueblo v. Martinez: Twenty-Five Years of Disparate Cultural Visions: An Essay Introducing the Case for Re-argument before the American Indian Nations Supreme Court', *Kansas Journal of Law & Pubic Policy*, 14(1) (2004), https://papers.ssrn.com/sol3/papers.cfm?abstract_id=2265961.

[32] *Santa Clara Pueblo v. Martinez* 436 US 49 (1978), at 73.

[33] Ibid., at 75.

[34] Ibid., 83.

[35] Alan Gewirth, 'The Rationality of Reasonableness', *Synthese*, 57(2) (1983): 225–247.

oppose women's claim for upholding their natural right to equality. After the *Martinez* decision, women who were denied tribal membership lost essential benefits including federal payments, education and medical care. Julia Martinez's daughter Audrey was denied medical treatment. Eventually, Audrey was able to secure health care but later died from strokes relating to her illness.[36] In the name of culture, the Pueblo should not deny women equal individual protections that every American citizen enjoys. Reconciling multiculturalism and liberalism requires invoking the Rawlsian Principle of Equal Liberty: each person has an equal right to the most extensive liberties compatible with similar liberties for all (Chapter 1). The state should provide education, minimum income and health care for all.[37]

By accentuating tribal sovereignty and narrowly interpreting the statutes in such a way that saw no urgency to interfere in the Pueblo affairs, the Supreme Court failed to appreciate Martinez's and other women's predicament. The court accorded respect for tribal sovereignty, protected the 'unique political, cultural, and economic needs of tribal governments'[38] and had deliberately chosen not to extend every provision of the Bill of Rights to tribes, thereby accepting the Pueblo claims. On the other hand, in balancing tribal sovereignty vis-à-vis gender rights my view decidedly favours the latter. It is the duty of the liberal state to protect the basic rights of vulnerable populations and not to leave women at the mercy of men who employ cultural justifications to harm them and undermine their existence. Gender equality and mutual respect should be promoted as vital values. Chauvinistic group discrimination should not enjoy any form of legitimacy. Granted that liberal institutions can only work if liberal beliefs have been internalized by the members of the self-governing society, education and dialogue should be implemented rather than granting legitimacy to unjust discrimination.

Principally, as Brian Barry noted, the Pueblo cannot run a sub-state that is religiously exclusive, certainly not in a liberal society. If the Pueblo want to retain their special political status, they should be required to observe the constraints on the use of political power that are imposed by liberal justice. They should have to accept that exercising political power cannot legitimately be used to foster religious and gender discrimination.[39] This is in line with the Convention on the Elimination of All Forms of Discrimination against Women, which holds (Article 16) that men and women have the same right to enter into marriage, and that both

---

[36] Christofferson, 'Tribal Courts' Failure to Protect Native American Women', 169.

[37] Rawls, A *Theory of Justice*, 302.

[38] *Santa Clara Pueblo v. Martinez*, at 62. For further discussion about the tensions between minority group rights and gender equality, and about conflicts over the culture defence in American criminal law, aboriginal membership rules, tribal sovereignty and polygamy, see Sarah Song, *Justice, Gender, and the Politics of Multiculturalism* (Cambridge: Cambridge University Press, 2007).

[39] Brian Barry, *Culture and Equality* (Cambridge, MA: Harvard University Press, 2001): 189.

spouses enjoy the same rights in respect of the ownership, acquisition, management, administration, enjoyment and disposition of property.[40]

Conversely, Chandran Kukathas supports group rights and autonomy even if they trump individual rights. He argues that the good society is a free society and a free society is one that upholds freedom of association.[41] In his extreme liberal view there are hardly any restrictions on what communities can do to their members. Kukathas simply mistrusts the government to act prudently without exploiting its powers. He assumes that any government intervention is likely to violate individuals' freedom of association and freedom of conscience and, therefore, a hands-off policy is warranted.

Kukathas' theory does not see 'cultural integration' or what he terms 'cultural engineering' as a part of the state's raison d'être. He rejects the idea of making the boundaries, the symbols and the cultural character of the state matters of justice.[42] Consequently, overarching tolerance is advocated regarding a wide array of controversial practices that include the denial of school education to children, arranged marriages, denial of medical care to members and the infliction of cruel punishment on members. All of this is possible in Kukathas' concept of toleration.[43] Kukathas explains at length why a free society should tolerate a variety of associations and practices, including those that do not value freedom or abide by the principle of toleration, and that embrace seemingly intolerable practices. While Kukathas acknowledges the importance of individual choice, he does not think it is important to ensure that the conditions within communities exist to ensure that individuals are free to make their own choices and live by them. In accordance with Kukathas' unconstrained and, indeed, unreasonable liberal theory, illiberal communities within liberal democracy can inflict all sorts of harm, physical and non-physical, on their own members.

Kukathas' theory is a perfect example for the urgent need to acknowledge the 'democratic catch' (Chapter 1). Liberal democracy perceives tolerance as a virtue. It embodies a normative stance geared to promote equal respect and self-determination when the latter results in an allocation of resources and involves some form of legal coercion. Respecting our fellow citizens entails that we should see them, in Kantian terms, as ends rather than means, appreciate diversity and differences, and not be quick to judge the others as 'strange' or 'peculiar' only because they adhere to a different way of life, or to a different conception of the good. Democratic government provides people with opportunities to develop themselves. However, tolerance should not provide carte blanche for abuse. Tolerance

---

[40] International Convention for Elimination of All Forms of Discrimination against Women (1967), www.ipu.org/PDF/publications/cedaw_en.pdf.

[41] Chandran Kukathas, *The Liberal Archipelago: A Theory of Diversity and Freedom* (Oxford: Oxford University Press, 2003): 76.

[42] Chandran Kukathas, 'Cultural Toleration', *Nomos*, 39 (1997): 69–104; Kukathas, *The Liberal Archipelago*, 15.

[43] Kukathas, *The Liberal Archipelago*, 134.

should not be exploited to enable gross abuse of human rights. I agree with Karl Popper that it is an absurd proposition to suggest that we should tolerate the intolerant with little or no regard to consequences.[44] The delicate task is to maintain a balance between group rights and the preservation of basic human rights, otherwise the very foundation of tolerance might provide the intolerant the tools for continued abuse.

Kukathas does not trust liberal justice because this concept of justice would lead to state interference and compulsion. Liberal justice cannot condone deep cultural diversity.[45] He acknowledges that clitoridectomy, the denial of blood transfusions and religious coercion are all oppressive. Yet he maintains that if the concern is oppression, 'there is just as much reason to hold (more) firmly to the principles of toleration – since the threat of oppression is as likely to come from outside the minority community as it is from within'.[46] Kukathas is more concerned with speculative future consequences of oppression than the here-and-now tangible oppression. Hypothetical fear of government abuse is more persuasive for him than present denial of basic rights. But silence and passivity will not stop abuse.

Kukathas concedes that there are cases where there is clear evidence of terrible practices. He believes that persuasion, rather than force, is the preferred, more effective and less damaging means of fostering change from the outside.[47] On this issue Kukathas and I agree. I also endorse deliberative democracy as the prime means to bring about change. But what if the leaders of the community are not open to debate and persuasion? Kukathas would then say, 'At least I tried', and leave the continuation of abuse intact, whereas I argue that there are instances where external argumentation might fall on deaf ears and then we should resort to action that is deemed necessary to end abuse and preserve basic human rights. Kukathas' arguments might be convincing in the realm of philosophy alone, not in reality.[48]

Unlike Kukathas, my liberal theory of just, reasonable multiculturalism perceives justice as a major, indeed indispensable, component. Applying Rawlsian reasoning (Chapter 1), conceptions that directly conflict with the principles of justice, or that wish to control the machinery of state and practices so as to coerce the citizenry by employing effective intolerance, should be excluded.[49] In view of the general facts

---

[44] Karl R. Popper, *The Open Society and Its Enemies* (London: Routledge and Kegan Paul, 1962): Vol. 1, 265.

[45] Kukathas, *The Liberal Archipelago*, 188.

[46] Ibid., 135–136.

[47] Ibid., 136–137.

[48] For further critique of Kukathas, see Jeff Spinner-Halev, *Surviving Diversity: Religion and Democratic Citizenship* (Baltimore, MD: Johns Hopkins University Press, 2000): 81–85; Barry, *Culture and Equality*, 239; Monique Deveaux, *Gender and Justice in Multicultural Liberal States* (Oxford: Oxford University Press, 2009): 41–53.

[49] Rawls, *A Theory of Justice*; John Rawls, 'The Priority of Right and Ideas of the Good', *Philosophy & Public Affairs*, 17(4) (1988): 251–276, at 266. Cf. John Rawls, *Political Liberalism* (New York: Columbia University Press, 1993): 140–144.

that characterize a democracy's public political culture and, in particular, the fact of *reasonable* pluralism, different political conceptions should be part of an overlapping consensus. Rawls assumes this consensus to consist of reasonable comprehensive doctrines likely to persist and gain adherents over time if the basic structure is just. The Pueblo that grew up in the United States have acquired a normally sufficient sense of justice so that they know they have the right to protest against unjust institutions. They appealed to the state courts. The liberal state and the illiberal indigenous groups need to come to some sort of *modus vivendi* compromise. This means that the majority should strive to prevent the violation of some individual rights within the minority community. The liberal state should not stand by and do nothing. Since an indigenous group which rules in an illiberal way acts unjustly, such that its norms would not be accepted by the Rawlsian veil of ignorance, liberals have a right – indeed a responsibility – to speak out against such injustice and to support any efforts the group makes to liberalize their culture. Since the most enduring forms of liberalization are those that result from internal reform, the primary focus for liberals outside the group should be to provide this sort of support.

In 2012, Santa Clara Pueblo's members voted to grant membership to the offspring of Pueblo women with men of other cultures. The non-member resident population was becoming more sizeable compared with the tribal member resident population, and the Tribal Council realized that and amended the discriminatory rule.[50] Indeed, preferably agitation for a more liberal order should come from within the indigenous community; however, change may be assisted by outside civil society groups. Incentives can be provided, in a non-coercive way, for further liberal reforms that would promote gender equality in a deliberative, consensual way, by emphasizing the merits of just distribution of resources, mutual respect and reasonable accommodations that value tradition and the inherent dignity of all members of the community, notwithstanding gender.

Another North American country, Canada, has also experienced similar challenges with its indigenous people. The following case is concerned with granting just and reasonable exit rights to those who wish to lead their lives independently of their community. Having an exit opportunity is vital for members who feel oppressed by their culture. As explained in Chapter 2, whether it is justified for the liberal state to intervene in affairs of an indigenous tribe that restricts its members' freedom of conscience depends on how the community in question is governed, that is, whether it is governed by a tyrannical leader who prevents members from leaving the community, or whether the tribal governance has broad support and religious dissidents are free to leave.

---

[50] Tom Sharpe, 'Santa Clara Pueblo Vote on Member Rules Leaves Loose Ends', *The New Mexican* (1 May 2012), www.santafenewmexican.com/news/local_news/santa-clara-pueblo-vote-on-member-rules-leaves-loose-ends/article_3ea83343–5059–5f87-aa25-a473d336aac1.html.

DENYING REASONABLE EXIT RIGHTS: *HOFER V. HOFER* AND *CANADA V. LAVELL*

Exiting a community is not easy. Uprooting demands sacrifice. Community moulds and shapes one's identity and provides home, shelter and a frame of reference. Often people define who they are in relation to their community. People who decide to make a significant change in their lives and leave their community should be able to retain their security and dignity. Barriers to exit include language, demanding a forfeit of accumulated lands or property, demanding that family and friends shun anyone who leaves the community, denying education or providing limited education.[51] Having a reasonable alternative is important. Opportunities for exit should be made available for members who cannot develop their capacities and who feel at a loss within their present community. Those who leave need to have a receptive community that would be willing to accept and accommodate them.

In Canada the relationship between the government and the Native peoples was marred by policies of genocide, countless broken treaties and Canada's ongoing failure to recognize the nationhood of Aboriginal peoples.[52] *Hofer v. Hofer* dealt with the powers of the Hutterite Church over its members.[53] The Hutterites are spiritual descendants of the Anabaptists. Anabaptists believe that baptism is valid only when candidates confess their faith in Christ and want to be baptized. They live in large agricultural communities called colonies, within which there is no private property. Members of the Hofer family, lifelong members of a Hutterite colony, were expelled for apostasy. They demanded their share of the colony's assets, which they had helped create with their years of labour. When the colony refused, the two ex-members sued in court. They objected to the fact that they had 'no right at any time in their life to leave the Colony where they are living unless they abandon literally everything ... even the clothes they are wearing'.[54] The Hutterites defended this practice on the grounds that freedom of religion protects a congregation's ability to live in accordance with its religious doctrine, even if this limits individual freedom. People who wished to leave the community were subjected to designated mechanisms of coercion to make their lives difficult, forcing them to reconsider their decision. Coercion was invoked through social pressure, with significant group penalties against dissenters. Are these internal restrictions just and reasonable?

The Canadian Supreme Court in a six to one decision accepted this Hutterite claim. The majority opinion (Cartwright C.J.C., Martland, Judson, Ritchie, Hall

---

[51] Jacob T. Levy, *The Multiculturalism of Fear* (New York: Oxford University Press, 2000): 113.

[52] Deveaux, *Gender and Justice in Multicultural Liberal States*, 129.

[53] *Hofer et al. v. Hofer et al.* (1970) S.C.R. 958.

[54] Ibid., 21. For further discussion, see William Janzen, *Limits of Liberty: The Experiences of Mennonite, Hutterite, and Doukhobour Communities in Canada* (Toronto: University of Toronto Press, 1990): 67. On exit rights, see Annamari Vitikainen, *The Limits of Liberal Multiculturalism: Towards an Individuated Approach to Cultural Diversity* (Houndmills: Palgrave, 2015): 127–150.

and Spence JJ.) did not regard this as a case in which the court can be asked to relieve against a forfeiture, for by the terms of the articles signed by the Hutterite members the appellant never had any individual ownership of any of the assets of the colony. Cartwright C.J.C. added that the 'principle of freedom of religion is not violated by an individual who agrees that if he abandons membership in a specified church he shall give up any claim to certain assets'.[55] Freedom of religion enables the community to live in accordance with its religious doctrine notwithstanding whether its way of life may limit individual freedom.

Yet again I side with the minority opinion. Justice Louis-Philippe Pigeon's dissent represents a just, liberal approach. Pigeon J. started by discussing the nature of the colony. He established that the colony was a commercial undertaking, not a church. The land was used essentially for growing crops and raising livestock. Its major part was sold to customers.[56] Therefore, the case should not be decided by the application of rules of law governing churches. Justice Pigeon acknowledged that the Hofer conduct was obviously of concern to the Hutterites and that the dispute was real and painful. The way to decide the dispute was through deciphering the principle of freedom of religion. Justice Pigeon noted that the usual liberal notion of freedom of religion 'includes the right of each individual to change his religion at will'.[57] Hence churches 'cannot make rules having the effect of depriving their members of this fundamental freedom'.[58] The proper scope of religious authority is therefore 'limited to what is consistent with freedom of religion as properly understood, that is, freedom for the individual not only to adopt a religion but also to abandon it at will'.[59] Pigeon J. thought that it was as nearly impossible as can be for people in a Hutterite community to reject irreligious teachings, due to the high cost of changing their religion, and so were effectively deprived of freedom of religion.[60]

Interestingly, four years later Justice Pigeon sided with the majority in the case of Jeanette Corbiere Lavell who lost her challenge to invalidate the Canadian Indian Act that provided that Native women who married non-Native men lost their status as Indian, as did their children. The Act did not penalize men in the same fashion. Under the Act, the only way a woman might regain status was to remarry a status man. After Lavell was notified that she had lost her status, she filed a lawsuit on the basis that this measure was in violation of the 1960 Canadian Bill of Rights because it discriminated against her based on gender. In 1971, the York County Court ruled

[55] *Hofer et al. v. Hofer et al.* (1970), 963.
[56] Ibid., 982.
[57] Ibid., 984.
[58] Ibid.
[59] Ibid. Brian Berry argues that the Hutterites were within their right to expel heretics. But the court erred in concluding that the ex-members' claim to some sort of compensation from the Hutterites should also fail. Barry, *Culture and Equality*, 163.
[60] *Hofer et al. v. Hofer et al.* (1970), 985. For a general discussion, see Yossi Katz and John Lehr, *The Hutterites in Canada and the United States* (Regina, SK: University of Regina Press, 2012).

that Lavell had not been deprived of equality under the law, since the Bill of Rights afforded her the same protections as other non-status women. Lavell then petitioned the Federal Court of Appeals that reversed the decision, holding that the Indian Act did not afford equality to indigenous women, and recommended that the Act be repealed for failing to adhere to the laws established in the Bill of Rights. In a narrow five to four decision, the Supreme Court of Canada reversed the Federal Court of Appeals' ruling, holding that the Indian Act did not violate the respondents' right to 'equality before the law' under the Canadian Bill of Rights.[61] Here, Pigeon J. did not wish to reach a firm conclusion as to whether the statutory provisions exhibited discrimination by reason of sex.[62]

Yet again, the court respected the structure created by the parliament for the internal administration of the life of Indians on their reserves and allowed the continued discrimination against women. The status provisions worked as an agent of disenfranchisement, which enabled the marginalization of indigenous women and institutionalized male privilege and an environment that oppressed women. In his dissent, Laskin J. said that the Canadian Bill of Rights dictates that laws of Canada shall operate without discrimination by reason of sex, and this provision cannot be ignored in the operation of the Indian Act.[63] Discriminatory treatment on the basis of race or colour or sex should be barred.

In a liberal democracy, people have a capacity to form and revise their conception of the good. Hence, the power of religious communities over their own members must be such that individuals can freely and effectively exercise that capacity. While liberals appreciate culture and tradition, perceiving them as a part of a chain that is important to members in any given culture, this consideration must be balanced against religious freedom. Religion and culture are matters of personal choice and include *freedom from religion and culture*. Citizens in a democracy should enjoy the ability to choose their way of life and to change it at will. The way to deal with people who wish to leave the community is through deliberation, not coercion; through compromise and mutual respect, not by showing contempt; by acknowledging members' contribution to the community, not by denying recognition; showing respect for their labour, not punishing and penalizing them. Fair distribution of assets is just and reasonable. People should have a share of the communal resources. A community that keeps its members through means of punishment and deterrence, that denies them mechanisms of deliberation and does not seek compromise when disagreement arises is not a model to follow, is certainly not in the confines of liberal democracy.

It is noted that Article 2 of the Declaration on the Elimination of All Forms of Intolerance and of Discrimination Based on Religion or Belief holds: 'No one shall

---

[61] *Canada (AG) v. Lavell* [1974] S.C.R. 1349.
[62] Ibid., 1390.
[63] Ibid., 1383.

be subject to discrimination by any State, institution, group of persons, or person on grounds of religion or other beliefs.'[64] Interestingly, when the United Nations adopted the Declaration on the Rights of Indigenous Peoples on 13 September 2007, Canada was one of four countries that voted against. The other three were Australia, New Zealand and the United States. The declaration that is very relevant to the four opposing countries establishes a universal framework of minimum standards for the survival, dignity and well-being of the indigenous peoples of the world. It recognizes and reaffirms that 'indigenous individuals are entitled without discrimination to all human rights recognized in international law, and that indigenous peoples possess collective rights which are indispensable for their existence, well-being and integral development as peoples'.[65] Using the term 'indigenous individuals' rather than indigenous groups aims to establish just, reasonable multiculturalism. Only in 2016 did Canada officially adopt the declaration.[66] Canada was the last of the four countries to reverse its position.[67]

ARRANGED AND FORCED MARRIAGES FOR GIRLS

We need to distinguish between arranged marriage in which families take a leading role, but the parties have the free will and choice to accept or decline the arrangement, and forced marriage where one or both people do not (or in cases of people with learning disabilities cannot) consent to the marriage and where pressure or abuse is used. While the latter is coercive the former is not. While forced marriages should be denounced as unjust, arranged marriages can be accepted. In England and Wales arranged marriage is permitted while forced marriage is illegal. Forced marriage includes taking someone overseas to force her to marry (whether or not the forced marriage takes place) or marrying someone who lacks the mental capacity to

---

[64] Declaration on the Elimination of All Forms of Intolerance and of Discrimination Based on Religion or Belief (25 November 1981), www.un.org/documents/ga/res/36/a36r055.htm.

[65] 61/295. *United Nations Declaration on the Rights of Indigenous Peoples* (13 September 2007).

[66] 'Canada Officially Adopts UN Declaration on Rights of Indigenous Peoples', *CBC* (10 May 2016), www.cbc.ca/news/indigenous/canada-adopting-implementing-un-rights-declaration-1 .3575272.

[67] The Australian government announced its support for the *united nations declaration* in 2009, www.humanrights.gov.au/our-work/aboriginal-and-torres-strait-islander-social-justice/projects/ un-declaration-rights. The New Zealand government officially endorsed the United Nations Declaration in April 2010, www.survivalinternational.org/news/5846, and the US government endorsed it in 2011: Announcement of U.S. Support for the United Nations Declaration on the Rights of Indigenous Peoples, U.S. DEP'T OF STATE 1–2 (12 January 2011), https://2009–2017 .state.gov/s/srgia/154553.htm. For further discussion, see Tsosie, 'Reconceptualizing Tribal Rights'; Avigail Eisenberg, 'Reasoning about the Identity of Aboriginal People', in Stephen Tierney (ed.), *Accommodating Cultural Diversity* (Aldershot: Ashgate, 2007): 79–97.

consent to the marriage.[68] It is estimated that 10 per cent of the arranged marriages are forced.[69]

Arranged marriages with adults for girls under 16 or 18 years old might constitute serious mischief to these girls. We can assume that such unequal marriage will result in subordination, discrimination, coercion and abuse. Commonly, such a marriage is between a grown-up man and a young female (I have never heard of a cultural phenomenon in which female adults marry young males).[70] In such a marriage the young female will have great difficulties in developing relationships that are built around values of equality, mutual respect and self-determination. Such inegalitarian arranged marriages are unreasonable in liberal terms. They gravely undermine children's/adolescent's ability to enjoy long-term basic human goods and relationships as they are hampered by a commitment decided for them by their families without their consent. The question is whether the state can and should intervene to prohibit them.

Consider the following scenarios:

1. Pado (42 years old) and Betu (8 years old) wish to register for marriage in Philadelphia. The Registrar will be justified in declining their request.
2. Abdul and Miah are a married couple. Abdul is thirty-four years older than Miah. In their culture in Yemen, such a marriage is common. When Miah is 18, the couple immigrate to a liberal society with their children. In this case, it is reasonable to hold that the liberal state should not intervene as the couple have built a life together. Miah is an adult. In a liberal society the option of divorce is available to her. It is only when Miah is coerced to continue the marriage against her will that the state should come to her assistance.
3. Saadi (42 years old) and Tohar (15 years old), another Yemenite married couple, immigrate to a liberal society. They have been living together for six years. Should liberal democracy recognize the marriage?

The last example is a hard case. It is harder if the couple has children. The line of reasoning I wish to pursue has principled as well as consequentialist dimensions. As usual, we need to examine whether the culture has historical claims, whether it

---

[68] Forced marriage, www.gov.uk/stop-forced-marriage. In the United Kingdom the Forced Marriage Unit (FMU) is a joint Foreign and Commonwealth Office and Home Office unit which leads on government policy, outreach and casework. Its jurisdiction includes the UK where support is provided to any individual and overseas where consular assistance is given to British nationals. The FMU operates a helpline to provide advice and support to forced marriage victims as well as to professionals. The assistance includes safety advice and helping 'reluctant sponsors'. In extreme circumstances the FMU assists with rescues of victims held against their will. See 'Forced Marriage', www.gov.uk/guidance/forced-marriage.

[69] Deveaux, *Gender and Justice in Multicultural Liberal States*, 164.

[70] There are, of course, individual cases where older women marry younger men, but this has nothing to do with group rites.

coerces others to follow its norm and whether children and their families have protected exit rights if they do not wish to follow the cultural norm. We need to weigh the rights of the child, the harms of separation and the pros and cons of state interference to the child and to the family at large. The liberal state should certainly reflect and consider, aiming to reach a solution through means of deliberation that would be just and reasonable. Let me demonstrate the relevant considerations by deliberating the behaviour of the Israeli establishment towards Jewish-Yemenite immigrants during the 1950s.

For these immigrants, who were Jewish observant, arrival in Israel presented a cherished opportunity to practice religion even more strongly in the sanctity of the Holy Land. They did not wish to break with tradition, their old customs or cultural heritage. They wished to maintain their traditional way of life, folkways and norms. They expected that the place of men and women, their status and honour, would be as it was in Yemen. At that time, testimonials were brought before the two chief rabbis of Israel, Rabbi Herzog and Rabbi Uziel, that young women were encouraged to leave their older husbands. This action was made upon the assumption that teenage girls were forced to marry older people in Yemen.[71] In 1950, the Marriage Age Law was passed, setting the minimum age at 17.[72] The motivation was well-intended. Israeli decision-makers wished to 'save' women from their 'locked' situation. The problem was that in many instances no action was taken to verify whether girls preferred to live with their husbands. Social workers and advisors took the liberty of interfering in this delicate issue of marital matters without checking other factors beside the age of the woman. The age factor, in their view, was the only significant consideration that justified intervention, aiming to break the marriage. This behaviour was a reflection of the then prevailing governmental attitude towards immigrants from Asia and Africa.[73] The absorbing elite believed that the best of the people and the best of the nation required paternalism; that they had to show 'the light' to the Yemenite immigrants, and that in due course these immigrants would thank them for this involvement. This was not the case. The immigrants perceived this paternalistic measure as an arrogant interference in their affairs, displaying ethnocentrism and misunderstanding of their norms. With due appreciation of the sincere motives on the part of the establishment, it was done in a crude way that disrespected the feelings of the people concerned, and probably resulted on

---

[71] Archives of the State of Israel, G5543/3631, file 607 (II). See also G5543/3631, file 607 (III).

[72] Marriage Age Law, 5710-1950. In 2013 the minimum age for marriage was raised to 18.

[73] Raphael Cohen-Almagor, 'Cultural Pluralism and the Israeli Nation-Building Ideology', *International Journal of Middle East Studies*, 27 (1995): 461–484; Bat-Sheva Margalit-Stern, 'Model Friendship', *Kathedra*, 118 (2006) (Hebrew): 115–144; Adia Menelson-Maoz, *Multiculturalism in Israel* (West Lafayette, IN: Purdue University Press, 2014); Seth J. Frantzman, 'The Tragedy and Shame of 1950s Israel's Treatment of Yemenite Children', *The Jerusalem Post* (29 December 2016), www.jpost.com/Opinion/The-tragedy-and-shame-of-1950s-Israels-treatment-of-Yemenite-children-476888; Yair Altman, 'Where Did the Assets of Yemenite Immigrants Disappear?', *Israel Hayom* (21 October 2018) (Israeli daily, Hebrew).

many occasions in more harm than good. Instead of opening channels of communication with the community, identifying desirable ends and seeking accommodation that would benefit first and foremost the women in question, the state behaved more as a bull in a china shop, dictating instead of deliberating, using its coercive authority rather than seeking constructive compromise. Women of course, young and old, should have the opportunity of opting out and asking for divorce. But their opinion should be sought and be considered.

Another pertinent issue was polygamy. In Yemenite culture polygamy was accepted, and the state of Israel could not have it. Freedom of choice is important provided it is not discriminatory. It is just to prohibit polygamy because it discriminates against women.[74] But if both men and women would be free to marry as many partners as they wish, meaning that both polygyny and polyandry were to be allowed in a certain community, then we may honour freedom of choice. Marriage between two individuals is normative, and norms may change. Indeed, norms have been changing. In this age, marriage between people of the same gender is becoming more acceptable. This idea was perceived as an aberration in previous centuries.[75] Today, most countries that permit polygamy are countries with a Muslim majority or with a sizeable Muslim minority. In India, polygamy is legal only for Muslims. In Russia and South Africa, polygamy is illegal but not criminalized.[76]

DISCRIMINATION AGAINST WOMEN IN JUDAISM

Numerous passages make it clear that women are not in the same category as men. The hierarchy between men and women is clear. It manifested itself from the very first story of the creation. First it is written in Genesis that God created mankind in his own image, 'in the image of God he created them; male and female he created them'.[77] But in the following chapter qualification and clarification are provided. God did not create man and woman together. Instead he created man and then he realized that Adam needed some assistance, 'a helper suitable for him'.[78] Wild

---

[74] Polygamy has been documented in 80 per cent of societies across the globe often to the detriment of women. In times of war, when many men are away and will possibly not return home, some women would rather share a man than have no man. See Dena Hassouneh-Phillips, 'Polygamy and Wife Abuse: A Qualitative Study of Muslim Women in America', *Health Care for Women International*, 22 (2001): 735–748. See also Salman Elbedour, Anthony J. Onwuegbuzie, Corin Caridine and Hasan Abu-Saad, 'The Effect of Polygamous Marital Structure on Behavioral, Emotional, and Academic Adjustment in Children: A Comprehensive Review of the Literature', *Clinical Child and Family Psychology Review*, 5 (2002): 255–271; House of Commons, *Polygamy* (London, 20 November 2018).

[75] Breana Noble, 'First Five Countries to Recognise Gay Marriage', *Newsmax* (15 June 2015), www.newsmax.com/FastFeatures/same-sex-marriage-legalized-countries/2015/06/15/id/650672/.

[76] Neel Burton, 'The Pros and Cons of Polygamy', *Psychology Today* (4 January 2018), www.psychologytoday.com/gb/blog/hide-and-seek/201801/the-pros-and-cons-polygamy.

[77] Genesis 1:27.

[78] Genesis 2:18.

animals and all the birds in the sky were provided for the man but no suitable helper was found for Adam. Thus, God decided to create a woman. In other words, the creation of the woman was decided after exhausting all other alternatives, and the woman's role on earth was decided from the start. Realizing that man needed help, God created a woman, but he did not create her in the same way that he created Adam. God formed a man from the dust of the ground and breathed into his nostrils the breath of life, while the woman was created from the man. God caused the man to fall into a deep sleep and while he was sleeping, he took one of the man's ribs and made a woman from the rib. The man said, 'This is now bone of my bones and flesh of my flesh; she shall be called "woman", for she was taken out of man.'[79] And when the woman disobeyed the words of God and ate from the tree of the knowledge of good and evil, her punishment included: 'Your desire will be for your husband, and he will rule over you.'[80]

Jewish law specifies the ways in which the wife must accept man's rule, tend to matters of the home and fulfil all the duties of practical daily life. She is obligated to serve her husband, revere him like a king and honour him exceedingly, obey him and do his will. She should 'fill for him his cup, make ready his bed and wash his face, hands and feet'.[81] A woman should raise her man up. 'When he is angry, she should calm him; when he is hurt, she should soothe him; when he has been done bad to, she should comfort him; when he is worried, she should restore him; when he is pressured, she should minimize requests; and cancel her will for her husband. She should diminish his sadness, his worry or anything which is hard on his heart.'[82] She must cook food for him and their children and provide clothing.[83]

According to *Halacha*, in the public sphere women cannot serve in power positions. They are excluded from the executive and judicial offices as well as from the spiritual sphere. The Torah dictates, 'be sure to appoint over you a king',[84] not a queen.[85] Women are invalid to serve as judges.[86] Women are invalid

---

[79] Genesis 2:23.

[80] Genesis 3:16. For further discussion, see Susannah Heschel, '"Wherever You See the Trace of Man, There I Stand Before You": The Complexities of God and Human Dignity within Judaism', in Dieter Grimm, Alexandra Kemmerer and Christoph Möllers (eds), *Human Dignity in Context* (Munich: Hart, 2018): 129–161.

[81] Babylonian Talmud: Tractate Kethuboth, Folio 61a, www.come-and-hear.com/kethuboth/kethuboth_61.html.

[82] Rabbi Forsythe, 'Shalom Bayis (Peaceful Marriage) Torah and Family Issues When Considering Divorce', www.shemayisrael.com/rabbiforsythe/shalombayis/issues.htm.

[83] Babylonian Talmud: Tractate Yebamoth, Folio 63a, www.come-and-hear.com/yebamoth/yebamoth_63.html; Bava Metzia 59, www.dafyomi.co.il/bmetzia/points/bm-ps-059.htm.

[84] Deuteronomy 17.

[85] Maimonides, *Laws of Kings and Wars*, http://halakhah.com/rst/kingsandwars.pdf.

[86] Shulchan Aruch/Choshen Mishpat/7, http://en.wikisource.org/wiki/Shulchan_Aruch/Choshen_Mishpat/7. Although Deborah led Israel as a judge. The opening of Judges 4:4–5 says: 'At that time Deborah, a prophetess, wife of Lappidoth, was judging Israel. She used to sit under the palm of Deborah between Ramah and Bethel in the hill country of Ephraim; and the Israelites came up to her for judgment.'

witnesses.[87] They cannot give evidence.[88] In the spiritual sphere, as noted above, women cannot read from the Torah in public. This is in order to protect public honour.[89] In the private sphere women are always under the authority of men. First, under the authority of their fathers, and once they wed they are subject to their husbands.[90]

The Talmud invokes the idea of *kevod ha-tsibbur*, 'dignity of the congregation',[91] or *zila milta*, maintenance of propriety/modesty within the community, to prevent women from being called to read the Torah in the synagogue. It is considered breach of propriety (*zila be-hu milta*) were women to assist the masses in fulfilling their obligation to read the Torah.[92] Essentially, the exclusion of women is designed to promote the dignity of both men and women. With this exclusion men can concentrate on reading religious texts while women can focus on doing other things, perceived by Jewish sages as more 'meaningful' to women. That women's dignity is violated by giving precedence to the dignity of the community is not a consideration.

According to Jewish law, a married woman has no money or property of her own, and she is fully subjugated to her husband. When a wife dies the husband inherits her belongings, but when the husband dies his wife does not inherit his belongings.[93] A daughter does not inherit unless there are no sons. It is expected that a certain amount of the father's property be designated for his daughter's dowry and may be claimed from the brother's inheritance.[94] Sixty-six per cent of the Israeli population who are not very religious or who are secular are required to abide by these discriminatory beliefs and practices.[95]

---

[87] Deuteronomy 19:17.

[88] Babylonian Talmud: Tractate Baba Kamma 88a, www.come-and-hear.com/babakamma/baba kamma_88.html.

[89] The sages said: 'a woman should not read from the Torah mipnei kevod hatzibbur – out of respect for the congregation'. See Natalie Bergner, 'Qeri'at ha-Torah: Public Torah Reading', *Women of the Wall*, http://womenofthewall.org.il/qeriat-ha-torah-public-torah-reading/.

[90] Babylonian Talmud: Tractate Kethuboth 48a, www.come-and-hear.com/kethuboth/kethu both_48.html. For further discussion, see Rachel Biale, *Women and Jewish Law: The Essential Texts, Their History, and Their Relevance for Today* (New York: Schocken, 1995).

[91] Masechet Megillah 23a.

[92] Rabbi Aryeh A. Frimer, 'Women's Megilla Reading', www.daat.ac.il/daat/english/tfila/frimer2 .htm.

[93] Tractate Bava Batra 111b and Maimonides, Laws of Inheritance, chap. 1, *Halacha* eight.

[94] Tirzah Meacham, 'Legal-Religious Status of the Jewish Female', *Jewish Women Encyclopedia*, http://jwa.org/encyclopedia/article/legal-religious-status-of-jewish-female.

[95] According to the 2019 Religion and State Index (Hiddush, Hebrew), 48 per cent of the population define themselves as secular, while 18 per cent define themselves as traditional, not very religious. For further discussion, see Raphael Cohen-Almagor, 'Discrimination against Jewish Women in *Halacha* (Jewish Law) and in Israel', *British Journal of Middle Eastern Studies*, 45(2) (2018): 290–310.

DENYING EDUCATION TO WOMEN

What degree of freedom should be allowed to communities in deciding their educational matters? What is the duty of the state to ensure that citizens receive an acceptable standard of education? These two questions are at the centre of the following discussion here and in Chapter 8.

Jewish law (*Halacha*) holds that women are different than men. Contra the liberal premises of this book of gender equality, of justice as fairness and of mutual respect, these differences lead to unjustified inequalities. Reconciling between Judaism and liberalism is possible only if there is awareness and recognition that biological gender differences should not serve as pretence for discrimination.

In defence of the 'separate but equal' policy, Jewish law holds that men and women have different qualities. Men, it is explained, are anatomically and spiritually external, and often view life from a more external viewpoint. Women, on the other hand, are anatomically and spiritually internal. They see the world from a more internal and holistic perspective.[96] Women should not try to be men. God has assigned men for particular tasks, and women for others. Jewish women have their own mission, their own identity, their own worth. The Torah commands that 'A man shall not wear a woman's garment', so equally it commands that a man's garment shall not be on a woman.[97] Neither men nor women 'carry out their G-d given tasks or achieve self-fulfillment by imitating the other. A woman has no reason to feel inferior to a man, and therefore she has no need to try to be as a man.'[98] Advocates of *Halacha* hold that the claims about discrimination against women and their subordination to men are false. Women should protest against those false claims which in essence rob them of their true identity. Policy of separate but equal is one thing. Discrimination and subordination are quite another.

Yet in *Halacha*, women are discouraged from pursuing higher education or religious pursuits. This is because women have frivolous minds[99] and also because they have important roles to fulfil in the home as wives and mothers.[100] Women have a vital role in establishing a creative marriage-relationship, shaping the atmosphere of the home and bringing up children in a spirit of warmth and mutuality.[101] As these tasks are very demanding, women are incapable of splitting their time

[96] Meir Goldberg, 'Moral Problems in Halacha: Women (2013)', http://truetorah.blogspot.com/2013/07/moral-problems-in-halacha-women-with.html.

[97] Deuteronomy 22:5.

[98] Cohen-Almagor, 'Discrimination against Jewish Women in *Halacha* (Jewish Law) and in Israel'.

[99] Tirzah Meacham, 'Legal-Religious Status of the Jewish Female', *Jewish Women Encyclopedia* (2009), http://jwa.org/encyclopedia/article/legal-religious-status-of-jewish-female.

[100] The Role of Women, *Judaism 101*, www.jewfaq.org/women.htm.

[101] Jonathan Sacks, 'The Role of Women in Judaism', in Peter Moore (ed.), *Man, Woman, and Priesthood* (London: Society for Promoting Christian Knowledge, 1978): 27–44.

between the home and pursuits of high education or religion to which they are ill-equipped; thus success in them would demand from them more effort, at the expense of caring for the home. Women must never neglect their husbands and children; thus, the priorities are clear. And because of these clear priorities, women are exempt from religious and other obligations.[102] The structured view of the world whereby men have certain roles, and women have certain roles, yields efficiency and constructive allocation of time for each gender to perform its duties. Many ultra-religious (*Haredi*) women have bought into this notion of separate but equal. These women experience what I termed internalized coercion (see Chapter 4).

However, this separate but 'equal' policy is problematic. In the liberal tradition people should be left to decide what they want to do. It is not God, or his believed directives, that should guide us all, but rather we, people, guide and direct our own lives as we see fit, and we should be free to do so as long as we do not harm others. *Tout court* denial of choice undermines women's ability to lead what they may perceive as a meaningful way of life.

Denying education has direct consequences for the welfare of women. Uneducated women have fewer opportunities to integrate in the job market, and when they do work it is usually in low-income, manual jobs.[103] Denial of education robs women of living life to the full and of a future that corresponds to abilities. The state should enhance and promote civic education which includes discussions on *mutual* respect. The upholding of the Kantian Respect for Others Principle and the Millian Harm Principle safeguards the rights of those who might find themselves in a disadvantageous position in society, in this case women. All segments of the population are entitled to the same rights and liberties. Accommodations and corrective mechanisms should be devised and implemented in every sphere where women are not accorded equal status.[104] Support for human rights and for liberal democracy necessitates equal rights for all citizens, notwithstanding gender, including children, the subject of Chapter 8.

In Israel, where secular Jews are the majority, while secular women are not equal to men in the job market, they are not denied education. Indeed, more than 50 per cent of the students in institutions of higher education are women.[105] Fifty-eight per cent of women in Israel in the young adult group (25–34 years old) have a college

---

[102] Rabbi Mark Goldfeder, 'Defining Equality in Judaism', http://morethodoxy.org/2012/10/25/defining-equality-in-judaism-by-rabbi-mark-goldfeder/.

[103] Amelia Josephson, 'The Average Salary by Education Level', *Smart Asset* (15 May 2018), https://smartasset.com/retirement/the-average-salary-by-education-level.

[104] See discussions on Jewish obligations to minorities in *Identities*, 3 (2013): 125–157 (Hebrew), especially the articles of Aviad Hacohen, Elyakim Rubinstein and Naftali Rotenberg.

[105] 'Women in Higher Education Institutions in Israel', *Report of the Committee for the Advancement and Representation of Women in Institutions of High Education* (Jerusalem, 2015, Hebrew).

education, compared to 38 per cent of men.[106] The picture is very different where *Haredi* women are concerned. In 2018–2019, the *Haredi* population was just over one million and of them 8,400 *Haredi* women attended Israeli institutions of higher education.[107] *Haredi* women tend to marry young and have large families. The average ultra-Orthodox household is 5.2 persons.[108] While there is a notable improvement in their education, forced by the facts that their husbands prefer to study in yeshivot (religious institutions where they study only Judaism), they lack educational opportunities that are opened for secular women. Ultra-Orthodox women are expected to first fulfil family roles in an optimal manner. The family comes first, and *Haredi* women prefer to work in their community and not in the larger secular job market.[109] The ideal of being 'the Queen of the House' is central to the traditional education rooted in the ultra-Orthodox community. Women have to juggle between their various demanding duties – taking care of their husbands, children and the home, and at the same time being the breadwinners of their large families.

The Global Gender Gap Report, published by the World Economic Forum, ranks countries according to participation by women in the workforce, their access to education and health, and opportunities for representation and promotion in politics. In 2020 Israel was ranked 64 out of the 153 countries rated. This ranking is explained by lack of representation and power for women in politics, reflected in the low number of parliamentarian women, their weak representation in government service, the substantial salary gap between women and men, and low participation of women in the labour force.[110]

CONCLUSION

The concept of reasonable multiculturalism is about inclusion as well as exclusion, about freedom of religion and freedom from religion, about providing

---

[106] Gil Gertel, 'Women are more educated than men, but earn less than them', *Sicha Mekomit* (12 September 2019, Hebrew), www.mekomit.co.il/אקדמאים-מרוויחים-יותר-הבעיה-שחצי-מהיש/.

[107] Gilad Malach and Lee Kahaner, *Yearbook of Haredi Society in Israel 2018* (Jerusalem: The Israel Democracy Institute, 2018) (Hebrew); Danny Zaken, 'Thanks to Women: The Standard of Living of Ultra-Orthodox Society is Steadily Rising', *Globes* (24 December 2019) (Hebrew). In her comments on a draft of this chapter, Yofi Tirosh notes that the vast majority of *Haredi* women acquired their education in conditions of gender segregation. This is not ideal but if this is the only way for *Haredi* women to acquire higher education then this might be a reasonable accommodation in order to facilitate self-development.

[108] Israel News Desk, 'Work more, earn less, pay much less taxes', *Israel National News* (30 December 2020), https://israelnational.news/work-more-earn-less-pay-much-less-taxes-2.html.

[109] Asaf Malhi and Miriam Abramovsky, *Integration of Family and Work among Ultra-Orthodox Women* (Jerusalem: Ministry of Economy, 2015) (Hebrew).

[110] *Global Gender Gap Report 2020*, World Economic Forum, www3.weforum.org/docs/WEF_GGGR_2020.pdf; Assaf Uni, 'Israel Slips 18 Places in Gender Gap Index', *Globes* (17 December 2019), https://en.globes.co.il/en/article-israel-slips-18-places-in-gender-gap-index-1001311453.

circumstances for people to promote their way of life as well as deserting it at will and having the ability to adopt another. The right to remain within the culture and the right of exit are equally important. Group members should be provided with reasonable conditions if and when they decide to leave their community and embark on a new chapter of life outside their community. But having an exit right is not in itself a sufficient guarantee for the preservation of basic human rights for it can be assumed that the most vulnerable members of a given community would find exit most difficult and therefore would remain in their unjust communities. A fair and reasonable balance needs to be maintained between individual rights and group rights.

In both the Hutterite and the Pueblo cases, the courts supported the claims of illiberal groups in the name of freedom of religion. The courts were reluctant to interfere in tribal affairs, viewing interference as an imposition of their own values on distinct minorities. The judges failed to realize that clinging to the principle of neutrality contradicts two other important liberal principles, those of gender equality and freedom. Hence, it seems that their judgements do not settle the disputes between liberal values and illiberal minorities. Tolerating tribal conduct had resulted in intolerant behaviour towards some tribe members. Since liberal tolerance is individual freedom-based, not group-based, it cannot justify internal restrictions that limit individual freedom of conscience. People should be free to move in and out of their cultural communities without penalties. They should not be coerced to stay in order to serve group interests.

In conflicting situations we need to weigh a plurality of interests with the aim of reaching compromises. But these compromises must be of common benefit. If benefit is the result of only one side or, worse, benefit of one is the detriment of the other, then protection of the weak and powerless is warranted. The protection of basic human and civil rights should be applied equally to both genders (and also to those with transient gender identity, i.e., transgenders). One gender should not be held superior to another. Human rights are aimed at sustaining and promoting the dignity of the person, and they are broadly classified as civil or social rights. They enshrine liberty and justice. Civil rights are essentially 'negative' rights, in the sense that they impose upon the state a duty to refrain from interference, and they derive from the principle of individual liberty. Social rights are 'positive' rights, in that they impose a duty of action upon the state and its agents, to advance the substantive equality of vulnerable groups in relation to basic conditions of existence (e.g., housing, food, work, education, social security and health), and they derive from the principle of justice. Both instruct the state to correct discrimination, whether individual or collective.[111]

---

[111] Carmel Shalev, 'Health Rights', in Raphael Cohen-Almagor (ed.), *Israeli Democracy at the Crossroads* (London: Routledge, 2005): 65–77, at 68. For further discussion, see Avigail

Israel is an economically developed democracy that strives to maintain a particular Jewish tradition and religious identity in a heterogeneous society. As a result of its distinct preference for Jewish orthodoxy, Israel has failed to adopt national standards for women that would bring Israeli law into compliance with international human rights. The constant challenge for Israeli democracy is to secure basic human rights for all. Improvement in women's status is possible if there is a growing egalitarian consciousness to counteract the coercive nature of Jewish orthodoxy supported by continued advancement of socioeconomic conditions.[112]

Finally, I argued that the state should come to the aid of women who are denied education. It is incumbent on the liberal state to help women when men use their authority to deny the right of education to women just because they can. Women should enjoy equal opportunities to develop themselves and become the persons they perceive in their dreams. Education is a key to self-development and to reaching interesting and fulfilling positions in society. These positions should be open to all, not just men. Cultural claims should not enable discrimination and coercion.

The principles of respecting others, and not harming others, require the state to intervene when basic human rights are violated. In Chapter 1 I spoke of dignity as recognition and dignity as liability. We should recognize the inner spark that women possess, their inherent quality qua persons. Dignity as liability requires the state to ensure that all people are accorded equal treatment from birth. Women have a right to develop themselves as autonomous human beings exactly as men do.

In Chapter 8 I examine whether the same (or similar) rationale that guides me on the problem of denying education to women is appropriate also when addressing the denial of education to children.

Eisenberg and Jeff Spinner-Halev (eds), *Minorities within Minorities: Equality, Diversity and Rights* (Cambridge: Cambridge University Press, 2009).

[112] 'Ensuring Equal Rights for Women in Israel', Israel Ministry of Foreign Affairs (31 December 2013), https://mfa.gov.il/MFA/AboutIsrael/State/Law/Pages/Ensuring-equal-rights-for-women-in-Israel.aspx; Ruth Halperin-Kaddari and Yaacov Yadgar, 'Between Universal Feminism and Particular Nationalism: Politics, Religion and Gender (In)equality in Israel', *Third World Quarterly*, 31(6) (2010): 905–920; R. Halperin-Kaddari, *Women in Israel: A State of Their Own* (Philadelphia: University of Pennsylvania Press, 2004).

8

Denying Education to Children

In some parts of the world, students are going to school every day. It's their normal life . . . But in other part[s] of the world, we are starving for education . . . it's like a precious gift. It's like a diamond.

Malala Yousafzai

Timothy Sauder left his Old Order Mennonite community and his family because he wanted to go to college and pursue a career in science. He could not be both an Old Order Mennonite and a college graduate because his community does not support higher education. Sauder used to dig televisions out of dumpsters to learn about the outside world. Finally, he was able to enrol, without a high school diploma, at the University of Pittsburgh-Greensburg and was later transferred to Columbia University.[1]

The Old Order Mennonite is a conservative branch of Christianity. People of the Order are Anabaptists who formed a wide variety of Christian churches in Europe and North America. The term 'Anabaptist' means 'rebaptiser' because the Order rejected the idea of infant baptism. As infants do not have the knowledge of good and evil, they cannot have sin. Like the Hutterite Church, the Order believes that baptism is valid only when candidates willingly confess their faith in Christ. Therefore, baptism should be conducted later in life, when people are capable of making a reasoned choice and decide their destiny.[2]

In the seventeenth century the Amish split off from the Mennonite. The Amish movement was founded in Switzerland by Jacob Ammann as a reform group.

[1] Olivia B. Waxman, 'Breaking Amish: One Ex-follower's True Story of Moving to the Big Apple', *Time* (9 September 2012), http://entertainment.time.com/2012/09/09/breaking-amish-one-ex-followers-true-story-of-moving-to-the-big-apple/.

[2] Donald B. Kraybill, Karen M. Johnson-Weiner and Steven M. Nolt, *The Amish* (Baltimore, MD: Johns Hopkins University Press, 2013); Steven M. Nolt, *The Amish* (Baltimore, MD: Johns Hopkins University Press, 2016).

FIGURE 8.1. Amish agriculture (Greg Pease/Stone/Getty Images).

Named after their leader Ammann, the Amish were among the early German settlers in Pennsylvania. During the eighteenth century the Amish who suffered persecution in Europe immigrated to the United States and Canada as both countries promised them religious freedom. Old Order Amish live in thirty-one states, four Canadian provinces, and two South American countries.[3] Though practice varies, today Amish and Mennonites share values of non-resistance, adult baptism and in some cases plain form of dress.[4]

The Amish believe that they must be separate from worldly sinful practices to receive salvation. They created small and distinctive communities that resist the modern way of life and maintain simple and austere living. They refrain from using electricity and use gas lamps instead. They strive to retain the customs and small-scale technologies that were common in rural society in the nineteenth century. The Amish live independently, forsake self-interest and submit to the authority of the church with humility (see Figure 8.1).[5]

---

3   'Amish State Guide', *Amish America*, http://amishamerica.com/amish-state-guide/.
4   'What's the difference between Amish and Mennonites?', *Amish America*, http://amishamerica
     .com/whats-the-difference-between-amish-and-mennonites/.
5   Steven M. Nolt, *The Amish*; James P. Choy, 'Religion and the Family: The Case of the Amish',
     The Warwick Economics Research Paper Series (TWERPS) (2016); Mindy Starns Clark, *Plain
     Answers about the Amish Life* (Eugene, OR: Harvest House publishers, 2011).

The Amish are a church, a spiritual union and an agricultural community that see spiritual worth in the universe in its natural form. Before 1950, most Amish children attended public schools. The Amish were comfortable with small rural schools and, indeed, some Amish fathers served on the boards of such public schools. Later, these schools were consolidated into large districts nationwide and the Amish lost control over the nurture of their children' education. Moreover, they considered formal study beyond the eighth grade unnecessary for their farming lifestyle.[6]

I have mentioned that a major attack on multiculturalism is that it is bad for democracy. Multiculturalism gives preference to group rights over individual rights. This chapter focuses on the Amish denial of education from their youth. The importance of the school cannot be underestimated. Schools play a formative role in shaping career choices, future professions, income level, ability to establish a family, place of residence, social circle and social status. As in Chapter 7, the question revolves around state intervention, whether a dominant culture has a right to interfere in the business of an illiberal cultural minority when its practices and norms are harmful to members of that same minority culture. While recognizing that government should not impose substantial burdens on minority cultures without compelling state interests, it is argued that state intervention to provide the Amish young education that prepares children for life in the broader society is justified as it is aimed at sustaining and promoting basic human rights. State interference does not reduce freedom but provides background conditions needed to secure freedom.

My study on denying education to Amish children raises a host of questions regarding culture and religion, education, morality and law. It is argued that the state should intervene in the Amish affairs in order to promote children's right to an open future, and in order to prevent abuse. In Chapter 6 I argued that parents should enable their children the greatest possible scope for exercising personal life choices in adulthood. When male circumcision is concerned, I think that the negative effects of circumcision are *de minimis*. This is not the case here. As for child abuse, I was surprised to read significant data about children and youth abuse. It was one of those occasions when one does research about a certain issue and discovers a different matter. Then one has to ask oneself whether that matter is relevant to the issue under scrutiny. Well, the matter is certainly relevant. In addition to non-physical harm, many Amish children seem to suffer physical abuse which makes state intervention even more necessary and urgent.

---

[6] 'Education', *Amish Studies*, https://groups.etown.edu/amishstudies/social-organization/education/.

AMISH EDUCATION

In the early 1970s the Amish wanted to withdraw their children from the state educational system before the age of sixteen, arguing that formal education beyond the eighth grade places the Amish children in an environment hostile to their beliefs, but also because it takes them away from their community, physically and emotionally, during the crucial and formative adolescence period of life. At the age of six, Amish children start first grade by attending a schoolhouse that includes grades one through eight. There are usually thirty to thirty-five children in a schoolhouse, and many are siblings and cousins. Amish children do not study science because it includes ideas contrary to their conception of the good such as evolution which is contrary to the Bible.[7] Amish education does not include computers because they reject modern technology. Nor does Amish education seek to create artists, scientists, musicians or actors.[8] The curriculum is limited to reading, spelling, grammar, penmanship, arithmetic, art, health, history (particularly Amish history), German and some geography.[9] Until age 13, most Amish children attend one-room schools. Believing that education leads to 'pride' and to a sense that one is better than those who have lesser education, the Amish require children to drop out after eighth grade and begin working.[10] The Amish educate for a life of 'goodness' rather than a life of intellect; 'wisdom, rather than technical knowledge; community welfare, rather than competition; and separation from, rather than integration with, contemporary worldly society'.[11] Amish education emphasizes the virtues of hard work, community life, group effort (individuality is not encouraged and individual merit is rarely singled out for awards of any kind), simplicity, sublimation of personal desire, surrender to God's will, humility, kindness, responsibility and caring.[12] School is usually within walking distance from home.[13] The timetable for lessons is constructed in such a way so as to allow children to help with seasonal farm work and take part in communal religious practices and ceremonies.[14] When the Amish complete eighth grade they join their parents at work, learning the

---

[7] Thomas J. Meyers, 'The Old Order Amish: To Remain in the Faith or to Leave', *The Mennonite Quarterly Review*, 68 (1994): 378–395; Karen Johnson-Weiner, *Train Up a Child: Old Order Amish and Mennonite Schools* (Baltimore, MD: Johns Hopkins University Press, 2007).

[8] 'A Look at Amish Education', www.exploring-amish-country.com/amish-education.html.

[9] Mark W. Dewalt, *Amish Education in the United States and Canada* (Lanham, MD: Rowman and Littlefield Education, 2006): 7, 188; Donald B. Kraybill, Karen M. Johnson-Weiner and Steven M. Nolt, *The Amish* (Baltimore, MD: Johns Hopkins University Press, 2013): chap. 14.

[10] David L. McConnell and Charles E. Hurst, 'No "Rip van Winkles" Here: Amish Education since *Wisconsin v. Yoder*', *Anthropology & Education Quarterly*, 37(3) (September 2006): 248. See also *Devil's Background, a Documentary about Amish Teenage Culture* (2002).

[11] *Wisconsin v. Yoder* 406 US 205, 92 S.Ct 1526 (1972): 211.

[12] Dewalt, *Amish Education in the United States and Canada*, 7–8, 113, 190, 194.

[13] 'A Look at Amish Education', www.exploring-amish-country.com/amish-education.html.

[14] Brian Barry, *Culture and Equality* (Cambridge, MA: Harvard University Press, 2001): 207.

required skills for contributing to the community economy. They learn the necessary skills to run a household, farm or small business.[15]

An independent school system isolates the children from the influences of the wider society. Undoubtedly, this severely limits the extent to which the children learn about the outside world. Heterogeneous school mixing teaches students about diversity, pluralism, the right to be different, equality and respect for people qua people. In contrast, the Amish schools are comprised only of Amish people. Students are not exposed to other people from the rich mix of American society. The Amish students are denied an opportunity to meet students of different backgrounds, with different systems of belief. They are handicapped in their knowledge of their surroundings. Furthermore, the limited curriculum puts the Amish at disadvantage if they were to pursue life outside the community. The curriculum inculcates Amish values and conceptions of the good and ensures that the significant other peer group is Amish. The large classes of children of different ages makes teaching a tough assignment as children between the ages of 6 and 13 have different learning capacities and needs.[16] By insisting on educating the young in one classroom within the community, the Amish prioritize the group over the individual. They deny children certain opportunities while providing them with a cohesive community. The Amish, like the Hutterites, defend this by arguing that freedom of religion protects a group's freedom to live in accordance with its doctrine, even if this limits the individual freedom of children.

The Amish insistence on a particular education curriculum for its children is understandable and, at the same time, challenging. The rationale is sensible from the Amish point of view as the community wishes to retain and perpetuate its culture. Amish theology is inward looking, distancing themselves from the materialistic and the so-called 'corrupt world'.[17] Does denial of opportunities provide a sufficient ground for state interference?

WISCONSIN V. YODER

The United States Supreme Court, in *Wisconsin v. Yoder*, dealt with the Amish refusal to send their children to public schools after the eighth grade.[18] It revolved around the question whether it is reasonable to deny Amish adolescents a standard American education. Wisconsin challenged the Amish way of life, insisting that the Amish integrate into American community to better serve the best interests of the young. The defendants, members of the Amish faith, refused to send their children, aged 14 and 15, to continue their education at public schools. The defendants were

---

[15] Dewalt, *Amish Education in the United States and Canada*, 7, 115, 190.
[16] For discussion on a typical teacher day in the Amish community, see ibid., 130–134.
[17] Choy, 'Religion and the Family'.
[18] *Wisconsin v. Yoder* 406 US 205, 92 S.Ct 1526 (1972).

convicted for violating Wisconsin's compulsory school attendance law requiring children to attend school until the age of 16.

The Amish do not have schools of higher learning. After the eighth grade, the children are taken out of school and go to work.[19] The Amish argued that forcing their children to study in American schools places them in an environment hostile to their way of life. The Wisconsin Circuit Court affirmed the Amish convictions. The Wisconsin Supreme Court, sustaining the defendants' claims that their First Amendment right to free exercise of religion had been violated, reversed the convictions.[20] Then the case reached the United States Supreme Court, which accepted the Amish claim in a six to one decision, with the majority opinion written by Chief Justice Warren Earl Burger.[21]

The state of Wisconsin argued that some degree of education is necessary to prepare citizens to participate effectively and intelligently in the open political system, 'if we are to preserve freedom and independence'.[22] Furthermore, the state maintained that 'education prepares individuals to be self-reliant and self-sufficient participants in society'.[23] The Supreme Court accepted these propositions yet sided with the idea that the Amish have group rights to decide their own education system, notwithstanding American law.

The Supreme Court upheld the principles of state non-interference in religious matters and of parental school choice. The court assigned more importance to children's integration into the Amish community than to their integration into the wider society. It acknowledged that the state has the power to impose reasonable regulations for the control and duration of basic education. Yet this paramount responsibility to provide universal education is not totally free from a balancing process when it impinges on fundamental rights and interests, such as those specifically protected by the Free Exercise Clause of the First Amendment, and the traditional interest of parents with respect to the religious upbringing of their children. Furthermore, the court was of the opinion that the values and programmes of the modern secondary school were in sharp conflict with the Amish mode of life. The mission of Amish education is to teach the skills that are needed to lead an Amish life while developing the ability to function independently and do business with the outside world. Enforcing state education would constitute the kind of objective danger to the free exercise of religion that the First Amendment was designed to prevent. It presented the Amish with the impossible choice of either abandoning belief and be assimilated into society at large, or be forced to migrate to

---

[19] John A. Hostetler, *Amish Society* (Baltimore, MD: Johns Hopkins University Press, 1993): 16.

[20] 49 Wis 2d 430, 182 NW2d 539.

[21] Powell and Rehnquist, JJ., did not participate.

[22] *Wisconsin v. Yoder* 406 US 205, 92 S.Ct 1526 (1972), at 221.

[23] Ibid. See also Ian Shapiro, 'Democratic Justice and Multicultural Recognition', in Paul Kelly (ed.), *Multiculturalism Reconsidered* (Cambridge: Polity, 2002): 174–183.

some other and more tolerant region. Both choices were deemed unreasonable, unjust and coercive.[24]

Undoubtedly, continuity is important to the Amish. In coming to analyse the court decision, it is first noted that the Amish wish to perpetuate their unique tradition and way of living by resisting the pressures of the external world. The need for continuity justifies paternalistic coercion (Chapter 4). Education of the young is the key to this. Amish education complements and reinforces church beliefs and values. It promotes community life rather than autonomy and self-expression. Excellence is secondary.[25] Amish education is the responsibility of the parents, the school and the entire community acting under the influence of the church.

Second, the Convention on the Rights of the Child voices its conviction that 'the family, as the fundamental group of society and the natural environment for the growth and well-being of all its members and particularly children, should be afforded the necessary protection and assistance so that it can fully assume its responsibilities within the community'.[26] Articles 3, 9, 18 and 21 of the convention emphasize that 'the best interests of the child shall be a primary consideration'.[27] Article 5 holds that

> States Parties shall respect the responsibilities, rights and duties of parents or, where applicable, the members of the extended family or community as provided for by local custom, legal guardians or other persons legally responsible for the child, to provide, in a manner consistent with the evolving capacities of the child, appropriate direction and guidance in the exercise by the child of the rights recognized in the present Convention.[28]

Indeed, generally speaking we should keep the integrity of the family and safeguard its privacy against state intrusion. There should be very compelling reasons to allow such interference.

Third, the United States is the only country in the world that has not ratified the convention because some critics argued that it would undermine parents' rights and 'give our children unrestricted access to abortion, pornography, gangs and the occult'.[29]

---

[24] *Wisconsin v. Yoder* 406 US 205, 92 S.Ct 1526 (1972), at 218.
[25] Dewalt, *Amish Education in the United States and Canada.*
[26] United Nations Human Rights, *Convention on the Rights of the Child*, adopted and opened for signature, ratification and accession by General Assembly resolution 44/25 of 20 November 1989 entry into force 2 September 1990, in accordance with article 49. Preamble. www.ohchr .org/en/professionalinterest/pages/crc.aspx.
[27] Ibid.
[28] Ibid.
[29] B. Shaw Drake and Megan Corrarino, 'U.S. Stands Alone: Not Signing U.N. Child Rights Treaty Leaves Migrant Children Vulnerable', *Huffington Post* (13 October 2015), www.huffpost .com/entry/children-migrants-rights_b_8271874.

PARENTHOOD

Furthermore, parents are the default decision-makers for their children. In many communities throughout the world, parents are responsible for the welfare of their children. Parents inculcate values. They provide guidance and a moral compass. They outline prospects for their children. They set standards and expectations. They instruct what is right and what is wrong. John Stuart Mill regarded education as a condition for people to exercise civil liberties and assigned responsibility for children's education to parents and state. The parent owes it to society to endeavour to make the child a good and valuable member. Mill wrote that to raise a child without a fair prospect of being able to provide food for its body and also instruction and training for its mind is 'a moral crime',[30] both against the unfortunate child and against society at large. Children have a claim against their parents to provide them with education, 'appliances and means' that 'will enable them to start with a fair chance of achieving by their own exertions a successful life'.[31] If the parent does not fulfil this obligation the state ought to ensure that it is fulfilled.

Mill said that democratic governments must provide proper facilities for education designed for the benefit of society as a whole, but it must not control all educational institutions: 'The case is one to which the reasons of the non-interference principle do not necessarily or universally extend.'[32] Nevertheless, the state must step in when children do not receive education adequate for their growth and self-development. Education meant for Mill the cultivation of the intellect, of moral powers and of aesthetics. A good government cultivates moral education; moral education makes human beings moral, thinking people who do not merely act as machines and, in the long run, makes people claim control over their own actions and inspires them to intensely seek the truth.[33]

The Amish assert their parental responsibility. Weighing the best interests of their children, and the best interests of their community, they adopted what they consider a reasonable Golden Mean. One may ask: Is the liberal way of life better than the

---

[30] J.S. Mill, *Utilitarianism, Liberty, and Representative Government* (London: J.M. Dent, 1948): 160; J.S. Mill, *Principles of Political Economy* (New York: D. Appleton, 1885): 201.

[31] Ibid.

[32] J.S. Mill, *Principles of Political Economy* (London: Longmans, Green, Reader and Dyer, 1869), Bk. V, 575. For different interpretations of Mill, see Richard S. Ruderman and R. Kenneth Godwin, 'Liberalism and Parental Control of Education', *The Review of Politics*, 62(3) (Summer 2000): 503–529; Raphael Cohen-Almagor, 'Between Autonomy and State Regulation: J.S. Mill's Elastic Paternalism', *Philosophy*, 87(4) (October 2012): 557–582.

[33] Mill, *Utilitarianism, Liberty, and Representative Government*, 202–208. Mill wrote: 'The very corner-stone of an education intended to form great minds, must be the recognition of the principle, that the object is to call forth the greatest possible quantity of intellectual power, and to inspire the intensest love of truth'. See Mill, 'Civilization, [1836]', (London: Longmans, Green, Reader & Dyer, 1859), available at http://ringmar.net/politicaltheoryfornomads/index .php/john-stuart-mill-civilization-1836-in-dissertations-and-discussions-political-philosophical-and-historical-london-j-w-parker-1859-160-205/.

Amish? Many would answer in the negative, highlighting the benefits of living in a coherent, supportive community with a strong cultural backbone, rich heritage and familiar way of life. There is something reassuring in having a sustained routine and strong family and community life in which roles, duties and privileges are clear. Undoubtedly, children need to be loved and cared for in a culturally coherent environment. There is a prima facie parental right to raise children according to the parents' own values.[34] Therefore, one may argue, the Amish parents are entitled to restrict their children's education.

But are parents *solely* responsible? Surely not. The same Supreme Court spoke in *Pierce* about subjecting parental rights to state regulations, offering a compromise between the rights of parents to choose education for their children and the state interests in sustaining public welfare.[35] In a unanimous decision, the court upheld parents' right to make educational decisions on behalf of their children while acknowledging the states' right to regulate education, even in non-public schools. The court held that parental rights are subject to the power of the state 'reasonably to regulate all schools, to inspect, supervise and examine them, their teachers and pupils; ... that certain studies plainly essential to good citizenship must be taught, and that nothing be taught which is manifestly inimical to the public welfare'.[36] Some may argue that education is a far too important an issue to be left only in the hands of parents. Liberalism invokes the personal autonomy argument against leaving the decision solely in the hands of the parents. And certainly, the Amish youth should have a voice in the dispute. John Rawls maintained that 'moral education is education for autonomy'.[37] To recall, the Rawlsian Principle of Equal Liberty holds that the state must provide education and training for the less well-off.[38]

The notion of autonomy involves one's ability to reflect upon beliefs and actions, and the ability to form an idea regarding them, so as to decide the way in which to lead a life (see Chapter 1). For by deciding between conflicting trends, agents consolidate their opinions more fully and review the ranking of values for themselves with a clear frame of mind. The Respect for Others Principle instructs us to enable self-development. It is important that children should have a real opportunity to become autonomous. This requires mandating autonomy-facilitating education.[39]

---

[34] Eamonn Callan, *Creating Citizens: Political Education and Liberal Democracy* (Oxford: Oxford University Press, 1997): 139; Allan J. Jacobs and Kavita Shah Arora, 'When May Government Interfere with Religious Practices to Protect the Health and Safety of Children?', *Ethics, Medicine and Public Health*, 5 (April–June 2018): 86–93. See also Charles Fried, *Right and Wrong* (Cambridge, MA: Harvard University Press, 1979).

[35] *Pierce v. Society of Sisters*, 268 U.S. 510 (1925), at 534, http://cdn.loc.gov/service/ll/usrep/usrep268/usrep268510/usrep268510.pdf.

[36] *Pierce v. Society of Sisters*, 268 U.S. 510 (1925).

[37] John Rawls, *A Theory of Justice* (Oxford: Oxford University Press, 1971): 516.

[38] Ibid., 302.

[39] Harry Brighouse, *School Choice and Social Justice* (Oxford: Oxford University Press, 2003): 111.

Amish adults are entitled to restrict their *own* self-development if so they choose in the spirit of maintaining tradition and culture. But are they also entitled to limit the self-development of their children?

VALUE OF EDUCATION

Amy Gutmann is arguably the most influential liberal thinker who probed the place of education in our life. Gutmann believes that parental influence should be limited by the state to achieve autonomy. Choice needs to be vindicated by its contribution to deliberative democracy essential for developing the necessary tools for taking part in public, democratic life. Gutmann endorses democratic education based on the contributions of the state, parents and educators to enable integration of the good insights of all. Such education will guarantee that future citizens are able to meaningfully share in self-consciously shaping the structure of their society.[40] Rob Reich's leading goal in his liberal theory of multicultural education is the cultivation of individual autonomy in children.[41] Similarly, Rawls' political liberalism requires that children's education include knowledge of their constitutional and civic rights to ensure that they will fully incorporate into society.[42]

Furthermore, the inculcation of deliberative character should be the main purpose of primary education because, Gutmann explains, 'Children must learn not just to behave in accordance with authority but to think critically about authority if they are to live up to the democratic ideal of sharing political sovereignty as citizens.'[43] The government should have the authority to impose common standards and to cultivate a common democratic culture upholding the principles of non-repression and non-discrimination without which 'despotism over the mind' might take place.[44] The United States Supreme Court forfeited these ideals once it gave precedence to Amish group rights at the expense of individual rights, allowing the Amish to be exempted from the required level of education.

Most other liberal democracies enforce a certain level of education. This compulsory education may seem to be an invasion on the individual's rights, but it can be defended on the grounds that, in final analysis, it may guarantee more freedom than it destroys. For if undemocratic curricula may be viewed as a sort of unfreedom, open education increases the number of alternatives for students to pursue their interests. This kind of governmental interference is justifiable as it opens for individuals more paths for liberty in the long run.

---

[40] Amy Gutmann, *Democratic Education* (Princeton, NJ: Princeton University Press, 1987): 46.

[41] Rob Reich, *Bridging Liberalism and Multiculturalism in American Education* (Chicago: University of Chicago Press, 2002).

[42] John Rawls, *Political Liberalism* (New York: Columbia University Press, 1993): 199.

[43] Gutmann, *Democratic Education*, 51.

[44] Ibid., 76. See also Stephen Macedo, *Diversity and Distrust: Civic Education in a Multicultural Democracy* (Cambridge, MA: Harvard University Press, 2000).

In support, Almond and Verba found in their comprehensive comparative research that higher education opens the minds of individuals to the secondary structures of their society, to dimensions of historical depth and to wider perspectives of the world scene. People learn how to gather information, better understand the working of the mass media and the formal structure of politics, as well as the importance of governmental and political institutions.[45]

While the Amish way of life may be appealing to most Amish people, it might not be appealing to all. Some of the Amish may wish to opt out. The concern I have is whether the independent Amish education system, designed to protect and promote the Amish community, not only restricts freedom of religion but also the options that the Amish have if they wish to opt out. The Supreme Court reflected on Thomas Jefferson who believed that some degree of education is necessary to prepare citizens to participate effectively and intelligently in the American open political system in order to preserve freedom and independence. The court acknowledged that education prepares individuals to be self-reliant and self-sufficient participants in society. However, the court said that the evidence 'persuasively' showed that an additional one or two years of formal high school for Amish children in place of their long-established programme of informal vocational education 'would do little to serve those interests'.[46] It is one thing to say that compulsory education for a year or two beyond the eighth grade may be necessary when its goal is the preparation for life in modern society; it is quite another if the goal of education be viewed as the 'preparation of the child for life in the separated agrarian community that is the keystone of the Amish faith'.[47] Thus, here the court had in mind the Amish adolescents who wish to remain in the community. It did not consider those who might wish to opt out, and the options presented to them if and when they leave the community.

The state of Wisconsin raised the issue of dissenters, arguing that the Amish education system was fostering ignorance and insisting that it is the role of the state to protect the children from such a policy. The state has a right to free children from ignorance. The Supreme Court accepted that the state has a duty to protect children from ignorance but maintained that 'this argument does not square with the facts disclosed in the record'.[48] The state argued that Amish children who leave their church would not be able to make their way in the world without the education available in the one or two additional years required by the state. The Supreme

---

[45] G. Almond and S. Verba, *The Civic Culture* (New York: Little, Brown & Company, 1965): 105, 317–318, 502.

[46] *Wisconsin v. Yoder*, at 222.

[47] Ibid.

[48] Ibid. For further discussion, see John A. Hostetler, 'The Amish and the Law: A Religious Minority and Its Legal Encounters', *Washington and Lee Law Review*, 41(1) (Winter 1984): 40–44.

Court dismissed this argument as 'highly speculative'.[49] The court found no evidence of the loss of Amish adherents by attrition, nor any showing that upon leaving the Amish community the dissenters would become burdens on society because of educational shortcomings. It seemed that the court and the state were speaking along parallel lines. The court said, 'not only do the Amish accept the necessity for formal schooling through the eighth grade level, but continue to provide what has been characterized by the undisputed testimony of expert educators as an "ideal" vocational education for their children in the adolescent years'.[50] But this 'ideal' education was for those who wished to remain in the Amish community, not for those who wished to leave it.

The Supreme Court raised another important issue relating to the question of traditional concepts of parental control over the religious upbringing and education of children, on the one hand, and to state intrusion into family decisions in the area of religious training, on the other. The court understood that if it were to interfere, this would give rise to questions relating to religious freedom.[51] The court felt that this interference is not merely about education but rather about the religious future of the Amish children and this, the court thought, was well outside the remit of reasonable interference. Weighing one against the other the state's interest in requiring two more years of compulsory education in the ninth and tenth grades versus the importance of the 'concededly sincere Amish religious practice to the survival of that sect',[52] the court was convinced that the latter outweighed the importance of the former.

Furthermore, courts 'are not school boards or legislatures, and are ill-equipped to determine the 'necessity' of discrete aspects of a state's programme of compulsory education'.[53] The court ruling was made, it was suggested, with great circumspection in performing the sensitive and most delicate task of weighing the state's legitimate social concern when faced with religious claims for exemption from generally applicable educational requirements.

However, a liberal court should weigh the conflicting considerations of autonomy and paternalism. Here the court observed the tension between parental paternalism and state paternalism but it ignored the agent's autonomy. The Supreme Court reasoning is inconsistent with basic liberal principles, and the conception/interpretation that the court gave to the right of freedom of religion is problematic and contested. The majority of the court defined freedom of religion primarily in terms of the group's ability to live in accordance with its doctrine, rather than the individual's ability to form and revise his or her religious beliefs.

[49] *Wisconsin v. Yoder*, at 224.
[50] Ibid., at 224.
[51] *Wisconsin v. Yoder*, at 231.
[52] Ibid., at 238.
[53] Ibid., at 235.

In previous decisions, the US Supreme Court has repeatedly affirmed the state's duty and legal power to protect children.[54] Not this time. Reflecting on *Yoder*, Kymlicka and I argued that the court never really even addressed that question systematically, since it defined freedom of religion in a non-liberal, group-based way. We were not saying that group-imposed restrictions on education are necessarily inconsistent with individual freedom of choice, but that for a liberal interpretation of freedom of religion this is what needs to be examined. The demands of the group must be consistent with the real and ongoing capacity for choice by individuals.[55]

Hence, my concern is with the test the court invoked to assess the Amish situation. Of course, one could argue that the Amish should be exempt from the usual liberal conception of freedom of religion, on the grounds that they do not fall under the jurisdiction of the Bill of Rights. But that was *not* the argument that the Amish made, nor was it the basis for the court's decision. So long as the Amish appeal to the right of freedom guaranteed in the constitution, the liberal state should interpret that as one which protects and defends the capacity of individuals to form and revise their religious beliefs.[56]

QUALITY OF EDUCATION

The court maintained: 'There is nothing in this record to suggest that the Amish qualities of reliability, self-reliance, and dedication to work would fail to find ready markets in today's society.'[57] The court also cited a study that indicated that Amish children in the eighth grade achieved comparably to non-Amish children in the basic skills.[58] This finding has been contested. The Amish teach very little science, history, social studies, art and music. Almost three-quarters of each day is spent on

---

[54] *Prince v. Massachusetts*, 321 U.S. 158 (1944); *Ginsberg v. New York*, 390 U.S. 629 (1968); *Parham v. J.R.*, 442 U.S. 584 (1979). For further discussion, see Carmen Green, 'Educational Empowerment: A Child's Right to Attend Public School', *Georgetown Law Journal*, 103 (2015): 1129–1130.

[55] Will Kymlicka and Raphael Cohen-Almagor, 'Ethnocultural Minorities in Liberal Democracies', in Maria Baghramian and Attracta Ingram (eds), *Pluralism: The Philosophy and Politics of Diversity* (London: Routledge, 2000): 228–250. For further discussion, see Tariq Modood, *Multiculturalism* (Cambridge: Polity, 2013). For a contrasting view, see Chandran Kukathas, *The Liberal Archipelago: A Theory of Diversity and Freedom* (Oxford: Oxford University Press, 2003).

[56] For further discussion of the court's (divided) reasoning on this case, see Richard Arneson and Ian Shapiro, 'Democratic Autonomy and Religious Freedom: A Critique of *Wisconsin v. Yoder*', in Ian Shapiro and Russell Hardin (eds), *Political Order: Nomos 38* (New York: New York University Press, 1996): 365–411, and Shelley Burtt's reply, 'In Defense of *Yoder*: Parental Authority and the Public Schools', in I. Shapiro and R. Hardin (eds), *Political Order*, 412–437.

[57] *Wisconsin v. Yoder*, at 224.

[58] *Wisconsin v. Yoder*, at 226, note 13.

reading, spelling and arithmetic.[59] Some Amish communities teach very little English.[60] Amish education has been based on the same textbooks for many years. Saloma Miller Furlong as a teacher taught from the same textbooks that she studied as a child.[61] The Amish curriculum is not comparable to that of an average American school.

If children arrive from school and tell their parents that today they learned creationism in biology class, parents might become concerned. It is one thing to study creationism as theology and quite another to learn it in science class. If children report that their science teacher taught them that one school of thought thinks the earth is flat, some parents might see this as a sign of openness, that the teacher entertains all schools of thought and plurality of ideas whereas other parents might perceive this as a sign of narrow-mindedness, that the teacher abuses authority to advance and promote a certain agenda that has been refuted a long time ago. Some parents might even ask to see the headmaster and complain about the level and quality of education their children receive at school. After all, so they may claim, they do not send their children to school to learn outdated ideas that science has disputed time and again. Conversely, the Amish are unlikely to complain. Some of the Amish children were taught to think that the earth is flat and that if they go too far they might fall.[62] Furthermore, Amish educators are not qualified teachers. Often their education does not extend beyond the eighth grade.[63] Many of the teachers are young, unmarried Amish women. Commonly they teach for three to five years and then get married and establish families. Community pressure is such that couples are expected to marry young and immediately start a family. Teacher turnover is a constant in the Amish community.[64]

PROTECTIVE COMMUNITY?

The Amish offer a very constricted framework of life. Life is simple and expected, with a well-known routine comprising limited education, a steady job, family and community. At least, one may think, the Amish offer its members a safe and protective life. They present themselves as a sheltered, self-sustaining community.

[59] William A. Fischel, 'Do Amish One-Room Schools Make the Grade? The Dubious Data of "Wisconsin v Yoder"', *University of Chicago Law Review*, 79(1) (2012): 107–129.

[60] 'Woman Who Left the Amish Community Opens Up to Megyn Kelly', *Megyn Kelly TODAY* (18 July 2018), www.youtube.com/watch?v=WvFaEM2uX8o.

[61] Saloma Miller Furlong, *Bonnet Strings* (Harrisonburg, VA: Herald Press, 2014): 197.

[62] 'Woman Who Left the Amish Community Opens Up to Megyn Kelly', *Megyn Kelly TODAY*; Candace Sutton, '"I Thought the Earth Was Flat": Teenage Girl's Escape from the Amish', *News.com* (3 August 2018), www.news.com.au/lifestyle/relationships/family-friends/i-thought-the-earth-was-flat-teenage-girls-escape-from-the-amish/news-story/ofccfec5ea82e975f00202a4f47b76c3.

[63] James A. Cates, *Serving the Amish* (Baltimore, MD: Johns Hopkins University Press, 2014): 63.

[64] Dewalt, *Amish Education in the United States and Canada*, 117, 195.

In school children study with staff and children they know. This, indeed, was the assumption in *Yoder*. The justices believed that Wisconsin's mandatory attendance statute was unnecessary for the protection of children as they would live their entire lives in sheltered communities.[65]

Amish families and communities love and cherish their children. Amish children are protected from many child welfare risks such as parental unemployment, divorce and homelessness. These are virtually non-existent in Amish communities. People who are vulnerable by age, health or ability are well cared for within their tightly knit social fabric. Children grow up in large families with strong ties to the other members. When a family experiences a hardship such as death, injury or illness, the community will rally around them.[66] I wanted to know what happens to those who wish to exit this way of life. Then, to what extent is Amish education sufficient, and how successful are those who choose to leave the community and who try to establish a new chapter in the wider American society? Some of the stories of those who left the Order are truly troubling. They reveal child abuse, sexual harassment, exploitation and cover up. James A. Cates, a psychologist who worked with the Amish, argues that all too often child abuse in the community occurs with impunity.[67] The Amish do not like to wash their dirty laundry outside, and they are protective of those who sin. As forgiveness is an essential value of their teachings, the Amish tend to forgive those who commit crimes. They shelter the abuser and fail to provide safety and protection to their young. Saloma Miller Furlong grew up in a home where her father often resorted to violence, confessed, and then reverted to violence. The cycle of violence continued unabated.[68] Only in rare instances where excommunication does not yield the right results do the Amish turn to external law enforcement, such as in the case of Chester Mast who was excommunicated three times for the rape of his younger cousins before he was finally reported and arrested. The alleged assaults took place for five years, between 2004 and 2009.[69]

In October 2018, 53-year-old Ora F. Troyer was sentenced to one term of fifteen to twenty-five years in prison and two terms of ten to fifteen years for sexually assaulting three girls multiple times during 2003–2018.[70] One may argue that sexual abuse

---

[65] *Wisconsin v. Yoder*, 210–211.

[66] Lisa Aronson Fontes and Jeanette Harder, 'Working with Amish Families on Child Abuse and Neglect', *Psychology Today* (18 May 2019).

[67] James A. Cates, *Serving the Amish*: 92.

[68] Miller Furlong, *Bonnet Strings*, 22, 51; Shelly Bradbury and Peter Smith, 'Forced Forgiveness: Plain Community Sexual Abuse Victims Sometimes Pressured to Take Offenders Back', *Post-Gazette* (28 May 2019), https://newsinteractive.post-gazette.com/coverings/mennonites-forgiveness-sexual-abuse-coverings-plain-amish-lancaster-county.

[69] Naimah Jabali-Nash, 'Amish Man Arrested in Two-State Child Sex Crimes Case', *CBS News* (10 June 2010), www.cbsnews.com/news/amish-man-arrested-in-two-state-child-sex-crimes-case/; Mike Devlin, '10 Weird Facts about the Amish', *Listverse* (29 August 2014), https://listverse.com/2014/08/29/10-weird-facts-about-the-amish/.

[70] Cole Waterman, 'Amish Man Faces 18 Counts of Sexual Assault Involving 3 Girls', *Bay City News* (16 August 2018), www.mlive.com/news/bay-city/index.ssf/2018/08/amish_man_faces_18_

crimes happen in many communities, not only in the Amish. The disturbing fact is that in this case the perpetrator got away with committing abuse over a fifteen-year period. In January 2019, two Amish brothers, Alfred N. Yoder (22) and Enos R. Yoder (22) faced multiple sexual charges in Daviess County. They allegedly performed sexual acts on two minors on multiple occasions. The alleged crimes took place between 2014 and 2018.[71]

'Mary B' grew up in an Old Order Amish family where isolation, secrecy and patriarchy masked repeated sexual assaults by her brothers that began when she was a 7 year old. By the age of 20, Mary alleged she had been raped more than 200 times. After years of pleading unsuccessfully with her mother and church officials to intervene, she sought therapy and help outside the Amish community. As a result, three of her brothers were incarcerated. Mary's family disowned her and she was banned from the Amish community, leaving the community with an eighth-grade education and little more than the clothes she was wearing.[72]

Misty Griffin published a book about her ordeal.[73] She describes the Amish community as a place of fear, animal cruelty and sexual abuse. Griffin was sexually abused by the bishop. Other books written by women who left the Amish portray similar if not identical troubling stories. One may question the reliability of books by disgruntled people who left the Amish. Still, we should not ignore these repeated examples of evidence. Saloma Miller Furlong published two books about her Amish experience. She was abused by both her father and her older brother.[74] Torah Bontrager was subjected to continued sexual abuse until she ran away. She did not find help within the Amish community.[75] Mary Byler was raped by several different attackers.[76] Byler was considered the villain by the Amish because she broke with the community and brought in outside authorities.[77] When charges are filed, Amish communities often refuse to cooperate with investigations, and witnesses are ordered not to testify. Victims find little support or opportunity for

counts_of_s.html; 'Michigan Amishman Gets 15–25 Years for Sexual Assault', *Amish America* (18 October 2018), http://amishamerica.com/michigan-amishman-gets-15–25-years-for-sexual-assault/.

71 Nick Sadowski, 'Amish Brothers Accused of Years-long Sexual Abuse of Minors in Daviess County', *KMZU* (24 January 2019) www.kmzu.com/amish-brothers-accused-of-years-long-sexual-abuse-of-minors-in-daviess-county/.

72 W.M. McGuigan and S.J. Stephenson, 'A Single-Case Study of Resiliency after Extreme Incest in an Old Order Amish Family', *Journal of Child Sexual Abuse*, 24(5) (2015): 526–537.

73 Misty Griffin, *Tears of the Silenced: A True Crime and an American Tragedy; Severe Child Abuse and Leaving the Amish* (La Vergne: Mango, 2018).

74 Saloma Miller Furlong, *Why I Left the Amish: A Memoir* (East Lansing: Michigan State University Press, 2011); Miller Furlong, *Bonnet Strings*.

75 Torah Bontrager, *An Amish Girl in Manhattan: A Memoir* (Know-T Publishing, 2018).

76 Jennifer Lavoie, 'Under Grace: Legal Isolation and the Children of the Old Order Amish', *The Modern American* (Spring 2006): 32–34.

77 'Sexual Abuse in the Amish Community', *ABC News* (10 December 2004), https://abcnews.go.com/2020/story?id=316371&page=1.

recovery and are punished for making their experiences public.[78] In 2017, a local bishop admitted to covering up sexual abuse in his community.[79]

The disturbing stories about sexual abuse have common features, as a result of the Amish culture and way of life. Amish men are dominant in this culture. From early on, girls are taught to be submissive to the men and boys. Most Amish do not educate their children about sex; therefore, girls can easily fall prey to sexual predators. The Amish rely on belief as the key to their living. Therefore, spiritual healing is required when sins are committed. Their emphasis on peace and consensus makes exposing violators more difficult. Cultural forces push victims into silence.[80] The Amish value non-violence, which is expressed as pacifism and leads them to avoid reporting crimes and avoid participating in court cases against people who have wronged them.[81] The books mentioned above reveal a repeated pattern. When sexual abuse is uncovered, the community shelters the predators rather than the children. They focus on the perpetrator's repentance rather than on the victim's welfare. They are given the opportunity to repent; in severe cases they are banned from the community for six weeks, and then return as if nothing happened. This allows paedophiles to continue living among their victims. This, of course, is very traumatic for the children. The community preference to shield the perpetrators leaves the victims in a state of helplessness and despair.[82]

If the abusers are reformed, while the victims still experience psychological torment, at least the physical danger is removed. But when the offenders continue with the abuse the vicious cycle can linger on. This explains why such crimes can last for many years. Reporting to the police is admitting that the Amish key to life, spiritual healing, has failed; failed to the extent that they need to appeal to worldly

---

[78] Ibid.

[79] Wesley Robinson, 'Amish Bishop Admits to Covering Up Sex Abuse, Sentenced to Probation', *Penn Live* (11 September 2017), www.pennlive.com/news/2017/09/amish_bishop_admits_to_coverin.html. See also 'Fighting Sexual Abuse in the Amish Community', *Fox43* (8 May 2013); David Wright, 'Abuse Case Dismissed against Highland County Amish Family', *The Times-Gazette* (24 November 2017), www.timesgazette.com/news/21744/abuse-case-dismissed-against-highland-county-amish-family.

[80] Cates, *Serving the Amish*, 91.

[81] Fontes and Harder, 'Working with Amish Families on Child Abuse and Neglect'.

[82] Peter Smith and Shelly Bradbury, 'Mennonites, Amish Face Growing Recognition of Widespread Sexual Abuse in their Communities', *Post-Gazette* (20 May 2019), https://newsinteractive.post-gazette.com/coverings/mennonite-amish-sexual-abuse-forgiveness-in-their-communities/; Shelly Bradbury and Peter Smith, 'After Years of Abuse, a Mennonite Couple Reconnects with Each Other and their Family', *Post-Gazette* (22 May 2019), https://newsinteractive.post-gazette.com/coverings/mennonites-burkholders-sexual-abuse-amish-cover ings/; Stephanie Strasburg and Peter Smith, 'Joanna's Journey', *Post-Gazette* (3 June 2019), https://newsinteractive.post-gazette.com/coverings/joanna-yoder-mennonite-child-sexual-abuse/; Peter Smith and Shelly Bradbury, 'Never Alone: Mennonite and Amish Sexual Abuse Victims Find Each Other and Find Their Voices', *Post-Gazette* (5 June 2019), https://newsinteractive.post-gazette.com/coverings/amish-mennonite-sexual-abuse-support-podcasts-advocacy-victims/. Peter Smith published dozens of similar articles. See https://muckrack.com/peter-smith-25/articles.

assistance. Thus, only in cases of repeated offences, after giving the offender a number of opportunities to repent, will the community surrender the offender to the police. But it takes long time until the Amish give up and appeal to the outside world. Meanwhile, the victims' traumas deepen and deepen.

The Amish look inside their communities for a spiritual solution, when the more appropriate solution would be to seek help from professionals who are trained to deal with psychological problems. The Amish are simply not sufficiently equipped to deal with these matters, and their isolation from mainstream society means that public services are largely out of reach, especially for children. The usual avenues for getting counsel are not available to them. They do not have access to emergency help and do not know where to turn. The social apparatus that exists in American schools that could potentially stop abuse and assist victims: police, teachers who receive training as to how to deal with abuse, mental health counsellors, psychologists and social workers – these professionals do not exist in the Amish communities. In society at large, abuses are first noticed and reported by school teachers but this is not the case in the Amish parochial schools. Hence, while sexual abuse is not unique to the Amish, it is easier for Amish abusers to continue their abuse. Even if people in the community know of abuse, they will usually not intervene on behalf of the children, because they do not want to be seen as meddling in other families' everyday lives, and they do not know how to deal with abuse. As aforesaid, sometimes the Amish blame the victims for the abuser's crime or for laundering dirty cloths outside the community. This leaves those Amish children who are being abused with few or no advocates, just when they need them the most.[83]

In January 2020, *Cosmopolitan* published a long report from an investigative journalist who spent a year researching sexual abuse among the Amish. The reporter, Sarah McClure, uncovered fifty-two cases, which include rape and incest, across seven American states over the past two decades. She argues that the full picture is much darker and more disturbing. Whenever she spoke with abused women they told her about dozens of other cousins and friends and family members who were victimized. Based on these conversations, McClure thinks there are a lot more victims in Amish country who never complained.[84]

McClure substantiated my research findings. Many of the perpetrators are family members who abuse family hierarchy that subordinates women to men to exploit daughters and sisters. The Amish community supports and shelters abusers, not the abused. Victims who sought to escape their lot and stop the abuse are subjected to threats. Sometimes they are shamed or shunned and are left with no place to go.

---

[83] 'Michigan Amishman Gets 15–25 Years for Sexual Assault', *Amish America* (18 October 2018), http://amishamerica.com/michigan-amishman-gets-15-25-years-for-sexual-assault/.

[84] Sarah McClure, 'The Amish Keep to Themselves: And They're Hiding a Horrifying Secret', *Cosmopolitan* (14 January 2020), www.cosmopolitan.com/lifestyle/amp30284631/amish-sexual-abuse-incest-me-too/?__twitter_impression=true&utm_campaign=todays_worldview&utm_medium=Email&utm_source=Newsletter&wpisrc=nl_todayworld&wpmm=1.

Even if they have left the community, their entire lives are turned upside down because they are not familiar with the outside world and do not receive the required support. It is extremely difficult for a young girl to go against her own family, father and brothers without any support. Sometimes the abusers are not sent away to allow breathing space for the abused; rather the victims are sent away. They are sent to special Amish or Mennonite mental health facilities, where they are drugged and become 'zombies'.[85] They are prescribed olanzapine, an antipsychotic medication that treats mental illnesses like schizophrenia, aiming to make them calm, 'submissive' and positive.[86] The complainants said that sexual abuse in their communities is an open secret spanning generations. The abuse is so widespread and accepted that one abuser said, in his defence, that he had sex with two of his daughters, insisting 'he made love to them at least three times each but didn't hurt them'.[87] Victims who wish this nightmare to stop and dare to complain to the outside world, something that the Amish consider 'un-Christian', do not even know the names of body parts. They are so young, so innocent and they are lacking sex education that explains the functioning of organs that equips young people with an understanding of what is right and what is wrong in family and communal affairs, and what are the moral boundaries of interference in private matters. The evidence suggests that in the Amish culture, women lack essential mechanisms of care and support to protect themselves against abuse.

QUALIFIED EXIT RIGHT

The Amish do provide their adolescents with the opportunity to change and revise their conception of the good, but this opportunity is limited. In their late teens or early twenties the Amish should accept baptism and the strict regulations of their order, known as the *Ordnung*. The *Ordnung* is based on biblical principles that were accepted and approved by the Amish in the sixteenth century as well as on the specific Amish community regulations that differentiate the community from the outside world.[88] Prior to this acceptance, some Amish communities give their adolescents an opportunity to taste outside life.[89] At the age of sixteen they experience a period of *Rumspringa*, 'running around', enjoying room to roam. Since the youth have not yet been baptized they are not subject to the church's rules about permitted and forbidden behaviours. During this period, which lasts between several months to several years, youngsters can drive cars, use modern technology, wear Western clothes, have sex and socialize with non-Amish. Nearly all youth continue

---

[85] Ibid.
[86] Ibid.
[87] Ibid.
[88] Dewalt, *Amish Education in the United States and Canada*, 20.
[89] Not all Amish communities allow *Rumspringa*. See Emma Gingerich, *Runaway Amish Girl: The Great Escape* (Progressive Rising Phoenix Press, 2014).

to live with their families. A minority of them leave home, find a job and self-sustain themselves.[90] The *Rumspringa* ends when the youngster agrees to be baptized into the church and take up the responsibilities attendant on being an adult member of the Amish community.[91] Indeed, the *Rumspringa* rite of passage demonstrates the prima facie voluntary nature of joining the church.

For the Amish community this is a calculated risk. The Amish know that they are going to lose some members but as long as the loss is not very significant, this is a price the Amish are willing to pay to maintain the Amish order. The majority of Amish youth have internalized the mechanisms of community order and control and thus opt to stay. Furthermore, as the Amish youth lack preparation for meaningful engagement with the outside world, being unqualified for many decent jobs and ineligible to pursue higher education, and because the Amish education system does not provide them with ample tools for social integration, the majority of Amish youth find the outside world too difficult and thus they return to the community after a year or so of running around. Leaving the Amish community entails uncertainty if not a solitary and harsh way of life. A cost–benefit analysis leads most youngsters back to the community, where they accept the *Ordnung* and settle down.[92] Those Amish adolescents who decide to leave the community have good reasons. Some of their stories are heart-wrenching and quite troubling.[93]

Those who wish to leave have a very low starting point because Amish education does not prepare the children to live in the larger American community and does not offer them a plurality of conceptions of the good. There is only one way: the Amish way. Thus, my view on Amish education comes close to that of the dissenting Justice William Orville Douglas who was of the opinion that the matter of education is not within the dispensation of parents alone. Douglas thought 'the children themselves have constitutionally protectible interests'.[94] In order to make an informed opinion, Douglas thought that the children should be entitled to be heard: 'While the parents, absent dissent, normally speak for the entire family, the

[90] Tom Shachtman, *Rumspringa: To Be or Not to Be Amish* (New York: North Point Press, 2007); William A. Fischel, 'Do Amish One-Room Schools Make the Grade? The Dubious Data of "Wisconsin v Yoder"', 113.

[91] Shachtman, *Rumspringa*; *Devil's Background, a Documentary about Amish Teenage Culture* (2002).

[92] Steven V. Mazie, 'Consenting Adults?: Amish Rumspringa and the Quandary of Exit in Liberalism', *Perspectives on Politics*, 3(4) (2005): 752.

[93] Misty Griffin, *Tears of the Silenced* (La Vergne: Mango, 2018); Waxman, 'Breaking Amish'; Laura DePinho, 'Confessions of a Shunned Amish Girl', *The Odyssey* (14 December 2016), www.theodysseyonline.com/confessions-of-shunned-amish-girl; '10 Amazing Stories of People Who Left the Amish Community', www.youtube.com/watch?v=t11ix1B3DtI; Ruth Irene Garrett, *Crossing Over: One Woman's Escape from Amish Life* (San Francisco: HarperOne, 2013); Mary Simms, 'Survivor Speaks Out against Amish Rape Culture ahead of Sentencing', *Huffpost* (4 October 2017), www.huffingtonpost.com/entry/survivor-speaks-out-against-amish-rape-culture-ahead_us_581e7b02e4b0334571e09cfd.

[94] *Wisconsin v. Yoder*, at 243.

education of the child is a matter on which the child will often have decided views. He may want to be a pianist or an astronaut or an oceanographer. To do so he will have to break from the Amish tradition.'[95] Interestingly, while Chief Justice Burger found 'no specific evidence of the loss of Amish adherents by attrition',[96] Justice Byron Raymond White in his concurring opinion,[97] and Justice Douglas in his dissenting opinion, noted evidence that a significant number of Amish children do leave the Old Order.[98] Both Justices White and Douglas presented the important liberal consideration of an agent's autonomy.

Justice White acknowledged that while possibly most Amish children may wish to continue living the rural life of their parents, others 'may wish to become nuclear physicists, ballet dancers, computer programmers, or historians',[99] and for attaining these occupations the Amish education system would not be sufficient. The state has 'a legitimate interest not only in seeking to develop the latent talents of its children but also in seeking to prepare them for the life style that they may later choose', and to provide them with an array of options.[100] In the circumstances of this case, Justice White was unable to say that the state demonstrated 'that Amish children who leave school in the eighth grade will be intellectually stultified or unable to acquire new academic skills later'.[101] White J. concurred with the majority of the court because he was impressed by the 'sincerity of the Amish religious policy', because the 'potentially adverse impact of the state requirement is great', and because the state's 'valid interest in education has already been largely satisfied by the eight years the children have already spent in school'.[102]

Justice Douglas thought that if the best interests of the Amish children are in mind, then the state of Wisconsin's stand should be accepted. Unlike White J. his view not only is consistent but it also adequately representing the liberal view. Douglas J wrote:

> It is the future of the student, not the future of the parents, that is imperiled by today's decision. If a parent keeps his child out of school beyond the grade school, then the child will be forever barred from entry into the new and amazing world of diversity that we have today. The child may decide that that is the preferred course, or he may rebel. It is the student's judgment, not his parents', that is essential if we are to give full meaning to what we have said about the Bill of Rights and of the right of students to be masters of their own destiny. If he is harnessed to the Amish way of life by those in authority over him and if his education is truncated, his entire

[95] Ibid., at 244–245. For further discussion, see Stephen T. Knudsen, 'The Education of the Amish Child', *California Law Review*, 62(5) (1974): 1506–1531.
[96] *Wisconsin v. Yoder*, at 224.
[97] Ibid., at 240.
[98] Ibid., at 245.
[99] *Wisconsin v. Yoder*, at 240.
[100] Ibid., at 240.
[101] Ibid., at 240.
[102] Ibid., at 241.

life may be stunted and deformed. The child, therefore, should be given an opportunity to be heard before the State gives the exemption which we honor today.[103]

Judged by practical results, retention rates after *Rumspringa* are high. Meyers' study of one Amish settlement from 1920 until 1969 shows that the percentage of Amish leaving their community varied from 5 per cent during 1960–1969 to 21 per cent during 1930–1939. The average defection across the decades was 13.8 per cent.[104] The study found that older siblings are more likely to defect, that the majority of those leaving were males, that Amish communities that have made the fewest concessions to modernity in agriculture and in laxity of discipline have the lowest percentage of defectors and that Amish pupils who attended Amish schools are less likely to defect than are those who have gone to public schools.[105] Choy, who studied three Amish communities, found that 36 per cent of New Order children, 14 per cent of Old Order children and 5 per cent of Andy Weaver children leave the church.[106] The strictest community is the last. Choy's evidence suggests that strict Amish regulations lead to low exit rates. Discipline and independent schooling are keys to keep the community together and maintaining higher retention rates. Fischel found that by the end of the *Rumspringa* 90 per cent of the Amish youth accept baptism and embrace the *Ordnung*.[107] The majority prefers to return to the familiar rather than continue to 'run around' aimlessly in a foreign environment which they do not really understand. Amish youth do not know what to look for or what distinctive ways of life are available. They cannot search for something they do not know. Filmmaker Lucy Walker, who directed *Devil's Playground*, an award-winning 2002 full-length documentary film about the culture of Amish teenagers as they reach their sixteenth birthday, also found that the retention rate was 90 per cent.

BALANCING INTERESTS

Balancing should consider the interests of the child, of the parents, of the community and of the state. The court should consider a long-term view of children's development. The word 'individuality' is not mentioned in the court judgement. The word 'autonomy' is mentioned once in the context of freedom of religious bodies, not of the child.[108] Consideration of the children's best interests was

---

[103] *Wisconsin v. Yoder*, at 245–246.
[104] Meyers, 'The Old Order Amish'.
[105] Ibid.
[106] Choy, 'Religion and the Family'.
[107] Fischel, 'Do Amish One-Room Schools Make the Grade? The Dubious Data of "Wisconsin v Yoder"'.
[108] *Wisconsin v. Yoder*, at 221.

mentioned once in passing[109] and the majority of the court failed to recognize the Amish children as an interested party whose future would be greatly affected by the judgement. Only Justice Douglas advocated the rights of the children, insisting that children should be given an opportunity to be heard.[110]

The term 'best interests' is tricky as many interests are involved, some of them are contradictory. They are subjective in the sense that different weight and importance is assigned to them by different stakeholders. Interests are hard to quantify and to prioritize in an objective fashion. Lord Justice Munby elucidated in this context:

> Evaluating a child's best interests involves a welfare appraisal in the widest sense, taking into account, where appropriate, a wide range of ethical, social, moral, religious, cultural, emotional and welfare considerations. Everything that conduces to a child's welfare and happiness or relates to the child's development and present and future life as a human being, including the child's familial, educational and social environment, and the child's social, cultural, ethnic and religious community, is potentially relevant and has, where appropriate, to be taken into account. The judge must adopt a holistic approach.[111]

Lord Justice Munby maintained that a child's welfare is to be judged by the standards of reasonable persons and with regard to the ever-changing nature of the world: 'changes in our understanding of the natural world, technological changes, changes in social standards and, perhaps most important of all, changes in social attitudes'.[112]

The goal of empowering children and helping them develop their potential is mentioned by Justice White who concurred with the decision. Justice White acknowledged that the state has an interest to expand children's knowledge, 'broaden their sensibilities, kindle their imagination, foster a spirit of free inquiry, and increase their human understanding and tolerance'.[113] However, most Amish children wish to continue living the rural life of their parents, in which case their school adequately equips them for their future role. But this is a problematic argument. It might be the case that the children wish to remain in the community because their education is restrictive and does not open them windows to know and

---

[109] Ibid., 232.

[110] In *Re G* [2012] EWCA Civ 1233, Lord Justice Munby wrote: (para. 43): 'Although a parent's views and wishes as to the child's religious upbringing are of great importance, and will always be seriously regarded by the court, just as the court will always pay great attention to the wishes of a child old enough to be able to express sensible views on the subject of religion, even if not old enough to take a mature decision, they will be given effect to by the court only if and so far as and in such manner as is in accordance with the child's best interests. In matters of religion, as in all other aspects of a child's upbringing, the interests of the child are the paramount consideration.'

[111] *Re G* [2012] EWCA (England and Wales Court of Appeal) Civ 1233, para. 27, www .familylawweek.co.uk/site.aspx?i=ed101479.

[112] Ibid., para. 33.

[113] *Wisconsin v. Yoder*, 239.

to think about matters that are outside the confines of the Amish community. It is not that the Amish education suffices for the life they choose but that Amish education, to a large extent, leads them to this choice. The Amish consciously restrict their children's open future (see Chapter 6). If they were to study the American curricula, maybe they would be encouraged to integrate into American life and to contribute to the wider society, not only the Amish. Thus, it is not that there is no need to insist on broader and longer education curricula because most Amish youth wish to remain in the community, but that most Amish youth are content to remain Amish because choice is restricted and the education system is designed for the purpose of perpetuating the community. Amish education does not introduce children to many conceptions of the good but only to one. It does not open their future but forecloses it, narrowing avenues to a single Amish avenue.

Bhikhu Parekh endorses the virtues of multicultural education and warns against closing of the mind by focusing on one so-called truth. Parekh rightly observes that one of the central aims of education should be to equip students with the ability to take part in a conversation between different conceptions of the good. Not only should the curricula include different religions and cultures but it should bring them into a fruitful dialogue. Thereby students are able to appreciate the complexity of truth and the irreducible diversity of interpretations. Multicultural education is an education in freedom, both in the sense of freedom from ethnocentric prejudices and biases as well as freedom to explore and learn from other cultures.[114] The uncompromising education of the Amish is the exact opposite. Not only is it not aimed to enrich contestation of truths but it also wishes to isolate the young from the larger American culture and society, trapping the young within the confines of one traditional belief system that is not suitable for all.

CONCLUSION

In *The Law of Peoples*, John Rawls explained that while liberal societies are pluralistic and peaceful, and are governed by reasonable people who protect basic human rights, minimal means of subsistence, security, liberty and personal property as well as formal equality and self-respect as expressed by the rules of natural justice, non-liberal societies adopt norms based on compulsion and coercion.[115] While liberal peoples are reasonable and rational, encouraging pluralism of ideas and providing avenues to empower opposition, and their conduct, laws and policies are guided by a sense of political justice,[116] authoritarian societies aggressively fight to undermine political opponents. Whereas liberal societies have no qualms to

---

[114] Bhikhu Parekh, *Rethinking Multiculturalism* (Houndmills: Palgrave, 2000): 229–230.

[115] John Rawls, *The Law of Peoples* (Cambridge, MA: Harvard University Press, 2002): 59–62. For further discussion, see Richard Rorty, 'Justice as a Larger Loyalty', *Ethical Perspectives*, 4 (1997): 139–151.

[116] Rawls, *The Law of Peoples*, 25.

present questions with no definite answers, to challenge common truisms, to present competing ideas, to admit human infallibility and to celebrate heresy, in contrast theocracy attempts to provide strict answers to all questions and concerns.

The clash between the liberal state and the Amish way of life is inevitable. The state has reasonable grounds to intervene and enforce the legitimate Wisconsin regulations designed to promote the rights of the child. The severity of children's rights violations justifies intervention. While the liberal state wishes to provide children with the tools to cultivate their talents and propensities, the Amish wish to restrict avenues and choices, putting the community well above the individual. In *Yoder*, the Amish were allowed to do this at the expense of the children. Group rights enjoyed precedence over individual rights. Appreciation of multiculturalism came at the expense of liberalism. I am unable to side with the majority of the Supreme Court because the liberal state has a legitimate interest in providing children with reasonable opportunities, intrigue their imagination, make them think, equip them with knowledge and tools to explain data and articulate their views on what they learn. The liberal state has an interest in seeking to develop the latent talents of its children and in preparing them for the lifestyle that they may later choose, or at least to provide them with an option other than the life they have led in the past. The societal concern for children's education is reasonable and legitimate. In the circumstances of this case, the Amish stifle intellectual progress and thinking and impede their ability to acquire academic skills.

Furthermore, it appears that the Amish have set internal restrictions that enable abuse of children in the name of sustaining community coherence. At the same time, the external protections – the right of a group against the larger society – make it difficult for those who are harmed by the community to reach out and ask for help. One of the main obligations of the liberal state is to protect vulnerable third parties. If the Amish do not provide a safe environment for their children, the state must step in. An aggravating factor in the specific Amish case is that the police and legal system are reluctant to get involved in Amish child abuse cases.[117]

This concern of potential child abuse is a forceful argument against the suggestion of homeschooling. Spinner-Halev argued that if the Amish were told that they had to send their children to schools outside their communities, the Amish might have decided to homeschool their children.[118] American agencies should be very cautious in granting such permissions.

The Amish insistence on its isolating education curriculum poses a real challenge to liberal democracy. The rational is sensible from their perspective as they wish to retain their group. While denying their children certain opportunities, the Amish provide them with a cohesive though not necessarily protective community.

---

[117] David Yoder, *Amish Deception* (Lulu, 2007).
[118] Jeff Spinner-Halev, *Surviving Diversity: Religion and Democratic Citizenship* (Baltimore, MD: Johns Hopkins University Press, 2000): 113.

Children are able to leave the community, although this is not easy as their starting point is very low. Balancing between the different interests, I would like to suggest the following:

- The Amish should be able to teach their own history, norms and tradition.
- The Amish should protect their children against abuse and provide opportunities to curious children who want to know more about the world. Stories of Amish adolescents who were able to build a life for themselves outside the community often include curiosity as a driving element. Saloma Miller Furlong, who left the Amish, said that she was labelled a chatterbox, a handful, stubborn and rebellious. For as long as she can remember, she was a misfit, also because she asked questions.[119] Linda Byler, who enrolled at Penn State University, said that she has always been a very curious person. She enjoyed school but what she learned seemed to her very limited. She spent a lot of her time studying with her older siblings, reading their textbooks. Once she started school, she learned about children in non-Amish schools who were learning more subjects. Byler said she 'felt like I was being cheated'.[120] The Amish should have a class for children who are deemed to be different, rebellious, curious and interested in the wider world, and for children whose parents wish for their children to have opportunities which they would not have under the Amish education system.
- Some Amish do send their children to public schools. This is more common in communities such as Holmes County, Ohio, or in northern Indiana. A few Amish homeschool their children. Yet the vast majority of Amish send their children to the local one-room schoolhouse.[121] Among the Amish, sending children to public schools is controversial as this act is deemed disloyal to the community.[122] Coercive restrictions on children's future in order to preserve familial, cultural and religious ties are highly problematic when the child is torn between different conceptions of the good. What is needed is a tolerant and supportive environment in which children feel safe to express their evolving beliefs. The Amish should openly allow children to study in regular American schools beyond the age of 13 without scapegoating them. Providing these opportunities to the young would not destroy the Amish community.

---

[119] Saloma Miller Furlong, *Bonnet Strings*, 11.

[120] Linda Byler, 'Growing up Amish', *Penn State Shenango* (nd), https://shenango.psu.edu/feature/growing-amish.

[121] 'Why Do Amish Only Go to School until 8th Grade?', *Amish America*, http://amishamerica.com/why-do-amish-only-go-to-school-until-8th-grade/; McConnell and Hurst, 'No "Rip van Winkles" Here', 244.

[122] David L. McConnell and Charles E. Hurst, Ibid.: 246.

Empowering younger generations would vitalize the entire community. Coping with change is a challenge but balancing between the interests of the community and the children's best interests, the change may be positive. It can be assumed that behind a veil of ignorance, people would opt to have these choices.

A study that examined the educational implications of the 1972 Supreme Court decision on an Ohio Amish community found that the Amish have adopted diverse educational pathways, including public schools, charter schools,[123] General Education Development (GED) programmes,[124] homeschooling and vocational courses.[125] The diverse ways in which the Amish continue to renegotiate social boundaries with their neighbours suggests the need for more attention to internal diversity within the Amish. Furthermore, to prevent potential abuse and to provide children with the safe environment they need, the state should show greater involvement in the Amish community and to subject them, as it does when other schools are concerned, to inspections and some form of monitoring. As many of the Amish teachers are young, they would benefit from impartial observers who would comment on their strengths and weaknesses, and who may suggest ways to improve.

Amish charter schools are already monitored by the state. Charter schools are accountable for academic results and for upholding the promises made in their charters. They must demonstrate good performance in the areas of academic achievement, financial management and organizational stability. If a charter school does not meet the set performance goals it then loses its charter and may be closed.

- The liberal state is required to protect vulnerable populations. At present, the American government neglects its duty of care. Abuse is more likely to happen in isolated communities because those communities do not have, or are lacking, the apparatus of prevention, deterrence and support that are commonly offered to prevent abuse and help victims. Indeed, the Amish is not the only community where child abuse takes place. In their comments on a draft of this chapter, Orit Ichilov and Allan Jacobs noted that such abuse took place in the

---

[123] *Charter schools* are semiautonomous schools of choice. They receive government funding, use certified teachers but operate independently of the established state school system in which they are located. Many Amish people sit on such school committees. Charter schools operate with more freedom over their budgets, staffing and curricula compared to regular schools, and with less strict regulations imposed upon district schools. For information on Ohio charter schools, see www.ohioschoolboards.org/sites/default/files/OSBAGuidetoCharterSchools.pdf.

[124] GED is an alternative to the US High school diploma. This is a group of four subject tests which, when passed, provide certification that the student has US high school-level academic skills.

[125] McConnell and Hurst, 'No "Rip van Winkles" Here', 236–254.

Catholic Church, in *Haredi* communities, in American prep schools and in the Israeli kibbutzim. All are closed, discrete communities that try to keep to themselves without involving the police when faced with the challenge of sexual abuse. Experience shows that self-regulation, where the community regulates itself, is often deficient. The Amish protect the abusers, not the abused. Sexual abuse, incest and paedophilia are not an 'internal, 'personal', 'group' problem. Liberal democracy is required to step in and help children in need. Otherwise the abuse might continue unabated for years, inflicting untold pain and suffering and destroying many lives. The Amish education system should include sex education, discussions on children rights, mental health counsellors, adequate child support, monitoring and reporting mechanisms and experienced external advisors who ensure that children are not exploited, sexually or otherwise.

- There is a clear gap between the Amish and American societies. The Amish do not know much about the American way of life, and Americans know little about the Amish. At times, when child welfare and legal professionals did intervene on behalf of abuse victims, they have harmed children through assessments, investigations and interventions that do not take into account the customs and values of the Amish way of life. Intervention should take place carefully and sensitively. Care workers and others should dress modestly, be mindful of gender issues (male professionals should not go into a house without a male family member present) and of the language barrier, build rapport and trust with Amish families, establish community liaisons and focus on common values such as children's safety.[126]

- The United States should open channels of communication with the Amish. Through deliberation and search for reasonable and constructive compromises, based on mutual respect and conducted in good faith, the state should balance competing interests: perpetuating the Amish community against children's self-development and children's right to an open future (see Chapter 6).[127] The liberal state should be concerned when parents pre-empt their children's future options and restrict the

[126] Fontes and Harder, 'Working with Amish Families on Child Abuse and Neglect'.
[127] Joel Feinberg, 'The Child's Right to an Open Future', in William Aiken and Hugh LaFollette (eds), *Whose Child?* (Totowa, NJ: Rowman & Littlefield, 1980): 124–153. See also, generally, Joel Feinberg, *Freedom and Fulfilment: Philosophical Essays* (Princeton, NJ: Princeton University Press, 1992). For a critique, see Joseph Millum, 'The Foundation of the Child's Right to an Open Future', *Journal of Social Philosophy*, 45(4) (2014): 522–538.

scope for their children's personal development. The state has an interest in empowering children to become equal citizens in society, enabling their integration into the wider society if they so wish.

The remainder of the book considers multiculturalism in two countries: France and Israel. Both exhibit discriminatory attitudes towards their respective minorities. As France is central to the history of liberalism, one would expect it to have a tolerant attitude to minorities. This is not the case. Chapter 9 explains this puzzle.

PART IV

Country Case Studies

9

Multiculturalism v. Security Considerations

Behind the French Veil of Ignorance

The tyranny of the majority is now generally included among the evils against which society requires to be on its guard.

J.S. Mill

Whatever system of governance is eventually adopted, it is important that it carries the people with it. We need to convey the message that safeguarding our common property, humankind, will require developing in each of us a new loyalty: a loyalty to mankind.

Joseph Rotblat

In the pre-COVID-19 era, suppose you entered a bus in London populated by people who were wearing anti-pollution masks. How would you feel?

Now suppose you enter a bus where many passengers are wearing crash helmets. How would you then feel?

Lastly, suppose you enter a bus where many women are wearing full facial veils. How would you feel?

While reflecting on these scenarios, ask yourself which scenario causes you the greatest discomfort, if any, and why.

Many people in the Western world, certainly before the COVID-19 epidemic, felt unease when they could not see people's faces. The more the face is covered, the greater our unease. This is because we assess situations vis-à-vis other people in large part by looking at their facial impressions. We look for clues and hints projected by eye and mouth movement. When people cover their faces we try to understand the reasons for hiding one's face. In the first scenario, we soon may have realized that the bus was occupied by a large group of tourists from the orient, where it is common to use anti-pollution masks as protection. In the second scenario, a motorcyclist club had prepared a surprise birthday party for one of their mates. He (and you) gasped when they all lifted their helmets and shouted 'surprise!' In the last scenario, you realize that the bus is populated with a large group of Muslim women who observe their tradition by wearing a veil. So there were perfectly good reasons for hiding people's faces. Is one justification more or less reasonable than another?

In previous chapters I tackled two main attacks against multiculturalism: that it is bad for women, and that it is also bad for democracy. I argue that multiculturalism as such is not bad for democracy. Quite the opposite. Multiculturalism enriches democracy. Abuse of power is bad for democracy. Multiculturalism and democracy are reconcilable provided that protective mechanisms to secure the fundamental rights of vulnerable populations are in place. While feminists and others who champion gender equality have been critical of cultural practices that, as seen from their perspective, discriminate against women or deny women the same degree of freedom afforded male members of the group, it is wrong to conclude that multiculturalism per se is bad for women. Liberal democratic societies must tolerate illiberal groups, so long as these groups conduct themselves in a manner that is just and reasonable, as outlined in the previous chapters. A fair balance must be struck between individual rights and group rights. The final part of this book examines these attacks as well as a further attack against multiculturalism: that it promotes terrorism and threatens national security. Populist leaders work on the human sentiment of fear to promote national unity and criticize multicultural divisions. I examine this attack in the context of two countries. This chapter examines France, while Chapter 10 studies Israel.

This chapter analyses French cultural policies in the face of what its government perceives as a challenge to its national raison d'être. Islam's way of life seems to challenge existing conventions. In recent years, tensions have been growing between the majority population and Muslim communities following a series of attacks carried out by Muslim terrorists. Those attacks shocked the French nation and widened negative sentiments of fear, resentment and suspicion regarding Islam and Muslims.

Debates over citizenship, immigration, colonial memory, the reform of the state, the historiography of modern France, terrorism and security and the complicated relationship between state and church have been exploited by politicians and galvanized society. Many of these debates have coalesced around the political concepts of republicanism, neutrality and the spirit of *laïcité* which structure the vocabulary of French political actors and of ordinary citizens. *Laïcité* describes a set of legislation, a state of affairs. It holds: we live in a secular state. *Laïcité* can be translated to English as secularity.

The tension between republicanism, neutrality and *laïcité*, on the one hand, and multiculturalism, on the other, has become the central battleground of contemporary French politics. Republicanism does not recognize minorities in the secular public space – conceptually, politically or legally. This tension highlights the differences between the French concept of liberalism as distinguished from the Anglo-Saxon understanding of liberalism.

Helena Rosenblatt argues that France invented liberalism in the early years of the nineteenth century. The French nobleman Charles de Montalembert (1810–1870) may have invented the term 'liberal democracy'. America took possession of liberalism only in the early twentieth century.[1] However, French republicanism is paternalistic, less suspicious of government, more supportive of government intervention in private matters and less pluralistic compared to Anglo-Saxon liberalism. The French endorse a strong unitary state whose role is to maintain citizenship that is independent of divisive cultural groups. Political liberties are more important than personal liberties. These stark features of French tradition, which at times supported the emergence of French republicanism, were evident during the second half of the twentieth century in the context of the controversy around the Muslim headscarf and dress. For some, the struggle against Muslim dress signifies secularism and freedom. For others, this struggle signifies intolerance and anti-Muslim sentiments. How come a Western democracy, said to be one of the foremothers of liberalism, is so obsessed with how people dress? Does this obsession go hand in hand with the values of the French Revolution (1789–1795)? What does this struggle tell us about the place of multiculturalism in France?

France has attempted to keep public space secular. The headscarf controversy erupted in 1989 when three Muslim girls who enrolled in Gabriel Havez, a state school in the town of Creil, arrived in school wearing the traditional headscarf, the hijab. That controversy was accompanied by a different yet related debate concerning school attendance of Jewish students on Shabbat (Saturday). In the following decades, state schools became the focal point of the debate. One of France's enshrined principles, *laïcité*, was questioned. In June 2003, President Jacques Chirac appointed an independent commission to study the implementation of secularity in public services, in the education system and in the workplace. Chirac tasked the committee to examine the neutrality of the public service, respect for pluralism, religious liberty, freedom of expression and the reinforcement of cohesion and brotherhood between citizens, equality of opportunity, rejection of discrimination, gender equality and the dignity of woman.[2] The committee, chaired by Bernard Stasi, conducted about 140 meetings. It heard testimonials from political, religious and union leaders, administrators, elected representatives, business leaders, education leaders, students and other members of the public. It also received hundreds of written contributions, and the twenty committee members travelled to other European countries to learn from their experiences.[3] The committee concluded that the principle of *laïcité* should be maintained in order to ensure

---

[1] Helena Rosenblatt, *The Lost History of Liberalism* (Princeton, NJ: Princeton University Press, 2018): 3.

[2] Robert O'Brien and Bernard Stasi, *The Stasi Report: The Report of the Committee of Reflection on the Application of the Principle of Secularity in the Republic* (Bufffalo, NY: William S. Hein, 2005): 8–9.

[3] Ibid., 36–37.

freedom of conscience and equality as well as to fight against discrimination.[4] More importantly, public order should be maintained.[5] The committee made a number of recommendations, the majority of which were never implemented. The commission opinion was unanimous with the exception of one abstention regarding the hijab ban at state schools. Both the recommendations that were accepted by the French government as well as those that were rejected were and are subjected to continued debate. That debate on secular school dress code is complex and requires a separate analysis beyond the scope of this chapter.[6]

Critiques of multiculturalism in France argue that multiculturalism is bad for democracy, is bad for the Republic, is bad for women and is undermining public order. I explain the reasoning of those who speak of compatibility between liberalism and French public secularity, or *laïcité*, and the criticism of *laïcité* as a non-liberal concept. The discussion is opened with background information about the crystallization of French values. I elucidate the alternative trinity that the French offered to replace the Father, the Son and the Holy Spirit: *liberté, égalité, fraternité*. This trinity became the motto of the Republic.

A fourth, no less important principle and value, very relevant to our discussion, is explored: *laïcité*. The French Revolution was anti-clerical. In the twentieth century these sentiments germinated into a form of secular religion. I examine the historical roots of *laïcité* and the extent to which *laïcité* can be reconciled with the principles of *liberté, égalité, fraternité*. I also explain how colonialism, immigration, multiculturalism and terrorism have shaped the present discourse.

A note on terminology is in order. The French use the words *foulard* (scarf/headscarf) and *voile* (veil) to describe all types of covering worn by Muslim women. These generic words for all kinds of head and face coverage create a lot of confusion.

---

[4] Ibid., 47–49.

[5] Ibid., 54.

[6] The complexity of the debate is manifested in the following studies: Patrick Weil, 'A Nation in Diversity: France, Muslims and the Headscarf', *Open Democracy* (25 March 2004), www .opendemocracy.net/en/article_1811jsp/; Johannes Willms, 'France Unveiled: Making Muslims into Citizens?', *Open Democracy* (26 February 2004), www.opendemocracy.net/en/ article_1753jsp/; Joan W. Scott, 'The Banning of Islamic Head Scarves in French Public Schools', *French Politics, Culture & Society*, 23(3) (Winter 2005): 106–127; Mohammad M. Idriss, 'Laïcité and the Banning of the "Hijab" in France', *Legal Studies*, 25(2) (April 2006): 260–295; John R. Bowen, *Why the French Don't Like Headscarves* (Princeton, NJ: Princeton University Press, 2007); Cécile Laborde, *Critical Republicanism: The Hijab Controversy and Political Philosophy* (Oxford: Oxford University Press, 2008); Sophie Heine, 'The Hijab Controversy and French Republicanism: Critical Analysis and Normative Propositions', *French Politics*, 7(2) (2009): 167–193; Guy Haarscher, 'Secularism, the Veil and "Reasonable Interlocutors": Why France Is Not That Wrong', *Penn State International Law Review*, 28(3) (2010): 367–382; Melanie Adrian, *Religious Freedom at Risk: The EU, French Schools, and Why the Veil Was Banned* (Berlin: Springer, 2015); Jean L. Cohen and Cécile Laborde (eds), *Religion, Secularism, and Constitutional Democracy* (New York: Columbia University Press, 2016); Murat Akan, *The Politics of Secularism: Religion, Diversity, and Institutional Change in France and Turkey* (New York: Columbia University Press, 2017).

FIGURE 9.1. Hijab (Colin Hawkins/Stone/Getty Images).

In the following discussion I use the term headscarf to refer only to the hijab, which is a head-covering scarf that some Muslim women wear in public. The hijab leaves the face uncovered (Figure 9.1).

Hair covering (hijab) has to be distinguished from different forms of face veiling. The burqa is the most extreme form of veiling. It completely hides the female behind a loose garment (Figure 9.2). A small mesh screen is available for her to see. The niqab, in turn, is a veil that conceals the face. It is worn along with a headscarf, leaving only the eyes exposed (Figure 9.3).

BACKGROUND

On 3 August 1787, the Marquis de Lafayette wrote to George Washington: 'The spirit of liberty is spreading in this country at a great rate ... Liberal ideas are cantering about from one end of the kingdom to the other.'[7] It seemed that the French were ready for a liberal system of government similar to America's.

On 14 July 1789, the French Revolution erupted. The Revolution was republican from the start. It proclaimed equal rights for all and collective sovereignty, and established representative powers. The constitution was no longer in the monarchy,

---

[7] Rosenblatt, *The Lost History of Liberalism*, 41.

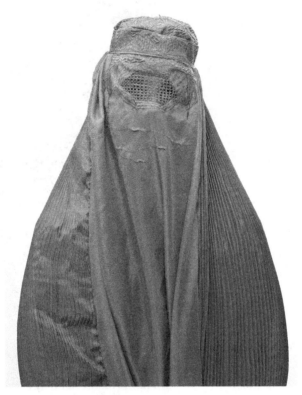

FIGURE 9.2. Burqa (Juanmonino/E+/Getty Images).

but the monarchy was in the constitution.[8] The principle of *liberté* was accentuated in one of the most important documents of liberal thought in general, and of France in particular. On 26 August 1789, the French National Constituent Assembly issued the *Déclaration des droits de l'homme et du citoyen* (Declaration of the Rights of Man and the Citizen) which defined individual and collective rights at the time of the Revolution. The declaration holds that 'Men are born and remain free and equal in respect of their rights.'[9] At a time when there was one law for the aristocracy and another law for the common people, when the king or his nobles could take others' liberty and life at will, this declaration was revolutionary. The declaration further explains that the aim of every political association is the protection of 'the

8   Patrice Gueniffey, 'The First Republic', in Edward Berenson, Vincent Duclert and Christophe Prochasson (eds), *The French Republic: History, Values, Debates* (Ithaca, NY: Cornell University Press, 2012): 21.
9   'Declaration of the Rights of Man and Citizen, decreed by the National Assembly in the sessions of 20th, 21st, 23rd, 24th and 26th August, 1789, accepted by the King.' At www.open .edu/openlearn/ocw/pluginfile.php/612270/mod_resource/content/1/rightsofman.pdf.

FIGURE 9.3. Niqab (Peter Dazeley/The Image Bank/Getty Images).

natural and imprescriptible rights of man; these rights are liberty, property, security and resistance to oppression'.[10] Article 4 of the declaration elucidates the meaning of liberty, saying: 'Liberty consists in being able to do whatever does not harm another. Thus, the exercise of each man's natural rights has no limits other than those which guarantee to the other members of society the enjoyment of these same rights; those limits can only be determined by the law.'[11] Specific importance is assigned to free expression of thoughts and opinions perceived as 'one of the most precious of the

[10] Ibid.
[11] Ibid.

FIGURE 9.4. The French Revolution (Photos.com/Getty Images Plus).

rights of man'.[12] The declaration aptly states that 'every citizen is therefore entitled to freedom of speech, of expression and of the press, save that he is liable for the abuse of this freedom in the circumstances laid down by the law' (see Figure 9.4).[13]

Freedom of religion is also important. Article 10 of the declaration postulates: 'No man must be penalised for his opinions, even his religious opinions, provided that their expression does not disturb the public order established by the law.'[14] As the Revolution was bloody and chaotic,[15] people were acutely aware of the need to secure public order by law. This need is accentuated time and again in French history.

In turn, Article 6 of the declaration had set forth the principle of *égalité*:

The law is the expression of the general will; all citizens have the right to participate in lawmaking, personally or through their representatives; the law must be the same

---

[12] Ibid.

[13] Ibid. See also Jeremy Jennings, 'Liberty', in Berenson et al., *The French Republic*, 95–102.

[14] Declaration of the Rights of Man and Citizen.

[15] Timothy Tackett, *The Coming of the Terror in the French Revolution* (Cambridge, MA: Harvard University Press, 2015); Marisa Linton, *Choosing Terror: Virtue, Friendship, and Authenticity in the French Revolution* (Oxford: Oxford University Press, 2015). See also Paul R. Hanson, 'Political History of the French Revolution since 1989', *Journal of Social History*, 52(3) (Spring 2019): 584–592.

for all, whether it protects or punishes. All citizens being equal in its eyes, are equally eligible for all public honours, positions and duties, according to their ability, and without any distinction other than those of their virtues and talents.[16]

The idea of 'the general will' stems from the philosophy of Jean-Jacques Rousseau. Indeed, Rousseau's philosophy is essential to the understanding of French social and political life. The mission of the state is to create a citizen in Rousseauian terms. Rousseau explained that the citizens are the sovereign. The citizens administer justice and govern the state.[17] They all commit themselves to observe the same conditions and they all should have the same rights. Thus, from the very nature of the social contract, every act of sovereignty – that is, 'every authentic act of the general will – obliges or favours all the citizens equally; so that the sovereign recognizes only the body of the nation and doesn't distinguish among the individuals of whom it is made up'.[18] Acts of the sovereign are just and reasonable because they are the making of equal citizens who share the general will; the union is as complete as it can be.[19] Laws benefit both the individual and the community at large.[20] That is to say, in addition to each individual's self-interest (the private will), the citizen has a collective interest in the well-being of the community. The 'general will' is the citizen body acting as a whole and freely adopting rules that apply equally to each individual. This idea stresses the importance of freely chosen social obligations as the basis of civic virtue. The citizen body is the only legitimate 'sovereign' of a political community.

According to Rousseau, sovereignty is unlimited and absolute. It requires total alienation of individual rights to the whole community. Rousseau acknowledged that this may seem drastic, but three features of the general will make it reasonable still:

1. Because each individual gives himself entirely, the result is the same for all and, therefore, no one has any interest in making things tougher.
2. Because the alienation is made without reserve, the union is as complete as it can be, and no associate has anything more to demand.
3. Each individual in giving himself to everyone gives himself to no one; 'the right over himself that the others get is matched by the right that he gets over each of them. So he gains as much as he loses, and also gains extra force for the preservation of what he has.'[21]

---

[16] Declaration of the Rights of Man and Citizen. See also Jeremy Jennings, 'Equality', in Berenson et al., *The French Republic*, 103–111.
[17] Jean-Jacques Rousseau, *Discourse on Inequality* (1755): 3.
[18] Jean-Jacques Rousseau, *The Social Contract* (Jonathan Bennett edition, 2017): 16, www .earlymoderntexts.com/assets/pdfs/rousseau1762.pdf.
[19] Ibid., 7.
[20] Ibid., 11.
[21] Ibid., 7.

Thus, in Rousseau's conception individuals immerse themselves in the collective without losing their identity. Assimilation brings about unity and justice. Collective decision-making serves and promotes public good. Equal participation in government requires minimal differences between citizens. Justice requires an equal, homogenous, other-regarding citizen body.[22] Each citizen puts his person and all his power in common under the supreme direction of the general will, and the collective receives each member as an indivisible part of the whole.

Article 3 of the Declaration of the Rights of Man and Citizen says that the 'fundamental source of all sovereignty resides in the nation; no body of men, no individual can exercise an authority which does not expressly derive therefrom'.[23] The nation's general will guarantees that the aims of the political association are accomplished. It emphasizes unity and equality between citizens. Anything that can disturb this unity is a threat to the nation and to the French nation-building enterprise. Therefore, there is little consideration for religious and cultural minorities. Ensuring diversity was not in the minds of the French nation-builders who wanted to create a cohesive republic. Conversely, diversity was perceived as a threat to the unity of the nation.

The third part of the Revolution motto, the principle of *fraternité*, is, on the one hand, at odds with the two others that are defined according to rights, statutes and contracts. On the other hand, fraternity depends on the extent of liberty and equality that exists in a given community. Fraternity – or brotherhood – is about moral obligations and harmony. It is a derivative of the general will, emphasizing the unity of the Republic and a sense of affinity for the national body and values. An understanding emerged that rights should be accompanied by a consideration for rights of others, and also by a willingness to accept reasonable adjustments.

In 1848, fraternity reappeared with a religious dimension when Catholic priests celebrated the brotherhood of Christ and blessed Liberty Trees planted at the time.[24] Since then the idea of fraternity has been frequently preached when social inequality was marked. During the nineteenth century it inspired humanitarians who claimed that this was a natural end for people, and that democracy aimed fundamentally at the progressive attainment of this objective. Fraternity emphasizes the interpersonal relation of mutual care and love for one another, since the basic value of human existence lies in communal, other-regarding relations. Individuals should not misuse their freedom but rather cooperate and help one another in creating a meaningful society. *Fraternité* implies a general sense of societal cooperation, depicts a picture in which members of society create, in the spirit of the family, a common framework – both material and mental – which is a necessary condition for

---

[22] L.R. Sorenson, 'Rousseau's Liberalism', *History of Political Thought*, 11(3) (Autumn 1990): 446. See also David Miller, 'Rousseau, Jean-Jacques', in D. Miller (ed.), *The Blackwell Encyclopaedia of Political Thought* (Oxford: Basil Blackwell, 1987): 457.

[23] Declaration of the Rights of Man and Citizen.

[24] National Motto of France, https://frenchmoments.eu/national-motto-of-france/.

the good life. Fraternity instructs treating others not simply as though they have rights equal to ours but with a loving concern for people's welfare, aiming to promote other's happiness, thus building a united family of mankind.[25]

The Revolution needed a new trinity; therefore, the motto *liberté, égalité, fraternité* became the values trademark of the French Republic. But hammering home the principle of anti-clericalism was no less important. One of the chief aims of the Revolution was to weaken the political, social and cultural influences of the Roman Catholic Church. Inspired and influenced by the ideas of the Enlightenment philosophers, Charles-Louis de Secondat, Baron de La Brède et de Montesquieu (1689–1755), Voltaire (1694–1778), Jean-Jacques Rousseau (1712–1778), Denis Diderot (1713–1784) and Jean Le Rond D'Alembert (1717–1783), the revolutionaries wished to promote scientific reasoning and to exclude religion from politics as they saw how religion was used as a tool for oppression. Clericalism was perceived as backward, superstitious and anti-rational. Clericalism, according to the revolutionary rationalism, was anything but reasonable as the motivations of those who upheld and promoted religion were partisan and suspect. French Catholicism had split into two parts: a Constitutional Church loyal to the revolution and a Refractory Church opposed to it.[26] Many Catholic priests opposed the Revolution and supported armed counter-revolutionary uprisings.

Montesquieu and Voltaire shared a bitter opposition to religious persecution and slavery, opposition to censorship, a deep scepticism regarding European imperialism and a commitment to judicial reforms and the rule of law.[27] In accordance with Montesquieu's *The Spirit of Laws*, freedom should not be unlimited. In societies directed by laws, 'liberty can consist only in the power of doing what we ought to will, and in not being constrained to do what we ought not to will'.[28] Montesquieu differentiated between independence and liberty. 'Liberty is a right of doing whatever the laws permit, and if a citizen could do what they forbid he would be no longer possessed of liberty, because all his fellow-citizens would have the same power.'[29] It is the role of the state, via its government and constitutional arrangements, to organize and regulate liberties. The government articulates to its citizens what they ought to do. Montesquieu emphasized that no society can subsist without a form of government. 'The united strength of individuals ... constitutes what we

[25] J.F. Stephen, *Liberty, Equality, Fraternity* (Cambridge: Cambridge University Press, 1967): 221–261; Ernest Barker, *Reflections of Government* (Oxford: Oxford University Press, 1942): 418–419; Anne-Claude Ambroise-Rendu, 'Fraternity', in Berenson et al., *The French Republic*, 112–118.

[26] Jean Baubérot, 'The Evolution of French Secularism', in Ranjan Ghosh, *Making Sense of the Secular* (New York: Routledge, 2013): 45. See, generally, Dorinda Outram, *The Enlightenment* (Cambridge: Cambridge University Press, 2019).

[27] Jacob T. Levy, *Rationalism, Pluralism and Freedom* (Oxford: Oxford University Press, 2014): 159.

[28] Montesquieu, *The Spirit of Laws* (Kitchener, ON: Batoche Books, 2001): Book 11, 172.

[29] Ibid.

call the body politic.'[30] And the body politic needs to be solidified and unified. Therefore, also in accordance with Rousseau's teachings, minorities needed to be incorporated into society and accept the general will once it was articulated. Interventionist and coercive Catholicism that penetrates all spheres of life was perceived as an obstacle to this desired integration. Anti-clericalism was invoked at the time of the French Revolution, when both the church and the aristocracy were under attack.

One should add that in the early nineteenth century the term 'Gallicanism' was coined, advocating restriction of papal power. Gallicanism consisted of three basic ideas: independence of the French king in the temporal order, superiority of an ecumenical council over the pope and union of clergy and king to limit the intervention of the pope within the kingdom. Gallicanists believed that the pope should be placed under the authority of the church as represented by the general council. They rejected the pope's assumed infallibility.[31]

LAÏCITÉ

Another term that was coined in the nineteenth century was *laïcité*. The first known usage of the noun *laïcité* was in a meeting of the Seine General Council on 8 November 1871, when two people from the doctrinal movement of *la Morale indépendante*, were said to have presented a 'proposition de *laïcité*' (proposal on *laïcité*). The context was a discussion on the exclusion of dogma in public educa-tion.[32] State *laïcité* emerged in opposition to the then vastly greater powers of coercion of the anti-republican Catholic Church in the eighteenth and nineteenth centuries. In order to unify the French nation and instil a sense of brotherhood among citizens, cultural pluralism and diversity could not have been tolerated. Viewed as a constitutional principle and even as a doctrine, *laïcité* postulates the existence of a secular ethics grounded in science and philosophy that acts as a civil religion and educational tool to implant tolerance.[33]

Laïcité was besought to prevent the encroachment of religious affiliations and instil civic values. Unity rather than cultural affiliation was emphasized. It was only

---

[30] Ibid, Book 1, 22.

[31] 'Gallicanism', *Encyclopaedia Britannica*, www.britannica.com/topic/Gallicanism.

[32] Sylvie Le Grand, 'The Origin of the Concept of Laïcité in Nineteenth Century France', in Marion Eggert and Lucian Hölscher (eds), *Religion and Secularity: Transformations and Transfers of Religious Discourses in Europe and Asia* (Leiden: Brill, 2013): 63.

[33] Jean Baubérot, 'The Evolution of Secularism in France: Between Two Civil Religions', in Linell E. Cady and Elizabeth Shakman Hurd (eds), *Comparative Secularism in a Global Age* (New York: Palgrave Macmillan, 2010): 57–68; Jeremy Jennings, 'Citizenship, Republicanism and Multiculturalism in Contemporary France', *British Journal of Political Science*, 30(4) (October 2000): 578. See, generally, Maurice Larkin, *Church and State after the Dreyfus Affair: The Separation Issue in France* (London: Macmillan, 1974); Jeremy Jennings, *Revolution and the Republic: A History of Political Thought in France since the Eighteenth Century* (Oxford: Oxford University Press, 2013).

as abstract individuals, divested of all particularity, that citizens could be treated equally.[34] The term *laïcité* means 'a separation between church and state that protects the freedom of religion and of non-religion, whose intention is to avoid any discrimination against people on the basis of their religious affiliation or lack thereof'.[35] *Laïcité* is *not* about the protection of religions from state interference. Conversely, the state has a very active and important role to play in the administration of *laïcité*.

There appears to be a paradox between a separation between church and state which protects the freedom of religion and, at the same time, lack of protection of religions from state interference. The resolution of this is the distinction between the private realm, where freedom of religion is protected, and the public realm, where the state has a regulatory duty in the name of the whole community.

I said that the seeds of *laïcité* were sown during the French Revolution. Catholic privileges were abolished. Papal influence was limited. French national sovereignty was proclaimed, independent of external influences. But while the Revolution was anti-clerical, it was *not* anti-religious. The widespread belief was that the state ought to have some religion. Some supported Catholicism in the French version which the pope did not accept as his authority was challenged. Others supported civil religion.[36]

Laïcité became the official doctrine of the Third Republic (1870–1940) when the secular state primary education system was established during the 1880s while the Catholic Church was disestablished in 1905.[37] In the First and Second Republics, *laïcité* was an idea. Thereafter, it became concrete. Secularity was made a cornerstone of the constitution. The law on the Separation of the Churches and State (*concernant la séparation des Églises et de l'État*) was passed by the Chamber of Deputies in December 1905.[38] The law, which was liberal in essence in the sense that it wanted to promote personal freedoms, inspired by the political philosophy of John Locke,[39] reflected strong anti-clericalism and established state secularity. It sought a compromise between a strengthened republican state and the Catholic Church. The law was built around four principles: furthering freedom of conscience, making religious choice a private matter, separating state and religion,

---

[34] Rita Chin, *The Crisis of Multiculturalism in Europe* (Princeton, NJ: Princeton University Press, 2017): 175.

[35] Shaira Nanwani, 'The Burqa Ban: An Unreasonable Limitation on Religious Freedom or a Justifiable Restriction?', *Emory International Law Review*, 25 (2011): 1431–1475.

[36] Discussion with Michel Troper, Paris (10 July 2019).

[37] Laborde, *Critical Republicanism*, 7.

[38] The Law of 1905, *Protestant Museum*, www.museeprotestant.org/en/notice/the-law-of-1905/.

[39] Comment made by Jean Bauberot. Email on 28 January 2020. Locke called religious societies churches. In *A Letter Concerning Toleration* (1689) he wrote: 'Just as the magistrate has no power to impose by his laws the use of any rites and ceremonies in any church, so also he has no power to forbid the use of any rites and ceremonies that are already accepted, approved, and practised by a church; because doing that would destroy the church itself as an institution whose sole purpose is to worship God freely in its own way.'

and granting equal respect to all faiths and beliefs.[40] The Republic does not recognize, fund or subsidize any religion. It guarantees free exercise of religion with the sole restriction decreed in the interest of public order. Tolerance of different religions was invoked as long as it did not interfere in public life. *Laïcité* was perceived as a compromise solution that attempted to heal a divisive political situation and to counteract the dominance of the Catholic Church in public affairs. The 1905 law prohibited faith-based discrimination. Consequently, crucifixes were not allowed in the classroom.[41] The law declared that all religious property were property of the state and local governments. Ownership of all church buildings built before 1905 was transferred to the state, and the French Republic took it upon itself to maintain them and allowed churches to use them. Public funds were used for the upkeep of churches and Jewish synagogues built before 1905.[42]

As a result of the separation between state and religion the Church lost positions of power it had formerly held. Public employees could not express religious beliefs while on duty. They have an obligation to political and religious neutrality.[43] The French adopted the liberal view on neutrality: government should be neutral regarding different conceptions of the good because otherwise bias would generate intolerance (see Chapter 1). Religion should not interfere with public and political affairs. Religion belongs to the private sphere.

Towards the end of the nineteenth century, republican ideas and values came to be institutionalized as part of the nation-building process that took place in the Third Republic.[44] Until 1918, France was Europe's only durable republic but it resisted acknowledging the particular interests of the working class. Emphasis was put on the nation as the only legitimate social entity.[45] As France was fragmented, there was a need to establish unity, to build a nation. Consequently, unitarianism (meaning the perception of a united, undivided republic) trumped cultural tolerance. National minorities were forced to accept unity. People were not allowed

[40] Othon Guerlac, 'The Separation of Church and State in France', *Political Science Quarterly*, 23(2) (1908): 259–296; Patrick Weil, 'Why the French Laïcité Is Liberal', *Cardozo Law Review*, 30(6) (2009): 2699–2714.

[41] Dominic McGoldrick, *Human Rights and Religion: The Islamic Headscarves Debate in Europe* (Oxford and Portland: Hart, 2006): 36–37.

[42] Because Islamic mosques did not exist in 1905 they are not supported by the state.

[43] 'Loi du 9 décembre 1905 concernant la séparation des Eglises et de l'Etat', www.legifrance .gouv.fr/texteconsolide/mcebw.htm. See also Alexandre Caeiro, 'Religious Authorities or Political Actors? The Muslim Leaders of the French Representative Body of Islam', in Jocelyne Cesari and Sean McLoughlin (eds), *European Muslims and the Secular State* (Abingdon: Routledge, 2016): 71–84, and David Saunders, 'France on the Knife-Edge of Religion: Commemorating the Centenary of the Law of 9 December 1905 on the Separation of Church and State', in G.B. Levey and T. Modood (eds), *Secularism, Religion and Multicultural Citizenship* (Cambridge: Cambridge University Press, 2009): 56–81.

[44] Emile Chabal, 'Writing the French National Narrative in the Twenty-First Century', *The Historical Journal*, 53(2) (2010): 499.

[45] Patrice Higonnet, 'Sociability, Social Structure, and the French Revolution', *Social Research*, 56(1) (Spring 1989): 122.

to speak their languages at school. And there was an ongoing battle between the Church and the Republic. In 1923 the reference to teaching duties towards God was dropped from the civic instruction programme and state education became officially non-religious.[46] The same year, 1923, relations between France and the Holy See, which were severed in 1904, were restored.

In 1945 the Catholic bishops decided that a positive meaning would be given to *laïcité*. A year later secularity was officially proclaimed and recognized by the Constitution of the Fourth Republic.[47] The present French Constitution was adopted in October 1958. It replaced the 1946 Constitution of the Fourth Republic. Article 1 of the Constitution holds: 'France shall be an indivisible, secular, democratic and social Republic. It shall ensure the equality of all citizens before the law, without distinction of origin, race or religion. It shall respect all beliefs.'[48] As a result of this clause, France's authorities do not collect information or publish statistics about religion. The word 'indivisible' is repeated in French constitutions from 1791 to 1958. The extent to which France respects all beliefs is open to interpretation and debate.

COLONIALISM

French colonialism during the nineteenth and twentieth centuries meant France had to deal, heads on, with different cultures, religions and nationalities. In the 1830s France invaded North Africa and, in the next decades, occupied Algeria, Tunisia and Morocco. France also expanded its empire deep into areas in West and Central Africa.[49] It welcomed people from North Africa to work in France. France slowly opened to the idea of becoming a polyethnic state. While appreciating the benefits of cheap labour, the French authorities were suspicious of Islam. Alexis de Tocqueville said: 'I must say that I emerged convinced that there are in the entire world few religions with such morbid consequences as that of Mohammed. To me it is the primary cause of the now visible decadence of the Islamic world.'[50]

Algeria was the most important colony in the French empire. It enjoyed a unique status as it was considered not only a colony but an integral part of France. Until its independence, Algeria was always administered by the Ministry of Interior, while Morocco and Tunisia were ruled from the Ministry of Foreign Affairs. In 1848, leaders of the Second Republic declared French territory in North Africa to be an

---

[46] Jennings, 'Citizenship, Republicanism and Multiculturalism in Contemporary France', 578.

[47] Baubérot, 'The Evolution of French Secularism', 47.

[48] France's constitution of 1958 with amendments through 2008, constituteproject.org.

[49] Robert Aldrich, *Greater France: A History of French Overseas Expansion* (London: Macmillan, 1996); Martin Thomas (ed.), *The French Colonial Mind: Mental Maps of Empire and Colonial Encounters* (Lincoln: Nebraska University Press, 2011).

[50] Tocqueville to Gobineau (22 October 1843), in John Lukacs (ed.), Alexis de Tocqueville (author), 'The European Revolution' and Correspondence with Gobineau (Westport, CT: Greenwood Press, 1974): 123.

extension of the Republic. Administratively and legally, Algeria was indivisible from France. In 1865, France extended nationality to all Muslim natives in Algeria. This status gave them the right to serve on equal terms in the French armed forces and civil service as well as the right to migrate to France.[51] However, prejudice against Islam persisted. Islam was perceived as a cause and effect of their inferiority.[52] By contrast, Jews in Algeria were automatically given citizenship by the 1870 Cremieux decree.[53] Only in 1961 did all Algerians become legally full French citizens.[54]

The Algerian War, also known as the Algerian War of Independence or the Algerian Revolution, was fought between France and the Algerian National Liberation Front (Front de Libération Nationale, FLN) from 1954 to 1962.[55] The war was bloody and brutal. Both France and the FLN used indiscriminate violence, terror and torture. French sources suggest that between 300,000 and 500,000 Algerians died in the war, while Algerian sources claim that as many as 1,500,000 had died.[56] The war caused the fall of six French governments, and led to the collapse of the Fourth Republic. The Algerian War sets the tone for decades of often tense relations, filled with hostility and suspicion between France and its former African colonies. Sentiments of guilt, resentment, suspicion and mistrust rose and prevailed. The Algerian War left deep scars in the national memories of both France and Algeria.[57] The conflict ended on 18 March 1962 in a military stalemate but in a political victory for the rebels as Algeria gained its independence from France.

IMMIGRATION

France is a land of immigrants. Late in the nineteenth century it absorbed many immigrants from Belgium and Italy. During the 1920s there was a wave of immigration from Eastern Europe that created Polish, Czech and Russian communities. During World War I France recruited migrants to work in war industries and in farms. More than 400,000 workers from Italy, Spain, Portugal, Greece, North Africa and Indochina arrived in France.[58] The flow of Algerians to France increased after World War I. In addition, between the two world wars, France absorbed large numbers of Jewish refugees from Eastern and Central Europe. The number of

[51] Chin, *The Crisis of Multiculturalism in Europe*, 37–38.
[52] Ibid., 40.
[53] Steven Uran, 'Crémieux Decree', in Norman A. Stillman (ed.), *Encyclopedia of Jews in the Islamic World* (Leiden: Brill, 2010).
[54] Bowen, *Why the French Don't Like Headscarves*, 36.
[55] Arnold Fraleigh, 'The Algerian War of Independence', *Proceedings of the American Society of International Law at Its Annual Meeting (1921–1969)*, 61 (27–29 April 1967): 6–12.
[56] 'The Algerian War of Independence', *Britannica* (2021), www.britannica.com/place/Algeria/The-Algerian-War-of-Independence.
[57] Alistair Horne, *A Savage War of Peace: Algeria 1954–1962* (New York: New York Review of Books, 2006).
[58] Mary Dewhurst Lewis, 'Immigration', in Berenson et al., *The French Republic*, 232–241.

immigrants was so great that by 1930 France had the highest rate of foreign population growth in the world.[59] The twentieth century also saw the establishment of other European and African communities, among them Portuguese and Spanish.[60] In the 1960s France opened its borders to workers from North Africa. The number of Algerian workers and their families increased from 350,000 in 1945 to 500,000 in 1964.[61] Immigration exacerbated the debates on the need to maintain one cohesive nation, statism and the unity of values. Immigration from Morocco and Tunisia took place during the 1970s. Later came immigrants from France's former colonies: Cameroon, Ivory Coast, Mali and Senegal. The most recent wave of immigration was from Eastern Europe and Turkey, with ongoing inflows from Turkey since the 1970s. The smallest group of immigrants come from Asia. Most of those immigrants originate from the former French colonies in South-East Asia: Cambodia, Laos and Vietnam.[62]

In the early 1970s, French leaders worried about higher numbers of foreigners and began to restrict immigration while striving to alleviate domestic tensions. French officials were primarily concerned with the size of the Algerian population. Recession caused resentment against Algerian workers perceived to be taking jobs away from native French. In 1974, French officials suspended labour migration from outside the European economic community.[63] This step represented the final turn away from a post-war policy that encouraged immigration from Southern Europe and the colonies.[64] At the same period of time, with the decline of the Communist Party and the weakening of a virulently anti-republican extreme right, the ideas of the Republic took a firm hold and became widespread and accepted.[65]

The scars of colonialism are real and concrete in France. While some steps were taken to celebrate cultural diversity (the production of TV programmes that showed cultures of different immigrant communities; provision that instructed schools to teach the languages of immigrants represented in different schools), these initiatives were not particularly successful but they laid the seeds for cultural recognition.[66]

---

[59] Chin, *The Crisis of Multiculturalism in Europe*, 25; Willms, 'France Unveiled'.
[60] Erik R. Vickstrom, *Pathways and Consequences of Legal Irregularity* (Cham: Springer, 2019); 'Which Countries Do French Immigrants Originate From?', www.worldatlas.com/articles/where-do-french-immigrants-come-from.html.
[61] O'Brien and Stasi, *The Stasi Report*, xvi.
[62] Yann Algan, Camille Landais and Claudia Senik, 'Cultural Integration in France', in Yann Algan, Alberto Bisin, Alan Manning and Thierry Verdier (eds), *Cultural Integration of Immigrants in Europe* (Oxford: Oxford Scholarship Online, 2013): chap. 2, www.oxfordscholarship.com/view/10.1093/acprof:oso/9780199660094.001.0001/acprof-9780199660094-chapter-2.
[63] Chin, *The Crisis of Multiculturalism in Europe*, 112; Bowen, *Why the French Don't Like Headscarves*, 67.
[64] Emile Chabal, 'French Political Culture in the 1970s', *Geschichte und Gesellschaft*, 42 (2016): 258.
[65] Ibid., 260; Chabal, *A Divided Republic*, 9.
[66] Chabal, 'French Political Culture in the 1970s', 260.

The claims of diversity and the right to be different, which received some recognition, have been replaced by strident assimilationist policies adopted by the political left as well as by the political right.[67] In 1987, President Jacques Chirac convened a Nationality Commission (Commission de la Nationalité) to provide a comprehensive reflection on the basis of social integration and national unity. This non-partisan independent committee of experts met for six months and in 1988 produced a two-volume report with recommendations.[68] The *Rapport de la Commission de la Nationalité* raised alarm that France's national future was endangered by the fundamentalist threat, especially by the Islamic practices of polygamy, gender inequality and arranged marriages, all irreconcilable with French values.

Algerian immigrants and Islam were the crucial challenge to French national identity. Islam was perceived as a cultural force that required from its adherents loyalty to the religious community above loyalty to the national community. Muslims were expected to accept the rules and the law of the Republic, including the idea of a secular state. The French state cannot renege on this demand.[69] To enter 'French civilization', Muslims who wished to become full French citizens with political rights were required to accept the absolute jurisdiction of the French legal code and reject the authority of religious courts. Many Muslim leaders did not object. For them as well as for many Jewish leaders, *laïcité* was not necessarily a negative thing. It can be perceived as positive as it means that there is no state religion. All religions are on a par.

In 1993 the 'Pasqua Law' was enacted in an effort to stop the immigration flow, specifically of North African/Arab immigrants, into France. Named after the French interior minister Charles Pasqua, the law reflected growing unease in the face of the increasing presence of Muslim communities in France. The law prohibited foreign graduates from accepting job offers by French employers and denying them a stable residence status, prevented the naturalizations and integration of African immigrants and increased the waiting period from one to two years for the non-national husbands and wives of French citizens before they could apply for naturalization.[70]

---

[67] Catherine Audard, 'The French Republic and the Claims of Diversity', in Carol Gould and Pasquale Pasquino (eds), *Cultural Identity and the Nation-State* (New York: Rowman & Littlefield, 2001): 89–108. In his comments on a draft of this chapter, Jonathan Fox noted that the far left and far right in Europe often advocate the same policies toward Muslims for very different reasons.

[68] La Commission de la Nationalité, une instance singulière (Entretien avec Jacqueline Costa-Lascoux), www.persee.fr/doc/remi_0765–0752_1988_num_4_1_1156.

[69] Marceau Long, *Être Français aujourd'hui et demain: Rapport de la Commission de la nationalité* (Paris: La Documentation Française, 1988); Naomi Davidson, *Only Muslim: Embodying Islam in Twentieth-Century France* (Ithaca, NY: Cornell University Press, 2012).

[70] Virginie Guiraudon, 'Immigration Policy in France', *Brookings* (1 July 2001), www.brookings .edu/articles/immigration-policy-in-france/; Eleonore Kofman, Madalina Rogoz and Florence Lévy, *Family Migration Policies in France* (Vienna: International Centre for Migration Policy Development, January 2010): 5.

During the 1990s and 2000s, public debate over France's colonial past became prominent. Slavery, the Algerian War, the treatment of indigenous people during the colonial period, colonial violence and responsibility for its conduct at home and abroad occupied the political discourse and were an integral part of neo-republicanism. French republicanism and France's civilizing mission were inextricably linked.[71] *Laïcité* was celebrated while Islamophobia crept in as a result of the headscarf and veil 'threats' to French civility and the Republic, the refugee crisis in Europe during the second decade of the twenty-first century and growing concerns regarding political Islam and its violent manifestations.

TERRORISM

A watershed in international relations was 11 September 2001. Al Qaeda's terror attack created havoc not only in the United States but in the world at large. Since then, the USA has been engaged in wars in Afghanistan and Iraq, and it has sent troops to other parts of the Middle East as part of the so-called 'war on terror'. French forces have been involved in the ongoing war in Afghanistan since October 2001. It also sent troops to the Central African Republic, Chad and Sudan.[72] To defend human rights, freedom and democracy, Western democracies have diminished freedom and democracy in their own countries. In the name of defeating terrorism, civil liberties have been undermined.[73] Yet the world has not become a safer place as a result. Quite the opposite. Terror attacks have become an integral part of reality in many parts of the world, including in Europe. Terror, coupled with vast waves of immigration and problems in the poor city suburbs, became a major concern in European social and political lives, especially in France.

France had experienced terror attacks prior to 2001, but after 9/11 sentiments of fear, insecurity and resentment pushed the French administration, on the one hand, and the French Muslim minority, on the other, to toughen their positions. After Al Qaeda's game-changer attack, a few thousand French-Algerian girls began arriving at school wearing head scarves. Many people saw this as the symbolic tip of an

---

[71] Emile Chabal, 'From the *Banlieue* to the Burkini: The Many Lives of French Republicanism', *Modern and Contemporary France*, 25(1) (2017): 68–74.

[72] Kelly Campbell, 'Central African Republic, Chad, and Sudan: Triangle of Instability?', *US Institute of Peace* (1 December 2006), www.usip.org/publications/2006/12/central-african-republic-chad-and-sudan-triangle-instability.

[73] Susan M. Akram and Kevin R. Johnson, 'Race, Civil Rights, and Immigration Law after 11 September 2001: The Targeting of Arabs and Muslims', NYU *Annual Survey of American Law*, 58 (2002): 295–356; A.C. Grayling, *Liberty in the Age of Terror: A Defence of Civil Liberties and Enlightenment Values* (New York and London: Bloomsbury, 2010); Derek McGhee, *The End of Multiculturalism* (Maidenhead: Open University Press, 2008); Ronald Dworkin, 'Terror and the Attack on Civil Liberties', *New York Review of Books*, 50(17) (6 November 2003): 1–20; Nanwani, 'The Burqa Ban'.

Islamist expansionist iceberg.[74] The 2004 law, known as the 'veil law' but should be called more appropriately the headscarf law, was the official rejection of what was perceived as religious extremism.[75] The law banned the wearing of all conspicuous religious symbols in state schools, including Muslim headscarves, Jewish skullcaps, Sikh turbans and large Christian crosses.[76] The law evoked heated debates.[77] The continued Palestinian strife resisting Israeli occupation, the wars in Afghanistan and Iraq, and universal jihadi terrorism have all influenced the French (and European discourse at large) to harden their stand on immigration and the relationships between the Christian majority and its religious minorities in France and in Western Europe at large. Since 2001 we have witnessed a remarkable rise in radical-right social and populist movements in Europe. In France, the right-wing *Front National* that in 2018 changed its name to The National Rally (Rassemblement national) has increased its strength as immigration concerns rose.[78] While once those populist right-wing parties were on the political fringes, in recent years they carry political weight in many countries, including France, Germany, Austria, Italy, Denmark, Finland, the Netherlands, Sweden, Greece and Spain.[79] Those movements wish to return Europe to Europeans and to discriminate against

---

[74] Jane Kramer, 'Behind France's Burka Ban', *The New Yorker* (15 July 2010), www.newyorker.com/news/news-desk/behind-frances-burka-ban.

[75] M. Akan, 'Laïcité and Multiculturalism: The Stasi Report in Context', *British Journal of Sociology*, 60(2) (2009): 237–256; Weil, 'A Nation in Diversity'.

[76] Will Adonis, 'Life in Blinkers', *Index on Censorship*, 4 (1 October 2003): 15–17; Scott, 'The Banning of Islamic Head Scarves in French Public Schools'; Stewart Motha, 'Veiled Women and the Affect of Religion in Democracy', *Journal of Law & Society*, 34(1) (March 2007): 139–162; C. Laborde, 'Secular Philosophy and Muslim Headscarves in Schools', *The Journal of Political Philosophy*, 13(3) (2005): 305–329.

[77] Weil, 'Why the French Laïcité Is Liberal'; Stéphanie Hennette Vauchez, 'Is French *Laïcité* Still Liberal? The Republican Project under Pressure (2004–15)', *Human Rights Law Review*, 17(2) (June 2017): 285–312; Elaine R. Thomas, 'Keeping Identity at a Distance: Explaining France's New Legal Restrictions on the Islamic Headscarf', *Ethnic and Racial Studies*, 29(2) (March 2006): 237–259; Nusrat Choudhury, 'From the Stasi Commission to the European Court of Human Rights: L'Affaire du Foulard and the Challenge of Protecting the Rights of Muslim Girls', *Columbia Journal of Gender and Law*, 16(1) (Winter 2007), www.questia.com/library/journal/1G1-162576736/from-the-stasi-commission-to-the-european-court-of.

[78] Joao Carvalho, *Impact of Extreme Right Parties on Immigration Policy: Comparing Britain, France and Italy* (London: Routledge, 2016).

[79] Piero Ignazi, *Extreme Right Parties in Western Europe* (Oxford: Oxford University Press, 2006); Andrea Mammone, Emmanuel Godin and Brian Jenkins (eds), *Mapping the Extreme Right in Contemporary Europe* (London: Routledge, 2012); Matthew Goodwin, 'Right Response: Understanding and Countering Populist Extremism in Europe', *Chatham House Report* (London, 2012); Ruth Wodak, Majid KhrosraviNik and Brigitte Mral (eds), *Right Wing Populism in Europe: Politics and Discourse* (London: Bloomsbury, 2013); M. Cutts and M. Goodwin, 'Getting Out the Right-Wing Extremist Vote: Extreme Right Party Support and Campaign Effects at a Recent British General Election', *European Political Science Review*, 6(1) (2014): 93–114.

immigrants, including those who have been settled in Europe for many years and received citizenship.

In France the discourse revolved in the main around the need for a united republic and fear of disintegration. Opposition to religious privileges have lingered since the Revolution. Citizens are not part of a distinct cultural or religious community. Rather, citizens are members of the nation as a whole. France should be one undivided community. Pierre-André Taguieff, a philosopher and sociologist who is a member of the Centre de recherche de sciences politiques, warned against the atomizing tendency of multiculturalism and spoke of the need to restore the French 'civic bond'. Taguieff uses the terms 'multiculturalism', 'multi-communautarisme' and 'tribalism' as synonyms and, for him, the prime threat is Islam or, more exactly, the 'Islamo-terrorist threat'. Societal breakdown will make space for militant Islam to grow and develop. The Republic should protect against outside threats and, at the same time, fight against internal fragmentation and disintegration.[80] The threat of terrorism and the continued debates about Islamic garb were exploited especially by the political right to warn against the Islamization of France.

In 2012 a terrorist attacked a Jewish school in Toulouse. A teacher and three children were killed.[81] In 2015 Paris was the target of two terrorist attacks: on 7 January against the satirical magazine *Charlie Hebdo* following publications that degraded Muhammad the Prophet,[82] and on 13 November against various locations in the French capital. French President François Hollande expressed fear over French identity, stating that the biggest threat that can affect the country would be to lose 'our soul', the identity 'we have inherited and that we need to carry forward for the future'.[83] The Muslim community was in the eye of the storm as public debate denounced 'perverted Islam' that negated the message of the Quran. Hollande posited 'us' versus 'them', French national identity against the terrorist other; the French Republic that stands for freedom vis-à-vis jihadist murderers who wish to challenge the spirit, unity and the values that enshrine the nation.[84]

On 14 July 2016, an Islamist terrorist rammed a lorry into crowds celebrating Bastille Day on the Promenade des Anglais in Nice. Eighty-six people were

---

[80] Pierre-André Taguieff, *Les contre-réactionnaires: le progressisme entre illusion et imposture* (Paris: Denoel, 2007); Pierre-André Taguieff, *La République enlisée: pluralisme, communautarisme et citoyenneté* (Paris: Syrtes 2005). See also Gilles Kepel, 'The Trail of Political Islam', *Open Democracy* (2 July 2002), www.opendemocracy.net/en/articlejspid526debateid5726arti cleid421/; Emile Chabal, 'Writing the French National Narrative in the Twenty-First Century', *The Historical Journal*, 53(2) (2010): 500–501; Chabal, A *Divided Republic*, 100–101; Alain Finkielkraut, 'La nation disparait au profits des tribus', *Le Monde* (13 July 1989).

[81] 'France Shooting: Toulouse Jewish School Attack Kills Four', *BBC* (19 March 2012), www.bbc .com/news/world-us-canada-17426313.

[82] Raphael Cohen-Almagor, 'Between Speech and Terror: The *Charlie Hebdo* Affair', The Great War Series (Part II), *The Critique* (7 January 2016).

[83] Ariane Bogain, 'Terrorism and the Discursive Construction of National Identity in France', *National Identities*, 21(3) (2019): 241–265.

[84] Ibid.

murdered and 450 others were injured in the attack.[85] The crudeness of the indiscriminate attack on the most important national holiday in France when the country celebrates the unity of the French people stunned the nation and, at the same time, solidified it. On 20 April 2017, an Islamist opened fire on police officers on the Champs-Elysees in Paris. One policeman was killed and two others were wounded.[86] On 23 March 2018, an ISIS terrorist killed four people and injured sixteen others in a prolonged terror incident.[87] On 11 December 2018, a terrorist opened fire outside the Strasbourg Christmas Market, killing five people and injuring eleven others.[88] In the wake of those terror attacks, yet again debates were vigorously held over France's colonial legacy, personal liberty, the need to preserve public order and security, civic culture and constitutional powers. Yet again, some circles in the political and intellectual elites set out to refound and strengthen the threatened Republic.[89]

In 2019, President Emmanuel Macron warned against 'stigmatizing' Muslims or linking the Islamic religion with the fight against terrorism and urged his people to stand together in solidarity with all fellow citizens. Macron called for a better understanding of the Muslim religion and condemned what he described as the 'fatal shortcut' of linking Islam with terrorism. 'Communalism is not terrorism', he said.[90] Even if minority communities do not wish to comply completely with the republican model, this does not make them terrorists.

[85] 'Attack on Nice: Who Was Mohamed Lahouaiej-Bouhlel?', *BBC* (19 August 2016), www.bbc.co.uk/news/world-europe-36801763; Alissa J. Rubin and Aurelien Breeden, 'France Remembers the Nice Attack: "We Will Never Find the Words"', *New York Times* (14 July 2017), www.nytimes.com/2017/07/14/world/europe/nice-attack-france-bastille-day.html.

[86] 'French Police Officer Killed in Shooting on Champs Élysées', *The Guardian* (21 August 2017), www.theguardian.com/world/2017/apr/20/paris-shooting-policeman-killed-on-champs-elysees.

[87] Angelique Chrisafis and Kim Willsher, 'French Supermarket Siege: Gendarme Dies After Taking Place of Hostage', *The Guardian* (24 March 2018), www.theguardian.com/world/2018/mar/23/french-police-called-to-trebes-supermarket-amid-hostage-reports-shootings.

[88] 'Strasbourg Shooting: What We Know', *BBC* (16 December 2018), www.bbc.co.uk/news/world-europe-46535862. For information about other attacks, see Kim Willsher, 'France's History of Terror: Islamic Extremist Attacks since 2015', *The Guardian* (23 March 2018), www.theguardian.com/world/2018/mar/23/heroic-gendarme-swapped-places-with-hostage-in-french-attack.

[89] Florence Faucher Laurie Boussaguet, 'The Politics of Symbols: Reflections on the French Government's Framing of the 2015 Terrorist Attacks', *Parliamentary Affairs*, 71(1) (January 2018): 169–195; 'France: New Terrorism Laws May Undercut Human Rights and Freedoms, Says UN Expert', *UN News* (25 May 2018), https://news.un.org/en/story/2018/05/1010721; Aurelien Breeden and Jeffrey Marcus, 'France Weighs Limits of Liberty, Equality and Citizenship', *New York Times* (30 March 2016). For further discussion, see Andrew Jainchill, *Reimagining Politics after the Terror: The Republican Origins of French Liberalism* (London: Cornell University Press, 2008); Marie Beauchamps, 'Perverse Tactics: "Terrorism" and National Identity in France', *Culture, Theory and Critique*, 58(1) (2017): 48–61.

[90] 'Macron Warning on Stigmatising Muslims amid France Veil Row', *BBC* (17 October 2019), www.bbc.com/news/world-europe-50079997. By 'communalism' Macron presumably meant allegiance to one's ethnic group rather than to the wider society.

BANNING THE BURQA AND THE NIQAB

The culmination and convergence of the concepts of the Republic, *liberté, égalité, fraternité, laïcité,* the meaning of being French, internalized coercion, imposed autonomy and fear of terrorism yielded a continued heated debate about Islamic dress. President Nicolas Sarkozy characterized the burqa as 'a sign of subservience' and 'a sign of debasement', declaring that France 'cannot accept that women be prisoners behind a screen, cut off from all social life, deprived of all identity'.[91] The burqa 'will not be welcome on the territory of the French Republic'.[92] His words received cross-party support. The very next day a committee chaired by André Gerin (La mission d'information sur la pratique du port du voile integral sur le territoire national) was established to investigate the use and practice of face veils. It concluded that the existing legislation did not provide a basis for prohibiting the face veil. Having said that, the majority of the Gerin Committee supported prohibitive legislation.[93] Its report characterized the full veil as 'contrary to the values of the Republic'.[94] The commission recommended that parliament adopt a resolution for enacting a law 'prohibiting the full veil as well as any other clothing entirely covering the face in public spaces, based upon the notion of public order'.[95]

Following the Parliamentary Commission's Report, Prime Minister François Charles Armand Fillon requested that the Conseil d'État examine the legal grounds for a ban on the burqa and niqab. In 2010, the Conseil d'État issued a report which 'found that no incontestable legal basis can be relied upon in support of a ban on wearing the full veil'.[96] However, it is possible to ban the full veil on the basis of public security. The 2010 law targeted veiling, that is, face covering. The public debate brought together anti-religious and anti-immigration sentiments as well as fears of terrorism. The debate accentuated the need for national unity, preservation of the Republic, secularity and paternalism. The questions were whether the general will should be asserted and multiculturalism should be rejected.

On 11 October 2010, France became the first European country to ban the full-face Islamic veil, the burqa and the niqab, in public places.[97] Wearing a full-face

---

[91] Associated Press, 'Sarkozy: Burqas "Not Welcome" in France', *CBS News* (22 June 2009), www.cbsnews.com/stories/2009/06/22/world/main5103076.shtml.

[92] Angelique Chrisafis, 'Nicolas Sarkozy Says Islamic Veils Are Not Welcome in France', *The Guardian* (22 June 2009), www.theguardian.com/world/2009/jun/22/islamic-veils-sarkozy-speech-france.

[93] H. Van Ooijen, *Religious Symbols in Public Function: Unveiling State Neutrality* (Utrecht: Utrecht University, 2012): 198.

[94] Nanwani, 'The Burqa Ban'.

[95] Ibid.

[96] 'Etude relative aux possibilités juridiques d'interdiction du port du voile integral' (25 March 2010), http://recherche.conseil-etat.fr/?rub=on&q=burqa.

[97] Loi n. 2010–1192 *interdisant la dissimulation du visage dans l'espace public* of 11 October 2010, JO (12 October 2010); 'The Islamic Veil Across Europe', *BBC* (31 May 2018), www.bbc.co.uk/news/world-europe-13038095.

veil that conceals one's face in a public space is punishable by a maximum fine of a €150 or by being required to take a class on the meaning of citizenship, or by both. The law also states that forcing a woman to wear a face-covering veil is punishable by one year of imprisonment or a €30,000 fine. If a person forces a minor to wear a face-covering veil, the possible fine is increased to €60,000.[98] The law defines 'public space' broadly to include public roads and spaces that are open to the public.[99]

Is this law socially just? Does it reasonably balance the preservation of societal values and freedom of conscience?

IS BANNING THE BURQA AND THE NIQAB JUST AND REASONABLE?

Many people try to isolate themselves from their surroundings. Some put on headphones, aiming to listen to whatever they wish and, at the same time, signal to others that they rather not engage in conversation. This does not seem to be problematic. People are free to wear headphones. Similarly, women who wear the burqa signal that they do not wish to engage with others, and that they wish to protect themselves from the gaze of others, especially of men. Lack of engagement is not the problem. Covering the face is. The wish to isolate is not the problem. The way people decide to do it is.

People concede that sometimes there are legitimate and reasonable reasons for covering one's face. Covering the face is legitimate when the reason is ecological. There is no problem in France regarding the wearing of ecological masks. Following the outbreak of the COVID-19, face masks became mandatory. Motorcyclists use safety helmets that cover their faces. People cover large parts of the faces in very cold days of winter. Many French people wear *passe-montagne*, a balaclava, when they jog in winter. Thus, concealment of the face as such is not the problem. The reason for it is. France does not accept concealment for religious reasons. The same reasoning – the national interest and good citizenship – serve to justify this duality. Muslims who cover their faces for religious reasons are liable to a fine and a citizenship course where they are taught the meaning of good citizenship. During the COVID-19 pandemic all were required to show 'good citizenship' and adopt 'barrier gestures' to protect the national community.[100] The fact that the scrutinized religion is Islam makes the debate more

---

[98] Loi n. 2010–1192 *interdisant la dissimulation du visage dans l'espace public* of 11 October 2010, JO (12 October 2010), art 4.

[99] Ibid., art 2; 'The Islamic veil across Europe'.

[100] James McAuley, 'France Mandates Masks to Control the Coronavirus: Burqas Remain Banned', *The Washington Post* (10 May 2020), www.washingtonpost.com/world/europe/france-face-masks-coronavirus/2020/05/09/6fbd50fc-8ae6-11ea-80df-d24b35a568ae_story.html?utm_campaign=wp_todays_worldview&utm_medium=email&utm_source=newsletter&wpisrc=nl_todayworld.

heated and hostile as deep-seated prejudices against Islam, as evinced by the de Tocqueville statement, linger on.

France has the largest Muslim population in Western Europe with an estimated five to six million Muslims (7–8 per cent of the population).[101] Studies showed that 1,900 women wore the niqab in France and no women wore the burqa. This number represented 0.04 per cent of the French Muslim population.[102] Data from 2015 showed that 1,546 fines had been imposed under the law.[103] These figures are mentioned to explain the scale of the phenomenon, not to justify or criticize the law. The numbers as such are not that important a consideration. I would object to one case of murder for family honour and would justify the law that bans it. The European Court of Human Rights upheld the burqa and niqab ban on 2 July 2014 after a case was brought by a 24-year-old French woman who argued that the ban violated her freedom of religion and expression. Most of the population – including most (but not all) Muslims – agree with the government when it describes the face-covering veil as an affront to society's values. Critics – chiefly outside France – say it is a violation of individual liberties.[104] Let me examine the arguments for the burqa and niqab ban.

Liberating Women and Re-establishing Their Dignity

The Constitutional Council upheld the law without mentioning *laïcité*. The council thought that the law was reasonable because it did not impose disproportionate punishment or prevent the free exercise of religion in a place of worship. The burqa and the niqab ban was described as necessary for liberating women and re-establishing their dignity. Supporters of the burqa and the niqab ban argued that these garments relegate women to an inferior status incompatible with the French ideas of equality and the dignity of the person.[105] According to supporters of the ban the burqa and the niqab represent sexism, coercive Islam and male religious chauvinism (other forms of chauvinism are a matter for another discussion). These uncomfortable, shapeless garments suppress women and emasculate femininity, and therefore they are offensive to those who believe in gender equality. They make women look suspicious and impolite. Veiled women deny their

---

[101] Nilufar Ahmed, 'How Many Muslim Women Actually Wear the Burka?', *Inews* (6 September 2019), https://inews.co.uk/opinion/comment/what-is-the-burqa-and-how-many-muslim-women-actually-wear-it-267209; Karina Piser, 'A New Plan to Create an "Islam of France"', *The Atlantic* (29 March 2018), www.theatlantic.com/international/archive/2018/03/islam-france-macron/556604/.

[102] Ahmed, 'How Many Muslim Women Actually Wear the Burka?'; 'France: Highlights of Parliamentary Report on the Wearing of the Full Veil (BURQA)', *Library of Congress*, www.loc.gov/law/help/france-veil.php.

[103] BBC, 'The Islamic Veil across Europe'.

[104] Ibid.

[105] Bernard-Henri Lévy, 'Why I Support a Ban on Burqas', *Hufflington Post* (25 May 2011).

existence in the public sphere and deprive themselves of social interaction. Such dresses undermine women's integration into French society.[106] The French establishment came to the rescue of Muslim women.

The French establishment decided to free Muslim women although at least some of them wished to wear the burqa and niqab, and there was no evidence of coercion. This form of paternalism gives Muslim women very limited credit in their abilities to decide for themselves what is good for them. No empirical evidence was provided to show that women's dignity is curtailed by wearing the burqa. France argued that radical practices undermining dignity and equality between men and women, such as the wearing of the full veil, were incompatible with the values of the French Republic and, therefore, appropriate means were implemented 'to ensure the effective protection of women who suffer duress or pressure, in particular those who are forced to wear a full veil'.[107]

Paternalism that holds noble ideas about freeing women from coercion is justified when women complain about their subjugation. We should help women who are subjected to *designated* coercion. As said in Chapter 1, it is from the concept of a person as an autonomous individual, whose actions are the product of choice and purpose, that the philosophy of a free society is constructed. But people's dubious assumptions about women's internalized coercion cannot constitute a reasonable justification for interference. We should engage with what women are saying, their concerns, their freedom of choice, their individuality and the way they express themselves. Respect for women means respecting their wishes and inhibitions. I cannot expect Muslim (and also some Jewish)[108] women to accept what I wish for them, and identification with a certain religion does not diminish women's universal entitlement to dignity and respect. *Dignity as liability* requires us all to respect persons qua persons (see Chapter 1). People are endowed with dignity and have the right to be treated with dignity.

Some French feminists support the burqa and niqab ban.[109] However, the feminist movement at large fights to enable women to express themselves in the way women see as appropriate. Some Muslim women wish to express themselves by wearing the burqa. Granted it is not a Western liberal dress; still not everyone needs

---

[106] Phyllis Chesler, 'Ban the Burqa? The Argument in Favor', *Middle East Quarterly* (Fall 2010): 44.

[107] *Sonia Yaker v. France*, at 11. Similar reasoning was invoked in *Miriana Hebbadj v. France*, at 9.

[108] Siobhan Kenna, '"Sickening" and "Radical": Why These Women Are So Controversial', 10 *Daily News* (24 December 2018), https://10daily.com.au/news/world/a181217kbh/sickening-and-radical-why-these-women-are-so-controversial-20181224.

[109] Ulrike Spohn, 'Sisters in Disagreement: The Dispute among French Feminists about the "Burqa Ban" and the Causes of Their Disunity', *Journal of Human Rights*, 12(2) (2013): 145–164; Christine Delphy, 'Feminists Are Failing Muslim Women by Supporting Racist French Laws', *The Guardian* (20 July 2015), www.theguardian.com/lifeandstyle/womens-blog/2015/jul/20/france-feminism-hijab-ban-muslim-women.

to accept the same dress code. Feminists encourage diversity. The burqa and niqab are part of the diverse ways by which women express themselves. Feminists criticize the enslavement of women to fashion. They reject that there is one ideal of beauty. They object to what they perceive as a highly sexualized public space where women are judged by their look and by their dress. If women were to wear the veil for non-religious reasons they would probably have been applauded by feminists. Feminists need to deal with their own biases and prejudices before they come to liberate women without proper deliberation and without seeking women's consent. The liberal motto is 'live and let live', not 'force them to be free'. Intervention is justified only for good reasons and, on this issue, the above reasons are far from being reasonable and convincing.

Feminists and women's rights activists should listen to what women say. Activists think that they come to help women, whereas in reality they are not helping them, nor liberating them. Quite the opposite. As was the case for Holt (Chapter 3), for some women their appearance is a defining matter. They are obliged to fulfil a divine commandment. Furthermore, for some girls and women, by wearing the veil they are allowed to go out of the home, to study and to work. By wearing the veil they set themselves apart from the non-Muslim world and signal their piety. The veil makes them feel secure. For some women the veil is a symbol of a disciplined and virtuous mind that aspires to higher spiritual beauty.[110] For some women the veil means freedom not only to go out and about but also freedom from men's intrusiveness; freedom from the sexualized public space; freedom from the extravagance of world fashion; freedom to be the person they want to be. The burqa and niqab ban could have the negative effects of confining women to their homes, impeding their access to public services and marginalizing them.[111] Women should not coerce other women to accept secular forms of dress in the name of freedom. And certainly, penalizing women for what they wear would put further hardship on them. 'Forcing women to be free' in line with Rousseau's reasoning[112] negates women's dignity no less than other forms of coercion as it denies women a voice. Women who wish to wear the traditional garb do not accept the burqa and niqab ban, and do not wish to be subjected to it because this law negates and does not reflect their free will.

---

[110] Natasha Bakht, 'Veiled Objections: Facing Public Opposition to the Niqab', in Lori G. Beaman (ed.), *Reasonable Accommodation* (Vancouver: UBC Press, 2012): 75; Jen'nan Ghazal Read and John P. Bartkowski. 'To Veil or Not to Veil? A Case Study of Identity Negotiation among Muslim Women in Austin, Texas', *Gender and Society* 14(3) (2000): 405.

[111] *Sonia Yaker v. France*, 18; *Miriana Hebbadj v. France*, 18. See also United Nations Human Rights Committee, 'France: Banning the Niqab Violated Two Muslim Women's Freedom of Religion – UN Experts' (23 October 2018), www.ohchr.org/EN/NewsEvents/Pages/DisplayNews.aspx?NewsID=23750&LangID=E.

[112] Rousseau, *The Social Contract*, 9.

Preserving French Identity and Unity

In the debate the underlying tone was concern for the changing face of the French Republic. Troubled by the increasing number of Muslims openly practising their religion in public, France felt the need to restore 'Frenchness' to their streets.[113] Secularity was invoked against Muslim reluctance to integrate into society and their attempt to advance distinctive communitarian conduct and values.[114] A French public intellectual, Bernard-Henri Lévy, wrote: 'This is not about the burqa, it's about Voltaire. What is at stake is the Enlightenment of yesterday and today, and the heritage of both, no less sacred than that of the three monotheisms.'[115] By invoking the Enlightenment, Lévy wished to convince us that his arguments are rational, reasonable, free from tradition and forward looking. Religion, on the other hand, is backward, irrational, superstitious, compulsive and coercive. Lévy wished to emancipate women whether they want it or not.

The distinction between private and public places is of relevance. The Commission de la Nationalité set the aim of achieving national integration, transforming foreigners into French citizens who speak the same language, share the same culture and civic values and participate in the national life. While in private these people may retain their religion and culture, in the public sphere all have to be French.[116] The ban on the burqa and the niqab is comprehensive, referring to adults and children in all public places that are not places of worship. France adopted restrictive, coercive illiberalism that negates individual freedom in general and freedom of choice in particular. In the name of liberating women of religious oppression, they coerce them. French oppression replaces alleged Muslim repression. Because individual interests are secondary to national interests, Muslim women are unable to express themselves in the dress of their choice.

Prior to the enactment of this law, the burqa and the niqab were already banned in specific places, including at school, in respect of students and staff; in public services, in respect of public officials; and in demonstrations.[117] Indeed, teachers and administrators need to be able to recognize students. They need to see students' faces clearly. Thus, it is unacceptable for students to cover their faces with a burqa, niqab or any other cloth or artefact. When there is a need to be identified, for example when one is conducting an exam, or wishes to issue a photo certificate, one

---

[113] Sandeep Gopalan, 'Behind the Burqa', *New York Times* (27 January 2010), www.nytimes.com/2010/01/28/opinion/28iht-edgopalan.html. In her comments on a draft of this chapter, Catherine Audard noted that Islam is a religion based on orthopraxy, not simply on orthodoxy, which means that it cannot be easily privatized and confined to the home or to religious halls.

[114] Jean-François Caron, 'Understanding and Interpreting France's National Identity: The Meanings of Being French', *National Identities*, 15(3) (2013): 223–237.

[115] Lévy, 'Why I Support a Ban on Burqas'.

[116] Chin, *The Crisis of Multiculturalism in Europe*, 172–174.

[117] Myriam Hunter-Henin, 'Why the French Don't Like the Burqa: Laïcité, National Identity and Religious Freedom': *International Comparative and Law Quarterly*, 61 (August 2012): 1–27.

then is required to reveal one's face. This is unobjectionable. Also, considerations of security and public order dictate that people should not drive with a face covering as the cover would inhibit the ability to drive carefully. While these considerations are reasonable and just, a *tout court* ban is not.

Generally speaking, a voluntary conduct is preferable and morally superior to a coercive one.[118] Context is relevant. In each and every society there are certain expected dress codes in public. In Japan I felt at unease upon witnessing large groups of people all wearing surgical masks. This was *my* problem. The Japanese are used to such scenes as it is a prevalent phenomenon. Behind the Rawlsian veil of ignorance women should be prima facie allowed to wear whatever *they* feel comfortable with. The burqa and niqab do not erode the two principles of justice. Banning such dress runs contrary to the principles of mutual respect. The preservation of individual rights and the dignity of the person as well as the emancipation of the individual from public control should mean that all people in a democracy enjoy the same equal rights. A person's liberty is significant for creating and maintaining her views and actions as long as she does not interfere with and damage the other's liberty.

Furthermore, the Rawlsian well-ordered liberal society would reject any sort of political and religious fundamentalism that urges that the best community is one in which only some preferred practices are allowed[119] (see Chapter 2) but Muslims in France do not try to coerce non-Muslims to wear the burqa. The principles of justice as fairness, respect for others and not harming others should dictate tolerance. Whoever exercises political power must respect the civil, religious and political rights of all members. If people feel uncomfortable witnessing women wearing full dress coverage, this is *their* problem and *they* need to deal with it.

Citizens should be allowed to follow their conceptions of the good as far as it is socially possible, rather than being coerced to forego their tradition. Freedom *of* religion is as valuable as freedom *from* religion. Imposition of secularity on people who wish to retain their religion subverts unity and restricts one's identity. Modesty is an important value that needs to be reckoned with. I wonder whether the French would similarly insist on such a ban if the headscarf and the veil were adopted by the Christianity of today.

Those who think that the ban promotes societal unity would find it difficult to substantiate their claim. There is no concrete evidence that the law lessens friction. On the other hand, there is evidence that a significant minority of French Muslims resent the law, finding it offensive and intrusive. Some burqa-wearing women suffered verbal and physical abuse.[120] In 2016, a poll conducted among French

---

[118] Virginia Held, 'Coercion and Coercive Offers', in J. Roland Pennock and John W. Chapman (eds), *Nomos XIV: Coercion* (Chicago and New York: Aldine – Atherton, Inc., 1972): 61.

[119] Rawls, *A Theory of Justice*, sect. 24.

[120] Hunter-Henin, 'Why the French Don't Like the Burqa'.

Muslim people found that 20 per cent of male Muslims and 28 per cent of females supported the wearing of the burqa.[121] Nilufar Ahmed wrote that forcing women not to wear the burqa is 'no different to the Taliban forcing women to wear it: it removes all control from the woman over her body, and is just part of the sexist narrative controlling women's dress in public places'.[122]

In 2014 the European Court of Human Rights upheld France's burqa ban, accepting the French government's argument that it encouraged citizens to 'live together'.[123] However, in October 2018 the United Nations Human Rights Committee considered the complaints of two women who were fined for wearing the niqab.[124] The women argued that the prohibition is not proportionate to its objective, as it is permanent, applies in all circumstances to all public spaces and its violation is a criminal offence. Both women contended that the prohibitive law negated their rights under articles 18 and 26 of the International Covenant on Civil and Political Rights.[125] Article 18(1) holds:

> Everyone shall have the right to freedom of thought, conscience and religion. This right shall include freedom to have or to adopt a religion or belief of his choice, and freedom, either individually or in community with others and in public or private, to manifest his religion or belief in worship, observance, practice and teaching.[126]

Article 18(2) maintains that 'No one shall be subject to coercion which would impair his freedom to have or to adopt a religion or belief of his choice.'[127] In turn, Article 26 prohibits any discrimination and guarantee to all persons equal and effective protection against discrimination on any ground including religion.[128] I should also mentioned that Article 27 of the covenant holds: 'In those States in which ethnic, religious or linguistic minorities exist, persons belonging to such minorities shall not be denied the right, in community with the other members of their group, to enjoy their own culture, to profess and practise their own religion, or to use their own language.'[129] Upon ratifying the covenant, France inserted a

---

[121] 'Poll: One in Four French Muslims Backs Burqa', *DW News* (18 September 2016), https://p.dw .com/p/1K4W6.

[122] Ahmed, 'How Many Muslim Women Actually Wear the Burka?'

[123] Kim Willsher, 'France's Burqa Ban Upheld by Human Rights Court', *The Guardian* (1 July 2014), www.theguardian.com/world/2014/jul/01/france-burqa-ban-upheld-human-rights-court.

[124] *Miriana Hebbadj v. France*, Human Rights Committee, CCPR/C/123/D/2807/2016 (17 October 2018), and *Sonia Yaker v. France*, Human Rights Committee, CCPR/C/123/D/2747/2016 (7 December 2018).

[125] *International Covenant on Civil and Political Rights* (1966), www.ohchr.org/en/professionalin terest/pages/ccpr.aspx.

[126] Ibid.

[127] Ibid.

[128] Ibid.

[129] Ibid.

qualification that in light of the French Constitution, Article 27 is not applicable to France.[130]

The Burqa and Niqab Undermine Public Safety and Public Order

Fear of terrorism was expressed in the media as an additional reason for the ban. Public security required this restriction as the burqa can assist terrorists in their operations.[131] France submitted that to ensure public safety and public order it needs to have the ability to identify individuals when necessary in order to avert threats to the security of persons or property and to combat identity fraud. The requirement that people reveal their faces is all the more crucial in the context of the global threat of terrorism.[132] This is in line with Article 18(3) of the International Covenant on Civil and Political Rights that postulates: 'Freedom to manifest one's religion or beliefs may be subject only to such limitations as are prescribed by law and are necessary to protect public safety, order, health, or morals or the fundamental rights and freedoms of others.'[133]

The United Nations Human Rights Committee accepted the two complaints, holding that France had violated their fundamental human rights. The committee found that the criminal ban on the niqab disproportionately harmed the petitioners' right to manifest their religious beliefs. The committee was not persuaded by France's claim that the ban was necessary and proportionate from a security standpoint or for attaining the goal of 'living together' in society. While France could require that individuals show their faces in specific circumstances for identification purposes, a general ban on the niqab was too sweeping for this purpose. France did not provide any public safety justification or explanation for why the burqa and niqab are prohibited while covering the face for numerous other purposes, including sporting, artistic and other traditional and religious purposes, is

---

[130] Human Rights Committee, 'Human Rights Committee Reviews the Report of France', *UN Human Rights* (10 July 2015), www.ohchr.org/EN/NewsEvents/Pages/DisplayNews.aspx?NewsID=16227&LangID=E; UN Doc CCPR/C/OP/3 (2002): 43, www.ohchr.org/Documents/Publications/SDecisionsVol3en.pdf.

[131] Daniel Pipes, 'Niqabs and Burqas as Security Threats', *Lion's Den* (12 October 2018), www.danielpipes.org/blog/2002/03/niqabs-and-burqas-as-security-threats; Hunter-Henin, 'Why the French Don't Like the Burqa'; Nanwani, 'The Burqa Ban'. See also Adam Taylor, 'Banning Burqas Isn't a Sensible Response to Terrorism', *Washington Post* (12 August 2016), www.washingtonpost.com/news/worldviews/wp/2016/08/12/banning-burqas-isnt-a-sensible-response-to-terrorism/?utm_term=.9c535e04a27f and Myriam Hunter-Henin, 'Living Together in an Age of Religious Diversity: Lessons from *Baby Loup* and *SAS*', *Oxford Journal of Law & Religion*, 4 (1) (February 2015): 94–118, which examines two decisions by the European Court of Human Rights and the French Cour de cassation: *SAS v France*, a challenge to the French ban on the full-face covering in the public space, and *Baby Loup*, in which a private nursery employee was dismissed for refusing to remove her non-face-covering Islamic veil.

[132] *Sonia Yaker v. France*, 12; *Miriana Hebbadj v. France*, at 10.

[133] *International Covenant on Civil and Political Rights* (1966). www.ohchr.org/en/professionalinterest/pages/ccpr.aspx

allowed. The committee further observed that France has not described any context, or provided any example, in which there was a specific and significant threat to public order and safety that would justify such a blanket ban.[134]

Indeed, the law is not proportional to the aim of promoting public safety. Daniel Pipes compiled incidents in which niqabs and burqas were used for terrorist incidents. He argues that both garments should be banned on security grounds.[135] However, there are many things that are used and abused but are not banned in democracies. Chemistry books are often used for very good, productive purposes but sometimes they are abused for terrorist bomb making. Motorcycle helmets are used to protect human lives but sometimes they are abused to rob banks and to serve antisocial purposes. The internet contains the best products of humanity, but it is also abused by terrorists, criminals and hate mongers. The telephone connects between families and friends, but it is also abused to concoct crimes. The fact that a dress is used and abused in different ways does not justify banning the dress.

Burqa and Niqab Are Offensive

Those who justify the ban on full-body cover argue that they find the garment offensive. The sight of women in burqas can be demoralizing and frightening to Westerners of all faiths.[136] But surely not everything that people might find offensive should be banned. If we were to ban all that some people may find offensive, then many kinds of dress, food, art and entertainment would have been banned. Those who find the burqa offensive, demoralizing and/or frightening should deal with their fears and suspicion. Again, this is *their* problem to sort, and the solution should not be simply to ban things that evoke negative sentiments. Many people are afraid of clowns. Should we ban clowns as well?

While I think the issue of offence should be taken seriously, we need to distinguish between profound offence that might be banned, and mere annoyance that might not be banned. Offence is behaviour that causes people upset and displeasure. People are offended when they suffer a disliked state of mind, attribute that state to the wrongful conduct of another and resent the other for her role in causing them to be in that state.[137] *Profound* offence amounts to an attack on one's sensibilities. It is real and deep, so much so that it might shatter the emotional structure of the affected individuals. Comparably, annoyance is a mild form of offence. It is no more than a nuisance. Elsewhere I developed the Offence to Sensibilities Argument, arguing that it should be taken seriously only when *profound* offences are at stake. The Offence to Sensibilities Argument will take precedence over freedom of

---

[134] *Sonia Yaker v. France*, 15; *Miriana Hebbadj v. France*, 15.
[135] Pipes, 'Niqabs and Burqas as Security Threats'.
[136] Chesler, 'Ban the Burqa?'
[137] Joel Feinberg, *Offense to Others* (New York: Oxford University Press, 1985): 2.

religion only in cases where profound and direct damage is inflicted upon the sensibilities of individuals, undermining their dignity, especially when the doer's intentions are to offend the individuals under circumstances in which the individuals cannot avoid.[138]

In the absence of a ban, individuals might be exposed to the burqa on the street. In this respect the burqa is unavoidable. However, the other ingredients of profound offence are missing: no one can claim that the burqa undermines another person's dignity. If at all, those who justify the ban argue that the burqa damages the dignity of the woman who wears it. Furthermore, women who opt to wear the burqa do not mean to offend anybody. There is no harmful intent in going around wearing the burqa. Rather, many women wear it to protect themselves from the gaze of the environment.

The Burqa and Niqab Cause Sensory Deprivation and Vitamin D Deficiency

Another curious argument in support of the burqa and niqab ban is that these forms of dress cause sensory deprivation and vitamin D deficiency from sunlight deprivation.[139] But if one is worried about people's health one should clarify one's position also on other unhealthy conduct such as smoking, vaping, consuming alcohol, sun bathing, artificial tan parlours, watching disturbing films that lead to sleep deprivation, professional boxing and the consumption of fatty food. This is only a preliminary list. Should the state interfere in all these matters to enhance public health? Liberalism endorses the maxim of 'live and let live' as long as people do not harm others. Such excessive interference in private matters would be considered by many as unreasonable, unjust and unwarranted. I wonder what is it in the burqa that evokes such paternalistic and caring feelings while other no less disconcerting conducts are perceived as private matters.

In sum, the burqa and niqab law is unjust and unreasonable. It erodes freedom of religion, and it offends the dignity of women who voluntarily opt to wear this garment for religious reasons in order to keep their modesty intact and also to protect themselves from strangers who might make them feel uncomfortable. Those who truly care for women's rights should invest in deliberation, education and persuasion, in the free exchange of ideas with both men and women of minority cultures. Those who truly care for women's rights should show respect for different conceptions of the good, for different reasoning about the place of women and sexuality in society and for differing attitudes to dress and for what dress symbolizes. While for some people the burqa is offensive, for others the miniskirt is offensive.

---

[138] I have tackled the issue of offence in *Speech, Media, and Ethics: The Limits of Free Expression* (Houndmills and New York: Palgrave, 2005): 3–23; *The Scope of Tolerance* (London and New York: Routledge, 2006): 77–122; and 'Taking Profound Offence Seriously: Freedom of Speech v. Human Dignity', *Journal of Hate Studies*, 16 (2020).

[139] Chesler, 'Ban the Burqa?'

While some people perceive the burqa as a health hazard because it is long, clumsy, cumbersome and restricts the wearer's movement,[140] other people perceive stiletto high-heels as a health hazard because they are uncomfortable, damaging to the spine, hips, knees, ankles and feet, and restrict the wearer's movement.[141] Wearing only the 'little black dress' on freezing weekends may also seem very dangerous to women who go out partying.

The legislators failed to recognize individuals as cultural beings. For some people, dress is *not* simply a matter of choice. Rather it is a matter of who I am. My identity defines my dress and the dress confirms and emboldens my identity. Furthermore, the legislators failed to recognize the possibility that the burqa and the niqab might be a liberating force for women. Either because of community norms, or because of their own beliefs as to the appropriate appearance in public, some women who are denied the ability to dress as they wish might opt, or be forced, to remain at home. Thus, the ban negates the abovementioned Article 4 of the Declaration of the Rights of Man and the Citizen as it inflicts distinct harm on some women because of their religious beliefs while they themselves did not inflict harm on others. The ban that was designed to liberate women actually increases their isolation. Because of this reason, the European Parliament adopted a resolution that member states should refrain from legislating against the burqa and the niqab. The European Parliament said that legal restrictions on wearing the burqa and the niqab may be justified where necessary, in particular for security purposes or where public or professional functions of individuals require their religious neutrality or that their face can be seen. However, 'a general prohibition of wearing the *burqa* and the *niqab* would deny women who freely desire to do so their right to cover their face'.[142]

Throughout the book I have emphasized the mechanisms of compromise and deliberation to mitigate tensions. Citizens, politicians and various groups should apply reason in deciding the political conceptions that would support the comprehensive, reasonable doctrines of justice. Dispute resolution mechanisms are required to institute just, reasonable multiculturalism and to settle differences and conflicts. Deliberative democracy facilitates communication and exchange of ideas as to how and why different conceptions of the good can coexist. Deliberative democracy evokes ideals of rational legislation, of participatory politics and of civic self-governance and autonomy (Chapter 3). It is essential to clarify terminology.

---

[140] Ibid., 33–45.

[141] Maxwell S. Barnish and Jean Barnish, 'High-Heeled Shoes and Musculoskeletal Injuries: A Narrative Systematic Review', *BMJ Open*, 6 (2016), https://bmjopen.bmj.com/content/bmjo pen/6/1/e010053.full.pdf; J.X. Moore, B. Lambert, G.P. Jenkins, et al., 'Epidemiology of High-Heel Shoe Injuries in U.S. Women: 2002 to 2012', *Journal of Foot and Ankle Surgery*, 54(4) (2015): 615–619; 'How High Heels Affect Your Body', *Advent Health*, www .thespinehealthinstitute.com/news-room/health-blog/how-high-heels-affect-your-body.

[142] European Parliament, Recommendation and Resolution no. 1743, 'Islam, Islamism and Islamophobia in Europe' (23 June 2010), para. 16, www.assembly.coe.int/nw/xml/XRef/Xref-XML2HTML-en.asp?fileid=17880&lang=en.

Each form of dress should be identified by its specific name: hijab, burqa, niqab, etc. Differences between them should be explained. Knowledge is the key to accommodating differences and for understanding difference. As Rawls explained, citizens' mutual knowledge of one another's religious and other doctrines freely expressed recognizes the roots of citizens' allegiance to their particular conceptions of the good. In this way, 'citizens' allegiance to the democratic ideal of public reason is strengthened for the right reasons'.[143]

Religion can be a barrier, but it can also be a bridge if and when people identify with the rationale for a certain conduct as beliefs transcend beyond a specific book of prayer. Thus, the reasons for wearing each dress should be made known. The prevalence of each dress in society should be acknowledged. The effects of the ban on Muslim women and families should be discussed and evaluated, followed by research that would shed light on the consequences of the ban. Data about instances in which people disturbed public order and caused violence while hiding behind the burqa in France (and possibly also in other places) should become public knowledge. Open debates between those endorsing and those opposing the ban should be held in public forums. Deliberations should be free of harassment and prejudice, and all parties should be substantially and formally equal, enjoying equal standing, equal ability and equal opportunity to table proposals, offer compromises, suggest solutions, support some motions and criticize others. Principled genuine compromises should be sought. Honesty is a must. What are the true motives behind the ban? As illustrated in Chapter 3, only frank conversations enable the tabling of genuine compromises. Mediators with good will in the form of human rights organizations (among others) may offer support to bridge gaps. Such public deliberations would enhance understanding of complicated issues, facilitate learning and create a vital and inclusive pluralistic democracy where citizens feel that they can make a difference, shaping and reshaping the decision-making processes. I have argued that the only meaningful democracy is participatory democracy.

BANNING THE BURKINI

From December 2014 until July 2016, France experienced a wave of terrorism that shocked the nation time and again.[144] The 14 July 2016 terror attack in Nice was especially tormenting. In the wake of that terror attack, armed policemen asked a Muslim woman to remove items of clothing because her clothing was deemed disrespectful to accepted customs and contravened rules of hygiene and of public safety.[145] During that same year, 2016, a controversial ban on women's full-body

---

[143] John Rawls, *The Law of Peoples* (Cambridge, MA: Harvard University Press, 2002): 153.
[144] 'Timeline: Attacks in France', *BBC* (26 July 2016), www.bbc.com/news/world-europe-33288542; 'Deadly Terror Attacks in France Since 2015', *Straits Times* (13 May 2018), www.straitstimes .com/world/europe/deadly-terror-attacks-in-france-since-2015.
[145] Conseil d'État, CE decision du 26 September 2016, no. 403578.

swimsuits, known as 'burkinis', was introduced by twenty-eight cities and communes on France's coast.[146] Mayor David Lisnard of the City of Cannes said he wanted to prohibit 'beachwear ostentatiously showing a religious affiliation while France and places of religious significance are the target of terror attacks' to avoid risks to public order.[147] A bylaw stated: anyone wearing swimwear deemed not to 'respect good customs and secularism' would be barred from visiting the resort's beaches or swimming.[148] A tribunal in Nice that upheld the ban said that it was 'necessary, appropriate and proportionate' to prevent public disorder.[149] Fines were imposed on women wearing burkinis in the towns of Cannes and Nice.[150] Prime Minister Manuel Valls supported the bans, saying burkinis are enslaving women and are 'the affirmation of political Islam in the public space'.[151] Former president Nicolas Sarkozy said that wearing a burkini is 'a political act, it's militant, a provocation', and that 'doing nothing' against the burkini would 'suggest France appears weak'.[152] The ridiculousness of the burkini ban is exemplified by the following comparison between the burkini (Figure 9.5) and a full swim suit (Figure 9.6).

The burkini ban was a strictly localized phenomenon, implemented by specific mayors in specific municipalities. It was rapidly struck down by the highest legal authority in France, the Conseil d'État. The Conseil d'État held that the burkini could be banned only if it triggers disturbances to public order, such as a brawl. The wearing of the burkini is perfectly legitimate. It does not constitute proselytism of a religion and it does not deny women freedom.[153]

[146] 'France Burkini Ban: Mayors Urged to Heed Court's Ruling', BBC (27 August 2016), WWW .BBC.CO.UK/NEWS/WORLD-EUROPE-37201888; David Chazan, 'French Towns Who Banned Burkini to Defy Court Ruling against Them', The Telegraph (28 August 2016), www .telegraph.co.uk/news/2016/08/28/french-towns-who-banned-burkini-to-defy-court-ruling-against-the/?utm_source=dlvr.it&utm_medium=twitter.

[147] Lizzie Dearden, 'Burkini Ban: Why Is France Arresting Muslim Women for Wearing Full-Body Swimwear and Why Are People So Angry?', The Independent (24 August 2016), www .independent.co.uk/news/world/europe/burkini-ban-why-is-france-arresting-muslim-women-for-wearing-full-body-swimwear-and-why-are-people-a7207971.html.

[148] Ibid.

[149] Ibid.

[150] Ibid. Will Worley, 'Burkini Ban: First French Muslim Women Fined for Wearing Garment on Beach in Cannes', The Independent (17 August 2016), www.independent.co.uk/news/world/europe/burkini-ban-first-french-muslim-women-fined-wearing-beach-cannes-a7196466.html.

[151] Asma T. Uddin, 'When a Swimsuit Is a Security Threat', New York Times (24 August 2016), www.nytimes.com/2016/08/24/opinion/when-a-swimsuit-is-a-security-threat.html?emc=edit_th_20160824&nl=todaysheadlines&nlid=33802468&_r=0; 'France Burkini Ban: Mayors Urged to Heed Court's Ruling', BBC (27 August 2016), www.bbc.co.uk/news/world-europe-37201888.

[152] Alexandra Sims, 'Wearing a Burkini Is a "Provocation", Says Former French President Nicolas Sarkozy', The Independent (25 August 2016), www.independent.co.uk/news/world/europe/wearing-a-burkini-is-a-provocation-says-former-french-president-nicolas-sarkozy-a7208251.html.

[153] Carl Hubert, 'Décision du Conseil d'État sur le burkini: la laïcité ne suffit pas pour protéger l'identité française de l'islamisation [rediffusion]', Polemia (7 August 2017) (in French), www .polemia.com/decision-du-conseil-detat-sur-le-burkini-la-laicite-ne-suffit-pas-pour-proteger-lidentite-francaise-de-lislamisation/.

FIGURE 9.5. Burkini (LiudmylaSupynska/iStock/Getty Images Plus).

FIGURE 9.6. Swim suit (Thomas Barwick/DigitalVision/Getty Images).

Unlike the ban on the hijab in French state schools,[154] the burkini ban cannot be taken as an example of a 'French' or 'national' policy. Instead, the burkini ban, imposed by French Riviera mayors in seaside resorts, reflected political dynamics in certain regions of France and the large autonomy that local municipalities have over citizens' behaviour. Local authorities wished to assert authority to implement anti-multicultural policies and they were subsequently corrected. The Conseil d'État made it clear that the ban did not promote women´s freedom but actually wished to deny that freedom, and that local governance lacked the ability to enforce discriminatory beach standards that targeted Muslim women.

Furthermore, arresting women on the beach due to their dress does not promote public order but disturbs it. Many people are upset by the sight of policemen harassing tranquil women who enjoy the sun and the beach as they see fit. The fight against terrorism has nothing to do with swimsuits. The police have far more important things to do, for instance, preventing crime and violent activities. Brayson argues that shifting legal justifications of gender oppression and national security obfuscate and enact a strategy of cultural and colonial assimilation that controls and regulates Islamic bodies in public space.[155] She sees this as analogous to French colonialism that strove to unveil Algerian women.[156]

Women's, and men's, choice of dress should be respected as much as it is possible. People should be left free to cover their bodies as they like. On the beach some people like to show off and to tan large portions of their bodies while some other people care more about their modesty. Some women are comfortable wearing the bikini. Other women feel comfortable wearing the burkini. Some women feel safer wearing the burkini as they do not wish to be the prey of ogling men.[157] This issue should remain a matter of personal choice.

CONCLUSION

Liberal democracy invokes neutrality between different conceptions of the good. Liberal neutrality means refraining from identification with a particular conception of the good and not compelling people to act in a way that might offend their religious beliefs. In France, neutrality is in itself a perfectionist principle that supersedes all other conceptions of the good. It is asserted in the service of the Republic to maintain national cohesion and secular equality. France restricts

---

[154] Mayanthi L. Fernando, *The Republic Unsettled: Muslim French and the Contradictions of Secularism* (Durham, NC: Duke University Press, 2014).

[155] Kimberley Brayson, 'Of Bodies and Burkinis: Institutional Islamophobia, Islamic Dress, and the Colonial Condition', *Journal of Law and Society*, 46(1) (2019): 57.

[156] Frantz Fanon, *A Dying Colonialism* (New York: Grove Press, 1965): 35–67.

[157] Carmen Fishwick and Guardian Readers, 'Why We Wear the Burkini: Five Women on Dressing Modestly at the Beach', *The Guardian* (31 August 2016), www.theguardian.com/world/2016/aug/31/why-we-wear-the-burkini-five-women-on-dressing-modestly-at-the-beach.

religious minorities in a manner that does not restrict the majority religion. The Christian majority not only accepts but relishes *laïcité*. France is certainly not neutral regarding the spirit and implementation of *laïcité*. Indeed, France is perfectionist in its adaptation of a very anti-religious secular ideology. In the Rousseauist spirit, French neutrality 'forces people to be free'. People are not free to follow *their* religious convictions as they wish. Faced with what Will Kymlicka defines as the classical dichotomy between 'integration' of the minority into the larger society and 'accommodation' of the minority culture into the majority,[158] France resolutely picked the former, employing majority coercion. However, it is reiterated that forcing people to be free against their will constitutes insensitive coercion. The boundaries of intervention in subculture's internal affairs should be delineated with great caution.

The French exhibit a strong nationalistic attitude that overrides liberty and fraternity. In the spirit of Montesquieu, liberty is the right to do whatever the laws permit, and it is the role of the state to organize and regulate liberties. The government articulates to its citizens what they ought to do and together all citizens make a unified body politic.[159] Religious liberties that might endanger the unison of the body politic are not tolerated. Solidarity means supporting each other as long as they accept the French way of life. All citizens should work for the good of the nation, and the good of the nation is achieved via conformity with the French way of life. In the French thinking, multiculturalism and multi-religions might lead to fragmentation and, therefore, they are a threat. The solution is *laïcité*.

I argued (Chapter 2) that liberal democracies that fail to accord substantial civil rights to members of minority cultures are deficient. Loss of cultural membership might inflict a profound harm on minority cultures. There is much resemblance between the anti-clericalism of the Revolution and modern *laïcité*. Both wish to put religion under check. Both object to the politicization of religion that might lead to coercion. Both wish to secure a public sphere that is free from religion.

Laïcité is the product of religious wars, colonialism, statism and nation building. Any dissent is deemed to be dangerous, divisive, threatening and challenging. Communitarianism and tribalism are described as enemies of the Republic. The three main arguments against multiculturalism – that it is bad for democracy, bad for women and linked to terror – are expressed with a French twist: multiculturalism is bad for the Republic rather than for democracy. France has been making an explicit effort to force the cultural practices and ways of life of minorities to converge with those of the majority and to conform to the 'general will'. In the name of the Republic, a new trinity has emerged: *indivisibilité*, *sécurité*, and *laïcité*. It is argued that in French society and politics we discern first- and second-order principles. The

---

[158] Will Kymlicka, 'The Internationalization of Minority Rights', *International Journal of Constitutional Law*, 6(1) (2008): 1–32, at 1.

[159] Montesquieu, *The Spirit of Laws*, Book 1, p. 22.

first-order principles are the traditional *liberté, égalité, fraternité*. The second-order principles are *indivisibilité, sécurité,* and *laïcité*. The second-order principles are superimposed on the traditional motto, and clear tensions have emerged between the two sets of principles. People should be French and leave their identities behind. Everyone is welcome provided that they embrace French republicanism. Republicanism is a synonym for Frenchness. Republicanism encapsulates the French ideal which is politically and culturally distinctive in its rejection of diversity. The Anglo-Saxon version of liberalism that appreciates pluralism and diversity is rejected as this means for the French majority individualism and even atomism, privatization, a free market economy and multiculturalism.[160] Individual rights are important, up to a point. While important they are secondary to the need to keep the Republic united.

Chapter 10 is concerned with Jewish–Arab relationships in Israel, a country that is no less fascinating and intriguing than France. In Israel, security eclipses all other considerations, and all-inclusive unity is not a goal. Israel has been striving to reconcile democracy and Judaism, with limited success. Non-Jews are at disadvantage. Israel, whose history is chequered with wars – 1948, 1956, 1967, 1973, 1982, 2006 – and with terrorism, is a country in a continued state of stress. The stress affects the relationships between the Jewish majority and the Arab/Palestinian minority often to the detriment of the latter. I present some accommodating reasonable proposals that, if adopted, would result in a more equitable and just multicultural society.

[160] Chabal, *A Divided Republic*, 105–128, 131–133, 158–160, 233–240, 245–248; Chin, *The Crisis of Multiculturalism in Europe*, 112–113.

10

Multiculturalism v. Security Considerations

Israeli Discrimination of Its Arab/Palestinian Citizens

Israel is not a state of all its citizens. According to the basic nationality law we passed, Israel is the nation state of the Jewish people – and only it.

Benjamin Netanyahu

Loving your neighbor as yourself is not a matter of right–left, Jewish–Arab, secular or religious, it is a matter of dialogue, of dialogue for peace, equality and tolerance for each other. The responsibility for such hope is on us to create a brighter future for our children.

Gal Gadot

In 2000, upon my return from a Fulbright year at the UCLA School of Law, I published a call for a new research assistant. There were some fifteen applicants and I chose the one who I thought would be the best assistant. I filled out the required forms and handed them to the departmental secretary for processing. She looked at the applicant's name and asked: 'What kind of a name is this?'

I answered:	'It's a perfectly good name. Why you ask?'
Secretary:	'It does not sound Jewish.'
RCA:	'So?'
Secretary:	'Is she Jewish?'
RCA:	'I don't know. Maybe she is not. Does it matter?'
Secretary:	'Aren't you afraid she might stab you in the back?'
RCA:	'I did not think about *this* until now. No, I don't.'

The aim of this chapter is to analyse coercion and discrimination applied by the Israeli Jewish majority over its Arab/Palestinian minority. I use the terms 'Israeli Arabs/Palestinians', Israeli Arabs and Israeli Palestinians interchangeably because some identify themselves as Palestinian, some as Arab, some as Israeli Arabs, some as

Palestinian Arabs and some as Palestinian Arabs in Israel.[1] The analysis opens with some background information. It proceeds by describing the Israeli vision, as pronounced by its leaders, and then probes reality, showing that there is quite a gap between vision and reality. It is argued that Israel cannot be described as a liberal democracy. At the same time, while acknowledging Jewish discrimination against its national minority, I reject the description of Israel as an apartheid state and explain that Israeli Arabs/Palestinians could better their condition if they accept upon themselves the same duties that Jewish citizens take upon themselves. I argue for accommodating the interests of the Israeli Arabs/Palestinians, and that Israel should strive to safeguard equal rights and liberties for all citizens – notwithstanding religion, race, culture, ethnicity, colour, gender, class or sexual orientation.

Because Israel is a relatively young democracy it lacks experience in dealing with the pitfalls involved in the working of the system. Like every young phenomenon, Israeli democracy needs to develop gradually, with great caution and care. I show that Israel struggles with issues pertaining to national, cultural and religious diversity. Like France, Israel is still searching for the right balance between the public and the private. It is struggling with what I term the 'democratic catch' (Chapter 1) and is very much concerned with its security. Unlike France, cultural and religious pluralism is very much part of the public sphere.

The litmus test for measuring the extent of democratization of any given society is the legal status of minorities and their enjoyment of equal civic and human rights. Lord Acton said that the most certain test by which we judge whether a country is really free is the amount of security enjoyed by its minorities.[2] The less discriminatory the society is against minorities, the more democratic it is. In this respect, Israel is struggling. Egalitarianism in terms of safeguarding basic civic and human rights for all is still in the making, something that Israel should aspire to achieve. Israel has navigated between liberalism, on the one hand, and promoting its religion and nationality as a Jewish state, on the other. Throughout the years, Israeli leaders have given precedence to Judaism and Jewishness over liberalism. While sometimes their language uttered liberal values, Israeli leaders' actions were perfectionist in essence, preferring one religion and one nation over others. While accommodations were sought and some compromises were made, the underlying motivation was not to achieve just egalitarianism.

BACKGROUND

In the nineteenth century there were more than 400,000 Arabs and some 25,000 Jews in Palestine under the Ottoman Empire.[3] Following World War I and the

---

[1] Sammy Smooha, *Still Playing by the Rules: Index of Arab–Jewish Relations in Israel 2017* (Jerusalem: Israel Democracy Institute, Data Israel, 2018): 222.

[2] Baron John Emerich Edward Dalberg Acton, *Essays on Freedom and Power* (Boston, MA: Beacon, 1948).

[3] Canadians for Justice and Peace in the Middle East, *Demographics of Historic Palestine Prior to 1948* (July 2004).

collapse of the Ottoman Empire, Palestine came under the control of the United Kingdom under a League of Nations' mandate. The British tried to govern Palestine and separate the two rivals, the Arabs and the Jews, who wished to have the upper hand and gain control over the territory. Their success was limited. Violence between the two sides reoccurred throughout the time of the mandate. Riots against Jews erupted in 1929 and again in 1936; the latter escalated into an Arab revolt against the Jews and the British Mandate (1936–1939).[4] At a time when antisemitism raged in Europe under Nazi influence, Britain limited Jewish immigration as a means of appeasing the Arabs.[5]

At the end of World War II the British decided that they could no longer govern Palestine. On 29 November 1947, the UN General Assembly adopted resolution 181 (II), approving with minor changes the Plan of Partition with Economic Union as proposed by the majority in the Special Committee on Palestine.[6] The plan included the creation of an Arab and a Jewish state; the town of Jaffa was to form an Arab enclave within Jewish territory, while Jerusalem was to be administered by the United Nations Trusteeship Council.[7] While the Jewish leadership in British Mandate Palestine accepted the decision with joy, the Arab leadership rejected it with contempt. Immediately thereafter the Palestinian Arabs, aided by volunteers from other countries, objected to the decision by fighting the Zionist forces. On 14 May 1948, Britain withdrew with the expiration of its mandate, and the state of Israel was proclaimed by Jewish Agency Chairman David Ben-Gurion. The next day, forces from Egypt, Transjordan, Syria, Lebanon and Iraq invaded the newly founded state. The bitter fighting continued for many months until 1949. When the war dust had settled, Israel had won the war.[8]

---

[4] David W. Lesch, *The Arab–Israeli Conflict: A History* (New York: Oxford University Press, 2008).

[5] British White Paper of 1939, the Avalon Project, https://avalon.law.yale.edu/20th_century/brwh1939.asp.

[6] In the Partition Plan the word 'Palestinian' is used to describe the citizenship identity of both the Arab and the Jewish citizens of Mandatory Palestine. See United Nations General Assembly, 'The Future Government of Palestine', at Sec. B, Part 1, Ch. B, art. 9, para. 2, which states: 'Qualified voters for each State for this election shall be persons [...] who are: (a) Palestinian citizens.' See Baruch Kimmerling and Joel S. Migdal, *The Palestinian People: A History* (Cambridge, MA: Harvard University Press, 2003): 135. For general reading, see Abdelaziz A. Ayyad, *Arab Nationalism and the Palestinians, 1850–1939* (Jerusalem: The Palestinian Academic Society for the Study of International Affairs, 1999); Rashid Khalidi, Lisa Anderson, Muhammad Muslih and Reeva S. Simon (eds), *The Origins of Arab Nationalism* (New York: Columbia University Press, 1991); Rashid Khalidi, *Palestinian Identity: The Construction of Modern National Consciousness* (New York: Columbia University Press, 1997); Youssef M. Choueiri, *Arab Nationalism – A History: Nation and State in the Arab World* (Oxford: Blackwell, 2001).

[7] Resolution 181 (II). Future Government of Palestine, United Nations, https://unispal.un.org/DPA/DPR/unispal.nsf/0/7F0AF2BD897689B785256C330061D253.

[8] Israel signed armistice agreements with Egypt on 24 February 1949, with Lebanon on 23 March 1949, with Jordan on 3 April 1949 and with Syria on 20 July 1949. No such agreement was signed with Iraq that also sent troops to fight against Israel. See, generally, Benny Morris, *1948: A History of the First Arab–Israeli War* (New Haven, CT: Yale University Press, 2009).

Since its establishment, Israel grew in size and population. Israel grew in size as a result of wars, most notably the 1967 Six Day War.[9] Israel grew in population as a result of a relatively high birth rate and Jewish immigration.[10] Israel is a country of immigration comprised mainly of Jews who came with different traditions, with many languages and with different ways of life. For one reason or another, they decided to make Israel their home.

In size, Israel is a relatively small country. Its size is roughly 22,072 square kilometres.[11] This is more or less the size of Wales (20,758 km^2)[12] and of the state of Massachusetts (21,456 km^2) which is ranked 45th among the fifty states of the United States.[13] In April 2020, Israel's population was 8,967,594,[14] of whom 74 per cent are Jewish and 21 per cent are Arab.[15] The Druze and the Bedouin are small minorities within the Palestinian Arab minority. Christians constitute 2 per cent of the Israeli population (175,000 in 2018); of them 77 per cent are Arabs and the rest came from the former Soviet Union.[16] Most of the Arabs reside in Galilee in north Israel. Smaller numbers live in the so-called Triangle area at the centre of Israel, and in the Negev desert in the south (mostly Bedouins).

The question of the legal status of Israel's Palestinian Arab citizens has been challenging since Israel was established, and even prior to that. Already in UN Resolution 181(II) (1947), which depicts the establishment of two independent democratic nation-based states in 'Mandatory Palestine',[17] that is, Arab and Jewish

---

[9]   Wm Roger Louis and Avi Shlaim (eds), *The 1967 Arab–Israeli War* (New York: Cambridge University Press, 2012).

[10] Immigration to Israel: Total Immigration, by Country of Origin (1948–Present), *Jewish Virtual Library*, www.jewishvirtuallibrary.org/jsource/Immigration/immigration_by_country.html.

[11] *Israel in Numbers* (Jerusalem: Israel Bureau of Statistics, 2020, Hebrew), https://old.cbs.gov.il/hodaot2020n/11_20_114t1.pdf.

[12] Wales Factfile, www.clickonwales.org/wp-content/uploads/1_Factfile_Geography.pdf.

[13] 'Massachusetts – Location, Size, and Extent', www.city-data.com/states/Massachusetts-Location-size-and-extent.html.

[14] Israel Bureau of Statistics, *Israel in Numbers* (Jerusalem, 2019, Hebrew), www.cbs.gov.il/he/pages/default.aspx.

[15] *Times of Israel* Staff, 'Israel's Population Tops 9 Million, Including 45% of World Jewry', *Times of Israel* (6 May 2019), www.timesofisrael.com/israels-population-tops-9-million-including-45-of-world-jewry/.

[16] Abigail Klein Leichman, 'Christians Comprise 2% of Israel's Population', *Israel 21C* (25 December 2018), www.israel21c.org/christians-comprise-2-of-israels-population/; Yoav Itiel, 'Residing in the North, with Two Children: For Christmas, Data about Christians in Israel', *Walla* (24 December 2018) (Hebrew), https://news.walla.co.il/item/3209231?utm_source=Generalshare&utm_medium=sharebuttonapp&utm_term=social&utm_content=general&utm_campaign=socialbutton.

[17] The term 'Mandatory Palestine' refers to the geographical area that was administered by the Mandate of the United Kingdom (hereinafter: the British Mandate), and was the area carved out of the southern area of Great Syria under the Ottoman Empire, that is, the territory of nowadays Jordan, Israel, as well as the West Bank and the Gaza Strip of the Palestinian Authority. See League of Nations, 'Mandate for Palestine' (24 July 1922), United Nations Information System on the Question of Palestine Documents Collections, https://web.archive.org/web/20131125014738/http://unispal.un.org/UNISPAL.NSF/0/2FCA2C68106F11AB0

states,[18] it was anticipated that Israel would be established as a Jewish and democratic state, in which an Arab/Palestinian minority would reside as full and equal citizens. Israel's 1948 Declaration of Independence[19] relies, *inter alia*, on the Partition Plan,[20] promising full and equal citizenship to the Arab/Palestinian residents of the state.

However, this pledge for equal citizenship is questioned by some Palestinian Arabs following the enactment of the 1994 Basic Law: Freedom of Occupation[21] and the 1992 Basic Law: Human Dignity and Liberty,[22] amended in 1994, where Israel was defined as a Jewish and democratic state, in this order.[23] First Jewish, then democratic, without due consideration to the inherent tension between them. Moreover, the recent legislation of Israel's 14th Basic Law: Israel as the Nation-State of the Jewish People (the Nation State Law), in 2018, has only muddied the waters, as it expressly emphasizes Israel's religious and national characteristics but omits to protect democratic values and rights, including the right to equality.[24]

Israel has a majority and a minority from two different peoples, and it is also polyethnic. It is multicultural as it has a significant national-cultural community and also because its Jewish population adheres to different conceptions of the good. The Jewish population does not agree on a single conception of 'the good life', but is largely

---

5256BCF007BF3CB. See also 'The Palestine Mandate', http://avalon.law.yale.edu/20th_century/palmanda.asp.

[18] United Nations General Assembly, Resolution 181, 'Future Government of Palestine' (29 November 1947), United Nations Information System on the Question of Palestine Documents Collections, https://unispal.un.org/DPA/DPR/unispal.nsf/0/7F0AF2BD89768 9B785256C330061D253.

[19] The declaration adopts the same terminology and merit of the Partition Plan. See 'The Declaration of the Establishment of the State of Israel' (14 May 1948), www.mfa.gov.il/mfa/foreignpolicy/peace/guide/pages/declaration%20of%20establishment%20of%20state%20of%20israel.aspx.

[20] The Declaration of Independence says: 'On 29th November, 1947, the United Nations General Assembly passed a resolution calling for the establishment of a Jewish State in Eretz-Israel; the General Assembly required the inhabitants of Eretz-Israel to take such steps as were necessary on their part for the implementation of that resolution. This recognition by the United Nations of the right of the Jewish people to establish their State is irrevocable ... Accordingly we, members of the People's Council, representatives of the Jewish Community of Eretz-Israel and of the Zionist Movement, are here assembled on the day of the termination of the British Mandate over Eretz-Israel and, by virtue of our natural and historic right and on the strength of the resolution of the United Nations General Assembly, hereby declare the establishment of a Jewish state in Eretz-Israel, to be known as the State of Israel.' http://mfa.gov.il/mfa/foreignpolicy/peace/guide/pages/declaration%20of%20establishment%20of%20state%20of%20israel.aspx.

[21] www.knesset.gov.il/laws/special/eng/basic4_eng.htm.

[22] www.knesset.gov.il/laws/special/eng/basic3_eng.htm.

[23] The law stipulates: 'The purpose of this Basic Law is to protect human dignity and liberty, in order to establish in a Basic Law the values of the State of Israel as a Jewish and democratic state.' The law is discussed below.

[24] Raoul Wootliff, 'Final Text of Jewish Nation-State Law, Approved by the Knesset Early on July 19', *Times of Israel* (19 July 2018), www.timesofisrael.com/final-text-of-jewish-nation-state-bill-set-to-become-law/.

united on seeing Israel as a Jewish state. By its very definition as a Jewish state, Israel follows a particular conception of the good. While some understand a Jewish state to be defined by its religious identity, others apply a cultural definition of what it means to be Jewish; but the vast majority wish Israel to remain Jewish, religiously and/or culturally. Israel prefers Judaism over other religions and often its aspiration to be a Jewish democracy faces inherent contradictions, where democracy withdraws under the duress of coercive Jewish nationalism. While I recognize the need for a home for the Jewish people, where Jews can decide their destiny and independently defend and promote their tradition and culture, it is argued that Israel should retain its democratic character. Democracy is not merely a majority rule. Democracy is about majority rule *while respecting the rights of minorities.* Both parts of this definition are necessary, and any part in itself is not sufficient. The second part of the definition is no less important than the first. Democracy should devise mechanisms to protect itself from any form of exploiting power; it should fight against and pre-empt the formation of any form of tyranny, majority and minority alike.[25] The right of the majority should not be considered as the rightness of the majority, as quantity alone does not make things right. Any form of unjustified discrimination should be opposed, whether the discrimination is based on sheer numbers, certain beliefs, custom or religion. Individuals should be able to fulfil their capacities and to establish their autonomy. Israel should provide open forums for debate and for practising alternative conceptions of the good. This can be done by adhering to the basic liberal principles of respect for others and not harming others. Government should respect the civil, religious and political rights of all citizens.

ISRAEL'S VISION

The Partition Plan is a significant official international document that recognizes Jewishness as a national identity, distinct from the concept of Judaism as a religious identity. It reflects what was envisioned by the 1917 'Balfour Declaration' as the establishment of 'a national home for the Jewish people'.[26] Such recognition is a prerequisite to granting the right to self-determination to any nation.[27]

---

[25] In *On Liberty*, J.S. Mill argued that 'the tyranny of the majority' is among the 'evils against which society requires to be on its guard'. https://socialsciences.mcmaster.ca/econ/ugcm/3ll3/mill/liberty.pdf.

[26] 'The Balfour Declaration', Israel Ministry of Foreign Affairs, www.mfa.gov.il/mfa/foreignpolicy/peace/guide/pages/the%20balfour%20declaration.aspx. This is a letter issued by the foreign secretary of the United Kingdom, Arthur James Balfour, to the leader of the British Jewish community, Lord Lionel Walter Rothschild, for transmission to the Federation of Great Britain and Ireland. Colin Shindler noted in his comments on a draft of this chapter that the term ' national home' in the Balfour Declaration was deliberately left ambiguous by the British so that they could reinterpret it after World War I.

[27] See the Montevideo Convention on the Rights and Duties of States, 26 December 1933, art. 1, which provides: '[T]he state as a person of international law should possess the following qualifications: (a) a permanent population; (b) a defined territory; (c) a government; and (d) the capacity to enter into relations with the other states.' 'Montevideo Convention on the

As far as a democratic regime is concerned, the Partition Plan stipulated that the nation-based states must apply substantive democratic regimes. It says: 'The Constituent Assembly of each State shall draft a democratic constitution for its State and choose a provisional government to succeed the Provisional Council of Government appointed by the Commission.'[28] The Partition Plan acknowledged the conceptual distinction between formal and substantive democracies (see Chapter 1) and aspired to the latter. The Partition Plan thus included a special chapter that guaranteed not only the equal constitutional protection of the remaining Arab minority in the newly emerging Jewish state, but also their linguistic, educational and religious rights as a national indigenous minority.[29]

Rights and Duties of States', International Law Students Association, www.ilsa.org/jessup/jessup15/Montevideo%20Convention.pdf. Shortly after World War II this principle had been accepted by the international community as the principle of self-determination. See the UN Charter, Cha. 1, art. 1, para. 2. For criticism on these criteria, see Jeffrey L. Dunoff, Steven R. Ratner and David Wippman, *International Law: Norms, Actors, Process: A Policy-Oriented Approach* (New York: Aspen Law and Business, 2002): 109–111.

[28] United Nations General Assembly, 'Future Government of Palestine', Sec. B(10), https://mfa.gov.il/MFA/ForeignPolicy/MFADocuments/Yearbook1/Pages/Future%20Government%20of%20Palestine-%20General%20Assembly%20R.aspx. Israel has not succeeded in adopting a full written constitution as mandated by the Partition Plan, Sec. B, Part 1, Ch. B, art. 9, para. 1. Eventually, by means of a political compromise, Israel adopted a series of incomplete Basic Laws intended, once enacted, to compose the constitution for Israel. Whereas the Knesset has never decided when such a project will be completed, thus establishing the full and final constitution, the contemporary Basic Laws that deal with human rights severely fail to include a straightforward constitutional protection for very basic human rights, otherwise included in the Partition Plan, e.g., freedom of expression and the right to equality. On the normative constitutional status of the basic laws, see Suzie Navot, *The Constitution of Israel: A Contextual Analysis* (Oxford: Hart Publishing, 2014), 4–12; Mohammed S. Wattad, 'Israel's Laws on Referendum: A Tale of Unconstitutional Legal Structure', *Florida Journal of International Law* 27(2) (2015): 213, 221–226. See also Aharon Barak's books, *Human Dignity* and *Proportionality: Constitutional Rights and Their Limitations* (Cambridge: Cambridge University Press, 2015, and 2012 respectively).

[29] Underlying this recognition is another implicit acknowledgment of the rights of the indigenous people of Mandatory Palestine – regardless of the question of who was first and who constituted a majority or a minority at different points of time. The idea is that indigenous citizens are more privileged in this regard, as compared with immigrant citizens. Whereas the latter decided to migrate from their homeland to another country, they are expected to accept the civil and national identity of the absorbing state; this is not the case for indigenous people. See and compare Will Kymlicka, *Multicultural Citizenship: A Liberal Theory of Minority Rights* (Oxford: Clarendon Press, 1995); Will Kymlicka and Raphael Cohen-Almagor, 'Ethnocultural Minorities in Liberal Democracies', in Maria Baghramian and Attracta Ingram (eds), *Pluralism: The Philosophy and Politics of Diversity* (London: Routledge, 2000): 228–250; Ilan Saban and Mohammad Amara, 'The Status of Arabic in Israel: Reflections on the Power to Produce Social Change', *Israel Law Review*, 36 (2002): 5; Sammy Smooha, 'The Model of Ethnic Democracy: Israel as a Jewish and Democratic State', *Nations and Nationalism*, 8(4) (October 2002): 475–503.

The Partition Plan envisioned welcoming Israel to the international community as a nation-based state, namely, a Jewish state. Second, this nation state has to be a constitutional democratic state. And third, a proper balance has to be established between Israel's Jewish identity and democracy, which reflects the particular circumstances of Mandatory Palestine and the expectations that its national indigenous minorities would become full legal citizens of the other nation state, that is, an Arab minority in the Jewish state and a Jewish minority in the Arab state.[30]

The Partition Plan was never adopted by the United Nations Security Council; therefore, it remains a non-binding resolution of the UN General Assembly.[31] The resolution was accepted by the Jewish Agency for Palestine. After the Holocaust, the goal was to found a safe haven for Jews all over the world so as to avoid the possibility of another horrific experience of that nature. Indeed, the United Nations acknowledged this goal. This creation, however, based on a specific conception of the good, discriminates against the Israeli Arabs/Palestinians who were perceived from the outset as a security threat.[32] Israel acknowledges the problematic aspects involved in the introduction of this religio-ethnic element in its framework of ruling. To assure an equal status for the Arab minority, the 1948 Declaration of Independence holds that Israel will foster the development of the country for the benefit of all its inhabitants; that it will be based on the foundations of liberty, justice and peace; that it will uphold complete equality of social and political rights to all of its citizens irrespective of religion, race or sex; and that it will guarantee freedom of religion, conscience, language, education and culture.[33]

Israel's first prime minister, David Ben-Gurion (who is often compared to George Washington), wrote to the French president, Charles de Gaulle, that 'the Arabs who reside in Eretz [Land of] Israel enjoy all the rights that residents in any democratic country enjoy, and a Jewish state is possible only as a democratic country'.[34] Ben-Gurion quoted from Leviticus 19: 'If a stranger sojourn with thee in your land, ye shall not do him wrong. The stranger that sojourneth with you shall be unto you as the home-born among you, and thou shalt love him as thyself; for ye were

---

[30] Benny Morris, *1948: A History of the First Arab–Israeli War* (New Haven, CT: Yale University Press, 2008): 66–67, 72–73, 75; Sami Hadawi, *Bitter Harvest: A Modern History of Palestine* (New York: Olive Branch Press, 1989): 76; United Nations, 'The Plan of Partition and End of the British Mandate', in *The Question of Palestine and the United Nations*, brochure DPI/2517/ Rev. 1, chap. 2, www.un.org/Depts/dpi/palestine/ch2.pdf.

[31] Liora Chartouni, '70 Years after UN Resolution 181: An Assessment', Jerusalem Center for Public Affairs (26 November 2017), http://jcpa.org/article/70-years-un-resolution-181-assessment/.

[32] Michael M. Karayanni, 'Two Concepts of Group Rights for the Palestinian-Arab Minority under Israel's Constitutional Definition as a "Jewish and democratic" State', *I.CON*, 10(2) (2012): 331.

[33] Israel's Declaration of Independence, http://mfa.gov.il/mfa/foreignpolicy/peace/guide/pages/ declaration%20of%20establishment%20of%20state%20of%20israel.aspx.

[34] David Ben-Gurion, Letter to De Gaulle, 6 December 1967, in *The Restored State of Israel* (Tel Aviv: Am Oved, 1975): Vol. 2, 842 (Hebrew).

strangers in the land of Egypt.'[35] Ben-Gurion pledged to President de Gaulle that the Jewish people is and will remain committed to the ideals of peace, human fraternity, justice and truth 'as ordered by our preachers'.[36]

Ben-Gurion saw no contradiction between the Jewish return to Zion and the Arab presence in Israel; thus, he regarded social-Zionism as a just movement. In 1928 Ben-Gurion declared: 'In accordance with my moral belief we do not have the right to deprive a single Arab child, even if our reward resulting from this deprivation would be the fulfillment of all our wishes.'[37] Ben-Gurion wrote that the Jewish state needs to behave towards its Arab citizens as if they were Jews, not just to give them equal rights but to constantly take steps to equate their life conditions with the economic and cultural conditions of Jews.[38]

Ze'ev Jabotinsky, founder of the Betar (Brith Joseph Trumpeldor) movement and leader of revisionist Zionism that forebears the Likud party, argued in *The Iron Wall* that his attitude to Arabs was determined by two principles: 'First of all, I consider it utterly impossible to eject the Arabs from Palestine. There will always be *two* nations in Palestine.'[39] And second, he believed in equality of rights for all nationalities living in the same state. Jabotinsky declared: 'I am prepared to take an oath binding ourselves and our descendants that we shall never do anything contrary to the principle of equal rights, and that we shall never try to eject anyone. This seems to me a fairly peaceful credo.'[40]

According to President of the Israel Supreme Court Aharon Barak, by virtue of the abovementioned Basic Law: Freedom of Occupation and Basic Law: Human Dignity and Liberty, human rights in Israel have become legal norms of preferred constitutional status. These laws are deemed to be of such significant importance that some, including Barak, described their legislation as no less than a constitutional revolution in the life of the country.[41]

The Declaration of Independence does not include the phrase 'Jewish and democratic state'; it also omits the word 'democracy'. However, as correctly held by the Supreme Court of Israel, a plausible interpretation of the declaration leaves no doubt as to the democratic nature of Israel.[42] Yet Israel must strike a just and

---

[35] *Leviticus* 19:33–34.

[36] David Ben-Gurion, Letter to De Gaulle, 6 December 1967, in *The Restored State of Israel*, 851.

[37] Quoted in Shabtai Teveth, *Ben Gurion and the Palestinian Arabs* (Jerusalem and Tel Aviv: Schocken, 1985): 258 (Hebrew).

[38] David Ben-Gurion, 'The Ways of the Jewish State', *Ba'Ma'aracha*, 1 (1957): 279–299 (Hebrew).

[39] Ze'ev (Vladimir) Jabotinsky, *The Iron Wall* (4 November 1923), www.jewishvirtuallibrary.org/jsource/Zionism/ironwall.html.

[40] Ibid. See also Arye Naor, 'Minorities in Israel and the Liberal Utopia of Jabotinsky', *Identities*, 3 (2013): 146–153 (Hebrew).

[41] Aharon Barak, 'A Constitutional Revolution: Israel's Basic Laws', *Yale Faculty Scholarship Series*, 3697 (1993), https://digitalcommons.law.yale.edu/fss_papers/3697. See also Navot, *The Constitution of Israel*.

[42] See *Kol Ha'am Co., Ltd. v. Minister of the Interior*, HCJ 73/53 and HCJ 87/53; 7(2) PD 871 (1953), 876–878.

reasonable balance between its Jewish identity and its democratic nature. People should adopt the Rawlsian veil of ignorance and apply the principles of justice to all, without distinction.

Israel expresses its Jewishness through the right of return,[43] the observance of official Jewish holidays and sanctioning Hebrew as the official state language.[44] As a Jewish state, Israel is the homeland of the Jewish nation, thus entitling all its members a special key to enter the house. However, within that house every legal citizen, whether a Jew or not, must be treated fairly and equitably.[45] As explicated in Chapter 2, people should have a share of the communal resources and the freedom to lead their conception of the good within their cultural community. Devolving greater power to local communities would enable Arabs to make certain decisions on their own. These external protections are consistent with democracy, and are necessary for just, reasonable multiculturalism. They would help put Arabs on a more equal footing and reduce the extent to which minorities are vulnerable to the larger society.[46]

SYMBOLS

Symbols are important in the life of a nation. As the only Jewish country in the world, Israel's symbols are expected to be Jewish. At the same time a significant Arab/ Palestinian minority resides in Israel and therefore some accommodation needs to be made with regard to them so that they feel part of the country. Here is a proposal that will provoke and promote debate. The methods of debate should be along the lines of deliberative democracy. Deliberative democracy accentuates processes and the transformation of preferences through open conversation, enabling free discussion to shape policies (see Chapter 3). This proposal should be perceived as a starting point, not as an ironclad scheme. Here is the proposal.

The *national emblem* of the state of Israel includes a menorah flanked by two olive branches. In antiquity the most commonly used symbol of Judaism was the menorah, the seven-branched candelabrum that stood in the Holy Temple in Jerusalem before it was destroyed by the Romans in 70 CE. The menorah was

---

[43] Law of Return 5710-1950, Israel Ministry of Foreign Affairs, http://mfa.gov.il/MFA/MFA-Archive/2001/Pages/The%20Law%20of%20Return-%201950.aspx.

[44] On the legal status of both the Arab and the Hebrew languages in Israel, see Article 82 of 'The Palestine Order in Council', United Nations Information System on the Question of Palestine Documents Collections, https://unispal.un.org/DPA/DPR/unispal.nsf/0/C7AAE196F41AA 05505 2565F50054E656. See also Meital Pinto, 'On the Intrinsic Value of Arabic in Israel – Challenging Kymlicka on Language Rights', *Canadian Journal of Law & Jurisprudence* 20(1) (2007): 143–172, https://papers.ssrn.com/sol3/papers.cfm?abstract_id=995507; opinion by Chief Justice Aharon Barak, in *Adalah and Association for Civil Rights in Israel v. Tel Aviv Municipality and Others*.

[45] Consider Opinion by Chief Justice Aharon Barak, in *Qa'adan et al. v. Israel Lands Administration et al.*, HCJ 6698/05, 54(1) PD 258 (2000), at the end of para. 31.

[46] Kymlicka and Cohen-Almagor, 'Ethnocultural Minorities in Liberal Democracies', 228–250.

FIGURE 10.1. The Menorah(Alexandra Krull/EyeEm/Getty Images).

adopted as the emblem of Israel by the decision of the Provisional Council of State on 11 Shevat 5709 in the Hebrew calendar (10 February 1949). This emblem should remain intact (Figure 10.1).

The *Israeli flag* is composed of blue stripes and a Star of David (Magen David). The blue stripes are intended to symbolize the stripes on a tallit, the traditional Jewish prayer shawl. The Magen David is a widely acknowledged symbol of the Jewish people and of Judaism. One of the earliest uses of the Star of David as a symbol of Jewish identity was in 1354, when King Charles IV of Bohemia granted the Jews of Prague the right to bear a red flag depicting the Star of David and Solomon's Seal (a Star of David within a circle). After Jews were emancipated following the French Revolution, many of their communities selected the Star of David as their emblem.[47] It should be noted that the six-pointed star is not uniquely a Jewish symbol. It was a common symbol in Islamic and Western occultism.[48] Muslims

---

[47] Ronen Shnidman, 'The Star of David: More than Just a Symbol of the Jewish People or Nazi Persecution', *Haaretz* (17 February 2014), www.haaretz.com/world-news/europe/the-star-of-david-isn-t-just-jewish-1.5323219.

[48] DHWTY, 'The Significance of the Sacred Seal of Solomon and Its Symbols', *Ancient Origins* (23 February 2016), www.ancient-origins.net/artifacts-other-artifacts/significance-sacred-seal-solomon-and-its-symbols-005401.

know the hexagram as the Seal of Solomon: both Solomon and David were prophets, and both are mentioned in the Quran. The hexagram appears in Islamic artefacts and decorations on mosques and other buildings worldwide. The Seal of Solomon was used by Muslims from India to Spain to adorn and decorate the bottom of drinking vessels and coins issued by various dynasties.[49] The flag should also remain intact.

Israel may consider amending the *national anthem*. Israel's Palestinian Arab citizens have been criticized for refusing to sing the words of the Israeli anthem. The argument has been that they must do so because they are citizens of the state of Israel. But then the anthem should relate to them and be meaningful to them. However, the anthem speaks of 'the Jewish spirit yearning deep in the heart'.[50] Currently the Israeli anthem appeals solely to Jewish hearts. It explicitly ignores the multicultural and multinational character of the state. Israel should learn from the lessons of other democracies that were bold enough to change their respective anthems in order to represent all factions of their populations (most notably South Africa, the 'rainbow' nation, after 1994. In 2018, Canada passed a bill to change the lyrics of its national anthem to remove gendered language following claims it is discriminatory.[51] The bill changes the phrase 'in all thy sons command' to 'in all of us command'). Israel need not necessarily adopt a different anthem. It may simply change a few words, mentioned above: instead of 'Zion' to speak of 'Israel' or 'our land'; instead of a 'Jew' to speak of a 'person' or 'citizen'. Such accommodations are steps in the right direction towards a more democratic society.

In this context let us mention that Canada, like Israel, struggles with national problems, for it embraces two nations; namely, the English and the French nations. Since French has become an official language, equal in status to English, the Canadian anthem was officially translated into French, in the following manner:

Ô Canada! Terre de nos aïeux, Ton front est ceint de fleurons glorieux! Car ton bras sait porter l'épée, Il sait porter la croix! Ton histoire est une épopée des plus brillants exploits. Et ta valeur, de foi trempée, Protégera nos foyers et nos droits; Protégera nos foyers et nos droits.

[O Canada! Land of our forefathers Thy brow is wreathed with a glorious garland of flowers. As in thy arm ready to wield the sword, So also is it ready to carry the cross. Thy history is an epic of the most brilliant exploits. Thy valour steeped in faith Will protect our homes and our rights Will protect our homes and our rights.]

---

[49] Khalid, 'Symbolism: Star of David or Solomon's Seal', *Baheyeldin Dynasty* (22 December 2004), https://baheyeldin.com/culture/star-of-david-solomons-seal.html.

[50] Quoted from the Israeli anthem 'Hatikva' ('The Hope').

[51] John Paul Tasker, 'Senate Passes Bill to Make O Canada Lyrics Gender Neutral', *CBC* (31 January 2018), www.cbc.ca/news/politics/anthem-bill-passes-senate-1.4513317.

The Canadian anthem in the French version speaks of 'So also is it ready to carry the cross'.[52] Many Canadian Jews argue against the French version of the anthem. They contend that the anthem must express their Canadian citizenship. Similarly, Israeli Palestinians may rightly object to an anthem that fails to embrace all Israeli citizens.

Israel has no official *national motto* and here is an opportunity to introduce something new that reflects the Israel of today, a motto that celebrates the mosaic of Israeli cultures, that celebrates diversity and pluralism, and that would unite all citizens around one unifying slogan with which all could identify.[53] The motto should preferably be selected from pertinent Arab proverbs, along the lines marked above regarding the beauty of multiculturalism and the need to create bridges and emphasize unity. United we stand. United is our strength. Any of the following values – peace, tolerance, power, freedom, truth, justice, charity and righteousness – may also be accentuated. For instance: 'Do not turn away a poor man . . . even if all you can give is half a date. If you love the poor and bring them near you' (Al-Tirmidhi, Hadith 1376). Adopting such a motto would be a step in the right direction.

Critiques might perceive these proposals as mere tokens rather than substantive changes. I believe that symbols do matter and may drive further positive changes. Respect for culture and heritage matter. I believe in incremental change, through compromise, deliberation and exchange of ideas: agree on what can be relatively easier to agree upon, and then move on to pursue further integrative steps that would reduce gaps of inequality and lead to integration and appreciation of society's cultural and religious mosaic. The suggestions are the starting point, not the end point. One scratch on the wall is just a scratch. Many scratches may change the shape of the wall. More scratches can eliminate it altogether. Every step aimed at increasing integration and reducing friction is a positive step in the right direction.

INEQUALITY AND DISCRIMINATION

The Palestinians who remained in Israel after its establishment in 1948 lived formally under military rule until November 1966. This policy of coercion was based on the perception of Arabs as an imminent threat to the state. That perception changed gradually until Israeli leaders realized that military rule needlessly punished Arabs who were not a security risk. Prime Minister Levy Eshkol thought that military rule might lead to Arab hostilities, that it prevented constructive cooperation

---

[52] The English version of the Canadian anthem does not speak of the 'cross': 'O Canada! Our home and native land! True patriot love in all thy sons command. With glowing hearts we see thee rise, The True North strong and free! From far and wide, O Canada, we stand on guard for thee. God keep our land glorious and free! O Canada, we stand on guard for thee. O Canada, we stand on guard for thee.'

[53] I am indebted to Bhikhu Parekh for this idea.

between Israeli Jews and Israeli Arabs, and that it was an obstacle to Arab integration into Israeli society. Ethical reasons also played a part as military rule coerced and discriminated against Arabs. Democracy should uphold basic human rights.[54]

The growing realization that the coercion policy might hamper Israel's security more than it enhanced it brought about an alternative approach that spoke of coexistence. The change in policy was not comprehensive but rather a collection of incremental steps towards 'normalization' and improving the living conditions of Arab citizens. The response of many Arabs was that 'existence precedes coexistence'. The alienation between Arab citizens and the state continued.[55] A fifth to a third of Arabs and Jews do not feel at ease when they share public spaces. In 2017, 30.3 per cent of Arabs felt uncomfortable speaking Arabic in Jewish places and 35.3 per cent of Jews felt unease upon hearing Arabic in their vicinity. Half of the Arabs said that they felt alien and rejected in Israel.[56] Asked whether there is a lot of discrimination against Arabs, 34 per cent agreed and 38.3 per cent were inclined to agree.[57] Asked 'How does the government today treat Arab citizens?' only 4.9 per cent said 'As equal citizens', while 40.3 per cent said 'As second-class citizens' and 25.4 per cent 'As hostile citizens who do not deserve equality'.[58]

Reasonableness consists in equitableness whereby individuals respect others' rights. Reasonableness includes patience and tolerance. Identification with a certain religion should not diminish one's entitlements (Chapter 2). The Israeli Democracy Index 2013 showed that the greatest share of respondents identified the tension between Jews and Arabs as the most serious area of friction in Israeli society.[59] Respondents continued to rank this tension as the highest in subsequent years up until 2018, where the tensions between left and right, and between religious and secular Jews, preceded the Arab–Jewish friction.[60] In 2019 the tension between Arabs and Jews was ranked highest.[61] The tensions

[54] Levy Eshkol, *Knesset Proceedings* (23 October 1963) (Hebrew).

[55] Amal Jamal, *Arab Minority Nationalism in Israel: The Politics of Indigeneity* (London: Routledge, 2011); Itzhak Galnoor and Dana Blander, *The Handbook of Israel's Political System* (Cambridge: Cambridge University Press, 2018); Sammy Smooha, 'Arabs and Jews in a Jewish and Democratic State: Mutual Disengagement from Responsibility', in Raphael Cohen-Almagor, Ori Arbel-Ganz and Asa Kasher (eds), *Public Responsibility in Israel* (Tel Aviv and Jerusalem: Hakibbutz Hameuchad and Mishkanot Shaananim, 2012): 527–551 (Hebrew).

[56] Sammy Smooha, *Still Playing by the Rules: Index of Arab–Jewish Relations in Israel 2017* (Jerusalem: Israel Democracy Institute, Data Israel, 2018): 43–44.

[57] Ibid., 208.

[58] Ibid., 221.

[59] Tamar Hermann et al., *Israeli Democracy Index 2013* (Jerusalem: The Israel Democracy Institute, 2013): 13, 150.

[60] Tamar Hermann et al., *The Israeli Democracy Index 2018* (Jerusalem: The Israel Democracy Institute, 2018): 138.

[61] Tamar Hermann Or Anabi, Ella Heller, Fadi Omar and William Cubbison, *A Conditional Partnership: Jews and Arabs, Israel 2019* ((Jerusalem: The Israel Democracy Institute, 2019) (Hebrew).

relate both to the Palestinians in the West Bank and Gaza as well as to the Palestinians inside the Green (1967) Line.[62]

In 2013 the Jewish public was divided as to whether Jewish citizens should be given more rights than non-Jewish citizens. The fact that roughly half of the respondents considered this to be an acceptable policy is extremely problematic as the preservation of equal rights is the essence of democracy. In 2018, 26.7 per cent strongly agreed or somewhat agreed that Jews should have more rights than non-Jews;[63] 52.3 per cent of Jews strongly agreed and 21.9 per cent somewhat agreed that 'Decisions crucial to the state on issues of peace and security should be made by a Jewish majority.'[64] Moreover, 35.5 per cent and 23.8 per cent strongly or somewhat agreed that 'Decisions crucial to the state regarding governance, economy, or society should be made by a Jewish majority.'[65] In 2013, 27.5 per cent of the Jews in the sample were said to 'Agree totally' and further 16.3 per cent 'Agree somewhat' with the statement: 'The government should encourage Arabs to emigrate from Israel.'[66] The survey also revealed that a majority of the Jewish public considered the Jews to be the 'chosen people' (50.1 per cent believe this 'Very strongly' and a further 14.2 per cent believe this 'Quite strongly').[67] This sense of 'chosenness' entails the exclusion of others.

According to government figures the 2013 budget for religious services for the Jewish population, including funding for religious councils, salaries for religious personnel, funding for the development of cemeteries and funding for the construction of synagogues and ritual baths, was approximately 418.8 million new Israeli shekels (NIS) ($120.7 million). Religious minorities (21 per cent of the population) received approximately NIS 79.1 million ($22.8 million), or 13 per cent of total funding, which included NIS 14.1 million ($4.1 million) for the development of religious sites and structures.[68] Proportionally this is not on a par with the resources allocated to the Jewish majority. The Mossawa Center, a civil society organization established to promote equality for Israeli Arab citizens, argues that the share of the Arab population in the budget has not changed significantly over the years. Analysis of the state budget for 2019 shows that systematic discrimination continues as a result of the government's strategy that has a strong bias in favour of Jews.[69]

---

[62] The Green Line is the demarcation line set in the 1949 Armistice Agreements between Israel and its enemies after the 1948 Arab–Israeli War.

[63] Tamar Hermann et al., *Israeli Democracy Index 2018*, 183, 225.

[64] Ibid., 187, 228.

[65] Ibid., 188, 228.

[66] Tamar Hermann et al., *Israeli Democracy Index 2013*, 148.

[67] Ibid., 152. For further discussion, see Raphael Cohen-Almagor and Amos Guiora, 'Democracy and Security in Israel', in Leonard Weinberg and Elizabeth Francis (eds), *Democracy and Security: A Handbook* (London and New York: Routledge, 2021): 172–190.

[68] US Department of State, 2013 *Report on International Religious Freedom: Israel and the Occupied Territories* (28 July 2014), www.state.gov/j/drl/rls/irf/2013/nea/222293.htm.

[69] Danny Zaken, 'Investment in Arab Society Will Benefit the Whole Economy', *Globes* (15 October 2019, Hebrew), www.globes.co.il/news/article.aspx?did=1001303029.

In Chapter 2 I argued that governments should work to prevent discrimination in the labour market and to combat prejudice against minorities. Officially Israeli Palestinians enjoy full equality before the law in many spheres. They have the right to vote and to be elected to state institutions. They have been serving in the Israeli parliament, the Knesset, and they enjoy religious and cultural autonomy. However, the Israeli Palestinian human rights organization Adalah compiled a Discriminatory Laws Database of over sixty-five Israeli laws that discriminate directly or indirectly against Palestinian citizens in Israel and/or Palestinian residents of the Occupied Palestinian Territory on the basis of their national belonging. The discrimination in these laws is either explicit or, more often, implicit. Those laws limit citizenship rights, land and housing rights, education rights, cultural and language rights, religious rights and due process rights during detention.[70]

In 2017 only 11 per cent of civil servants were Palestinians. This is less than two-thirds of the Arab percentage of the Israeli population.[71] Only 2.5 per cent of university faculty members were Palestinians.[72] In 2019, 76 per cent of Arabs believed that Jews will always be accepted for study or work placements before Arabs, even if the Arab candidate is better suited.[73] Arab citizens are discriminated against in having access to land, in land planning, in rural and urban development and in housing provisions. Arabs own only 3.5 per cent of Israel's lands[74] and they lack the ability to acquire the majority of Israeli land. While over 1,000 Jewish settlements have been established since 1948, the Arab community has remained almost at a standstill.[75]

The lack of town plans and planning permissions for Palestinian towns is one of the main causes of inequality and of the failure of the Palestinian citizens to fulfil

---

[70] Adalah, 'The Discriminatory Laws Database' (25 September 2017), www.adalah.org/en/content/view/7771.

[71] Citizens' Empowerment Center in Israel (2017) (Hebrew); Tamar Harmann's personal communication (27 June 2019).

[72] Education, Culture and Sport Committee, the Knesset, Protocol No. 564 (19 February 2018) (Hebrew). See also Rebecca Vikomerson, *Public Policy in Divided Societies* (Nazareth: Dirasat, 2011): 6–7; Shlomit Kagya, Ola Nabwani, Avital Manor, Nabil Khattab and Sami Miaari, 'Social Justice in Jewish–Arab Relations in Israel', Israel Democracy Institute (22 April 2013), https://en.idi.org.il/articles/11760.

[73] Tamar Hermann et al., *A Conditional Partnership.*

[74] Sammy Smooha's comment on a draft of this chapter. Email dated 18 January 2020.

[75] Menachem Mautner, *Law and Culture in Israel at the Threshold of the Twenty-First Century* (Tel Aviv: Am Oved, 2008): 295–296 (Hebrew); Kais Nasser, *Severe Housing Distress and Destruction of Arab Homes: Obstacles and Recommendations for Change* (Nazareth: Dirasat, Arab Center for Law and Policy, 2012): 85–86. For further discussion, see Yosef Jabareen, 'Controlling Land and Demography in Israel: The Obsession with Territorial and Geographic Dominance', in Nadim N. Rouhana and Sahar S. Huneidi (eds), *Israel and Its Palestinian Citizens: Ethnic Privileges in the Jewish State* (Cambridge: Cambridge University Press, 2017): 238–265.

their economic potential.[76] As Israeli governments refused to issue building plans for Arab communities, Arabs took the initiative and established new villages that are not recognized by Israeli law. Some thirty-six Bedouin settlements in the Negev are unrecognized and consequently some 45,000 structures are at risk of demolition.[77] Arab municipalities are not allocated comparable funding granted to Jewish municipalities.[78]

The Bedouins, who comprise 12 per cent of the Palestinian Arab citizens of Israel, are particularly discriminated against. Between 1968 and 1989, half of the Bedouin population was transferred into townships in the north-east part of the Negev desert. The rest remained in unrecognized villages built by the Bedouins for their own welfare and needs, with no basic utilities such as electricity or water. Now more than half of the Bedouins, about 90,000 of 170,000 people, are deprived of their ancestral lands, living in what the Israeli government terms 'illegally constructed villages', still without public utilities or basic services.[79] More than 1,000 Bedouin homes were demolished in 2011 and dozens more in 2012.[80] More recently, Israeli authorities designated the Umm al-Hiran village for demolition, expelling its community and building a Jewish settlement in its place.[81]

Around 40 per cent of the Israeli Arab/Palestinian population lives in poverty. The poverty rate among Arab families significantly increased during the 1990s, rising from 35 per cent in 1990 to 45 per cent in 2002.[82] In 2017, 38 per cent of poor families in Israel were Arab.[83] Arabs are on the periphery of the job market. They are among the first to be dismissed in hard times for the economy, and the last to re-enter the job market when it revives. Generally speaking they hold the low-skilled, low-wage jobs in the Israeli economy. A decade ago Arab men earned on average 60 per cent of the national average wage, while Arab women earned 70 per cent of the average

[76] Baroness Warsi, 'Israel: Arab Citizens', *House of Lords Official Report, Hansard*, 741(84) (13 December 2012): 1232.

[77] Nasser, *Severe Housing Distress and Destruction of Arab Homes*, 84.

[78] Peleg and Waxman, *Israel's Palestinians*, 43; Raphael Cohen-Almagor, 'Israeli Democracy and the Rights of Its Palestinian Citizens', *Ragion Pratica*, 45 (December 2015): 351–368.

[79] Lord Bishop of Exeter right reverend Prelate, 'Israel: Arab Citizens', *House of Lords Official Report, Hansard*, 741(84) (13 December 2012): 1203.

[80] Baroness Uddin, 'Israel: Arab Citizens', *House of Lords Official Report, Hansard*, 741(84) (13 December 2012): 1222.

[81] Kamel Hawwash, 'Bedouins' Endless Suffering in Israel', *The Arab Weekly* (25 February 2018), https://thearabweekly.com/bedouins-endless-suffering-israel. For historical background and legal analysis of the Bedouin systematic discrimination, see Alexander Kedar, Ahmad Amara and Oren Yiftachel, *Emptied Lands: A Legal Geography of Bedouin Rights in the Negev* (Stanford: Stanford University Press, 2018).

[82] Ilan Peleg and Dov Waxman, *Israel's Palestinians* (New York: Cambridge University Press, 2011): 35. See also Gadi Hitman, 'Israel's Policy towards Its Arab Minority, 1990–2010', *Israel Affairs*, 25(1) (2019): 149–164.

[83] Myers, JDC and Brookdale, *Poverty in Israel – Facts and Figures* (January 2018), https://brookdale.jdc.org.il/wp-content/uploads/2018/02/Facts_and_Figures_Poverty_in_Israel_2018.pdf.

wage.[84] The situation has not changed much since then. According to the data of the Central Bureau of Statistics for 2017, the average monthly salary of a Jewish employee is NIS 10,701 whereas an Arab employee earns 64 per cent of this salary (NIS 6,896). The average hourly pay has improved for both Jews and Arabs but the gap did not narrow: NIS 40.7 for Arabs and NIS 62.3 for Jews.[85] Thus, the schism between Jews and Arabs was and remains very significant.

For many years the majority of Israeli Palestinians did not feel that they were fully integrated into Israel because it is a Jewish state and due to continued discrimination in many spheres of life. Many do not feel at home in Israel. According to the 2015 Democracy Index, 32.4 per cent of the Israeli Palestinians greatly feel a part of the state and its problems (of whom a mere 8 per cent responded 'very much', and 24.4 per cent 'quite a lot'); 45.7 per cent of the Palestinians in the sample answered the question 'To what extent do you feel part of the State of Israel and its problems?' 'Not so much' while 21.1 per cent answered 'Not at all'.[86]

In the 2018 Democracy Index, 68 per cent of the Israeli Muslim and Christian respondents said that Israel is not democratic towards its Arab citizens; 64 per cent of the Druze expressed the same opinion.[87] In 2019, while 71 per cent of Jews thought Israel is also democratic for Arabs, only 55 per cent of Arabs thought so.[88] What is greatly disappointing is that Jews lack awareness with regard to the state of the Arabs in the country. While a mere 6.4 per cent of the Arabs in the 2018 survey strongly agreed with the statement 'The regime in Israel is also democratic for Arab citizens', 40.3 per cent of the Jews strongly agreed with this statement.[89]

Multiculturalism is grounded in a specific set of sociopolitical realities and is developed out of a broadly accepted framework of norms, policies and politics.[90] An important distinction has to be made between *formal* citizenship and *full* citizenship. Israeli Jews can be said to enjoy full citizenship: they enjoy equal respect as individuals, and they are entitled to equal treatment by law and in its administration. The situation is different with regard to the Israeli Palestinians, the Bedouin and the Druze.[91] Although they are formally considered to enjoy liberties equally with the

---

[84] Israel Central Statistics Bureau, *Arab Population 2008* (Jerusalem: Israel Central Statistics Bureau, 2008, Hebrew); Peleg and Waxman, *Israel's Palestinians*, 36–37.

[85] Israel Central Bureau of Statistics (2018).

[86] Tamar Hermann et al., *The Israeli Democracy Index 2015* (Jerusalem: The Israel Democracy Institute, 2015): 27, 109, http://en.idi.org.il/media/4256544/democracy_index_2015_eng.pdf.

[87] Tamar Hermann et al., *The Israeli Democracy Index 2018* (Jerusalem: The Israel Democracy Institute, 2018): 70.

[88] Hermann et al., *A Conditional Partnership*.

[89] Ibid., 234.

[90] Tariq Modood, *Multiculturalism* (Cambridge: Polity, 2013): 113.

[91] Kais M. Firro, 'Reshaping Druze Particularism in Israel', *Journal of Palestine Studies*, 30(3) (Spring 2001): 40–53; Kais M. Firro, *The Druzes in the Jewish State: A Brief History* (Leiden: Brill, 1999).

Jewish community, in practice they do not share and enjoy the same rights and liberties.

On 30 December 2015, the Israeli government approved a much-needed five-year plan worth fifteen billion NIS (approximately £2.62 billion) for social and employment development designed to improve the Arab community position in society. The money was designed to improve the life of Israeli Arabs in many spheres, including housing, education, health, infrastructure, water and sewage, transportation, employment, community services and culture.[92] This was an important initiative on the route to narrowing the gaps and promoting equality in Israeli society. This route, however, is long and winding. Far more is needed to assure equality to all. It is sad and disappointing that only recently are such measures being taken to ensure just allocation of budgets to Israeli Palestinians in accordance with their proportion in society.

THE NATION STATE LAW (2018)

In 2018 the Knesset passed the Nation State Law which, in effect, gives Jewish values supremacy over Israel's democratic commitments and jeopardizes Israel as a democratic state. This law degrades Israel's moral legitimacy. The law anchors the state's menorah emblem, Jerusalem as Israel's capital and 'Hatikvah' ('The Hope') as the state anthem.[93] The state flag is white, with two blue stripes near the edges and a blue Star of David in the centre.[94] The Hebrew calendar is the official calendar of the state and alongside it is the Gregorian calendar to be used as the official calendar. The Sabbath and the festivals of Israel are the established days of rest in the state. Non-Jews have a right to maintain days of rest on their Sabbaths and festivals.[95] Many of these principles are similar to the principles of the French Fifth Republic Constitution of 1958.[96]

---

[92] Government Resolution 922. Kobi Gideon, 'Changes to Israel's Budget Allocation to Arab Communities', *BICOM* (8 January 2016), www.bicom.org.uk/analysis/28151/.

[93] Raoul Wootliff, 'Final Text of Jewish Nation-State Law, Approved by the Knesset Early on July 19', *The Times of Israel* (19 July 2018), www.timesofisrael.com/final-text-of-jewish-nation-state-bill-set-to-become-law/.

[94] Ibid.

[95] Ibid.

[96] Article 2 of the French Constitution holds: 'The language of the Republic shall be French.

- National flag. The national emblem shall be the blue, white and red tricolour flag.
- National anthem. The national anthem shall be La Marseillaise.
- National motto. The maxim of the Republic shall be "Liberty, Equality, Fraternity".
- Reference to fraternity/solidarity. The principle of the Republic shall be: government of the people, by the people and for the people.'

However, the controversial parts of the law are the following:

1. Basic principles
C. The right to exercise national self-determination in the State of Israel is unique to the Jewish people.[97]

The word 'unique' should be uniquely used, when it is of absolute necessity. This phrase ignores the non-Jewish minorities in Israel. Unfortunately there is a need to repeat time and again: democracy is about majority rule while respecting the rights of minorities.

3. The capital of the state
   Jerusalem, complete and united, is the capital of Israel.[98]

The words 'complete and united' are problematic as Israeli sovereignty over East Jerusalem is disputed. There would have been no problem if the wording was: Jerusalem is the capital of Israel.

4. Language
A. The state's language is Hebrew.
B. The Arabic language has a special status in the state; regulating the use of Arabic in state institutions or by them will be set in law.
C. This clause does not harm the status given to the Arabic language before this law came into effect.[99]

Of course it does. Arabic has been demoted in importance from official language to a 'special status'.[100] I spoke of the importance of language in Chapter 2. Language shapes life in a distinctive way. It is the way people communicate their identity, thoughts, experiences and sentiments. As a state with a significant Arab minority, Arabic should be taught at every Israeli primary and high school together with English. Language is a key factor in creating bridges between people – Israeli Jews and Israeli Arabs/Palestinians, and between Jews and Arabs in general. Judaic studies should be available in every Jewish primary and high school. They should be made compulsory for two or three years and then be optional. Studies of other religions that exist in Israel should also be made available. Similarly, studies of Islam should be part of the curricula of Muslim schools while studies of Christianity should be taught in Christian schools. Mixed Arab/Jewish schools should teach all religions represented in these schools. Signposts should be written in Hebrew and in Arabic. Key signposts should also be written in English (as now is the case) for tourists.

---

[97] Wootliff, 'Final Text of Jewish Nation-State Law, Approved by the Knesset Early on July 19'.
[98] Ibid.
[99] Ibid.
[100] Arguably contrary to Article 82 of *Dvar Ha-Melikh Be-Moa'tsato* ('King's Order-in-Council') (originally published in 1922, as the Palestinian Order-in-Council, upon establishing the British Mandate on Mandatory Palestine, on 10 August 1922), which declares Arabic as an official language in Israel, https://en.wikisource.org/wiki/Palestine_Order-in-Council.

The Nation State Law also contains a clause that legally sanctions segregated communities in Israel, enabling discrimination against various groups, including non-Jews. Section 7 – Jewish settlement states: 'A. The state views the development of Jewish settlement as a national value and will act to encourage and promote its establishment and consolidation.'[101] The development of Jewish settlements is fine. The development of Jewish settlements in the occupied territories is contested.

DISCRIMINATION NOT APARTHEID

Israel has been accused of resembling the notorious South African apartheid regime. Apartheid is defined as a system of discrimination and segregation based on race. The resettlement of some Arab citizens from Jerusalem to the West Bank is deemed reminiscent of the Group Areas Act of the apartheid regime. The separate roads in the West Bank for Jews and others for Palestinians as well the arbitrary checkpoints that agonize Palestinian life resemble aspects of the apartheid transport arrangements.[102]

Critics of Israel should clearly distinguish between the Israeli occupation of the West Bank, where Palestinians are separated from Israelis who reside there and where Palestinians are routinely subjected to oppressive regulations of the occupation, and the condition of Israeli Palestinians inside the Green Line.[103] It is reiterated that brute forms of oppression are manifestly unjust. But, as far as Israel's Arab/Palestinian citizens are concerned, the apartheid argument does not stand. The Supreme Court protected various rights granted to the Arab minority, including the right to vote, the right to establish political parties, freedom of expression, religious autonomy and separate educational systems. This should not be understood as a trivial process, nor should it be perceived as self-evident.

While Israeli Palestinians do not always receive equal treatment and they *de facto* do not have the same rights and liberties as Israeli Jews, Israeli Palestinians do not live under anything that resembles the South African apartheid. Discrimination is one thing and apartheid is another. The situation is problematic as is and there is no need to exaggerate its severity. Those who claim that Israel is an apartheid state know

[101] Wootliff, 'Final Text of Jewish Nation-State Law, Approved by the Knesset Early on July 19'. For further critique of the law, see Dov Waxman and Ilan Peleg, 'The Nation-State Law and the Weakening of Israeli Democracy', *Israel Studies*, 25(3) (2020): 185–200; Orit Kamir, 'Basic Law: Israel as Nation-State – National Honor Defies Human Dignity and Universal Human Rights', *Israel Studies*, 25(3) (2020): 213–227.

[102] Lord Steel of Aikwood, 'Israel: Arab Citizens', *House of Lords Official Report, Hansard*, 741(84) (13 December 2012): 1208. A former Israeli prime minister acknowledged the arbitrariness of the checkpoints and the agony that they are creating in the West Bank. Ehud Olmert, *In First Person* (Tel Aviv: Yedioth Ahronoth, 2018): 827 (Hebrew).

[103] Raphael Cohen-Almagor, 'Fifty Years of Israeli Occupation', *E-International Relations* (14 October 2017), www.e-ir.info/2017/10/14/fifty-years-of-israeli-occupation/.

very little about Israel and South Africa.[104] Israeli multiculturalism yields schisms and leads to discrimination against minorities, similar to the kinds based on age, sexual orientation and/or gender. While the government can surely do more in closing the gaps, acts of discrimination have not been legitimized. Those who bluntly practice policies of discrimination are penalized and reprimanded by the courts. The courts reiterated that identification with the Arab/Palestinian heritage and tradition should not diminish citizens' universal entitlement to dignity and respect.

Mortality rates among Israeli Arabs/Palestinians have fallen by over two-thirds since the establishment of Israel, while life expectancy has increased by thirty years, reaching 78.5 (women 80.7, men 76.3) in 2009. Infant mortality rates have similarly been significantly reduced from 56 per 1,000 live births in 1950 to 6.5 in 2008. As for education, adult illiteracy rates among Israeli Arabs/Palestinians dropped from 57.2 per cent (79 per cent among women) to 7.7 per cent (11.7 per cent among women). In 1961, less than half of Arab children attended school, with only 9 per cent acquiring secondary or higher education. By 1999, 97 per cent of Arab children attended schools. Fifty years ago, a mere 4 per cent of Arab teachers held academic degrees; by 1999 the figure had vaulted to 47 per cent.[105] In 2017, Arab students accounted for 16.1 per cent of all students in bachelor's degree programmes, up from 10.2 per cent in 2010.[106]

One of the Supreme Court justices is an Arab,[107] and there are many other Arabs in lower courts. Arab nationals hold distinguished governmental positions, including in the Prime Minister's Office.[108] Israeli Arabs/Palestinians enjoy freedom of association and are able to establish political parties; they have their own seats in parliament; they have their own political newspapers;[109] they have their own voice. Israel has been implementing a policy of affirmative action towards the Arab population in the public service.[110]

---

[104] Benjamin Pogrund, *Drawing Fire: Investigating the Accusations of Apartheid in Israel* (New York: Rowman & Littlefield, 2014).

[105] Efraim Karsh, 'Israel's Arabs: Deprived or Radicalized?', *Israel Affairs* (January 2013): 1–19, www .meforum.org/3423/israel-arabs-deprived-radicalized.

[106] Cary Nelson, *Israel Denial* (Bloomington: Indiana University Press, 2019): 337.

[107] Justice George Karra. Prior to him Justice Saleem Gubran served at the court; there he was promoted, based on seniority, to the position of deputy president of the court.

[108] For instance, Member of the Knesset (MK) Majalli Whbee served as deputy minister in the Prime Minister's Office, deputy minister of education, culture, and sport, and deputy minister of foreign affairs. Other Israeli Arabs held, and hold, other parliamentary positions in the Israeli Knesset, as well as sensitive governmental positions. MK Mohammad Barakeh served as deputy speaker of the Knesset.

[109] Among other leading Arab newspapers in Israel, these are: *Al-Senarah, Kol El-Arab, Al-Etihad* and *Panorama*.

[110] See article 15A of *Hok Shirot Ha-Mdina (Minoyeem)* ('The State Service (Appointments)') of 1959. See also: HCJ (High Court of Justice) 6427/02. *The Movement for Quality Government in Israel et al. v. The Knesset et al.* (not published yet) (decided on 11 May 2006); HCJ (High Court of Justice) 11163/03 *The National Committee for the Heads of the Arab Local Authorities in Israel*

The Supreme Court gave Mr Mohammed Bakri, an Arab film producer, the constitutional protection to screen his movie *Jenin Jenin*, which accuses Israeli soldiers of crimes against humanity during their military activity in the Palestinian city Jenin, following a bloody terrorist attack on Israeli civilians.[111] The court entitled Mr Adel Qaadan, an Israeli Arab/Palestinian, to buy a plot of land in a Jewish communal settlement, deciding that a policy that calls for segregation is unconstitutional.[112] The court also granted constitutional protection to Israeli Arabs/ Palestinians who aspired to become members of parliament, even when their political proposals voiced stern criticism of the state of Israel, including the expression of grave doubts regarding its basic legitimacy. All attempts by Jewish-Zionist political parties to deprive these Israeli Arabs/Palestinians of their right to be elected to parliament were met with the Supreme Court's objection.[113] The state of Israel also established three Inquiry Commissions regarding the relationship between the state and Arab nationals, being citizens of Israel,[114] residents of the Occupied Territories[115] or citizens of a neighbouring country.[116]

However, the picture is not all rosy; there are many gaps to bridge. As is the case in France, Israeli leaders wish to put the minority population in check. Israeli leaders have limited the liberties and capabilities of the Palestinian population because they think that unqualified liberty and tolerance might endanger the very existence of the

---

et al. v. The Prime Minister of the State of Israel (not published yet) (decided on 27 February 2006); HCJ (High Court of Justice) 6924/98 *The Association for Civil Rights in Israel v. The Israeli Government*, 58(5) P.D. 15 (decided on 9 July 2001).

[111] See HCJ (High Court of Justice) 316/03 *Bakri et al. v. Israel Film Council et al.*, 58(1) P.D. 249 (decided on 11 November 2003). After Israeli Defense Force (IDF) operations against the terror infrastructure in Jenin (a Palestinian city) in April 2002 ('Operation Defensive Wall'), Mohammed Bakri filmed the responses of local Palestinians and edited them into the film *Jenin, Jenin*. After advance screenings, both domestically and abroad, and in anticipation of the film's domestic commercial screening, Bakri requested the approval of the Israel Film Council. The council denied its approval. Bakri claimed that this decision violated fundamental constitutional rights and Israeli administrative law. The court held that that freedom of speech constitutes one of the fundamental principles of a democratic society. The court decided that, under the circumstances, the decision of the Israel Film Council unlawfully infringed the constitutional rights of the petitioners.

[112] See the *Qa'adan* case, mentioned above. The court held that the state of Israel may not discriminate Israeli Arabs against Israeli Jews in allocating lands for settlement, even when these lands were initially allocated by the Jewish Agency.

[113] EA (Election Appeal) 131/03. *The Central Election Commission for the 16th Knesset v. MP Ahmad Tibi and MP Azmi Besharah*, 57(4) P.D. 1 (decided on 15 May 2003).

[114] *Or Commission* of 2000 (investigating the reasons for and the consequences of the death of thirteen Israeli Arabs, allegedly killed by Israeli policemen, during a violent protest of Israeli Arabs against a prominent politician, Ariel Sharon, upon his provocative visit to the Temple Mount).

[115] *Shamgar Commission* of 1995 (investigating the massacre committed by a Jewish Israeli terrorist against innocent Arab Muslims during their religious pray).

[116] *Kahan Commission* of 1982 (investigating the alleged massacre committed against Arab Lebanese in times of war, by Israeli military forces, in the Lebanese villages of *Sabra* and *Shatila*).

Israeli state (the 'democratic catch'). In the competition of scarce resources against a potentially challenging group, Israel preferred to qualify democracy and its liberalism and not to risk the Jewish character of the nation. As is the case in France, Israeli leaders fear that the Arab/Palestinian minority might undermine the state, perceiving Arabs as a fifth column. In Israel, too, multiculturalism has been associated with terrorism. In Israel, like in France, a delicate balance needs to be maintained: the government should provide opportunities for freedom and at the same time maintain law and order.

On the day of the 2015 elections, Prime Minister Benjamin Netanyahu, who sought to secure another term in office, urged the Jewish public to vote by warning that the Arabs were voting in high numbers.[117] Jews should flock the polls to counteract Arab mobilization and secure the Likud a continued regime. The anti-Arab rhetoric was repeated, successfully from Netanyahu's viewpoint. Netanyahu effectively focused the agenda on security, making political gains by delegitimizing the Arab minority.

In 2019, Prime Minister Netanyahu warned against a narrow coalition of his political rivals that would include Arabs. Netanyahu said at a rally broadcast on TV that Knesset members from the Arab Joint List want to destroy the state and that a government in which they are part would be an 'existential threat to Israel'.[118] President Reuven Rivlin spoke out strongly against Netanyahu's delegitimating campaign of Arab citizens. Rivlin said that Israel is a Jewish and democratic state that must ensure equal rights for all. He asked 'everyone who cares about the State of Israel to stop these ugly statements once and for all'.[119]

Following the 2020 close elections in which the predominantly Arab Joint List won nearly 582,000 votes and fifteen seats in the Knesset, Netanyahu immediately delegitimized the party by saying that it includes lawmakers who support terrorism and oppose Israel's self-definition as a Jewish state. He warned against comprising a coalition that would include the Arab party and declared that this party is 'not part of the equation'.[120] The Joint List, he said, 'attacks our soldiers and opposes the State of Israel'.[121] President Reuven Rivlin again criticized Prime Minister Netanyahu for his

---

[117] Mairav Zonszein, 'Binyamin Netanyahu: "Arab Voters Are Heading to the Polling Stations in Droves"', *The Guardian* (17 March 2015), www.theguardian.com/world/2015/mar/17/binyamin-netanyahu-israel-arab-election.

[118] TOI Staff, 'Rivlin Rebukes Netanyahu for "Ugly" Comments Branding Arab Lawmakers a "Threat"', *Times of Israel* (19 November 2019),), www.timesofisrael.com/rivlin-rebukes-netanyahu-for-ugly-comments-branding-arab-lawmakers-a-threat/.

[119] Ibid.

[120] David M. Halbfinger, 'Israel Faces a Defining Question: How Much Democracy Should Arabs Get?', *New York Times* (13 March 2020), www.nytimes.com/2020/03/12/world/middleeast/israel-arabs-vote.html?action=click&module=moreIn&pgtype=Article&region=Footer.

[121] Ibid.

racist and discriminatory remarks by saying, 'There are no semi-citizens in Israel. There are strong disagreements but not semi-citizens.'[122]

I should note that there is a very limited basis for making associations between Israeli Palestinian-Arabs and terrorism. As is the case in France, the populist assertion is exaggerated and hyped. There is a grain of truth in associating Israeli Arabs/Palestinians with terrorism, but only a grain. Of the 161 incidents of suicide terrorism between 2000 and 2005, one incident involved an Israeli Palestinian.[123] Since September 2015, Israel has experienced a wave of terror that included hundreds of attacks. Just two of them involved Israeli Palestinians.[124] To associate Israeli Palestinian-Arabs with terror is like associating women who wear burqas with terrorism.

In the Israeli Democracy Index 2018, a significant minority – 18.9 per cent and 21.7 per cent of the Jewish respondents – either strongly agreed or somewhat agreed that 'Israel's Arab citizens pose a threat to the country's security'.[125] Among Jews there is a widespread perception that Israeli Arabs are part of the Arabs of the Middle East, hostile to the Jews and carriers of a backward culture.[126] Populist leaders promote fear in the service of their narrow political interests.

THE RIGHTS AND DUTIES OF CITIZENSHIP

Citizenship entails many benefits. Citizens enjoy political and social rights. They are entitled to basic social security and to basic health privileges. However, reasonableness also includes reciprocity. The existing state of affairs in which large sectors of the population do not fulfil their civic duties is unacceptable and unfair to those who share the burden. People should not only take from the state; they should also invest in it and contribute to it. Israel cannot afford to have such an exemption phenomenon. It cannot afford it when Arabs are concerned, and it cannot afford it when ultra-religious Jews are concerned. Both sectors are significant, and both pose challenges to the idea of full citizenship.

Israel has exempted the majority of its Arab citizens from army service. The exception relates to Druze men who are required to serve in the Israeli Defense Force (IDF) since 1956 and, consequently, the majority of Druze men are drafted.[127]

---

[122] Gil Hoffman and Rachel Wolf, 'Rivlin Calls on Likud, Blue and White to Compromise on Unity', *Jerusalem Post* (11 March 2020), www.jpost.com/Israel-News/President-Reuven-Rivlin-receives-election-results-WATCH-LIVE-620521.

[123] Gideon Aran, *The Smile of the Human Bomb* (Ithaca, NY and London: Cornell University Press, 2018): 53–55.

[124] Israeli Ministry of Foreign Affairs, *Wave of Terror 2015–2019* (19 February 2019), https://mfa.gov .il/MFA/ForeignPolicy/Terrorism/Palestinian/Pages/Wave-of-terror-October-2015.aspx.

[125] Hermann et al., *Israeli Democracy Index 2018*, 197, 235.

[126] Sammy Smooha, *Still Playing by the Rules: Index of Arab–Jewish Relations in Israel 2017*: 42.

[127] 'Druze', *Ministry of Defence* (Hebrew), www.noar.mod.gov.il/DruzeAndCircassians/Pages/ Druze.aspx; 'IDF Minority Service of Minorities in the IDF and in Civil-National Service',

Other Arab communities largely embrace the exemption. This exemption, however, is a double-edged sword as it serves as a pretence for discrimination. The argument being made by those opposing equality of rights to all Israeli citizens is that Arabs do not serve in the army and do not carry the same duties and obligations as Jews; therefore, they should not enjoy the same rights and privileges. It is in Arab interest to silence this line of argumentation. Citizens who have a problem serving in the army for religious, moral or national reasons, and citizens who refuse to serve in order to avoid a situation by which they might confront their Palestinian brothers on the enemy side, should commit themselves to do national (or civil) service for the required period of time (from July 2020, thirty months for men; twenty-four months for women) in their own communities, or in other communities, working to better the conditions of their own group. Palestinian Arabs should do national (civil) service if this is their wish in their own neighbourhoods. They could volunteer to work in charity, welfare and relief organizations, the fire brigades, medical service, etc. Conscientious objectors could contribute to Israel in various ways other than serving in the army. All should take part in this important societal duty. As long as Israel's very existence is disputed by powerful players, such as Iran, pacifism is a luxury that Israel cannot afford.

In 2010, only 600 non-Jews served in Israel's national service programme. In 2017, 4,500 non-Jews were doing national service.[128] While this is not a very substantive number, and most Arabs still refuse to do national service, the trend is positive and reassuring. Asked whether Arab citizens should fulfil 'a duty of any kind of service to the state', 14.8 per cent agreed and 23.5 per cent were inclined to agree.[129]

CONCLUSION

A multicultural society cannot ignore the demands of diversity. Diversity is an inescapable part of the collective life. It cannot be pushed aside or suppressed without coercion. Since we are attached to and shaped by our culture, the basic respect we owe to our fellow human beings extends to their culture. Bhikhu Parekh notes that respect for culture also earns loyalty, gives people the confidence and courage to interact with other cultures, and facilitates their integration into wider society. Cultural diversity is thus desirable for society and represents a valuable collective asset.[130]

Equity in Burden Commission, the Knesset (16 December 2013, Hebrew), https://oknesset.org/meetings/5/4/544608.html.

[128] Dov Lieber, 'More Arab Israelis Join National Service, Discovering State Benefits, Patriotism', *Times of Israel* (15 August 2016), www.timesofisrael.com/more-arab-israelis-join-national-service-discovering-state-benefits-patriotism/.

[129] Smooha, *Still Playing by the Rules*, 214.

[130] Bhikhu Parekh, *Rethinking Multiculturalism* (Houndmills: Palgrave, 2000): 196.

Israel is a multicultural democracy. Israeli democracy is majoritarian and procedural. As Sammy Smooha suggests, it is an ethnic rather than liberal democracy.[131] The situation of its Palestinian minority is tricky and sensitive. Palestinians do not have national rights. These rights are reserved only to Jews. The raison d'être of the state is to be a magnet and a place of refuge for Jews from all over the world. In Israel, Jews can live life free of antisemitism, persecution and pogroms. This, however, does not mean that Jews in Israel are safe. Situated in a hostile region, some of Israel's neighbours have not come to terms with its very existence. Hamas, the Islamic Jihad, Hezbollah and Iran are among the parties that perceive Israel as a bone in their throats and wish to undo the Zionist revolution. The ongoing conflict puts the Israeli Palestinians in a very tenuous position.

Israel perceives its Palestinian citizens with suspicion and mistrust. It employs perfectionist policies that elevate Jewish religio-national values above liberalism. Many liberals would find anathema the perfectionist's suggestion that one of the appropriate functions of the state is to favour and promote ideals of the good that it judges to be excellent, worthy or virtuous.[132] As a democracy, Israel recognizes that all its citizens should enjoy basic human rights. This does not mean egalitarian implementation of rights. Israeli policies vis-à-vis the Palestinian minority involve coercion, limiting their access to power positions, putting them on constant check as the Palestinians are seen as a security threat and posing an alternative to the existent reality. The Palestinians are not part of the Zionist enterprise and do not share the Jewish vision and aspirations. Their national movement was in competition with Zionism, offering an alternative that would have ended the Zionist dream. Israeli policies regarding the Palestinians have aimed to answer the dual challenges of security and demography. Both are very much on the mind of Israeli decision-makers.[133]

Consequently, Israel is willing to accommodate Palestinian interests to an extent; concessions are measured and discrimination against Israeli Arabs/Palestinians is prevalent in many spheres of life, including land allocation, municipality budgets, employment, urban development and basic civil rights. There is an unhealthy discrepancy between official statements which are not backed by deeds. The Arab/Palestinians do not enjoy the same rights and liberties. The symbols of the Jewish state ignore its minorities.

---

[131] Sammy Smooha, 'Types of Democracy and Modes of Conflict-Management in Ethnically Divided Societies', *Nations and Nationalism*, 8(4) (October 2002): 423–431; Sammy Smooha, 'Is Israel Western?', in Eliezer Ben-Rafael and Yitzhak Sternberg (eds), *Comparing Modernities: Pluralism versus Homogeneity – Essays in Homage to Shmuel N. Eisenstadt* (Leiden and Boston: Brill Academic Publishers, 2005): 413–442. See also Smooha, 'Israel70: The Global Enigma', *Fathom* (July 2018), http://fathomjournal.org/israel70-the-global-enigma/.

[132] Collis Tahzib, 'Perfectionism: Political not Metaphysical', *Philosophy & Public Affairs*, 47(2) (2019): 176.

[133] Charles D. Freilich, *Israel National Security* (New York: Oxford University Press, 2018).

Since 1994, Israeli governments have been taking affirmative action measures to enhance the integration of Arab, Bedouin, Druze and Circassian populations into the civil service, including issuing legislative amendments and publishing tenders for mid-level positions solely to members of minority communities.[134] While the data indicate a steady increase in the rates of Arab, Druze and Circassian employees in the civil service, minorities are still significantly underrepresented. In December 2012, 8.4 per cent of all the civil service employees were Arabs, including Bedouins, Druze and Circassians in comparison to 6.17 per cent in 2007. Representation of Arab and Druze women has also improved. In 2011 there was an increase of 30.6 per cent in the rate of Arab and Druze women employed in the civil service in comparison to 2008.[135]

In Chapter 1 I noted that participation in the political processes and representation of the public are essential for the working of democracy. Substantive democracy respects majority rule and at the same time guarantees that minorities are protected against abuse. Israeli Arabs are entitled to take part in decision-making processes that concern them. However, Arabs are underrepresented in power positions. To date there have been only three Arab ministers: Salah Tarif, a Druze Israeli politician who was appointed minister without portfolio by Ariel Sharon (2001–2002); Raleb Majadele who was appointed minister without portfolio in 2007 and a few months later became minister of culture, sport and science – Majadele served in this role for two years until 2009; and Ayoob Kara is an Israeli Druze politician who served as minister of communications and minister in the Prime Minister's Office (2017–2019). No Palestinian has ever served in a senior position in the Israeli government. This should be corrected. At the same time, Israel would like to see from all its citizens, without exception, a real and strong commitment to the state, to peace and to the struggle against terror.

Israel is a nationally divided society. It struggles to maintain Jewish democracy, currently giving precedence to Judaism and Jewishness over democracy. It is argued that the reverse should be the case. Any form of tyranny, minority and majority alike, is repugnant. The decision of one to discriminate against the other due to religion is awful. The decision of many to discriminate against the minority, just because they can, makes the situation equally terrible, and cruder. This is bullying. Israel should develop and promote mechanisms for the self-realization of all individuals, notwithstanding their religion, race, ethnicity, colour, gender, class or sexual orientation. These mechanisms, which include compromise, open debate, mutual respect and

---

[134] J.S. Mill wrote in his *Autobiography*: 'Minorities, so long as they remain minorities, are, and ought to be outvoted; but under arrangements which enable any assemblage of voters, amounting to a certain number, to place in the legislature a representative of its own choice, minorities cannot be suppressed', www.earlymoderntexts.com/assets/pdfs/mill1873e.pdf.

[135] Human Rights Council, 'National Report Submitted in Accordance with Paragraph 5 of the Annex to Human Rights Council Resolution 16/21', Working Group on the Universal Periodic Review, Seventeenth Session, Geneva, 21 October–1 November 2013, Israel: 7.

democratic deliberation, should be aptly employed at all state levels: symbolic, declarative, governmental and practical.

The prominence of security considerations in the Israeli psyche and politics hampers civic rights. The Arab–Israeli conflict continues to overshadow all civil and social issues, rendering them secondary in importance and allowing the perpetuation of discriminatory and coercive treatment of Arabs in Israel. By adhering to an ethno-religious credo, Israel has failed to establish a just, reasonable multicultural liberal democracy, where the rights of all are respected and where egalitarianism is accepted and promoted as an enshrined value.

It is reasonable to assume that ending the Israeli occupation of the West Bank, resolving the Israeli Palestinian conflict and achieving a just peace with all Israeli neighbours will have a positive effect on the social and political status of Israeli Palestinians. Israel signed peace accords with Egypt in 1979 and with Jordan in 1994. Israel started a positive peace process with the Palestinian Liberation Organization (PLO) in 1993 but this process did not result in a sustained, comprehensive and much-desired peace.[136] A two-state solution that would resolve the tensions between Israel, on the one hand, and the PLO and Hamas, on the other, is the least bloody and most just solution to the wide Israeli Palestinian conflict,[137] a conflict that concerns the brethren of Israeli Palestinian citizens.

In addition, Israel needs to strive for equality in the allocation of resources and in the fight against racism, bigotry and discrimination, and introduce important changes to accommodate the interests of Israeli Arabs/Palestinians so that people 'feel at home' in their own country. In the Rawlsian conception of a reasonable and well-ordered society, people are disposed to cooperate with each other by virtue of their basic concern and respect for each other, or by virtue of one's attachment to an identity or project one shares with the other (Chapter 1). The Palestinians/Arabs find it difficult to identify with the Zionist project that until now gave clear precedence to Jews over Arabs. Studies of all religions that exist in Israel should be made available.

Israel should promote principles of substantive democracy by lending itself to liberal values. Recalling the distinction between formal and substantive democracies (Chapter 1), it is notable that, especially during recent years, government officials perceive democracy as nothing but a means to fulfil the needs and the wishes of the electoral majority, notwithstanding how immoral they might be. This is a wrong and dangerous approach.

Being a multicultural society, Israel should strive to become a better place for its minorities, a state where all citizens feel a sense of belonging, perceiving Israel as a home. Israel should keep and promote its democratic character, otherwise it will

---

[136] Raphael Cohen-Almagor, 'The Oslo Peace Process: Interview with Joel Singer', *Israel Affairs*, 24(5) (2018): 733–766.

[137] Raphael Cohen-Almagor, 'In Support of Two-State Solution', *Youth Law Journal* (12 November 2018), www.theylj.co.uk/in-support-of-two-state-solution/.

slide and become like any other theocracy. Let us recall the holy scripture, where The Lord said to Israel:

> I have a greater task for you, my servant.
> Not only will you restore to greatness
> the people of Israel who have survived,
> but I will also make you a light to the nations –
> so that all the world may be saved.[138]

The conversation with the departmental secretary that opened this chapter illustrates the level of suspicion that Israeli Palestinians, and those who associate with them, encounter regularly. September 2000 was a tough month for Israel, as the Al Aqsa Intifada has just erupted. Still, to think that a young female law student at the University of Haifa might choose to stab me in the back was quite astonishing. At least to me. With all its faults, Israel is a democracy. As it turned out, the chosen applicant was the best research assistant I have ever had. She remained in this position until she completed her studies, became a lawyer and worked at the Attorney General Office.

Let me end on a positive note as there are winds of change that are quite promising. In 2019 the majority of Arabs in a sample (57 per cent) reported feeling part of Israeli society, compared with 84 per cent of Jews.[139] In 2020, as Israel much like the rest of the world was faced with the coronavirus crisis, the Jewish People Policy Institute's in its Pluralism Index for 2020 noted a significant change in the way Israeli Arabs identify themselves. According to the survey, about a quarter of Israeli minorities (23 per cent) defined themselves primarily as 'Israeli' (compared to 5 per cent in the previous year), half (51 per cent) self-identified as 'Israeli Arab', while only 7 per cent defined themselves as 'Palestinian', down from 18 per cent the previous year. Significantly, answering whether they 'feel like a real Israeli', most Arabs responded that they either agreed completely (65 per cent) or somewhat agreed (33 per cent) with the statement.[140] Several explanations may be suggested for this significant positive change. First, the government has been investing more resources in the Arab minority. Second, in the March 2020 elections to the 23rd Knesset, Arab turnout surged to 64.7 per cent and the United Arab Party received fifteen seats in parliament, making it the third largest party in parliament. This achievement is instrumental for making a minority feel represented, part of the

---

[138] Isaiah 49, www.biblegateway.com/passage/?search=Isaiah+49&version=GNT.

[139] Hermann et al., *A Conditional Partnership*.

[140] Idan Zonshine, 'Only 7% of Israeli Arabs Define Themselves as 'Palestinian'', *Jerusalem Post* (21 April 2020), www.jpost.com/arab-israeli-conflict/only-7-percent-of-israeli-arabs-define-themselves-as-palestinian-625285?utm_source=VeryGoodNewsIsrael+List&utm_campaign=66850b7564-EMAIL_CAMPAIGN_2020_04_25_08_11&utm_medium=email&utm_term=0_57ad33723e-66850b7564-83850093.

nation social fabric. Third, during the COVID-19 crisis a genuine sense of comradeship and partnership between Arabs and Jews, essential for fighting the lethal virus, emerged. All were fighting against the virus that does not discriminate between people. Arab medical professionals and pharmacists excelled in their dedicated work to save life just as Jews did. Arabs comprise 17 per cent of Israel's doctors, 24 per cent of nurses and 48 per cent of pharmacists.[141] This crisis showed that different communities can see beyond religious and cultural differences and unite in the face of a challenge that endangers human life.

[141] Joshua Mitnick, 'In Israeli War on Coronavirus, Arab Doctors Rush to the Front', *Christian Science Monitor* (16 April 2020), www.csmonitor.com/World/Middle-East/2020/0416/In-Israeli-war-on-coronavirus-Arab-doctors-rush-to-the-front?utm_source=VeryGoodNewsIsrael+List&utm_campaign=3460ead321-EMAIL_CAMPAIGN_2020_05_02_08_27&utm_medium=email&utm_term=0_57ad33723e-3460ead321–83850093.

Conclusion

Difference is of the essence of humanity. Difference is an accident of birth and it should therefore never be the source of hatred or conflict. The answer to difference is to respect it. Therein lies a most fundamental principle of peace: respect for diversity.

John Hume

By liberty I mean the assurance that every man shall be protected in doing what he believes is his duty against the influence of authority and majorities, custom and opinion.

John Dalberg-Acton

Democracies are associations of free and equal persons. Such an association is structured by relations of mutual recognition in which each individual is respected as free and equal. The politics of recognition is a basic element of justice. In a multicultural society a basic level of recognition is required to enable political communication aimed at solving problems justly.[1] I spoke of the value and importance of participatory democracy where all citizens take part in decisions that may potentially affect their lives. People engage in a deliberative process in which they sustain and promote their own conceptions of the good. Having diverse ideals, in light of which people lead different ways of life, is the normal condition. This variety can be positive and beneficial to society at large. We benefit and take pleasure from the complementary nature of our developed inclinations.

Awareness of the 'democratic catch' necessitates the introduction of boundaries. I have argued that a liberal democracy is justified in interfering in the business of its minority cultures when their excessive norms subvert the basic principles upon which a liberal society is founded. That is, democracy has the right to curtail norms that disrespect and cause harm to other persons (who may live inside or outside the

---

[1] Iris Marion Young, *Inclusion and Democracy* (Oxford: Oxford University Press, 2000): 61; Charles Taylor, 'The Politics of Recognition', in Amy Gutmann (ed.), *Multiculturalism: Examining the Politics of Recognition* (New Jersey: Princeton University Press, 1994): 25–73.

given cultural community). While many people recognize the need to prevent inflicting significant physical harm on group members in the name of culture and tradition, the issues are more difficult and complicated when members endure non-physical harm. All too often, women and children are denied basic human rights in the name of culture. I argued that liberal democracy should step in to protect people and to ensure their rights. Considerations of substance (extent of harm) and context (time and place) must be taken into account, and these may require the introduction of constraints.

A democratic government has to play the role of umpire both in the sense of applying just considerations when reviewing different conceptions and also in trying to reconcile conflicting interests, trends and claims. This is a delicate task that demands integrity as well as impartiality: to refrain from identifying with one group rather than with the other; not to exploit its own role for self-advantage; bearing in mind when making decisions the relevant considerations and demands which concern society as a whole, and not only one or some fractions of it.

I rejected the claims that multiculturalism is bad for democracy and that it is conducive to terrorism. Multiculturalism enriches democracy and is not necessarily bad for women. If protections are in place to secure human rights for all, then multiculturalism can serve the best interests of all. There is nothing inherently wrong in multiculturalism. Like most concepts it can be used and abused. While every idea possesses a claim to equal validity within a democratic society, considerations of context and intentions must be taken into account, and they may require some accommodation. Via mechanisms of deliberative democracy, compromise and, if needed, coercion, just, reasonable multiculturalism is within reach. As Joseph Raz says, liberal multiculturalism as a normative principle affirms that, in the circumstances of contemporary societies, a political attitude of fostering and encouraging the prosperity of cultural groups within a society, and respecting their identity, is justified by considerations of freedom and human dignity.[2]

Cultures may restrict choice in order to maintain and protect their group. Education is a key factor. Minority groups should have the right to decide their curricula in a way that would benefit both the community and the young. They can set reasonable targets and decide the scope of studies. The question is whether the choices and restrictions are reasonable and measured. We acknowledge that religions restrict the choices made by their members, and the choices of outsiders. We respect groups that prohibit their members from certain pursuits, for instance studying certain subjects in schools. All societies do not teach their young *every-thing*. All societies set priorities and have agendas. British schools do not teach Danish history and American public schools do not teach Hebrew grammar. We also appreciate restricting membership in religious bodies to members of the

---

[2]   Joseph Raz, *Ethics in the Public Domain: Essays in the Morality of Law and Politics* (Oxford: Clarendon Press, 1995): 189.

religion. If Jews were to accept Christians to the Rabbinate, or if the Anglican Church would admit Muslim priests, religion would change, lose its distinctiveness and become something different. While this mix might be appealing to some, it is very likely to raise serious objections among others.

British education curricula include sex education in primary schools and discussing same sex marriage and the changing face of the family. These issues are sensitive and problematic in the eyes of some religious groups. Orthodox Judaism objects to sex education in primary schools, and to homosexuality in general. Now suppose that Ofsted[3] would demand teaching these subjects in Orthodox religious schools in order to conform to the values of the British nation. Such a demand would be resisted by the schools. They would argue that while they accept the British education curricula on the whole, they cannot teach these subjects in their schools. They would request some autonomy in deciding what subjects they should teach, balancing their religious views against wider societal considerations. They would argue that Orthodox Jews marry young anyway, usually before the age of twenty, and that people would receive all the sexual information they need from the rabbi or from his wife. They would further argue that teaching same sex marriage legitimizes homosexuality, something they are not willing to do as this sexual practice is forbidden according to Jewish law,[4] and that in any event the community would not approve same sex marriage. They would further argue that if the authorities insist, the demand would push them to trick the system as they cannot abandon their set of values. Such insistence ignores who they are, and what they believe in. They would stress the importance of religion, of tolerance, of respecting difference, of non-coercion and of cultural autonomy.

Indeed, such insistence seems to be unwise. Allowing minorities to have some latitude in deciding their curricula in a way that would respect their conception of the good is in line with liberalism and thus with British values. A limited scope for educational autonomy would not undermine British culture. Similarly, a limited scope for Amish autonomy would not undermine the American culture. A balance needs to be struck between competing interests and values in a way that would respect diversity. Compromise is important for living together and for just, reasonable multiculturalism. Cultures should be respected. Parents should be able to educate their young about the reasons that have perpetuated their group sometimes for many generations. But it is also important that the curricula include chapters about the history and traditions of the larger society in which they live. We need to learn about the other in order to understand different ways of life, develop respect and appreciation of difference and establish solidarity that is the glue of a

---

[3] Ofsted is the Office for Standards in Education, Children's Services and Skills in Britain. It inspects and regulates services that care for children and young people, and services providing education and skills for learners of all ages.

[4] Leviticus 18–20.

well-ordered society. Liberal multiculturalism celebrates plurality of colours, tastes, smells, dresses, textures and voices. Liberal multiculturalism embraces differences and out of them makes a rainbow that is rich and empowering.

Neutrality is a liberal mechanism to enable the development of the valuable and moral mosaic of many conceptions of the good. France and Israel, however, present perfectionist models. President Sarkozy boldly set the terms of integration into French society: 'If you come to France, you accept to melt into a single community, which is the national community ... And if you do not want to accept that, you cannot be welcome in France.'[5]

Sarkozy assumed that some cultural minorities lack common grounds that would enable constructive discussion and enable channels of communication to facilitate integration. Their conception of the good, their cultural and political norms, their moral codes, are so different that the gap between that culture and France becomes unbridgeable. Sarkozy represents a widespread French belief that upholds unity and conformity, opposing the view that civilization should encourage differences and celebrate pluralism. Sarkozy represents the belief that the national-building process that started with the Revolution is still ongoing, and the French national identity is still threatened; therefore, France should take the necessary precautions to defend itself. The fear of disintegration is very much alive and it is exacerbated by the fear of terrorism.

French republicanism differs from Anglo-Saxon liberalism in some crucial respects: it promotes statism and trust in government; it accentuates national building, national unity and national identity; it resents multiculturalism, perceived to negate unity; tolerance in the public sphere and diversity are not cherished values; communities do not receive recognition as there is only one community – the French nation. Communitarianism in France is a pejorative expression that suggests a failed multicultural model. It is contrasted with the cherished model of republic-anism. In French republicanism, individuals are members of the nation and there is a perpetual need to maintain order because of the threats of multiculturalism, seen as a source of disorder and chaos.[6] In France, the general will of the state is more important and compelling. This abstract general will is imposed on the body politic with all its variety, leading to coercive conformity in the public place and to fear of diversity and cultural differences. Jonathan Fox argues that the secular gods are jealous of those who follow religious ideologies that contradict their secular ideals. Thus, the liberal ideal of religious freedom is often trumped by secular ideology and beliefs.[7]

---

[5] 'France's Sarkozy: Multiculturalism Has Failed', *CBN News* (11 February 2011), www.cbn.com/cbnnews/world/2011/february/frances-sarkozy-multiculturalism-has-failed/?mobile=false.

[6] Paul May, 'French Cultural Wars: Public Discourses on Multiculturalism in France (1995–2013)', *Journal of Ethnic and Migration Studies*, 42(8) (2016): 1334–1352.

[7] Jonathan Fox, *Thou Shalt Have No Other Gods before Me: Why Governments Discriminate against Religious Minorities* (New York: Cambridge University Press, 2020): 7.

Analysing the Jewish–Arab relationships in Israel, I argued for accommodating the interests of the Israeli Arabs/Palestinians, that Israel should strive to safeguard equal rights and liberties for all citizens notwithstanding religion, race, ethnicity, colour, gender, class or sexual orientation. Israel needs to ensure that minorities have full citizenship. It is argued that delegates of the Arab/Palestinian minority should be represented, in accordance with their size in society, in the parliament and in the government. Symbols of the state should be accommodated to give expression to all citizens of Israel. Since Israel is defined as a Jewish *and democratic* state, there is a responsibility to embrace all Israeli citizens. In doing so, Israel does not negate the essence of its being Jewish. Furthermore, studies of *all* religions that exist in Israel should be made available.

Until now Israel has fallen way short when it comes to treating its Arab/Palestinian citizens as equals, neither affording them the full citizenship rights they are promised in law nor taking steps to ensure that they receive, as Dworkin puts it, 'equal concern and respect' from the state. Israel needs to do what it reasonably can to end Arab second-class citizenship by ensuring equal rights, doing more to provide symbolic acknowledgement of their full membership in the state and spending more equally on Arab communities. But it seems that for the time being the fundamental disconnect in Israeli democracy will remain: Israel will be a Jewish state with Arab citizens. And so, it is likely that a significant part of its Arab/Palestinian citizens will always feel estranged from the state, even if the state treats them fairly. It is one thing to be at home in your own house, another to feel at home in the house of another. No matter how often a guest is told to 'make herself at home', she knows that it is not her house. If Israeli leaders will perceive democracy as at least as important as religion, perhaps then future generations of Israeli Palestinians will feel reasonably accommodated and will regard the country as their own.

GOVERNANCE AND POWER STRUGGLE

Many of the tensions within multicultural societies arise as a result of power imbalance. Native Americans in North America, Muslim minorities in Europe or Israeli Palestinians/Arabs in Israel are objectively weak. They lack access to resources, wealth, elite status, state power and political patronage. They are marginalized by the majority and develop political identities that try to keep some independent distance from that which is dictated by the majority. Power is exercised through many means – ideological, historical, political, economical, structural, geographical, symbolic.

It is possible to distinguish between situations (1) where minorities wish to integrate in society and (2) where minorities wish to remain distinct from the majority culture. This is the case, for instance, of the Amish in the United States, of the Hutterites in Canada and of the ultra-Orthodox Hassidic Jewish communities all over the world. Both (1) and (2) present to the liberal state requests and demands for recognition of their cultural norms. They should be distinguished from cases (3) where radical groups wish to contest the values of society. They do not seek integration but wish to *see their value system prevail within society*. These radical groups pose the greatest challenge for liberal democracies and they threaten the viability of pluralism and multiculturalism. Because of those radical groups, opposition to multiculturalism is growing, wrongly associating multiculturalism with destructive forces. In France, much of the debate on multiculturalism is driven by fears of Muslim radicalization and coercion. In Israel, fear of Palestinian nationalism and Islam underpins the state's relationship with its minorities.

Liberals promote the development of regional or international mechanisms for protecting human rights. Many national minorities have expressed a willingness to abide by international declarations of human rights, and to answer to international tribunals for complaints of rights violations within their community. Indeed, minorities have often shown greater willingness to accept this kind of international review than majority groups, which jealously guard their sovereignty in domestic affairs.[8] I support a deliberative process by which communal gaps are bridged and agreements replace division.

THE VEIL CONTROVERSY

We should distinguish between *objective and directly harmful* and *subjective and indirectly harmful* practices. Murder for family honour belongs to the first category. Wearing a headscarf belongs to the second. It is a contentious issue whether the girls who wear headscarves are coerced to do so. It is a sweeping generalization to claim that *all* Muslim women who wear headscarves are harmed by it. There is strong evidence to suggest that for some women the headscarf is a manifestation of their identity as women.[9] For other women, the headscarf provides a sense of security. During the COVID-19 pandemic, people wear face mask also for security reasons.

Democracies' attitudes towards the headscarf issue differ widely on a continuum that goes from the French integrationist ideal to the multicultural model in the United Kingdom. The French solution is by no means the only strategy implemented in order to square the circle of relations between liberal democracies and 'group-differentiated' rights. The balance between 'integration' and 'accommodation' has been interpreted in various ways and with different nuances across the Western world. And, if it is inappropriate to see the French decision on the headscarf issue as another sign of the current crisis of liberal democracy, in which 'democracy is invoked to legitimate violations of individual freedom and

---

[8] Kymlicka and Cohen-Almagor, 'Democracy and Multiculturalism', 89–118.
[9] See, e.g., BBC, *Islam, Women and Me* (2018), www.bbc.co.uk/iplayer/episode/b09r8kdt/islam-women-and-me.

liberty',[10] nonetheless there are countries in which this problem has been effectively solved without resorting to legislation. On a delicate subject such as intercultural coexistence more informal and less ideological tools can prove at least as effective as the strategy implemented in France.

Legal Ban

Belgium followed France by introducing a ban on full-face veils in 2011. It outlaws any clothing that obscures one's face in public places. Veiled women can be jailed for up to seven days or forced to pay a €1,378 fine.[11] The European Court of Human Rights has consistently backed these bans, upholding France's in 2014 and Belgium's in 2017,[12] and choosing to give each country significant leeway in determining what it needs to do to ensure public safety and social cohesion.[13]

In Austria, a law was enacted in 2017 stating that faces must be visible from hairline to chin in public places. This is related to the burqa and niqab as well as to off-slope ski masks and surgical masks outside of hospitals. Austrian police are allowed to use force to make people show their face and can impose fines of €150.[14]

In August 2018, a law that bans any 'garment that hides the face in public' came into force in Denmark. Justice Minister Søren Pape Poulsen called the niqab 'incompatible with the values in Danish society'.[15]

Partial Ban

While a total ban is excessive, time, manner and place regulations may be reasonable. In the Netherlands around 5 per cent of the sixteen million residents are Muslims. In 2018 it approved a ban on the Islamic full veil in public places such as schools and hospitals, and on public transport. The niqab and the burka full-face veils were included in the ban along with face coverings such as ski masks and

---

[10] Stewart Motha, 'Veiled Women and the *Affect* of Religion in Democracy', *Journal of Law and Society*, 34(1) (2007): 139–162, at 145.

[11] Radhika Sanghani, 'Burka Bans: The Countries Where Muslim Women Can't Wear Veils', *The Telegraph* (17 August 2017), www.telegraph.co.uk/women/life/burka-bans-the-countries-where-muslim-women-cant-wear-veils/.

[12] 'The Islamic Veil Across Europe', *BBC* (31 May 2018), www.bbc.co.uk/news/world-europe-13038095.

[13] Sigal Samuel, 'Banning Muslim Veils Tends to Backfire: Why Do Countries Keep Doing It?', *The Atlantic* (3 August 2018), www.theatlantic.com/international/archive/2018/08/denmark-burqa-veil-ban/566630/.

[14] Mike Wright and Associated Press, 'Austria's "Burka Ban" Comes into Force, Prohibiting Face Veils in Public Places', *The Telegraph* (1 October 2017), www.telegraph.co.uk/news/2017/10/01/austrias-burka-ban-comes-force-prohibiting-face-veils-public/.

[15] Samuel, 'Banning Muslim Veils Tends to Backfire'.

helmets. Offenders are fined up to €410.[16] The ban does not apply to public streets, although police can ask an individual to remove face-covering clothing for identification.[17]

In Norway, burqas and niqabs are banned in schools.[18] In Germany, the southern state of Bavaria has banned the full-face veil and elsewhere in the country it is outlawed while driving.[19]

In Spain, the city of Barcelona announced in 2010 a ban on full Islamic face veils in some public spaces such as municipal offices, public markets and libraries. Barcelona's city council said the partial ban targeted any headwear that impeded identification, including motorbike helmets and balaclavas. Other smaller towns in Catalonia have also imposed bans. But a ban in the town of Lleida was overturned by Spain's Supreme Court in February 2013. It ruled that it was an infringement of religious liberties.[20]

Since 2017, the Quebec Bill 62 is 'An act to foster adherence to State religious neutrality and, in particular, to provide a framework for requests for accommodations on religious grounds in certain bodies'.[21] The Act requires Quebec residents to keep their faces uncovered while giving or receiving a provincial or municipal service, a requirement that extends to libraries, schools, hospitals, universities and public transit.[22] Justice Minister Stéphanie Vallée explained that 'Having your face uncovered is a legitimate question of communication, identification and security', and that the Bill was not aimed at any specific religious group.[23]

Non-legal Means

In the United Kingdom there is no ban on Islamic dress, but schools are allowed to decide their own dress code after a 2007 directive which followed several high-

---

[16] 'The Islamic Veil across Europe'; Raf Casert and Aleksandar Furtula, 'Netherlands Approves Limited Ban on "Face Covering Clothing" Like Niqabs and Burqas', *The Independent* (26 June 2018), www.independent.co.uk/news/world/europe/netherlands-burqa-niqab-ban-public-health-education-islam-a8418551.html.

[17] Casert and Furtula, 'Netherlands Approves Limited Ban on "Face Covering Clothing" Like Niqabs and Burqas'. See also Sanghani, 'Burka Bans'. For further discussion, see Maarten P. Vink, 'Dutch "Multiculturalism" beyond the Pillarisation Myth', *Political Studies Review*, 5 (3) (2007): 337–350.

[18] Chris Harris, 'Where in Europe is the Islamic Full-Face Veil Banned?', *Euronews* (12 August 2018), www.euronews.com/2018/08/08/where-in-europe-is-the-islamic-full-face-veil-banned-.

[19] Ibid.

[20] 'The Islamic Veil Across Europe'.

[21] Bill 62, www2.publicationsduquebec.gouv.qc.ca/dynamicSearch/telecharge.php?type=5&file=2017C19A.PDF.

[22] Ibid.

[23] Graeme Hamilton, 'Quebec Passes Bill Banning Niqab, Burka While Receiving Public Services', *National Post* (18 October 2017), https://nationalpost.com/news/politics/quebec-passes-bill-62.

profile court cases.[24] Muslim women's right to wear the veil in public places is granted by law, although there have been several attempts at limiting it.[25] Following a classical liberal approach, British authorities deal with the headscarf issue by resorting to non-legal means. According to the governmental Commission on Integration and Cohesion, which was created ad hoc in 2006, relations with minority cultures must be dealt with by 'developing practical solutions for local communities based on the best existing practice', thus 'push[ing] further against perceived barriers to cohesion and integration'.[26]

The creation of a multicultural society, pluralizing the concept of equality and attempting to respect difference and accommodate cultures, is the British way of reconciling between liberalism and multiculturalism. The British try to balance between competing interests: cultural needs and public order. They seek compromise via deliberation and try to accommodate rather than coerce. An illustrative example is the *Denbigh* case. A student wished to wear a long garment, the jihab, to school. She refused to wear one of the approved uniforms which other Muslim women wore. The House of Lords was impressed with the school's care in designing its uniform policy: it consulted on what would be an appropriate uniform for Muslim students, and communicated its policy clearly to prospective students and their families.[27] When challenged by the Muslim student, the school took advice and concluded that its uniform policy should be maintained. Some other Muslim students in the same school resisted the introduction of the jihab and the school feared introducing it would highlight and encourage religious distinctions among Muslim students. Also, of significance was the fact that many of the persons involved in running this school were themselves of the Muslim faith. Care was given to strike a balance between conflicting interests. This sort of dialogue is to be encouraged. The House of Lords concluded that the school was fully justified in acting the way it did.

INTEGRATION AND ACCOMMODATION

Article 9 of the European Convention on Human Rights holds: 'Freedom to manifest one's religion or beliefs shall be subject only to such limitations ...

---

[24] 'The Islamic Veil across Europe'.

[25] A lawyer wearing a full-face veil, for instance, was told by a judge that she could not represent a client because he could not hear her; a teacher wearing the same kind of veil was dismissed from school. See Jane Perlez, 'Muslims' Veils Test Limits of Britain's Tolerance', *New York Times* (22 June 2007).

[26] Shane Brighton, 'British Muslim, Multiculturalism and UK Foreign Policy: "Integration" and "Cohesion" in and beyond the State', *International Affairs*, 83(1) (2007): 1–17, at 4. See, generally, James A. Beckford, 'Public Responses to Religious Diversity in Britain and France', in Lori G. Beaman (ed.), *Reasonable Accommodation* (Vancouver: UBC Press, 2012): 109–138.

[27] *R v. Headteacher and Governors of Denbigh High School* [2006] UKHL 15 (22 March 2006).

necessary in a democratic society in the interests of public safety, for the protection of public order, health or morals, or for the protection of the rights and freedoms of others.'[28] Furthermore, the Convention on the Elimination of All Forms of Discrimination against Women recalls that 'discrimination against women violates the principles of equality of rights and respect for human dignity, is an obstacle to the participation of women, on equal terms with men, in the political, social, economic and cultural life of their countries'.[29] Such discrimination 'hampers the growth of the prosperity of society and the family, and makes more difficult the full development of the potentialities of women in the service of their countries and of humanity'.[30] Therefore, states should take active measures in all fields of life to ensure the full development and advancement of women, for the purpose of guaranteeing them the exercise and enjoyment of human rights and fundamental freedoms on a basis of equality with men and mutual respect. Harming women in the name of culture should not be part of this place.

A focus on deliberative discourse is one way to resolve cultural dilemmas. Resolving tensions between individual and group rights will not be done easily but much can be done by mediators and facilitators who promote principles of non-discrimination, substantive and contextualized interpretations of rights and a democratic discourse on the understanding of rights.[31] We should strive to engage in a dialogue in order to understand one another. Communication makes that which is far nearer, and what is strange familiar.

Still, we have to deal with the complex reality of social alert when it comes to coexistence with radical, fundamentalist groups whose conception of the good is foreign to liberal values and principles. We have to keep in mind that no 'accommodation' is acceptable when it comes to violating the core values of democracy, respecting others as human beings and not harming others. The balance between 'integration' and 'accommodation' must be handled carefully in order to avoid intra-group tensions and preserve the underpinning values of liberal democracies.

In this light, it is difficult to agree with the view that would urge, for instance, adopting Sharia law and/or Jewish law in the British system to maintain social cohesion. Citizens, immigrant citizens among them, are entitled to retain their cultural and religious norms if they do not contradict the state's laws. Democracies should enable multiculturalism and religious freedoms, but it is not incumbent on them to transform their set of laws. At the same time, citizens have both rights and

---

[28] European Convention on Human Rights (1950), www.echr.coe.int/Documents/Convention_ENG.pdf.

[29] Adopted and opened for signature, ratification and accession by UN General Assembly resolution 34/180 of 18 December 1979; entry into force 3 September 1981, www.ohchr.org/documents/professionalinterest/cedaw.pdf.

[30] Ibid.

[31] Koen De Feyter and George Pavlakos (eds), *The Tension between Group Rights and Human Rights* (Oxford and Portland, OR: Hart Publishing, 2008): 145–146.

duties towards the state: loyalty to the state, in this context, should be a precondition for citizenship.

In his discussion of the overlapping consensus concept, Rawls acknowledges that such a consensus is not always possible. Indeed, we have little empirical reason to believe that all of the diverse conceptions of the good that people embrace provide the overlapping consensus of which Rawls speaks. Nevertheless, Rawls thinks that through this idea we may be able to show how, despite a diversity of doctrines, convergence on a political conception of justice may be achieved and social unity sustained in a long-term equilibrium, that is, over time from one generation to the next. Rawls writes that 'when basic institutions satisfy a political conception of justice mutually acknowledged by citizens affirming comprehensive doctrines in a reasonable overlapping consensus, this fact confirms that those institutions allow sufficient space for ways of life worthy of citizens' devoted support'.[32] The consolidation of any long-lasting consensus inevitably necessitates some forms of compromise and coercion. Both compromise and coercion are essential to democratic governance, especially to the work of legislators and government officials who are tasked with devising and implementing public policies and bridge over disputes and disagreements.

INSIGHTS AND LESSONS

Throughout the book I have been arguing that just, reasonable multiculturalism, reconcilable with liberalism, is possible. Good education should be enabling and respectful. Reasonableness dictates taking into consideration the composition of the community. Thus, we should respect Muslim teachers who wish to pray on Friday by organizing their teaching in a way that would free their time to pray. Reasonableness brings us to think that Jewish teachers and students should enjoy Shabbat as their day of rest. Reasonableness would also suggest that we should not schedule sad events on the Chinese New Year if part of the community is Chinese, and that we should not organize happy events on the Jewish Yom Kippur when part of the community is Jewish. It is a good idea to devise a multicultural calendar in which all cultures and religions represented in school or on campus are clearly noted, so organizers are able to consult the calendar before planning events. I have initiated such a calendar at the University of Hull.

Research and thinking for this book showed me, once again, the timelessness and validity of the theories of Immanuel Kant, John Stuart Mill, John Rawls and Jürgen Habermas. I have been using their theories in many of my research projects, in different contexts, and always discover some new facets, new ideas and new ways to apply the theories to different case studies, addressing diverse dilemmas. While deontology is too demanding to be realistic and humane, and utilitarianism can

---

[32] Rawls, *Political Liberalism*: 187.

be pushed to unacceptable crudeness, elements of these theories have helped in shaping the theory of just, reasonable multiculturalism without subscribing to a single philosophy as a whole. Following Kant, we ought to respect others as autonomous human beings who exercise self-determination to live according to their own life plans; we should respect people as self-developing beings who are able to develop their inherent faculties as they choose. Following Mill, we should exercise power carefully, enable individual autonomy and avoid harming others without proper justification. Following Rawls, moral and religious freedoms stem from the Principle of Equal Liberty, and, assuming the priority of this principle, the only grounds for denying equal liberties is to avoid an even greater injustice, an even greater loss of liberty. Individual liberty is valuable as we wish to secure an extensive system of overall liberties for everyone. Following Habermas, Mill and Rawls, we should prefer open deliberation and constructive all-inclusive debate to coercion. Their scholarship helped me in my attempt to chart a way forward for liberals who are concerned with the argument that liberalism is insensitive to the importance of group membership. The theoretical part of this book discusses mechanisms for determining what liberals can tolerate without violating their fundamental commitments and what they are not obliged to endure in the name of multiculturalism.

I have been thinking of the challenges of multiculturalism for a long time. I grew up in a multicultural family whose roots stretch to Eastern Europe, Africa, Asia and South America. Many members of my family are secular. Some are very religious. I studied in Israel, the United States and the United Kingdom. I have deep appreciation for cultural pluralism, for religion and for the richness and beauty of traditions that I experienced from a young age. I am also acutely aware of the gender discrimination phenomenon that I witnessed in many countries. I have merged my general interest and scholarly research into the field of multiculturalism since 1992. During this considerable length of time I have studied many pertinent practices and court cases. In crafting this book, I had to decide what issues should enter the book, which should be mentioned in passing and which topics are to be excluded. On physical harm, I decided to start the conversation with the 'easy' or least controversial cases: suttee and murder for family honour. Even staunch multiculturalists who oppose any government interference in cultural affairs may be convinced that these grave issues require interference. Boundaries need to be drawn. I wanted to make people aware that strong claims for cultural autonomy and strong claims for liberal neutrality might result in great suffering. Another consideration that prompted me of the need for such a discussion is the inclusion of culture as a potential mitigating factor in criminal defences of those violent cases, especially at the level of sentencing. Attempts at condoning those practices or presenting them as 'private matters' that should not concern the legal authorities are reprehensible. Throughout the book I reiterate time and again that it is the duty of the liberal state to protect vulnerable people.

FGM

I re-evaluated my position on female circumcision and FGM. My research forced me to reconsider differences and similarities between male and female circumcision. As liberal democracy does not have overriding justifications to ban male circumcision, so it does not have strong justifications to outlaw mild forms of female circumcision. Engaging with communities through means of deliberative democracy is one thing. Enforcing a ban on communities that strongly believe in upholding such symbolic rituals is another. At the same time, liberal democracy should be resolute in its absolute objection to torture, including FGM. Undoubtedly, excessive forms of FGM are repulsive, alien to any humanistic thinking and should have no place in a liberal society. This is why, quite appropriately, the term FGM is used with regard to those excessive forms and not the term circumcision. The practice mutilates the young female body and causes girls prolonged suffering for the rest of their lives. FGM is a psychologically damaging and oppressive tradition designed to subjugate women and their sexuality. My research confirmed that FGM remains a challenge for liberal democracies and other societies, a challenge that needs to be addressed adequately and resolved.

After completing the first draft of my book I had a discussion with experts on multiculturalism who questioned my position on FGM. They criticized my approach to FGM by raising several objections. First, they object to the use of the term 'mutilation', saying that this physical harm is not mutilation.

Second, sex is not such an important thing. At some point, it becomes boring. You repeat the same movement time and again and once you get accustomed to it, sex loses its attraction.

Third, society is not to guarantee people all pleasures. We need to accept that some pleasures are denied to us and, surely, society has no duty to provide people with all causes for pleasures.

Fourth, what if an adult woman wishes to have FGM at a late stage of her life, voluntarily, without pressure? Why do you want to deny her the FGM experience if this is what she wants?

In response, mutilation means to injure a body part to the extent that it is permanently damaged, detached or disfigured. The Latin root *mutilare* literally means 'with a part cut off'. To mutilate is to cripple. The term is not subjective. It is an objective description of the consequences of female genital practice that is done for no health or other reasonable justification. FGM is an abhorrent practice. At the same time, I reiterate the difference between FGM and female circumcision, and that moderate form of cutting, similar to male circumcision, may be reasonable and acceptable in the name of culture.

Second, arguing that sex is not important is a subjective statement that reflects a particular viewpoint about sex that is not widely shared. Sex is a human urge that most of us wish to experience time and again for a variety of reasons, the obvious one being in order to establish a family. But most people have sex not only for procreation. People have sex for many physical and emotional reasons. When the body is damaged, then this has an effect not only on the body but also on the psyche and on the ability to have a fulfilling relationship, and intimacy, with one's partner. A study that investigated why people have sex identified 237 expressed reasons for having sex, ranging from the mundane (e.g., 'I wanted to experience physical pleasure') to the spiritual (e.g., 'I wanted to get closer to God'), from altruistic (e.g., 'I wanted the person to feel good about himself/herself') to vengeful (e.g., 'I wanted to get back at my partner for having cheated on me').[33] Participants in the study were asked to evaluate the degree to which each of the 237 reasons had led them to have sexual intercourse. Four large factors and thirteen subfactors were identified: (1) physical reasons which include stress reduction, pleasure, physical desirability, and experience seeking; (2) goal attainment reasons which include resources, social status, revenge and the promotion of one's happiness and the happiness of others; (3) emotional reasons which include love, commitment and expression; and (4) insecurity reasons which include self-esteem boost, duty/pressure and mate guarding.[34] The study revealed significant gender differences. Women exceeded men in endorsing certain of the emotional motivations for sex, such as 'I wanted to express my love for the person' and 'I realized that I was in love'. Women, more than men, prefer sex within the context of an ongoing committed relationship, and feelings or expressions of love provide signals of that commitment. It is important to note, however, that most of the emotional motivations for engaging in sex were not endorsed more frequently by women. Both men and women at times desire intimacy and emotional connectedness from sexual activity.[35] Thus, if you deprive women of the ability to enjoy sex to the fullest, you harm not only women but also men and partner relationships as the desire for intimacy and emotional connectedness from sexual activity might be infringed by FGM.

Third, of course society is not to guarantee people all pleasures. I enjoy cruises, French cuisine and fast cars. Society is not obliged to sponsor my lucrative tastes by arranging for me annual cruises to the Caribbean, weekly dinners at three-Michelin star restaurants and a Lamborghini in the courtyard. The analogy between these lucrative things and having a healthy, natural and intimate relationship between husband and wife (or partners) is false. Sex is a basic need that can be the source of enormous pleasure with no extravagant expense. To enjoy it we need to have functioning organs. Mutilating women's organs beyond repair (e.g., by cutting the clitoris) deny this basic ability to enjoy what is naturally given to you.

[33] Cindy M. Meston and David M. Buss, 'Why Humans Have Sex', *Archives of Sexual Behavior*, 36 (2007): 477–507.
[34] Ibid.
[35] Ibid.

Fourth, we need to engage with adult women who wish to have FGM. Through deliberation we need to enquire about the reasons that bring a woman to ask for this practice, why she wishes to damage her body beyond repair, what does she actually know about FGM, what exact procedure she has in mind and whether this wish is the result of internal thinking or external pressure. We need to explain to her the consequences of FGM and how the procedure will affect her life. After such an extensive deliberation, if a woman still insists that she wants to experience FGM then she is free to travel to an illiberal place, outside liberal democracy, where FGM is not illegal. But a liberal society cannot permit FGM as it does not permit torture. Consented torture is likened to consented slavery. Both are not just or reasonable. Both are outside the scope of tolerance.

Male Circumcision

This is a very sensitive issue of which I am fully aware as a Jewish father. For Orthodox Jews, male circumcision is of utmost importance. In writing this chapter I consulted many scholars and authorities in the field, including the president of the World Medical Association, the president of British Medical Association and a retired justice of the Israel Supreme Court who is also an Orthodox Jew, the leading halachic authority in Israel who is the author of the *Encyclopedia of Jewish Medical Ethics* for which he was awarded the prestigious Israel Prize in 1999, and who is also a senior paediatric neurologist at the Shaare Zedek Medical Center in Jerusalem where he directs the Medical Ethics Unit. I also consulted Orthodox and Reform rabbis, a Muslim paediatrician, medical consultants in the fields of anaesthesia and neonatology and circumcisers. I drafted and redrafted my proposal for well over a year, learning the intricacies, agreements and disagreements across cultures and medical professions. The issue was more complex than I initially expected. Studying the religious and medical aspects of the procedure was fascinating and enriching. I hope my detailed proposal will lead to an open debate with the communities, where the need for adequate analgesia is explained, and the rights of the child are safeguarded. An open discussion, conducted in civility and with mutual respect, would promote understanding of cultural needs while protecting the rights of all in aiming to secure a just and reasonable multicultural society. I also hope the WHO and liberal democracies will learn the proposal and adopt at least some aspects of it.

Gender Discrimination

The Canadian *Hofer v. Hofer*, which dealt with the powers of the Hutterite Church over its members and the denial of property from members who were expelled for apostasy, and the American *Wisconsin v. Yoder* concerning the power of the Amish community over its members, are clear examples of clashes between group rights and individual rights. Will Kymlicka and I have worked on these concerns in the past and here I revisited my reasoning, arguing that the court rulings failed to offer just, reasonable compromises to accommodate between liberalism and multiculturalism at the service of weak groups. Just and reasonable multiculturalism requires defending basic individual rights when these are infringed in the name of culture.

The Amish

My research on Amish education and what happens to Amish people when they leave their community and start a new chapter in American society brought me, quite unexpectedly, to consider child abuse, a problem that affects many closed societies, as we have seen with the Catholic and Anglican churches. One by one, the stories of Amish women who left the community revealed a repeated pattern of violence and abuse. The image of the Amish as a peaceful community that is protective of its youth was shaken. It seems that lack of external involvement; a culture that fails to establish reasonable and moral sexual boundaries; religious legitimacy of gender inequality; the Amish reluctance to wash their dirty linen in public; the community values of forgiveness and repentance; the economic structure where families are very much dependent on men's labour and therefore the community is reluctant to inflict significant penalties on perpetrators; lack of sex education; the fact that Amish teachers tend to be young, inexperienced women of the same community; the lack of mental health and safety provisions at schools; and the Amish isolation from the larger society that allows them self-governance and cultural autonomy in which the norm is to punish the victim rather than the abuser, have all contributed to this troubling phenomenon of violence and abuse of young Amish. The urgency of opening the gates for integrating Amish education into American society and subjecting it to reasonable monitoring standards is accentuated when one reads those troubling and horrifying stories. The limitations posed by the Amish on their members deny adolescents not only chances for an autonomous open future and self-development but also, in a significant number of cases, deny them healthy and safe growth.

In this context, may I mention Article 19 of the Convention on the Rights of the Child, which holds:

1. States Parties shall take all appropriate legislative, administrative, social and educational measures to protect the child from all forms of physical or mental violence, injury or abuse, neglect or negligent treatment, maltreatment or exploitation, including sexual abuse, while in the care of parent(s), legal guardian(s) or any other person who has the care of the child.

2. Such protective measures should, as appropriate, include effective procedures for the establishment of social programmes to provide necessary support for the child and for those who have the care of the child, as well

as for other forms of prevention and for identification, reporting, referral, investigation, treatment and follow-up of instances of child maltreatment described heretofore, and, as appropriate, for judicial involvement.[36]

It is unacceptable to allow a situation in which anguished victims have to continue living with their tormentors in constant fear. Liberal democracy has a duty of care towards exposed third parties. As the Amish culture protects abusers and neglects its responsibilities towards their young, the liberal state must step in. The Amish education system should include discussions about Amish history and culture, religion, agriculture, group rights and individual rights and the need to find a reasonable balance between them. Issues such as private and public, human rights including children's and women's rights, respect and the dignity of the person, sex education, the harm in incest and paedophilia, and the boundaries of liberty and tolerance (the 'democratic catch') should be part of the curricula. The education system should also provide children with the much-needed expert and specialized support to escape victimhood. There are too many stories of girls who were subjected to inappropriate touching, groping, fondling, exposure to genitals, penetration, oral sex, anal sex and rape, all at the hands of their own family members, neighbours and church leaders.[37] The subjection of girls and women to this brute reality is unacceptable. Unwittingly, *Wisconsin v. Yoder* has shielded a reality in which girls, and sometimes boys, have nowhere to turn when they need.[38] *Yoder* has to be revisited.

Laïcité

My research on *laïcité* revealed the complexity of the relationship between state and religion in France. During my fieldwork in France I was surprised to hear that some of my interviewees did not know the difference between hijab, niqab and burqa. It is easier to criticize the *foulard* without knowing what it is. Many people in France do not know what exactly the pertinent laws are and to what kind of dress they refer. My research also revealed the problematic nature of Rousseau's concept of the general

---

[36] Article 19 of the Convention on the Rights of the Child. Adopted and opened for signature, ratification and accession by General Assembly resolution 44/25 of 20 November 1989, entry into force 2 September 1990, in accordance with article 49, www.ohchr.org/en/professionalin terest/pages/crc.aspx.

[37] Sarah McClure, 'The Amish Keep to Themselves: And They're Hiding a Horrifying Secret', *Cosmopolitan* (14 January 2020); Michel Martin, 'Investigation Into Child Sex Abuse in Amish Communities', *NPR* (19 January 2020); Leah Simpson, 'Horrifying Record of Child Sex Abuse in Amish Communities with More than 50 Cases in Seven States as Victims Tell of Being Shunned or Sent to "Mental Health" Facilities If They Complained', *The Daily Mail* (15 January 2020), www.cosmopolitan.com/lifestyle/amp30284631/amish-sexual-abuse-incest-me-too/?__twitter_impression=true%26utm_campaign=todays_worldview%26utm_medium=Email%26utm_source=Newsletter%26wpisrc=nl_todayworld%26wpmm=1

[38] *Wisconsin v. Yoder* 406 US 205, 92 S.Ct 1526 (1972).

will as it is opened to coercive interpretations. I very much wanted to relate also to the hijab controversy but this intricate and multifaceted issue requires further in-depth deliberation and another, separate discussion. Reading and communicating with two members of the Stasi Committee, Patrick Weil who agreed with the hijab ban in public schools, and Jean Baubérot who abstained, reveal some of the complexities.[39] Indeed, delving into the various arguments on both sides of the debate for and against the hijab in public schools, in a way that would do justice to protagonists and antagonists who advance well-reasoned philosophical and empirical arguments, would require at least another lengthy chapter on France.

Personally, I never had an occasion to hear a lecturer who chooses to address her audience in a niqab or burqa. I suspect that I would feel estranged from her unless this dress choice was pertinent to her lecture: 'Women in Islam', 'Coercion in Islam', 'Muslim Women and Feminism', 'The Right to Choose', 'Multiculturalism in France' or 'Behind the Veil of Ignorance'. Then I would perceive the dress as a physical statement that serves a purpose in delivering the lecture.

I taught at several universities in the United Kingdom, Israel, the United States and India. I never had a student who chose to come to class wearing a burqa or niqab; I have had plenty of students who were wearing the hijab. Their dress did not bother me. This was their choice. Mutual respect is the guiding rule. I would be disturbed if they were denied the right to wear the hijab. I think I would feel uncomfortable if students were to wear niqab or burqa because it is important for me to have communication with students. Eye contact and facial expressions are important. Students give signals about their engagement with lectures. These signals affect me as a lecturer. They tell me when students understand or do not understand, when they are interested and when they lose interest. My ability to be attentive to such signals would be dramatically reduced when students' faces are largely or completely covered. Similarly, up until the 2020 coronavirus epidemic I thought I would feel estranged if Christian or Jewish students arrived to class fully covered, if male students covered their faces with helmets or scarves, or if students came to class with surgical masks to protect themselves from environmental hazards. The epidemic brought me to reconsider the issue. Humans have an incredible ability to adjust to new circumstances. Things that we may have found difficult to consider in the past quickly might become the new reality. When I was in Japan in

---

[39] 'A Conversation between Jean Baubérot and Sarah Fainberg', and Jean Baubérot, 'Laïcité and Freedom of Conscience in Pluricultural France', both in Jacques Berlinerblau, Sarah Fainberg and Aurora Nou (eds), *Secularism on the Edge: Rethinking Church–State Relations in the United States, France, and Israel* (Houndmills: Palgrave Macmillan, 2014): 85–94, 103–111, respectively; Patrick Weil, 'Lifting the Veil', *French Politics, Culture and Society*, 22(3) (2003): 142–149, and Patrick Weil, 'Why the French Laïcité Is Liberal', *Cardozo Law Review*, 30(6) (2009): 2699–2714.

2009 it was strange for me to see so many people wearing ecological masks. In 2020 this is no longer strange. Circumstances change, and we change with them.

As said, while time, manner and place regulations may be reasonable, a comprehensive ban on the burqa and niqab is not. Throughout this book, I have argued that we should respect people's life decisions because each course of life has intrinsic value, and we respect individual reasoning, *so long as people do not harm others*. The experiences of many nations have shown that multiculturalism is enriching and stimulating. It should be nourished and encouraged.

Minority Rights in Israel

My research into majority and minority relationships in Israel pushed me to probe deeper for just, reasonable compromises that would promote meaningful multiculturalism and substantive forms of democracy that would be more egalitarian in nature. Applying the Rawlsian veil of ignorance brings us to conclude that egalitarian fairness should be the guiding rule, notwithstanding one's religion, culture or gender. At the same time, Israeli citizens should insist on mutual respect and on a collective effort to preserve and promote national security. Security is the most important value in Israeli society for understandable reasons and therefore the burden of security should be shared by all. But security should not overshadow every other consideration and should not serve as a pretext for discrimination. Democracies should aspire for overlapping consensus where mutual respect, toleration and reasonableness are the norms. Such a consensus is moral in its reasoning and is affirmed by different religious and cultural doctrines in a just multicultural democracy.

Cécile Laborde argues that all liberal democracies are characterized by a basic separation between state and religion. All adopted a minimal 'anti-theocratic' principle that makes it impermissible for the state to constitutively associate itself with religious institutions and appeal to specifically religious ends in political justification.[40] Israel, however, did not adopt this 'anti-theocratic' principle. In Israel there are inherent contradictions between the religious and the existing liberal worldviews. Many believe that in order to survive as a Jewish state, the Jewish character of the state should be preserved and promoted even if that entails inequitable treatment of the other.[41]

In Israel, internal conflicts were and remain secondary to the Arab–Israeli conflict. From Prime Minister Ben-Gurion onwards, Jewish unity (as distinct from

---

[40] Cécile Laborde, 'Conclusion: Is Religion Special?', in Jean L. Cohen and Cécile Laborde (eds), *Religion, Secularism, and Constitutional Democracy* (New York: Columbia University Press, 2016): 424.
[41] Yehezkel Dror, *Israeli Statecraft: National Security Challenges and Responses* (London and New York: Routlege, 2011): 20.

all-inclusive national unity) against external threats is being perceived by all prime ministers as most important. In the name of Jewish unity basic rights and freedoms are undermined. Due to power politics considerations, secular leaders who, on the whole, wish to retain the Jewish character of the state do not push hard for separation between state and religion.

Religion is a powerful sentiment. One of Karl Marx's greatest mistakes was that he underestimated the power of religion, thinking that economy is a more powerful consideration in the eyes of the masses. Because religion is so powerful it needs to be confined to boundaries that would enable living together, in a community composed of a plurality of cultures and religion, possible. The distinction between private and public, emphasized by the French, is too restrictive as some people continue to practice their religion wherever they are, also when they leave their homes and places of prayer. A more just and reasonable accommodation is to insist that religion does not enter the political realm. Separation between state and religion in the political sphere would make all people recognize that in the shared political domain one's religious views do not necessarily and directly prevail. As Catherine Audard notes, then people would start to acknowledge the plurality of competing views as well as the principle of democratic legitimacy, the authority of political principles beyond their own community of justification in order to regulate these conflicts.[42] Reasonableness dictates that a just political system should be independent from any religious or other comprehensive doctrine and thus acceptable to all.

FINAL WORDS

Culture and religion are powerful. They affect many millions of lives. People voluntarily adopt certain values and norms. Democracies should be sensitive to these powers. They should strive to reconcile between their basic values and the values of different cultures.

Developing a comprehensive liberal theory of just, reasonable multiculturalism is of the utmost importance for the future of healthy relationships between the majority and minorities in liberal and other democracies. Liberalism and multiculturalism are reconcilable within certain boundaries, set by liberal democracy as a general framework for human interaction. But this book offers not only a theory of just, reasonable multiculturalism. It also suggests practical mechanisms to make harmonious living together in a heterogeneous liberal democracy possible. Liberal democracies should enhance cross-cultural, deliberative engagement in order to make sustainable progress while securing civic and human rights for all. This book provides guidelines in the liberal direction that help secure group

---

[42] Catherine Audard, 'Pluralism and the Possibility of a Liberal Political Consensus', in Ingrid Salvatore and Volker Kaul (eds), *What Is Pluralism?* (London: Routledge, 2020).

rights and, at the same time, compel us to acknowledge the need for setting adequate limitations on both the power of groups over their members and on state interference in the cultural affairs of minorities. Governments have dual responsibility to ensure that certain groups are not discriminated against and that individuals within groups are also protected. A delicate balance between individual rights and group rights needs to be maintained. While this task of having a rich, just and reasonable multicultural society is difficult, it is doable and well worthy of the effort.

Select Bibliography

GENERAL

Abizadeh, Arash, 'Democratic Theory and Border Coercion: No Right to Unilaterally Control Your Own Borders', *Political Theory*, 36 (2008): 37–65.

'Democratic Legitimacy and State Coercion: A Reply to David Miller', *Political Theory*, 38 (2010): 121–130.

Ackerman, Bruce A., *Social Justice in the Liberal State* (New Haven, CT and London: Yale University Press, 1980).

Ahdar, Rex, and Lan Leigh, *Religious Freedom in the Liberal State* (Oxford: Oxford University Press, 2005).

Airaksinen, Timo, *Ethics of Coercion and Authority* (Pittsburgh, PA: University of Pittsburgh Press, 1988).

Alexander, Jeffrey C., *The Civic Sphere* (New York: Oxford University Press, 2006).

Almond G., and S. Verba, *The Civic Culture* (New York: Little, Brown & Company, 1965).

Anderson, Scott, 'The Enforcement Approach to Coercion', *Journal of Ethics and Social Philosophy*, 5(1) (2010): 1–31.

'Coercion', *Stanford Encyclopedia of Philosophy* (2011), https://plato.stanford.edu/entries/coercion/.

Arneson, R.J., 'Mill versus Paternalism', *Ethics*, 90 (1980): 470–489.

Ashbee, Edward, *American Society Today* (Manchester: Manchester University Press, 2002).

Audard, Catherine, 'Pluralism and the Possibility of a Liberal Political Consensus', in Ingrid Salvatore and Volker Kaul (eds), *What Is Pluralism?* (London: Routledge, 2020): 99–121.

Audi, Robert, 'The Separation of Church and State and the Obligations of Citizenship', *Philosophy & Public Affairs*, 18(3) (1989): 259–296.

Augsberg, Ino, '"The Moral Feeling within Me": On Kant's Concept of Human Freedom and Dignity as Auto-heteronomy', in Dieter Grimm, Alexandra Kemmerer and Christoph Möllers (eds), *Human Dignity in Context* (Munich: Hart, 2018), 55–68.

Avineri, Shlomo, and Avner de-Shalit (eds), *Communitarianism and Individualism* (Oxford: Clarendon Press, 1992).

Bächtiger, André, et al. (eds), *The Oxford Handbook of Deliberative Democracy* (Oxford: Oxford University Press, 2018).

Baghramian, Maria, and Attracta Ingram (eds), *Pluralism: The Philosophy and Politics of Diversity* (London: Routledge, 2000).

Baker, Judith (ed.), *Group Rights* (Toronto: University of Toronto Press, 1994).

Baker Reynolds, Holly, book review of *Sati: Widow Burning in India*, *Harvard Women's Law Journal*, 12 (1989): 277–86.

Barber, Jennifer S., 'Community Social Context and Individualistic Attitudes toward Marriage', *Social Psychology Quarterly*, 67(3) (2004): 236–256.

Barker, Ernest, *Reflections of Government* (Oxford: Oxford University Press, 1942).

Barry, Brian, *Theories of Justice* (London: Harvester, 1989).

   Culture and Equality: An Egalitarian Critique of Multiculturalism (Cambridge: Polity 2000).

   Culture and Equality: An Egalitarian Critique of Multiculturalism, 2nd ed. (Cambridge, MA: Harvard University Press, 2001).

Baubock, Rainer (ed.), *From Aliens to Citizens: Redefining the Legal Status of Immigrants* (Aldershot: Avebury, 1994).

Baum, Bruce, and Robert Nichols (eds), *Isaiah Berlin and the Politics of Freedom: 'Two Concepts of Liberty' 50 Years Later* (London: Routledge, 2015).

Beaman, Lori G. (ed.), *Reasonable Accommodation* (Vancouver: UBC Press, 2012).

Bejan, Teresa M., *Mere Civility: Disagreement and the Limits of Toleration* (Cambridge, MA: Harvard University Press, 2017).

Bell, Daniel, *Communitarianism and Its Critics* (Oxford: Clarendon Press, 1993).

   'Communitarianism', Stanford Encyclopedia of Philosophy (2016), https://plato.stanford.edu/entries/communitarianism/.

Bellamy, Richard, *Liberalism and Pluralism* (London and New York: Routledge, 1999).

Benhabib, Seyla, 'Deliberative Rationality and Models of Democratic Legitimacy', *Constellations*, 1 (1994): 26–52.

   The Claims of Culture: Equality and Diversity in the Global Era (Princeton, NJ: Princeton University Press, 2002).

   The Rights of Others: Aliens, Residents, and Citizens (New York: Cambridge University Press, 2004).

Benjamin, Martin, *Splitting the Difference* (Lawrence: University Press of Kansas, 1990).

Berlin, Isaiah, *Concepts and Categories* (Oxford: Oxford University Press, 1980).

   Liberty (Oxford: Oxford University Press, 2002).

   The Crooked Timber of Humanity (Princeton, NJ: Princeton University Press, 2013).

Bessette, Joseph, *The Mild Voice of Reason: Deliberative Democracy and American National Government* (Chicago: University of Chicago Press, 1994).

Biale, Rachel, *Women and Jewish Law: The Essential Texts, Their History, and Their Relevance for Today* (New York: Schocken, 1995).

Bilimoria, Purushottama, 'The Jaina Ethic of Voluntary Death', *Bioethics*, 6(4) (1992): 331–355.

   'The Enlightenment Paradigm of Native Right and Hybridity of Cultural Rights in British India', in Michael Barnhardt (ed.), *Varieties of Ethical Reflection: New Directions for Ethics in a Global Context* (Lanham, MD: Lexington Books, 2002): 235–262.

Bird, Graham (ed.), *A Companion to Kant* (Oxford: Blackwell, 2006).

Bohman, James, 'Public Reason and Cultural Pluralism', *Political Theory*, 23(2) (1995): 253–279.

Bollinger, Lee C., *The Tolerant Society* (Oxford: Clarendon Press, 1986).

Borowitz, Eugene, and Francs Schwartz, *Touch of the Sacred: A Theologian's Informal Guide to Jewish Belief* (Woodstock, VT: Jewish Lights Publishing, 2009).

Brett, Nathan, 'Language Laws and Collective Rights', *Canadian Journal of Law and Jurisprudence*, 4(2) (1991): 347–360.

Bricker, David, 'Autonomy and Culture: Will Kymlicka on Cultural Minority Rights', *Southern Journal of Philosophy*, 36 (1998): 47–59.

Brighouse, Harry, *School Choice and Social Justice* (Oxford: Oxford University Press, 2003).

Brighton, Shane, 'British Muslims, Multiculturalism and UK Foreign Policy: "Integration" and "Cohesion" in and beyond the State', *International Affairs*, 83(1) (2007): 1–17.

Brooks, Thom, *Becoming British: UK Citizenship Examined* (London: Biteback, 2016).

Brown, D.G., 'Mill on Harm to Others' Interests', *Political Studies*, 26 (1978): 395–399.

Brugger, W., and M. Karayanni (eds), *Religion in the Public Sphere: A Comparative Analysis of German, Israeli, American and International Law* (Berlin: Max Plank, 2007).

Bryce, James, *Modern Democracies* (London and New York: Macmillan, 1924),.

Bryson, Valerie, *Feminist Political Theory* (London: Palgrave, 2016).

Budde, Rebecca, and Urszula Markowska-Manista (eds), *Childhood and Children's Rights between Research and Activism* (Weisbaden: Springer, 2020).

Callan, Eamonn, *Creating Citizens: Political Education and Liberal Democracy* (Oxford: Oxford University Press, 1997).

Cameron, David, 'Speech on Radicalisation and Islamic Extremism', *New Statesman* (5 February 2011), www.newstatesman.com/blogs/the-staggers/2011/02/terrorism-islam-ideology.

Carr, Craig L., 'Coercion and Freedom', *American Philosophical Quarterly*, 25(1) (January 1988): 59–67.

Carter, April, *Direct Action and Liberal Democracy* (London: Routledge & Kegan Paul, 1973).

Carvalho, Joao, *Impact of Extreme Right Parties on Immigration Policy: Comparing Britain, France and Italy* (London: Routledge, 2016).

Cassatella, Andrea, 'Multicultural Justice: Will Kymlicka and Cultural Recognition', *Ratio Juris*, 19(1) (2006): 80–100.

Castiglione, Dario (ed.), *Toleration, Neutrality and Democracy* (Dordrecht: Springer, 2011).

Chaplin, Jonathan, 'How Much Cultural and Religious Pluralism Can Liberalism Tolerate?', in J. Horton (ed.), *Liberalism, Multiculturalism and Toleration* (New York: St. Martin's Press, 1993): 32–49.

Chappell, Zsuzsanna, *Deliberative Democracy* (Houndmills: Palgrave Macmillan, 2012).

Chin, Rita, *The Crisis of Multiculturalism in Europe: A History* (Princeton, NJ: Princeton University Press, 2017).

Christman, John, 'Autonomy in Moral and Political Philosophy', *The Stanford Encyclopedia of Philosophy* (Spring 2018 Edition), Edward N. Zalta (ed.), https://plato.stanford.edu/archives/spr2018/entries/autonomy-moral/.

Claude, I., *National Minorities: An International Problem* (Cambridge, MA: Harvard University Press, 1955).

Cohen, Asher, and Bernard Susser, 'Religious Pressure Will Increase in the Future', *Israel Studies Review*, 27(1) (Summer 2012): 16–20.

Cohen, Jean L., and Cécile Laborde (eds) *Religion, Secularism, and Constitutional Democracy* (New York: Columbia University Press, 2016).

Cohen, Joshua, 'Procedure and Substance in Deliberative Democracy', in James Bohman and William Rehg (eds), *Deliberative Democracy: Essays on Reason and Politics* (Cambridge, MA and London: MIT Press, 1997): 407–438.

'Deliberation and Democratic Legitimacy', in Alan Hamlin and Philip Petit (eds), *The Good Polity: Normative Analysis of the State* (Oxford: Basil Blackwell, 1998): 17–34.

Cohen-Almagor, Raphael, *The Boundaries of Liberty and Tolerance* (Gainesville: University Press of Florida, 1994).

'Between Neutrality and Perfectionism', *The Canadian Journal of Law and Jurisprudence*, 7 (2) (1994): 217–236.

'Disqualification of Lists in Israel (1948–1984): Retrospect and Appraisal', *Law and Philosophy*, 13(1) (1994): 43–95.

'Liberalism, and the Limits of Pluralism', *Terrorism and Political Violence*, 7(2) (1995): 25–48.

'Disqualification of Political Parties in Israel: 1988–1996', *Emory International Law Review*, 11(1) (1997): 67–109.

Speech, Media, and Ethics (Houndmills and New York: Palgrave Macmillan, 2005).

The Scope of Tolerance (London: Routledge, 2006).

'On Compromise and Coercion', *Ratio Juris*, 19(4) (December 2006): 434–455.

'Between Autonomy and State Regulation: J.S. Mill's Elastic Paternalism', *Philosophy*, 87 (4) (October 2012): 557–582.

Confronting the Internet's Dark Side: Moral and Social Responsibility on the Free Highway (New York and Washington, DC: Cambridge University Press and Woodrow Wilson Center Press, 2015).

'JS Mill's Boundaries of Freedom of Expression: A Critique', *Philosophy*, 92(4) (October 2017): 565–596.

'Tolerating Racism and Hate Speech: A Critique of C.E. Baker's "Almost" Absolutism', in Mitja Sardoc (ed.), *The Palgrave Handbook of Toleration* (London: Palgrave, 2021).

Cohen-Almagor, Raphael (ed.), *Challenges to Democracy: Essays in Honour and Memory of Professor Sir Isaiah Berlin* (Aldershot: Ashgate, 2000).

(ed.), *Liberal Democracy and the Limits of Tolerance: Essays in Honor and Memory of Yitzhak Rabin* (Ann Arbor: University of Michigan Press, 2000).

Cohen-Almagor, Raphael, and Marco Zambotti, 'Liberalism, Tolerance and Multiculturalism: The Bounds of Liberal Intervention in Affairs of Minority Cultures', in Krzysztof Wojciechowski and Jan C. Joerden (eds), *Ethical Liberalism in Contemporary Societies* (Frankfurt am Main: Peter Lang, 2009): 79–98.

Convention on the Rights of the Child (1990), www.ohchr.org/en/professionalinterest/pages/crc.aspx.

Craiutu, Aurelian, *Faces of Moderation* (Philadelphia: University of Pennsylvania Press, 2017).

Dalberg-Acton, John Emerich Edward, Baron, *Essays on Freedom and Power* (Boston, MA: Beacon, 1948).

Dallmayr, Fred, and Seyla Benhabib (eds), *The Communicative Ethics Controversy* (Cambridge, MA: MIT Press, 1990).

Daniels, Norman (ed.), *Reading Rawls* (Oxford: Blackwell, 1975).

Darwall, Stephen, 'Two Kinds of Respect', *Ethics*, 88 (1977): 36–49.

'Honor, History, and Relationship: Essays in Second-Personal Ethics II', *Oxford Scholarship Online* (January 2014).

Declaration on the Elimination of all Forms of Intolerance and of Discrimination Based on Religion or Belief (1981), www.ohchr.org/EN/ProfessionalInterest/Pages/ReligionOrBelief.aspx.

Declaration of the Rights of the Child, G.A. res. 1386 (XIV), 14 U.N. GAOR Supp. (No. 16) at 19, U.N. Doc. A/4354 (1959), http://hrlibrary.umn.edu/instree/k1drc.htm.

De Feyter, Koen, and George Pavlakos (eds), *The Tension between Group Rights and Human Rights* (Oxford and Portland, OR: Hart Publishing, 2008).

De Marneffe, Peter, 'Liberalism, Liberty, and Neutrality', *Philosophy & Public Affairs*, 19(3) (1990): 253–274.

De Tocqueville, Alexis, *Democracy in America* (The Pennsylvania State University, 2002), http://seas3.elte.hu/coursematerial/LojkoMiklos/Alexis-de-Tocqueville-Democracy-in-America.pdf.

Deveaux, Monique, *Cultural Pluralism and Dilemmas of Justice* (Ithaca, NY: Cornell University Press, 2000).

Gender and Justice in Multicultural Liberal States (Oxford: Oxford University Press, 2009).

Dewey, John, *Freedom and Culture* (New York: G.P. Putnam's Sons, 1939).

Dobel, Patrick, *Compromise and Political Action* (Savage, MD: Rowman and Littlefield, 1990).

Doppelt, Gerald, 'Is Rawls's Kantian Liberalism Coherent and Defensible?', *Ethics*, 99(4) (1989): 815–851.

Downie, R. S., and Elizabeth Telfer, *Respect for Persons* (London: George Allen and Unwin, 1969).

Dryzek, John S., *Deliberative Democracy and Beyond* (Oxford: Oxford University Press, 2002).

Foundations and Frontiers of Deliberative Governance (Oxford: Oxford University Press, 2012).

Dworkin, Gerald, *The Theory and Practice of Autonomy* (Cambridge: Cambridge University Press, 1988).

Dworkin, Ronald M., *Taking Rights Seriously* (London: Duckworth, 1977).

A Matter of Principle (Oxford: Clarendon Press, 1985).

Sovereign Virtue (Cambridge, MA: Harvard University Press, 2000).

'Terror and the Attack on Civil Liberties', *New York Review of Books*, 50(17) (6 November 2003): 1–20.

Justice for Hedgehogs (Cambridge, MA: Belknap, 2011).

Religion without God (Cambridge, MA: Harvard University Press, 2013).

Dwyer, James G., *Religious Schools v. Children's Rights* (Ithaca, NY: Cornell University Press, 1998).

Eggert, Marion, and Lucian Hölscher, *Religion and Secularity: Transformations and Transfers of Religious Discourses in Europe and Asia* (Leiden: Brill, 2013).

Eisenberg, Avigail, and Jeff Spinner-Halev (eds), *Minorities within Minorities: Equality, Diversity and Rights* (Cambridge: Cambridge University Press, 2009).

Elbedour, Salman, Anthony J. Onwuegbuzie, Corin Cardidine and Hasan Abu-Saad, 'The Effect of Polygamous Marital Structure on Behavioral, Emotional, and Academic Adjustment in Children: A Comprehensive Review of the Literature', *Clinical Child and Family Psychology Review*, 5 (2002): 255–271.

Elster, Jon, *Deliberative Democracy* (Cambridge: Cambridge University Press, 1998).

Ely, John H., *Democracy and Distrust* (Cambridge, MA: Harvard University Press, 1980).

European Convention on Human Rights (1950), www.echr.coe.int/Documents/Convention_ENG.pdf.

European Framework Convention for the Protection of National Minorities (Strasbourg, 1995), www.coe.int/en/web/conventions/full-list/-/conventions/rms/090000168007cdac.

Feinberg, Joel, *Rights, Justice, and the Bounds of Liberty* (Princeton, NJ: Princeton University Press, 1980).

'The Child's Right to an Open Future', in William Aiken and Hugh LaFollette (eds), *Whose Child?* (Totowa, NJ: Rowman & Littlefield, 1980): 124–153.

Offense to Others (New York: Oxford University Press, 1985).

Freedom and Fulfilment: Philosophical Essays (Princeton, NJ: Princeton University Press, 1992).

Festenstein, Matthew, *Negotiating Diversity: Culture, Deliberation, Trust* (Cambridge: Polity, 2005).

Fisher, Roger and William Ury, *Getting to Yes: Negotiating Agreement without Giving in* (London: Random House, 1991).

Fishkin, James S., *Democracy and Deliberation* (New Haven, CT: Yale University Press, 1993).

Fishkin, James S., and Peter Laslett, *Debating Deliberative Democracy* (Oxford: Wiley-Blackwell, 2003).

Fisk, Robert, 'The Crimewave That Shames the World', *The Independent* (7 September 2010), www.independent.co.uk/voices/commentators/fisk/robert-fisk-the-crimewave-that-shames-the-world-2072201.html.

Forst, Rainer, 'A Critical Theory of Multicultural Toleration', in Anthony Simon Laden and David Owen (eds), *Multiculturalism and Political Theory* (Cambridge: Cambridge University Press, 2007): 292–311.

Forsythe, Frederick P. (ed.), *Encyclopedia of Human Rights* (New York: Oxford University Press, 2009).

Fox, Jonathan, *Thou Shalt Have No Other Gods before Me: Why Governments Discriminate against Religious Minorities* (New York: Cambridge University Press, 2020).

Fraser, N. and A. Honneth, *Redistribution or Recognition? A Political–Philosophical Exchange* (London: Verso, 2003).

Galston, W., 'Two Concepts of Liberalism', *Ethics*, 105(3) (1995): 516–535.

Garve, Roland, et al., 'Scarification in Sub-Saharan Africa: Social Skin, Remedy and Medical Import', *Tropical Medicine & International Health*, 22(6) (2017), www.researchgate.net/publication/315800896_Scarification_in_sub-Saharan_Africa_Social_skin_remedy_and_medical_import.

Gewirth, Alan, 'The Rationality of Reasonableness', *Synthese*, 57(2) (1983): 225–247.

Ghimire, Dirgha J., William G. Axinn, Scott T. Yabiku and Arland Thornton, 'Social Change, Premarital Nonfamily Experience, and Spouse Choice in an Arranged Marriage Society', *The American Journal of Sociology*, 111(4) (2006): 1181–1218.

Gisbertz, Philipp, 'Overcoming Doctrinal School Thought: A Unifying Approach to Human Dignity', *Ratio Juris*, 31(2) (2018): 196–207.

Grayling, A.C., *Liberty in the Age of Terror: A Defence of Civil Liberties and Enlightenment Values* (New York and London: Bloomsbury, 2010).

Green, Carmen, 'Educational Empowerment: A Child's Right to Attend Public School', *Georgetown Law Journal*, 103 (2015): 1089–1133.

Greenawalt, Kent, *Religious Convictions and Political Choice* (Oxford: Oxford University Press, 1988).

Grill, Kalle, and Jason Hanna (eds), *Routledge Handbook of the Philosophy of Paternalism* (London: Routledge, 2018).

Grimm, Dieter, Alexandra Kemmerer and Christoph Möllers (eds), *Human Dignity in Context* (Munich: Hart, 2018).

Gutmann, Amy, 'Children, Education and Autonomy: A Liberal Argument', *Philosophy and Public Affairs*, 9(4) (1980): 338–358.

Democratic Education (Princeton, NJ: Princeton University Press, 1987).

Identity in Democracy (Princeton, NJ: Princeton University Press, 2003).

Gutmann, Amy, and Dennis F. Thompson, *Democracy and Disagreement* (Cambridge, MA: Belknap Press, 1998).

Why Deliberative Democracy? (Princeton, NJ: Princeton University Press, 2004).

The Spirit of Compromise (Princeton, NJ: Princeton University Press, 2012).

Gutmann, Amy (ed.), *Multiculturalism: Examining the Politics of Recognition* (Princeton, NJ: Princeton University Press, 1994).

(ed.), *Associational Life* (Princeton, NJ: Princeton University Press, 1997).

Guyer, Paul, *Kant's System of Nature and Freedom* (Oxford: Clarendon Press, 2005).

Habermas, Jürgen, *Theory of Communicative Action* (Cambridge: Polity, 1986).

The Structural Transformations of the Public Sphere (Cambridge: MIT Press, 1989).

Moral Consciousness and Communicative Action (Cambridge, MA: MIT Press, 1990).

'Reconciliation through the Public Use of Reason: Remarks on John Rawls's Political Liberalism', *Journal of Philosophy*, 92 (1995): 109–131.

Between Facts and Norms (Cambridge: Polity, 1996).

'Equal Treatment of Cultures and the Limits of Postmodern Liberalism', *Journal of Political Philosophy*, 13(1): (2005): 1–28.

'Religion in the Public Sphere', *The European Journal of Philosophy*, 14(1) (2006): 1–25.

Hamlin, Alan, and Philip Petit (eds), *The Good Polity* (Oxford: Blackwell, 1989).

Hardy, Henry (ed.), *The Crooked Timber of Humanity* (London: John Murray, 1990).

Harvard Law Review Note, 'Developments in the Law: Religion and the State', *Harvard Law Review*, 100(7) (May 1987): 1606–1781.

Hassoun, Nicole, 'Coercion, Legitimacy and Global Justice', *Carnegie Mellon University Research Showcase* (2009).

Hassouneh-Phillips, Dena, 'Polygamy and Wife Abuse: A Qualitative Study of Muslim Women in America', *Health Care for Women International*, 22 (2001): 735–748.

Hawley, John Stratton (ed.), *Sati, the Blessing and the Curse: The Burning of Wives in India* (New York: Oxford University Press, 1994).

Hayek, F.A., 'Individual and Collective Aims', in S. Mendus and David Edwards (eds), *On Toleration* (Oxford: Clarendon Press, 1987): 35–47.

Henderson, Carol E., *Scarring the Black Body: Race and Representation in African American Literature* (Columbia: University of Missouri Press, 2002).

Henkin, Louis, *The Age of Rights* (New York: Columbia University Press, 1990).

Hertting, Nils, and Clarissa Kugelberg (eds), *Local Participatory Governance and Representative Democracy* (London: Routledge, 2017).

Heyd, David (ed.), *Toleration: An Elusive Virtue* (Princeton, NJ: Princeton University Press, 1996).

Heyman, Steven J., *Free Speech and Human Dignity* (New Haven, CT: Yale University Press, 2008).

Hill, Thomas, *Autonomy and Self-respect* (Cambridge: Cambridge University Press, 1991).

Hobhouse, L.T., *Liberalism* (London: Oxford University Press, 1945).

Hodson, John D., 'Mill, Paternalism and Slavery', *Analysis*, 41 (1981): 60–62.

Holt v. Hobbs, 574 US 352, 135 S. Ct. 853 (2015).

Horton, John (ed.), *Liberalism, Multiculturalism and Toleration* (New York: St. Martin's Press, 1993).

Horton, John, and Susan Mendus (eds), *Toleration, Identity and Difference* (Houndmills: Macmillan, 1999).

Hurka, Thomas, *Perfectionism* (Oxford: Oxford University Press, 1993).

Hutler, Brian, 'Compromise and Religious Freedom', *Law and Philosophy*, 39 (2020): 177–202.

Idriss, Mohammad M., and Tahir Abbas (eds), *Honour, Violence, Women and Islam* (London: Routledge, 2010).

International Convention for Elimination of All Forms of Discrimination against Women (1967), www.ipu.org/PDF/publications/cedaw_en.pdf.

International Covenant on Civil and Political Rights (1966), www.ohchr.org/en/professiona linterest/pages/ccpr.aspx.

International Covenant of Economic, Social and Cultural Rights (1966), www.ohchr.org/EN/ Professionalinterest/Pages/CESCR.aspx.

Jacobs, Allan J., and Kavita Shah Arora, 'When May Government Interfere with Religious Practices to Protect the Health and Safety of Children?', *Ethics, Medicine and Public Health*, 5 (April–June 2018): 86–93.

Jacobs, Louis, *The Book of Jewish Belief* (Springfield, NJ: Behrman House Inc, 1984).

Jafri, Amir H., *Honour Killing* (Oxford: Oxford University Press, 2008).

Jaggar, Alison M., *Feminist Politics and Human Nature* (Totowa, NJ: Rowman & Allanheld, 1983).

Johnson, J., 'Why Respect Culture?', *American Journal of Political Science*, 44(3) (2000): 405–418.

Jones, Peter, 'Group Rights', in *Stanford Encyclopedia of Philosophy* (17 March 2016), https:// plato.stanford.edu/entries/rights-group/.

Jones, Peter, and Ian O'Flynn, 'Can a Compromise Be Fair?', *Politics, Philosophy & Economics*, 12(2) (2012): 115–135.

Joppke, Christian, 'The Retreat of Multiculturalism in the Liberal State: Theory and Policy', *British Journal of Sociology*, 55(2) (2004): 237–257.

Is Multiculturalism Dead? Crisis and Persistence in the Constitutional State (Cambridge: Polity, 2016).

Joppke, Christian, and Steven Lukes (eds), *Multicultural Questions* (Oxford: Oxford University Press, 1999).

Jost, Lawrence, and Julian Wuerth (eds), *Perfecting Virtue: New Essays on Kantian Ethics and Virtue Ethics* (Cambridge: Cambridge University Press, 2011).

Kant, Immanuel, *Kant on Education: Ueber Pädagogik* (Boston: D.C. Health & Co. Publishers 1900).

Foundations of the Metaphysics of Morals and What Is Enlightenment? (Indianapolis: Bobbs-Merrill Educational Publishing, 1959).

Foundations of the Metaphysics of Morals, trans. Lewis White Beck, with critical essays (Indianapolis: Bobbs-Merrill Educational Publishers, 1969).

Critique of Pure Reason (1781) (Jonathan Bennett, 2017), www.earlymoderntexts.com/assets/ pdfs/kant1781part1.pdf.

Toward Perpetual Peace: A Philosophical Sketch (Jonathan Bennett, 2017), www.earlymo- derntexts.com/assets/pdfs/kant1795_1.pdf.

Kappel, Klemens, 'How Moral Disagreement May Ground Principled Moral Compromise', *Politics, Philosophy and Economics*, 17(1) (2017): 75–96.

Katz, Jacob, *Exclusiveness and Tolerance* (New York: Oxford University Press, 1961).

Kelly, Paul (ed.), *Multiculturalism Reconsidered: Culture and Equality and Its Critics* (Cambridge: Polity Press, 2002).

Kern, Soeren, 'The Netherlands to Abandon Multiculturalism', Gatestone Institute (23 June 2011), www.gatestoneinstitute.org/2219/netherlands-abandons-multiculturalism.

Knight, Jack (ed.), *Nomos LIX: Compromise* (New York: New York University Press, 2018).

Koopmans, Ruud, *Contested Citizenship: Immigration and Cultural Diversity in Europe* (Minneapolis: University of Minnesota Press, 2005).

Kühler, Michael, 'Can a Value-Neutral Liberal State Still Be Tolerant?', *Critical Review of International Social and Political Philosophy* (2019), https://doi.org/10.1080/13698230 .2019.1616878.

Kukathas, Chandran, 'Cultural Toleration', *Nomos*, 39 (1997): 69–104.

The Liberal Archipelago: A Theory of Diversity and Freedom (Oxford: Oxford University Press, 2003).

'Is Multiculturalism Bad for Democracy?', www.academia.edu/12540718/Is_multicultural ism_bad_for_democracy.

Kukathas, Chandran, and Philip Pettit, *Rawls: A Theory of Justice and Its Critics* (Cambridge: Polity Press, 1990).

Kymlicka, Will, *Liberalism, Community, and Culture* (Oxford: Clarendon Press, 1989).

'Federalismo, Nacionalismo y Multiculturalismo', *Revista Internacional de Filosofia Politica*, 7 (1996): 20–54.

'Do We Need a Liberal Theory of Minority Rights? Reply to Carens, Young, Parekh and Forst', *Constellations*, 4(1) (1997): 72–87.

Multicultural Citizenship: A Liberal Theory of Minority (Oxford: Oxford University Press, 2000).

Alternative Conceptions of Civil Society (Princeton, NJ: Princeton University Press, 2002).

'Liberal Theories of Multiculturalism', in Lukas Meyer, Stanley Paulson and Thomas Pogge (eds), *Rights, Culture and the Law* (Oxford: Oxford University Press, 2003): 229–250.

'The New Debate on Minority Rights (and Postscript)', in Anthony Simon Laden and David Owen (eds), *Multiculturalism and Political Theory* (Cambridge: Cambridge University Press, 2007): 25–59.

'The Internationalization of Minority Rights', *International Journal of Constitutional Law*, 6(1) (2008): 1–32.

'The Rise and Fall of Multiculturalism? New debates on Inclusion and Accommodation in Diverse Societies', *International Social Science Journal* (November 2010): 97.

'The Essential Critique of Multiculturalism: Theories, Policies, Ethos', in Varun Uberoi and Tariq Modood (eds), *Multiculturalism Rethought: Interpretations, Dilemmas and New Directions* (Edinburgh: Edinburgh University Press, 2015): 209–249.

'Liberal Multiculturalism as a Political Theory of State-Minority Relations', *Political Theory* (2017): https://doi.org/10.1177/0090591717696021.

Kymlicka, Will, and Raphael Cohen-Almagor, 'Democracy and Multiculturalism', in R. Cohen-Almagor (ed.), *Challenges to Democracy*: 89–118. Reprinted as 'Ethnocultural Minorities in Liberal Democracies', in Maria Baghramian and Attracta Ingram (eds), *Pluralism: The Philosophy and Politics of Diversity* (London: Routledge, 2000): 228–250.

Kymlicka, Will, and Ruth Rubio Marin, 'Liberalism and Minority Rights: An Interview', *Ratio Juris*, 12(2) (1999): 133–152.

Kymlicka, Will (ed.) *The Rights of Minority Cultures* (Oxford: Oxford University Press, 1997).

Kymlicka, Will, and Bashir Bashir (eds), *The Politics of Reconciliation in Multicultural Societies* (New York: Oxford University Press, 2010).

Laden, Anthony Simon, and David Owen (eds), *Multiculturalism and Political Theory* (Cambridge: Cambridge University Press, 2007).

Laforest, Guy, and Roger Gibbins (eds), *Beyond the Impasse: Toward Reconciliation* (Montreal: Institute for Research in Public Policy, 1998).

Laski, Harold J., *The Rise of European Liberalism: An Essay in Interpretation* (London: Unwin Books, 1962).

Laslett, P., and J. Fishkin (eds), *Philosophy, Politics, and Society* (Oxford: Basil Blackwell, 1979).

Leiter, Brian, *Why Tolerate Religion?* (Princeton, NJ: Princeton University Press, 2014).

Levey, Geoffrey Brahm, 'Equality, Autonomy, and Cultural Rights', *Political Theory*, 25(2) (April 1997): 215–248.

'Liberal Autonomy as a Pluralistic Value', *The Monist*, 95(1) (2012): 103–126.

Levey, Geoffrey Brahm, and Tariq Modood (eds), *Secularism, Religion and Multicultural Citizenship* (Cambridge: Cambridge University Press, 2009).

Levy, Jacob T., *The Multiculturalism of Fear* (Oxford: Oxford University Press, 2000).

Rationalism, Pluralism and Freedom (Oxford: Oxford University Press, 2014).

Lipjhart, Arend, *Patterns of Democracy: Government Forms and Performance in Thirty-Six Countries* (New Haven, CT: Yale University Press, 2012).

Ludbrook, Robert, 'The Child's Ability to Bodily Integrity', *Current Issues in Criminal Justice*, 7(2) (1995): 123–132.

Lukic, Reneo, and Michael Brint (eds), *Culture, Politics and Nationalism in the Age of Globalization* (Aldershot: Ashgate, 2018).

Macedo, Stephen, 'Liberal Civic Education and Religious Fundamentalism: The Case of God v. John Rawls?', *Ethics*, 105 (April 1995): 468–496.

Deliberative Politics: Essays on Democracy and Disagreement (New York: Oxford University Press, 1999).

Diversity and Distrust: Civic Education in a Multicultural Democracy (Cambridge, MA: Harvard University Press, 2000).

Macpherson, C.B., *The Real World of Democracy* (Oxford: Clarendon Press, 1972).

Democratic Theory: Essays in Retrieval (Oxford: Clarendon Press, 1973).

The Life and Times of Liberal Democracy (Oxford: Oxford University Press, 1977).

Maffettone, Sebastiano, 'Political Liberalism: Reasonableness and Democratic Practice', *Philosophy and Social Criticism*, 30(5–6) (2004): 541–577.

Mahajan, Gurpreet, 'Multiculturalism in the Age of Terror: Confronting the Challenges', *Political Studies Review*, 5 (2007): 317–336.

Accommodating Diversity (Oxford: Oxford University Press, 2011).

Maimonides, Moses, A *Guide for the Perplexed* (1186), https://oll.libertyfund.org/titles/maimonides-a-guide-for-the-perplexed.

Maimonides, *Laws of Kings and Wars*, http://halakhah.com/rst/kingsandwars.pdf.

Malik, Kenan, 'The Failure of Multiculturalism', *Foreign Affairs*, (March/April 2015), www.foreignaffairs.com/articles/western-europe/failure-multiculturalism.

Mangini, Michele, 'Toward a Theory of Reasonableness', *Ratio Juris*, 31(2) (2018): 208–230.

March, Andrew F., 'Liberal Citizenship and the Search for an Overlapping Consensus: The Case of Muslim Minorities', *Philosophy and Public Affairs*, 34(4) (2006): 373–402.

Margalit, Avishai, *On Compromise and Rotten Compromise* (Princeton, NJ: Princeton University Press, 2010).

'Indecent Compromise, Decent Peace', *The Tanner Lectures on Human Values*, Stanford University (4–5 May 2005), https://tannerlectures.utah.edu/_documents/a-to-z/m/Margalit_2006.pdf.

Margalit, Avishai and Moshe Halbertal, 'Liberalism and the Right to Culture', *Social Research*, 61(3) (1994): 491–510.

Maris, Cees, and Sawitri Saharso, 'Honour Killing: A Reflection on Gender, Culture and Violence', *Netherlands Journal of Social Sciences*, 37(1) (2001): 52–73.

May, Simon Cabulea, 'Principled Compromise and the Abortion Controversy', *Philosophy & Public Affairs*, 33(4) (September 2005): 317–348.

'Moral Compromise, Civic Friendship, and Political Reconciliation', *Critical Review of International Social and Political Philosophy*, 14(5) (2011): 581–602.

McBride, Cillian, 'Deliberative Democracy and the Politics of Recognition', *Political Studies*, 53(3) (2005): 497–515.

McCloskey, H.J., 'Coercion: Its Nature and Significance', *Southern Journal of Philosophy*, 18(3) (Fall 1980): 335–351.

McCrudden, Christopher (ed.), *Understanding Human Dignity* (Oxford: Oxford University Press, 2015).

McDonald, Michael, 'Should Communities Have Rights? Reflections on Liberal Individualism', *Canadian Journal of Law and Jurisprudence*, 4(2) (1991): 217–37.

McGhee, Derek, *The End of Multiculturalism* (Maidenhead: Open University Press, 2008).

McMurrin, Sterling M. (ed.), *The Tanner Lectures on Human Values* (Cambridge: Cambridge University Press, 1987).

Menser, Michael, *We Decide! Theories and Cases in Participatory Democracy* (Philadelphia: Temple University Press, 2018).

Meyer, Lukas, Stanley Paulson and Thomas Pogge (eds), *Rights, Culture and the Law* (Oxford: Oxford University Press, 2003).

Mill, J.S., *Dissertations and Discussions* (London: Longmans, Green, Reader & Dyer, 1859). *Principles of Political Economy* (New York: D. Appleton, 1885).

Utilitarianism, Liberty, and Representative Government (London: J.M. Dent, 1948), Everyman's edition.

'The Subjection of Women', in *Three Essays* (Oxford: Oxford University Press, 1975): 427–548.

Miller, David (ed.), *The Blackwell Encyclopaedia of Political Thought* (Oxford: Basil Blackwell, 1987).

Miller, David, 'Democracy's Domain', *Philosophy and Public Affairs*, 37 (2009): 201–228.

'Why Immigration Controls Are Not Coercive: A Reply to Arash Abizadeh', *Political Theory*, 38 (2010): 111–120.

Millum, Joseph, 'The Foundation of the Child's Right to an Open Future', *Journal of Social Philosophy*, 45(4) (2014): 522–538.

Mnookin, Robert, *Bargaining with the Devil* (New York: Simon and Schuster, 2011).

Modood, Tariq, 'Moderate Secularism, Religion as Identity and Respect for Religion', *Political Quarterly*, 81(1) (2010): 4–14.

Multiculturalism (Cambridge: Polity, 2013).

Essays on Secularism and Multiculturalism (London: ECPR Press, 2019).

Moore, Margaret, 'On Reasonableness', *Journal of Applied Philosophy*, 13(2) (1996): 167–178.

Moore, Peter (ed.), *Man, Woman, and Priesthood* (London: Society for Promoting Christian Knowledge, 1978).

Morgenbesser, Sidney, Patrick Suppes and Morton White (eds), *Philosophy, Science, and Method: Essays in Honor of Ernest Nagel* (New York: St. Martin's Press, 1969).

Morley, John, *On Compromise* (London: Macmillan, 1923).

Multani v. Commission scolaire Marguerite-Bourgeoys, [2006] 1 S.C.R. 256, 2006 SCC 6.

Murray, Jane, Beth Blue Swadener and Kylie Smith (eds), *The Routledge International Handbook of Young Children's Rights* (London: Routledge, 2019).

Narasimhan, Sakuntala, *Sati: Widow Burning in India* (New York: Anchor, 1998).

Narveson, Jan, 'Collective Rights?', *Canadian Journal of Law & Jurisprudence*, 4(2) (1991): 329–345.

Nino, C.S., *The Constitution of Deliberative Democracy* (New Haven, CT: Yale University Press, 1996).

Nozick, Robert, 'Coercion', in Sidney Morgenbesser, Patrick Suppes and Morton White (eds), *Philosophy, Science, and Method: Essays in Honor of Ernest Nagel* (New York: St. Martin's Press, 1969): 440–472.

Anarchy, State and Utopia (New York: Basic Books, 1974).

Nussbaum, Martha C., *Sex and Social Justice* (New York: Oxford University Press, 2000).
  Women and Human Development: The Capabilities Approach (Cambridge: Cambridge University Press, 2000).
Nye, Andrea, *Feminist Theory and the Philosophies of Man* (London: Croom Helm, 1988).
Okin, Susan Moller, 'Feminism, Women's Human Rights, and Cultural Differences', *Hypatia*, 13(2) (Spring 1998): 32–52.
  'Feminism and Multiculturalism: Some Tensions', *Ethics*, 108 (1998): 661–684.
  'Is Multiculturalism Bad for Women?', in Joshua Cohen, Matthew Howard and Martha C. Nussbaum (eds), *Is Multiculturalism Bad for Women?* (Princeton, NJ: Princeton University Press, 1999): 9–24.
  '"Mistresses of Their Own Destiny": Group Rights, Gender, and Realistic Rights of Exit', *Ethics*, 112(2) (2002): 205–230.
Outram, Dorinda, *The Enlightenment* (Cambridge: Cambridge University Press, 2019).
Parekh, Bhikhu, 'Dilemmas of a Multicultural Theory of Citizenship', *Constellations*, 4(1) (1997): 35–87.
  Rethinking Multiculturalism (Houndmills: Palgrave, 2000).
  Debating India: Essays on Indian Political Discourse (Oxford University Press, 2016).
  Ethnocentric Political Theory (Cham: Palgrave, 2019).
Parkinson, John, and Jane Mansbridge (eds), *Deliberative Systems* (Cambridge: Cambridge University Press, 2012).
Passerin, Maurizio, *Democracy as Public Deliberation* (Piscataway, NJ: Transaction Publishers, 2006).
Pateman, Carole, *Participation and Democratic Theory* (Cambridge: Cambridge University Press, 1970).
Patten, Alan, 'Liberal Neutrality: A Reinterpretation and Defense', *Journal of Political Philosophy*, 20(3) (2012): 249–272.
  Equal Recognition: The Moral Foundations of Minority Rights (Princeton, NJ: Princeton University Press, 2014).
Pearlman, Wendy, and Boaz Atzili, *Triadic Coercion* (New York: Columbia University Press, 2018).
Pennock, J. Roland, and John W. Chapman (eds), *Nomos XIV: Coercion* (Chicago and New York: Aldine – Atherton, Inc., 1972).
  (eds), *Nomos XXI: Compromise in Ethics, Law and Politics* (New York: New York University Press, 1979).
Phillips, Anne, *Multiculturalism without Culture* (Princeton, NJ: Princeton University Press, 2007).
  'What Makes Culture Special?', *Political Theory*, 46(1) (2018): 92–98.
Popper, Karl R., *The Open Society and Its Enemies* (London: Routledge & Kegan Paul, 1962), Vols 1, 2.
Poulter, Sebastian, 'Ethnic Minority Customs, English Law, and Human Rights', *International and Comparative Law Quarterly*, 36(3) (1987): 589–615.
Raday, Frances, 'Self-Determination and Minority Rights', *Fordham International Law Journal*, 26(3) (2002): 453–499.
  'Culture, Religion and Gender', *International Journal of Constitutional Law*, 1 (2003): 663–715.
  'Sacralising the Patriarchal Family in the Monotheistic Religions: "To No Form of Religion Is Woman Indebted for One Impulse of Freedom"', *International Journal of Law in Context*, 8(2) (2012): 211–230.

Rauscher, Frederick, 'Kant's Social and Political Philosophy', *Stanford Encyclopedia of Philosophy* (2016), https://plato.stanford.edu/entries/kant-social-political/.

Rawls, John, *A Theory of Justice* (Oxford: Oxford University Press, [1971] 1986).

'Fairness to Goodness', *Philosophical Review*, 84 (1975): 536–554.

'A Well-Ordered Society', in P. Laslett and J. Fishkin, (eds), *Philosophy, Politics, and Society* (Oxford: Basil Blackwell, 1979): 6–20.

'Representation of Freedom and Equality', *Journal of Philosophy*, 77(9) (1980): 535–554.

'Justice as Fairness: Political not Metaphysical', *Philosophy & Public Affairs*, 14(3) (1985): 223–251.

'The Idea of an Overlapping Consensus', *Oxford Journal of Legal Studies*, 7(1) (1987): 1–25.

'The Priority of Right and Ideas of the Good', *Philosophy & Public Affairs*, 17(4) (1988): 251–276.

'The Domain of the Political and Overlapping Consensus', *New York University Law Review*, 64(2) (May 1989): 233–255.

Political Liberalism (New York: Columbia University Press, 1993).

The Law of Peoples (Cambridge, MA: Harvard University Press, 2002).

Raz, Joesph, *The Morality of Freedom* (Oxford: Clarendon Press, 1986).

'Multiculturalism: A Liberal Perspective', *Dissent*, 4 (Winter 1994): 67–79.

Ethics in the Public Domain: Essays in the Morality of Law and Politics (Oxford: Clarendon Press, 1995).

'Multiculturalism', *Ratio Juris*, 11(3) (1998): 197.

Value, Respect, and Attachment (Cambridge: Cambridge University Press, 2001).

Réaume, Denise G., 'Justice between Cultures: Autonomy and the Protection of Cultural Affiliation', *UBC Law Review*, 29(1) (1995): 117–141.

Reich, Rob, *Bridging Liberalism and Multiculturalism in American Education* (Chicago: University of Chicago Press, 2002).

Reingold, Rebecca B., and Lawrence O. Gostin, 'Women's Health and Abortion Rights: Whole Woman's Health v Hellerstedt', *JAMA*, 316(9) (2016): 925–926.

Reitz, Jeffrey, and Raymond Breton, *Multiculturalism and Social Cohesion: Potentials and Challenges of Diversity* (New York: Springer, 2009).

Richardson, Henry S., *Democratic Autonomy: Public Reasoning about the Ends of Policy* (Oxford: Oxford University Press, 2002).

Rimalt, Noya, 'When Rights Don't Talk: Abortion Law and the Politics of Compromise', *Yale Journal of Law and Feminism*, 28 (2016–2017): 327–379.

Ripstein, Arthur, 'Authority and Coercion', *Philosophy & Public Affairs*, 32(1) (January 2004): 2–35.

Roach, Kent, 'National Security, Multiculturalism and Muslim Minorities', *University of Toronto Legal Studies Series*, Research Paper No. 938451 (October 2006).

Robertson, John A., 'Whole Woman's Health v. Hellerstedt and the Future of Abortion Regulation', *UC Irvine Law Review*, 7 (2017): 623–651.

Roe v. Wade, 410 U.S. 113 (1973).

Rorty, Richard, 'Justice as a Larger Loyalty', *Ethical Perspectives*, 4 (1997): 139–151.

Rosenblatt, Helena, *The Lost History of Liberalism* (Princeton, NJ: Princeton University Press, 2018).

Rostbøll, Christian F., and Theresa Scavenius (eds), *Compromise and Disagreement in Contemporary Political Theory* (London: Routledge, 2017).

Rubinstein, Amnon, 'The Decline, but Not Demise, of Multiculturalism', *Israel Law Review*, 40(3) (Winter 2007): 763–810.

Ruderman, Richard S. and R. Kenneth Godwin, 'Liberalism and Parental Control of Education', *The Review of Politics*, 62(3) (Summer 2000): 503–529.

Ryan, Cheyney C., 'The Normative Concept of Coercion', *Mind*, 89(356) (October 1980): 481–498.

Sacks, Jonathan, 'The Role of Women in Judaism', in Peter Moore (ed.), *Man, Woman, and Priesthood* (London: Society for Promoting Christian Knowledge, 1978): 27–44.

    One People? Tradition, Modernity, and Jewish Unity (Oxford: Littman Library of Jewish Civilization, 2008).

Sassoon, Isaac, *The Status of Women in Jewish Tradition* (New York: Cambridge University Press, 2011).

Saunders, Ben, 'Reformulating Mill's Harm Principle', *Mind*, 125(500) (October 2016): 1005–1032.

Scanlon, Thomas, 'Contractualism and Utilitarianism', in Amartya Kumar Sen and Bernard Arthur Owen Williams (eds), *Utilitarianism and Beyond* (Cambridge: Cambridge University Press, 1982): 103–110.

Scanlon, T.M., *The Difficulty of Tolerance* (Cambridge: Cambridge University Press, 2003).

Scheffler, Samuel, 'Immigration and the Significance of Culture', *Philosophy and Public Affairs*, 35(2) (2007): 93–125.

Schubring, Walther, *The Doctrine of the Jainas: Described after the Old Sources* (Dehli: Motilal Banarsidass, 1962).

Schulze, Kirsten, Martin Stokes and Colm Campbell (eds), *Nationalism, Minorities and Diasporas: Identities and Rights in the Middle East* (London: I.B. Tauris, 1996).

Scruton, Roger, *Kant* (Oxford: Oxford University Press, 1982).

Sen, Amartya Kumar and Bernard Arthur Owen Williams (eds), *Utilitarianism and Beyond* (Cambridge: Cambridge University Press, 1982).

Shachar, Ayelet, 'Group Identity and Women's Rights in Family Law: The Perils of Multicultural Accommodation', *Journal of Political Philosophy*, 6(3) (1998): 285–305.

    Multicultural Jurisdictions: Cultural Differences and Women's Rights (Cambridge: Cambridge University Press, 2001).

    'Feminism and Multiculturalism: Mapping the Terrain', in Anthony Simon Laden and David Owen (eds), *Multiculturalism and Political Theory* (Cambridge: Cambridge University Press, 2007): 115–147.

Shapiro, Ian, 'Democratic Justice and Multicultural Recognition', in Paul Kelly (ed.), *Multiculturalism Reconsidered* (Cambridge: Polity, 2002): 174–183.

Shapiro, Ian, and Russell Hardin (eds), *Political Order: Nomos 38* (New York: New York University Press, 1996).

Shapiro, Ian, and Will Kymlicka (eds), *Ethnicity and Group Rights* (New York: NYU Press, 2000).

Sher, George, *Beyond Neutrality* (Cambridge: Cambridge University Press, 1997).

Smooha, Sammy, 'Types of Democracy and Modes of Conflict-Management in Ethnically Divided Societies', *Nations and Nationalism*, 8(4) (October 2002): 423–431.

    'How Do Western Democracies Cope with the Challenge of Societal Diversity?', *Nations and Nationalism*, 24(2) (2018): 215–236.

Song, Sarah, *Justice, Gender, and the Politics of Multiculturalism* (Cambridge: Cambridge University Press, 2007).

Special Rapporteur on Torture and Other Cruel, Inhuman or Degrading Treatment or Punishment, 'Promotion and Protection of All Human Rights, Civil, Political, Economic, Social and Cultural Rights, Including the Right to Development', Report, UN Human Rights Council (15 January 2008).

Spinner-Halev, Jeff, *Surviving Diversity: Religion and Democratic Citizenship* (Baltimore, MD: Johns Hopkins University Press, 2000).

'Feminism, Multiculturalism, Oppression, and the State', *Ethics*, 112 (October 2001): 84–113.

Squires, Judith, 'Culture, Equality and Diversity', in Paul Kelly (ed.), *Multiculturalism Reconsidered* (Cambridge: Polity, 2002): 114–132.

Stanton, Graham N., and Guy G. Stroumsa (eds), *Tolerance and Intolerance in Early Judaism and Christianity* (Cambridge: Cambridge University Press, 2008).

Stavropoulos, Nicos, 'The Relevance of Coercion: Some Preliminaries', *Ratio Juris*, 22(3) (September 2009): 339–358.

Steiner, Hillel, *Essay on Rights* (Oxford: Blackwell, 1994).

Stephen, J.F., *Liberty, Equality, Fraternity* (Cambridge: Cambridge University Press, 1967).

Stolzenberg, Nomi Maya, '"He Drew a Circle That Shut Me Out": Assimilation, Indoctrination, and the Paradox of a Liberal Education', *Harvard Laq Review*, 106 (1993): 581–667.

Stouffer, Samuel, *Community, Conformity, and Civil Liberties* (New York: Doubleday, 1955).

Sumner, L.W., *The Moral Foundations of Rights* (Oxford: Oxford University Press, 1987).

Tahzib, Collis, 'Perfectionism: Political not Metaphysical', *Philosophy and Public Affairs*, 47 (2) (2019): 144–178.

Tam, Henry, *Communitarianism: A New Agenda for Politics and Citizenship* (Basingstoke: Macmillan, 1998).

Taylor, Charles, *Multiculturalism and the Politics of Recognition* (Princeton, NJ: Princeton University Press, 1992).

'The Politics of Recognition', in Amy Gutmann (ed.), *Multiculturalism: Examining the Politics of Recognition* (Princeton, NJ: Princeton University Press, 1994): 25–73.

Thompson, Dennis F., *Why Deliberative Democracy?* (Princeton, NJ: Princeton University Press, 2004).

Thompson, Edward, *Suttee: A Historical and Philosophical Enquiry into the Hindu Rite of Widow-Burning* (New York: Houghton Mifflin, 1928).

Tierney, Stephen (ed.), *Accommodating Cultural Diversity* (Aldershot: Ashgate, 2007).

Triandafyllidou, Anna, and Tariq Modood (eds), *The Problem of Religious Diversity* (Edinburgh: Edinburgh University Press, 2017).

Tully, James, *Strange Multiplicity: Constitutionalism in an Age of Diversity* (Cambridge: Cambridge University Press, 1995).

Turner, G.A., 'Some of the Tribal Marks of the South African Native Races', paper read before the Transvaal Medical Society, *Transvaal Medical Journal* (February 1911): 1–15.

Uberoi, Varun, and Tariq Modood (eds), *Multiculturalism Rethought: Interpretations, Dilemmas and New Directions* (Edinburgh: Edinburgh University Press, 2015).

United Nations Human Rights Council, 'Promotion and Protection of All Human Rights, Civil, Political, Economic, Social and Cultural Rights, Including the Right to Development', *Report of the Special Rapporteur on Torture and Other Cruel, Inhuman or Degrading Treatment or Punishment*, A/HRC/7/3 (15 January 2008).

United Nations Human Rights, Convention on the Rights of the Child, adopted and opened for signature, ratification and accession by General Assembly resolution 44/25 of 20 November 1989 entry into force 2 September 1990, in accordance with article 49, www.ohchr.org/en/professionalinterest/pages/crc.aspx.

Universal Declaration of Human Rights (1948), www.un.org/en/universal-declaration-human-rights/.

Valadez, Jorge, *Deliberative Democracy, Political Legitimacy, and Self-Determination in Multicultural Societies* (London: Routledge, 2018).

Van Dyke, Vernon, 'Collective Rights and Moral Rights: Problems in Liberal-Democratic Thought', *Journal of Politics*, 44 (1982): 21–40.

Vink, Maarten P., 'Dutch "Multiculturalism" beyond the Pillarisation Myth', *Political Studies Review*, 5(3) (2007): 337–350.

Vitikainen, Annamari. *The Limits of Liberal Multiculturalism: Towards an Individuated Approach to Cultural Diversity* (Houndmills: Palgrave, 2015).

Waldron, Jeremy, *The Harm in Hate Speech* (Cambridge, MA: Harvard University Press, 2012).

Walzer, Michael, 'The Moral Standing of States', *Philosophy and Public Affairs*, 9(2) (1980): 209–229.

  Spheres of Justice: A Defence of Pluralism and Equality (New York: Basic Books, 1983).

Weinstock, Daniel, 'On the Possibility of Principled Moral Compromise', *Critical Review of International Social and Political Philosophy*, 16(4) (2013): 537–556.

Wertheimer, Alan, *Coercion* (Princeton, NJ: Princeton University Press, 1987).

West, G.C., 'Liberty and Education: J.S. Mill's Dilemma', *Philosophy*, 40 (April 1965): 129–142.

Whole Woman's Health v. Hellerstedt, 136 S. Ct. 2292 (2016).

Wilhelm, Cornelia (ed.), *Migration, Memory, and Diversity: Germany from 1945 to the Present* (New York: Berghahn Books, 2018).

Williams, Raymond, *Culture and Society 1780–1950* (Harmondsworth: Penguin, 1971).

Wodak, Ruth, *The Politics of Fear* (London: Sage, 2015).

Wojciechowski, Krzysztof, and Jan C. Joerden (eds), *Ethical Liberalism in Contemporary Societies* (Frankfurt am Main: Peter Lang, 2009).Wolff, Robert Paul (ed.), *Kant* (London: Macmillan, 1968).

Young, Iris M., *Justice and the Politics of Difference* (Princeton, NJ: Princeton University Press, 1990).

  Inclusion and Democracy (Oxford: Oxford University Press, 2000).

Young, Shaun (ed.), *Reasonableness in Liberal Political Philosophy* (London: Routledge, 2008).

Ziegler, Ruvi, 'Asylum Seekers Are Now Political Pawns in a Disharmonious EU', *The Conversation* (13 June 2018), https://theconversation.com/asylum-seekers-are-now-polit ical-pawns-in-a-disharmonious-eu-98260.

Zittel, Thomas, and Dieter Fuchs (eds), *Participatory Democracy and Political Participation* (London: Routledge, 2006).

AMISH

Aronson Fontes, Lisa, and Jeanette Harder, 'Working with Amish Families on Child Abuse and Neglect', *Psychology Today* (18 May 2019).

Cates, James A., *Serving the Amish* (Baltimore, MD: Johns Hopkins University Press, 2014).

Choy, James P., 'Religion and the Family: The Case of the Amish', *The Warwick Economics Research Paper Series (TWERPS)* (2016).

Clark, Mindy Starns, *Plain Answers about the Amish Life* (Eugene, OR: Harvest House publishers, 2011).

Dewalt, Mark W., *Amish Education in the United States and Canada* (Lanham, MD: Rowman and Littlefield Education, 2006).

Fischel, William A., 'Do Amish One-Room Schools Make the Grade? The Dubious Data of "Wisconsin v Yoder"', *University of Chicago Law Review*, 79(1) (2012): 107–129.

Furlong, Saloma Miller, *Why I Left the Amish: A Memoir* (East Lansing: Michigan State University Press, 2011).

Bonnet Strings (Harrisonburg, VA: Herald Press, 2014).

Garrett, Ruth Irene, *Crossing Over: One Woman's Escape from Amish Life* (New York: HarperOne, 2003).

Gingerich, Emma, *Runaway Amish Girl: The Great Escape* (Progressive Rising Phoenix Press, 2014).

Griffin, Misty, *Tears of the Silenced: A True Crime and an American Tragedy; Severe Child Abuse and Leaving the Amish* (La Vergne: Mango, 2018).

Hostetler, John A., 'The Amish and the Law: A Religious Minority and Its Legal Encounters', *Washington and Lee Law Review*, 41(1) (Winter 1984): 33–47.

Amish Society (Baltimore, MD: Johns Hopkins University Press, 1993).

Johnson-Weiner, Karen, *Train Up a Child: Old Order Amish and Mennonite Schools* (Baltimore, MD: Johns Hopkins University Press, 2007).

Knudsen, Stephen T., 'The Education of the Amish Child', *California Law Review*, 62(5) (1974): 1506–1531.

Kraybill, Donald B., Karen M. Johnson-Weiner and Steven M. Nolt, *The Amish* (Baltimore, MD: Johns Hopkins University Press, 2013).

Lavoie, Jennifer, 'Under Grace: Legal Isolation and the Children of the Old Order Amish', *The Modern American* (Spring 2006): 32–34.

Mazie, Steven V., 'Consenting Adults?: Amish Rumspringa and the Quandary of Exit in Liberalism', *Perspectives on Politics*, 3(4) (2005): 745–757.

McConnell, David L., and Charles E. Hurst, 'No "Rip van Winkles" Here: Amish Education since *Wisconsin v. Yoder*', *Anthropology & Education Quarterly*, 37(3) (September 2006): 236–254.

McGuigan, W.M., and S.J. Stephenson, 'A Single-Case Study of Resiliency after Extreme Incest in an Old Order Amish Family', *Journal of Child Sexual Abuse*, 24(5) (2015): 526–537.

Meyers, Thomas J., 'The Old Order Amish: To Remain in the Faith or to Leave', *The Mennonite Quarterly Review*, 68 (1994): 378–395.

Nolt, Steven M., *The Amish* (Baltimore, MD: Johns Hopkins University Press, 2016).

Re G [2012] EWCA Civ 1233, www.familylawweek.co.uk/site.aspx?i=ed101479.

Shachtman, Tom, *Rumspringa: To Be or Not to Be Amish* (New York: North Point Press, 2007).

Shapiro, Ian, 'Democratic Justice and Multicultural Recognition', in Paul Kelly (ed.), *Multiculturalism Reconsidered* (Cambridge: Polity, 2002): 174–183.

Wisconsin v. Yoder 406 U.S. 205 (1972).

FEMALE CIRCUMCISION AND FEMALE GENITAL MUTILATION (FGM)

Abdulcadir, Jasmine, et al., 'Sexual Anatomy and Function in Women with and without Genital Mutilation: A Cross-Sectional Study', *Journal of Sexual Medicine*, 13(2) (2016): 226–237.

Abu Sahlieh, Sami A. Aldeeb, 'To Mutilate in the Name of Jehovah or Allah: Legitimization of Male and Female Circumcision', *Medicine and Law*, 13(4) (1994): 575–622.

Almroth, L., et al., 'Primary Infertility after Genital Mutilation in Girlhood in Sudan: A Case-Control Study', *Lancet*, 366(9483) (2005): 385–391.

American Academy of Pediatrics, Committee on Bioethics, 'Ritual Genital Cutting of Female Minors', *Pediatrics*, 125(5) (May 2010), http://pediatrics.aappublications.org/content/125/5/1088.

Applebaum, Julia, et al., 'Symptoms of Posttraumatic Stress Disorder after Ritual Female Genital Surgery among Bedouin in Israel: Myth or Reality?', *Primary Care Companion to the Journal of Clinical Psychiatry*, 10(6) (2008): 453–456.

Arora, Kavita Shah, and Jacobs Allan J., 'Female Genital Alteration: A Compromise Solution', *Journal of Medical Ethics*, 42(3) (2016): 148–154, www.researchgate.net/publication/280238965_Female_Genital_Alteration_-_A_Compromise_Solution.

Asali A., et al., 'Ritual Female Genital Surgery among Bedouin in Israel', *Archives of Sexual Behavior*, 24(5) (1995): 571–575.

Avalos, Lisa R., 'Female Genital Mutilation and Designer Vaginas in Britain: Crafting an Effective Legal and Policy Framework', *Vanderbilt Journal of Transnational Law* (1 May 2015), www.thefreelibrary.com/Female+genital+mutilation+and+designer+vaginas+in+Britain%3A+crafting. . .-a0421625965.

Baillot, Helen, Nina Murray, Elaine Connelly and Natasha Howard, 'Addressing Female Genital Mutilation in Europe: A Scoping Review of Approaches to Participation, Prevention, Protection, and Provision of Services', *International Journal for Equity in Health*, 17(1) (2018): 21, https://equityhealthj.biomedcentral.com/articles/10.1186/s12939-017-0713-9.

Belmaker, R.H., 'Successful Cultural Change: The Example of Female Circumcision among Israeli Bedouins and Israeli Jews from Ethiopia', *Israel Journal of Psychiatry and Related Sciences*, 49(3) (2012): 178–183.

Boddy, Janice, 'Womb as Oasis: The Symbolic Context of Pharaonic Circumcision in Rural Northern Sudan', *American Ethnologist*, 9(4) (November 1982): 682–698.

Boulware-Miller, Kay, 'Female Circumcision: Challenges to the Practice as a Human Rights Violation', *Harvard Women's Law Journal*, 8 (1985): 155–177.

Broussard, Patricia A., 'The Importation of Female Genital Mutilation to the West: The Cruelest Cut of All', *University of San Francisco Law Review*, 44 (2010): 787–824.

Cardenas, Amanda, 'Female Circumcision: The Road to Change', *Syracuse Journal of International Law and Commerce*, 26 (1999): 291–313.

Cohen-Almagor, Raphael, 'Female Circumcision and Murder for Family Honour among Minorities in Israel', in Kirsten Schulze, Martin Stokes and Colm Campbell (eds), *Nationalism, Minorities and Diasporas: Identities and Rights in the Middle East* (London: I.B. Tauris, 1996): 171–187.

Davar, Binaifer A., 'Women: Female Genital Mutilation', *Texas Journal of Women and the Law*, 6 (1997): 257–271.

Duivenbode, Rosie, and Aasim I. Padela, 'Female Genital Cutting (FGC) and the Cultural Boundaries of Medical Practice', *American Journal of Bioethics*, 19(3) (2019): 3–6.

'The Problem of Female Genital Cutting: Bridging Secular and Islamic Bioethical Perspectives', *Perspectives in Biology and Medicine*, 62(2) (Spring 2019): 273–300.

Earp, Brian D., 'Female Genital Mutilation and Male Circumcision: Toward an Autonomy-Based Ethical Framework', *Medicolegal and Bioethics*, 5 (2015): 89–104.

'Between Moral Relativism and Moral Hypocrisy: Reframing the Debate on "FGM"', *Kennedy Institute of Ethics Journal*, 26(2) (July 2016): 105–144.

'Protecting Children from Medically Unnecessary Genital Cutting without Stigmatizing Women's Bodies: Implications for Sexual Pleasure and Pain', *Archives of Sexual Behavior* (April 2020), www.researchgate.net/publication/337971788_Protecting_chil

dren_from_medically_unnecessary_genital_cutting_without_stigmatizing_women%
27s_bodies_implications_for_sexual_pleasure_and_pain.

'Tolerance for Genital Mutilation: A Review of Moral Justifications', *Current Sexual Health Reports* (2021).

Ergas, Yasmine, 'Regulating Religion beyond Borders: The Case of FGM/C', in Jean L. Cohen, and Cécile Laborde (eds), *Religion, Secularism, and Constitutional Democracy* (New York: Columbia University Press, 2016): 66–88.

European Institute for Gender Equality (EIGE), *Female Genital Mutilation in the European Union and Croatia* (Belgium: EIGE, 2013).

Gillia, Beth Ann, 'Female Genital Mutilation: A Form of Persecution', *New Mexico Law Review*, 27 (1997): 579–614.

Gomaa, Ali, 'The Islamic View on Female Circumcision', *African Journal of Urology*, 19(3) (September 2013): 123–126, www.sciencedirect.com/science/article/pii/S1110570413000313.

Grisaru, Nimrod, Simcha Lezer and R.H. Belmaker, 'Ritual Female Genital Surgery among Ethiopian Jews', *Archives of Sexual Behavior*, 26(2) (1997): 211–215.

Gruenbaum, Ellen, 'Socio-Cultural Dynamics of Female Genital Cutting: Research Findings, Gaps, and Directions', *Culture, Health & Sexuality*, 7(5) (September–October, 2005): 429–441.

Hellsten, S.K., 'Rationalising Circumcision: from Tradition to Fashion, from Public Health to Individual Freedom – Critical Notes on Cultural Persistence of the Practice of Genital Mutilation', *Journal of Medical Ethics*, 30 (2004): 248–253.

Hernlund, Ylva K., and Bettina K. Shell-Duncan (eds), *Transcultural Bodies: Female Genital Cutting in Global Context* (Piscataway, NJ: Rutgers University Press, 2007).

Israel Ministry of Justice, 'Female Genital Mutilation', *Response by the State of Israel to the Questionnaire for Member States Following Human Rights Council Resolution 27/22* (17 December 2014).

Jacobs, Allan J., and Kavita Shah Arora, 'Punishment of Minor Female Genital Ritual Procedures: Is the Perfect the Enemy of the Good?', *Developing World Bioethics*, 17(2) (2017): 134–140.

James, Stephen A., 'Reconciling International Human Rights and Cultural Relativism: The Case of Female Circumcision', *Bioethics*, 8(1) (January 1994): 7–10.

Johnsdotter, Sara, 'Meaning Well while Doing Harm: Compulsory Genital Examinations in Swedish African Girls', *Sexual and Reproductive Health Matters*, 27(2) (2019): 1–13.

Jones-Bibbs, Tiajuana, 'United States Follows Canadian Lead and Takes an Unequivocal Position against Female Genital Mutilation: In re Fauziya Kasinga', *Tulsa Journal of Comparative and International Law*, 4 (1997): 275–304.

Kandala, Ngianga-Bakwin, et al., 'Secular Trends in the Prevalence of Female Genital Mutilation/Cutting among Girls: A Systematic Analysis', *BMJ Global Health*, 3(5) (2018), https://gh.bmj.com/content/3/5/e000549.

Kavita Shah Arora, and Allan J. Jacobs, 'Female Genital Alteration: A Compromise Solution', *Journal of Medical Ethics*, 42(3) (2016): 148–154.

Kelson, Gregory A., 'Female Circumcision in the Modern Age: Should Female Circumcision Now Be Considered Grounds for Asylum in the United States?', *Buffalo Human Rights Law Review*, 4 (1998): 185–209.

Kimani, Samuel, et al., 'Female Genital Mutilation/Cutting: Innovative Training Approach for Nurse-Midwives in High Prevalent Settings', *Obstetrics and Gynecology International* (2018), https://doi.org/10.1155/2018/5043512.

Kutscher, Jens, 'Towards a Solution Concerning Female Genital Mutilation? An Approach from Within According to Islamic Legal Opinions', *Scripta Instituti Donneriani Aboensis*, 23 (2011): 216–236.

Lee, Kirsten, 'Female Genital Mutilation: Medical Aspects and the Rights of Children', *The International Journal of Children's Rights*, 2(1) (1994): 35–44.

Levin, Roy J., 'The Clitoris – An Appraisal of Its Reproductive Function during the Fertile Years: Why Was It, and Still Is, Overlooked in Accounts of Female Sexual Arousal?', *Clinical Anatomy* (5 November 2019).

Leye, Els, et al., 'An Analysis of the Implementation of Laws with Regard to Female Genital Mutilation in Europe', *Crime, Law and Social Change*, 47 (2007): 1–31.

Liu, Joanne A., 'When Law and Culture Clash: Female Genital Mutilation, a Traditional Practice Gaining Recognition as a Global Concern', *New York International Law Review*, 11 (1998): 71–95.

Mackay, R.D. 'Is Female Circumcision Unlawful?', *Criminal Law Review* (November 1983): 717–722.

Mathews, Ben, 'Female Genital Mutilation: Australian Law, Policy and Practical Challenges for Doctors', *Medical Journal of Australia*, 194(3) (2011): 139–141, www.mja.com.au/journal/2011/194/3/female-genital-mutilation-australian-law-policy-and-practical-chal lenges-doctors.

Messito, Carol M., 'Regulating Rites: Legal Responses to Female Genital Mutilation in the West', *In the Public Interest*, 16 (1997–1998): 33–77.

Meston, Cindy M., and David M. Buss, 'Why Humans Have Sex', *Archives of Sexual Behavior*, 36 (2007): 477–507.

Mishori, Ranit, Nicole Warren and Rebecca Reingold, 'Female Genital Mutilation or Cutting', *American Family Physician*, 97(1) (January 2018): 49–52B.

Muthumbi, Jane, Joar Svanemyr, Elisa Scolaro, Marleen Temmerman and Lale Say, 'Female Genital Mutilation: A Literature Review of the Current Status of Legislation and Policies in 27 African Countries and Yemen', *African Journal of Reproductive Health*, 19(3) (2015): 32–40.

Ndikom, Chizoma Millicent, Feyintoluwa Anne Ogungbenro and Olajumoke Adetoun Ojeleye, 'Perception and Practice of Female Genital Cutting among Mothers in Ibadan, Nigeria', *International Journal of Nursing & Health Science*, 4(6) (2017): 71–80.

NHS, 'Female Genital Mutilation (FGM)' (16 June 2016), www.nhs.uk/conditions/female-genital-mutilation-fgm/.

Oosterveld, Valerie, 'Refugee Status for Female Circumcision Fugitives: Building a Canadian Precedent', *University of Toronto Faculty of Law Review*, 51(2) (Spring 1993): 277–303.

Puppo, Vincenzo, 'Female Genital Mutilation and Cutting: An Anatomical Review and Alternative Rites', *Clinical Anatomy*, 30(1) (January 2017): 81–88.

Reisel, Dan, and Sarah. M. Creighton, 'Long Term Health Consequences of Female Genital Mutilation (FGM)', *Maturitas*, 80(1) (2015): 48–51.

Shahvisi, Arianne, and Brian D. Earp, 'The Law and Ethics of Female Genital Cutting', in S. Creighton and L.-M. Liao (eds) *Female Genital Cosmetic Surgery: Solution to What Problem?* (Cambridge: Cambridge University Press, 2019), www.researchgate.net/publi cation/322287554_The_law_and_ethics_of_female_genital_cutting.

Smith, Robyn Cenry, 'Female Circumcision: Bringing Women's Perspectives into the International Debate', *Southern California Law Review*, 65 (1992): 2449–2504.

Stern, Amy, 'Female Genital Mutilation: United States Asylum Laws Are in Need of Reform', *American University Journal of Gender and the Law*, 6 (1997): 89–111.

Sussman, Erika, 'Contending with Cultures: An Analysis of the Female Genital Mutilation Act of 1996', *Cornell International Law Journal*, 31 (1998): 193–250.

The Public Policy Advisory Network on Female Genital Surgeries in Africa, 'Seven Things to Know about Female Genital Surgeries in Africa', *Hastings Center Report*, 6 (2012): 19–27.

Turillazzi, E., and V. Fineschi, 'Female Genital Mutilation: The Ethical Impact of the New Italian Law', *Journal of Medical Ethics*, 33 (2007): 98–101.

UNICEF, *The Dynamics of Social Change: Towards the Abandonment of Female Genital Mutilation/Cutting in Five African Countries* (Florence: UNICEF, 2010), www.unicefirc .org/publications/pdf/fgm_insight_eng.pdf.

United Nations Population Fund, 'Female Genital Mutilation (FGM) Frequently Asked Questions' (February 2018), www.unfpa.org/resources/female-genital-mutilation-fgm-fre quently-asked-questions.

Webber, Sarah and Toby Schonfeld, 'Cutting History, Cutting Culture: Female Circumcision in the United States', *American Journal of Bioethics*, 3(2) (2003): 65–66.

Whitehorn, J., O. Ayonrinde and S. Maingay, 'Female Genital Mutilation: Cultural and Psychological Implications', *Sexual & Relationship Therapy*, 17(2) (May 2002): 161–170.

WHO, 'Female Genital Mutilation', *Fact Sheet* (February 2017), www.who.int/mediacentre/ factsheets/fs241/en/.

  Global Strategy to Stop Health-Care Providers from Performing Female Genital Mutilation (Geneva: WHO, 2010).

FRANCE

Adrian, Melanie, *Religious Freedom at Risk: The EU, French Schools, and Why the Veil Was Banned* (Berlin: Springer, 2015).

Akan, Murat, 'Laïcité and Multiculturalism: The Stasi Report in Context', *British Journal of Sociology*, 60(2) (2009): 237–256.

  The Politics of Secularism: Religion, Diversity, and Institutional Change in France and Turkey (New York: Columbia University Press, 2017).

Aldrich, Robert. *Greater France: A History of French Overseas Expansion* (London: Macmillan, 1996).

Algan, Yann, Camille Landais and Claudia Senik, 'Cultural Integration in France', in Yann Algan, Alberto Bisin, Alan Manning and Thierry Verdier (eds), *Cultural Integration of Immigrants in Europe* (Oxford: Oxford Scholarship Online, 2013): 1–32, www .oxfordscholarship.com/view/10.1093/acprof:oso/9780199660094.001.0001/acprof-9780199660094-chapter-2.

Aston, Nigel, *Religion and Revolution in France, 1780–1804* (Houndmills and New York: Palgrave Macmillan, 2000).

Audard, Catherine, 'The French Republic and the Claims of Diversity', in Carol Gould and Pasquale Pasquino (eds), *Cultural Identity and the Nation-State* (New York: Rowman & Littlefield, 2001): 89–108.

Baker, Donald N., and Patrick J. Harrigan (eds), *The Making of Frenchmen: Current Directions in the History of Education in France, 1679–1979* (Ontario: Historical Reflections, 1980), Vol. 7, Nos 2–3.

Bakht, Natasha, 'Veiled Objections: Facing Public Opposition to the Niqab', in Lori G. Beaman (ed.), *Reasonable Accommodation* (Vancouver: UBC Press, 2012): 70–108.

Baubérot, Jean, 'The Evolution of Secularism in France: Between Two Civil Religions', in Linell E. Cady and Elizabeth Shakman Hurd (eds), *Comparative Secularism in a Global Age* (New York: Palgrave Macmillan, 2010): 57–68.

Beauchamps, Marie, 'Perverse Tactics: "Terrorism" and National Identity in France', *Culture, Theory and Critique*, 58(1) (2017): 48–61.

Berenson, Edward, Vincent Duclert and Christophe Prochasson (eds), *The French Republic: History, Values, Debates* (Ithaca, NY: Cornell University Press, 2012).

Berlinerblau, Jacques, Sarah Fainberg and Aurora Nou (eds), *Secularism on the Edge: Rethinking Church–State Relations in the United States, France, and Israel* (Houndmills: Palgrave Macmillan, 2014).

Bogain, Ariane, 'Terrorism and the Discursive Construction of National Identity in France', *National Identities*, 21(3) (2019): 241–265.

Bowen, John R., *Why the French Don't Like Headscarves* (Princeton, NJ: Princeton University Press, 2007).

Brayson, Kimberley, 'Of Bodies and Burkinis: Institutional Islamophobia, Islamic Dress, and the Colonial Condition', *Journal of Law and Society*, 46(1) (2019): 55–82.

Brems, Eva, 'Diversity in the Classroom: The Headscarf Controversy in European Schools', *Peace & Change*, 31(1) (2006): 117–131.

Caporali, Arianna, 'Educational Policies: France', *Population Europe Resource Finder and Archive* (2014), www.perfar.eu/policy/education/france.

Caron, Jean-François, 'Understanding and Interpreting France's National Identity: The Meanings of Being French', *National Identities*, 15(3) (2013): 223–237.

Carvalho, Joao, *Impact of Extreme Right Parties on Immigration Policy: Comparing Britain, France and Italy* (London: Routledge, 2016).

CBN News, 'France's Sarkozy: Multiculturalism Has Failed', *CBN News* (11 February 2011), www.cbn.com/cbnnews/world/2011/february/frances-sarkozy-multiculturalism-has-failed/?mobile=false.

Cesari, Jocelyne, and Sean McLoughlin (eds), *European Muslims and the Secular State* (Abingdon: Routledge, 2016).

Chabal, Emile, 'Writing the French National Narrative in the Twenty-First Century', *The Historical Journal*, 53(2) (2010): 495–516.

   A *Divided Republic: Nation, State and Citizenship in Contemporary France* (Cambridge: Cambridge University Press, 2015).

   'French Political Culture in the 1970s', *Geschichte und Gesellschaft*, 42 (2016): 243–265.

   'From the *Banlieue* to the Burkini: The Many Lives of French Republicanism', *Modern and Contemporary France*, 25(1) (2017): 68–74.

Chabal, Emile (ed.), *France since the 1970s* (London: Bloomsbury, 2015).

Chesler, Phyllis, 'Ban the Burqa? The Argument in Favor', *Middle East Quarterly* (Fall 2010): 33–45.

Chirac, Jacques, president of the French Republic, on respecting the principle of secularism, Paris (17 December 2003). www.jacqueschirac-asso.fr/archives-elysee.fr/elysee/elysee.fr/anglais/speeches_and_documents/2003/fi004414.html.

Choudhury, Nusrat, 'From the Stasi Commission to the European Court of Human Rights: L'Affaire du Foulard and the Challenge of Protecting the Rights of Muslim Girls', *Columbia Journal of Gender and Law*, 16(1) (Winter 2007), www.questia.com/library/journal/1G1-162576736/from-the-stasi-commission-to-the-european-court-of.

Cohen, Jean L. and Cécile Laborde (eds) *Religion, Secularism, and Constitutional Democracy* (New York: Columbia University Press, 2016).

Cohen-Almagor, Raphael, 'Between Speech and Terror: The Charlie Hebdo Affair', The Great War Series (Part II), *The Critique* (7 January 2016).

Corbett, Anne, and Bob Moon (eds), *Education in France: Continuity and Change in the Mitterrand Years 1981–1995* (London: Routledge, 1996).

Davidson, Naomi, *Only Muslim: Embodying Islam in Twentieth-Century France* (Ithaca, NY: Cornell University Press, 2012).

De Clermont-Tonnerre, Stanislas-Marie-Adélaïde, 'Speech on Religious Minorities and Questionable Professions (23 December 1789)', *Liberty, Equality, Fraternity*, http://chnm.gmu.edu/revolution/d/284.

De Tocqueville, Alexis, *The Old Regime and the Revolution* (New York: Harper, 1856), https://soth.alexanderstreet.com/cgi-bin/SOTH/hub.py?type=getdoc&docid=S10019251-D000020.

    Democracy in America (Pennsylvania State University, 2002), http://seas3.elte.hu/coursematerial/LojkoMiklos/Alexis-de-Tocqueville-Democracy-in-America.pdf.

Fanon, Frantz, *A Dying Colonialism* (New York: Grove Press, 1965).

Faucher, Florence, and Laurie Boussaguet, 'The Politics of Symbols: Reflections on the French Government's Framing of the 2015 Terrorist Attacks', *Parliamentary Affairs*, 71(1) (January 2018): 169–195.

Fernando, Mayanthi L., *The Republic Unsettled: Muslim French and the Contradictions of Secularism* (Durham, NC: Duke University Press, 2014).

Fraleigh, Arnold, 'The Algerian War of Independence', *Proceedings of the American Society of International Law at Its Annual Meeting (1921–1969)*, 61 (27–29 April 1967): 6–12.

Fuga, Artan, 'Multiculturalism in France: Evolutions and Challenges', *Eurosphere Working Paper* 12 (2008): 1–9.

Galton, A.H., *Church and State in France 1300–1870* (London: Edward Arnold, 1907).

Ghosh, Ranjan, *Making Sense of the Secular* (New York: Routledge, 2013).

Gordon, Daniel, 'Democracy and the Deferral of Justice in France and the United States', *Yale French Studies*, 100, France/USA: The Cultural Wars (2001): 65–87.

Guardian Editorial, '*The Guardian* View on France's "Burkini Bans": Ugly Politics on the Beach' (24 August 2016), www.theguardian.com/commentisfree/2016/aug/24/the-guardian-view-on-frances-burkini-bans-ugly-politics-on-the-beach.

Guérard de Latour, Sophie, 'Is Multiculturalism Un-French? Towards a Neo-Republican Model of Multiculturalism', in P. Balint and Sophie Guérard de Latour (eds), *Liberal Multiculturalism and the Fair Terms of Integration* (Basingstoke: Palgrave Macmillan, 2013): 139–156.

    'Cultural Insecurity and Political Solidarity: French Republicanism Reconsidered', in Emile Chabal (ed.), *France in an Age of Uncertainty* (London: Bloomsbury, 2014): 245–262.

Guerlac, Othon, 'The Separation of Church and State in France', *Political Science Quarterly*, 23(2) (1908): 259–296.

Guiraudon, Virginie, 'Immigration Policy in France', *Brookings* (1 July 2001), www.brookings.edu/articles/immigration-policy-in-france/.

Gunn, T. Jeremy, 'Religious Freedom and Laicite: A Comparison of the United States and France', *BYU Law Review*, 2 (2004): 419–506.

Haarscher, Guy, 'Secularism, the Veil and "Reasonable Interlocutors": Why France Is Not That Wrong', *Penn State International Law Review*, 28(3) (2010): 367–382.

Hanson, Paul R., 'Political History of the French Revolution since 1989', *Journal of Social History*, 52(3) (Spring 2019): 584–592.

Hazareesingh, Sudhir, *Political Traditions in Modern France* (Oxford: Oxford University Press, 1998).

How the French Think: An Affectionate Portrait of an Intellectual People (London: Penguin, 2016).

Healey, Robert M., 'The Year of the Debre Law', *Journal of Church and State*, 12(2) (Spring 1970): 213–235.

Heine, Sophie, 'The Hijab Controversy and French Republicanism: Critical Analysis and Normative Propositions', *French Politics*, 7(2) (2009): 167–193.

Higonnet, Patrice, 'Sociability, Social Structure, and the French Revolution', *Social Research*, 56(1) (Spring 1989): 99–125.

Horne, Alistair, *A Savage War of Peace: Algeria 1954–1962* (New York: New York Review of Books, 2006).

Hunter-Henin, Myriam, 'Why the French Don't Like the Burqa: Laïcité, National Identity and Religious Freedom', *International Comparative and Law Quarterly*, 61 (August 2012): 1–27.

'Living Together in an Age of Religious Diversity: Lessons from Baby Loup and SAS', *Oxford Journal of Law and Religion*, 4(1) (February 2015): 94–118.

Hurd, Elizabeth Shakman, *The Politics of Secularism in International Relations* (Princeton, NJ: Princeton University Press, 2008).

Idriss, Mohammad M., 'Laïcité and the Banning of the "Hijab" in France', *Legal Studies*, 25 (2) (April 2006): 260–295.

Jennings, Jeremy, 'Citizenship, Republicanism and Multiculturalism in Contemporary France', *British Journal of Political Science*, 30(4) (October 2000): 575–597.

Revolution and the Republic: A History of Political Thought in France since the Eighteenth Century (Oxford: Oxford University Press, 2013).

Joppke, Christian, *Veil: Mirror of Identity* (Cambridge: Polity, 2009).

Kepel, Gilles, 'The Trail of Political Islam', *Open Democracy* (2 July 2002), www .opendemocracy.net/en/articlejspid526debateid5726articleid421/.

Killian, Caitlin, 'The Other Side of the Veil: North African Women in France Respond to the Headscarf Affair', *Gender and Society*, 17(4) (2003): 567–590.

Klausen, Jytte, *The Islamic Challenge: Politics and Religion in Western Europe* (Oxford: Oxford University Press, 2005).

Kofman, Eleonore, Madalina Rogoz and Florence Lévy, *Family Migration Policies in France* (Vienna: International Centre for Migration Policy Development, January 2010).

Kramer, Jane, 'Behind France's Burka Ban', *New Yorker* (15 July 2010), www.newyorker.com/news/news-desk/behind-frances-burka-ban.

Laborde, Cécile, 'Secular Philosophy and Muslim Headscarves in Schools', *The Journal of Political Philosophy*, 13(3) (2005): 305–329.

Critical Republicanism: The Hijab Controversy and Political Philosophy (Oxford: Oxford University Press, 2008).

'Liberal Neutrality, Religion, and the Good', in Jean L. Cohen and Cécile Laborde (eds), *Religion, Secularism, and Constitutional Democracy* (New York: Columbia University Press, 2016): 249–272.

Liberalism's Religion (Cambridge, MA: Harvard University Press, 2017).

Larkin, Maurice, *Church and State after the Dreyfus Affair: The Separation Issue in France* (London: Macmillan, 1974).

Lefebvre, G., *The French Revolution: From Its Origins to 1793* (New York: Columbia University Press, 1962).

Le Grand, Sylvie, 'The Origin of the Concept of Laïcité in Nineteenth Century France', in Marion Eggert and Lucian Hölscher (eds), *Religion and Secularity: Transformations and Transfers of Religious Discourses in Europe and Asia* (Leiden: Brill, 2013): 59–76.

Lévy, Bernard-Henri, 'Why I Support a Ban on Burqas', *Hufflington Post* (25 May 2011).

Linton, Marisa, *Choosing Terror: Virtue, Friendship, and Authenticity in the French Revolution* (Oxford: Oxford University Press, 2015).

Mancini, Susanna, and Michel Rosenfeld (eds), *Constitutional Secularism in an Age of Religious Revival* (New York and Oxford: Oxford University Press, 2014).

May, Paul, 'French Cultural Wars: Public Discourses on Multiculturalism in France (1995–2013)', *Journal of Ethnic and Migration Studies*, 42(8) (2016): 1334–1352.

McGoldrick, Dominic, *Human Rights and Religion: The Islamic Headscarves Debate in Europe* (Oxford and Portland, OR: Hart, 2006).

Miriana Hebbadj v. France, Human Rights Committee, CCPR/C/123/D/2807/2016 (17 October 2018).

Montesquieu, Baron de La Brède et de, *The Spirit of Laws* (Kitchener, ON: Batoche Books, 2001).

Moruzzi, Norma Claire, 'A Problem with Headscarves: Contemporary Complexities of Political and Social Identity', *Political Theory*, 22(4) (1994): 653–672.

Motha, Stewart, 'Veiled Women and the Affect of Religion in Democracy', *Journal of Law & Society*, 34(1) (March 2007): 139–162.

Nanwani, Shaira, 'The Burqa Ban: An Unreasonable Limitation on Religious Freedom or a Justifiable Restriction?', *Emory International Law Review*, 25 (2011): 1431–1475.

O'Brien, Robert, and Bernard Stasi, *The Stasi Report: The Report of the Committee of Reflection on the Application of the Principle of Securlarity in the Republic* (Bufffalo, NY: William S. Hein, 2005).

Pipes, Daniel, 'Niqabs and Burqas as Security Threats', *Lion's Den* (12 October 2018), www .danielpipes.org/blog/2002/03/niqabs-and-burqas-as-security-threats.

Plender, Richard, 'The New French Nationality Law', *The International and Comparative Law Quarterly*, 23(4) (October 1974): 709–747.

Rousseau, Jean-Jacques, *The Social Contract* (Jonathan Bennett, 2017), www .earlymoderntexts.com/assets/pdfs/rousseau1762.pdf.

  Discourse on Inequality (1755) Translated by G.D.H. Cole, www.aub.edu.lb/fas/cvsp/ Documents/DiscourseonInequality.pdf879500092.pdf.

Safran, William, 'State, Nation, National Identity, and Citizenship: France as a Test Case', *International Political Science Review/Revue internationale de science politique*, 12(3) (July 1991): 219–238.

Saunders, David, 'France on the Knife-Edge of Religion: Commemorating the Centenary of the Law of 9 December 1905 on the Separation of Church and State', in G.B. Levey and T. Modood (eds), *Secularism, Religion and Multicultural Citizenship* (Cambridge: Cambridge University Press, 2009): 56–81.

Scott, Joan W., 'The Banning of Islamic Head Scarves in French Public Schools', *French Politics, Culture & Society*, 23(3) (Winter 2005): 106–127.

Shusterman, Noah, *The French Revolution* (New York: Routledge, 2013).

Sonia Yaker v. France, Human Rights Committee, CCPR/C/123/D/2747/2016 (7 December 2018).

Sorenson, L.R., 'Rousseau's Liberalism', *History of Political Thought*, 11(3) (Autumn 1990): 443–466.

Stephen, J.F., *Liberty, Equality, Fraternity* (Cambridge: Cambridge University Press, 1967).

Tackett, Timothy, *The Coming of the Terror in the French Revolution* (Cambridge, MA: Harvard University Press, 2015).

Telegraph, 'Nicolas Sarkozy Declares Multiculturalism Had Failed', *The Telegraph* (11 February 2011), www.telegraph.co.uk/news/worldnews/europe/france/8317497/Nicolas-Sarkozy-declares-multiculturalism-had-failed.html.

Thomas, Elaine R., 'Keeping Identity at a Distance: Explaining France's New Legal Restrictions on the Islamic Headscarf', *Ethnic and Racial Studies*, 29(2) (March 2006): 237–259.

Thomas, Martin (ed.), *The French Colonial Mind: Mental Maps of Empire and Colonial Encounters* (Lincoln: Nebraska University Press, 2011), 2 vols.

Troper, Michel, 'French Secularism or Laïcité', *Cardozo Law Review*, 21 (2000): 1266–1284.

'Sovereignty and Laïcité', *Cardozo Law Review*, 30(6) (2009): 2560–2574.

'Republicanism and Freedom of Religion in France', in Jean L. Cohen, and Cécile Laborde (eds) *Religion, Secularism, and Constitutional Democracy* (New York: Columbia University Press, 2016): 316–337.

United Nations Human Rights Committee, 'France: Banning the Niqab Violated Two Muslim Women's Freedom of Religion – UN Experts' (23 October 2018), www.ohchr .org/EN/NewsEvents/Pages/DisplayNews.aspx?NewsID=23750&LangID=E.

Van Ooijen, H., *Religious Symbols in Public Function: Unveiling State Neutrality* (Utrecht: Utrecht University, 2012).

Vauchez, Stéphanie Hennette, 'Is French *Laïcité* Still Liberal? The Republican Project under Pressure (2004–15)', *Human Rights Law Review*, 17(2) (June 2017): 285–312.

Vickstrom, Erik R., *Pathways and Consequences of Legal Irregularity* (Cham: Springer, 2019).

Wallerstein, Immanuel, 'The French Revolution as a World-Historical Event', *Social Research*, 56(1) (Spring 1989): 33–52.

Weil, Patrick, 'Lifting the Veil', *French Politics, Culture and Society*, 22(3) (2003): 142–149.

'A Nation in Diversity: France, Muslims and the Headscarf', *Open Democracy* (25 March 2004), www.opendemocracy.net/en/article_1811jsp/.

'Why the French Laïcité Is Liberal', *Cardozo Law Review*, 30(6) (2009): 2699–2714.

Wiles, Ellen, 'Headscarves, Human Rights, and Harmonious Multicultural Society: Implications of the French Ban for Interpretations of Equality', *Law & Society Review*, 41(3) (2007): 699–736.

Willms, Johannes, 'France Unveiled: Making Muslims into Citizens?', *Open Democracy* (26 February 2004), www.opendemocracy.net/en/article_1753jsp/.

INDIGENOUS PEOPLE

Brown, Ray A., 'The Indian Problem and the Law', *Yale Law Journal*, 39(3) (1930): 307–331.

Canada (AG) v. Lavell [1974] S.C.R. 1349.

Christofferson, Carla, 'Tribal Courts' Failure to Protect Native American Women: A Reevaluation of the Indian Civil Rights Act', *Yale Law Journal*, 101(1) (1991): 169–185.

Hofer et al. v. Hofer et al. (1970) 13 DLR (3d) 1.

Holder, C.L., and J.J. Corntassel, 'Indigenous Peoples and Multicultural Citizenship: Bridging Collective and Individual Rights', *Human Rights Quarterly*, 24(1) (2002): 126–151.

Janzen, William, *Limits of Liberty: The Experiences of Mennonite, Hutterite, and Doukhobour Communities in Canada* (Toronto: University of Toronto Press, 1990).

Johnson v. M'Intosh, 21 U.S. (8 Wheat.) 543 (1823).

Katz, Yossi and John Lehr, *The Hutterites in Canada and the United States* (Regina, SK: University of Regina Press, 2012).

Newton, Nell Jessup, 'Federal Power over Indians: Its Sources, Scope and Limitations', *University of Pennsylvania Law Review*, 132(2) (1984): 195–288.

Resnik, Judith, 'Dependent Sovereigns: Indian Tribes, States, and the Federal Courts', *University of Chicago Law Review*, 56 (1989): 671–759.

Santa Clara Pueblo v. Martinez 436 US 49 (1978).

Saucedo, Everett, 'Curse of the New Buffalo: A Critique of Tribal Sovereignty in the Post-Igra World', *St. Mary's Law Review on Minority Issues* (Fall, 2000): 71–113.

Shachar, Ayelet, *Multicultural Jurisdictions: Cultural Differences and Women's Rights* (Cambridge: Cambridge University Press, 2001).

Svensson, Frances, 'Liberal Democracy and Group Rights: The Legacy of Individualism and Its Impact on American Indian Tribes', *Political Studies*, 27(3) (1979): 421–439.

Tierney, Stephen (ed.), *Accommodating Cultural Diversity* (Aldershot: Ashgate, 2007).

Tomasi, John, 'Kymlicka, Liberalism, and Respect for Aboriginal Cultures', *Ethics*, 105(3) (1995): 580–603.

Tsosie, Rebecca, 'Reconceptualizing Tribal Rights: Can Self-Determination Be Actualized within the U.S. Constitutional Structure?', *Lewis & Clark Law Review*, 15(4) (2011): 923–950.

Valencia-Weber, Gloria, 'Santa Clara Pueblo V. Martinez: Twenty-Five Years of Disparate Cultural Visions an Essay Introducing the Case for Re-argument before the American Indian Nations Supreme Court', *Kansas Journal of Law & Pubic Policy*, 14(1) (2004), https://papers.ssrn.com/sol3/papers.cfm?abstract_id=2265961.

'Three Stories in One: The Story of Santa Clara Pueblo v. Martinez', in C. Goldberg, K.K. Washburn and P.P. Frickey (eds), *Indian Law Stories* (New York: Thomson Reuters/ Foundation Press 2011), https://papers.ssrn.com/sol3/papers.cfm?abstract_id=2265946.

Wilkins, D.E., '*Johnson v. M'Intosh Revisited:* Through the Eyes of *Mitchel v. United States*', *American Indian Law Review*, 19(1) (1994): 159–181.

Williams Jr., R., 'Sovereignty, Racism, Human Rights: Indian Self-Determination and the Postmodern World Legal System', *Review of Constitutional Studies*, 2 (1995): 146–202.

ISRAEL

Aran, Gideon, *The Smile of the Human Bomb* (Ithaca, NY and London: Cornell University Press, 2018).

Ayyad, Abdelaziz A., *Arab Nationalism and the Palestinians, 1850–1939* (Jerusalem: The Palestinian Academic Society for the Study of International Affairs, 1999).

Barak, Aharon, 'A Constitutional Revolution: Israel's Basic Laws', *Yale Faculty Scholarship Series*, 3697 (1993), https://digitalcommons.law.yale.edu/fss_papers/3697.

Proportionality: Constitutional Rights and Their Limitations (Cambridge: Cambridge University Press, 2012).

Human Dignity (Cambridge: Cambridge University Press, 2015).

Ben-Gurion, David, *The Restored State of Israel* (Tel Aviv: Am Oved, 1975) (Hebrew).

Caplan, Neil, *The Israel–Palestine Conflict: Contested Histories* (Chichester: Wiley-Blackwell, 2010).

Cherlow, Yuval, '"Jewish" and "Democratic": Can They Coexist?', *Justice*, 49 (Fall 2011): 8–9.

Choueiri, Youssef M., *Arab Nationalism – A History: Nation and State in the Arab World* (Oxford: Blackwell, 2001).

Cohen, Asher, and Bernard Susser, 'Religious Pressure Will Increase in the Future', *Israel Studies Review*, 27(1) (Summer 2012): 16–20.

Cohen-Almagor, Raphael, 'Cultural Pluralism and the Israeli Nation-Building Ideology', *International Journal of Middle East Studies*, 27 (1995): 461–484.

'Israeli Democracy, Religion and the Practice of *Halizah* in Jewish Law', *UCLA Women's Law Journal*, 11(1) (Fall/Winter 2000): 45–65.

'Avoiding the Destruction of the Third Temple: Separating State and Religion', in Yossi Goldstein (ed.), *Religion Nationalism: The Struggle for Modern Jewish Identity, an Interdisciplinary Annual* (Ariel: Ariel University, 2014): 170–189.

'Israeli Democracy and the Rights of Its Palestinian Citizens', *Ragion Pratica*, 45 (December 2015): 351–368.

'The Monopoly of Jewish Orthodoxy in Israel and Its Effects on the Governance of Religious Diversity', in Anna Triandafyllidou and Tariq Modood (eds), *The Problem of Religious Diversity* (Edinburgh: Edinburgh University Press, 2017): 250–272.

'Fifty Years of Israeli Occupation', *E-International Relations* (14 October 2017), www.e-ir.info/2017/10/14/fifty-years-of-israeli-occupation/.

'Discrimination against Jewish Women in *Halacha* (Jewish Law) and in Israel', *British Journal of Middle Eastern Studies*, 45(2) (2018): 290–310.

'In Support of Two-State Solution', *Youth Law Journal* (12 November 2018), www.theylj.co.uk/in-support-of-two-state-solution/.

Cohen-Almagor, Raphael, and Amos Guiora, 'Democracy and Security in Israel', in Leonard Weinberg and Elizabeth Francis (eds), *Democracy and Security: A Handbook* (London and New York: Routledge, 2020).

Cohen-Almagor, Raphael, and Mohammed S. Wattad, 'The Legal Status of Israeli-Arabs/Palestinians', *GNLU Law & Society Review*, 1 (March 2019): 1–28.

Cohen-Almagor, Raphael (ed.), *Israeli Democracy at the Crossroads* (London: Routledge, 2005).

(ed.), *Israeli Institutions at the Crossroads* (London: Routledge, 2005).

Cohen-Almagor, Raphael, Ori Arbel-Ganz and Asa Kasher (eds), *Public Responsibility in Israel* (Tel Aviv and Jerusalem: Hakibbutz Hameuchad and Mishkanot Shaananim, 2012) (Hebrew).

Dror, Yehezkel, *Israeli Statecraft: National Security Challenges and Responses* (London and New York: Routlege, 2011).

Feldheim, Miriam, 'Balancing Women's Rights and Religious Rights: The Issue of Bus Segregation', *Shofar*, 31(2) (2013): 73–94.

Firro, Kais M., *The Druzes in the Jewish State: A Brief History* (Leiden: Brill, 1999).

'Reshaping Druze Particularism in Israel', *Journal of Palestine Studies*, 30(3) (Spring 2001): 40–53.

Freedman, Edwin, 'Family Law in Israel: Overview', *Practical Law* (2017), https://uk.practicallaw.thomsonreuters.com/5-564-7346?transitionType=Default&contextData=(sc.Default)&firstPage=true&comp=pluk&bhcp=1.

Freilich, Charles D., *Israel National Security* (New York: Oxford University Press, 2018).

Galnoor, Itzhak, and Dana Blander, *The Handbook of Israel's Political System* (Cambridge: Cambridge University Press, 2018).

Gera Margaliot, Michal, and Miriam Zalkind, 'Feminism in Israel: Contesting Social Exclusion in Israel', *Fathom* (February 2018), http://fathomjournal.org/feminism-in-israel-contesting-social-exclusion-in-israel/.

Gilbert, Martin, *Israel: A History* (New York: Harpercollins, 2008).

Goldstein, Yossi (ed.), *Religion Nationalism: The Struggle for Modern Jewish Identity, an Interdisciplinary Annual* (Ariel: Ariel University, 2014).

Halila S., et al., 'Disappearance of Female Genital Mutilation from the Bedouin Population of Southern Israel', *Journal of Sexual Medicine*, 6(1) (2009): 70–73.

Halperin-Kaddari, Ruth, 'Women, Religion and Multiculturalism in Israel', *UCLA Journal of International Law and Foreign Affairs*, 5(2) (2000–2001): 339–366.

Women in Israel: A State of Their Own (Philadelphia: University of Pennsylvania Press, 2004).

Halperin-Kaddari, Ruth, and Tamar Adelstein-Zekback, *Pi Project: Supervision Enforcement and Implementation of Family Law in Israel* (Ramat Gan: The Rackman Center for the Advancement of the Status of Women, 2011) (Hebrew).

Halperin-Kaddari, Ruth, and Yaacov Yadgar, 'Between Universal Feminism and Particular Nationalism: Politics, Religion and Gender (In)equality in Israel', *Third World Quarterly*, 31(6) (2010): 905–920.

Hermann, Tamar, et al., *Israeli Democracy Index 2013* (Jerusalem: The Israel Democracy Institute, 2013).

et al., *Israeli Democracy Index 2015* (Jerusalem: The Israel Democracy Institute, 2015).

et al., *Israeli Democracy Index 2018* (Jerusalem: The Israel Democracy Institute, 2018).

Hermann, Tamar, Or Anabi, Ella Heller, Fadi Omar and William Cubbison, *A Conditional Partnership: Jews and Arabs, Israel 2019* (Jerusalem: The Israel Democracy Institute, 2019) (Hebrew).

Hermann, Tamar, and Chanan Cohen, 'Reform and Conservative Jews in Israel: A Profile and Attitudes', Israel Democracy Institute (30 June 2013), http://en.idi.org.il/analysis/articles/the-reform-and-conservative-movements-in-israel-a-profile-and-attitudes.

Herr, Moshe David, 'Retreat in the Position of Women in Halacha', *New Directions*, 27 (November–December 2012): 61–81 (Hebrew).

Hiddush, 2016 Israel Religion and State Index (September 2016).

Hitman, Gadi, 'Israel's Policy towards Its Arab Minority, 1990–2010', *Israel Affairs*, 25(1) (2019): 149–164.

Israel-Cohen, Yael, *Between Feminism and Orthodox Judaism* (Leiden: Brill, 2015).

Jabotinsky, Ze'ev (Vladimir), *The Iron Wall* (4 November 1923), www.jewishvirtuallibrary.org/jsource/Zionism/ironwall.html.

Jamal, Amal, *Arab Minority Nationalism in Israel: The Politics of Indigeneity* (London: Routledge, 2011).

Jobani, Yuval, and Nahshon Perez, *Women of the Wall: Navigating Religion in Sacred Sites* (Oxford: Oxford University Press, 2017).

Kagya, Shlomit, Ola Nabwani, Avital Manor, Nabil Khattab and Sami Miaari, 'Social Justice in Jewish–Arab Relations in Israel', Israel Democracy Institute (22 April 2013), https://en.idi.org.il/articles/11760.

Kamir, Orit, 'Basic Law: Israel as Nation-State – National Honor Defies Human Dignity and Universal Human Rights', *Israel Studies*, 25(3) (2020): 213–227.

Kaplan, Yehiel S., 'Enforcement of Divorce Judgments in Jewish Courts in Israel: The Interaction between Religious and Constitutional Law', *Middle East Law and Governance*, 4 (2012): 1–68.

Karayanni, Michael M., 'Two Concepts of Group Rights for the Palestinian-Arab Minority under Israel's Constitutional Definition as a 'Jewish and democratic' State', *I.CON*, 10(2) (2012): 304–339.

Karsh, Efraim, 'Israel's Arabs: Deprived or Radicalized?', *Israel Affairs* (January 2013): 1–19, www.meforum.org/3423/israel-arabs-deprived-radicalized.

Kedar, Alexander, Ahmad Amara and Oren Yiftachel, *Emptied Lands: A Legal Geography of Bedouin Rights in the Negev* (Stanford: Stanford University Press, 2018).

Khalidi, Rashid, *Palestinian Identity: The Construction of Modern National Consciousness* (New York: Columbia University Press, 1997).

Kimmerling, Baruch, and Joel S. Migdal, *The Palestinian People: A History* (Cambridge, MA: Harvard University Press, 2003).

Kretzmer, David, *The Legal Status of the Arabs in Israel* (Boulder: Westview Press, 1987).

Lesch, David W., *The Arab–Israeli Conflict: A History* (New York: Oxford University Press, 2008).

Lustick, Ian, *Arabs in the Jewish State: Israel's Control of a National Minority* (Austin: University of Texas Press, 1980).

Malach, Gilad, and Lee Kahaner, *Yearbook of Haredi Society in Israel 2018* (Jerusalem: The Israel Democracy Institute, 2018) (Hebrew).

Malhi, Asaf, and Miriam Abramovsky, *Integration of Family and Work among Ultra-Orthodox Women* (Jerusalem: Ministry of Economy, 2015) (Hebrew).

Mautner, Menachem, *Law and Culture in Israel at the Threshold of the Twenty First Century* (Tel Aviv: Am Oved, 2008) (Hebrew).

'From "Honor" to "Dignity": How Should a Liberal State Treat Non-liberal Cultural Groups?', *Theoretical Inquiries in Law*, 9 (2008): 609–642.

Menelson-Maoz, Adia, *Multiculturalism in Israel* (West Lafayette, IN: Purdue University Press, 2014).

Merin, Yuval, "The Right to Family Life and (Civil) Marriage – International and Local Law," in Yoram Rabin and Yuval Shany (eds.), *Economic, Social and Cultural Rights in Israel* (Tel Aviv: Ramot, 2004) (Hebrew): 663–724.

Morris, Benny, *1948: A History of the First Arab–Israeli War* (New Haven, CT: Yale University Press, 2009).

Navot, Suzie, *The Constitution of Israel: A Contextual Analysis* (Oxford: Hart Publishing, 2014).

Nelson, Cary, *Israel Denial* (Bloomington: Indiana University Press, 2019).

Olmert, Ehud, *In First Person* (Tel Aviv: Yedioth Ahronoth, 2018) (Hebrew).

Peled, Yoav and Horit Herman Peled, *The Religionization of Israeli Society* (London and New York: Routledge, 2019).

Peleg, Ilan, and Dov Waxman, *Israel's Palestinians* (New York: Cambridge University Press, 2011).

Pew Research Center, 'Israel's Religiously Divided Society', *Pew* (8 March 2016), www.pewforum.org/2016/03/08/israels-religiously-divided-society/.

Pinto, Meital, 'On the Intrinsic Value of Arabic in Israel: Challenging Kymlicka on Language Rights', *Canadian Journal of Law & Jurisprudence*, 20(1) (2007): 143–172.

Pogrund, Benjamin, *Drawing Fire: Investigating the Accusations of Apartheid in Israel* (New York: Rowman & Littlefield, 2014).

Raday, Frances, 'Religion, Multiculturalism and Equality: The Israeli Case', *Israel Yearbook on Human Rights*, 25 (1995): 193–241.

Raday, Frances, Carmel Shalev and Michal Liban Kooby (eds), *Women's Status in Israeli Law and Society* (Tel-Aviv: Schocken, 1995).

Refaeli v. Refaeli, 51(1) (1997) 198 (Hebrew).

Regev, Uri, 'The 2019 Religion-and-State Index', *Hiddush* (2019) (Hebrew).

Rouhana, Nadim N., and Sahar S. Huneidi (eds), *Israel and Its Palestinian Citizens: Ethnic Privileges in the Jewish State* (Cambridge: Cambridge University Press, 2017).

Sassoon, Isaac, *The Status of Women in Jewish Tradition* (New York: Cambridge University Press, 2011).

Schafferman, Karin Tamar, 'Milestones in Legislation and Judgments', Israel Democracy Institute (5 March 2008), https://en.idi.org.il/articles/9786.

Sezgin, Yuksel, 'The Israeli Millet System: Examining Legal Pluralism through Lenses of Nation-Building and Human Rights', *Israel Law Review*, 43 (2010): 631–633.

Shakdiel, Leah, 'Women of the Wall: Radical Feminism as an Opportunity for a New Discourse in Israel', *Journal of Israeli History*, 21(1) (2002): 126–163.

Shapira, Anita, *Israel: A History* (London: Weidenfeld and Nicolson, 2012).

Sharfman, Daphna, *Living without a Constitution* (Armonk, New York: M.E. Sharpe, 1993).

Shoham, Giora, and Anthony Grahame (eds), *Israel Studies in Criminology* (Tel-Aviv: Turtledove Press, 1979).

Smooha, Sammy, 'Types of Democracy and Modes of Conflict-Management in Ethnically Divided Societies', *Nations and Nationalism*, 8(4) (October 2002): 423–431.

'The Model of Ethnic Democracy: Israel as a Jewish and Democratic State', *Nations and Nationalism*, 8(4) (October 2002): 475–503.

'Is Israel Western?', in Eliezer Ben-Rafael and Yitzhak Sternberg (eds), *Comparing Modernities: Pluralism versus Homogeneity: Essays in Homage to Shmuel N. Eisenstadt* (Leiden and Boston: Brill Academic Publishers, 2005): 413–442.

'How Do Western Democracies Cope with the Challenge of Societal Diversity?', *Nations and Nationalism*, 24(2) (2018): 215–236.

'Israel70: The Global Enigma', *Fathom* (July 2018), http://fathomjournal.org/israel70-the-global-enigma/.

Still Playing by the Rules: Index of Arab–Jewish Relations in Israel 2017 (Jerusalem: Israel Democracy Institute, Data Israel, 2018).

Stopler, Gila, 'Religious Establishment, Pluralism and Equality in Israel: Can the Circle Be Squared?', *Oxford Journal of Law & Religion* (2012): 1–25.

Triger, Zvi, 'Freedom from Religion in Israel: Civil Marriage and Cohabitation of Jews Enter the Rabbinical Courts', *Israel Studies Review*, 27(2) (2012): 1–17.

United Nations Human Rights Council, 'National Report Submitted in Accordance with Paragraph 5 of the Annex to Human Rights Council Resolution 16/21', Working Group on the Universal Periodic Review, Seventeenth Session, Geneva, 21 October–1 November 2013, Israel.

US Department of State, *2013 Report on International Religious Freedom: Israel and the Occupied Territories* (28 July 2014), www.state.gov/j/drl/rls/irf/2013/nea/222293.htm.

Wattad, Mohammed S., 'Israel's Laws on Referendum: A Tale of Unconstitutional Legal Structure', *Florida Journal of International Law*, 27(2) (2015): 213–260.

Waxman, Dov, and Ilan Peleg, 'The Nation-State Law and the Weakening of Israeli Democracy', *Israel Studies*, 25(3) (2020): 185–200;.

World Economic Forum, *Global Gender Gap Report 2018* (Geneva, 2018).

MALE CIRCUMCISION

American Academy of Family Physicians, *Position Paper on Neonatal Circumcision* (Leawood, Kansas, 14 February 2002), www.cirp.org/library/statements/aafp2002/.

Benatar, Michael, and David Benatar, 'Between Prophylaxis and Child Abuse: The Ethics of Neonatal Male Circumcision', *American Journal of Bioethics*, 3(2) (2003): 35–48.

Ben-Yami, Hanoch, 'Circumcision: What Should Be Done?', *Journal of Medical Ethics*, 39 (7) (2013): 459–462.

Bezaleli Fisher, Rabbi Uri, 'Circumcision with Anaesthesia', *Toraland*, 115 (nd), www .toraland.org.il/הרדמה-סם-ע-מילה-ברית/והלכה/רפואה-ורפואה-טכנולוגיה/מאמרים / (Hebrew).

Boyle, Gregory J., 'Circumcision of Infants and Children: Short-Term Trauma and Long-Term Psychosexual Harm', *Advances in Sexual Medicine*, 5(2) (2015): 22–38.

Boyle, G.J., R. Goldman, J.S. Svoboda and E. Fernandez, 'Male Circumcision: Pain, Trauma and Psychosexual Sequelae', *Journal of Health Psychology*, 7(3) (2002): 329–343.

Brigman, William E., 'Circumcision as Child Abuse: The Legal and Constitutional Issues', *Journal of Family Law*, 23(3) (1984–1985): 337–357.

British Medical Association, 'The Law and Ethics of Male Circumcision: Guidance for Doctors', *Journal of Medical Ethics*, 30(3) (2004): 259–263.

Brussels Collaboration on Bodily Integrity, 'Medically Unnecessary Genital Cutting and the Rights of the Child: Moving toward Consensus', *American Journal of Bioethics*, 19(10) (2019): 17–28.

Cooper, David A., Alex D. Wodak and Brian J. Morris, 'The Case for Boosting Infant Male Circumcision in the Face of Rising Heterosexual Transmission of HIV', *The Medical Journal of Australia*, 193 (2010): 318–319.

Darby, Robert, J.L., 'The Child's Right to an Open Future: Is the Principle Applicable to Non-therapeutic Circumcision?', *Journal of Medical Ethics*, 39 (2013): 463–468.

Davis D., 'Ancient Rites and New Laws: How Should We Regulate Religious Circumcision of Minors?', *Journal of Medical Ethics*, 39(7) (July 2013): 456–458.

Decision Support in Medicine, 'Anesthesiology: Circumcision', *Clinical Pain Advisor* (2017), www.clinicalpainadvisor.com/home/decision-support-in-medicine/anesthesiology/circumcision/.

Dekkers, Wim, Cor Hoffer and Jean-Pierre Wils, 'Bodily Integrity and Male and Female Circumcision', *Medicine Health Care and Philosophy*, 8(2) (2005): 179–191.

Denniston, George C., Frederick Mansfield Hodges and Marilyn Fayre Milos (eds), *Male and Female Circumcision: Medical, Legal and Ethical Considerations in Pediatric Practice* (New York: Kluwer Academic/Plenum Publishers, 1999).

Dunsmuir, W.D., and E.M. Gordon, 'The History of Circumcision', *BJU International*, 83, Suppl. 1 (1999): 1–12.

Earp, Brian D., 'The Ethics of Infant Male Circumcision', *Journal of Medical Ethics*, 39(7) (2013): 418–420.

'In Defence of Genital Autonomy for Children', *Journal of Medical Ethics*, 41(3) (2016): 158–163.

'The Child's Right to Bodily Integrity', in David Edmonds (ed.), *Ethics and the Contemporary World* (Abingdon and New York: Routledge, 2019): 217–235.

Earp, Brian D., V. Allareddy, V. Allareddy and A.T. Rotta, 'Factors Associated with Early Deaths Following Neonatal Male Circumcision in the United States, 2001–2010', *Clinical Pediatrics*, 57(13) (2018): 1532–1540.

Earp, Brian D., and R. Darby, 'Does Science Support Infant Circumcision?', *The Skeptic*, 25 (3) (2015): 23–30.

Earp, Brian D., and D.M. Shaw, 'Cultural Bias in American Medicine: The Case of Infant Male Circumcision', *Journal of Pediatric Ethics*, 1(1) (2017): 8–26.

El Bcheraoui, Charbel, et al., 'Rates of Adverse Events Associated with Male Circumcision in US Medical Settings, 2001 to 2010', *JAMA Pediatrics*, 168(7) (2014): 625–634.

Elhaik, Eran, 'Neonatal Circumcision and Prematurity Are Associated with Sudden Infant Death Syndrome (SITS)', *Journal of Clinical and Translational Research*, 4(2) (2019): 136–151, www.jctres.com/media/filer_public/94/aa/94aafcfa-dbe0-4275-8f7c-fb149ab0 daf9/elhaik2018jclintranslres_epub.pdf.

Fateh-Moghadam, Bijan, 'Criminalizing Male Circumcision? Case Note: Landgericht Cologne, Judgment of 7 May 2012 – No. 151, Ns 169/11', *German Law Journal*, 13(9) (2012): 1131–1145.

Fox, Marie, Michael Thomson, 'A Covenant with the Status Quo? Male Circumcision and the New BMA Guidance to Doctors', *Journal Med Ethics*, 31 (2005): 463–469.

Fox, Marie, Michael Thomson and Joshua Warburton, 'Non-therapeutic Male Genital Cutting and Harm: Law, Policy and Evidence from U.K. Hospitals', *Bioethics*, 33 (2019): 467–474.

Frisch, Morten, and Brian D. Earp, 'Circumcision of Male Infants and Children as a Public Health Measure in Developed Countries: A Critical Assessment of Recent Evidence', *Global Public Health*, 13(5) (2018): 626–641.

Germann, Michael, and Clemens Wackernagel, 'The Circumcision Debate from a German Constitutional Perspective', *Oxford Journal of Law and Religion*, 4 (2015): 442–468.

Gollaher, David, *Circumcision: A History of the World's Most Controversial Surgery* (New York: Basic Books, 2000).

Goodman, J., 'Jewish Circumcision: An Alternative Perspective', *BJU International*, 83 Supp. 1 (1999): 22–27.

Hutson, J.M., 'Circumcision: A Surgeon's Perspective', *Journal of Medical Ethics*, 30 (2004): 238–240.

Jacobs, Allan J., and Kavita S. Arora, 'Ritual Male Infant Circumcision and Human Rights', *American Journal of Bioethics*, 15(2) (2015): 30–39.

Johnsdotter, Sara, 'Discourses on Sexual Pleasure After Genital Modifications: The Fallacy of Genital Determinism (a Response to J. Steven Svoboda', *Global Discourse*, 3(2) (2013): 256–265.

Johnson, Matthew, 'Male Genital Mutilation: Beyond the Tolerable?', *Ethnicities*, 10(2) (2010): 181–207.

Johnson, Matthew Thomas, 'Religious Circumcision, Invasive Rites, Neutrality and Equality: Bearing the Burdens and Consequences of Belief', *Journal of Medical Ethics*, 39(7) (2013): 450–455.

Klausner, Jeffrey D., and Brian J. Morris, 'Benefits of Male Circumcision', *JAMA*, 307(5) (2012): 455–456.

Landgericht Cologne, 'Judgment of 7 May 2012 – No. 151, Ns 169/11', *German Law Journal*, 13 (9) (2012): 1131–1145.

Larke, Natasha L., Sara L. Thomas, Isabel dos Santos Silva and Helen A. Weiss, 'Male Circumcision and Penile Cancer: A Systematic Review and Meta-analysis', *Cancer Causes Control*, 22(8) (2011): 10097–1110.

Lenhart, J.G., N.M. Lenhart, A. Reid and B.K. Chong, 'Local Anesthesia for Circumcision: Which Technique Is Most Effective?', *The Journal of the American Board of Family Practice*, 10(1) (1997):13–19.

Levey, Geoffrey Brahm, 'Thinking about Infant Male Circumcision after the Cologne Court Decision', *Global Discourse*, 3(2) (2013): 326–331.

Marcell, Arik V., 'Greater Benefits of Infant Circumcision', *Johns Hopkins Medicine* (15 October 2012), www.hopkinsmedicine.org/news/articles/greater-benefits-of-infant-circumcision.

Mazor, Joseph, 'The Child's Interests and the Case for the Permissibility of Male Infant Circumcision', *Journal of Medical Ethics*, 39(7) (2013): 421–428.

'On the Strength of Children's Right to Bodily Integrity: The Case of Circumcision', *Journal of Applied Philosophy*, 36(1) (February 2019): 1–16.

Mendus, Susan, 'Infant Male Circumcision in the Public Square: Applying the Public Reason of John Rawls (a Reply to Robert Van Howe)', *Global Discourse*, 3(2) (2013): 230–233.

Merkel, Reinhard, and Holm Putzke, 'After Cologne: Male Circumcision and the Law – Parental Right, Religious Liberty or Criminal Assault?', *Journal of Medical Ethics*, 39(7) (2013): 444–449.

Morris, Brian J., et al., 'Early Infant Male Circumcision: Systematic Review, Risk–Benefit Analysis, and Progress in Policy', *World Journal of Clinical Pediatrics*, 6(1) (8 February 2017): 89–102.

Morris, Brian J., John N. Krieger, Jeffrey D. Klausner and Beth E. Rivin, 'The Ethical Course Is to Recommend Infant Male Circumcision: Arguments Disparaging American Academy of Pediatrics Affirmative Policy Do Not Withstand Scrutiny', *Journal of Law, Medicine & Ethics*, 45 (2017): 647–663.

Morris, Brian J., Stephen Moreton and John N Krieger, 'Critical Evaluation of Arguments Opposing Male Circumcision: a Systematic Review', *Journal of Evidence-Based Medicine* (September 2019): 1–28.

Morris, Brian J., Richard G. Wamai, Esther B. Henebeng et al., 'Estimation of Country-Specific and Global Prevalence of Male Circumcision', *Population Health Metrics*, 14(4) (2016), https://pophealthmetrics.biomedcentral.com/articles/10.1186/s12963-016-0073-5.

Morris, Brian J., Jake H. Waskett, Joya Banerjee et al., 'A "Snip" in Time: What Is the Best Age to Circumcise?', *BMC Pediatrics*, 12 (2012): 20, www.ncbi.nlm.nih.gov/pmc/articles/PMC3359221/.

Munzer, Stephen R., 'Examining Nontherapeutic Circumcision', *Health Matrix: Journal of Law-Medicine*, 28 (2018): 1–78.

Myers, A., and B.D. Earp, 'What Is the Best Age to Circumcise? A Medical and Ethical Analysis', *Bioethics* (February 2020), www.researchgate.net/publication/337720859_What_is_the_best_age_to_circumcise_A_medical_and_ethical_analysis.

Olapade-Olaopa, Emiola Oluwabunmi, Mudasiru Adebayo Salami and Taiwo Akeem Lawal, 'Male Circumcision and Global HIV/AIDS Epidemic Challenges', *African Journal of Urology*, 25 (November 2019): 3, https://link.springer.com/article/10.1186/s12301-019-0005-2.

Paix, B.R., and S.E. Peterson, 'Circumcision of Neonates and Children without Appropriate Anaesthesia Is Unacceptable Practice', *Anaesthesia and Intensive Care*, 40 (2012):511–516.

Razmus, Ivy S., Madelyn E. Dalton and David Wilson, 'Pain Management for Newborn Circumcision', *Pediatric Nursing*, 30(5) (January 2004): 414–417.

Reichman, Edward, and Fred Rosner, 'The Use of Anesthesia in Circumcision: A Re-evaluation of the Halakhic Sources', *Tradition: A Journal of Orthodox Jewish Thought*, 34(3) (Fall 2000): 6–26.

Rosen, Michael, 'Anesthesia for Ritual Circumcision in Neonates', *Paediatrics Anaesthesia*, 20 (2010): 1124–1127.

Royal Dutch Medical Association (KNMG), *Non-therapeutic Circumcision of Male Minors* (Amsterdam: KNMG, May 2010), www.knmg.nl/circumcision/.

Sarajlic, Eldar, 'Can Culture Justify Infant Circumcision?', *Res Publica*, 20(4) (November 2014): 327–343.

Sharara-Chami, Rana, Zavi Lakissian, Lama Charafeddine, Nadine Milad and Yaser El-Hout, 'Combination Analgesia for Neonatal Circumcision: A Randomized Controlled Trial', *Pediatrics*, 140(6) (December 2017), https://pediatrics.aappublications.org/content/140/6/e20171935.

Short, R.V., 'Male Circumcision: A Scientific Perspective', *Journal of Medical Ethics*, 30(3) (2004): 241.

Silverman, Eric K., 'Anthropology and Circumcision', *Annual Review of Anthropology*, 33 (2004): 419–445.

Somerville, Margaret A., *The Ethical Canary: Science, Society and the Human Spirit* (Toronto: Viking, 2000).

Steinberg, Avraham, 'Anaesthesia in Circumcision, Medical and Halachic Perspectives', *Shana Be'Shana* (2001) (Hebrew), www.daat.ac.il/he-il/kitveyet/shana_beshana/mehab rim/steinberg-hardama.htm.

Svoboda, J. Steven, 'Circumcision of Male Infants as a Human Rights Violation', *Journal of Medical Ethics*, 39 (7) (2013): 469–474.

'Promoting Genital Autonomy by Exploring Commonalities between Male, Female, Intersex, and Cosmetic Female Genital Cutting', *Global Discourse*, 3(2) (2013): 237–255.

Taddio, A., J. Katz, A.L. Ilersich and G. Koren, 'Effect of Neonatal Circumcision on Pain Response during Subsequent Routine Vaccination', *The Lancet*, 349 (1997): 599–603.

Task Force on Circumcision, 'Male Circumcision', *Pediatrics*, 130(3) (September 2012), http://pediatrics.aappublications.org/content/130/3/e756.

Taylor, J.R., A.P. Lockwood and A.J. Taylor, 'The Prepuce: Specialized Mucosa of the Penis and Its Loss to Circumcision', *British Journal of Urology*, 77(2) (1996): 291–295.

Tobian, A.A.R., and R.H. Gray, 'The Medical Benefits of Male Circumcision', *JAMA*, 306(13) (2011): 1479–1480.

Ungar-Sargon, Eliyahu, 'On the Impermissibility of Infant Male Circumcision: A Response to Mazor', *Journal of Medical Ethics*, 41(2) (2015): 186–190.

University of Oxford, 'Babies Feel Pain "Like Adults": Most Babies Not Given Pain Meds for Surgery', *Science Daily* (21 April 2015).

Vadnal, Julie, 'Why Fewer Guys Are Getting Circumcised', *Cosmopolitan* (21 August 2018), www.cosmopolitan.com/sex-love/a22094429/why-fewer-guys-are-getting-circumcised/.

Van Howe, Robert, 'Infant Male Circumcision in the Public Square: Applying the Public Reason of John Rawls', *Global Discourse*, 3(2) (2013): 214–229.

Weiss, Helen A., Maria A. Quigley and Richard J. Hayes, 'Male Circumcision and Risk of HIV Infection in Sub-Saharan Africa: A Systematic Review and Meta-analysis', *AIDS*, 14 (2002): 2361–2370.

Weiss, Helen A., Natasha Larke, Daniel Halperin, et al., 'Complications of Circumcision in Male Neonates, Infants and Children: A Systematic Review', *BMC Urology*, 10 (2010): 2, www.ncbi.nlm.nih.gov/pmc/articles/PMC2835667/.

Wheeler, Robert, and Pat Malone, 'Male Circumcision: Risk versus Benefit', *Archives of Disease in Childhood*, 98 (2013): 321–322.

WHO, *Male Circumcision: Global Trends and Determinants of Prevalence, Safety and Acceptability*, World Health Organization and Joint United Nations Programme on HIV/AIDS (2007).

Manual for Male Circumcision under Local Anaesthesia, Version 3.1 (December 2009), www.who.int/hiv/pub/malecircumcision/who_mc_local_anaesthesia.pdf.

Neonatal and Child Male Circumcision: A Global Review (April 2010).

Wolbarst, A., 'Circumcision and Penile Cancer', *The Lancet*, 1(5655) (16 January 1932): 150–153.

MURDER FOR FAMILY HONOUR

Abu-Rabia, Aref, 'Family Honor Killings: Between Custom and State Law', *The Open Psychology Journal*, 4 Suppl. 1-M4 (2011): 34–44.

Amnesty International, 'The Horror of "Honor Killings", Even in US' (nd), www.amnestyusa
.org/the-horror-of-honor-killings-even-in-us/.

Baker, Nancy V., Peter R. Gregware and Margery A. Cassidy, 'Family Killing Fields: Honor Rationales in the Murder of Women', *Violence Against Women*, 5(2) (1999): 164–184.

Chesler, Phyllis, 'Worldwide Trends in Honor Killings', *Middle East Quarterly*, 17(2) (Spring 2010): 3–11.

Cohen-Almagor, Raphael, 'Female Circumcision and Murder for Family Honour among Minorities in Israel', in Kirsten Schulze, Martin Stokes and Colm Campbell (eds), *Nationalism, Minorities and Diasporas: Identities and Rights in the Middle East* (London: I.B. Tauris, 1996): 171–187.

Ginat, Joseph, *Blood Disputes among Bedouin and Rural Arabs in Israel* (Pittsburgh: University of Pittsburgh Press, in cooperation with Jerusalem Institute for Israel Studies, 1987).

Blood Revenge (Tel Aviv: Haifa University Press and Zmora-Bitan, 2000) (Hebrew).

Glazer, Ilsa M., and Wahiba Abu Ras, 'On Aggression, Human Rights, and Hegemonic Discourse: The Case of a Murder for Family Honor in Israel', *Sex Roles: A Journal of Research*, 30(3–4) (1994): 269–288.

Hasan, Manar, 'The Politics of Honor: Patriarchy, the State and the Murder of Women in the Name of Family Honor', *Journal of Israeli History*, 21(1–2) (2002): 1–37.

Husseini, Rana, *Murder in the Name of Honor* (London: Oneworld, 2009).

Idriss, Mohammad M., and Tahir Abbas (eds), *Honour, Violence, Women and Islam* (London: Routledge, 2010).

Jabareen, Yosef, 'Controlling Land and Demography in Israel', in Nadim N. Rouhana and Sahar S. Huneidi (eds), *Israel and Its Palestinian Citizens: Ethnic Privileges in the Jewish State* (Cambridge: Cambridge University Press, 2017): 238–265.

Kressel, G.M., 'Sororicide/Filiacide: Homicide for Family Honour', *Current Anthropology*, 22 (2) (1981): 141–158.

Kressel, Gideon M., and Unni Wikan, 'More on Honour and Shame', *Man*, 23(1) (March 1988): 167–170.

Maris, Cees, and Sawitri Saharso, 'Honour Killing: A Reflection on Gender, Culture and Violence', *Netherlands Journal of Social Sciences*, 37(1) (2001): 52–73.

Meetoo, Veena, and Heidi Safia Mirza, 'There Is Nothing "Honourable" about Honour Killings': Gender, Violence and the Limits of Multiculturalism', *Women's Studies International Forum*, 30 (2007): 187–200.

Peristiany, J.G. (ed.), *Honour and Shame: The Values of Mediterranean Society* (London: Weidenfeld & Nicholson, 1965).

Stewart, Frank H., *Honor* (Chicago: University of Chicago Press, 1994).

Taha Najar v. State of Israel. Criminal Appeal 10828/03. Israel Supreme Court (2 May 2005).

Index

substantive, 98, 304–5
system of government, 26
young, 278
democratic catch, the, 8, 12, 14, 23, 39, 42–3, 60, 85,
    108, 126, 188, 278, 300, 308, 324
demography, 303
deontology, 318
Deveaux, Monique, 15, 84
Diderot, Denis, 247
dignity, 28, 35, 40, 67, 72, 86, 93, 160, 190–1, 203,
    265, 298, 309, 324, *See also* Kant, Immanuel
  as liability, 37, 204, 262
  as recognition, 37, 115, 120, 204
  as recognition and as liability, 36
  equal, 180
  inherent, 120
  of the congregation, 199
  of the indigenous peoples of the world, 194
  of woman, 73, 120, 239, 261–3, 269
discrimination, 187, 195, 204, 277, 282, 292, 305,
    309, 326
  against Israeli-Arabs, 290–1, 294, 302
  against minorities, 298, 304
  against non-Orthodox Jews, 104
  against women, 111, 193, 197, 200, 317
  and segregation, 297
  faith-based, 250
  gender, 179, 183–4, 187, 319, 322
  group, 187
  in the labour market, 292
  individual or collective, 203
  institutional, 19
  of women, 143
  religious, 18, 249, 266
  sex, 193
dispute resolution, 52, 64, 67, 186, 270
diversity, 10, 248, 263, 302, 311
  a threat, 246
  cultural, 253
  internal, 231
  of doctrines, 318
  rejection of, 276
divorce, 104
  bill of, 106
dorsal penile nerve block (DPNB), 169, 173. *See
    also* anaesthesia
Douglas, William Orville, Justice, 224–5, 227
Druze, 121, 280, 294, 301, 304
Dryzek, John, 15
Dworkin, Ronald, 36, 39, 53, 312

Earp, Brian, 127, 132, 147, 155, 160
education, 29, 187
  a key factor, 309

aims of, 228
Amish, 208
Amish denial of, 207, 213
children, 16
civic, 86
compulsory, 96, 97, 214–16
democratic, 214
denial of, 4, 16, 188, 191, 200–1
essential for good government, 96
for autonomy, 213
goal of, 215
higher, 215
in France, 97
in Israel, 298
is essential, 125
key to self-development, 204
mandatory, 97
moral, 212
multicultural, 214, 228
restrictions on, 217
sex, 223, 232, 310, 323–4
state, 210, 251
traditional, 202
universal, 210
value of, 214
vocational, 216
women, 201
women are discouraged from, 200
egalitarian fairness, 326
Egalitarianism, 278, 305
égalité, 240, 244, 247, 259
Eidelman, Leonid, 170–1
Enlightenment, The, 264
equality
  basic moral, 5
  before the law, 9, 28, 193, 292
  between citizens, 246
  between men and women, 262
  and freedom, 41
  formal, 228
  French, 261
  gender, 11, 13, 79, 125, 180, 187, 190, 200, 203,
      238–9, 261
  in allocation of resources, 305
  in education, 79
  in housing, 312
  legal, 24
  moral, 138
  natural right to, 187
  of all citizens, 251
  of opportunity, 30
  of rights, 285, 302, 317
  of social and political rights, 284
  political, 80, 84